The CISSP® Prep Guide, Second Edition: Mastering the CISSP and ISSEP™ Exams

Ronald L. Krutz and Russell Dean Vines

WILEY

Wiley Publishing, Inc.

The CISSP Prep Guide, Second Edition
Published by
Wiley Publishing Inc.
10475 Crosspoint Boulevard
Indianapolis, IN 46256
www.wiley.com

To Jean Vines, in memory of her son, Denny Jones —RDV

To each of my loved ones . . . always keep a happy heart—RLK

Credits

Vice President and Executive Group Publisher
Richard Swadley

Vice President and Executive Publisher
Robert Ipsen

Vice President and Publisher
Joseph B. Wikert

Executive Editorial Director
Mary Bednarek

Executive Editor
Carol Long

Editorial Manager
Kathryn A. Malm

Development Editor
Sharon Nash

Senior Production Manager
Fred Bernardi

Senior Production Editor
Angela Smith

Media Development Specialist
Travis Silvers

Permissions Editor
Laura Moss

Project Coordinator
Kristie Rees

Proofreading and Indexing
Publication Services

Text Design and Composition
Wiley Composition Services

Contents at a Glance

Contents

● ●

Part III: Appendices   649

Acknowledgments

The authors would like to thank those who contributed changes, updates, corrections, and ideas for this second edition and especially Carol Long, Wiley Executive Editor, Angela Smith, Senior Production Editor, and Sharon Nash, Wiley Developmental Editor.

Again, I want to thank my wife, Hilda, for her continuing support and encouragement during this project.

I, also, want to express my thanks to Russell Dean Vines for the opportunity to work with him in developing our texts. Russ is a true professional and valued friend.

—RLK

Thanks to all of my friends, family, and associates who supported me throughout the process of producing this book. I would especially like to thank Lance Kostrobala and Howard Weiner; Jonathan Krim; Diane Moser; Dom Moio; Sid Jacobs; Fred, Phyllis, and Ben Stimler; Lena Kolb; John Mueller and Sheila Roman; and Elzy Kolb, Irene Cornell Meenan, and the rest of the Roundup Grrls.

—RDV

The authors would also like to thank Barry C. Stauffer for contributing the Foreword to this edition.

Special Thanks

We would also like to include a special thank you to Benjamin S. Blanchard for allowing us to include an appendix from his title, *System Engineering Management*, 3rd Edition (Wiley, ISBN: 0-471-29176-5), as our Appendix E, "The Cost Analysis Process."

Foreword

The advent of the computer age brought us the ability to gather and process large quantities of information in ever decreasing time. Unfortunately, this new age also arrived with a host of new challenges. First Grace Hooper identified the first computer bug, and, I might add, successfully repaired the problem. Then soon afterward we discovered that some users had learned to use the computer systems to exploit the information to their own desires. Similarly we discovered that other well-meaning users and information system managers had inadvertently caused equally challenging problems. Thus we learned to develop methods and procedures to preserve the confidentiality of the information, maintain the integrity of the data, ensure the availability of the information systems, and to enforce the accountability of the users and processes. A cadre of information systems security professionals quickly rose to the challenge and began to identify and then attempt to solve the security issues.

Our early attempts first sought to identify the threats, vulnerabilities, and risk through risk assessments, certification and accreditation, vulnerability testing, penetration testing, red and black teams and a host of other methods to identify the security issues. Then like our medieval kings we built fortresses (firewalls) to protect our enclaves by walling off our information and systems from outside intruders. However, like the medieval leaders that too late discovered the fundamental management error in allowing the first Trojan Horse into their enclave, our IT management professionals continue to be faced with challenging issues. While some of the security community advocates new technology as the solution to all security, others continue to advocate the timeless process of security evaluations and assessments. Neither by themselves will be sufficient. We certainly need the technological advances of intrusion detection and prevention systems, security operations centers, and incident response tools, but this technology does not hold all the answers. Similarly we must learn to conduct the proper evaluations and assessments in a manner that not just produces a report but also instead leads to actionable recommendations. The security problem has raised to the attention of both industry and government leaders. The U.S. Congress has mandated that government leaders address, and report, their progress on resolving the security issues. The U.S. government is also searching for ways to successfully motivate industry leaders to the security challenges in the private sector.

Today's Information Technology managers are faced with ever increasing issues. Many have hundreds, and some tens of thousands, of systems and applications. Yet many of us as security professionals continue to attack the issues on a system-by-system basis with the same tools we have always used. Instead we must address the hard management issues of developing enterprise level security architectures, configuration control, patch management, user management, and user training. The challenge facing us as security professionals is now to bring both the technology and management processes to bear on the security problems in a synergistic approach by providing security solutions, not more system-level assessments.

Our IT managers have long recognized the need for more experienced and well-rounded security professionals. Thus the need arose for a method to identify qualified security professionals. At one level this rests with qualifications such as the Certified Information Systems Security Professional (CISSP) and now at the next level for the government with the Information System Security Engineering Professional (ISSEP) certification. Our new ISSEPs will be knowledgeable of the U.S. government information assurance regulations, practices, and procedures as well as the latest security technology. These qualifications provide one path for managers to identify those security professionals that have taken the initiative to advance their careers with independent study and have proven themselves with their certifications.

I wish each of you the best success as you move forward in your security career.

Barry C. Stauffer

December 2003

Mr. Stauffer is the Chief Information Assurance Officer of BAE SYSTEMS and the founder and former CEO of Corbett Technologies, Inc. In 1981 Mr. Stauffer entered the security community as a Naval Officer on the Department of Defense Joint Staff. Since that time he has been involved in both industry and government in the development of security practices, procedures and management approaches. He led the development of the DITSCAP and NIACAP and has been directly involved in the certification and accreditation of numerous systems and the development of large-scale Government security programs.

Introduction

The need to protect information resources has produced a demand for information systems security professionals. Along with this demand came a need to ensure that these professionals possess the knowledge to perform the required job functions. To address this need, the Certified Information Systems Security Professional (CISSP) certification emerged. This certification guarantees to all parties that the certified individual meets the standard criteria of knowledge and continues to upgrade that knowledge in the field of information systems security. The CISSP initiative also serves to enhance the recognition and reputation of the field of information security.

For the CISSP who wishes to concentrate in information systems security for U.S. federal information systems, the CISSP Information System Security Engineering Professional (ISSEP) concentration certification has been established. This certification is particularly relevant for efforts in conjunction with the National Security Agency (NSA) and with other U.S. government agencies.

The (ISC)² Organization

The CISSP certification is the result of cooperation among a number of North American professional societies in establishing the International Information Systems Security Certification Consortium (ISC)² in 1989. The (ISC)² is a nonprofit corporation whose sole function is to develop and administer the certification program. The organization defined a common body of knowledge (CBK) that defines a common set of terms for information security professionals to use to communicate with each other and to establish a dialogue in the field. This guide was created based on the most recent CBK and skills, as described by (ISC)² for security professionals. At this time, the domains in alphabetical order are as follows:

- ✦ Access Control Systems and Methodology
- ✦ Application and Systems Development Security
- ✦ Business Continuity and Disaster Recovery Planning
- ✦ Cryptography
- ✦ Law, Investigation, and Ethics
- ✦ Operations Security
- ✦ Physical Security
- ✦ Security Architecture and Models
- ✦ Security Management Practices
- ✦ Telecommunications and Networking Security

The ISSEP concentration address four additional areas related to U.S. government information assurance, particularly NSA information assurance. These four areas are:

✦ Systems Security Engineering

✦ Certification and Accreditation

✦ Technical Management

✦ U.S. Government Information Assurance Regulations

The (ISC)[2] conducts review seminars and administers examinations for information security practitioners who seek the CISSP and ISSEP certifications. Candidates for the CISSP examination must attest that they have three to five years' experience in the information security field and that they subscribe to the (ISC)[2] Code of Ethics. The seminars cover the CBK from which the examination questions originate. The seminars are not intended to teach the examination.

A candidate for the ISSEP examination must have the CISSP certification as a prerequisite.

New Candidate CISSP Requirements

Beginning June 1, 2002, the (ISC)[2] has divided the credentialing process into two steps: examination and certification. Once a CISSP candidate has been notified of passing the examination, he or she must have the application endorsed by a qualified third party before the CISSP credential is awarded. Another CISSP, the candidate's employer, or any licensed, certified, or commissioned professional can endorse a CISSP candidate.

After the examination scoring and the candidate receiving a passing grade, a notification letter advises the candidate of his or her status. The candidate has 90 days from the date of the letter to submit an endorsement form. If the endorsement form is not received before the 90-day period expires, the application is void and the candidate must resubmit to the entire process. Also, a percentage of the candidates who pass the examination and submit endorsements are randomly subjected to audit and are required to submit a resume for formal review and investigation.

You can find more information regarding this process at www.isc2.org.

The CISSP Examination

The examination questions are from the CBK and aim at the level of a three-to-five-year practitioner in the field. The examination consists of 250 English language questions, of which 25 are not counted. The 25 are trial questions that might be used on future exams. The 25 are not identified, so there is no way to tell which questions they are. The questions are not ordered according to domain but are randomly arranged. There is no penalty for candidates answering questions of which they are unsure. Candidates have six hours for the examination.

The examination questions are multiple choice with four possible answers. No acronyms appear without an explanation. It is important to read the questions carefully and thoroughly and to choose the best possible answer of the four. As with any conventional test-taking strategy, a good approach is to eliminate two of the four answers and then choose the best answer of the remaining two. The questions are not of exceptional difficulty for a knowledgeable person who has been practicing in the field. Most professionals are not usually involved with all 10 domains in their work, however. It is uncommon for an information security practitioner to work in all the diverse areas that the CBK covers. For example, specialists in physical security might not be required to work in depth in the areas of computer law or cryptography as part of their job descriptions. The examination questions also do not refer to any specific products or companies. Approximately 70 percent of the people taking the examination score a passing grade.

The ISSEP Concentration Examination

The ISSEP examination is similar in format to that of the CISSP examination. The questions are also multiple choice with the examinee being asked to select the best answer of four possible answers.

The examination comprises 150 questions, 25 of which are experimental questions that are not counted. The candidate is allotted 3 hours to complete the examination.

The Approach of This Book

Based on the experience of the authors, who have both taken and passed the CISSP examination and one who has taken and passed the ISSEP examination, there is a need for a single, high-quality reference source that the candidate can use to prepare for the CISSP and ISSEP examinations. This text is also useful if the candidate is taking the (ISC)² CISSP or ISSEP training seminars. Prior to this text, the candidate's choices were the following:

1. To buy numerous expensive texts and use a small portion of each in order to cover the breadth of the 10 CISSP domains and 4 ISSEP domains

2. Acquire and attempt to digest the myriad of NIST, NSA, and U.S. government standards applicable to the ISSEP concentration

3. To purchase a so-called single source book that focused on areas in the domains not emphasized in the CBK or that left gaps in the coverage of the CBK

Chapters 11 through 14 emphasize material that is directly relevant to the ISSEP certification examination. In addition, the authors have used an ISSEP icon in the margin of the updated and enhanced CISSP 10-domain material to indicate content that is directly applicable to the ISSEP certification examination.

Organization of the Book

We organize the text into the following parts:

Part I: Focused Review of the CISSP Ten Domains

Chapter 1: Security Management Practices

Chapter 2: Access Control Systems

Chapter 3: Telecommunications and Network Security

Chapter 4: Cryptography

Chapter 5: Security Architecture and Models

Chapter 6: Operations Security

Chapter 7: Applications and Systems Development

Chapter 8: Business Continuity Planning and Disaster Recovery Planning

Chapter 9: Law, Investigation, and Ethics

Chapter 10: Physical Security

Part II: The Information Systems Security Engineering Professional (ISSEP) Concentration

Chapter 11: Systems Security Engineering

Chapter 12: Certification and Accreditation (C&A)

Chapter 13: Technical Management

Chapter 14: U.S. Government Information Assurance (IA) Regulations

Part III: Appendices

Appendix A: Answers to Assessment Questions

Appendix B: Glossary of Terms and Acronyms

Appendix C: Sample SSAA

Appendix D: Excerpts from the Common Criteria

Appendix E: The Cost Analysis Process

Appendix F: National Information Assurance (IA) Glossary

Appendix G: What's on the CD-ROM

CD-ROM

For details about the CD-ROM accompanying this title, please refer to Appendix G.

What the Icons Mean

Throughout this book, you will find icons in the margins that highlight special or important information. Keep an eye out for the following icons:

A Note icon highlights interesting or supplementary information and often contains extra bits of technical information about a subject.

The ISSEP icon highlights important information about ISSEP topics. The information is not separated from the regular text as with Note icons.

Who Should Read This Book?

There are three main categories of readers for this comprehensive guide:

1. Candidates for the CISSP or ISSEP examinations who are studying on their own or those who are taking the CISSP or ISSEP review seminars will find this text a valuable aid in their preparation plan. The guide provides a no-nonsense way of obtaining the information needed without having to sort through numerous books covering portions of the CBK or U.S. government information assurance domains and then filtering their content to acquire the fundamental knowledge needed for the exam. The assessment questions provided will acclimate the reader to the type of questions that he or she will encounter on the exams, and the answers serve to cement and reinforce the candidate's knowledge.

2. Candidates with the CISSP certification that will be working on information assurance with U.S. federal government agencies and in particular, with the NSA.

3. Students attending information system security certification programs offered in many of the major universities will find this text a valuable addition to their reference library. For the same reasons cited for the candidate preparing for the CISSP or ISSEP exam, this book is a single-source repository of fundamental and emerging information security knowledge. It presents the information at the level of the experienced information security professional and thus is commensurate with the standards that universities require for their certificate offerings.

   The material contained in this book is of practical value to information security professionals in performing their job functions. The professional, certified or not, will refer to the text as a refresher for information security basics as well as for a guide to the application of emerging methodologies.

Summary

The authors sincerely believe that this text will provide a cost-effective and time-saving means of preparing for the CISSP and ISSEP certification examinations. By using this reference, the candidate can focus on the fundamentals of the material instead of spending time deciding upon and acquiring numerous expensive texts and the overwhelming number of U.S. government information assurance publications. It also provides the breadth and depth of coverage to avoid gaps in the CBK and U.S. government information assurance requirements that are present in other "single" references.

We present the information security material in the text in an organized, professional manner that is a primary source of information for students in the information security field as well as for practicing professionals.

New Material for the Second Edition

We've made extensive additions and revisions for this Second Edition of the CISSP Prep Guide. In addition to corrections and updates, we include new security information — especially in the areas of law, cryptography, U.S. government information assurance topics, and wireless technology.

Also, the ISSEP assessment questions will be particularly helpful to all readers of this text, and the new, focused appendices will help the reader expand his or her comfort with the material.

About the Authors

RONALD L. KRUTZ, Ph.D., P.E., CISSP, ISSEP. Dr. Krutz is a Senior Information Security Researcher in the Advanced Technology Research Center of Sytex, Inc. In this capacity, he works with a team responsible for advancing the state of the art in information systems security. He has more than 40 years of experience in distributed computing systems, computer architectures, real-time systems, information assurance methodologies, and information security training.

He has been an information security consultant at REALTECH Systems Corporation and BAE Systems, an associate director of the Carnegie Mellon Research Institute (CMRI), and a professor in the Carnegie Mellon University Department of Electrical and Computer Engineering. Dr. Krutz founded the CMRI Cybersecurity Center and was founder and director of the CMRI Computer, Automation, and Robotics Group. He is a former lead instructor for the (ISC)^2 CISSP Common Body of Knowledge review seminars. Dr. Krutz is also a Distinguished Special Lecturer in the Center for Forensic Computer Investigation at the University of New Haven, a part-time instructor in the University of Pittsburgh Department of Electrical and Computer Engineering, and a Registered Professional Engineer.

Dr. Krutz is the author of five best-selling publications in the area of information systems security and is a consulting editor for John Wiley & Sons for its information security book series. Dr. Krutz holds B.S., M.S., and Ph.D. degrees in Electrical and Computer Engineering.

RUSSELL DEAN VINES, CISSP, CISM, Security +, CCNA, MCSE, MCNE. Mr. Vines is president and founder of The RDV Group Inc. (www.rdvgroup.com), a New York–based security consulting services firm. He has been active in the prevention, detection, and remediation of security vulnerabilities for international corporations, including government, finance, and new media organizations, for many years. Mr. Vines is a specialist in cybercounterterrorism, recently focusing on energy and telecommunications vulnerabilities in New York State.

He holds high-level certifications in Cisco, 3Com, Ascend, Microsoft, and Novell technologies and is trained in the National Security Agency's ISSO Information Assessment Methodology. He has headed computer security departments and managed worldwide information systems networks for prominent technology, entertainment, and nonprofit corporations based in New York. He is the author of six best-selling information system security publications and is a consulting editor for John Wiley & Sons for its information security book series.

Mr. Vines' early professional years were illuminated not by the flicker of a computer monitor but by the bright lights of Nevada casino show rooms. After receiving a *Down Beat* magazine scholarship to Boston's Berklee College of Music, he performed as a sideman for a variety of well-known entertainers, including George Benson, John Denver, Sammy Davis Jr., and Dean Martin. Mr. Vines composed and arranged hundreds of pieces of jazz and contemporary music recorded and performed by his own big band and others. He also founded and managed a scholastic music publishing company and worked as an artist-in-residence for the *National Endowment for the Arts* (NEA) in communities throughout the West. He still performs and teaches music in the New York City area and is a member of the American Federation of Musicians Local #802.

Preface to the 2nd Edition

When I met Ron Krutz at a security seminar in Brooklyn, N.Y., in December 1999, neither of us had any idea what was ahead of us.

We became friendly enough to lunch together at Junior's, a long-time NYC landmark, renowned for its New York–style cheesecake. When the class was done, we returned to our respective home bases and kept in touch.

Ron and I had discussed writing a book that would aid CISSP candidates in scaling the huge mountain of study material required to prepare for the CISSP exam, and with the help and patience of Carol Long the "CISSP Prep Guide" came to fruition.

During those months of writing the text, we never imagined the impact this book would have. When the book was published in August 2001, it immediately became a nonfiction bestseller. It stayed on the Amazon Hot 100 list for more than four months and was the top-selling computer book of the year.

The information systems security community's endorsement of the book was heartening, and we were very pleased to receive feedback from readers, that ran along the lines of:

> ". . . this book is the key to the kingdom."

> ". . . is exactly what CISSP candidates need to prepare for the exam."

> "I've been teaching the CISSP material for some time now and will make this our new text. This is a GREAT book - must have"

> "This book is a great review book. It's easy-to-read."

> ". . . very detailed, more organized, and overall a better preparation for the exam than [another] book."

> "The authors got right to the point, which when studying for this test can save you hours upon hours."

> ". . . written in a very clear style that flows well."

> ". . . the additional information provided in each appendix make this not only a required study tool, but also a 'must have' reference."

> "Consider it required reading."

> "I passed the test the first time and I attribute that fact to this book."

The "Prep Guide" has spawned a raft of information systems security material including six additional books between us; translations of these books into Korean, Finnish, Japanese, two Chinese dialects, and other languages; the creation of Wiley's popular security certification book series; and the development of our new security certification training seminars (for more information see www.rdvgroup.com).

But since that time, some things have endured and flourished, not the least being my continuing friendship with Ron Krutz. His professionalism and integrity have been an example for me, especially through the dark days after 9/11 and into our continuing work combating cyberterrorism.

But the most important thing we have recognized is this: The fundamental tenets of computer security must be understood by everyone who works in information technology, not just those with a security background. We feel genuine satisfaction that we're helping others learn how to protect computing infrastructure globally.

Through the "CISSP Prep Guide," a computer professional can get his or her feet wet in the many disparate domains that comprise the world of information systems security. We're happy to have played a part.

And we're still crazy about Junior's cheesecake.

Russell Dean Vines

December 15, 2003

Focused Review of the CISSP Ten Domains

]

Security Management Practices

In our first chapter, we enter the domain of Security Management. Throughout this book, you will see that many Information Systems Security domains have several elements and concepts that overlap. Although all other security domains are clearly focused, this domain introduces concepts that we extensively touch upon in both the Operations Security (Chapter 6) and Physical Security (Chapter 10) domains. A CISSP professional will be expected to know the following:

+ Basic security management concepts

+ The difference between policies, standards, guidelines, and procedures

+ Security awareness concepts

+ Risk management (RM) practices

+ Data classification levels

We will examine the InfoSec domain of Security Management by using the following elements:

+ Concepts of Information Security Management

+ The Information Classification process

+ Security Policy implementation

+ The roles and responsibilities of Security Administration

+ Risk Management Assessment tools

+ Security Awareness training

Note   Throughout the book we have footnotes that will help direct the reader to additional study sources.

Domain Definition

The InfoSec domain of Security Management incorporates the identification of information data assets with the development and implementation of policies, standards, guidelines, and procedures. It defines the management practices of data classification and risk management. It also addresses confidentiality, integrity, and availability by identifying threats, classifying the organization's assets, and rating their vulnerabilities so that effective security controls can be implemented.

Management Concepts

Under the heading of Information Security Management concepts, we will discuss the following:

✦ The big three: Confidentiality, Integrity, and Availability

✦ The concepts of identification, authentication, accountability, authorization, and privacy

✦ The objective of security controls (to reduce the impact of threats and the likelihood of their occurrence)

System Security Life Cycle

Security, like other aspects of an IT system, is best managed if planned for throughout the IT system life cycle. There are many models for the IT system life cycle, but most contain five basic phases: initiation, development/acquisition, implementation, operation, and disposal.

Chapter 11 in the ISSEP study section describes systems security engineering in more detail, but let's get to know the basic steps of the system security life cycle. The order of these phases is*:

1. *Initiation phase*. During the initiation phase, the need for a system is expressed and the purpose of the system is documented.

2. *Development/acquisition phase*. During this phase, the system is designed, purchased, programmed, developed, or otherwise constructed.

3. *Implementation phase*. During implementation, the system is tested and installed or fielded.

---

*Source: NIST Special Publication 800-14, "Generally Accepted Principles and Practices for Securing Information Technology Systems."

4. *Operation/maintenance phase.* During this phase, the system performs its work. The system is almost always being continuously modified by the addition of hardware and software and by numerous other events.

5. *Disposal phase.* The disposal phase of the IT system life cycle involves the disposition of information, hardware, and software.

The Big Three

Throughout this book, you will read about the three tenets of InfoSec: Confidentiality, Integrity, and Availability (C.I.A.), as shown in Figure 1-1. These concepts represent the three fundamental principles of information security. All of the information security controls and safeguards and all of the threats, vulnerabilities, and security processes are subject to the C.I.A. yardstick.

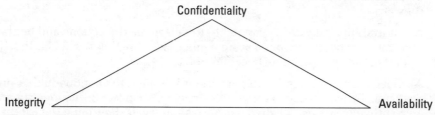

Figure 1-1: The C.I.A. triad.

Confidentiality. The concept of confidentiality attempts to prevent the intentional or unintentional unauthorized disclosure of a message's contents. Loss of confidentiality can occur in many ways, such as through the intentional release of private company information or through a misapplication of network rights.

Integrity. The concept of integrity ensures that:

- Modifications are not made to data by unauthorized personnel or processes

- Unauthorized modifications are not made to data by authorized personnel or processes

- The data is internally and externally consistent; in other words, that the internal information is consistent among all subentities and that the internal information is consistent with the real-world, external situation

Availability. The concept of availability ensures the reliable and timely access to data or computing resources by the appropriate personnel. In other words, availability guarantees that the systems are up and running when needed. In addition, this concept guarantees that the security services that the security practitioner needs are in working order.

Note The reverse of confidentiality, integrity, and availability is disclosure, alteration, and destruction (D.A.D.).

Other Important Concepts

There are also several other important concepts and terms that a CISSP candidate must fully understand. These concepts include identification, authentication, accountability, authorization, and privacy, and are found frequently throughout the book:

Identification. The means by which users claim their identities to a system. Most commonly used for access control, identification is necessary for authentication and authorization.

Authentication. The testing or reconciliation of evidence of a user's identity. It establishes the user's identity and ensures that the users are who they say they are.

Accountability. A system's capability to determine the actions and behaviors of a single individual within a system and to identify that particular individual. Audit trails and logs support accountability.

Authorization. The rights and permissions granted to an individual or process that enable access to a computer resource. Once a user's identity and authentication are established, authorization levels determine the extent of system rights that a user can hold.

Privacy. The level of confidentiality and privacy protection given to a user in a system. This is often an important component of security controls. Privacy not only guarantees the fundamental tenet of confidentiality of a company's data, but also guarantees the data's level of privacy, which is being used by the operator.

NIST 33 Security Principles

In June 2001, the National Institute of Standards and Technology's (NIST) Information Technology Laboratory (ITL) published NIST Special Publication (SP) 800-27, "Engineering Principles for Information Technology Security (EP-ITS)" to assist in the secure design, development, deployment, and life cycle of information systems. It presents 33 security principles that start at the design phase of the information system or application and continue until the system's retirement and secure disposal. Some of the 33 principles that are most applicable to security management are*:

Principle 1. Establish a sound security policy as the foundation for design.

Principle 2. Treat security as an integral part of the overall system design.

---

*Source: NIST SP 800-27, "Engineering Principles for Information Technology Security (A Baseline for Achieving Security)," and "Federal Systems Level Guidance for Securing Information Systems," James Corrie, August 16, 2001.

Principle 5. Assume that external systems are insecure.

Principle 6. Identify potential trade-offs between reducing risk and increased costs and decreases in other aspects of operational effectiveness.

Principle 7. Implement layered security; ensure there is no single point of vulnerability (see sidebar).

Principle 11. Minimize the system elements to be trusted.

Principle 16. Isolate public access systems from mission critical resources (e.g., data, processes, etc.).

Principle 17. Use boundary mechanisms to separate computing systems and network infrastructures.

Principle 22. Authenticate users and processes to ensure appropriate access control decisions both within and across domains.

Principle 23. Use unique identities to ensure accountability.

Principle 24. Implement least privilege.

Trade-Off Analysis (TOA)

The simplest examples of a trade-off analysis are the choices we make every minute of every day, often subconsciously, weighing the pros and cons of any action and the benefit versus the cost of each decision. In security management, this cost versus benefit analysis is a very important process. The need for, or value of, a particular security control must be weighed against its impact or resource allocation drain and its usefulness. Any company can have exemplary security with an infinite budget, but there is always a point of diminishing returns, when the security demands interfere with the primary business. Making the financial case to upper management for various security controls is a very important part of a security manager's function.

Layered Security Architecture

Security designs should consider a layered approach to address or protect against a specific threat or to reduce vulnerability. For example, the use of a packet-filtering router in conjunction with an application gateway and an intrusion detection system combine to increase the work-factor an attacker must expend to successfully attack the system. The need for layered protections is important when commercial-off-the-shelf (COTS) products are used. The current state-of-the-art for security quality in COTS products does not provide a high degree of protection against sophisticated attacks. It is possible to help mitigate this situation by placing several controls in levels, requiring additional work by attackers to accomplish their goals.

(Source: NIST SP 800-27, "Engineering Principles for Information Technology Security (A Baseline for Achieving Security)")

A trade-off analysis can be formal or informal, depending upon the audience and the intent of the analysis. If the audience of the TOA is higher management or a client, often a formalized TOA, supported by objective evidence, documentation, and reports will be necessary. If the TOA is intended to be examined by internal staff or department, often it can be less formal. But the fundamental concepts and principles still apply in either case.

TOA Elements

The steps in a TOA are similar to the steps in the systems engineering methodology (see Chapter 11). The general steps in the TOA (formal or informal) are:

1. *Define the Objective*. The TOA is started by identifying the requirements that the solution must fulfill. These requirements can be expressed in terms of measures of effectiveness (MOEs).

2. *Identify Alternatives*. An effort must be made to identify the possible potential courses of action and include all promising candidate alternatives. Any course of action or possible candidate solution that fails to comply with any essential requirement should be rejected.

3. *Compare Alternatives*. The candidate solutions should be compared with one another with respect to each of the MOEs. The relative order of merit is judged by the cumulative rating of all the MOEs.

The detailed steps in a formal trade-off analysis process include:

1. Define the objectives.
2. Identify viable alternatives.
3. Define the selection criteria.
4. Assign weighing factors to selection criteria.
5. Assign value ratings for alternatives.
6. Calculate competitive scores.
7. Analyze the results.
8. Create the TOA report.

Objectives of Security Controls

The objective of security controls is to reduce vulnerabilities to a tolerable level and minimize the effect of an attack. To achieve this, the organization must determine the impact that an attack might have on an organization and the likelihood that the loss could occur. The process that analyzes various threat scenarios and produces a representative value for the estimated potential loss is constituted in the Risk Analysis (RA).

Controls function as countermeasures for vulnerabilities. There are many kinds, but generally they are categorized into four types*:

✦ *Deterrent controls* reduce the likelihood of a deliberate attack.

✦ *Preventative controls* protect vulnerabilities and make an attack unsuccessful or reduce its impact. Preventative controls inhibit attempts to violate security policy.

✦ *Corrective controls* reduce the effect of an attack.

✦ *Detective controls* discover attacks and trigger preventative or corrective controls. Detective controls warn of violations or attempted violations of security policy and include such controls as audit trails, intrusion detection methods, and checksums.

To visualize the effect of security controls, it might help to create a matrix, wherein the y-axis represents the level of impact of a realized threat and the x-axis represents the likelihood of the threat being realized. When the matrix is created, it produces the graph shown in Figure 1-2. A properly implemented control should move the plotted point from the upper right — the threat value defined before the control was implemented — to the lower left (that is, toward 0,0) after the control is implemented. This concept is also useful when determining a control's cost/benefit ratio.

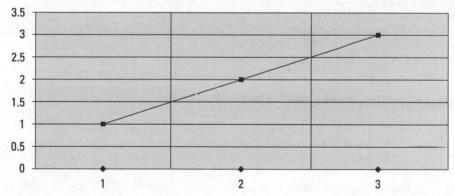

Figure 1-2: Simple threat matrix.

Therefore, an improperly designed or implemented control will show very little to no movement in the point before and after the control's implementation. The point's movement toward the 0,0 range could be so small (or in the case of badly designed controls, in the opposite direction) that it does not warrant the expense of implementation.

---

*Source: *Introduction to Risk Analysis*, C & A Security Risk Analysis Group and NIST Special Publication 800-30, "Risk Management Guide for Information Technology Systems."

OMB Circular A-130

The Office of Management and Budget Circular A-130, revised November 30, 2000, requires that a review of the security controls for each major government application be performed at least every three years. For general support systems, OMB Circular A-130 requires that the security controls either be reviewed by an independent audit or self review. Audits can be self-administered or independent (either internal or external). The essential difference between a self-audit and an independent audit is objectivity; however, some systems may require a fully independent review. More information on auditing can be found in Chapter 6.

The goal, the 0,0 point (no threat with no likelihood), is obviously impossible to achieve because a very unlikely threat could still exist and have some measurable impact. For example, the possibility that a flaming pizza delivery van will crash into the operations center is extremely unlikely; however, this situation would likely have a fairly serious impact on the availability of computing resources.

Information Classification Process

The first major process that we examine in this chapter is the concept of Information Classification. The Information Classification process is related to the domain of Business Continuity Planning and Disaster Recovery Planning because both focus on business risk and data valuation, yet it is still a fundamental concept in its own right — one that a CISSP candidate must understand.

Information Classification Objectives

There are several good reasons to classify information. Not all data has the same value to an organization. Some data is more valuable to the people who are making strategic decisions because it aids them in making long-range or short-range business direction decisions. Some data, such as trade secrets, formulas, and new product information, is so valuable that its loss could create a significant problem for the enterprise in the marketplace by creating public embarrassment or by causing a lack of credibility.

For these reasons, it is obvious that information classification has a higher, enterprise-level benefit. Information can have an impact on a business globally, not just on the business unit or line operation levels. Its primary purpose is to enhance confidentiality, integrity, and availability and to minimize the risks to the information. In addition, by focusing the protection mechanisms and controls on the information areas that need it the most, you achieve a more efficient cost-to-benefit ratio.

Information classification has the longest history in the government sector. Its value has long been established, and it is a required component when securing trusted systems. In this sector, information classification is used primarily to prevent the unauthorized disclosure of information and the resultant failure of confidentiality.

You can also use information classification to comply with privacy laws or to enable regulatory compliance. A company might wish to employ classification to maintain a competitive edge in a tough marketplace. There might also be sound legal reasons for a company to employ information classification, such as to minimize liability or to protect valuable business information.

Information Classification Benefits

In addition to the reasons mentioned previously, employing information classification has several clear benefits to an organization. Some of these benefits are as follows:

✦ Demonstrates an organization's commitment to security protections

✦ Helps identify which information is the most sensitive or vital to an organization

✦ Supports the tenets of confidentiality, integrity, and availability as it pertains to data

✦ Helps identify which protections apply to which information

✦ Might be required for regulatory, compliance, or legal reasons

Information Classification Concepts

The information that an organization produces or processes must be classified according to the organization's sensitivity to its loss or disclosure. These data owners are responsible for defining the sensitivity level of the data. This approach enables the security controls to be properly implemented according to the classification scheme.

Classification Terms

The following definitions describe several governmental data classification levels ranging from the lowest level of sensitivity to the highest:

1. *Unclassified.* Information designated as neither sensitive nor classified. The public release of this information does not violate confidentiality.

2. *Sensitive but Unclassified (SBU).* Information designated as a minor secret but might not create serious damage if disclosed. Answers to tests are an example of this kind of information. Health care information is another example of SBU data.

3. *Confidential.* Information designated to be of a confidential nature. The unauthorized disclosure of this information could cause some damage to the country's national security. This level applies to documents labeled between SBU and Secret in sensitivity.

4. *Secret*. Information designated of a secret nature. The unauthorized disclosure of this information could cause serious damage to the country's national security.

5. *Top Secret*. The highest level of information classification. The unauthorized disclosure of Top Secret information will cause exceptionally grave damage to the country's national security.

In all of these categories, in addition to having the appropriate clearance to access the information, an individual or process must have a "need to know" the information. Thus, an individual cleared for Secret or below is not authorized to access Secret material that is not needed for him or her to perform assigned job functions.

In addition, the following classification terms are also used in the private sector (see Table 1-1):

1. *Public*. Information that is similar to unclassified information; all of a company's information that does not fit into any of the next categories can be considered public. While its unauthorized disclosure may be against policy, it is not expected to impact seriously or adversely the organization, its employees, and/or its customers.

2. *Sensitive*. Information that requires a higher level of classification than normal data. This information is protected from a loss of confidentiality as well as from a loss of integrity due to an unauthorized alteration. This classification applies to information that requires special precautions to assure the integrity of the information by protecting it from unauthorized modification or deletion. It is information that requires a higher-than-normal assurance of accuracy and completeness.

3. *Private*. This classification applies to personal information that is intended for use within the organization. Its unauthorized disclosure could seriously and adversely impact the organization and/or its employees. For example, salary levels and medical information are considered private.

4. *Confidential*. This classification applies to the most sensitive business information that is intended strictly for use within the organization. Its unauthorized disclosure could seriously and adversely impact the organization, its stockholders, its business partners, and/or its customers. This information is exempt from disclosure under the provisions of the Freedom of Information Act or other applicable federal laws or regulations. For example, information about new product development, trade secrets, and merger negotiations is considered confidential.

An organization may use the high, medium, or low classification scheme based upon its C.I.A. needs and whether it requires high, medium, or low protective controls. For example, a system and its information may require a high degree of integrity and availability, yet have no need for confidentiality.

Table 1-1 Private/Commercial Sector Information Classification Scheme	
Definition	**Description**
Public Use	Information that is safe to disclose publicly
Internal Use Only	Information that is safe to disclose internally but not externally
Company Confidential	The most sensitive need-to-know information

The designated owners of information are responsible for determining data classification levels, subject to executive management review. Table 1-2 shows a simple H/M/L data classification for sensitive information.

Table 1-2 H/M/L Data Classification	
Category	**Description**
High	Could cause loss of life, imprisonment, major financial loss, or require legal remediation if the information is compromised.
Medium	Could cause noticeable financial loss if the information is compromised.
Low	Would cause only minor financial loss or require minor administrative action for correction if the information is compromised

(Source: NIST Special Publication 800-26, "Security Self-Assessment Guide for Information Technology Systems.")

Classification Criteria

Several criteria may be used to determine the classification of an information object:

Value. Value is the number one commonly used criteria for classifying data in the private sector. If the information is valuable to an organization or its competitors, it needs to be classified.

Age. The classification of information might be lowered if the information's value decreases over time. In the Department of Defense, some classified documents are automatically declassified after a predetermined time period has passed.

Useful Life. If the information has been made obsolete due to new information, substantial changes in the company, or other reasons, the information can often be declassified.

Personal Association. If information is personally associated with specific individuals or is addressed by a privacy law, it might need to be classified. For example, investigative information that reveals informant names might need to remain classified.

Information Classification Procedures

There are several steps in establishing a classification system. These are the steps in priority order:

1. Identify the administrator and data custodian.

2. Specify the criteria for classifying and labeling the information.

3. Classify the data by its owner, who is subject to review by a supervisor.

4. Specify and document any exceptions to the classification policy.

5. Specify the controls that will be applied to each classification level.

6. Specify the termination procedures for declassifying the information or for transferring custody of the information to another entity.

7. Create an enterprise awareness program about the classification controls.

Distribution of Classified Information

External distribution of classified information is often necessary, and the inherent security vulnerabilities will need to be addressed. Some of the instances when this distribution is necessary are as follows:

Court order. Classified information might need to be disclosed to comply with a court order.

Government contracts. Government contractors might need to disclose classified information in accordance with (IAW) the procurement agreements that are related to a government project.

Senior-level approval. A senior-level executive might authorize the release of classified information to external entities or organizations. This release might require the signing of a confidentiality agreement by the external party.

Information Classification Roles

The roles and responsibilities of all participants in the information classification program must be clearly defined. A key element of the classification scheme is the role that the users, owners, or custodians of the data play in regard to the data. These roles are important to remember.

Various officials and organizational offices are typically involved with computer security. They include the following groups:

✦ Senior management

✦ Program managers

✦ Application owners

✦ Computer security management

✦ Technology providers

✦ Supporting organizations

✦ Users

Senior management has the final responsibility through due care and due diligence to preserve the capital of the organization and further its business model through the implementation of a security program. While senior management does not have the functional role of managing security procedures, it has the ultimate responsibility to see that business continuity is preserved.

Owner

An information owner might be an executive or manager of an organization. This person is responsible for the information assets that must be protected. An owner is different from a custodian. The owner has the final corporate responsibility of data protection, and under the concept of due care the owner might be liable for negligence because of the failure to protect this data. The actual day-to-day function of protecting the data, however, belongs to a custodian.

The responsibilities of an information owner could include the following:

✦ Making the original decision about what level of classification the information requires, which is based upon the business needs for the protection of the data

✦ Reviewing the classification assignments periodically and making alterations as the business needs change

✦ Delegating the responsibility of the data protection duties to the custodian

The information owner for information stored within, processed by, or transmitted by a system may or may not be the same as the System Owner. Also, a single system may utilize information from multiple Information Owners. The Information Owner is responsible for establishing the rules for appropriate use and protection of the subject data/information (rules of behavior). The Information Owner retains that responsibility even when the data/information are shared with other organizations.*

---

*Source: NIST Special Publication 800-18, "Guide for Developing Security Plans for Information Technology Systems."

The System Owner is responsible for ensuring that the security plan is prepared and for implementing the plan and monitoring its effectiveness. The System Owner is responsible for defining the system's operating parameters, authorized functions, and security requirements.

Custodian

The owner of information delegates the responsibility of protecting that information to the information custodian. IT systems personnel commonly execute this role. The duties of a custodian might include the following:

✦ Running regular backups and routinely testing the validity of the backup data

✦ Performing data restoration from the backups when necessary

✦ Maintaining those retained records IAW the established information classification policy

The custodian might also have additional duties, such as being the administrator of the classification scheme.

User

In the information classification scheme, an end user is considered to be anyone (such as an operator, employee, or external party) who routinely uses the information as part of his or her job. This person can also be considered a consumer of the data — someone who needs daily access to the information to execute tasks. The following are a few important points to note about end users:

✦ Users must follow the operating procedures defined in an organization's security policy, and they must adhere to the published guidelines for its use.

✦ Users must take "due care" to preserve the information's security during their work (as outlined in the corporate information use policies). They must prevent "open view" from occurring (see sidebar).

✦ Users must use company computing resources only for company purposes and not for personal use.

Organizations should ensure an effective administration of users' computer access to maintain system security, including user account management, auditing, and the timely modification or removal of system access.* This includes:

User Account Management. Organizations should have a process for requesting, establishing, issuing, and closing user accounts, tracking users and their respective access authorizations, and managing these functions.

---

*Source: NIST Special Publication 800-14, "Generally Accepted Principles and Practices for Securing Information Technology Systems."

Management Reviews. It is necessary to periodically review user accounts. Reviews should examine the levels of access each individual has, conformity with the concept of least privilege, whether all accounts are still active, whether management authorizations are up-to-date, and whether required training has been completed.

Detecting Unauthorized/Illegal Activities. Mechanisms besides auditing and analysis of audit trails should be used to detect unauthorized and illegal acts, such as rotating employees in sensitive positions, which could expose a scam that required an employee's presence, or periodic re-screening of personnel.

Employee Termination

Although actually under the purview of Human Resources, it's important that the ISO understand the impact of employee terminations on the integrity of the computer systems. Normally there are two types of terminations, friendly and unfriendly, and both require specific actions.

Friendly terminations should be accomplished by implementing a standard set of procedures for outgoing or transferring employees.* This normally includes:

✦ The removal of access privileges, computer accounts, authentication tokens.

✦ The briefing on the continuing responsibilities for confidentiality and privacy.

✦ The return of company computing property, such as laptops.

✦ The continued availability of data. In both the manual and the electronic worlds this may involve documenting procedures or filing schemes, such as how documents are stored on the hard disk and how they are backed up. Employees should be instructed whether or not to "clean up" their PC before leaving.

✦ If cryptography is used to protect data, the availability of cryptographic keys to management personnel must be ensured.

Given the potential for adverse consequences during an unfriendly termination, organizations should do the following:

✦ System access should be terminated as quickly as possible when an employee is leaving a position under less-than-friendly terms. If employees are to be fired, system access should be removed at the same time (or just before) the employees are notified of their dismissal.

✦ When an employee notifies an organization of the resignation and it can be reasonably expected that it is on unfriendly terms, system access should be immediately terminated, or as soon as is feasible.

---

*Source: NIST Special Publication 800-14, "Generally Accepted Principles and Practices for Securing Information Technology Systems."

Open View

The term *open view* refers to the act of leaving classified documents in the open where an unauthorized person can see them, thus violating the information's confidentiality. Procedures to prevent open view should specify that information is to be stored in locked areas or transported in properly sealed containers, for example.

✦ During the *notice of termination* period, it may be necessary to assign the individual to a restricted area and function. This may be particularly true for employees capable of changing programs or modifying the system or applications.

✦ In some cases, physical removal from the offices may be necessary.

In either scenario, network access and system rights must be strictly controlled.

Security Policy Implementation

Security policies are the foundation of a sound security implementation. Often organizations will implement technical security solutions without first creating this foundation of policies, standards, guidelines, and procedures, unintentionally creating unfocused and ineffective security controls.

We discuss the following questions in this section:

✦ What are policies, standards, guidelines, and procedures?

✦ Why do we use policies, standards, guidelines, and procedures?

✦ What are the common policy types?

Policies, Standards, Guidelines, and Procedures

A policy is one of those terms that can mean several things. For example, there are security policies on firewalls, which refer to the access control and routing list information. Standards, procedures, and guidelines are also referred to as policies in the larger sense of a global information security policy.

A good, well-written policy is more than an exercise created on white paper — it is an essential and fundamental element of sound security practice. A policy, for example, can literally be a lifesaver during a disaster, or it might be a requirement of a governmental or regulatory function. A policy can also provide protection from liability due to an employee's actions, or it can control access to trade secrets.

NIST categorizes computer system security policies into three basic types:

✦ *Program policy*—used to create an organization's computer security program

✦ *Issue-specific policies*—used to address specific issues of concern to the organization

✦ *System-specific policies*—technical directives taken by management to protect a particular system

Program policies and issue-specific policies both address policy from a broad level, usually encompassing the entire organization. Program policy is traditionally more general and strategic; for example, the organization's overall computer security program may be defined in a program policy. An issue-specific policy is a nontechnical policy addressing a single or specific issue of concern to the organization, such as the procedural guidelines for checking disks brought to work or email privacy concerns. Issue-specific policies are similar to program policies, in that they are not technically focused.

However, program policy and issue-specific policies do not provide sufficient information or direction, for example, to be used in establishing an access control list or in training users on what actions are permitted. System-specific policies fill this need. A system-specific policy is technically focused and addresses only one computer system or device type.

Table 1-3 helps illustrate the difference between these three types of NIST policies.

Table 1-3 NIST Security Policy Types		
Policy Type	**Description**	**Example**
Program policy	High-level program policy	Senior-level management statement
Issue-specific policy	Addresses single issue	Email privacy policy
System-specific policy	Single-system directives	Router access control lists

(Source: National Institute of Standards and Technology, "An Introduction to Computer Security: The NIST Handbook Special Publication 800-12.")

Policy Types

In the corporate world, when we refer to specific polices rather than a group policy, we generally refer to those policies that are distinct from the standards, procedures, and guidelines. As you can see from the policy hierarchy chart in Figure 1-3, policies are considered the first and highest level of documentation, from which the lower level elements of standards, procedures, and guidelines flow. This order, however, does not mean that policies are more important than the lower elements. These higher-level policies, which are the more general policies and statements, should be created first in the process for strategic reasons, and then the more tactical elements can follow.

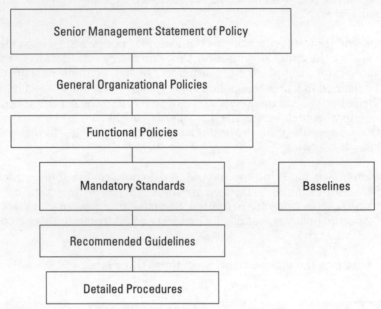

Figure 1-3: Security Policy Hierarchy.

Senior Management Statement of Policy. The first policy of any policy creation process is the Senior Management Statement of Policy. This is a general, high-level statement of a policy that contains the following elements:

- An acknowledgment of the importance of the computing resources to the business model
- A statement of support for information security throughout the enterprise
- A commitment to authorize and manage the definition of the lower-level standards, procedures, and guidelines

Regulatory. Regulatory policies are security policies that an organization must implement due to compliance, regulation, or other legal requirements. These companies might be financial institutions, public utilities, or some other type of organization that operates in the public interest. These policies are usually very detailed and are specific to the industry in which the organization operates.

Regulatory polices commonly have two main purposes:

1. To ensure that an organization is following the standard procedures or base practices of operation in its specific industry

2. To give an organization the confidence that it is following the standard and accepted industry policy

Advisory. Advisory policies are security polices that are not mandated to be followed but are strongly suggested, perhaps with serious consequences defined for failure to follow them (such as termination, a job action warning, and so forth). A company with such policies wants most employees to consider these policies mandatory. Most policies fall under this broad category.

Advisory policies can have many exclusions or application levels. Thus, these policies can control some employees more than others, according to their roles and responsibilities within that organization. For example, a policy that requires a certain procedure for transaction processing might allow for an alternative procedure under certain, specified conditions.

Informative. Informative policies are policies that exist simply to inform the reader. There are no implied or specified requirements, and the audience for this information could be certain internal (within the organization) or external parties. This does not mean that the policies are authorized for public consumption but that they are general enough to be distributed to external parties (vendors accessing an extranet, for example) without a loss of confidentiality.

Especially high visibility should be afforded the formal issuance of security policy. This is because nearly all employees at all levels will in some way be affected, major organizational resources will be addressed, and many new terms, procedures, and activities will be introduced.

Including security as a regular topic at staff meetings at all levels of the organization can be helpful. Also, providing visibility through such avenues as management presentations, panel discussions, guest speakers, question/answer forums, and newsletters can be beneficial.

Senior Management Commitment

Fundamentally important to any security program's success is the senior management's high-level statement of commitment to the information security policy process and the senior management's understanding of how important security controls and protections are to the enterprise's continuity. Senior management must be aware of the importance of security implementation to preserve the organization's viability (and for their own "due care" protection) and must publicly support that process throughout the enterprise.

Standards, Guidelines, and Procedures

The next level down from policies is the three elements of policy implementation: standards, guidelines, and procedures. These three elements contain the actual details of the policy, such as how it should be implemented and what standards and procedures should be used. They are published throughout the organization via manuals, the intranet, handbooks, or awareness classes.

It is important to know that standards, guidelines, and procedures are separate yet linked documents from the general polices (especially the senior-level statement). Unfortunately, companies will often create one document that satisfies the needs of all of these elements. This situation is not good. There are a few good reasons why they should be kept separate:

✦ Each of these elements serves a different function and focuses on a different audience. Also, physical distribution of the policies is easier.

✦ Security controls for confidentiality are different for each policy type. For example, a high-level security statement might need to be available to investors, but the procedures for changing passwords should not be available to anyone who is not authorized to perform the task.

✦ Updating and maintaining the policy is much more difficult when all the policies are combined into one voluminous document. Mergers, routine maintenance, and infrastructure changes all require that the policies be routinely updated. A modular approach to a policy document will keep the revision time and costs down.

Standards. Standards specify the use of specific technologies in a uniform way. This standardization of operating procedures can be a benefit to an organization by specifying the uniform methodologies to be used for the security controls. Standards are usually compulsory and are implemented throughout an organization for uniformity.

Guidelines. Guidelines are similar to standards; they refer to the methodologies of securing systems, but they are only recommended actions and are not compulsory. Guidelines are more flexible than standards and take into consideration the varying nature of the information systems. Guidelines can be used to specify the way standards should be developed, for example, or to guarantee the adherence to general security principles.

Procedures. Procedures embody the detailed steps that are followed to perform a specific task. Procedures are the detailed actions that personnel must follow. They are considered the lowest level in the policy chain. Their purpose is to provide detailed steps for implementing the policies, standards, and guidelines previously created. *Practices* is also a term that is frequently used in reference to procedures.

Baselines. Once a consistent set of baselines has been created, we can design the security architecture of an organization and develop standards. Baselines take into consideration the difference between various operating systems, for example, to ensure that the security is being uniformly implemented throughout the enterprise.

Roles and Responsibilities

Although members of an organization frequently wear multiple hats, defined roles and responsibilities are important in the security administration process. Also, roles and responsibilities are central to the *separation of duties* concept — the concept that security is enhanced through the division of responsibilities in the production cycle. Therefore, it is important that individual roles and responsibilities are clearly communicated and understood (see Table 1-4).

Table 1-4 Roles and Responsibilities	
Role	**Description**
Senior Manager	Has the ultimate responsibility for security
InfoSec Officer	Has the functional responsibility for security
Owner	Determines the data classification
Custodian	Preserves the information's CIA
User/Operator	Performs IAW the stated policies
Auditor	Examines security

Some of these roles are:

Senior Management. Executive or senior-level management is assigned the overall responsibility for the security of information. Senior management might delegate the function of security, but they are viewed as the end of the food chain when liability is concerned.

Information Systems Security Professionals. Information systems security professionals are delegated the responsibility for implementing and maintaining security by the senior-level management. Their duties include the design, implementation, management, and review of the organization's security policy, standards, guidelines, and procedures.

Data Owners. As we previously discussed in the section titled "Information Classification Roles," data owners are primarily responsible for determining the data's sensitivity or classification levels. They can also be responsible for maintaining the information's accuracy and integrity.

Users. As we previously discussed in the section titled "Information Classification Roles," users are responsible for following the procedures set out in the organization's security policy during the course of their normal daily tasks.

Information Systems Auditors. Information systems auditors are responsible for providing reports to the senior management on the effectiveness of the security controls by conducting regular, independent audits. They also examine whether the security policies, standards, guidelines, and procedures effectively comply with the company's stated security objectives.

Risk Management

A major component of InfoSec is Risk Management (RM). RM's main function is to mitigate risk. Mitigating risk means to reduce risk until it reaches a level that is acceptable to an organization. We can define RM as the identification, analysis, control, and minimization of loss that is associated with events.

The identification of risk to an organization entails defining the following basic elements:

✦ The actual threat

✦ The possible consequences of the realized threat

✦ The probable frequency of the occurrence of a threat

✦ The extent of how confident we are that the threat will happen

Many formulas and processes are designed to help provide some certainty when answering these questions. We should point out, however, that because life and nature are constantly evolving and changing, we cannot consider every possibility. RM tries as much as possible to see the future and to lower the possibility of threats impacting a company.

 Note   It's important to remember that the risk to an enterprise can never be totally eliminated; that would entail ceasing operations. Risk management means finding out what level of risk the enterprise can safely tolerate and still continue to function effectively.

Principles of Risk Management

The RM task process has several elements, primarily including the following:

✦ Performing a Risk Analysis, including the cost-benefit analysis of protections

✦ Implementing, reviewing, and maintaining protections

To enable this process, you will need to determine some properties of the various elements, such as the value of assets, threats, and vulnerabilities and the likelihood of events. A primary part of the RM process is assigning values to threats and estimating how often (or how likely) that threat will occur. To perform this task, several formulas and terms have been developed, and the CISSP candidate must fully understand them. The terms and definitions listed in the following section are ranked in the order that they are defined during the Risk Analysis (RA).

The Purpose of Risk Analysis

The main purpose of performing a Risk Analysis is to quantify the impact of potential threats — to put a price or value on the cost of a lost business functionality. The two main results of an RA — the identification of risks and the cost/benefit justification of the countermeasures — are vitally important to the creation of a risk mitigation strategy.

There are several benefits to performing an RA. It creates a clear cost-to-value ratio for security protections. It also influences the decision-making process dealing with hardware configuration and software systems design. In addition, it helps a company focus its security resources where they are needed most. Furthermore, it can influence planning and construction decisions, such as site selection and building design.

Terms and Definitions

The following are RA terms that the CISSP candidate will need to know:

> **Asset.** An asset is a resource, process, product, computing infrastructure, and so forth that an organization has determined must be protected. The loss of the asset could intangibly affect confidentiality, integrity, or availability, or it could have a tangible dollar value. It could also affect the ability of an organization to continue in business. The value of an asset is composed of all of the elements that are related to that asset — its creation, development, support, replacement, public credibility, considered costs, and ownership values.

> **Threat.** Simply put, the presence of any potential event that causes an undesirable impact on the organization is called a threat. As we will discuss in the Operations Domain, a threat could be man-made or natural and could have a small or large effect on a company's security or viability.

> **Vulnerability.** The absence or weakness of a safeguard constitutes a vulnerability. A minor threat has the potential to become a greater or more frequent threat because of a vulnerability. Think of a vulnerability as the threat that gets through a safeguard into the system. Combined with the terms asset and threat, vulnerability is the third part of an element that is called a *triple* in risk management.

> **Safeguard.** A safeguard is the control or countermeasure employed to reduce the risk associated with a specific threat or group of threats.

> **Exposure Factor (EF).** The EF represents the percentage of loss that a realized threat event would have on a specific asset. This value is necessary to compute the Single Loss Expectancy (SLE), which in turn is necessary to compute the Annualized Loss Expectancy (ALE). The EF can be a small percentage, such as the effect of a loss of some hardware, or a very large percentage, such as the catastrophic loss of all computing resources.

Single Loss Expectancy (SLE). An SLE is the dollar figure that is assigned to a single event. It represents an organization's loss from a single threat and is derived from the following formula:

Asset Value (\$) × Exposure Factor (EF) = SLE

For example, an asset valued at \$100,000 that is subjected to an exposure factor of 30 percent would yield an SLE of \$30,000. While this figure is defined primarily in order to create the Annualized Loss Expectancy (ALE), it is occasionally used by itself to describe a disastrous event for a Business Impact Assessment (BIA).

Annualized Rate of Occurrence (ARO). The ARO is a number that represents the estimated frequency with which a threat is expected to occur. The range for this value can be from 0.0 (never) to a large number (for minor errors, such as misspellings of names in data entry). How this number is derived can be very complicated. It is usually created based upon the likelihood of the event and the number of employees that could make that error occur. The loss incurred by this event is not a concern here, only how often it occurs.

For example, a meteorite damaging the data center could be estimated to occur only once every 100,000 years and will have an ARO of .00001. In contrast, 100 data entry operators attempting an unauthorized access attempt could be estimated at six times a year per operator and will have an ARO of 600.

Annualized Loss Expectancy (ALE). The ALE, a dollar value, is derived from the following formula:

Single Loss Expectancy (SLE) × Annualized Rate of Occurrence (ARO) = ALE

In other words, an ALE is the annually expected financial loss to an organization from a threat. For example, a threat with a dollar value of \$100,000 (SLE) that is expected to happen only once in 1,000 years (ARO of .001) will result in an ALE of \$100. This example helps to provide a more reliable cost-benefit analysis. Remember that the SLE is derived from the asset value and the Exposure Factor (EF). Table 1-5 shows these formulas.

Table 1-5
Risk Analysis Formulas

Concept	Derivation Formula
Exposure Factor (EF)	Percentage of asset loss caused by threat
Single Loss Expectancy (SLE)	Asset Value x Exposure Factor (EF)
Annualized Rate of Occurrence (ARO)	Frequency of threat occurrence per year
Annualized Loss Expectancy (ALE)	Single Loss Expectancy (SLE) x Annualized Rate of Occurrence (ARO)

Overview of Risk Analysis

We now discuss the four basic elements of the Risk Analysis process:

1. Quantitative Risk Analysis
2. Qualitative Risk Analysis
3. Asset Valuation Process
4. Safeguard Selection

Quantitative Risk Analysis

The difference between quantitative and qualitative RA is fairly simple: Quantitative RA attempts to assign independently objective numeric values (hard dollars, for example) to the components of the risk assessment and to the assessment of potential losses. Qualitative RA addresses more intangible values of a data loss and focuses on other issues, rather than on the pure, hard costs.

When all elements (asset value, impact, threat frequency, safeguard effectiveness, safeguard costs, uncertainty, and probability) are measured, rated, and assigned values, the process is considered to be fully quantitative. Fully quantitative risk analysis is not possible, however, because qualitative measures must always be applied. Thus, you should be aware that just because the figures look hard on paper does not mean it is possible to foretell the future with any certainty.

A quantitative risk analysis process is a major project, and as such it requires a project or program manager to manage the main elements of the analysis. A major part of the initial planning for the quantitative RA is the estimation of the time required to perform the analysis. In addition, you must also create a detailed process plan and assign roles to the RA team.

A Preliminary Security Examination (PSE) is often conducted before the actual quantitative RA. The PSE helps to gather the elements that you will need when the actual RA takes place. A PSE also helps to focus an RA. Elements that are defined during this phase include asset costs and values, a listing of various threats to an organization (in terms of threats to both the personnel and the environment), and documentation of the existing security measures. The PSE is normally then subject to a review by an organization's management before the RA begins.

Any combination of the following techniques can be used in gathering information relevant to the IT system within its operational boundary*:

> **Questionnaire.** The questionnaire should be distributed to the applicable technical and nontechnical management personnel who are designing or supporting the IT system.

---

*Source: NIST Special Publication 800-30, "Risk Management Guide for Information Technology Systems."

On-Site Interviews. On-site visits also allow risk assessment personnel to observe and gather information about the physical, environmental, and operational security of the IT system.

Document Review. Policy documents, system documentation, and security-related documentation can provide good information about the security controls used by and planned for the IT system.

Automated Scanning Tools. Proactive technical methods can be used to collect system information efficiently.

Risk Analysis Steps

The three primary steps in performing a risk analysis are similar to the steps in performing a Business Impact Assessment (see Chapter 8). A risk analysis is commonly much more comprehensive, however, and is designed to be used to quantify complicated, multiple-risk scenarios.

The three primary steps are as follows:

1. Estimate the potential losses to assets by determining their value.
2. Analyze potential threats to the assets.
3. Define the Annualized Loss Expectancy (ALE).

Estimate Potential Losses

To estimate the potential losses incurred during the realization of a threat, the assets must be valued by commonly using some sort of standard asset valuation process (we describe this task in more detail later). This process results in an assignment of an asset's financial value by performing the EF and the SLE calculations.

Analyze Potential Threats

Here, we determine what the threats are and how likely and often they are to occur. To define the threats, we must also understand the asset's vulnerabilities and perform an ARO calculation for the threat and vulnerabilities.

Automated Risk Analysis Products

There are several good automated risk analysis products on the market. The main objective of these products is to minimize the manual effort expended to create the risk analysis and to provide the capability to forecast expected losses quickly and with differing input variations. The creation of a database during an initial automated process enables the operator to rerun the analysis by using different parameters to create a what-if scenario. These products enable the users to perform calculations quickly in order to estimate future expected losses, thereby determining the benefit of their implemented safeguards.

All types of threats should be considered in this section, no matter whether they seem likely or not. It might be helpful to organize the threat listing into the types of threats by source or by their expected magnitude. In fact, some organizations can provide statistics on the frequency of various threats that occur in your area. In addition, the other domains of InfoSec discussed in this book have several varied listings of the categories of threats.

Some of the following categories of threats could be included in this section:

Data Classification. Data aggregation or concentration that results in data inference, covert channel manipulation, a malicious code/virus/Trojan horse/worm/logic bomb, or a concentration of responsibilities (lack of separation of duties).

Information Warfare. Technology-oriented terrorism, malicious code or logic, or emanation interception for military or economic espionage.

Personnel. Unauthorized or uncontrolled system access, misuse of technology by authorized users, tampering by disgruntled employees, or falsified data input.

Application/Operational. An ineffective security application that results in procedural errors or incorrect data entry.

Criminal. Physical destruction or vandalism, the theft of assets or information, organized insider theft, armed robbery, or physical harm to personnel.

Environmental. Utility failure, service outage, natural disasters, or neighboring hazards.

Computer Infrastructure. Hardware/equipment failure, program errors, operating system flaws, or a communications system failure.

Delayed Processing. Reduced productivity or a delayed funds collection that results in reduced income, increased expenses, or late charges.

Define the Annualized Loss Expectancy (ALE)

Once we have determined the SLE and ARO, we can estimate the ALE by using the formula that we previously described.

Results

After performing the Risk Analysis, the final results should contain the following:

✦ Valuations of the critical assets in hard costs

✦ A detailed listing of significant threats

✦ Each threat's likelihood and possible occurrence rate

✦ Loss potential by a threat — the dollar impact that the threat will have on an asset

✦ Recommended remedial measures and safeguards or countermeasures

Remedies

There are three generic remedies to risk that might take the form of either one or a combination of the following three:

Risk Reduction. Taking measures to alter or improve the risk position of an asset throughout the company

Risk Transference. Assigning or transferring the potential cost of a loss to another party (like an insurance company)

Risk Acceptance. Accepting the level of loss that will occur and absorbing that loss

The remedy chosen will usually be the one that results in the greatest risk reduction while retaining the lowest annual cost necessary to maintain a company.

Qualitative Risk Analysis

As we mentioned previously, a qualitative RA does not attempt to assign hard and fast costs to the elements of the loss. It is more scenario-oriented, and as opposed to a quantitative RA, a purely qualitative risk analysis is possible. Threat frequency and impact data are required to do a qualitative RA, however.

In a qualitative risk assessment, the seriousness of threats and the relative sensitivity of the assets are given a ranking, or qualitative grading, by using a scenario approach and creating an exposure rating scale for each scenario.

During a scenario description, we match various threats to identified assets. A scenario describes the type of threat and the assets facing potential loss and selects safeguards to mitigate the risk.

Qualitative Scenario Procedure

After the threat listing has been created, the assets for protection have been defined, and an exposure level rating is assigned, the qualitative risk assessment scenario begins. See Table 1-6 for a simple exposure rating scale.

Table 1-6
Simple Exposure Rating Level Scale

Rating Level	Exposure Percentage
Blank or 0	No measurable loss
1	20% loss
2	40% loss
3	60% loss
4	80% loss
5	100% loss

The procedures in performing the scenario are as follows:

✦ A scenario is written that addresses each major threat.

✦ The business unit managers review the scenario for a reality check.

✦ The RA team recommends and evaluates the various safeguards for each threat.

✦ The RA team works through each finalized scenario by using a threat, asset, and safeguard.

✦ The team prepares their findings and submits them to management.

After the scenarios have all been played out and the findings are published, management must implement the safeguards that were selected as being acceptable and begin to seek alternatives for the safeguards that did not work.

Asset Valuation Process

There are several elements of a process that determine the value of an asset. Both quantitative and qualitative RA (and Business Impact Assessment) procedures require a valuation to be made of the asset's worth to the organization. This valuation is a fundamental step in all security auditing methodologies. A common universal mistake made by organizations is not accurately identifying the information's value before implementing the security controls. This situation often results in a control that is ill suited for asset protection, is not financially effective, or is protective of the wrong asset. Table 1-7 demonstrates quantitative versus qualitative RA.

Table 1-7
Quantitative versus Qualitative RA

Property	Quantitative	Qualitative
Cost/benefit analysis	Yes	No
Financial hard costs	Yes	No
Can be automated	Yes	No
Guesswork involved	Low	High
Complex calculations	Yes	No
Volume of information required	High	Low
Time/work involved	High	Low
Ease of communication	High	Low

Reasons for Determining the Value of an Asset

Here are some additional reasons to define the cost or value that we previously described:

✦ The asset valuation is necessary to perform the cost-benefit analysis.

✦ The asset's value might be necessary for insurance reasons.

✦ The asset's value supports safeguard selection decisions.

✦ The asset valuation might be necessary to satisfy due care and prevent negligence and legal liability.

Elements that Determine the Value of an Asset

Three basic elements determine an information asset's value:

1. The initial and ongoing cost (to an organization) of purchasing, licensing, developing, and supporting the information asset

2. The asset's value to the organization's production operations, research and development, and business model viability

3. The asset's value established in the external marketplace and the estimated value of the intellectual property (trade secrets, patents, copyrights, and so forth)

Safeguard Selection Criteria

Once the risk analysis has been completed, safeguards and countermeasures must be researched and recommended. There are several standard principles that are used in the selection of safeguards to ensure that a safeguard is properly matched to a threat and to ensure that a given safeguard most efficiently implements the necessary controls. Important criteria must be examined before selecting an effective countermeasure.

Cost-Benefit Analysis

The number one safeguard selection criteria is the cost effectiveness of the control to be implemented, which is derived through the process of the cost-benefit analysis. To determine the total cost of the safeguard, many elements need to be considered (including the following):

✦ The purchase, development, and/or licensing costs of the safeguard

✦ The physical installation costs and the disruption to normal production during the installation and testing of the safeguard

✦ Normal operating costs, resource allocation, and maintenance/repair costs

The simplest calculation to compute a cost-benefit for a given safeguard is as follows:

(ALE before safeguard implementation) – (ALE after safeguard implementation) – (annual safeguard cost) = value of safeguard to the organization

For example, if an ALE of a threat has been determined to be $10,000, the ALE after the safeguard implementation is $1,000, and the annual cost to operate the safeguard totals $500, then the value of a given safeguard is thought to be $8,500 annually. This amount is then compared against the startup costs, and the benefit or lack of benefit is determined.

This value can be derived for a single safeguard or can be derived for a collection of safeguards though a series of complex calculations. In addition to the financial cost-benefit ratio, other factors can influence the decision of whether to implement a specific security safeguard. For example, an organization is exposed to legal liability if the cost to implement a safeguard is less than the cost resulting from the threat realized and the organization does not implement the safeguard.

Level of Manual Operations

The amount of manual intervention required to operate the safeguard is also a factor in the choice of a safeguard. In case after case, vulnerabilities are created due to human error or an inconsistency in application. In contrast, automated systems require fail-safe defaults to allow for manual shutdown capability in case a vulnerability occurs. The more automated a process, the more sustainable and reliable that process will be.

In addition, a safeguard should not be too difficult to operate, and it should not unreasonably interfere with the normal operations of production. These characteristics are vital for the acceptance of the control by operating personnel and for acquiring the all-important management support required for the safeguard to succeed.

Auditability and Accountability Features

The safeguard must allow for the inclusion of auditing and accounting functions. The safeguard must also have the capability for auditors to audit and test it, and its accountability must be implemented to effectively track each individual who accesses the countermeasure or its features.

Recovery Ability

The safeguard's countermeasure should be evaluated with regard to its functioning state after activation or reset. During and after a reset condition, the safeguard must provide the following:

✦ No asset destruction during activation or reset

✦ No covert channel access to or through the control during reset

✦ No security loss or increase in exposure after activation or reset

✦ No operator access or rights in the default state until the controls are fully operational

Back Doors

A back door, maintenance hook, or trap door is a programming element that gives application maintenance programmers access to the internals of the application, thereby bypassing the normal security controls of the application. While this function is valuable for the support and maintenance of a program, the security practitioner must be aware of these doors and provide a means of control and accountability during their use.

Vendor Relations

The credibility, reliability, and past performance of the safeguard vendor must be examined. In addition, the openness (open source) of the application programming should also be known in order to avoid any design secrecy that prevents later modifications or allows unknown applications to have a back door into the system. Vendor support and documentation should also be considered.

Security Awareness

Although this section is our last for this chapter, it is not the least important. Security awareness is often an overlooked element of security management because most of a security practitioner's time is spent on controls, intrusion detection, risk assessment, and proactively or reactively administering security.

It should not be that way, however. People are often the weakest link in a security chain because they are not trained or generally aware of what security is all about. Employees must understand how their actions, even seemingly insignificant actions, can greatly impact the overall security position of an organization.

Employees must be aware of the need to secure information and to protect the information assets of an enterprise. Operators need training in the skills that are required to fulfill their job functions securely, and security practitioners need training to implement and maintain the necessary security controls.

All employees need education in the basic concepts of security and its benefits to an organization. The benefits of the three pillars of security awareness training — awareness, training, and education — will manifest themselves through an improvement in the behavior and attitudes of personnel and through a significant improvement in an enterprise's security.

The purpose of computer security awareness, training, and education is to enhance security by:

✦ Improving awareness of the need to protect system resources

✦ Developing skills and knowledge so computer users can perform their jobs more securely

✦ Building in-depth knowledge, as needed, to design, implement, or operate security programs for organizations and systems

An effective computer security awareness and training program requires proper planning, implementation, maintenance, and periodic evaluation. In general, a computer security awareness and training program should encompass the following seven steps*:

1. Identify program scope, goals, and objectives.

2. Identify training staff.

3. Identify target audiences.

4. Motivate management and employees.

5. Administer the program.

6. Maintain the program.

7. Evaluate the program.

Making computer system users aware of their security responsibilities and teaching them correct practices helps users change their behavior. It also supports individual accountability because without the knowledge of the necessary security measures and to how to use them, users cannot be truly accountable for their actions.

Awareness

As opposed to training, security awareness refers to an organization's personnel being generally, collectively aware of the importance of security and security controls. In addition to the benefits and objectives we previously mentioned, security awareness programs also have the following benefits:

✦ Make a measurable reduction in the unauthorized actions attempted by personnel.

✦ Significantly increase the effectiveness of the protection controls.

✦ Help to avoid the fraud, waste, and abuse of computing resources.

---

*Source: NIST Special Publication 800-14, "Generally Accepted Principles and Practices for Securing Information Technology Systems."

The Need for User Security Training

All personnel using a system should have some kind of security training that is specific either to the controls employed or to general security concepts. Training is especially important for those users who are handling sensitive or critical data. The advent of the microcomputer and distributed computing has created an opportunity for the serious failures of confidentiality, integrity, and availability.

Personnel are considered "security aware" when they clearly understand the need for security, how security impacts viability and the bottom line, and the daily risks to computing resources.

It is important to have periodic awareness sessions to orient new employees and refresh senior employees. The material should always be direct, simple, and clear. It should be fairly motivational and should not contain a lot of techno-jargon, and you should convey it in a style that the audience easily understands. The material should show how the security interests of the organization parallel the interest of the audience and how they are important to the security protections.

Let's list a few ways that security awareness can be improved within an organization without a lot expense or resource drain:

Live/interactive presentations. Lectures, videos, and computer-based training (CBT).

Publishing/distribution. Posters, company newsletters, bulletins, and the intranet.

Incentives. Awards and recognition for security-related achievement.

Reminders. Login banner messages and marketing paraphernalia such as mugs, pens, sticky notes, and mouse pads.

One caveat here: It is possible to oversell security awareness and to inundate personnel with a constant barrage of reminders. This will most likely have the effect of turning off their attention. It is important to find the right balance of selling security awareness. An awareness program should be creative and frequently altered to stay fresh.

Training and Education

Training is different from awareness in that it utilizes specific classroom or one-on-one training. The following types of training are related to InfoSec:

✦ Security-related job training for operators and specific users

✦ Awareness training for specific departments or personnel groups with security-sensitive positions

✦ Technical security training for IT support personnel and system administrators

✦ Advanced InfoSec training for security practitioners and information systems auditors

✦ Security training for senior managers, functional managers, and business unit managers

In-depth training and education for systems personnel, auditors, and security professionals is very important and is considered necessary for career development. In addition, specific product training for security software and hardware is vital to the protection of the enterprise.

A good starting point for defining a security training program could be the topics of policies, standards, guidelines, and procedures that are in use at an organization. A discussion of the possible environmental or natural hazards or a discussion of recent common security errors or incidents — without blaming anyone publicly — could work. Motivating the students is always the prime directive of any training, and their understanding of the value of security's impact to the bottom line is also vital. A common training technique is to create hypothetical security vulnerability scenarios and then to get the students' input on the possible solutions or outcomes.

✦　　✦　　✦

Assessment Questions

You can find the answers to the following questions in Appendix A.

1. Which choice below is an incorrect description of a control?

    a. Detective controls discover attacks and trigger preventative or corrective controls.

    b. Corrective controls reduce the likelihood of a deliberate attack.

    c. Corrective controls reduce the effect of an attack.

    d. Controls are the countermeasures for vulnerabilities.

2. Which statement below is accurate about the reasons to implement a layered security architecture?

    a. A layered security approach is not necessary when using COTS products.

    b. A good packet-filtering router will eliminate the need to implement a layered security architecture.

    c. A layered security approach is intended to increase the work-factor for an attacker.

    d. A layered approach doesn't really improve the security posture of the organization.

3. Which choice below represents an application or system demonstrating a need for a high level of confidentiality protection and controls?

    a. Unavailability of the system could result in inability to meet payroll obligations and could cause work stoppage and failure of user organizations to meet critical mission requirements. The system requires 24-hour access.

    b. The application contains proprietary business information and other financial information, which if disclosed to unauthorized sources, could cause an unfair advantage for vendors, contractors, or individuals and could result in financial loss or adverse legal action to user organizations.

    c. Destruction of the information would require significant expenditures of time and effort to replace. Although corrupted information would present an inconvenience to the staff, most information, and all vital information, is backed up by either paper documentation or on disk.

    d. The mission of this system is to produce local weather forecast information that is made available to the news media forecasters and the general public at all times. None of the information requires protection against disclosure.

4. Which choice below is NOT a concern of policy development at the high level?

    a. Identifying the key business resources

    b. Identifying the type of firewalls to be used for perimeter security

    c. Defining roles in the organization

    d. Determining the capability and functionality of each role

5. Which choice below is NOT an accurate statement about the visibility of IT security policy?

    a. The IT security policy should not be afforded high visibility.

    b. The IT security policy could be visible through panel discussions with guest speakers.

    c. The IT security policy should be afforded high visibility.

    d. The IT security policy should be included as a regular topic at staff meetings at all levels of the organization.

6. Which question below is NOT accurate regarding the process of risk assessment?

    a. The likelihood of a threat must be determined as an element of the risk assessment.

    b. The level of impact of a threat must be determined as an element of the risk assessment.

    c. Risk assessment is the first process in the risk management methodology

    d. Risk assessment is the final result of the risk management methodology.

7. Which choice below would NOT be considered an element of proper user account management?

    a. Users should never be rotated out of their current duties.

    b. The users' accounts should be reviewed periodically.

    c. A process for tracking access authorizations should be implemented.

    d. Periodically re-screen personnel in sensitive positions.

8. Which choice below is NOT one of NIST's 33 IT security principles?

    a. Implement least privilege.

    b. Assume that external systems are insecure.

    c. Totally eliminate any level of risk.

    d. Minimize the system elements to be trusted.

9. How often should an independent review of the security controls be performed, according to OMB Circular A-130?

    a. Every year

    b. Every three years

    c. Every five years

    d. Never

10. Which choice below BEST describes the difference between the System Owner and the Information Owner?

    a. There is a one-to-one relationship between system owners and information owners.

    b. One system could have multiple information owners.

    c. The Information Owner is responsible for defining the system's operating parameters.

    d. The System Owner is responsible for establishing the rules for appropriate use of the information.

11. Which choice below is NOT a generally accepted benefit of security awareness, training, and education?

    a. A security awareness program can help operators understand the value of the information.

    b. A security education program can help system administrators recognize unauthorized intrusion attempts.

    c. A security awareness and training program will help prevent natural disasters from occurring.

    d. A security awareness and training program can help an organization reduce the number and severity of errors and omissions.

12. Who has the final responsibility for the preservation of the organization's information?

    a. Technology providers

    b. Senior management

    c. Users

    d. Application owners

13. Which choice below is NOT an example of an issue-specific policy?

    a. Email privacy policy

    b. Virus-checking disk policy

    c. Defined router ACLs

    d. Unfriendly employee termination policy

14. Which statement below is NOT true about security awareness, training, and educational programs?

   a. Awareness and training help users become more accountable for their actions.

   b. Security education assists management in determining who should be promoted.

   c. Security improves the users' awareness of the need to protect information resources.

   d. Security education assists management in developing the in-house expertise to manage security programs.

15. Which choice below is an accurate statement about standards?

   a. Standards are the high-level statements made by senior management in support of information systems security.

   b. Standards are the first element created in an effective security policy program.

   c. Standards are used to describe how policies will be implemented within an organization.

   d. Standards are senior management's directives to create a computer security program.

16. Which choice below is a role of the Information Systems Security Officer?

   a. The ISO establishes the overall goals of the organization's computer security program.

   b. The ISO is responsible for day-to-day security administration.

   c. The ISO is responsible for examining systems to see whether they are meeting stated security requirements.

   d. The ISO is responsible for following security procedures and reporting security problems.

17. Which statement below is NOT correct about safeguard selection in the risk analysis process?

   a. Maintenance costs need to be included in determining the total cost of the safeguard.

   b. The best possible safeguard should always be implemented, regardless of cost.

   c. The most commonly considered criteria is the cost effectiveness of the safeguard.

   d. Many elements need to be considered in determining the total cost of the safeguard.

18. Which choice below is usually the number-one-used criterion to determine the classification of an information object?

    a. Value

    b. Useful life

    c. Age

    d. Personal association

19. What are high-level policies?

    a. They are recommendations for procedural controls.

    b. They are the instructions on how to perform a Quantitative Risk Analysis.

    c. They are statements that indicate a senior management's intention to support InfoSec.

    d. They are step-by-step procedures to implement a safeguard.

20. Which policy type is MOST likely to contain mandatory or compulsory standards?

    a. Guidelines

    b. Advisory

    c. Regulatory

    d. Informative

21. What does an Exposure Factor (EF) describe?

    a. A dollar figure that is assigned to a single event

    b. A number that represents the estimated frequency of the occurrence of an expected threat

    c. The percentage of loss that a realized threat event would have on a specific asset

    d. The annual expected financial loss to an organization from a threat

22. What is the MOST accurate definition of a safeguard?

    a. A guideline for policy recommendations

    b. A step-by-step instructional procedure

    c. A control designed to counteract a threat

    d. A control designed to counteract an asset

23. Which choice MOST accurately describes the differences between standards, guidelines, and procedures?

   a. Standards are recommended policies, whereas guidelines are mandatory policies.

   b. Procedures are step-by-step recommendations for complying with mandatory guidelines.

   c. Procedures are the general recommendations for compliance with mandatory guidelines.

   d. Procedures are step-by-step instructions for compliance with mandatory standards.

24. What are the detailed instructions on how to perform or implement a control called?

   a. Procedures

   b. Policies

   c. Guidelines

   d. Standards

25. How is an SLE derived?

   a. (Cost – benefit) × (% of Asset Value)

   b. AV × EF

   c. ARO × EF

   d. % of AV – implementation cost

26. What is a noncompulsory recommendation on how to achieve compliance with published standards called?

   a. Procedures

   b. Policies

   c. Guidelines

   d. Standards

27. Which group represents the MOST likely source of an asset loss through inappropriate computer use?

   a. Crackers

   b. Hackers

   c. Employees

   d. Saboteurs

28. Which choice MOST accurately describes the difference between the role of a data owner versus the role of a data custodian?

    a. The custodian implements the information classification scheme after the initial assignment by the owner.

    b. The data owner implements the information classification scheme after the initial assignment by the custodian.

    c. The custodian makes the initial information classification assignments, whereas the operations manager implements the scheme.

    d. The custodian implements the information classification scheme after the initial assignment by the operations manager.

29. What is an ARO?

    a. A dollar figure assigned to a single event

    b. The annual expected financial loss to an organization from a threat

    c. A number that represents the estimated frequency of an occurrence of an expected threat

    d. The percentage of loss that a realized threat event would have on a specific asset

30. Which formula accurately represents an Annualized Loss Expectancy (ALE) calculation?

    a. $SLE \times ARO$

    b. Asset Value (AV) $\times EF$

    c. $ARO \times EF - SLE$

    d. % of $ARO \times AV$

Access Control Systems

The information security professional should be aware of access control requirements and their means of implementation to ensure a system's, confidentiality, integrity, and availability. In the world of networked computers, this professional should understand the use of access control in distributed as well as centralized architectures.

The professional should also understand the threats, vulnerabilities, and risks associated with the information system's infrastructure and the preventive and detective measures that are available to counter them. In addition, the InfoSec professional should understand the application of penetration testing tools.

Rationale

Controlling access to information systems and associated networks is necessary for the preservation of their confidentiality, integrity, and availability. Confidentiality ensures that the information is not disclosed to unauthorized persons or processes. We address integrity through the following three goals:

1. Prevention of the modification of information by unauthorized users

2. Prevention of the unauthorized or unintentional modification of information by authorized users

3. Preservation of the internal and external consistency:

   a. Internal consistency ensures that internal data is consistent. For example, assume that an internal database holds the number of units of a particular item in each department of an organization. The sum of the number of units in each department should equal the total number of units that the database has recorded internally for the whole organization.

b. External consistency ensures that the data stored in the database is consistent with the real world. Using the example previously discussed in (a), external consistency means that the number of items recorded in the database for each department is equal to the number of items that physically exist in that department.

Availability ensures that a system's authorized users have timely and uninterrupted access to the information in the system. The additional access control objectives are reliability and utility.

These and other related objectives flow from the organizational security policy. This policy is a high-level statement of management intent regarding the control of access to information and the personnel who are authorized to receive that information.

Three things that you must consider for the planning and implementation of access control mechanisms are the threats to the system, the system's vulnerability to these threats, and the risk that the threats might materialize. We further define these concepts as follows:

Threat. An event or activity that has the potential to cause harm to the information systems or networks

Vulnerability. A weakness or lack of a safeguard that can be exploited by a threat, causing harm to the information systems or networks

Risk. The potential for harm or loss to an information system or network; the probability that a threat will materialize

Controls

Controls are implemented to mitigate risk and reduce the potential for loss. Controls can be *preventive, detective,* or *corrective*. Preventive controls are put in place to inhibit harmful occurrences; detective controls are established to discover harmful occurrences; and corrective controls are used to restore systems that are victims of harmful attacks.

To implement these measures, controls can be administrative, logical or technical, and physical.

✦ Administrative controls include policies and procedures, security awareness training, background checks, work habit checks, a review of vacation history, and increased supervision.

✦ Logical or technical controls involve the restriction of access to systems and the protection of information. Examples of these types of controls are encryption, smart cards, access control lists, and transmission protocols.

✦ Physical controls incorporate guards and building security in general, such as the locking of doors, the securing of server rooms or laptops, the protection of cables, the separation of duties, and the backing up of files.

Controls provide accountability for individuals who are accessing sensitive information. This accountability is accomplished through access control mechanisms that require identification and authentication and through the audit function. These controls must be in accordance with and accurately represent the organization's security policy. Assurance procedures ensure that the control mechanisms correctly implement the security policy for the entire life cycle of an information system.

In general, a group of processes that share access to the same resources is called a *protection domain*.

Models for Controlling Access

Controlling access by a subject (an active entity such as an individual or process) to an object (a passive entity such as a file) involves setting up access rules. These rules can be classified into three categories or models:

Mandatory Access Control. The authorization of a subject's access to an object depends upon labels, which indicate the subject's *clearance*, and the *classification* or *sensitivity* of the object. For example, the military classifies documents as unclassified, confidential, secret, and top secret. Similarly, an individual can receive a clearance of confidential, secret, or top secret and can have access to documents classified at or below his or her specified clearance level. Thus, an individual with a clearance of "secret" can have access to secret and confidential documents with a restriction. This restriction is that the individual must have a *need to know* relative to the classified documents involved. Therefore, the documents must be necessary for that individual to complete an assigned task. Even if the individual is cleared for a classification level of information, the individual should not access the information unless there is a need to know. *Rule-based access control* is a type of mandatory access control because rules determine this access (such as the correspondence of clearance labels to classification labels), rather than the identity of the subjects and objects alone.

Discretionary Access Control. The subject has authority, within certain limitations, to specify what objects are accessible. For example, access control lists can be used. An access control list (ACL) is a list denoting which users have what privileges to a particular resource. For example, a *tabular listing* would show the subjects or users who have access to the object, FILE X, and what privileges they have with respect to that file. An *access control triple* consists of the user, program, and file with the corresponding access privileges noted for each user. This type of access control is used in local, dynamic situations where the subjects must have the discretion to specify what resources certain users are permitted to access. When a user within certain limitations has the right to alter the access control to certain objects, this is termed as user-directed discretionary access control. An identity-based access control is a type of discretionary access control based on an individual's identity. In some instances, a hybrid approach is used, which combines the features of user-based and identity-based discretionary access control.

Non-Discretionary Access Control. A central authority determines which subjects can have access to certain objects based on the organizational security policy. The access controls might be based on the individual's role in the organization (role-based) or the subject's responsibilities and duties (task-based). In an organization where there are frequent personnel changes, non-discretionary access control is useful because the access controls are based on the individual's role or title within the organization. These access controls do not need to be changed whenever a new person takes over that role. Another type of non-discretionary access control is *lattice-based access control*. In this type of control, a lattice model is applied. In a lattice model, there are pairs of elements that have the least upper bound of values and greatest lower bound of values. To apply this concept to access control, the pair of elements is the subject and object, and the subject has the greatest lower bound and the least upper bound of access rights to an object.

Access control can also be characterized as *context-dependent* or *content-dependent*. Context-dependent access control is a function of factors such as location, time of day, and previous access history. It is concerned with the environment or context of the data. In content-dependent access control, access is determined by the information contained in the item being accessed.

Control Combinations

By combining preventive and detective control types with administrative, technical (logical), and physical means of implementation, the following pairings are obtained:

✦ Preventive/administrative

✦ Preventive/technical

✦ Preventive/physical

✦ Detective/administrative

✦ Detective/technical

✦ Detective/physical

Next, we discuss these six pairings and the key elements that are associated with their control mechanisms.

Preventive/Administrative

In this pairing, we place emphasis on "soft" mechanisms that support the access control objectives. These mechanisms include organizational policies and procedures, pre-employment background checks, strict hiring practices, employment agreements, friendly and unfriendly employee termination procedures, vacation scheduling, labeling of sensitive materials, increased supervision, security aware-ness training, behavior awareness, and sign-up procedures to obtain access to information systems and networks.

Preventive/Technical

The preventive/technical pairing uses technology to enforce access control poli-cies. These technical controls are also known as logical controls and can be built into the operating system, can be software applications, or can be supplemental hardware/software units. Some typical preventive/technical controls are protocols, encryption, smart cards, biometrics (for authentication), local and remote access control software packages, call-back systems, passwords, constrained user inter-faces, menus, shells, database views, limited keypads, and virus scanning software. Protocols, encryption, and smart cards are technical mechanisms for protecting information and passwords from disclosure. Biometrics apply technologies such as fingerprint, retina, and iris scans to authenticate individuals requesting access to resources, and access control software packages manage access to resources hold-ing information from subjects local to the information system or from those at remote locations. *Callback systems* provide access protection by calling back the number of a previously authorized location, but this control can be compromised by call forwarding. Constrained user interfaces limit the functions that a user can select. For example, some functions might be "grayed-out" on the user menu and cannot be chosen. Shells limit the system-level commands that an individual or process can use. *Database views* are mechanisms that restrict the information that a user can access in a database. Limited keypads have a small number of keys that the user can select. Thus, the functions that are intended not to be accessible by the user are not represented on any of the available keys.

Preventive/Physical

Many preventive/physical measures are intuitive. These measures are intended to restrict the physical access to areas with systems holding sensitive information. A circular security perimeter that is under access control defines the area or zone to be protected. Preventive/physical controls include fences, badges, multiple doors (a man-trap that consists of two doors physically separated so that an individual can be "trapped" in the space between the doors after entering one of the doors), magnetic card entry systems, biometrics (for identification), guards, dogs, environ-mental control systems (temperature, humidity, and so forth), and building and access area layout. Preventive/physical measures also apply to areas that are used for storage of the backup data files.

Detective/Administrative

Several detective/administrative controls overlap with preventive/administrative controls because they can be applied for the prevention of future security policy violations or to detect existing violations. Examples of such controls are organiza-tional policies and procedures, background checks, vacation scheduling, the label-ing of sensitive materials, increased supervision, security awareness training, and behavior awareness. Additional detective/administrative controls are job rotation, the sharing of responsibilities, and reviews of audit records.

Detective/Technical

The detective/technical control measures are intended to reveal violations of security policy by using technical means. These measures include intrusion detection systems and automatically generated violation reports from audit trail information. These reports can indicate variations from "normal" operation or detect known signatures of unauthorized access episodes. In order to limit the amount of audit information flagged and reported by automated violation analysis and reporting mechanisms, clipping levels can be set. Using *clipping levels* refers to setting allowable thresholds on a reported activity. For example, a clipping level of three can be set for reporting failed logon attempts at a workstation. Three or fewer logon attempts by an individual at a workstation would not be reported as a violation, thus eliminating the need for reviewing normal logon entry errors.

Due to the importance of the audit information, audit records should be protected at the highest level of sensitivity in the system.

Detective/Physical

Detective/physical controls usually require a human to evaluate the input from sensors or cameras to determine whether a real threat exists. Some of these control types are motion detectors, thermal detectors, and video cameras.

Access Control Attacks

It is important for the information security professional to understand and identify the different types of access control attacks. These attacks are summarized in the following sections.

Denial of Service/Distributed Denial of Service (DoS/DDoS)

A *denial of service* attack consumes an information system's resources to the point where it cannot handle authorized transactions. A distributed DoS attack on a computing resource is launched from a number of other host machines. Attack software is usually installed on a large number of host computers, unbeknownst to their owners, and then activated simultaneously to launch communications to the target machine of such magnitude as to overwhelm the target machine.

Specific examples of DoS attacks are:

Buffer Overflow. A process receives much more data than expected. If the process has no programmed routine to deal with this excessive amount of data, it acts in an unexpected way that the intruder can exploit. A Ping of Death exploits ICMP by sending an illegal ECHO packet of >65K octets of data, which can cause an overflow of system variables and lead to a system crash.

SYN Attack. In this attack, an attacker exploits the use of the buffer space during a Transmission Control Protocol (TCP) session initialization handshake. The attacker floods the target system's small in-process queue with connection requests, but it does not respond when a target system replies to those requests. This causes the target system to time out while waiting for the proper response, which makes the system crash or become unusable.

Teardrop Attack. The length and fragmentation offset fields in sequential Internet Protocol (IP) packets are modified. The target system then becomes confused and crashes after it receives contradictory instructions on how the fragments are offset on these packets.

Smurf. This attack involves IP spoofing and ICMP to saturate a target network with traffic, thereby launching a DoS attack. It consists of three elements — the source site, the bounce site, and the target site. The attacker (the source site) sends a spoofed ping packet to the broadcast address of a large network (the bounce site). This modified packet contains the address of the target site. This causes the bounce site to broadcast the misinformation to all of the devices on its local network. All of these devices now respond with a reply to the target system, which is then saturated with those replies.

Back Door

A back door attack takes place using dial-up modems or asynchronous external connections. The strategy is to gain access to a network through bypassing of control mechanisms by getting in through a back door such as a modem.

Spoofing

Intruders use IP spoofing to convince a system that it is communicating with a known, trusted entity in order to provide the intruder with access to the system. IP spoofing involves an alteration of a packet at the TCP level, which is used to attack Internet-connected systems that provide various TCP/IP services. The attacker sends a packet with an IP source address of a known, trusted host instead of its own IP source address to a target host. The target host may accept the packet and act upon it.

Man-in-the-Middle

The man-in-the-middle attack involves an attacker, A, substituting his or her public key for that of another person, P. Then, anyone desiring to send an encrypted message to P using P's public key is unknowingly using A's public key. Therefore, A can read the message intended for P. A can then send the message on to P, encrypted in P's real public key and P will never be the wiser. Obviously, A could modify the message before resending it to P

Replay

The replay attack occurs when an attacker intercepts and saves old messages and then tries to send them later, impersonating one of the participants. One method of making this attack more difficult to accomplish is through the use of a random number or string called a *nonce*. If Bob wants to communicate with Alice, he sends a nonce along with the first message to Alice. When Alice replies, she sends the nonce back to Bob, who verifies that it is the one he sent with the first message. Anyone trying to use these same messages later will not be using the newer nonce. Another approach to countering the replay attack is for Bob to add a timestamp to his message. This timestamp indicates the time that the message was sent. Thus, if the message is used later, the timestamp will show that an old message is being used.

TCP Hijacking

As an example of this type of attack, an attacker hijacks a session between a trusted client and network server. The attacking computer substitutes its IP address for that of the trusted client and the server continues the dialog believing it is communicating with the trusted client. Simply stated, the steps in this attack are as follows:

1. Trusted client connects to network server.

2. Attack computer gains control of trusted client.

3. Attack computer disconnects trusted client from network server.

4. Attack computer replaces the IP address of trusted client with its own IP address and spoofs the client's sequence numbers.

5. Attack computer continues dialog with network server. (Network server believes it is still communicating with trusted client.)

Social Engineering

This attack uses social skills to obtain information such as passwords or PIN numbers to be used against information systems. For example, an attacker may impersonate someone in an organization and make phone calls to employees of that organization requesting passwords for use in maintenance operations. The following are additional examples of social engineering attacks:

✦ Emails to employees from a cracker requesting their passwords to validate the organizational database after a network intrusion has occurred

✦ Emails to employees from a cracker requesting their passwords because work has to be done over the weekend on the system

✦ Email or phone call from a cracker impersonating an official who is conducting an investigation for the organization and requires passwords for the investigation

✦ Improper release of medical information to individuals posing as doctors and requesting data from patients' records

✦ A computer repair technician convinces a user that the hard disk on his or her PC is damaged and unrepairable and installs a new hard disk for the user. The technician then takes the hard disk, extracts the information, and sells the information to a competitor or foreign government.

The best defense against social engineering attacks is an information security policy addressing such attacks and educating the users about these types of attacks.

Dumpster Diving

Dumpster diving involves the acquisition of information that is discarded by an individual or organization. In many cases, information found in trash can be very valuable to a cracker. Discarded information may include technical manuals, password lists, telephone numbers, and organization charts. It is important to note that one requirement for information to be treated as a trade secret is that the information be protected and not revealed to any unauthorized individuals. If a document containing an organization's trade secret information is inadvertently discarded and found in the trash by another person, the other person can use that information since it was not adequately protected by the organization.

Password Guessing

Because passwords are the most commonly used mechanism to authenticate users to an information system, obtaining passwords is a common and effective attack approach. Gaining access to a person's password can be obtained by physically looking around their desk for notes with the password, "sniffing" the connection to the network to acquire unencrypted passwords, social engineering, gaining access to a password database, or outright guessing. The last approach can be done in a random or systematic manner.

Brute Force

Brute force password guessing means just that, trying a random approach by attempting different passwords and hoping that one works. Some logic can be applied by trying passwords related to the person's name, job title, hobbies, or other similar items.

Dictionary Attack

A dictionary attack is one in which a dictionary of common passwords is used in an attempt to gain access to a user's computer and network. One approach is to copy an encrypted file that contains passwords and, applying the same encryption to a dictionary of commonly used passwords, compare the results.

Software Exploitation

Vulnerabilities in software can be exploited to gain unauthorized access to information systems' resources and data. Some examples of software exploitation are:

Novell Web Server. An attacker can cause a DoS buffer overflow by sending a large GET request to the remote administration port. This causes the data being sent to overflow the storage buffer and reside in memory as executable code.

AIX Operating System. Passwords can be exposed by diagnostic commands.

IRIX Operating System. A buffer overflow vulnerability enables an attacker to gain root access.

Windows 9x. A vulnerability enables an attacker to locate system and screen-saver passwords, thereby providing the attacker with means to gain unauthorized logon access.

Windows NT. Privilege exploitation software used by attacker can gain administrative access to the operating system.

Trojan Horses

Trojan Horses hide malicious code inside a host program that seems to do something useful. Once these programs are executed, the virus, worm, or other type of malicious code hidden in the Trojan horse program is released to attack the workstation, server, or network, or to allow unauthorized access to those devices. Trojans are common tools used to create backdoors into the network for later exploitation by crackers.

Trojan horses can be carried via Internet traffic such as FTP downloads or downloadable applets from Web sites, or distributed through email.

Common Trojan horses and ports are:

✦ Trinoo: ports 1524, 27444, 27665, 31335

✦ Back Orifice: port 31337

✦ NetBus: port 12345

✦ SubSeven: ports 1080, 1234, 2773

Some Trojans are programmed to open specific ports to allow access for exploitation. If a Trojan is installed on a system it often opens a high-numbered port. Then the open Trojan port could be scanned and located enabling an attacker to compromise the system. Malicious scanning is discussed later in this chapter.

System Scanning

No computer system connected to a public network is immune from malicious or indiscriminate scanning. System *scanning* is a process used to collect information about a device or network to facilitate an attack on the system. Attackers use it to discover what ports are open, what services are running, and what system software is being used. Scanning enables an attacker to more easily detect and exploit known vulnerabilities within a target machine.

Rather than an end in its own right, scanning is often one element of a network attack plan, consisting of:

Network Reconnaissance. Through scanning, an intruder can find out valuable information about the target network such as:

- Domain names and IP blocks
- Intrusion detection systems
- Running services
- Platforms and protocols
- Firewalls and perimeter devices
- General network infrastructure

Gaining System Access. Gaining access to a system can be achieved many ways, such as by:

- Session hijacking
- Password cracking
- Sniffing
- Direct physical access to an uncontrolled machine
- Exploiting default accounts
- Social engineering

Removing Evidence of the Attack. After the attack, traces of the attack can be eliminated by:

- Editing and clearing security logs
- Compromising the Syslog server
- Replacing system files by using rootkit tools
- Creating legitimate accounts
- Leaving backdoor Trojan viruses, such as SubSeven or NetBus

Security administrators should also use scanning to determine any evidence of compromise and identify vulnerabilities. Because scanning activity is often a prelude to a system attack, detecting malicious scans should be accompanied by monitoring and analysis of the logs and by blocking of unused and exposed ports.

Penetration Testing

Penetration testing can be employed in order to evaluate the resistance of an information system to attacks that can result in unauthorized access. In this approach, the robustness of an information system's defense in the face of a determined cracker is evaluated. The *penetration test*, or *ethical hacking* as it is sometimes known, is conducted to obtain a high level evaluation of a system's defense or to perform a detailed analysis of the information system's weaknesses. A penetration test can determine how a system reacts to an attack, whether or not a system's defenses can be breached, and what information can be acquired from the system. There are three general types of penetration tests:

1. *Full knowledge test.* The penetration testing team has as much knowledge as possible about the information system to be evaluated. This type of test simulates the type of attack that might be mounted by a knowledgeable employee of an organization.

2. *Partial knowledge test.* The testing team has knowledge that might be relevant to a specific type of attack. The testing personnel will be provided with some information that is related to the specific type of information vulnerability that is desired.

3. *Zero knowledge test.* The testing team is provided with no information and begins the testing by gathering information on its own initiative.

Another category used to describe penetration test types is open-box or closed-box testing. In an *open-box* test, the testing team has access to internal system code. Open box testing is appropriate for use against general-purpose operating systems such as Unix or Linux. Conversely, in *closed-box* testing, the testing team does not have access to internal code. This type of testing is applied to specialized systems that do not execute user code.

Obviously, the team conducting the penetration test must do so with approval of the sponsoring organization and ensure that the test does not go beyond the limits specified by the organization. The penetration test should never cause damage or harm to the information system or its data.

Penetration tests comprise the following phases:

1. *Discovery.* Information and data relevant to the organization and system to be evaluated is obtained through public channels, databases, Web sites, mail servers, and so on.

2. *Enumeration.* The penetration testing team works to acquire network information, versions of software running on the target system, IDs, user names, and so on.

3. *Vulnerability mapping.* The testing team profiles the information system environment and identifies its vulnerabilities.

4. *Exploitation.* The testing team attempts to exploit the system vulnerabilities and gain access privileges to the target system.

Identification and Authentication

Identification and authentication are the keystones of most access control systems. *Identification* is the act of a user professing an identity to a system, usually in the form of a logon ID to the system. Identification establishes user accountability for the actions on the system. *Authentication* is verification that the user's claimed identity is valid, and it is usually implemented through a user password at logon time. Authentication is based on the following three factor types:

> **Type 1.** Something you know, such as a personal identification number (PIN) or password.
>
> **Type 2.** Something you have, such as an ATM card or smart card.
>
> **Type 3.** Something you are (physically), such as a fingerprint or retina scan.

Sometimes a fourth factor, something you do, is added to this list. Something you do might be typing your name or other phrases on a keyboard. Conversely, something you do can be considered something you are.

Two-Factor Authentication refers to the act of requiring two of the three factors to be used in the authentication process. For example, withdrawing funds from an ATM machine requires a two-factor authentication in the form of the ATM card (something you have) and a PIN number (something you know).

Passwords

Passwords can be compromised and must be protected. In the ideal case, a password should be used only once. This "one-time password" provides maximum security because a new password is required for each new logon. A password that is the same for each logon is called a *static password*. A password that changes with each logon is termed a *dynamic password*. The changing of passwords can also fall between these two extremes. Passwords can be required to change monthly, quarterly, or at other intervals, depending on the criticality of the information needing protection and the password's frequency of use. Obviously, the more times a password is used, the more chance there is of it being compromised. A *passphrase* is a sequence of characters that is usually longer than the allotted number for a password. The passphrase is converted into a virtual password by the system.

Tokens in the form of credit card–sized memory cards or smart cards, or those resembling small calculators, supply static and dynamic passwords. These types of tokens are examples of something you have. An ATM card is a memory card that stores your specific information. *Smart cards* provide even more capability by incorporating additional processing power on the card. The following are the four types of smart cards:

✦ Static password tokens

- The owner authenticates himself to the token.
- The token authenticates the owner to an information system.

✦ Synchronous dynamic password tokens

- The token generates a new, unique password value at fixed time intervals (this password could be the time of day encrypted with a secret key).

- The unique password is entered into a system or workstation along with an owner's PIN.

- The authentication entity in a system or workstation knows an owner's secret key and PIN, and the entity verifies that the entered password is valid and that it was entered during the valid time window.

✦ Asynchronous dynamic password tokens

- This scheme is similar to the synchronous dynamic password scheme, except the new password is generated asynchronously and does not have to fit into a time window for authentication.

✦ Challenge-response tokens

- A workstation or system generates a random challenge string, and the owner enters the string into the token along with the proper PIN.

- The token generates a response that is then entered into the workstation or system.

- The authentication mechanism in the workstation or system then determines whether the owner should be authenticated.

In all these schemes, a front-end authentication device and a back-end authentication server, which services multiple workstations or the host, can perform the authentication.

Biometrics

An alternative to using passwords for authentication in logical or technical access control is *biometrics*. Biometrics is based on the Type 3 authentication mechanism—something you are. Biometrics is defined as an automated means of identifying or authenticating the identity of a living person based on physiological or behavioral characteristics. In biometrics, identification is a one-to-many search of an individual's characteristics from a database of stored images. Authentication in biometrics is a one-to-one search to verify a claim to an identity made by a person. Biometrics is used for identification in physical controls and for authentication in logical controls.

There are three main performance measures in biometrics:

False Rejection Rate (FRR) or Type I Error. The percentage of valid subjects that are falsely rejected.

False Acceptance Rate (FAR) or Type II Error. The percentage of invalid subjects that are falsely accepted.

Crossover Error Rate (CER). The percent in which the FRR equals the FAR.

Almost all types of detection permit a system's sensitivity to be increased or decreased during an inspection process. If the system's sensitivity is increased, such as in an airport metal detector, the system becomes increasingly selective and has a higher FRR. Conversely, if the sensitivity is decreased, the FAR will increase. Thus, to have a valid measure of the system performance, the CER is used. We show these concepts in Figure 2-1.

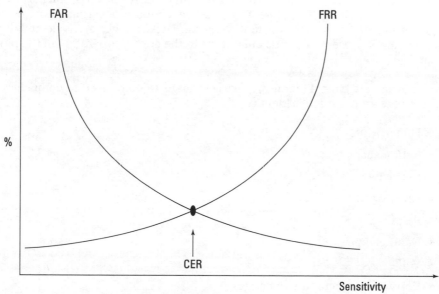

Figure 2-1: Crossover Error Rate (CER).

In addition to the accuracy of the biometric systems, there are other factors that must be considered. These factors include the enrollment time, the throughput rate, and acceptability. *Enrollment time* is the time that it takes to initially register with a system by providing samples of the biometric characteristic to be evaluated. An acceptable enrollment time is around two minutes. For example, in fingerprint systems the actual fingerprint is stored and requires approximately 250KB per finger for a high-quality image. This level of information is required for one-to-many searches in forensics applications on very large databases. In finger-scan technology, a full fingerprint is not stored; rather, the features extracted from this fingerprint are stored by using a small template that requires approximately 500 to 1,000 bytes of storage. The original fingerprint cannot be reconstructed from this template. Finger-scan technology is used for one-to-one verification by using smaller databases. Updates of the enrollment information might be required because some biometric characteristics, such as voice and signature, might change with time.

The *throughput rate* is the rate at which the system processes and identifies or authenticates individuals. Acceptable throughput rates are in the range of 10 subjects per minute. *Acceptability* refers to considerations of privacy, invasiveness, and psychological and physical comfort when using the system. For example, a concern with retina scanning systems might be the exchange of body fluids on the eyepiece. Another concern would be the retinal pattern, which could reveal changes in a person's health, such as diabetes or high blood pressure.

Collected biometric images are stored in an area referred to as a *corpus*. The corpus is stored in a database of images. Potential sources of error are the corruption of images during collection and mislabeling or other transcription problems associated with the database. Therefore, the image collection process and storage must be performed carefully with constant checking. These images are collected during the enrollment process and thus are critical to the correct operation of the biometric device.

The following are typical biometric characteristics that are used to uniquely authenticate an individual's identity:

✦ Fingerprints

✦ Retina scans

✦ Iris scans

✦ Facial scans

✦ Palm scans

✦ Hand geometry

✦ Voice

✦ Handwritten signature dynamics

Single Sign-On (SSO)

Single Sign-On (SSO) addresses the cumbersome situation of logging on multiple times to access different resources. A user must remember numerous passwords and IDs and might take shortcuts in creating passwords that might be open to exploitation. In SSO, a user provides one ID and password per work session and is automatically logged on to all the required applications. For SSO security, the passwords should not be stored or transmitted in the clear. SSO applications can run either on a user's workstation or on authentication servers. The advantages of SSO include having the ability to use stronger passwords, easier administration of changing or deleting the passwords, and requiring less time to access resources. The major disadvantage of many SSO implementations is that once a user obtains access to the system through the initial logon, the user can freely roam the network resources without any restrictions.

The Open Group has defined functional objectives in support of a user SSO interface. These objectives include the following:

✦ The interface shall be independent of the type of authentication information handled.

✦ It shall not predefine the timing of secondary sign-on operations.

✦ Support shall be provided for a subject to establish a default user profile.

Authentication mechanisms include items such as smart cards and magnetic badges. Strict controls must be placed to prevent a user from changing configurations that another authority sets. The scope of the Open Group SSO Standards is to define services in support of the following:

✦ "The development of applications to provide a common, single end-user sign-on interface for an enterprise"

✦ "The development of applications for the coordinated management of multiple user account management information bases maintained by an enterprise"

SSO can be implemented by using scripts that replay the users' multiple logins or by using authentication servers to verify a user's identity and encrypted authentication tickets to permit access to system services.

Enterprise Access Management (EAM) provides access control management services to Web-based enterprise systems that include SSO. SSO can be provided in a number of ways. For example, SSO can be implemented on Web applications residing on different servers in the same domain by using nonpersistent, encrypted cookies on the client interface. This task is accomplished by providing a cookie to each application that the user wishes to access. Another solution is to build a secure credential for each user on a reverse proxy that is situated in front of the Web server. The credential is then presented at each instance of a user attempting to access protected Web applications.

Kerberos, SESAME, KryptoKnight, and NetSP are authentication server systems with operational modes that can implement SSO.

Kerberos

Kerberos is a trusted, third party authentication protocol developed under Project Athena at the Massachusetts Institute of Technology (MIT). In Greek mythology, Kerberos is a three-headed dog that guards the entrance to the underworld.

Using symmetric key cryptography, Kerberos authenticates clients to other entities on a network of which a client requires services. The rationale and architecture behind Kerberos can be illustrated by using a university environment as an example. In such an environment, there are thousands of locations for workstations, local networks, and PC computer clusters. Client locations and computers are not secure; thus, one cannot assume that the cabling is secure. Messages, therefore, are not secure from interception. A few specific locations and servers can be secured, however, and can serve as trusted authentication mechanisms for every client and service on that network. These centralized servers implement the Kerberos-trusted Key Distribution Center (KDC), Kerberos Ticket Granting Service (TGS), and Kerberos Authentication Service (AS). Windows 2000 provides Kerberos implementations.

The basic principles of Kerberos operation are as follows:

1. The KDC knows the secret keys of all clients and servers on the network.

2. The KDC initially exchanges information with the client and server by using these secret keys.

3. Kerberos authenticates a client to a requested service on a server through TGS and by issuing temporary symmetric session keys for communications between the client and KDC, the server and the KDC, and the client and server.

4. Communication then takes place between the client and the server by using those temporary session keys.

Table 2-1 explains this detailed procedure using the Kerberos terminology and symbols.

Table 2-1 Kerberos Items and Symbols	
Kerberos Item	**Symbol**
Client	C
Client secret key	K_c
Client network address	A
Server	S
Client/TGS session key	$K_{c,\,tgs}$
TGS secret key	K_{tgs}
Server secret key	K_s
Client/server session key	$K_{c,\,s}$

Kerberos Item	Symbol
Client/TGS ticket	$T_{c,tgs}$
Client to server ticket	$T_{c,s}$
Client to server authenticator	$A_{c,s}$
Starting and ending time ticket is valid	V
Timestamp	T
M encrypted in secret key of x	$[M] K_x$
Ticket Granting Ticket	TGT
Optional, additional session key	Key

Kerberos Operation

Next, we examine in more detail the exchange of messages among the client, TGS Server, Authentication Server, and the server that is providing the service.

Client-TGS Server: Initial Exchange

To initiate a request for service from a server (or servers), the user enters an ID and password on the client workstation. The client temporarily generates the client's secret key (K_c) from the password by using a one-way hash function. (The one-way hash function performs a mathematical encryption operation on the password that cannot be reversed.) The client sends a request for authentication to the TGS server by using the client's ID in the clear. Note that no password or secret key is sent. If the client is in the Authentication Server database, the TGS server returns a client/TGS session key ($K_{c,tgs}$), which is encrypted in the secret key of the client, and a Ticket Granting Ticket (TGT) encrypted in the secret key (K_{tgs}) of the TGS server. Thus, neither the client nor any other entity except the TGS server can read the contents of the TGT because only the TGS server knows the K_{tgs}. The TGT consists of the client ID, the client network address, the starting and ending time that the ticket is valid (v), and the client/TGS session key. Symbolically, these initial messages from the TGS server to the client are represented as follows:

```
[K_c, tgs]K_c
TGT = [c, a, v, K_c, tgs]K_tgs
```

The client decrypts the message containing the session key ($K_{c,tgs}$) with its secret key (K_c) and now uses this session key to communicate with the TGS server. Then, the client erases its stored secret key to avoid compromising the secret key.

Client to TGS Server: Request for Service

When requesting access to a specific service on the network from the TGS server, the client sends two messages to the TGS server. In one message, the client submits the previously obtained TGT, which is encrypted in the secret key (K_{tgs}) of the TGS server, and an identification of the server (s) from which service is requested. The other message is an authenticator that is encrypted in the assigned session key ($K_{c, tgs}$). The authenticator contains the client ID, a timestamp, and an optional additional session key. These two messages are as follows:

```
TGT = s, [c, a, v, K_{c, tgs}]K_{tgs}
Authenticator = [c, t, key]K_{c, tgs}
```

TGS Server to Client: Issuing of Ticket for Service

After receiving a valid TGT and an authenticator from the client requesting a service, the TGS server issues a ticket ($T_{c, s}$) to the client that is encrypted in the server's secret key (K_s) and a client/server session key ($K_{c, s}$) that is encrypted in the client/TGS session key ($K_{c, tgs}$). These two messages are as follows:

```
Ticket T_{c, s} = s, [c, a, v, K_{c, s}]K_s
[K_{c, s}]K_{c, tgs}
```

Client to Server Authentication: Exchange and Providing of Service

To receive service from the server (or servers), the client sends the ticket ($T_{c, s}$) and an authenticator to the server. The server decrypts the message with its secret key (K_s) and checks the contents. The contents contain the client's address, the valid time window (v), and the client/server session key ($K_{c, s}$), which will now be used for communication between the client and server. The server also checks the authenticator, and if that timestamp is valid, it provides the requested service to the client. The client messages to the server are as follows:

```
Ticket T_{c, s} = s, [c, a, v, K_{c, s}]K_s
Authenticator = [c, t, key]K_{c, s}
```

Kerberos Vulnerabilities

Kerberos addresses the confidentiality and integrity of information. It does not directly address availability and attacks, such as frequency analysis. Furthermore, because all the secret keys are held and authentication is performed on the Kerberos TGS and the authentication servers, these servers are vulnerable to both physical attacks and attacks from malicious code. Replay can be accomplished on

Kerberos if the compromised tickets are used within an allotted time window. Because a client's password is used in the initiation of the Kerberos request for the service protocol, password guessing can be used to impersonate a client.

The keys used in the Kerberos exchange are also vulnerable. A client's secret key is stored temporarily on the client workstation and can be compromised as well as the session keys that are stored at the client's computer and at the servers.

SESAME

To address some of the weaknesses in Kerberos, the Secure European System for Applications in a multi-vendor Environment (SESAME) project uses public key cryptography for the distribution of secret keys and provides additional access control support. It uses the Needham-Schroeder protocol and a trusted authentication server at each host to reduce the key management requirements. SESAME employs the MD5 and crc32 one-way hash functions. In addition, SESAME incorporates two certificates or tickets. One certificate provides authentication as in Kerberos, and the other certificate defines the access privileges assigned to a client. One weakness in SESAME is that it authenticates by using only the first block of a message and not the complete message. SESAME is also subject to password guessing (like Kerberos).

KryptoKnight

The IBM KryptoKnight system provides authentication, SSO, and key distribution services. It was designed to support computers with widely varying computational capabilities. KryptoKnight uses a trusted Key Distribution Center (KDC) that knows the secret key of each party. One of the differences between Kerberos and KrytpoKnight is that there is a peer-to-peer relationship among the parties and the KDC. To implement SSO, the KDC has a party's secret key that is a one-way hash transformation of their password. The initial exchange from the party to the KDC is the user's name and a value, which is a function of a nonce (a randomly-generated, one-time use authenticator) and the password. The KDC authenticates the user and sends the user a ticket encrypted with the user's secret key. The user decrypts this ticket and can use it for authentication to obtain services from other servers on the system. NetSP is a product that is based on KryptoKnight and uses a workstation as an authentication server. NetSP tickets are compatible with a number of access control services, including the Resource Access Control Facility (RACF).

Access Control Methodologies

Access control implementations are as diverse as their requirements. However, access control can be divided into two domains: centralized access control and decentralized/distributed access control. In the following sections, we summarize the mechanisms to achieve both types.

Centralized Access Control

Dial-up users can use the standard Remote Authentication and Dial-In User Service (RADIUS). RADIUS incorporates an authentication server and dynamic passwords. Users can also use Callback. In Callback, a remote user dials in to the authentication server, provides an ID and password, and then hangs up. The authentication server looks up the caller's ID in a database of authorized users and obtains a phone number at a fixed location. (Note that the remote user must be calling from that location.) The authentication server then calls the phone number, the user answers, and then the user has access to the system. In some Callback implementations, the user must enter another password upon receiving a Callback. The disadvantage of this system is that the user must be at a fixed location whose phone number is known to the authentication server. A threat to Callback is that a cracker can arrange to have the call automatically forwarded to their number, enabling access to the system.

Another approach to remote access is the *Challenge Handshake Authentication Protocol* (CHAP). CHAP protects the password from eavesdroppers and supports the encryption of communication.

For networked applications, the *Terminal Access Controller Access Control System* (TACACS) employs a user ID and a static password for network access. TACACS+ provides even stronger protection through the use of tokens for two-factor, dynamic password authentication.

Decentralized/Distributed Access Control

A powerful approach to controlling the access of information in a decentralized environment is through the use of databases. In particular, the relational model developed by E. F. Codd of IBM (circa 1970) has been the focus of much research in providing information security. Other database models include models that are hierarchical, networked, object-oriented, and object-relational. The relational and object-relational database models support queries while the traditional file systems and the object-oriented database model do not. The object-relational and object-oriented models are better suited to managing complex data, such as what is required for computer-aided design and imaging. Because the bulk of information security research and development has focused on relational databases, this section emphasizes the relational model.

Relational Database Security

A relational database model has three parts:

✦ Data structures called tables or relations

✦ Integrity rules on allowable values and value combinations in the tables

✦ Operators on the data in the tables

A database can be defined as a persistent collection of interrelated data items. *Persistency* is obtained through the preservation of integrity and through the use of nonvolatile storage media. The description of the database is a *schema*, and a Data Description Language (DDL) defines the schema. A *database management system* (DBMS) is the software that maintains and provides access to the database. For security, you can set up the DBMS so that only certain subjects are permitted to perform certain operations on the database. For example, a particular user can be restricted to certain information in the database and will not be allowed to view any other information.

A *relation* is the basis of a relational database and is represented by a two-dimensional table. The rows of the table represent records or tuples, and the columns of the table represent the attributes. The number of rows in the relation is referred to as the cardinality, and the number of columns is the degree. The domain of a relation is the set of allowable values that an attribute can take. For example, a relation might be PARTS, as shown in Table 2-2, or ELECTRICAL ITEMS, as shown in Table 2-3.

Table 2-2
PARTS Relation

Part Number	Part Name	Part Type	Location
E2C491	Alternator	Electrical	B261
M4D326	Idle Gear	Mechanical	C418
E5G113	Fuel Gauge	Electrical	B561

Table 2-3
ELECTRICAL ITEMS Relation

Serial Number	Part Number	Part Name	Part Cost
S367790	E2C491	Alternator	$200
S785439	E5D667	Control Module	$700
S677322	E5W459	Window Motor	$300

In each table, a *primary key* is required. A primary key is a unique identifier in the table that unambiguously points to an individual tuple or record in the table. A primary key is a subset of candidate keys within the table. A *candidate key* is an attribute that is a unique identifier within a given table. In Table 2-2, for example, the primary key would be the Part Number. If the Location of the part in Table 2-2 were unique to that part, it might be used as the primary key. Then, the Part Numbers and Locations would be considered candidate keys and the primary key would be taken from one of these two attributes. Now, assume that the Part Number attributes in

Table 2-2 are the primary keys. If an attribute in one relation has values matching the primary key in another relation, this attribute is called a *foreign key*. A foreign key does not have to be the primary key of its containing relation. For example, the Part Number attribute E2C491 in Table 2-3 is a foreign key because its value corresponds to the primary key attribute in Table 2-2.

Entity and Referential Integrity

Continuing with the example, if we designate the Part Number as the primary key in Table 2-2, then each row in the table must have a Part Number attribute. If the Part Number attribute is NULL, then Entity Integrity has been violated. Similarly, the Referential Integrity requires that for any foreign key attribute, the referenced relation must have a tuple with the same value for its primary key. Thus, if the attribute E2C491 of Table 2-3 is a foreign key of Table 2-2, then E2C491 must be a primary key in Table 2-2 to hold the referential integrity. Foreign key to primary key matches are important because they represent references from one relation to another and establish the connections among these relations.

Relational Database Operations

A number of operations in a relational algebra are used to build relations and operate on the data. Five of these operations are primitives, and the other operations can be defined in terms of those five. Later, we discuss in greater detail some of the more commonly applied operations. The operations include the following:

- ✦ Select (primitive)
- ✦ Project (primitive)
- ✦ Union (primitive)
- ✦ Difference (primitive)
- ✦ Product (primitive)
- ✦ Join
- ✦ Intersection
- ✦ Divide
- ✦ Views

For clarification, the Select operation defines a new relation based on a formula (for example, all the electrical parts whose cost exceeds $300 in Table 2-3). The Join operation selects tuples that have equal numbers for some attributes; for example, in Tables 2-2 and 2-3, Serial Numbers and Locations can be joined by the common Part Number. The Union operation forms a new relation from two other relations (for example, for relations that we call X and Y, the new relation consists of each tuple that is in either X or Y or both).

An important operation related to controlling the access of database information is the View. A *View* is defined from the operations of Join, Project, and Select. A View does not exist in a physical form, and it can be considered as a virtual table that is derived from other tables. (A relation that actually exists in the database is called a *base relation*.) These other tables could be tables that exist within the database or previously defined Views. You can think of a View as a way to develop a table that is going to be frequently used although it might not physically exist within the database. Views can be used to restrict access to certain information within the database, to hide attributes, and to implement content-dependent access restrictions. Thus, an individual requesting access to information within a database will be presented with a View containing the information that the person is allowed to see. The View will then hide the information that individual is not allowed to see. In this way, the View can be thought of as implementing *Least Privilege*.

In developing a query of the relational database, an optimization process is performed. This process includes generating query plans and selecting the best (lowest in cost) of the plans. A *query pl*an is comprised ofimplementation procedures that correspond to each of the low-level operations in that query. The selection of the lowest-cost plan involves assigning costs to the plan. Costs might be a function of disk accesses and CPU usage.

In statistical database queries, a protection mechanism that is used to limit *inferencing* of information is the specification of a minimum query set size, but prohibiting the querying of all but one of the records in the database. This control thwarts an attack of gathering statistics on a query set size M, equal to or greater than the minimum query set size, and then requesting the same statistics on a query set size of M + 1. The second query set would be designed to include the individual whose information is being sought surreptitiously. When querying a database for statistical information, individually identifiable information should be protected. Thus, requiring a minimum size for the query set (greater than one) offers protection against gathering information on one individual.

A *bind* is also applied in conjunction with a plan to develop a query. A bind creates the plan and fixes or resolves the plan. Bind variables are placeholders for literal values in a Structured Query Language (SQL) query being sent to the database on a server. The SQL statement is sent to the server for parsing, and then later values are bound to the placeholders and sent separately to the server. This separate binding step is the origin of the term *bind variable*.

Data Normalization

Normalization is an important part of database design that ensures that attributes in a table depend only on the primary key. This process makes it easier to maintain data and to have consistent reports.

Normalizing data in the database consists of three steps:

1. Eliminating any repeating groups by putting them into separate tables

2. Eliminating redundant data (occurring in more than one table)

3. Eliminating attributes in a table that are not dependent on the primary key of that table

SQL

Developed at IBM, SQL is a standard data manipulation and relational database definition language. The SQL Data Definition Language creates and deletes views and relations (tables). SQL commands include Select, Update, Delete, Insert, Grant, and Revoke. The latter two commands are used in access control to grant and revoke privileges to resources. Usually, the owner of an object can withhold or transfer GRANT privileges related to an object to another subject. If the owner intentionally does not transfer the GRANT privilegesthat are relative to an object to the individual A, however, A cannot pass on the GRANT privileges to another subject. In some instances, though, this security control can be circumvented. For example, if A copies the object, A essentially becomes the owner of that object and thus can transfer the GRANT privileges to another user, such as user B.

SQL security issues include the granularity of authorization and the number of different ways you can execute the same query.

Object-Oriented Databases (OODB)

Relational database models are ideal for business transactions where most of the information is in text form. Complex applications involving multimedia, computer-aided design, video, graphics, and expert systems are more suited to an object-oriented database (OODB). For example, an OODB places no restrictions on the types or sizes of data elements, as is the case with relational databases. An OODB has the characteristics of ease of reusing code and analysis, reduced maintenance, and an easier transition from analysis of the problem to design and implementation. Its main disadvantages are a steep learning curve, even for experienced traditional programmers, and a high overhead of hardware and software required for development and operation.

Object-Relational Databases

The object-relational database is the marriage of object-oriented and relational technologies and combines the attributes of both. This model was introduced in 1992 with the release of the UniSQL/X unified relational and object-oriented database system. Hewlett Packard then released OpenODB (later called Odapter), which extended its AllBase relational Database Management System.

Intrusion Detection

An Intrusion Detection System (IDS) is a system that monitors network traffic or monitors host audit logs in order to determine whether any violations of an organization's security policy have taken place. An IDS can detect intrusions that have circumvented or passed through a firewall or that are occurring within the local area network behind the firewall.

A truly effective IDS will detect common attacks as they occur, which includes distributed attacks. This type of IDS is called a *network-based* IDS because it monitors network traffic in real time. Conversely, a *host-based* IDS resides on centralized hosts.

Network-Based IDS

A network-based IDS usually provides reliable, real-time information without consuming network or host resources. A network-based IDS is passive when acquiring data. Because a network-based IDS reviews packets and headers, it can also detect denial of service (DoS) attacks. Furthermore, because this IDS is monitoring an attack in real time, it can also respond to an attack in progress to limit damage.

A problem with a network-based IDS system is that it will not detect attacks against a host made by an intruder who is logged in at the host's terminal. If a network IDS along with some additional support mechanism determines that an attack is being mounted against a host, it is usually not capable of determining the type or effectiveness of the attack being launched.

Host-Based IDS

A host-based IDS can review the system and event logs in order to detect an attack on the host and to determine whether the attack was successful. (It is also easier to respond to an attack from the host.) Detection capabilities of host-based ID systems are limited by the incompleteness of most host audit log capabilities.

IDS Detection Methods

An IDS detects an attack through two major mechanisms: a signature-based ID or a statistical anomaly–based ID. These approaches are also termed Knowledge-based and Behavior-based ID, respectively, and are reinforced in Chapter 3.

Signature-Based ID

In a signature-based ID, signatures or attributes that characterize an attack are stored for reference. Then, when data about events are acquired from host audit logs or from network packet monitoring, this data is compared with the attack signature database. If there is a match, a response is initiated. A weakness of this approach is the failure to characterize slow attacks that extend over a long time period. To identify these types of attacks, large amounts of information must be held for extended time periods.

Another issue with signature-based IDs is that only attack signatures that are stored in their databases are detected.

Statistical Anomaly–Based ID

With this method, an IDS acquires data and defines a normal usage profile for the network or host that is being monitored. This characterization is accomplished by taking statistical samples of the system over a period of normal use. Typical characterization information used to establish a normal profile includes memory usage, CPU utilization, and network packet types. With this approach, new attacks can be detected because they produce abnormal system statistics. Some disadvantages of a statistical anomaly–based ID are that it will not detect an attack that does not significantly change the system operating characteristics, or it might falsely detect a non-attack event that has caused a momentary anomaly in the system.

Some Access Control Issues

As we discussed earlier in this chapter, the cost of access control must be commensurate with the value of the information being protected. The value of this information is determined through qualitative and quantitative methods. These methods incorporate factors such as the cost to develop or acquire the information, the importance of the information to an organization and its competitors, and the effect on the organization's reputation if the information is compromised.

Access control must offer protection from an unauthorized, unanticipated, or unintentional modification of information. This protection should preserve the data's internal and external consistency. The confidentiality of the information must also be similarly maintained, and the information should be available on a timely basis. These factors cover the integrity, confidentiality, and availability components of information system security.

Accountability is another facet of access control. Individuals on a system are responsible for their actions. This accountability property enables system activities to be traced to the proper individuals. Accountability is supported by audit trails that record events on the system and on the network. Audit trails can be used for intrusion detection and for the reconstruction of past events. Monitoring individual activities, such as keystroke monitoring, should be accomplished in accordance with the company policy and appropriate laws. Banners at logon time should notify the user of any monitoring being conducted.

The following measures compensate for both internal and external access violations:

✦ Backups

✦ RAID (Redundant Array of Independent Disks) technology

✦ Fault tolerance

✦ Business continuity planning

✦ Insurance

✦   ✦   ✦

Assessment Questions

You can find the answers to the following questions in Appendix A.

1. The goals of integrity do NOT include:

    a. Accountability of responsible individuals

    b. Prevention of the modification of information by unauthorized users

    c. Prevention of the unauthorized or unintentional modification of information by authorized users

    d. Preservation of internal and external consistency

2. Kerberos is an authentication scheme that can be used to implement:

    a. Public key cryptography

    b. Digital signatures

    c. Hash functions

    d. Single Sign-On (SSO)

3. The fundamental entity in a relational database is the:

    a. Domain

    b. Relation

    c. Pointer

    d. Cost

4. In a relational database, security is provided to the access of data through:

    a. Candidate keys

    b. Views

    c. Joins

    d. Attributes

5. In biometrics, a "one-to-one" search to verify an individual's claim of an identity is called:

    a. Audit trail review

    b. Authentication

    c. Accountability

    d. Aggregation

6. Biometrics is used for identification in the physical controls and for authentication in the:

    a. Detective controls

    b. Preventive controls

    c. Logical controls

    d. Corrective controls

7. Referential integrity requires that for any foreign key attribute, the referenced relation must have:

    a. A tuple with the same value for its primary key

    b. A tuple with the same value for its secondary key

    c. An attribute with the same value for its secondary key

    d. An attribute with the same value for its other foreign key

8. A password that is the same for each logon is called a:

    a. Dynamic password

    b. Static password

    c. Passphrase

    d. One-time pad

9. Which one of the following is NOT an access attack?

    a. Spoofing

    b. Back door

    c. Dictionary

    d. Penetration test

10. An attack that uses a detailed listing of common passwords and words in general to gain unauthorized access to an information system is BEST described as:

    a. Password guessing

    b. Software exploitation

    c. Dictionary attack

    d. Spoofing

11. A statistical anomaly–based intrusion detection system:

    a. Acquires data to establish a normal system operating profile

    b. Refers to a database of known attack signatures

    c. Will detect an attack that does not significantly change the system's operating characteristics

    d. Does not report an event that caused a momentary anomaly in the system

12. Which one of the following definitions BEST describes system scanning?

    a. An attack that uses dial-up modems or asynchronous external connections to an information system in order to bypass information security control mechanisms.

    b. An attack that is perpetrated by intercepting and saving old messages and then sending them later, impersonating one of the communicating parties.

    c. Acquisition of information that is discarded by an individual or organization

    d. A process used to collect information about a device or network to facilitate an attack on an information system

13. In which type of penetration test does the testing team have access to internal system code?

    a. Closed box

    b. Transparent box

    c. Open box

    d. Coding box

14. A standard data manipulation and relational database definition language is:

    a. OOD

    b. SQL

    c. SLL

    d. Script

15. An attack that can be perpetrated against a remote user's callback access control is:

    a. Call forwarding

    b. A Trojan horse

    c. A maintenance hook

    d. Redialing

16. The definition of CHAP is:

    a. Confidential Hash Authentication Protocol

    b. Challenge Handshake Authentication Protocol

    c. Challenge Handshake Approval Protocol

    d. Confidential Handshake Approval Protocol

17. Using symmetric key cryptography, Kerberos authenticates clients to other entities on a network and facilitates communications through the assignment of:

    a. Public keys

    b. Session keys

    c. Passwords

    d. Tokens

18. Three things that must be considered for the planning and implementation of access control mechanisms are:

    a. Threats, assets, and objectives

    b. Threats, vulnerabilities, and risks

    c. Vulnerabilities, secret keys, and exposures

    d. Exposures, threats, and countermeasures

19. In mandatory access control, the authorization of a subject to have access to an object is dependent upon:

    a. Labels

    b. Roles

    c. Tasks

    d. Identity

20. The type of access control that is used in local, dynamic situations where subjects have the ability to specify what resources certain users can access is called:

    a. Mandatory access control

    b. Rule-based access control

    c. Sensitivity-based access control

    d. Discretionary access control

21. Role-based access control is useful when:

    a. Access must be determined by the labels on the data.

    b. There are frequent personnel changes in an organization.

    c. Rules are needed to determine clearances.

    d. Security clearances must be used.

22. Clipping levels are used to:

    a. Limit the number of letters in a password.

    b. Set thresholds for voltage variations.

    c. Reduce the amount of data to be evaluated in audit logs.

    d. Limit errors in callback systems.

23. Identification is:

    a. A user being authenticated by the system

    b. A user providing a password to the system

    c. A user providing a shared secret to the system

    d. A user professing an identity to the system

24. Authentication is:

    a. The verification that the claimed identity is valid

    b. The presentation of a user's ID to the system

    c. Not accomplished through the use of a password

    d. Applied only to remote users

25. An example of two-factor authentication is:

    a. A password and an ID

    b. An ID and a PIN

    c. A PIN and an ATM card

    d. A fingerprint

26. In biometrics, a good measure of the performance of a system is the:

    a. False detection

    b. Crossover Error Rate (CER)

    c. Positive acceptance rate

    d. Sensitivity

27. In finger scan technology:

    a. The full fingerprint is stored.

    b. Features extracted from the fingerprint are stored.

    c. More storage is required than in fingerprint technology.

    d. The technology is applicable to large, one-to-many database searches.

28. An acceptable biometric throughput rate is:

    a. One subject per two minutes

    b. Two subjects per minute

    c. Ten subjects per minute

    d. Five subjects per minute

29. Which one of the following is NOT a type of penetration test?

    a. Sparse knowledge test

    b. Full knowledge test

    c. Partial knowledge test

    d. Zero knowledge test

30. Object-Oriented Database (OODB) systems:

    a. Are ideally suited for text-only information

    b. Require minimal learning time for programmers

    c. Are useful in storing and manipulating complex data, such as images and graphics

    d. Consume minimal system resources

Telecommunications and Network Security

The Telecommunications and Network Security domain is the most detailed and comprehensive domain of study for the CISSP test.

Caveat: If you're an experienced network engineer, some of this information may seem simplistic or out-of-date. This is not the latest and greatest network security info, but this information is what you'll need to know to study for the CISSP exam.

The professional should fully understand the following:

- ✦ Communications and network security as it relates to voice, data, multimedia, and facsimile transmissions in terms of local area, wide area, and remote access networks

- ✦ Communications security techniques to prevent, detect, and correct errors so that integrity, availability, and the confidentiality of transactions over networks may be maintained

- ✦ Internet/intranet/extranet in terms of firewalls, routers, gateways, and various protocols

- ✦ Communications security management and techniques, which prevent, detect, and correct errors so that the confidentiality, integrity, and availability of transactions over networks may be maintained

Domain Definition

The Telecommunications and Network Security domain includes the structures, transmission methods, transport formats, and security measures that provide confidentiality, integrity, availability, and authentication for transmissions over private and public communications networks and media. This domain is the information security domain that is concerned with protecting data, voice, and video communications, and ensuring the following:

> **Confidentiality.** Making sure that only those who are supposed to access the data can access it. Confidentiality is the opposite of *disclosure*.
>
> **Integrity.** Making sure that the data has not been changed due to an accident or malice. Integrity is the opposite of *alteration*.
>
> **Availability.** Making sure that the data is accessible when and where it is needed. Availability is the opposite of *destruction*.

The Telecommunications Security Domain of information security is also concerned with the prevention and detection of the misuse or abuse of systems, which poses a threat to the tenets of Confidentiality, Integrity, and Availability (C.I.A.).

The C.I.A. Triad

The fundamental information systems security concept of C.I.A. relates to the Telecommunications domain in the following three ways.

Confidentiality

Confidentiality is the prevention of the intentional or unintentional unauthorized disclosure of contents. Loss of confidentiality can occur in many ways. For example, loss of confidentiality can occur through the intentional release of private company information or through a misapplication of network rights.

Some of the elements of telecommunications used to ensure confidentiality are:

✦ Network security protocols

✦ Network authentication services

✦ Data encryption services

Integrity

Integrity is the guarantee that the message sent is the message received and that the message is not intentionally or unintentionally altered. Loss of integrity can occur either through an intentional attack to change information (for example, a Web site defacement) or by the most common type (data is altered accidentally by an operator). Integrity also contains the concept of nonrepudiation of a message source, which we will describe later.

Some of the elements used to ensure integrity are:

✦ Firewall services

✦ Communications Security Management

✦ Intrusion detection services

Availability

This concept refers to the elements that create reliability and stability in networks and systems. It ensures that connectivity is accessible when needed, allowing authorized users to access the network or systems. Also included in that assurance is the guarantee that security services for the security practitioner are usable when they are needed. The concept of availability also tends to include areas in Information Systems (IS) that are traditionally not thought of as pure security (such as guarantee of service, performance, and up time) yet are obviously affected by an attack like a Denial of Service (DoS).

Some of the elements that are used to ensure availability are:

✦ Fault tolerance for data availability, such as backups and redundant disk systems

✦ Acceptable logins and operating process performances

✦ Reliable and interoperable security processes and network security mechanisms

You should also know another point about availability: The use of ill-structured security mechanisms can also affect availability. Over-engineered or poorly designed security systems can impact the performance of a network or system as seriously as an intentional attack.

The C.I.A. triad is often represented by a triangle, as shown in Figure 3-1.

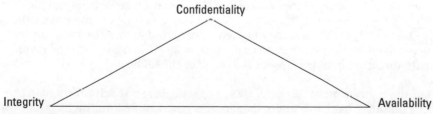

Figure 3-1: The C.I.A. triad.

Before we start to look at the various infrastructure devices and elements, we need to take a quick look at the OSI model and the TCP/IP protocol suite. These devices use many different protocols at varying OSI model layers, and the CISSP candidate will need to know one from another.

Protocols

In this section, we will examine the OSI and the TCP/IP layered models and the protocols that accompany each of these models.

A *protocol* is a standard set of rules that determine how computers communicate with each other across networks. When computers communicate with one another, they exchange a series of messages. A protocol describes the format that a message must take and the way in which computers must exchange messages. Protocols enable different types of computers, such as Macintosh, PC, Unix, and so on, to communicate in spite of their differences. They communicate by describing a standard format and communication method and by adhering to a layered architecture model.

The Layered Architecture Concept

Layered architecture is a conceptual blueprint of how communications should take place. It divides communication processes into logical groups called layers.

There are many reasons to use a layered architecture:

✦ To clarify the general functions of a communications process rather than focusing on the specifics of how to do it

✦ To break down complex networking processes into more manageable sublayers

✦ To enable interoperability by using industry-standard interfaces

✦ To change the features of one layer without changing all of the programming code in every layer

✦ To make for easier troubleshooting

How Data Moves through a Layered Architecture

Data is sent from a source computer to a destination computer. In a layered architecture model, the data passes downward through each layer from the highest layer (the Application Layer 7 in the OSI model) to the lowest layer (the Physical Layer 1 of the OSI model) of the source. It is then transmitted across the medium (cable) and is received by the destination computer, where it is passed up the layers in the opposite direction from the lowest (Layer 1) to the highest (Layer 7).

Each of the various protocols operates at specific layers. Each protocol in the source computer has a job to do: Each one is responsible for attaching its own unique information to the data packet when it comes through its own layer. When the data packet reaches the destination computer, it moves up the model. Each protocol on the destination computer also has a job to do: Each protocol detaches and examines only the data that was attached by its protocol counterpart at the source computer, then it sends the rest of the packet up the protocol stack to the next highest layer. Each layer at each destination sees and deals only with the data that was packaged by its counterpart on the sending side.

Layered Models

Layered models serve to enhance the development and management of a network architecture. While they primarily address issues of data communications, they also include some data processing activities at the upper layers. These upper layers address applications software processes, the presentation format, and the establishment of user sessions. Each independent layer of a network architecture addresses different functions and responsibilities. All of these layers work together to maximize the performance of the process and interoperability. Examples of the various functions addressed are data transfer, flow control, sequencing, error detection, and notification.

Open Systems Interconnect (OSI) Model

In the early 1980s, the Open Systems Interconnection (OSI) reference model was created by the International Standards Organization (ISO) to help vendors create interoperable network devices. The OSI reference model describes how data and network information are communicated from one computer through a network media to another computer.

The OSI reference model breaks this approach into seven distinct layers. Layering divides a piece of data into functional groups that permit an easier understanding of each piece of data. Each layer has a unique set of properties and directly interacts with its adjacent layers. The process of *data encapsulation* wraps data from one layer around a data packet from an adjoining layer.

The Seven Layers

The OSI reference model is divided into seven layers, which we will examine here. (I've always used the old chestnut: "All People Seem to Need Data Processing" (APSTNDP), to remember the names of the OSI layers.)

> **Application Layer (Layer 7).** The Application Layer of the OSI model supports the components that deal with the communication aspects of an application. The Application Layer is responsible for identifying and establishing the availability of the intended communication partner. It is also responsible for determining whether sufficient resources exist for the intended communication. This layer is the highest level and is the interface to the user. The following are some examples of Application Layer applications:
>
> - World Wide Web (WWW)
> - File Transfer Protocol (FTP)
> - Trivial File Transfer Protocol (TFTP)
> - Line Printer Daemon (LPD)
> - Simple Mail Transfer Protocol (SMTP)

Data Encapsulation

Data encapsulation is the process in which the information from one data packet is wrapped around or attached to the data of another packet. In the OSI reference model, each layer encapsulates the layer immediately above it as the data flows down the protocol stack. The logical communication, which happens at each layer of the OSI reference model, does not involve several physical connections because the information that each protocol needs to send is encapsulated within the protocol layer.

Presentation Layer (Layer 6). The Presentation Layer presents data to the Application Layer. It functions essentially as a translator, such as Extended Binary-Coded Decimal Interchange Code (EBCDIC) or American Standard Code for Information Interchange (ASCII). Tasks like data compression, decompression, encryption, and decryption are all associated with this layer. This layer defines how the applications can enter a network. When you are surfing the Web, most likely you are frequently encountering some of the following Presentation Layer standards:

- Hypertext Transfer Protocol (HTTP)
- Tagged Image File Format (TIFF) — A standard graphics format
- Joint Photographic Experts Group (JPEG) — Standard for graphics defined by the Joint Photographic Experts Group
- Musical Instrument Digital Interface (MIDI) — A format used for digitized music
- Motion Picture Experts Group (MPEG) — The Motion Picture Experts Group's standard for the compression and coding of motion video.

Session Layer (Layer 5). The Session Layer makes the initial contact with other computers and sets up the lines of communication. It formats the data for transfer between end nodes, provides session restart and recovery, and performs the general maintenance of the session from end to end. The Session Layer offers three different modes: simplex, half duplex, and full duplex. It also splits up a communication session into three different phases: connection establishment, data transfer, and connection release. Some examples of Session Layer protocols are:

- Network File System (NFS)
- Structured Query Language (SQL)
- Remote Procedure Call (RPC)

Transport Layer (Layer 4). The Transport Layer defines how to address the physical locations and/or devices on the network, how to make connections between nodes, and how to handle the networking of messages. It is responsible for maintaining the end-to-end integrity and control of the session. Services located in the Transport Layer both segment and reassemble the data from upper-layer applications and unite it onto the same data stream, which provides end-to-end data transport services and establishes a logical connection between the sending host and destination host on a network. The Transport Layer is also responsible for providing mechanisms for multiplexing upper-layer applications, session establishment, and the teardown of virtual circuits. Examples of Transport Layer protocols are:

- Transmission Control Protocol (TCP)
- User Datagram Protocol (UDP)
- Sequenced Packet Exchange (SPX)

Network Layer (Layer 3). The Network Layer defines how the small packets of data are routed and relayed between end systems on the same network or on interconnected networks. At this layer, message routing, error detection, and control of node data traffic are managed. The Network Layer's primary function is the job of sending packets from the source network to the destination network. Therefore, the Network Layer is primarily responsible for routing. Examples of Network Layer protocols are:

- Internet Protocol (IP)
- Open Shortest Path First (OSPF)
- Internet Control Message Protocol (ICMP)
- Routing Information Protocol (RIP)

Data Link Layer (Layer 2). The Data Link Layer defines the protocol that computers must follow in order to access the network for transmitting and receiving messages. Token Ring and Ethernet operate within this layer. This layer establishes the communications link between individual devices over a physical link or channel. It also ensures that messages are delivered to the proper device and translates the messages from layers above into bits for the Physical Layer to transmit. It also formats the message into data frames and adds a customized header that contains the hardware destination and source address. The Data Link Layer contains the Logical Link Control Sublayer and the Media Access Control (MAC) Sublayer. Bridging is a Data Link Layer function. Examples of Data Link Layer protocols are:

- Address Resolution Protocol (ARP)
- Serial Line Internet Protocol (SLIP)
- Point-to-Point Protocol (PPP)

Physical Layer (Layer 1). The Physical Layer defines the physical connection between a computer and a network and converts the bits into voltages or light impulses for transmission. It also defines the electrical and mechanical aspects of the device's interface to a physical transmission medium, such as twisted pair, coax, or fiber. Communications hardware and software drivers are found at this layer as well as electrical specifications, such as EIA-232 (RS-232) and Synchronous Optical NETwork (SONET). The Physical Layer has only two responsibilities: It sends bits and receives bits. Signal regeneration and repeating is primarily a Physical Layer function. The Physical Layer defines standard interfaces like:

- EIA/TIA-232 and EIA/TIA-449
- X.21
- High-Speed Serial Interface (HSSI)

OSI Security Services and Mechanisms

OSI defines six basic security services to secure OSI communications. A security service is a collection of security mechanisms, files, and procedures that help protect the network. They are:

1. Authentication
2. Access control
3. Data confidentiality
4. Data integrity
5. Nonrepudiation
6. Logging and monitoring

In addition, the OSI model defines eight security mechanisms. A security mechanism is a control that is implemented in order to provide the six basic security services. These are:

1. Encipherment
2. Digital signature
3. Access control
4. Data integrity
5. Authentication
6. Traffic padding
7. Routing control
8. Notarization

Transmission Control Protocol/Internet Protocol (TCP/IP)

Transmission Control Protocol/Internet Protocol (TCP/IP) is the common name for the suite of protocols originally developed by the Department of Defense (DoD) in the 1970s to support the construction of the Internet. The Internet is based on TCP/IP, which are the two best-known protocols in the suite. A CISSP candidate should be familiar with the major properties of TCP/IP and should know which protocols operate at which layers of the TCP/IP protocol suite.

Application Layer. This layer isn't really in TCP/IP; it's made up of whatever application is trying to communicate using TCP/IP. TCP/IP views everything above the three bottom layers as the responsibility of the application, so that the Application, Presentation, and Session Layers of the OSI model are considered folded into this top layer. Therefore, the TCP/IP suite primarily operates in the Transport and Network Layers of the OSI model.

Host-to-host layer. The host-to-host layer is comparable to the OSI Transport Layer. It defines protocols for setting up the level of transmission service. It provides for reliable end-to-end communications, ensures the error-free delivery of the data, handles packet sequencing of the data, and maintains the integrity of the data. The primary host-to-host layer protocols are:

- Transmission Control Protocol (TCP)
- User Datagram Protocol (UDP)

Internet layer. The Internet layer corresponds to the OSI Network Layer. It designates the protocols relating to the logical transmission of packets over the network. It gives network nodes an IP address and handles the routing of packets among multiple networks. It also controls the communication flow between hosts. The primary Internet layer protocols are:

- Internet Protocol (IP)
- Address Resolution Protocol (ARP)
- Reverse Address Resolution Protocol (RARP)
- Internet Control Message Protocol (ICMP)

Network access layer. At the bottom of the TCP/IP model, the network access layer monitors the data exchange between the host and the network. The equivalent of the Data-Link and Physical Layers of the OSI model, it oversees hardware addressing and defines protocols for the physical transmission of data.

TCP/IP Protocols

Let's look at the various protocols that populate the TCP/IP model. Table 3-1 lists some important TCP/IP protocols and their related layers.

Table 3-1 TCP/IP Protocols	
Layer	Protocol
Host-to-host	Transmission Control Protocol (TCP)
Host-to-host	User Datagram Protocol (UDP)
Internet	Internet Protocol (IP)
Internet	Address Resolution Protocol (ARP) I
Internet	Reverse Address Resolution Protocol (RARP)
Internet	Internet Control Message Protocol (ICMP)

Figure 3-2 shows OSI model layers mapped to their TCP/IP protocols.

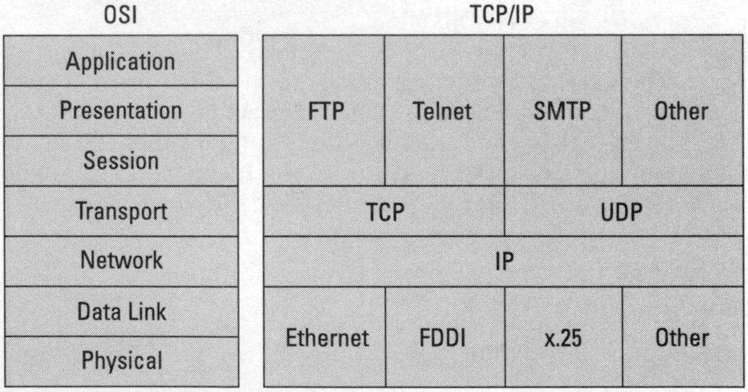

Figure 3-2: OSI model layers mapped to TCP/IP protocols.

Transmission Control Protocol (TCP)

TCP provides a full-duplex, connection-oriented, reliable connection. Incoming TCP packets are sequenced to match the original transmission sequence numbers. Because any lost or damaged packets are retransmitted, TCP is very costly in terms of network overhead and is slower than UDP. Reliable data transport is addressed by TCP to ensure that the following goals are achieved:

✦ An acknowledgment is sent back to the sender upon the reception of delivered segments.

✦ Any unacknowledged segments are retransmitted.

✦ Segments are sequenced back in their proper order upon arrival at their destination.

✦ A manageable data flow is maintained in order to avoid congestion, overloading, and data loss.

User Datagram Protocol (UDP)

UDP is similar to TCP but gives only a "best effort" delivery, which means it offers no error correction, does not sequence the packet segments, and does not care in which order the packet segments arrive at their destination. Consequently, it's referred to as an unreliable protocol.

UDP does not create a virtual circuit and does not contact the destination before delivering the data. Thus, it is also considered a connectionless protocol. UDP imposes much less overhead, however, which makes it faster than TCP for applications that can afford to lose a packet now and then, such as streaming video or audio. Table 3-2 illustrates the differences between the TCP and the UDP protocols.

TCP and UDP must use port numbers to communicate with the upper layers. Port numbers are used to keep track of the different conversations that are simultaneously crossing the network. Originating source port numbers dynamically assigned by the source host are usually some number greater than 1,023.

Table 3-2 TCP versus UDP Protocol	
TCP	*UDP*
Sequenced	Unsequenced
Connection-oriented	Connectionless
Reliable	Unreliable
High overhead	Low overhead
Slower	Faster

Connection-Oriented versus Connectionless Network Services

The traditional telephone-versus-letter example might help you to understand the difference between a TCP and a UDP. Calling someone on the phone is like TCP because you have established a virtual circuit with the party at the other end. That party may or may not be the person you want to speak to (or might be an answering machine), but you know whether or not you spoke to them. Alternatively, using UDP is like sending a letter. You write your message, address it, and mail it. This process is like UDP's connectionless property. You are not really sure it will get there, but you assume the post office will provide its best effort to deliver it.

Internet Protocol (IP)

All hosts on the Internet have a logical ID called an IP address. On the Internet, and in networks using the IP protocol, each data packet is assigned the IP address of the sender and the IP address of the recipient. Each device then receives the packet and makes routing decisions based upon the packet's destination IP address. Each device then receives the packet and makes routing decisions based upon the packet's destination IP address.

IP provides an unreliable datagram service, meaning that it does not guarantee that the packet will be delivered at all, that it will be delivered only once, or that it will be delivered in the order in which it was sent.

Address Resolution Protocol (ARP)

IP needs to know the hardware address of the packet's destination so it can send it. ARP is used to match an IP address to a Media Access Control (MAC) address. ARP allows the 32-bit IP address to be matched up with this hardware address.

A MAC address is a 6-byte, 12-digit hexadecimal number subdivided into two parts. The first three bytes (or first half) of the MAC address is the manufacturer's identifier (see Table 3.3). This can be a good troubleshooting aid if a network device is acting up, as it will isolate the brand of the failing device.*

---

*Source: *Mastering Network Security* by Chris Brenton (Sybex, 1999). The second half of the MAC address is the serial number the manufacturer has assigned to the device.

Table 3.3
Common Vendors' MAC Addresses

First Three Bytes	Manufacturer
00000C	Cisco
0000A2	Bay Networks
0080D3	Shiva
00AA00	Intel
02608C	3COM
080007	Apple
080009	Hewlett-Packard
080020	Sun
08005A	IBM

ARP interrogates the network by sending out a broadcast seeking a network node that has a specific IP address and then asking it to reply with its hardware address. ARP maintains a dynamic table (known as the ARP cache) of these translations between IP addresses and MAC addresses, so that it has to broadcast a request to every host only the first time it is needed. Figure 3-3 shows a flow chart of the ARP decision process.

Reverse Address Resolution Protocol (RARP)

In some cases the MAC address is known but the IP address needs to be discovered. This is sometimes the case when diskless machines are booted onto the network. The RARP protocol sends out a packet that includes its MAC address along with a request to be informed of which IP address should be assigned to that MAC address. A RARP server responds with the answer.

Internet Control Message Protocol (ICMP)

ICMP is a management protocol and messaging service provider for IP. ICMP's primary function is to send messages between network devices regarding the health of the network. It can inform hosts of a better route to a destination if there is trouble with an existing route, and it can help identify the problem with a route. PING is an ICMP utility used to check the physical connectivity of machines on a network.

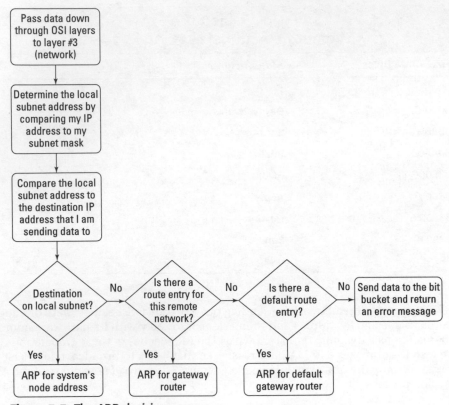

Figure 3-3: The ARP decision process.

Other TCP/IP Protocols

Telnet. Telnet's function is terminal emulation. It enables a user on a remote client machine to access the resources of another machine. Telnet's capabilities are limited to running applications; it cannot be used for downloading files.

File Transfer Protocol (FTP). FTP is the protocol that facilitates file transfer between two machines. FTP is also employed to perform file tasks. It enables access for both directories and files and can accomplish certain types of directory operations. However, FTP cannot execute remote files as programs.

Trivial File Transfer Protocol (TFTP). TFTP is a stripped-down version of FTP. TFTP has no directory-browsing abilities; it can do nothing but send and receive files. Unlike FTP, authentication does not occur, so it is insecure. Some sites choose not to implement TFTP due to the inherent security risks.

Network File System (NFS). NFS is the protocol that supports file sharing. It enables two different types of file systems to interoperate.

Simple Mail Transfer Protocol (SMTP). SMTP is the protocol/process used to send and receive Internet email. When a message is sent, it is sent to a mail queue. The SMTP server regularly checks the mail queue for messages and delivers them when they are detected.

Line Printer Daemon (LPD). The LPD daemon, along with the Line Printer (LPR) program, enables print jobs to be spooled and sent to a network's shared printers.

X Window. X Window defines a protocol for the writing of graphical user interface–based client/server applications.

Simple Network Management Protocol (SNMP). SNMP is the protocol that provides for the collection of network information by polling the devices on the network from a management station. This protocol can also notify network managers of any network events by employing agents that send an alert called a *trap* to the management station. The databases of these traps are called Management Information Bases (MIBs).

Bootstrap Protocol (BootP). When a diskless workstation is powered on, it broadcasts a BootP request to the network. A BootP server hears the request and looks up the client's MAC address in its BootP file. If it finds an appropriate entry, it responds by telling the machine its IP address and the file from which it should boot. BootP is an Internet Layer protocol.

LAN Technologies

A Local Area Network (LAN) (see Figure 3-4) is a discrete network that is designed to operate in a specific, limited geographic area like a single building or floor. LANs connect workstations and file servers together so that they can share network resources like printers, email, and files. LAN devices connect to one another by using a type of connection medium (such as copper wire or fiber optics), and they use various LAN protocols and access methods to communicate through LAN devices (such as bridges or routers). LANs can also be connected to a public switched network.

LAN media access methods control the use of a network (its Physical and Data Link Layers). Now, we will discuss the basic characteristics of Ethernet, ARCnet, Token Ring, and FDDI—the LAN technologies that account for virtually all deployed LANs.

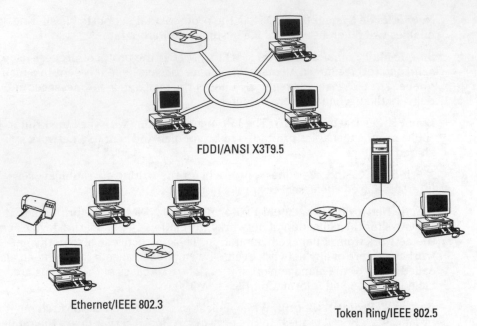

FDDI/ANSI X3T9.5

Ethernet/IEEE 802.3

Token Ring/IEEE 802.5

Figure 3-4: Local Area Networks (LANs).

Ethernet

The Ethernet media access method transports data to the LAN by using CSMA/CD. Currently, this term is often used to refer to all CSMA/CD LANs. Ethernet was designed to serve on networks with sporadic, occasionally heavy traffic requirements. Ethernet defines a BUS-topology LAN. Figure 3-5 shows an Ethernet network segment, and Table 3-4 lists the various Ethernet types.

Ethernet Segment

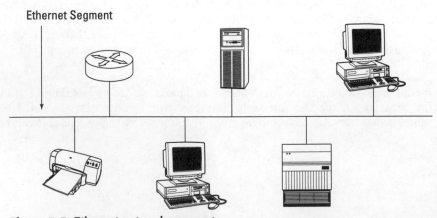

Figure 3-5: Ethernet network segment.

Table 3-4 Ethernet Types			
Ethernet Type	*Cable Type*	*Rated Speed*	*Rated Distance*
10Base2	Thinnet Coax	10 Mbps	185 meters
10Base5	Thicknet Coax	10 Mbps	500 Meters
10BaseT	UTP	10 Mbps	300 meters
100BaseT (TX, T4, Fast Ethernet)	UTP	100 Mbps	300 meters
1000BaseT (Gigabit Ethernet)	UTP	100 Mbps	300 meters

ARCnet

ARCnet is one of the earliest LAN technologies. It uses a token-passing access method in a STAR technology on coaxial cable. ARCnet provides predictable, if not fast, network performance. One issue with ARCnet stations is that the node address of each station has to be manually set during installation, thus creating the possibility of duplicate, conflicting nodes.

Token Ring

IBM originally developed the Token Ring network in the 1970s. It is second only to Ethernet in general LAN popularity. The term Token Ring refers both to IBM's Token Ring network and to IEEE 802.5 networks. All end stations are attached to a device called a Multistation Access Unit (MSAU). One station on a Token Ring network is designated the *active monitor*. The active monitor makes sure that there is not more than one token on the ring at any given time. If a transmitting station fails, it probably cannot remove a token as it makes it way back onto the ring. In this case, the active monitor will step in and remove the token and generate a new one.

Fiber Distributed Data Interface (FDDI)

Like Token Ring, FDDI is a token-passing media access topology. It consists of a dual Token Ring LAN that operates at 100 Mbps or more over fiber-optic cabling. FDDI employs a token-passing media access with dual counter-rotating rings, with only one ring active at any given time. If a break or outage occurs, the ring will then wrap back the other direction, keeping the ring intact. The following are the major advantages of FDDI:

✦ It can operate over long distances, at high speeds, and with minimal electromagnetic or radio frequency interference present.

✦ It provides predictable, deterministic delays and permits several tokens to be present on the ring concurrently.

Dueling Ethernets

Digital, Intel, and Xerox teamed up to create the original Ethernet I standard in 1980. In 1984, they followed up with the release of Ethernet II. The Institute of Electrical and Electronic Engineers (IEEE) founded the 802.3 subcommittee to create an Ethernet standard that was almost identical to the Ethernet II version. These two standards differ only in their descriptions of the Data Link Layer: Ethernet II has a "Type" field, whereas 802.3 has a "Length" field. Otherwise, both are the same in their Physical Layer specifications and MAC addressing.

The major drawbacks of FDDI are its expense and the expertise needed to implement it properly.

A variation of FDDI called Copper Distributed Data Interface (CDDI) uses a UTP cable to connect servers or other stations into the ring instead of using fiber optic cable. Unfortunately, this introduces the basic problems that are inherent with the use of copper cabling (length and interference problems).

Cabling Types

Network cabling commonly comes in three types: twisted pair, coaxial, and fiber optic, as shown in Figure 3-6.

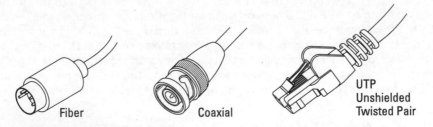

Fiber   Coaxial   UTP
Unshielded
Twisted Pair

Figure 3-6: Cabling types.

Coaxial Cable (Coax)

Coax consists of a hollow outer cylindrical conductor that surrounds a single, inner wire conductor. Two types of coaxial cable are currently used in LANs: 50-ohm cable, which is used for digital signaling, and 75-ohm cable, which is used for analog signaling and high-speed digital signaling. Coax requires fixed spacing between connections.

Coax is more expensive, yet it is more resistant to electromagnetic interference (EMI) than twisted pair cabling and can transmit at a greater bandwidth and distance. However, twisted pair cabling is so ubiquitous that most installations rarely use coax except in special cases, such as broadband communications.

Coax can come in two types for LANs:

1. *Thinnet* — (RG58 size)
2. *Thicknet* — (RG8 or RG11 size)

There are two common types of coaxial cable transmission methods:

1. *Baseband* — The cable carries only a single channel. Baseband is a transmission method that is accomplished by applying a direct current to a cable. The currents, or signals, hold binary information. Higher voltage usually represents the binary value of 1, whereas lower voltage represents the binary value of 0. Ethernet is baseband.
2. *Broadband* — The cable carries several usable channels, such as data, voice, audio, and video. Broadband includes leased lines (T1 and T3), ISDN, ATM, DSL, Broadband wireless, and CATV.

Baseband uses the full cable for its transmission, whereas broadband usually divides the cable into channels so that different types of data can be transmitted at the same time. Baseband permits only one signal to be transmitted at a time, whereas broadband carries several signals over different channels.

Twisted Pair

Twisted pair cabling is a relatively low-speed transmission medium, which consists of two insulated wires that are arranged in a regular spiral pattern. The wires can be shielded (STP) or unshielded (UTP). UTP cabling is a four-pair wire medium used in a variety of networks. UTP does not require the fixed spacing between connections that is necessary with coaxial-type connections.

UTP comes in several categories. The category rating is based on how tightly the copper cable is wound within the shielding: the tighter the wind, the higher the rating and its resistance against interference and attenuation. In fact, UTP Category 3 wire was often used for phone lines, but now the Category 5 wire is the standard, and even higher categories are available. Eavesdroppers can more easily tap UTP cabling than the other cable types. The categories of UTP are:

✦ **Category 1 UTP** — Used for telephone communications and not suitable for transmitting data

✦ **Category 2 UTP** — Specified in the EIA/TIA-586 standard to be capable of handling data rates of up to 4 million bits per second (Mbps)

✦ **Category 3 UTP** — Used in 10BaseT networks and specified to be capable of handling data rates of up to 10 Mbps

✦ **Category 4 UTP**—Used in Token Ring networks and can transmit data at speeds of up to 16 Mbps

✦ **Category 5 UTP**—Specified to be capable of handling data rates of up to 100 Mbps, and is currently the UTP standard for new installations

✦ **Category 6 UTP**—Specified to be capable of handling data rates of up to 155 Mbps

✦ **Category 7 UTP**—Specified to be capable of handling data rates of up to 1 billion bits per second (Gbps)

Table 3-5 shows the UTP categories and their rated performance.

Table 3-5
UTP Categories of Performance

UTP Cat	Rated Performance	Common Applications
Cat1	Under 1 MHz	Analog Voice, older ISDN BRI
Cat2	1 MHz	IBM 3270, AS/400/Apple LocalTalk
Cat3	16 MHz	!0BaseT, 4 Mbps Token Ring
Cat4	20 MHz	16 Mbps Token Ring
Cat5	100 MHz	100BaseT

Fiber-Optic Cable

Fiber-optic cable is a physical medium that is capable of conducting modulated light transmission. Fiber-optic cable carries signals as light waves, thus allowing higher transmission speeds and greater distances due to less attenuation. This type of cabling is much more difficult to tap than other cabling and is the most resistant to interference, especially EMI. It is sometimes called optical fiber.

Fiber-optic cable is usually reserved for the connections between backbone devices in larger networks. In some very demanding environments, however, fiber-optic cable connects desktop workstations to the network or links to adjacent buildings. Fiber-optic cable is the most reliable cable type, but it is also the most expensive to install and terminate.

Fiber-optic cable has three basic physical elements:

✦ *Core*—The core is the innermost transmission medium, which can be glass or plastic.

✦ *Cladding*—The next outer layer, the cladding is also made of glass or plastic but has different properties. It helps reflect the light back into the core.

✦ *Jacket*—The outermost layer, the jacket provides protection from heat, moisture, and other environmental elements.

Figure 3-7 shows a cross-section of a fiber optic-cable and its layers.

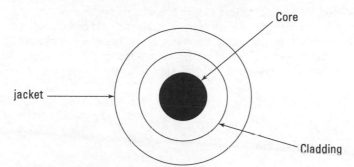

Figure 3-7: Fiber-optic cable cross-section.

Cabling Vulnerabilities

Failures and issues with cables often comprise a large part of the network's problems. The CISSP candidate should be aware of a few of them.

Coaxial cabling has two primary vulnerabilities: cable failure and length issues. All network devices attached to the same length of coax in a bus topology are vulnerable to disconnection from the network if the cable is broken or severed. This was one reason the star and ring topologies overtook the bus topology in installed base. Also, exceeding the specified effective cable length can be a source of cabling failures.

Twisted Pair cables currently have two categories in common usage: CAT3 and CAT5. The fundamental difference between these two types is how tightly the copper wires are wound. This tightness determines the cable's resistance to interference, the allowable distance it can be pulled between points, and the data's transmission speed before attenuation and crosstalk begins to affect the signal. CAT3 is an older specification with a shorter effective distance, and it can contribute to failure due to exceeding the specified effective cable length (100 meters in most cases).

UTP does not require the fixed spacing between connections that is necessary with some coaxial-type connections. UTP also is not as vulnerable to failure due to cable breaks as coax, but eavesdroppers can more easily tap UTP cabling than either coax or fiber.

Fiber-optic cable is immune to the effects of noise and electromagnetic interference (EMI) and therefore has a much longer effective usable length (up to 2 kilometers in some cases). It can carry a heavy load of activity much more easily than the copper types, and as such it is commonly used for infrastructure backbones, server farms, or connections that need large amounts of bandwidth. The primary drawbacks of this cable type are its cost of installation and the high level of expertise needed to have it properly terminated.

Asynchronous and Synchronous Communications

Asynchronous communication transfers data by sending bits of data sequentially. Start and stop bits mark the beginning and the end of each transfer. Communications devices must operate at the same speed to communicate asynchronously. Asynchronous communication is the basic language of modems and dial-up remote access systems. Synchronous communication is characterized by very high-speed transmission rates governed by electronic clock timing signals.

Cable failure terms to remember are:

✦ *Attenuation* — The loss of signal strength as the data travel through the cable. The higher the frequency and the longer the cable, the greater the risk of attenuation.

✦ *Crosstalk* — Because it uses less insulation than other cabling, UTP is more susceptible to crosstalk, a condition where the data signals mix.

✦ *Noise* — Environmental electromagnetic radiation from various sources can corrupt and interfere with the data signal.

Transmission Types

In addition, a CISSP candidate should know the difference between analog and digital transmission. Figure 3-8 shows the difference between an analog and digital signal, and Table 3-6 shows the difference between analog and digital technologies.

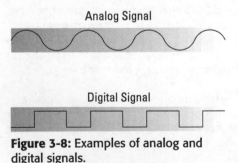

Figure 3-8: Examples of analog and digital signals.

Table 3-6 Analog versus Digital Technologies	
Analog	**Digital**
Infinite wave form	Saw-tooth wave form
Continuous signal	Pulses
Varied by amplification	On-off only

Network Topologies

A network topology defines the manner in which the network devices are organized to facilitate communications. A LAN topology defines this transmission manner for a Local Area Network. There are five common LAN topologies: BUS, RING, STAR, TREE, and MESH.

BUS

In a BUS topology, all the transmissions of the network nodes travel the full length of cable and are received by all other stations (see Figure 3-9). Ethernet primarily uses this topology. This topology does have some faults. For example, when any station on the bus experiences cabling termination errors, the entire bus can cease to function.

Figure 3-9: A BUS topology.

RING

In a RING topology, the network nodes are connected by unidirectional transmission links to form a closed loop (see Figure 3-10). Token Ring and FDDI both use this topology.

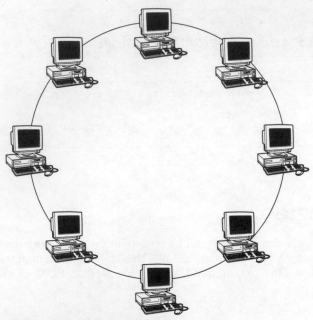

Figure 3-10: A RING topology.

STAR

In a STAR topology, the nodes of a network are connected directly to a central LAN device (see Figure 3-11). Here is where it gets a little confusing: The logical BUS and RING topologies that we previously described are often implemented physically in a STAR topology. Although Ethernet is logically thought of as a BUS topology (its first implementations were Thinnet and Thicknet on a BUS), 10BaseT is actually wired as a STAR topology, which provides more resiliency for the entire topology when a station experiences errors.

TREE

The TREE topology (as shown in Figure 3-12) is a BUS-type topology where branches with multiple nodes are possible.

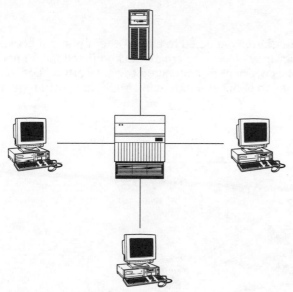

Figure 3-11: A STAR topology.

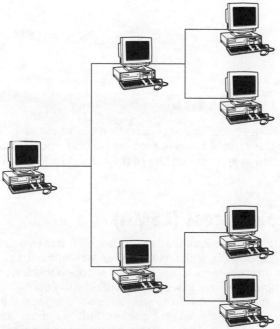

Figure 3-12: A TREE topology.

MESH

In a MESH topology, all the nodes are connected to every other node in a network (see Figure 3-13). This topology may be used to create backbone-redundant networks. A full MESH topology has every node connected to every other node. A partial MESH topology may be used to connect multiple full MESH networks together.

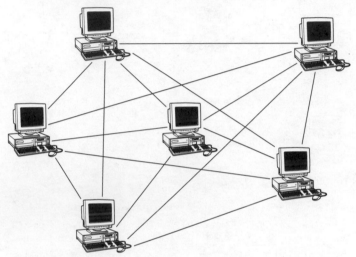

Figure 3-13: A MESH topology.

LAN Transmission Protocols

LAN Transmission Protocols are the rules for communication between computers on a LAN. These rules oversee the various steps in communicating, such as the formatting of the data frame, the timing and sequencing of packet delivery, and the resolution of error states.

Carrier-Sense Multiple Access (CSMA)

This is the foundation of the Ethernet communications protocol. It has two functional variations: CSMA/CA and CSMA/CD, which is the Ethernet standard. In CSMA, a workstation continuously monitors a line while waiting to send a packet, and then transmits the packet when it thinks the line is free. If the workstation doesn't receive an acknowledgment from the destination to which it sent the packet, it assumes a collision has occurred, and it resends the packet. This is defined as *persistent carrier sense*. Another version of CSMA is called *non-persistent carrier sense*, which is where a workstation waits a random amount of time before resending a packet, thus resulting in fewer errors.

Carrier-Sense Multiple Access with Collision Avoidance (CSMA/CA)

In this variation of CSMA, workstations are attached to two coaxial cables. Each coax cable carries data signals in one direction only. A workstation monitors its receive cable to determine whether the carrier is busy. It then communicates on its transmit cable if it detects no carrier. Thus, the workstation transmits its intention to send when it feels the line is clear due to a precedence that is based upon preestablished tables. Pure CSMA does not have a feature to avoid the problem of one workstation dominating a conversation.

Carrier-Sense Multiple Access with Collision Detection (CSMA/CD)

Under the Ethernet CSMA/CD media-access process, any computer on a CSMA/CD LAN can access the network at any time. Before sending data, CSMA/CD hosts listen for traffic on the network. A host wanting to send data waits until it does not detect any traffic before it transmits. Ethernet enables any host on a network to transmit whenever the network is quiet. In addition, the transmitting host constantly monitors the wire to make sure that no other hosts begin transmitting. If the host detects another signal on the wire, it then sends out an extended jam signal that causes all nodes on the segment to stop sending data. These nodes respond to that jam signal by waiting a bit before attempting to transmit again.

CSMA/CD was created to overcome the problem of collisions that occur when packets are simultaneously transmitted from different nodes. Collisions occur when two hosts listen for traffic, and upon hearing none they both transmit simultaneously. In this situation, both transmissions are damaged and the hosts must retransmit at a later time.

Polling

In the polling transmission method, a primary workstation checks a secondary workstation regularly at predetermined times to determine whether it has data to transmit. Secondary workstations cannot transmit until the primary host gives them permission. Polling is commonly used in large mainframe environments where hosts are polled to determine whether they need to transmit. Because polling is very inexpensive, low-level and peer-to-peer networks also use it.

Token-Passing

Used in Token Ring, FDDI, and Attached Resource Computer Network (ARCnet) networks, stations in token-passing networks cannot transmit until they receive a special frame called a token. This arrangement prevents the collision problems that are present in CSMA. Token-passing networks will work well if large, bandwidth-consuming applications are commonly used on the network.

Token Ring and IEEE 802.5 are two principal examples of token-passing networks. Token-passing networks move a small frame, called a token, around the network. Possession of this token grants the right to transmit. If a node that is receiving the token has no information to send, it passes the token to the next end station. Each station can then hold the token for a maximum period of time, as determined by the 802.5 specification.

Unlike CSMA/CD networks (such as Ethernet), token-passing networks are deterministic, which means that it is possible to calculate the maximum time that will pass before any end station can transmit. This feature and the fact that collisions cannot occur make Token Ring networks ideal for applications where the transmission delay must be predictable and robust network operation is important. Factory automation environments are examples of such applications.

Also, there are three flavors of LAN transmission methods:

✦ *Unicast*—The packet is sent from a single source to a single destination address.

✦ *Multicast*—The source packet is copied and sent to specific multiple destinations on the network.

✦ *Broadcast*—The packet is copied and sent to all of the nodes on a network or segment of a network.

Networking Devices

Many networking devices co-exist on the Internetwork. These devices provide communications between hosts, computers and other network devices. Let's look at the major categories of these devices.

Hubs and Repeaters

Repeaters and hubs operate at the Physical Layer of the OSI model. Repeaters amplify the data signal to extend the length of a network segment, and they help compensate for signal deterioration due to attenuation. Hubs and repeaters are used to connect multiple LAN devices, such as servers and workstations. They do not add much intelligence to the communications process, however, as they don't filter packets, examine addressing, or alter the data packet. Figure 3-14 shows a repeater or hub amplifying the network signal.

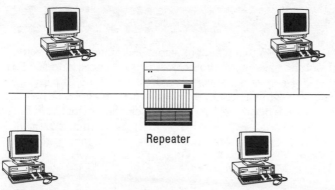

Figure 3-14: A hub or repeater.

Bridges

Like hubs, bridges also amplify the data signals, but they make intelligent decisions as to where to forward the data. A bridge forwards the data to all other network segments if the Media Access Control (MAC) of the destination computer is not on the local network segment. If the destination computer is on the local network segment, it does not forward the data.

Because bridges operate at the Data Link Layer, Layer 2, they do not use IP addresses (IP information is attached in the Network Layer, Layer 3). Because a bridge automatically forwards any broadcast traffic to all ports, an error state known as a *broadcast storm* can develop, overwhelming the network devices. Figure 3-15 shows a bridged network.

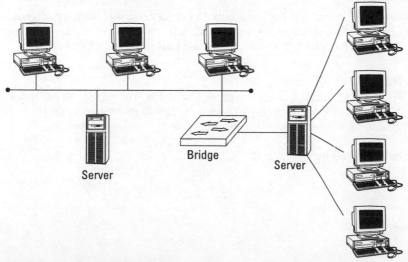

Figure 3-15: A bridged network.

Broadcasts

A broadcast is a data packet (FF.FF.FF.FF) that is sent to all network stations at the same time. Broadcasts are an essential function built into all protocols. When servers need to send data to all the other hosts on the network segment, network broadcasts are useful. If a lot of broadcasts are occurring on a network segment, however, network performance can be seriously degraded. It is important to use these devices properly and to segment the network correctly.

Spanning Tree

To prevent broadcast storms and other unwanted side effects of looping, Digital Equipment Corporation created the Spanning Tree Protocol (STP), which has been standardized as the 802.1d specification by the Institute of Electrical and Electronic Engineers (IEEE).

A spanning tree uses the *spanning tree algorithm* (STA), which senses that the switch has more than one way to communicate with a node and determines which way is best. It blocks out the other paths but keeps track of them in case the primary path becomes unavailable.

Switches

A switch is similar to a bridge or a hub, except that a switch will send the data packet only to the specific port where the destination MAC address is located, rather than to all ports that are attached to the hub or bridge. A switch relies on the MAC addresses to determine the source and destination of a packet, which is Layer 2 networking.

Switches primarily operate at the Data Link Layer, Layer 2, although intelligent Layer 3 switching techniques (combining, switching, and routing) are being more frequently used (see "Layer 3 Switching," below). Figure 3-16 shows a switched network.

Transparent Bridging

Most Ethernet LAN switches use transparent bridging to create their address lookup tables. Transparent bridging allows a switch to learn everything it needs to know about the location of nodes on the network.

Transparent bridging has five steps:

1. Learning
2. Flooding
3. Filtering
4. Forwarding
5. Aging

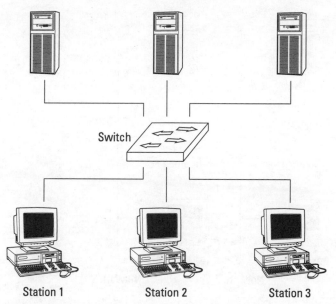

Figure 3-16: A switched network.

Routers

Routers add more intelligence to the process of forwarding packets. When a router receives a packet, it looks at the Network Layer source and destination addresses (IP address) to determine the path the packet should take, and forwards the packet only to the network to which the packet was destined.

This prevents unnecessary network traffic from being sent over the network by blocking broadcast information and traffic to unknown addresses. Routers operate at the Network Layer, Layer 3 of the OSI protocol model. Routers are necessary when communicating between VLANs. Figure 3-17 shows a routed network.

Routing Methodologies

Three fundamental routing methodologies exist, and other routing protocols and methods expand on these.

- ✦ Static routing
- ✦ Distance vector routing
- ✦ Link state routing

Static routing refers to the definition of a specific route in a configuration file on the router and does not require the routers to exchange route information dynamically.

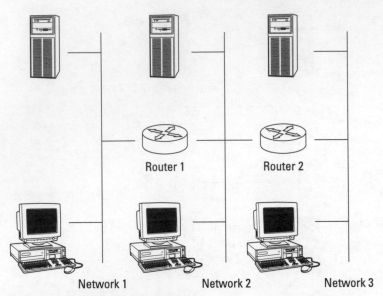

Figure 3-17: A routed network.

Distance vector routing uses the Routing Information Protocol (RIP) to maintain a dynamic table of routing information, which is updated regularly. RIP bases its routing path on the distance (number of hops) to the destination. RIP maintains optimum routing paths by sending out routing update messages if the network topology changes (see Figure 3-18).

For example, if a router finds that a particular link is faulty, it will update its routing table, and then send a copy of the modified table to each of its neighbors. It is the oldest and most common type of dynamic routing, and it commonly broadcasts its routing table information to all other routers every minute. RIP is the earliest and the most commonly found Interior Gateway Protocol (IGP).

Link state routers function like distance vector routers, but they use only first-hand information when building routing tables by maintaining a copy of every other router's Link State Protocol (LSP) frame. This helps to eliminate routing errors and considerably lessens convergence time.

The *Open Shortest Path First* (OSPF) is a link-state hierarchical routing algorithm intended as a successor to RIP. It features least-cost routing, multipath routing, and load balancing.

The *Internet Gateway Routing Protocol* (IGRP) is a Cisco protocol that uses a composite metric as its routing metric, including bandwidth, delay, reliability, loading, and maximum transmission unit.

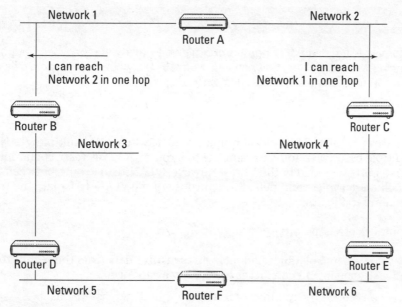

Figure 3-18: Distance vector routing.

Layer 3 Switching

Although most standard switches operate at the Data Link Layer, Layer 3 switches operate at the Network Layer and function like a router by incorporating some router features. The pattern matching and caching on Layer 3 switches is similar to the pattern matching and caching on a router. Both use a routing protocol and routing table to determine the best path. However, a big difference between a router and a Layer 3 switch is that Layer 3 switches have optimized hardware to pass data as fast as Layer 2 switches.

Also, a Layer 3 switch has the ability to reprogram the hardware dynamically with the current Layer 3 routing information, providing much faster packet processing. The information received from the routing protocols is used to update the hardware caching tables.

Within the LAN environment, a Layer 3 switch is usually faster than a router because it is built on switching hardware. Many of Cisco's Layer 3 switches, like the Cisco Catalyst 6000, are actually routers that operate faster because they are built on switching hardware with customized chips inside the box.

VLANs

A *Virtual Local Area Network* (VLAN) allows ports on the same or different switches to be grouped so that traffic is confined to members of that group only. It also restricts broadcast, unicast, and multicast traffic. A VLAN is a collection of nodes that are grouped together in a single broadcast domain in a switch and are based on something other than physical segment location.

Broadcast Domain

A broadcast domain is a network (or portion of a network) that will receive a broadcast packet from any node located within that network. Normally everything on the same side of the router is all part of the same broadcast domain.

A VLAN creates an isolated broadcast domain, and a switch with multiple VLANs creates multiple broadcast domains, similarl to a router. A VLAN restricts flooding to only those ports included in the VLAN. However VLANs can't route between each other. Such routing would defeat the purpose of the VLAN, to isolate the traffic from the general traffic flow.

Some advantages of VLANs are:

✦ VLANs can aid in isolating segments with sensitive data from the rest of the broadcast domain and can increase security assurance.

✦ VLANs can reduce the number of router hops and increase the usable bandwidth.

✦ A VLAN reduces routing broadcasts as ACLs control which stations receive what traffic.

✦ A VLAN is segmented logically, rather than physically.

✦ VLANs may be created to segregate job or department functions that require heavy bandwidth, without affecting the rest of the network.

VLANs can span across multiple switches, and you can have more than one VLAN on each switch. For multiple VLANs on multiple switches to be able to communicate via a single link between the switches, you must use a process called *trunking*. Trunking is the technology that allows information from multiple VLANs to be carried over just one link between switches. The VLAN Trunking Protocol (VTP) is the protocol that switches use to communicate among themselves about VLAN configuration.

When a VLAN is implemented with private-port, or single-user, switching, it provides fairly stringent security because broadcast vulnerabilities are minimized. A *closed* VLAN authenticates a user to an access control list on a central authentication server, where they are assigned authorization parameters to determine their level of network access.

Brouters

Brouters are hybrid bridge/router devices. Instead of dropping an undeliverable packet, as a router would do, a brouter attempts to bridge the packet using its MAC address.

Gateways

Gateways are primarily software products that you can run on computers or other network devices. They can be multi-protocol (link different protocols) and can examine the entire packet. Mail gateways are used to link dissimilar mail programs. Gateways can also be used to translate between two dissimilar network protocols.

LAN Extenders

A LAN extender is a remote-access, multi-layer switch that connects to a host router (see Figure 3-19). LAN extenders forward traffic from all the standard network-layer protocols (such as IP, IPX, and Appletalk) and filter traffic based on the MAC address or network-layer protocol type. LAN extenders scale well because the host router filters out unwanted broadcasts and multicasts. LAN extenders, however, are not capable of segmenting traffic or creating security firewalls.

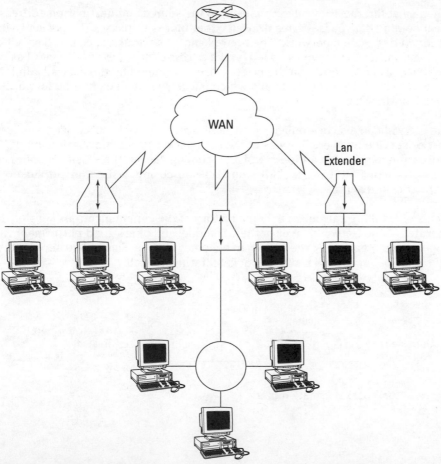

Figure 3-19: LAN extenders.

Firewall Types

Another important type of network device is a firewall. A CISSP candidate will need to know the basic types of firewalls and their functions, which firewalls operate at which protocol layer, and the basic variations of firewall architectures.

Firewalls act as perimeter access-control devices and are classified into three common types:

1. Packet-level filtering firewalls
2. Proxy firewalls, such as application level or circuit level
3. Stateful inspection firewalls

Packet Filtering Firewalls

The packet filtering firewall examines both the source and destination address of the incoming data packet. This firewall either blocks or passes the packet to its intended destination network. The firewall can allow or deny access to specific applications and/or services based on the *Access Control Lists* (ACLs). ACLs are database files that reside on the firewall, are maintained by the firewall administrator, and tell the firewall specifically which packets can and cannot be forwarded to certain addresses.

The firewall can also be configured to allow access for only authorized application port or service numbers. It looks at the data packet to get information about the source and destination addresses of an incoming packet, the session's communications protocol (TCP, UDP, or ICMP), and the source and destination application port for the desired service.

A packet level firewall doesn't keep a history of the communications session. It operates at the Network Layer of the OSI model and offers good performance. Ongoing maintenance of the ACLs can become an issue. Figure 3-20 shows an external router being used as a simple packet filtering firewall.

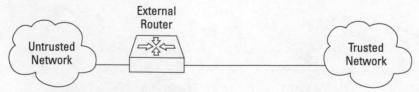

Figure 3-20: A packet filtering router.

Application Level Firewalls

An application level firewall (see Figure 3-21) is commonly a host computer that is running proxy server software, making it a proxy server. This firewall works by transferring a copy of each accepted data packet from one network to another, thereby masking the data's origin. A proxy server can control which services a workstation uses on the Internet, and it aids in protecting the network from outsiders who may be trying to get information about the network's design.

Also called an application layer gateway, it is commonly used with a dual-homed host. It operates at the OSI protocol Layer seven, the Application Layer. It is more secure because it examines the packet at the Application Layer, but it does so at the expense of performance.

As opposed to packet firewalls, proxy firewalls capture some session history. Proxy firewalls have higher protocols carried on low-level protocols, like email or HTML.

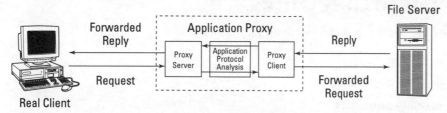

Figure 3-21: Application level proxy firewall process.

Circuit Level Firewalls

Like an application level firewall, a circuit level firewall is used as a proxy server. It is similar to the application level firewall in that it functions as a proxy server, but it differs in that special proxy application software is not needed

This firewall creates a virtual circuit between the workstation client (destination) and the server (host). It also provides security for a wide variety of protocols and is easier to maintain.

Stateful Inspection Firewalls

A stateful inspection firewall intercepts incoming packets at the Network Layer, and then uses an *inspection engine* to extract state-related information from upper layers. It maintains the information in a *dynamic state table* and evaluates subsequent connection attempts. Stateful inspection firewalls keep low-protocol records at the IP level.

Dynamic Packet Filtering Firewalls

A dynamic packet filtering firewall employs a technology that enables the modification of the firewall security rule. This type of technology is used mostly for providing limited support for UDP. For a short period of time, this firewall remembers all of the UDP packets that have crossed the network's perimeter, and it decides whether to enable packets to pass through the firewall.

The packets are queued and then analyzed at all OSI layers against the state table. By examining the *state* and *context* of the incoming data packets, protocols that are considered "connectionless," such as UDP-based applications and Remote Procedure Calls (RPCs), can be tracked more easily.

Firewall Architectures

The four basic types of firewall architectures are:

✦ Packet-filtering

✦ Screened hosts

✦ Dual-homed hosts

✦ Screened subnet firewalls

Note　Keep in mind that some of these architectures are specifically associated with one of the previously discussed firewall types while other architectures can be a combination of types.

Packet-Filtering Routers

A packet-filtering router is the most common and oldest firewall device in use. A packet-filtering router sits between the private "trusted" network and the "untrusted" network or network segment. This firewall architecture is used as a packet-filtering firewall, described above. A packet-filtering router is sometimes used to directly manage access to a demilitarized zone (DMZ) network segment.

Screened-Host Firewalls

Like a dual-homed host, a screened-host firewall uses two network cards to connect to the trusted and untrusted networks, but adds a screening router between the host and the untrusted network (see Figure 3-22). It provides both network-layer (routing) and application-layer (proxy) services. This type of firewall system requires an intruder to penetrate two separate systems before he or she can compromise the trusted network.

The host is configured between the local trusted network and untrusted network. Because the firewall can be the focus of external attacks, it is sometimes called the *sacrificial lamb*.

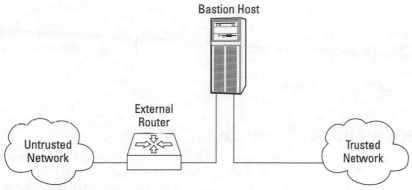

Figure 3-22: A screened-host firewall.

Dual-Homed Host Firewalls

Another very common firewall architecture configuration is the Dual-Homed Host (see Figure 3-23). A dual-homed host has two NICs but no screening router. It uses two NICs to attach to two separate networks, commonly a trusted network and an untrusted network.

This architecture is a simple configuration that consists of a single computer (the host) with two NICs: One is connected to the local trusted network and the other is connected to the Internet or an untrusted external network. A dual-homed host firewall usually acts to block or filter some or all of the traffic trying to pass between the networks.

IP traffic forwarding is usually disabled or restricted; all traffic between the networks and the traffic's destination must pass through some kind of security inspection mechanism.

The host's routing capabilities must be disabled so that it does not unintentionally enable internal routing, which will connect the two networks together transparently and negate the firewall's function. Many systems come with routing enabled by default, such as IP forwarding, which makes the firewall useless.

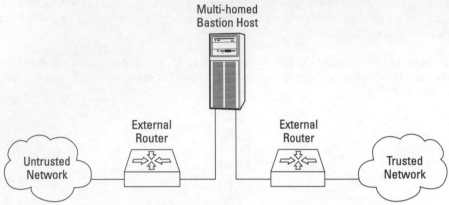

Figure 3-23: A dual-homed firewall.

Screened-Subnet Firewalls

One of the most secure implementations of firewall architectures is the screened-subnet firewall. A screened-subnet firewall also uses two NICs, but it has two screening routers with the host acting as a proxy server on its own network segment. One screening router controls traffic local to the network, while the second monitors and controls incoming and outgoing Internet traffic.

It employs two packet-filtering routers and a bastion host. Like a screened-host firewall, this firewall supports both packet filtering and proxy services yet it can also define a *demilitarized zone* (DMZ).

A DMZ is a network added between an internal network and an external network in order to provide an additional layer of security. Sometimes it is also called a *perimeter network*. The DMZ creates a small network between the untrusted network and the trusted network where the bastion host and other public Web services exist. The outside router provides protection against external attacks while the inside router manages the private network access to a DMZ by routing it through the bastion host.

Bastion Host

A bastion host is any computer that is fully exposed to attack by being on the public side of the demilitarized zone (DMZ), unprotected by a firewall or filtering router. Firewalls and routers, anything that provides perimeter access-control security, can be considered bastion hosts. Other types of bastion hosts can include Web, mail, DNS, and FTP servers. Often a bastion host is used as a sacrificial lamb. Due to their exposure, a great deal of effort must be put into designing and configuring bastion hosts to minimize the chances of penetration.

Many firewalls allow you to place a network in the demilitarized zone (DMZ). Figure 3-24 shows a common firewall implementation employing a DMZ.

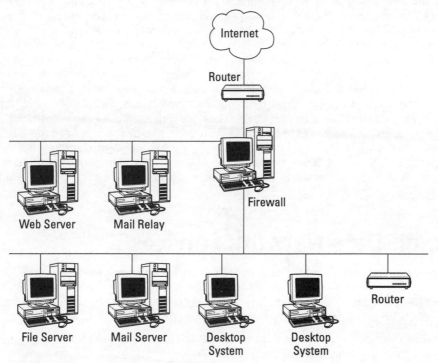

Figure 3-24: Common firewall implementation.

SOCKS

A SOCKS server provides another variation of firewall protection. Socket Security (SOCKS) is a Transport Layer, secure networking proxy protocol. SOCKS replaces the standard network systems calls with its own calls. These calls open connections to a SOCKS proxy server for client authentication transparently to the user. Common network utilities, like Telnet or FTP, need to be SOCKS-ified, or have their network calls altered to recognize SOCKS proxy calls.

This is a circuit-level proxy server that does not require the server resource overhead of conventional proxy servers. SOCKS uses port 1080 and is used both for outbound host access by a workstation and to allow a host outside of a firewall to connect transparently and securely through the firewall.

As a consequence, some sites may have port 1080 opened for incoming connections to a system running a SOCKS daemon. One of the more common uses of SOCKS is to allow ICQ traffic to hosts that are behind a firewall.

A Word about Network Architectures

Network architecture refers to the communications products and services that ensure that the various components of a network, such as devices, protocols, and access methods, work together. Originally, a manufacturer's network system often did not interoperate within its own product line, much less enable connectivity with the products of other manufacturers. Although IBM's Systems Network Architecture (SNA) and Digital Equipment Corporation's DECnet were seen as an advance in solving these problems within the vendor's product line, they still did not interoperate outside of that product line. The Open Systems Interconnection (OSI) model by the International Standardization Organizations (ISO) was a big step in solving this problem. Other network architecture examples include the Xerox Networking System (XNS) and the Advanced Research Projects Agency Network (ARPANET), the originator of the Internet. These and other standard computer network architectures divide and subdivide the various functions of data communications into isolated layers, which makes it easier to create products and standards that can interoperate.

Common Data Network Services

Some of the common services that a data network provides are:

✦ *File services* — Sharing data files and subdirectories on file servers. We look at these in more detail below.

✦ *Mail services* — Sending and receiving email internally or externally through an email gateway device.

✦ *Print services* — Printing documents to a shared printer or a print queue/spooler.

✦ *Client/Server services* — Allocating computing power resources among workstations with some shared resources centralized in a file server.

✦ *Domain Name Service (DNS)* — Resolving hostnames to IP addresses. DNS matches Internet Uniform Resource Locator (URL) requests with the actual address or location of the server that provides that URL. It is a distributed database system that maps host names to IP addresses.

File Transfer Services

A server providing File Transfer Protocol (FTP) services can allow fully anonymous login without requiring passwords, or it can be set up to require a valid username/password pair. FTP servers provide a simple interface resembling a standard Unix file directory. Users can retrieve files and then view or execute the files later, if they have the appropriate applications.

FTP and Firewall Proxy

Applications gateways may require a proxy for FTP services to be supported through the firewall. All incoming requests for FTP network services should go through the appropriate proxy on the firewall regardless of which host on the internal network will be the final destination. These application level firewalls should be configured such that outbound network traffic appears as if the traffic had originated from the firewall (i.e., only the firewall is visible to outside networks). In this manner, direct access to network services on the internal network is not allowed.

However, if an FTP server is not configured correctly, it can provide access to any file found on the host computer or even on the network connected to the host computer. FTP servers should be restricted to accessing a limited directory space and should require the use of passwords whenever feasible.

Sometimes an organization may wish to support an anonymous FTP server to allow all external users the ability to download nonsensitive information without using strong authentication. In this case, FTP should be hosted outside the firewall or on a service network not connected to corporate networks that contain sensitive data. Table 3-7 shows a sample of such an FTP policy.

Table 3-7
Sample FTP Service Policy

Policy Statement	Non-Anonymous FTP service	Anonymous FTP service
Require FTP server outside the firewall	N	Y
Require FTP server on the service network	N	Y
Require FTP server on protected network	Y	N
Require FTP server on the firewall itself	N	N
FTP server will be accessed by Internet	N	Y

SFTP

SFTP (Secure File Transfer Protocol) is replacing the File Transfer Protocol (FTP) because it includes strong encryption and authentication. SFTP is a FTP-style client that can be used to exchange files over a network and is an encryption-based replacement for the insecure FTP. SFTP provides secure file transfer functionality using SSH or SSH-2; it is the standard file transfer protocol for use with the SSH-2 protocol.

Although SFTP is designed to primarily provide file transfer services, it can provide secure file system access to a remote server. An SFTP server can be designed to provide only file transfer access, or it can provide system command access as well. SFTP can restrict users to their home directories, is not vulnerable to the "flashfxp" transfer utility (which allows an unknown third-party to use the network for file transfer to a remote location), and is much less vulnerable to remote exploitation than standard FTP. It can be configured to authorize users with certificates as well as passwords. MacSFTP is a Macintosh application used to transfer files over TCP/IP using SFTP.

SSH/SSH-2

Secure Shell (SSH) is a set of protocols that are used primarily for remote access over a network by establishing an encrypted tunnel between an SSH client and an SSH server. This protocol can be used to authenticate the client to the server. In addition, it can also provide confidentiality and integrity services. It is composed of a Transport Layer protocol, a User Authentication protocol, and a Connection protocol. A number of SSH software programs are available on the Internet for free, such as OPENSSH.

Secure Shell version 2 (SSH-2) contains security enhancements over the original SSH and should be used in place of SSH. SSH-2 is not strictly a VPN product, but it can be used like one. SSH opens a secure, encrypted shell (command line) session from the Internet through a firewall to the SSH server. After the connection is established, it can be used as a terminal session or for tunneling other protocols.

SSH-2 should be used instead of Telnet when connecting to remote hosts. Tunneling features available in SSH-2 can be utilized for providing secure connections to applications that are connected to a remote server, such as connecting to a POP3 email server.

TFTP

Trivial File Transfer Protocol (TFTP) is a stripped-down version of FTP. TFTP has no directory browsing abilities; it can do nothing but send and receive files. TFTP is commonly used to capture router configuration files by logging a terminal session during a configuration session and then storing that configuration on a TFTP server. The TFTP server is then accessed during the configuration session to save or retrieve configuration information to the network device. However, unlike FTP, session authentication does not occur, so it is insecure. Some sites choose not to implement TFTP due to the inherent security risks.

Data Network Types

A CISSP candidate will also need to know the basics of the data network structures — the types of cabling, the various network access methods and topologies, and the differences between various LANs and WANs.

Saving Configuration Files and Trivial File Transfer Protocol

Sometimes when a network device fails, the configuration programmed into it is also lost. This can especially happen to routers. The procedure that is used to prevent this from occurring consists of capturing the configuration files by logging a terminal session during a configuration session and then storing that configuration on floppies or installing a Trivial File Transfer Protocol (TFTP) server. The TFTP server is then accessed during the configuration session to save or retrieve configuration information to the network device. As TFTP is very insecure, this server must be located in a secure area.

A *data network* consists of two or more computers that are connected for the purpose of sharing files, printers, data, and so forth. To communicate on the network, every workstation must have an NIC inserted into the computer, a transmission medium (such as copper, fiber, or wireless), a Network Operating System (NOS), and a LAN device of some sort (such as a hub, bridge, router, or switch) to physically connect the computers together.

In addition to the local area network we described, two other common types of LANs are:

✦ *Campus Area Network* (CAN) — A typically large campus network that connects multiple buildings with each other across a high-performance, switched backbone on the main campus.

✦ *Metropolitan Area Network* (MAN) — Although not often used as a description, essentially a LAN that extends over a citywide metropolitan area. It's commonly a backbone network that connects business to WANs, often using SONET or FDDI rings provided by telecommunications vendors.

Wide Area Networks

A Wide Area Network (WAN) is a network of subnetworks that are physically or logically interconnected over a larger geographic area than LANs.

A WAN might be privately operated for a specific user community, might support multiple communication protocols, or might provide network connectivity and services via interconnected network segments (extranets, intranets, and VPNs). We'll examine WAN technologies in more detail later.

Internet

The Internet is a WAN that was originally funded by the DoD, which uses TCP/IP for data interchange. The term *Internet* is used to refer to any and all kinds of Advanced Research Projects Agency Network (ARPANET), Department of Defense Research

SONET

Synchronous Optical Network (SONET) is a standard for telecommunications transmission over fiber optics. SONET network rings transmit voice and data over fiber optic networks. Multiple varying-speed SONET rings often communicate with each other. SONET is a self-healing technology, meaning that it can recover from a break by employing a redundant ring, making the technology fault tolerant.

Projects Agency Network (DARPANET), Defense Data Network (DDN), or DoD Internets. It specifically refers to the global network of public networks and ISPs throughout the world. Either public or private networks (with a VPN) can utilize the Internet.

Intranet

An intranet is an Internet-like logical network that uses a firm's internal, physical network infrastructure. Because it uses TCP/IP and HTTP standards, it can use low-cost Internet products like Web browsers. A common example of an intranet would be a company's human resource department publishing employee guidelines that are accessible by all company employees on the intranet. An intranet provides more security and control than a public posting on the Internet.

Extranet

Like an intranet, an extranet is a private network that uses Internet protocols. Unlike an intranet, users outside the company (partners, vendors, and so forth) can access an extranet but the general public cannot. An example of someone using this type of network is a company's supplier accessing a company's private network (via a VPN or Internet connection with some kind of authentication) but only having access to the information that he or she needs.

WAN Technologies

To become more familiar with the various types of WAN technologies, you must understand WAN protocols, topologies, and devices. Like LAN protocols, WAN protocols are the rules for communicating between computers on a WAN. Because the WAN is more often used for connecting diverse networks than a LAN, these protocols address the issues involved with communications between many large and disparate networks.

Dedicated Lines

A dedicated line is a communications line that is indefinitely and continuously reserved for transmission, rather than being switched on and off as transmission is required. A dedicated link can be a *leased line* or a *point-to-point link*. When a communications carrier reserves a dedicated line for a customer's private use, this is called a leased line.

Dedicated lines are also called point-to-point links, and use private circuits. Private circuits evolved before packet-switching networks. A private circuit network is a dedicated analog or digital point-to-point connection joining geographically diverse networks.

T-carriers

T-carriers are dedicated lines that carry voice and data information over trunk lines. Types and speeds of various T-carriers and dedicated lines are:

✦ *Digital Signal Level 0 (DS-0)* — The framing specification used in transmitting digital signals over a single channel at 64 Kbps on a T1 facility

✦ *Digital Signal Level 1 (DS-1)* — The framing specification used in transmitting digital signals at 1.544 Mbps on a T1 facility (in the United States) or at 2.108 Mbps on an E1 facility (in Europe)

✦ *Digital Signal Level 3 (DS-3)* — The framing specification used for transmitting digital signals at 44.736 Mbps on a T3 facility

✦ *T1* — Transmits DS-1-formatted data at 1.544 Mbps through a telephone-switching network

✦ *T3* — Transmits DS-3-formatted data at 44.736 Mbps through a telephone-switching network

✦ *E1* — A wide-area digital transmission scheme predominantly used in Europe that carries data at a rate of 2.048 Mbps

✦ *E3* — The same as E1 (both can be leased for private use from common carriers), but carries data at a rate of 34.368 Mbps

WAN Switching

When the network grows and needs more than a single point-to-point connection, WAN switching is required. There are two main flavors of WAN switching: circuit switching and packet switching.

Circuit-Switched Networks

Circuit switching is defined as a switching system in which a dedicated physical circuit path must exist between the sender and receiver for the duration of the transmission or the "call." A circuit-switched network describes a type of WAN that consists of a physical, permanent connection from one point to another. This technology is older than packet switching, which we discuss next, but it is the main choice for communications that need to be "on" constantly and have a limited scope of distribution (one transmission path only). This network type is used heavily in telephone company networks. ISDN is an example of a circuit-switched network.

Packet-Switched Networks

Packet switching is defined as a networking method where nodes share bandwidth with each other by sending small data units called *packets*. A packet-switched network (PSN) or PSDN is a network that uses packet-switching technology for data transfer. Unlike circuit-switched networks, the data in packet-switched networks is broken up into packets and then sent to the next destination based on the router's understanding of the best available route. At that destination, the packets are reassembled based on their originally assigned sequence numbers. Although the data is manhandled a lot in this process, it creates a network that is very resistant to error. Table 3-8 lists some of the basic differences between circuit and packet switching.

Table 3-8
Circuit Switching versus Packet Switching

Circuit Switching	Packet Switching
Constant traffic	Bursty traffic
Fixed delays	Variable delays
Connection-oriented	Connectionless
Sensitive to loss of connection	Sensitive to loss of data
Voice-oriented data	Data-oriented data

Packet-Switched Technologies

Packet-switched networks can be far more cost effective than dedicated circuits because they create virtual circuits, which are used as needed, rather than supplying a continuous dedicated circuit. Examples of packet-switching networks are X.25, Link Access Procedure-Balanced (LAPB), Frame Relay, Switched Multimegabit Data

Service (SMDS), Asynchronous Transfer Mode (ATM), and Voice over IP (VoIP) (Source: *Communications Systems and Networks* by Ray Horak, M&T Books, 2000).

X.25. X.25 defines an interface to the first commercially successful connection-oriented packet-switching network, in which the packets travel over virtual circuits. X.25 defines the point-to-point communication between Data Terminal Equipment (DTE), Data Circuit-Terminating Equipment (DCE, commonly a modem), or a Data Service Unit/Channel Service Unit (DSU/CSU), which supports both switched virtual circuits (SVCs) and permanent virtual circuits (PVCs). X.25 defines how WAN devices are established and maintained. X.25 was designed to operate effectively regardless of the type of systems that are connected to the network. It has become an international standard and is currently much more prevalent overseas than in the United States.

Link Access Procedure-Balanced (LAPB). Created for use with X.25, LAPB defines frame types and is capable of retransmitting, exchanging, and acknowledging frames as well as detecting out-of-sequence or missing frames.

Frame Relay. Frame Relay is a high-performance WAN protocol that operates at the Data Link Layer of the OSI model. Originally designed for use across ISDN interfaces, it is currently used with a variety of other interfaces and is a major standard for high-speed WAN communications. Frame Relay is a successor to X.25 and LAPB. It is the fastest of the WAN protocols listed because of its simplified framing approach, which utilizes no error correction. Frame Relay uses SVCs, PVCs, and Data Link Connection Identifiers (DLCIs) for addressing. Because it requires access to a high-quality digital network infrastructure, it is not available everywhere.

Switched Multimegabit Data Service (SMDS). SMDS is a high-speed, connectionless, packet-switched public network service that extends LAN-like performance to a metropolitan area network (MAN) or a wide area network (WAN). It's generally delivered over a SONET ring with a maximum effective service radius of around 30 miles. It provides bandwidth to companies that need to exchange large amounts of data with other enterprises over WANs on a bursty or non-continuous basis, by providing connectionless bandwidth upon demand.

Asynchronous Transfer Mode (ATM). ATM is a high-bandwidth, low-delay technology that uses both switching and multiplexing. It uses 53-byte, fixed-size cells instead of frames like Ethernet. It can allocate bandwidth upon demand, making it a solution for bursty applications. ATM requires a high-speed, high-bandwidth medium like fiber optics. ATM was developed from an outgrowth of ISDN standards and is a fast-packet, connection-oriented, cell-switching technology.

Voice over IP (VoIP). VoIP is one of several digital, multi-service access IP technologies that combine many types of data (such as voice, audio, and video) into a single IP packet, which provides major benefits in the areas of cost, interoperability, and performance.

Virtual Circuits

Frame relay uses virtual circuits to forward packets. Switched virtual circuits (SVCs) are virtual circuits that are dynamically established on demand and are torn down when transmission is complete. SVCs are used in situations where data transmission is sporadic. SVCs have three phases: circuit establishment, data transfer, and circuit termination (teardown). Permanent virtual circuits (PVCs) are virtual circuits that are permanently connected. PVCs save the bandwidth that is associated with circuit establishment and teardown. A PVC provides the frame relay customer with guaranteed bandwidth.

Other WAN Protocols

Synchronous Data Link Control (SDLC). SDLC is a protocol that IBM created to make it easier for its mainframes to connect to the remote offices. SDLC defines and uses a polling media-access method. It consists of a primary station, which controls all communications, and one or more secondary stations. SDLC is based on dedicated, leased lines with permanent physical connections, and it has evolved into the HDLC and Link Access Procedure-Balanced (LAPB) protocols. This protocol operates at the Data Link Layer.

High-Level Data Link Control (HDLC). Derived from SDLC, HDLC specifies the data encapsulation method on synchronous serial links by using frame characters and checksums. The ISO created the HDLC standard to support both point-to-point and multi-point configurations. Vendors often implement HDLC in different ways, which sometimes makes the HDLC protocol incompatible. It also operates at the Data Link Layer.

High-Speed Serial Interface (HSSI). HSSI is a DTE/DCE interface that was developed to address the need for high-speed communications over WAN links. It defines the electrical and physical interfaces that DTE/DCEs use and operates at the Physical Layer of the OSI model.

Common WAN Devices

WAN devices enable the use of WAN protocols and topologies. The following are examples of these device types:

Routers. Although previously described as a LAN device, routers are extremely important in the WAN environment — especially for IP Internet traffic.

Multiplexers. Commonly referred to as a *mux*, a multiplexer is a device that enables more than one signal to be sent out simultaneously over one physical circuit.

WAN Switches. WAN Switches are multi-port networking devices that are used in carrier networks. They operate at the Data Link Layer and typically switch Frame Relay, X.25, and SMDS. These switches connect private data over public data circuits by using digital signals.

Access Servers. An access server is a server that provides dial-in and dial-out connections to the network. These are typically asynchronous servers that enable users to dial in and attach to the LAN. Cisco's AS5200 series of communication servers are an example of such devices.

Modems. A modem is a device that interprets digital and analog signals, which enables data to be transmitted over voice-grade telephone lines. The digital signals are then converted to an analog form, which is suitable for transmission over an analog communications medium. These signals are then converted back to their digital form at the destination.

Channel Service Unit (CSU)/Data Service Unit (DSU). This digital interface device terminates the physical interface on a DTE device (such as a terminal) to the interface of a DCE device (such as a switch) in a switched carrier network. These devices connect to the closest telephone company switch in a central office (CO).

Figure 3-25 shows a network that allows Internet access with several different devices.

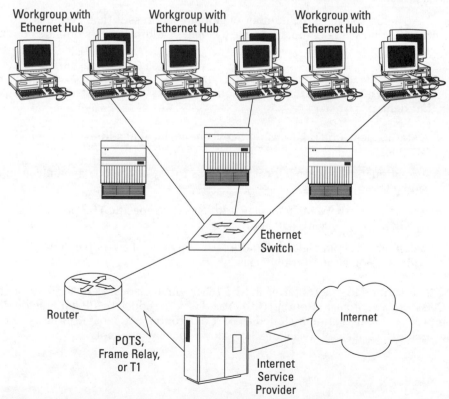

Figure 3-25: Shared Internet access with WAN and LAN devices.

Network Address Translation (NAT)

Generically, NAT (Network Address Translation) describes the process of converting an IP address valid within one network to a different IP address valid within another network. More specifically, NAT converts a private IP address on the inside, trusted network to a registered "real" IP address seen by the untrusted, outside network.

The Internet Assigned Numbers Authority (IANA) has reserved three blocks of the IP address space for private Internets:

✦ 10.0.0.0 to 10.255.255.255

✦ 172.16.0.0 to 172.31.255.255

✦ 192.168.0.0 to 192.168.255.255

Employing these internal addresses through NAT enhances security by hiding the true IP address of the packet's origin. As each incoming or outgoing packet is converted by NAT, the request may be authenticated.

Also, NAT helps conserve the number of global IP addresses that a company requires and allows the company to use a single IP address for its outside communications.

NAT can be statically defined or it can be configured to dynamically use a group of IP addresses. For example, Cisco's version of NAT lets an administrator create policies that define:

✦ A static one-to-one relationship between one local IP address and one global IP address

✦ A relationship between a local IP address to any of one of a dynamic group of global IP addresses

✦ A relationship between a local IP address and a specific TCP port to a static or dynamic group of global IP addresses

✦ A conversion from a global IP address to any one of a group of local IP addresses on a round-robin basis

NAT is described in general terms in RFC 1631, which discusses NAT's relationship to Classless Interdomain Routing (CIDR) as a way to reduce the IP address depletion problem. NAT is often included as part of a router, and most firewall systems now include NAT capability. Figure 3-26 shows the NAT concept.

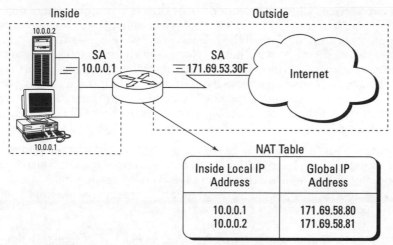

Figure 3-26: Network Address Translation (NAT).

Remote Access Technologies

Remote access technologies can be defined as those data networking technologies that are uniquely focused on providing the remote user (telecommuter, Internet/intranet user, or extranet user/partner) with access into a network, while striving to maintain the principle tenets of Confidentiality, Availability, and Integrity.

There are many obvious advantages to employing secure remote network access, such as the following:

✦ Reducing networking costs by using the Internet to replace expensive dedicated network lines

✦ Providing employees with flexible work styles such as telecommuting

✦ Building more efficient ties with customers, suppliers, and employees

Remote Access Types

While several of these remote access types share common WAN protocols, we list them here to indicate their importance in the area of remote access security.

Asynchronous Dial-Up Access. This method is how most everyone accesses the Internet. It is the most common remote access method for personal remote users because it uses the existing public switched telephone network to access an ISP.

Integrated Services Digital Network (ISDN). ISDN is a combination of digital telephony and data transport services that telecommunications carriers offer. ISDN consists of a digitization of the telephone network by permitting voice and other digital services (data, music, video, and so forth) to be transmitted over existing telephone wires. The more popular xDSL types have overtaken it in general use. ISDN has two interface types: Basic Rate Interface (BRI), which is composed of two B channels and one D channel, and Primary Rate Interface (PRI), which consists of a single 64 Kbps D channel plus 23 (T1) or 30 (E1) B channels for voice or data.

XDSL. Digital Subscriber Line (xDSL) uses existing twisted pair telephone lines to transport high bandwidth data to remote subscribers. It consists of a point-to-point public network that is accessed through an in-home copper phone wire. It is rapidly becoming the standard for inexpensive remote connectivity. Examples of various flavors of xDSL are:

- *Asymmetric Digital Subscriber Line (ADSL)* — ADSL is designed to deliver more bandwidth downstream (from the central office to the customer site) than upstream. Downstream rates range from 1.5 to 9 Mbps whereas upstream bandwidth ranges from 16 to 640 Kbps. ADSL transmissions work at distances of up to 18,000 feet over a single copper twisted pair (although 14,400 feet is the maximum practical length).

- *Single-Line Digital Subscriber Line (SDSL)* — SDSL delivers 1.544 Mbps both downstream and upstream over a single copper twisted pair. This use of a single twisted pair limits the operating range of SDSL to 10,000 feet.

- *High-Rate Digital Subscriber Line (HDSL)* — HDSL delivers 1.544 Mbps of bandwidth each way over two copper twisted pairs. Because HDSL provides T1 speed, telephone companies have been using HDSL to provide local access to T1 services whenever possible. The operating range of HDSL is limited to 12,000 feet.

- *Very-High Data Rate Digital Subscriber Line (VDSL)* — VDSL delivers 13 to 52 Mbps downstream and 1.5 to 2.3 Mbps upstream over a single twisted copper pair. The operating range of VDSL is limited to 1,000 to 4,500 feet.

Cable Modems. A cable modem provides high-speed access to the Internet by the cable company. All cable modems share a single coax line to the Internet; therefore, throughput varies according to how many users are currently using the service. It is also considered one of the most insecure of the remote access types because the local segment is typically not filtered or firewalled.

Remote Access Security Methods

Let's look at some common methods for securing remote access devices:

Restricted Address. This procedure filters out unauthorized users based on their source protocol address (IP or other LAN protocol). It enables incoming calls only from specific addresses on an approved list. You should remember, however, that this procedure authenticates the node; it is not a user authentication method.

Caller ID. Caller ID checks the incoming phone number of the caller against an approved phone list before accepting the session. This is one of the most common security methods because it is very hard to defeat. Its major drawback is that it is hard to administer for traveling users (such as users calling from a different hotel every night).

Callback. In a callback scenario, a user attempting to initiate the session supplies a password or some type of identifying code. The access server then hangs up and calls the user back at a predetermined phone number. Again, this procedure authenticates the node, not the user, and is difficult to administer in traveling situations.

Virtual Private Networking (VPN)

A virtual private network (VPN) is created by building a secure communications link between two nodes by emulating the properties of a point-to-point private link. A VPN can be used to facilitate secure remote access into a network, securely connect two networks together, or create a secure data tunnel within a network.

The portion of the link in which the private data is encapsulated is known as the *tunnel*. It may be referred to as a secure, encrypted tunnel, although it's more accurately defined as an encapsulated tunnel, as encryption may or may not be used. To emulate a point-to-point link, data is encapsulated, or wrapped, with a header that provides routing information. Most often the data is encrypted for confidentiality. This encrypted part of the link is considered the actual virtual private network connection. Figure 3-27 shows a common VPN configuration for remote access into a company intranet through the Internet.

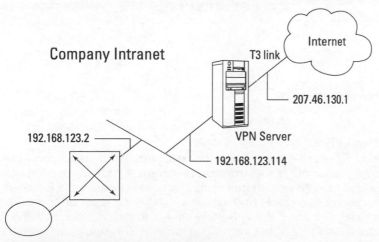

Figure 3-27: A common VPN configuration.

VPN Examples

Let's look at some common VPN configurations:

- ✦ Remote access VPNs
- ✦ Network-to-network VPNs
- ✦ Intranet access VPNs

Remote Access VPNs

A VPN can be configured to provide remote access to corporate resources over the public Internet to maintain confidentiality and integrity. This configuration allows the remote user to utilize whatever local ISP is available to access the Internet without forcing the user to make a long distance or 800 call to a third-party access provider. Using the connection to the local ISP, the VPN software creates a virtual private network between the dial-up user and the corporate VPN server across the Internet. Figure 3-28 shows a remote user VPN connection.

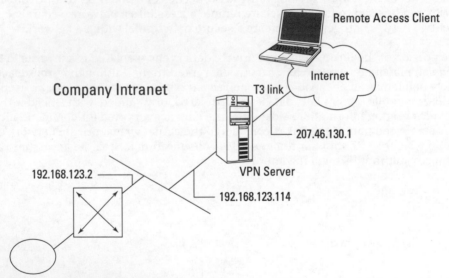

Figure 3-28: A remote access VPN.

Network to Network VPNs

A VPN is commonly used to connect two networks, perhaps the main corporate LAN and a remote branch office LAN, through the Internet. This connection can either use dedicated lines to the Internet or dial-up connections to the Internet. However, the corporate hub router that acts as a VPN server must be connected to a local ISP with a dedicated line if the VPN server needs to be available 24/7. The VPN software uses the connection to the local ISP to create a VPN tunnel between the branch office router and the corporate hub router across the Internet. Figure 3-29 shows a remote branch office connected to the corporate main office using a VPN tunnel through the Internet.

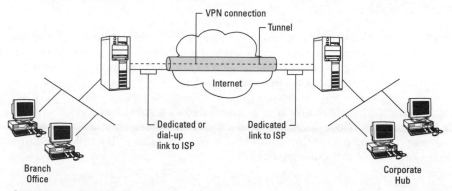

Figure 3-29: A network-to-network VPN.

Intranet Access VPNs

If remote users need to access sensitive data on a LAN physically disconnected from the rest of the corporate network, a VPN may provide the solution. A VPN allows the LAN with the sensitive data to be physically connected to the corporate Internetwork but separated by a VPN server, as shown in Figure 3-30. This ensures that only authorized users on the corporate network can establish a VPN with the VPN server and gain access to the sensitive data.

In this case, the VPN server is not acting as a router between the corporate Internetwork and the department LAN, as a router would connect the two networks, thus allowing everyone access to the sensitive LAN.

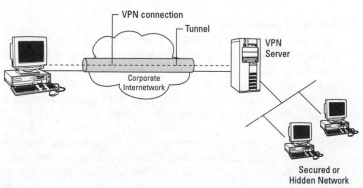

Figure 3-30: An intranet access VPN.

VPN Tunneling

Tunneling is a method of transferring data from one network to another network by encapsulating the packets in an additional header. The additional header provides routing information so that the encapsulated payload can traverse the intermediate networks, as shown in Figure 3-31.

For a tunnel to be established, both the tunnel client and the tunnel server must be using the same tunneling protocol. Tunneling technology can be based on either a Layer 2 or a Layer 3 tunneling protocol. These layers correspond to the Open Systems Interconnection (OSI) Reference Model.

Tunneling, and the use of a VPN, is not intended as a substitute for encryption/decryption. In cases where a high level of security is necessary, the strongest possible encryption should be used within the VPN itself, and tunneling should serve only as a convenience.

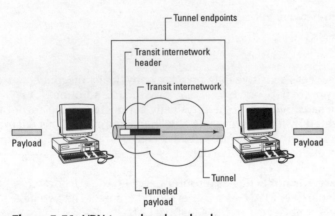

Figure 3-31: VPN tunnel and payload.

VPN and Remote Access Protocols

Both the Point-to-Point Tunneling Protocol (PPTP) and the Layer Two Tunneling Protocol (L2TP) are Layer 2 tunneling protocols using Data Link Layer formatting and encapsulating the payload in a Point-to-Point Protocol (PPP) frame (see "Remote Access protocols," below). Layer 3 protocols correspond to the Network Layer and use packets. IPSec tunnel mode is an example of a Layer 3 tunneling protocol that encapsulates IP packets in an additional IP header.

Layer 3 tunneling technologies generally assume that all of the configuration issues are preconfigured, often by manual processes. For these protocols, there may be no tunnel maintenance phase. For Layer 2 protocols, however, a tunnel must be created, maintained, and then terminated.

Point-to-Point Tunneling Protocol (PPTP)

Point-to-Point Tunneling Protocol (PPTP) works at the Data Link Layer of the OSI model. It is designed for individual client-to-server connections as it allows only a single point-to-point connection per session. PPTP is commonly used by Windows clients for asynchronous communications. PPTP uses the native PPP authentication and encryption services.

PPTP allows IP, IPX, or NetBEUI traffic to be encrypted and then encapsulated in an IP header to be sent across a corporate IP Internetwork or a public IP Internetwork, such as the Internet. PPTP uses a TCP connection for tunnel maintenance and a modified version of Generic Routing Encapsulation (GRE) to encapsulate PPP frames for tunneled data. The payloads of the encapsulated PPP frames can be encrypted and/or compressed.

Layer 2 Tunneling Protocol (L2TP)

Layer 2 Tunneling Protocol (L2TP) is a combination of PPTP and the earlier Layer 2 Forwarding Protocol (L2F) and also works at the Data Link Layer. L2TP is an accepted tunneling standard for VPNs. Dial-up VPNs also use this standard frequently. Like PPTP, it was designed for single point-to-point client-to-server connections. Like PPTP, L2TP allows IP, IPX, or NetBEUI traffic to be encrypted and then sent over any medium that supports point-to-point datagram delivery, such as:

✦ IP

✦ X.25

✦ Frame Relay

✦ ATM

L2TP supports TACACS+ and RADIUS, but PPTP does not. L2TP running over IP networks uses UDP and a series of L2TP messages for tunnel maintenance. L2TP also uses UDP to send L2TP-encapsulated PPP frames as the tunneled data. The payloads of encapsulated PPP frames can be encrypted and/or compressed.

Internet Protocol Security (IPSec)

IPSec operates at the Network Layer and allows multiple simultaneous tunnels. IPSec contains the functionality to encrypt and authenticate IP data. While PPTP and L2TP are aimed more at dial-up VPNs, IPSec also encompasses network-to-network connectivity.

Although IPSec operates at the Network Layer and enables multiple simultaneous tunnels, it is not multi-protocol. IPSec has the functionality to encrypt and authenticate IP data. It is built into the new IPv6 standard and is used as an add-on to the current IPv4. IPSec tunnel mode allows IP packets to be encrypted and then encapsulated in an IP header to be sent across a corporate IP Internetwork or a public IP Internetwork, such as the Internet.

IPSec uses an authentication header (AH) to provide source authentication and integrity without encryption, and it uses the Encapsulating Security Payload (ESP) to provide authentication and integrity along with encryption. With IPSec, only the sender and recipient know the key. If the authentication data is valid, the recipient knows that the communication came from the sender and that it was not changed in transit.

Serial Line Internet Protocol (SLIP)

Serial Line Internet Protocol (SLIP) is a TCP/IP protocol and early de facto standard for asynchronous dial-up communication. An ISP may provide a SLIP connection for Internet access. PPP is now preferred over SLIP because it can handle synchronous as well as asynchronous communication. PPP can share a line with other users, and it has error detection that SLIP lacks.

Point-to-Point Protocol (PPP)

The Point-to-Point Protocol (PPP) defines an encapsulation method to transmit multiprotocol packets over Layer 2 point-to-point links, such as a serial interface. PPP is a full-duplex protocol that can be used on various physical media, including twisted pair or fiber optic lines or satellite transmissions. It uses a variation of High Speed Data Link Control (HDLC) for packet encapsulation.

A user may connect to a network access server (NAS) through ISDN, ADSL, dialup POTS, or another service and then run PPP over that connection. Most implementations of PPP provide limited authentication methods, including:

✦ Password Authentication Protocol (PAP)

✦ Challenge Handshake Authentication Protocol (CHAP)

✦ Microsoft Challenge Handshake Authentication Protocol (MS-CHAP)

Password Authentication Protocol

The Password Authentication Protocol (PAP) is a basic clear-text authentication scheme. The NAS requests the username and password, and PAP returns them in clear text, unencrypted. PAP user authentication is often used on the Internet, which simply sends a username and password to a server where they are compared with a database of authorized users. While the user database may be kept in encrypted form, each ID and password is sent unencrypted.

This authentication scheme is not secure because a third party could capture the user's name and password and use it to get subsequent access to the NAS and all of the resources provided by the NAS. PAP provides no protection against replay attacks or remote client impersonation once the user's password is compromised. A better variation on this method is the Challenge Handshake Authentication Protocol (CHAP).

Challenge Handshake Authentication Protocol

The Challenge Handshake Authentication Protocol (CHAP) is an encrypted authentication mechanism that avoids transmission of the actual password on the connection.

The NAS sends a challenge, which consists of a session ID and an arbitrary challenge string, to the remote client. The remote client must use the MD5 one-way hashing algorithm to return the username and an encryption of the challenge, the session ID, and the client's password. The username is sent unhashed.

CHAP is an improvement over PAP because the clear-text password is not sent over the link. Instead, the password is used to create an encrypted hash from the original challenge. The server knows the client's clear-text password and can, therefore, replicate the operation and compare the result to the password sent in the client's response. CHAP protects against replay attacks by using an arbitrary challenge string for each authentication attempt. CHAP protects against remote client impersonation by unpredictably sending repeated challenges to the remote client throughout the duration of the connection.

During the CHAP process, a three-way handshake occurs:

1. A link is established, and then the server agent sends a message to the machine originating the link.

2. This machine then computes a hash function from the challenge and sends it to the server.

3. The server determines whether this is the expected response and, if so, authenticates the connection.

At any time, the server can request the connected party to send a new challenge message. Because CHAP identifiers are changed frequently and because authentication can be requested by the server at any time, CHAP provides more security than PAP. Both CHAP and PAP are defined in RFC1334.

MS-CHAP

The Microsoft Challenge Handshake Authentication Protocol (MS-CHAP) is an encrypted authentication mechanism very similar to CHAP. As in CHAP, the NAS sends a challenge, which consists of a session ID and an arbitrary challenge string, to the remote client. The remote client must return the username and an encrypted form of the challenge string, the session ID, and the MD4-hashed password. This design, which uses a hash of the MD4 hash of the password, provides an additional level of security because it allows the server to store hashed passwords instead of clear-text passwords.

MS-CHAP also provides additional error codes, including a password expired code, and additional encrypted client-server messages that permit users to change their passwords. In MS-CHAP, both the access client and the NAS independently generate an initial key for subsequent data encryption by MPPE. Therefore, MS-CHAP authentication is required to enable MPPE-based data encryption.

MS-CHAP version 2

MS-CHAP version 2 (MS-CHAP v2) is an updated encrypted authentication mechanism that provides stronger security. The NAS sends a challenge to the access client that consists of a session identifier and an arbitrary challenge string. The remote access client sends a response that contains the following:

✦ The username

✦ An arbitrary peer challenge string

✦ An encrypted form of the received challenge string

✦ The peer challenge string

✦ The session identifier

✦ The user's password

The NAS checks the response from the client and sends back a response containing an indication of the success or failure of the connection attempt and an authenticated response based on the sent challenge string, the peer challenge string, the encrypted response of the client, and the user's password. The remote access client verifies the authentication response and, if correct, uses the connection. If the authentication response is not correct, the remote access client terminates the connection.

Using this process, MS-CHAP v2 provides mutual authentication; the NAS verifies that the access client has knowledge of the user's password, and the access client verifies that the NAS has knowledge of the user's password. MS-CHAP v2 also determines two encryption keys, one for data sent and one for data received.

Extensible Authentication Protocol

Because most implementations of PPP provide very limited authentication methods, the Extensible Authentication Protocol (EAP) was designed to allow the dynamic addition of authentication plug-in modules at both the client and server ends of a connection

EAP is an extension to PPP that allows for arbitrary authentication mechanisms for the validation of a PPP connection. This allows vendors to supply a new authentication scheme at any time, providing the highest flexibility in authentication uniqueness and variation. EAP is supported in Microsoft Windows 2000 and is defined in RFC 2284.

EAP Transport Level Security

EAP Transport Level Security (EAP-TLS) is an IETF standard (RFC 2716) for a strong authentication method based on public-key certificates. With EAP-TLS, a client presents a user certificate to the dial-in server, and the server presents a server certificate to the client. The client provides strong user authentication to the server, and the server provides assurance that the user has reached the server that he or she expected. Both systems rely on a chain of trusted authorities to verify the validity of the offered certificate.

EAP-TLS is the specific EAP method implemented in Microsoft Windows 2000. Like MS-CHAP and MS-CHAP v2, EAP-TLS returns an encryption key to enable subsequent data encryption by MPPE.

Wireless VPNs

Wireless LANs can especially benefit from a VPN. A VPN can be used to act as a gateway between the WLAN and the network and can supplement the WEP's authentication and encryption functions. All traffic between the wired and wireless network should travel through the VPN tunnel and be encrypted with the IPSec protocol. IPSec thwarts sniffer attacks launched using applications such as AirSnort.

When a VPN client needs to access the network, it will connect to a VPN server, and the server will authenticate the client. Once authenticated, the VPN server will provide the client with an IP address and an encryption key. All communications will be carried out through this IP address. Every packet that passes through this secure tunnel between the client and server will be encrypted.

Consequently, an attacker cannot simply hijack an IP address to gain access, because he or she will not possess the encryption key. The VPN server will simply reject all connections from the attacker.

Guidelines for wireless VPN implementation include:

✦ Use VPN clients on wireless devices to enforce strong encryption and require positive authentication via hardware tokens.

✦ For wireless applications within the company, use a wireless VPN solution that supports a FIPS-approved data encryption algorithm to ensure data confidentiality in a WLAN environment.

✦ Ensure that each endpoint of the VPN remains under company control. When possible, install WLAN network APs and wVPN gateways behind network perimeter security mechanisms (e.g., firewall, IDS, etc.), so that wireless access to the internal wired network can be controlled and monitored.

More detail about wireless technologies can be found later in the chapter.

RADIUS and TACACS

As the demand for large remote access networks increases, remote access authentication systems have emerged to provide better network access security for remote clients. The two most common remote access authentication systems are Remote Authentication Dial-In User Server (RADIUS) and Terminal Access Controller Access Control System + (TACACS+), which is TACACS with additional features, including the use of two-factor authentication.

TACACS and RADIUS are *standards-based*, which means that they are interoperable with other systems of the same type. Some of these systems provide a centralized database that maintains user lists, passwords, and user profiles that remote access equipment on a network can access to authenticate clients.

Remote Authentication Dial-in User Service (RADIUS)

The Remote Authentication Dial-in User Service (RADIUS) protocol is a lightweight, UDP-based protocol used for managing remote user authentication and authorization. It is a fully open protocol, is distributed in source code format, and can be modified to work with any security system that is currently available on the market.

RADIUS is a distributed client/server system wherein the clients send their authentication requests to a central RADIUS server that contains all of the user authentication and network service access information (network ACLs). RADIUS servers can be located anywhere on the network, and they provide authentication and authorization for network access servers and VPNs.

RADIUS can be used with TACACS+ and Kerberos to provide CHAP remote node authentication. It provides similar user authentication (including the use of dynamic passwords) and password management as a TACACS+-enabled system.

Because RADIUS does not support all protocols, it is often used as a stepping-stone to a more robust TACACS+ system. Also, RADIUS does not provide two-way authentication and therefore is not commonly used for router-to-router authentication. Figure 3-32 shows a RADIUS server performing authentication within a company intranet for VPN and remote access server (RAS) clients.

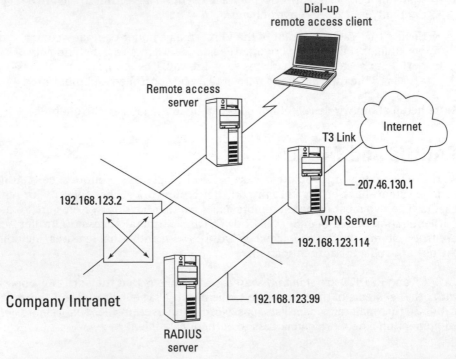

Figure 3-32: A RADIUS VPN.

Wireless RADIUS

Several 802.11 access points offer RADIUS authentication, which gives wireless clients access to network resources after supplying a username and password to a RADIUS server. Such user-based authentication provides a centrally managed method of verifying users who attempt to access the wireless network. Most RADIUS servers can handle this VPN client authentication functionality.

Some RADIUS implementations also allow the user to be authenticated via a digital key system, and they restrict access to preauthorized areas by the user. For example, Cisco's RADIUS server makes it possible to establish access by time and date.

Terminal Access Controller Access Control System (TACACS)

TACACS is an authentication protocol that provides remote access authentication and related services, such as event logging. In a TACACS system, user passwords are administered in a central database rather than in individual routers, which provides an easily scalable network security solution. A TACACS-enabled network device prompts the remote user for a username and static password, and then the TACACS-enabled device queries a TACACS server to verify that password. TACACS does not support prompting for a password change or for the use of dynamic password tokens.

TACACS+ has superseded TACACS. TACACS+ provides the following additional features:

✦ The use of two-factor password authentication

✦ The ability for a user to change his or her password

✦ The capability for resynchronizing security tokens

✦ Better audit trails and session accounting

Network Availability

This section defines those elements that can provide for or threaten network availability. Network availability can be defined as an area of the Telecommunications and Network Security domain that directly affects the Information Systems Security tenet of availability.

RAID

RAID stands for *redundant array of inexpensive disks*. It is also commonly referred to as the *redundant array of independent disks*. Its primary purpose is to provide fault tolerance and protection against file server hard disk failure and the resultant loss of availability and data. Some RAID types secondarily improve system performance by caching and distributing disk reads from multiple disks that work together to save files simultaneously.

Simply put, RAID separates the data into multiple units and stores it on multiple disks by using a process called *striping*. It can be implemented either as a hardware or a software solution; each type of implementation has its own issues and benefits.

The RAID Advisory Board has defined three classifications of RAID:

✦ Failure Resistant Disk Systems (FRDS)
✦ Failure Tolerant Disk Systems
✦ Disaster Tolerant Disk Systems

RAID Levels

RAID is implemented in one or a combination of several ways, called *levels*. They are:

RAID Level 0 creates one large disk by using several disks. This process is called *striping*. It stripes data across all disks (but provides no redundancy) by using all of the available drive space to create the maximum usable data volume size and to increase the read/write performance. One problem with this level of RAID is that it actually lessens the fault tolerance of the disk system rather than increasing it; the entire data volume is unusable if one drive in the set fails.

RAID Level 1 is commonly called *mirroring*. It mirrors the data from one disk or set of disks by duplicating the data onto another disk or set of disks. This process is often implemented by a one-for-one disk-to-disk ratio; each drive is mirrored to an equal drive partner that is continually being updated with current data. If one drive fails, the system automatically gets the data from the other drive. The main issue with this level of RAID is that the one-for-one ratio is very expensive, resulting in the highest cost per megabyte of data capacity. This level effectively doubles the amount of hard drives you need; therefore, it is usually best for smaller-capacity systems.

RAID Level 2 consists of bit-interleaved data on multiple disks. The parity information is created by using a hamming code that detects errors and establishes which part of which drive is in error. It defines a disk drive system with 39 disks—32 disks of user storage and seven disks of error recovery coding. This level is not used in practice and was quickly superseded by the more flexible levels of RAID that follow.

RAID Levels 3 and 4 are discussed together because they function in the same way. The only difference is that level 3 is implemented at the byte level and level 4 is usually implemented at the block level. In this scenario, data is striped across several drives and the parity check bit is written to a dedicated parity drive. This process is similar to RAID 0. They both have a large data volume, but the addition of a dedicated parity drive provides redundancy. If a hard disk fails, the data can be reconstructed by using the bit information on the parity drive. The main issue with these levels of RAID is that the constant writes to the parity drive can create a performance hit. In this implementation, spare drives can be used to replace crashed drives.

RAID Level 5 stripes the data and the parity information at the block level across all the drives in the set. It is similar to RAID 3 and 4 except that the parity information is written to the next-available drive rather than to a dedicated drive by using an interleave parity. This feature enables more flexibility in the implementation and increases fault tolerance because the parity drive is not a single point of failure, as it is in RAID 3 and 4. The disk reads and writes are also performed concurrently, thereby increasing performance over levels 3 and 4. The spare drives that replace the failed drives are usually *hot swappable*, meaning they can be replaced on the server while the system is up and running. This is probably the most popular implementation of RAID today.

Vendors created various other implementations of RAID to combine the features of several RAID levels, although these levels are less common. Level 6 is an extension of Level 5 that allows for additional fault tolerance by using a second independent distributed parity scheme, i.e., two-dimensional parity. Level 10 is created by combining level 0 (striping) with level 1 (mirroring). Level 15 is created by combining level 1 (mirroring) with level 5 (interleave). Level 51 is created by mirroring entire level 5 arrays. Table 3-9 shows the various levels of RAID with terms you will need to remember.

Table 3-9
RAID Level Descriptions

RAID Level	Description
0	Striping
1	Mirroring
2	Hamming Code Parity
3	Byte Level Parity
4	Block Level Parity
5	Interleave Parity
6	Second Independent Parity
7	Single Virtual Disk
10	Striping Across Multiple Pairs (1+0)
15	Striping With Parity Across RAID 5 Pairs (1+5)
51	Mirrored RAID 5 Arrays With Parity (5+1)

High Availability and Fault Tolerance

The concept of high availability refers to a level of fault tolerance and redundancy in transaction processing and communications. While these processes are not used solely for disaster recovery, they are often elements of a larger disaster recovery plan. If one or more of these processes are employed, the ability of a company to get back on-line is greatly enhanced.

Some concepts employed for high availability and fault tolerance are:

Electronic vaulting. Electronic vaulting refers to the transfer of backup data to an off-site location. This is primarily a batch process of dumping the data through communications lines to a server at an alternate location.

Remote journaling. Remote journaling consists of the parallel processing of transactions to an alternate site, as opposed to a batch dump process like electronic vaulting. A communications line is used to transmit live data as they occur. This feature enables the alternate site to be fully operational at all times and introduces a very high level of fault tolerance.

Database shadowing. Database shadowing uses the live processing advantages of remote journaling, but it creates even more redundancy by duplicating the database sets to multiple servers.

Redundant Servers. A redundant server implementation takes the concept of RAID 1 (mirroring) and applies it to a pair of servers. A primary server mirrors its data to a secondary server, thus enabling the primary to "roll over" to the secondary in the case of primary server failure (the secondary server steps in and takes over for the primary server). This rollover can be hot or warm (that is, the rollover may or may not be transparent to the user), depending upon the vendor's implementation of this redundancy. This process is also known as *server fault tolerance*. Figure 3-33 demonstrates redundant servers.

Server Clustering. A server cluster is a group of independent servers that are managed as a single system, providing higher availability, easier manageability, and greater scalability. The concept of server clustering is similar to the redundant server implementation previously discussed, except that all the servers in the cluster are online and take part in processing service requests. By enabling the secondary servers to provide processing time, the cluster acts as an intelligent entity and balances the traffic load to improve performance. The cluster looks like a single server from the user's point of view. If any server in the cluster crashes, processing continues transparently; however, the cluster suffers some performance degradation. This implementation is sometimes called a *server farm*. Figure 3-34 shows a type of server clustering.

Redundant communications lines. T1 and other communications lines need redundancy, as the severing of a T1 line or another type of loss of the line can cause a failure of availability. ISDN BRI is commonly used as a backup for a T1. An organization may use multiple telecommunications vendors for fault tolerance.

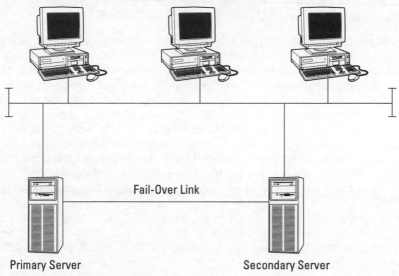

Figure 3-33: Redundant servers.

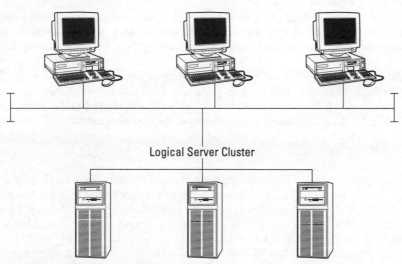

Figure 3-34: Server clustering.

Backup Concepts

A CISSP candidate will also need to know the basic concepts of data backup. The candidate might be presented with questions regarding file selection methods, tape format types, and common problems.

Backup Method Example

A full backup was made on Friday night. This full backup is just what it says—it copied every file on the file server to the tape regardless of the last time any other backup was made. This type of backup is common for creating full copies of the data for off-site archiving or in preparation for a major system upgrade. On Monday night, another backup was made. If the site uses the Incremental Backup method, Monday, Tuesday, Wednesday, and Thursday's backup tapes contain only those files that were altered during that day (Monday's incremental backup tape has only Monday's data on it, Tuesday's backup tape has only Tuesday's on it, and so on). All backup tapes might be required to restore a system to its full state after a system crash because some files that changed during the week might exist only on one tape. If the site is using the Differential Backup method, Monday's tape backup has the same files that the incremental tape has (Monday is the only day that the files have changed so far). However, on Tuesday, rather than only backing up that day's files, it also backed up Monday's files—creating a longer backup. Although this increases the time required to perform the backup and increases the amount of tapes needed, it does provide more protection from tape failure and speeds up recovery time (see Table 3-10).

Tape Backup Methods

The purpose of a tape backup method is to protect and/or restore lost, corrupted, or deleted information—thereby preserving the data's integrity and ensuring network availability. There are several varying methods of selecting files for backup.

Most backup methods use the Archive file attribute to determine whether the file should be backed up or not. The backup software determines which files need to be backed up by checking to see whether the Archive file attribute has been set and then resets the Archive bit value to null after the backup procedure.

The three most common methods are:

1. *Full Backup Method*—This backup method makes a complete backup of every file on the server every time it is run. A full or complete backup backs up all files in all directories stored on the server regardless of when the last backup was made and whether the files have already been backed up. The Archive file attribute is changed to mark that the files have been backed up, and the tapes or tapes will have all data and applications on it or them. The method is primarily run for system archive or baselined tape sets.

2. *Incremental Backup Method*—The incremental backup method backs up files that have been created or modified only since the last backup was made, or in other words files whose Archive file attribute is reset. This can result in the backup operator needing several tapes to do a complete restoration, as every tape with changed files as well as the last full backup tape will need to be restored.

3. *Differential Backup Method*—The differential backup method backs up files that have been created or modified only since the last backup was made, like

an incremental backup. However, the difference between an incremental backup and a differential backup is that the Archive file attribute is not reset after the differential backup is completed. Therefore the changed file is backed up every time the differential backup is run. The backup set grows in size until the next full backup as these files continue to be backed up during each subsequent differential backup. The advantage of this backup method is that the backup operator should need only the full backup and the one differential backup to restore the system.

Table 3-10
Differential versus Incremental Tape Backup

Backup Method	Monday	Tuesday	Wednesday	Thursday	Friday
Full Backup	Not Used	Not Used	Not Used	Not Used	All files
Differential	Changed File A	Changed Files A & B	Files A, B, & C	Files A, B, C, & D	Not Used
Incremental	Changed File A	Changed File B	Changed File C	Changed File D	Not Used

Other Backup Formats

Compact Disc (CD) optical media. Write once, read many (WORM) optical disk "jukeboxes" are used for archiving data that does not change. This is a very good format to use for a permanent backup. Companies use this format to store data in an accessible format that may need to be accessed at a much later date, such as legal data. The shelf life of a CD is also longer than a tape. Rewritable and erasable (CDR/W) optical disks are sometimes used for backups that require short-time storage for changeable data but require faster file access than tape. This format is used more often for very small data sets.

Zip/Jaz drives, SyQuest, and Bernoulli boxes. These types of drives are frequently used for the individual backups of small data sets of specific application data. These formats are very transportable and are often the standard for data exchange in many businesses.

Tape Arrays. A Tape Array is a large hardware/software system that uses the RAID technology we discussed earlier in a large device with multiple (sometimes 32 or 64) tapes, configured as a single array. These devices require very specific hardware and software to operate, but they provide a very fast backup and a multi-tasking backup of multiple targets with considerable fault tolerance.

Hierarchical Storage Management (HSM). HSM provides a continuous online backup by using optical or tape "jukeboxes," similar to WORMs. It appears as an infinite disk to the system and can be configured to provide the closest version of an available real-time backup. This is commonly employed in very large data retrieval systems.

Common Backup Issues and Problems

All backup systems share common issues and problems, whether they use a tape or a CD-ROM format. There are three primary backup concerns:

Slow data transfer of the backup. All backups take time, especially tape backup. Depending upon the volume of data that needs to be copied, full backups to tape can take an incredible amount of time. In addition, the time required to restore the data must also be factored into any disaster recovery plan. Backups that pass data through the network infrastructure must be scheduled during periods of low network utilization, which are commonly overnight, over the weekend, or during holidays. This also requires off-hour monitoring of the backup process.

Server disk space utilization expands over time. As the amount of data that needs to be copied increases, the length of time to run the backup proportionally increases, and the demand on the system grows as more tapes are required. Sometimes the data volume on the hard drives expands very quickly, thus overwhelming the backup process. Therefore, this process must be monitored regularly.

The time the last backup was run is never the time of the server crash. With noncontinuous backup systems, data that was entered after the last backup prior to a system crash will have to be recreated. Some systems have been designed to provide online fault tolerance during backup (the old Vortex Retrochron was one), yet because backup is a post-processing batch process, some data re-entry will need to be performed.

Wireless Technologies

Wireless technology is probably the fastest-growing area of network connectivity. Experts estimate that the number of Internet-connected PDAs, such as the Palm Pilot, will eclipse the number of personal computers in use in a few years. Security is an extreme concern here because all wireless technologies (mobile phones, satellite transmissions, and so forth) are inherently susceptible to interception and eavesdropping. Encryption standards are rapidly being developed to combat this problem.

IEEE Wireless Standards

IEEE 802.11 refers to a family of specifications for wireless local area networks (WLANs) developed by a working group of the Institute of Electrical and Electronics Engineers (IEEE). 802.11 also generically refers to the IEEE Committee responsible for setting the various wireless LAN standards. This standards effort began in 1989 with the focus on deployment in large enterprise networking environments, effectively a wireless equivalent to Ethernet. The IEEE accepted the specification in 1997.

The 802.11 specification identifies an over-the-air interface between a mobile device wireless client and a base station or between two mobile device wireless clients. To date, there are four completed specifications in the family: 802.11, 802.11a, 802.11b, and 802.11g, with a fifth, 802.11e, in development as a draft standard. All four existing standards use the Ethernet protocol and carrier sense multiple access with collision avoidance (CSMA/CA) for path sharing.

There are several specifications in the 802.11 family, including:

✦ **802.11** — The original IEEE wireless LAN standard that provides 1 or 2 Mbps transmission speed in the 2.4 GHz band, using either FHSS or DSSS (see "Spread Spectrum Technologies"). The modulation used in 802.11 is commonly phase-shift keying (PSK).

✦ **802.11a** — An extension to the original IEEE 802.11 wireless LAN standard that provides up to 54 Mbps in the 5 GHz band. 802.11a uses an orthogonal frequency division multiplexing encoding scheme rather than FHSS or DSSS.

✦ **802.11b** — An extension to the 802.11 wireless LAN standard, it provides 11 Mbps transmission speed (but that automatically slows down to 5.5 Mbps, 2 Mbps, or 1 Mbps speeds in the 2.4 GHz band based upon the strength of the signal). 802.11b uses only DSSS. 802.11b, a 1999 ratification to the original 802.11 standard, provides wireless functionality comparable to Ethernet; it is also referred to as 802.11 High Rate or Wi-Fi.

✦ **802.11g** — A newer IEEE wireless standard that applies to wireless LANs, 802.11g provides 20 Mbps to 54 Mbps in the 2.4 GHz band.

✦ **802.11e** — The latest IEEE draft extension to provide QoS features and multimedia support for home and business wireless environments.

✦ **802.15** — IEEE 802.15 defines Wireless Personal Area Networks (WPAN), such as Bluetooth, in the 2.4-2.5 GHz band.

✦ **802.16** — Another wireless 802 standard called IEEE 802 Broadband Wireless Access (802.WBA or 802.16) is under development. IEEE 802.16 standardizes the air interface and related functions associated with the wireless local loop (WLL) for wireless broadband subscriber access. Three working groups have been chartered to produce 802.16 standards: IEEE 802.16.1, air interface for 10 to 66 GHz; IEEE 802.16.2, coexistence of broadband wireless access systems; and IEEE 802.16.3, air interface for licensed frequencies, 2 to 11 GHz.

802.1x

The IEEE drafted the 802.1x Port Based Network Access Control standard in 2001 to provide enhanced security for users of 802.11b wireless LANs. It provides port-level authentication for any wired or wireless Ethernet client system. This supplement to ISO/IEC 15802-3:1998 (IEEE Std 802.1D-1998) defines the changes necessary to the operation of a MAC Bridge in order to provide port-based network access control capability.

Originally designed as a standard for wired Ethernet, 802.1x is applicable to WLANs. It leverages many of the security features used with dial-up networking; for example, it uses encryption keys that are unique for each user and each network session, and it supports 128-bit key lengths. It has a key management protocol built into its specification, which provides keys automatically. Keys can also be changed rapidly at set intervals. It will also support the use of Remote Authentication Dial-in User Service (RADIUS) and Kerberos. The 802.1x standard can be used to provide link-layer authentication, making employee authentication by active directories and databases easier.

The standard defines a client/server-based access control and authentication protocol that restricts unauthorized devices from connecting to a LAN through publicly accessible ports. The authentication server verifies each client connected to a switch port before making available any services offered by the switch or the LAN. Until the client has been authenticated, 802.1x access control allows only Extensible Authentication Protocol over LAN (EAPOL) traffic through the port to which the client is connected. Once the client has been authenticated, normal traffic can pass through the port.

Cisco Systems has implemented 802.1x in its Aironet series of cards, and Microsoft has added the feature to WinXP. The goal of 802.1x is to provide a level of authentication comparable to that of the wired network. Using 802.1x, any appropriated wireless network interface cards (NICs) no longer pose a threat because the network now authenticates the user, not the hardware.

When the user (called the *supplicant*) wants to use the network service, he or she will connect to the access point (called the *authenticator*), and a RADIUS server (the authentication server) at the other end will receive the request and issue a challenge. If the supplicant can provide a correct response, it is allowed access.

Cisco introduced the Lightweight Extensible Authentication Protocol (LEAP) for its Aironet devices. Using LEAP, client devices dynamically generate a new WEP key as part of the login process instead of using a static key. In the Cisco model, the supplicant and authentication server change roles and attempt mutual communication. Using this method of authentication, the risk of authenticating to a rogue access point is minimized. After authentication, the authentication server and the supplicant determine a WEP key for the session. This gives each client a unique WEP for every session.

Spread-Spectrum Technologies

The de facto communication standard for wireless LANs is spread spectrum, a wideband radio frequency technique originally developed by the military for use in secure, mission-critical communications systems[1]. Spread spectrum uses a radio transmission mode that broadcasts signals over a range of frequencies. The receiving mobile device must know the correct frequency of the spread-spectrum signal being broadcast.

Two different spread spectrum technologies for 2.4 GHz wireless LANs currently exist: direct-sequence spread spectrum (DSSS) and frequency-hopping spread spectrum (FHSS).

Direct Sequence Spread Spectrum (DSSS)

DSSS is a wideband spread-spectrum transmission technology that generates a redundant bit pattern for each bit to be transmitted. DSSS spreads the signal over a wide frequency band in which the source transmitter maps each bit of data into a pattern of chips. At the receiving mobile device, the original data is recreated by mapping the chips back into a data bit. The DSSS transmitter and receiver must be synchronized to operate properly. A DSSS signal appears as low-power wideband noise to a non-DSSS receiver and therefore is ignored by most narrowband receivers.

DSSS spreads across the spectrum, but the number of independent, non-overlapping channels in the 2.4 GHz band is small (typically only three). Therefore, only a very limited number of collocated networks can operate without interference. Some DSSS products enable users to deploy more than one channel in the same area by separating the 2.4 GHz band into multiple subbands, each of which contains an independent DSSS network.

Frequency-Hopping Spread Spectrum (FHSS)

FHSS uses a narrowband carrier that continually changes frequency in a known pattern. The FHSS algorithm spreads the signal by operating on one frequency for a short duration and then "hopping" to another frequency. The minimum number of frequencies engaged in the hopping pattern and the maximum frequency dwell time (how long it stays on each frequency before it changes) are restricted by the FCC, which requires that 75 or more frequencies be used with a maximum dwell time of 400 ms.

The source mobile device's transmission and the destination mobile device's transmission must be synchronized so that they are on the same frequency at the same time. When the transmitter and receiver are properly synchronized, it maintains a single logical communications channel. Similar to DSSS, FHSS appears to be noise of a short duration to a non-FHSS receiver and hence is ignored.

FHSS makes it possible to deploy many non-overlapping channels. Because there are a large number of possible sequences in the 2.4 GHz band, FHSS products enable users to deploy more than one channel in the same area by implementing separate channels with different hopping sequences.

WLAN Operational Modes

The IEEE 802.11 wireless networks operate in one of two operational modes: ad hoc or infrastructure mode. Ad hoc mode is a peer-to-peer type of networking, whereas infrastructure mode uses access points to communicate between the mobile devices and the wired network.

Ad Hoc Mode

In ad hoc mode, each mobile device client communicates directly with the other mobile device clients within the network. That is, no access points are used to connect the ad hoc network directly with any WLAN. Ad hoc mode is designed so that only the clients within transmission range (within the same cell) of each other can communicate. If a client on an ad hoc network wants to communicate outside the cell, a member of the cell must operate as a gateway and perform a routing service. Figure 3-35 shows a wireless session in ad hoc mode.

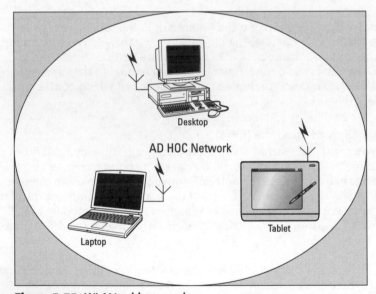

Figure 3-35: WLAN ad hoc mode.

Infrastructure Mode

Each mobile device client in infrastructure mode sends all of its communications to a network device called an *access point* (*AP*). The access point acts as an Ethernet bridge and forwards the communications to the appropriate network, either the WLAN or another wireless network. Figure 3-36 shows access points attached to a wired LAN to create an Infrastructure Mode 802.11b WLAN.

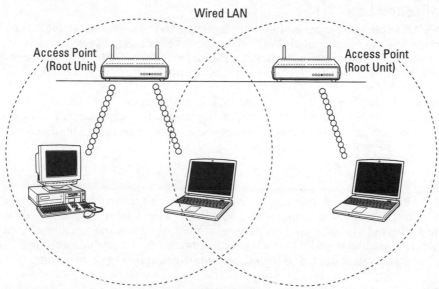

Figure 3-36: Infrastructure Mode 802.11b WLAN.

Wireless Application Protocol (WAP)

Wireless Application Protocol (WAP) was developed as a set of technologies related to HTML but tailored to the small screens and limited resources of handheld, wireless devices. The most notable of these technologies is the Handheld Device Markup Language (HDML). HDML looks similar to HTML but has a feature set and programming paradigm tailored to wireless devices with small screens. HDML and other elements of this architecture eventually became the Wireless Markup Language (WML) and the architecture of WAP.

Since its initial release, WAP has evolved twice. Releases 1.1 and 1.2 of the specification have the same functionality as 1.0 but with added features to align with what the rest of the industry is doing. Version 1.3 is used most often in WAP products as of this writing.

In August 2001, the WAP Forum approved and released the specifications for WAP 2.0 for public review, and Ericsson, Nokia, and Motorola all announced support for WAP 2.0. The WAP 2.0 specification contains new functionality that enables users to send sound and moving pictures, among other things, over their telephones. WAP 2.0 will also provide a toolkit for easy development and deployment of new services, including XHTML.

The WAP architecture is loosely based on the OSI model, but unlike the seven layers of OSI or the four layers of the TCP/IP model, WAP has five layers: application, session, transaction, security, and transport.

Application Layer

The WAP application layer is the direct interface to the user and contains the wireless application environment (WAE). This top layer consists of several elements, including a microbrowser specification for Internet access, the Wireless Markup Language (WML), WMLScript, and wireless telephony applications (WTA).

It encompasses devices, content, development languages (WML and WMLScript), wireless telephony APIs (WTA) for accessing telephony functionality from within WAE programs, and some well-defined content formats for phone book records, calendar information, and graphics.

Session Layer

The WAP session layer contains the Wireless Session Protocol (WSP), which is similar to the Hypertext Transfer Protocol (HTTP) because it is designed for low-bandwidth, high-latency wireless networks. WSP facilitates the transfer of content between WAP clients and WAP gateways in a binary format. Additional functionalities include content push and the suspension/resumption of connections.

The WSP layer provides a consistent interface to WAE for two types of session services: a connection mode and a connectionless service. This layer provides the following:

✦ Connection creation and release between the client and server

✦ Data exchange between the client and server by using a coding scheme that is much more compact than traditional HTML text

✦ Session suspend and release between the client and server

Transaction Layer

The WAP transaction layer provides the Wireless Transactional Protocol (WTP), which provides functionality similar to TCP/IP in the Internet model. WTP is a lightweight transactional protocol that provides reliable request and response transactions and supports unguaranteed and guaranteed push.

WTP provides transaction services to WAP. It handles acknowledgments so that users can determine whether a transaction has succeeded. It also provides a retransmission of transactions in case they are not successfully received, and it removes duplicate transactions. WTP manages different classes of transactions for WAP devices — unreliable one-way requests, reliable one-way requests, and reliable two-way requests. An unreliable request from a WAP device means that no precautions are taken to guarantee that the request for information makes it to the server.

Security Layer

The security layer contains Wireless Transport Layer Security (WTLS). WTLS is based on Transport Layer Security (TLS, similar to the Secure Sockets Layer, or SSL) and can be invoked in a manner similar to HTTPS in the Internet world. It provides data integrity, privacy, authentication, and DoS protection mechanisms. See the section following for more detail on the function of WTLS.

WAP privacy services guarantee that all transactions between the WAP device and gateway are encrypted. Authentication guarantees the authenticity of the client and application server. DoS protection detects and rejects data that comes in the form of unverified requests.

Transport Layer

The bottom WAP layer, the transport layer, supports the Wireless Datagram Protocol (WDP), which provides an interface to the bearers of transportation. It supports the CDPD, GSM, *Integrated Digital Enhanced Network* (iDEN), CDMA, TDMA, SMS, and FLEX protocols.

WDP provides a consistent interface to the higher layers of the WAP architecture, meaning that it does not matter which type of wireless network on which the application is running. Among other capabilities, WDP provides data error correction. The bearers, or wireless communications networks, are at WAP's lowest level.

Figure 3-37 shows the layers of WAP.

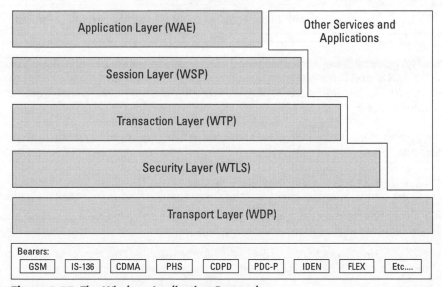

Figure 3-37: The Wireless Application Protocol.

Wireless Security

Wireless is one of the newest communications technology frontiers, offering the possibility of always-on, instant mobile communications. However, the vulnerabilities inherent to wireless computing present daunting hurdles. These vulnerabilities — eavesdropping, session hijacking, data alteration and manipulation, in conjunction with an overall lack of privacy — are major challenges posed by wireless technologies.

Typically, when a new technology emerges, standards are created and a rush commences to develop the technology without a thorough security vetting. This has been the case with wireless, too. The result is that much work is now devoted to retrofitting security into the existing models and protocols and designing new models and protocols with better security features. Progress is being made, as standards like 802.1x and newer versions of WAP show. Network infrastructure design, such as implementation of VPNs and RADIUS, also can help create secure pipes for wireless sessions.

Wireless Transport Layer Security Protocol

The Wireless Transport Layer Security Protocol (WTLS), is WAP's communications security protocol. It operates above the Transport Protocol layer and provides the upper-level layer of the WAP with a secure transport service interface. The interface preserves the transport interface below it and presents methods to manage secure connections. The primary purpose of the WTLS is to provide privacy, data integrity, and authentication for WAP applications to enable safe connections to other clients.

The WTLS supports a group of algorithms to meet privacy, authentication, and integrity requirements.

Currently, privacy is implemented using block ciphers, such as DES-CBC, IDEA, and RC5-CBC. RSA- and Diffie-Hellman–based key exchange suites are supported to authenticate the communicating parties. Integrity is implemented with SHA-1 and MD5 algorithms.

For secure wireless communications, the client and the server must be authenticated and the connection encrypted. WTLS provides three classes of security:

✦ *Class 1: Anonymous Authentication* — In this mode, the client logs on to the server, but neither the client nor the server can be certain of the other's identity.

✦ *Class 2: Server Authentication* — The server is authenticated to the client, but the client is not authenticated to the server.

✦ *Class 3: Two-Way Client and Server Authentication* — The server is authenticated to the client, and the client is authenticated to the server.

WTLS is based on the Transport Layer Security (TLS) security layer used on the Internet but with a number of modifications to accommodate the nature of wireless networks. For one, it has been optimized for low-bandwidth networks with relatively long latency. And because of the limited processing power and memory of mobile devices, fast algorithms are implemented in the algorithm suite. In addition, restrictions on export and the using of cryptography must be observed.

The WTLS is the first attempt to provide a secure end-to-end connection for the WAP. The most common protocols, such as TLS v1.0 and SSL v3.0, were adopted as a basis of the WTLS. WTLS incorporates features such as datagram support, optimized packet size and handshake, and dynamic key refreshing.

WEP Encryption

An option in IEEE 802.11b, Wired Equivalent Privacy (WEP), uses a 40-bit shared secret key, a Rivest Code 4 (RC4) pseudorandom number generator (PRNG) encryption algorithm, and a 24-bit initialization vector (IV) to provide data encryption. The basic process works as follows:

1. A checksum of the message is computed and appended to the message.

2. A shared secret key and the IV are fed to the RC4 algorithm to produce a key stream.

3. An exclusive OR (XOR) operation of the key stream with the message and checksum grouping produces ciphertext.

4. The IV is appended to the ciphertext to form the encrypted message, which is sent to the intended recipient.

5. The recipient, who has a copy of the same shared key, uses it to generate an identical key stream.

6. XORing the key stream with the ciphertext yields the original plaintext message.

You can find more details about WEP in Chapter 4, "Cryptography."

Wireless Vulnerabilities

Many vulnerabilities exist in wireless networks; let's look at a few.

Denial-of-Service Attacks

A denial-of-service (DoS) attack is an example of the failure of the tenet of availability. A DoS attack occurs when an adversary causes a system or a network to become unavailable to legitimate users or causes services to be interrupted or delayed. Consequences can range from a measurable reduction in performance to the complete failure of the system. An example from the wireless world could be an external signal jamming the wireless channel. There is little that can be done to keep a determined adversary from mounting a DoS attack because, as noted, wireless LANs are susceptible to interference and interception and hence often can be easily jammed.

Wireless networks are vulnerable to DoS attacks due to the nature of the wireless transmission medium. If an attacker makes use of a powerful transceiver, enough interference can be generated to prevent wireless devices from communicating with one another. DoS attack devices do not have to be next to the devices being attacked, either; they need only to be within range of the wireless transmissions.

Examples of techniques used to deny service to a wireless device are:

✦ Requests for authentication at such a frequency as to disrupt legitimate traffic.

✦ Requests for deauthentication of legitimate users. These requests may not be refused according to the current 802.11 standard.

✦ Mimics the behavior of an access point and convinces unsuspecting clients to communicate with it.

✦ Repeatedly transmits RTS/CTS frames to silence the network.

The 2.4-GHz frequency range, within which 802.11b operates, is shared with other wireless devices such as cordless telephones, baby monitors, and Bluetooth-based devices. All of these devices can contribute to the degradation and interruption of wireless signals. In addition, a determined and resourceful attacker with the proper equipment can flood the frequency with artificial noise and completely disrupt wireless network operation.

The "WAP GAP"

A specific security issue that is associated with WAP is the "WAP GAP." A WAP GAP results from the requirement to change security protocols at the carrier's WAP gateway from the wireless WTLS to SSL for use over the wired network. At the WAP gateway, the transmission, which is protected by WTLS, is decrypted and then re-encrypted for transmission using SSL. Thus, the data is temporarily in the clear on the gateway and can be compromised if the gateway is not adequately protected (See Figure 3-38).

In order to address this issue, the WAP Forum has put forth specifications that will reduce this vulnerability and thus support e-commerce applications. These specifications are defined in WAP 1.2 as WMLScript Crypto Library and the WAP Identity Module (WIM). The WMLScript Crypto Library supports end-to-end security by providing for cryptographic functions to be initiated on the WAP client from the Internet content server. These functions include digital signatures originating with the WAP client and encryption and decryption of data. The WIM is a tamper-resistant device, such as a smart card, that cooperates with WTLS and provides cryptographic operations during the handshake phase.

Take special precautions to avoid the compromise of sensitive information caused by the WAP GAP. WAP-enabled PEDs should not use commercial wireless network service provider gateways to access company Web servers unless end-to-end data encryption is provided.

However, the safest implementation of a WAP gateway is for companies to install the gateway in their own networks. A company WAP gateway reduces the risk of data compromise because the WTLS-to-SSL conversion required to access company Web servers would occur on a company-controlled and protected network, and connections may be monitored by IDS.

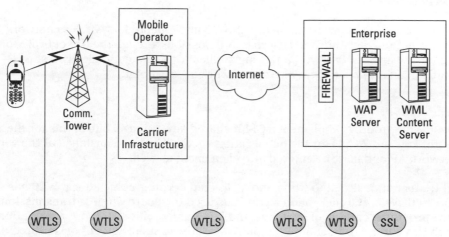

Figure 3-38: A WAP gateway.

Insertion Attacks

In an insertion attack, unauthorized devices are deployed in order to gain access to an existing network. Laptops or PDAs can be configured to attempt access to networks simply by installing wireless network cards and setting up near a target network. If password authentication is not enabled on the network, it's a simple matter to get a connection to an access point and network resources.

Rogue Access Points

An insertion attack could be facilitated by the deployment of rogue access points, either by a hacker or by well-meaning internal employees seeking to enhance wireless coverage. Hacker-controlled access points can be used to entice authorized wireless clients to connect to a hacker's access point rather than to the network's intended access points. In addition, access points not authorized by the network administrator have the potential to be improperly configured and thus vulnerable to outside attack. This raises the risk of the interception of login IDs and passwords for future direct attacks on a network. The risk can be magnified if rogue access points are deployed behind the corporate firewall.

Typically, an access point has one or several methods available to control access to a wireless LAN, typically including use of a common SSID, to allow access based on a MAC address, and WEP. Because the default authentication in 802.11 is open authentication, most systems will authenticate any user who requests connection. Shared key authentication is described but not mandated in 802.11, and it can be defeated.

Another common issue with 802.11b networks is that the access points have been designed for easy installation. So, though security features may be present, in most cases the default settings are for the features to be turned off so the network can be up and running as quickly as possible. Network administrators who leave their equipment with the default settings intact are particularly vulnerable, as hackers are likely to try known passwords and settings when attempting to penetrate wireless networks.

Also, even when password authentication is implemented on wireless network access points, unauthorized access is still possible through the use of brute-force dictionary attacks. Password-cracking applications can methodically test passwords in an attempt to break in to a network access point.

WEP Weaknesses

Most WEP products implement a 64-bit shared key, using 40 bits of this for the secret key and 24 bits for the initialization vector. The key is installed at the wired network AP and must be entered into each client as well.

WEP was not designed to withstand a directed cryptographic attack. WEP has well-known flaws in the encryption algorithms used to secure wireless transmissions. Two programs capable of exploiting the RC4 vulnerability, AirSnort, and WEPCrack, both run under Linux, and both require a relatively small amount of captured data.

A number of researchers have investigated attacks on WEP:

✦ University of California, Berkeley, and Zero-Knowledge Systems researchers released a paper outlining the vulnerability of key stream reuse caused by the mismanagement of IVs. In their paper it was noted that all possible IVs could be exhausted in as little as five hours.

✦ A paper written in 2000 by Scott Fluhrer, Itsik Mantin, and Adi Shamir exposed two significant weaknesses of RC4 in the key scheduling algorithm (KSA). They found that a small portion of the secret key determines a large portion of the initial KSA output, and the secret key can be easily derived by looking at the key stream used with multiple IVs.

✦ Rice University and AT&T Lab researchers put the aforementioned Fluhrer theory into practice by cracking encrypted packets and successfully demonstrating the severity of the flaw.

✦ In 2001, Nikita Borisov and a group of researchers from the University of California, Berkeley, published a paper regarding weaknesses in the WEP RC4 stream cipher. They found that if two messages used the same key stream, it might reveal information about both messages.

✦ Adam Stubblefield, an intern at AT&T Labs, was the first person to implement the Fluhrer attack mentioned above. He noted that an extra 802.2 header is added in IP traffic, making the attack easier as every IP packet has the same first plaintext byte.

WEP Encryption Workarounds

To address WEP encryption issues, some vendors have implemented several enhanced 802.11b security methods, such as:

Secure key derivation. The original shared secret secure key derivation is used to construct responses to the mutual challenges. It undergoes irreversible one-way hashes that make password-replay attacks impossible. The hash values sent over the wire are useful for one time at the start of the authentication process, but never again.

Initialization vector changes. The Cisco Aironet wireless security solution also changes the initlalization vector (IV) on a per-packet basis so that hackers can find no predetermined sequence to exploit. This capability, coupled with the reduction in possible attack windows, greatly mitigates exposure to hacker attacks due to frequent key rotation. In particular, this makes it difficult to create table-based attacks based on the knowledge of the IVs seen on the wireless network.

Dynamic WEP Keys. Several vendors are offering products that eliminate the use of static keys and instead implement per-user/per-session keys combined with RADIUS authentication. Clients must authenticate with a RADIUS server using network credentials, and WEP keys are dynamically distributed securely to the client.

Service Set Identifier (SSID) Issues

The service set identifier (SSID) is an identification value programmed in the access point or group of access points to identify the local wireless subnet. This segmentation of the wireless network into multiple networks is a form of an authentication check. If a wireless station does not know the value of the SSID, access is denied to the associated access point. When a client computer is connected to the access point, the SSID acts as a simple password, which provides a measure of security.

The wireless access point is configured to broadcast its SSID. When enabled, any client without a SSID is able to receive it and have access to the access point. Users are also able to configure their own client systems with the appropriate SSID because they are widely known and easily shared. A problem caused by the fact that most access points broadcast the SSID in their signals is that several of these access points use default SSIDs provided by the manufacturers, and a list of those default SSIDs is available for download on the Internet. This means that it's very easy for a hacker to determine a network's SSID and gain access to it via software tools.

Wireless Scanning and Eavesdropping

Wireless technology is also vulnerable to eavesdropping, especially because intruders do not have to physically tap into a network. Whether on a different floor, across the room, or outside the building, an intruder can passively "sniff" your network traffic without gaining physical access as long as he or she has a WLAN network card that has a promiscuous mode (that is, has the capability to capture every packet on the segment of the LAN). Covert monitoring of wireless LANs is simple.

Unless specifically configured to prevent another WLAN device from joining the network, a WLAN device will accept communications from any device within its range.

Furthermore, the 802.11 protocol inherently leaves the Physical Layer header unencrypted, providing critical information to the attacker. Therefore, data encryption is the critical layer of defense, but often data is transmitted unencrypted. Using wireless packet sniffers, an attacker can passively intercept wireless network traffic and, through packet analysis, determine login IDs and passwords, as well as collect other sensitive data.

War Driving

War driving (also war walking) is a term used to describe a hacker who, armed with a laptop and a wireless adapter card, and traveling via a car, bus, subway train, or other form of transport, goes around sniffing for WLANs.

The concept of war driving is simple: Using a device capable of receiving an 802.11b signal, a device capable of locating itself on a map, and software that will log data from the second when a network is detected by the first, the hacker moves from place to place, letting these devices do their job. Over time, the hacker builds up a database comprising the network name, signal strength, location, and ip/namespace in use. Via SNMP, the hacker may even log packet samples and probe the access point for available data. The hacker may also mark the location of the vulnerable wireless network with chalk on the sidewalk or building itself. This is called *war-chalking*, and alerts other intruders that an exposed WLAN is nearby.

Common war driving exploits find many wireless networks with WEP disabled and using only the SSID for access control. And, as noted earlier, the SSID for wireless networks can be found quickly. This vulnerability makes these networks susceptible to what's called the *parking lot attack*, where at a safe distance from the building's perimeter, an attacker gains access to the target network.

Wireless Packet Sniffers and Scanners

Wireless packet analyzers, or sniffers, basically work the same way as wired network packet analyzers: They capture packets from the data stream and allow the user to open them up and look at, or decode, them. Some wireless scanners don't employ full decoding tools but show existing WLANs and SSIDs.

A few of the wireless sniffers available are:

AirMagnet. AirMagnet is a wireless tool originally developed for WLAN inventory, but it has developed into a useful wireless security assessment utility.

NetStumbler. NetStumbler is a shareware program for locating WLAN SSIDs. It attempts to identify the WLAN vendor, and when coupled with a GPS, NetStumbler can provide directional information.

AiroPeek. WildPackets' AiroPeek is a packet analyzer for IEEE 802.11b wireless LANs, supporting all higher-level network protocols such as TCP/IP,

AppleTalk, NetBEUI, and IPX. AiroPeek is used to isolate security problems by decoding 802.11b WLAN protocols and by analyzing wireless network performance with an identification of signal strength, channel, and data rates.

Sniffer Wireless. McAfee Sniffer Wireless is also a packet analyzer for managing network applications and deployments on Wireless LAN 802.11a and 802.11b networks. It has the ability to decrypt Wired Equivalent Privacy–based traffic (WEP).

PDA Security Issues

PDAs have not been designed to the same standards nor exposed to the same rigorous examination as desktop operating systems, such as the functional requirements spelled out in the ISO standard 15408, the Common Criteria. When compared with the OS against security requirements described in these and other standards, most PDAs receive a very poor rating.

+ PDA operating systems do not have provisions to separate one user's data from another, which are required to support Discretionary Access Control (DAC).

+ They lack audit capabilities.

+ They have no support for object reuse control through the implementation of Identification and Authentication (I&A).

+ They do not provide data integrity protection.

+ Even when the OS is password-locked, applications can be installed onto the PalmOS without the owner's knowledge.

Confidentiality Loss

Even if a PDA is password-protected, a malicious user can retrieve the password of a target PDA by using the Palm debug mode. The password can then be decoded by using simple tools such as the PalmCrypt tool.

Once the password has been bypassed, all of the information on the PDA is fully readable by the malicious user. Security administrators currently do not have the ability to determine whether this type of attack has occurred, nor do they have any method to determine who was responsible for the attack.

Physical Loss

Probably the most common threat to a PDA is caused by the physical loss of the device. Although some technical solutions are available to protect against some of the OS security deficiencies we just mentioned, none provide a countermeasure to the physical security concerns associated with the use of PDAs. The devices are so small and portable that the loss of the device and any information contained on it is common. They are smaller, lighter, and their mode of use puts them at a greater risk because they are generally used in uncontrolled environments.

Intrusion Detection and Response

The number of reported computer intrusion incidents is constantly on the rise, from 9,859 in 1999 to 82,094 in 2002 (Source: CERT Coordination Center [CERT/CC], www.cert.org). Intrusion Detection (ID) and Response is the task of monitoring systems for evidence of an intrusion or an inappropriate usage and responding to the intrusion. ID is the detection of inappropriate, incorrect, or anomalous activity. ID is not a preventative control; it is a detective control.

Types of ID Systems

ID systems that operate on a specific host and detect malicious activity only on that host are called *host-based* ID systems. ID systems that operate on network segments and analyze that segment's traffic are called *network-based* ID systems. Since there are pros and cons to each, an effective IDS should use a combination of both network- and host-based intrusion detection systems.

Host-Based ID systems

Host-based ID systems employ small software programs called *intelligent agents*. They reside on a host computer, monitor the operating system, and continually write to log files and trigger alarms. They detect inappropriate activity only on the host computer; they do not monitor the entire network segment.

Host-based ID systems:

- ✦ Monitor accesses and changes to critical system files and changes in user privileges

- ✦ Detect trusted-insider attacks better than network-based IDS

- ✦ Are relatively effective for detecting attacks from the outside

- ✦ Can be configured to look at all network packets, connection attempts, or login attempts to the monitored machine, including dial-in attempts or other non-network–related communication ports

Network-Based ID systems

Network-based ID systems commonly reside on a discrete network segment and monitor the traffic on that network segment. They usually consist of a network appliance with a Network Interface Card (NIC) that is operating in promiscuous mode and is intercepting and analyzing the network packets in real time

Network-based ID involves looking at the packets on the network as they pass by some sensor. The sensor can see only the packets that happen to be carried on the network segment it's attached to. Network traffic on other segments, and traffic on other means of communication (like phone lines), can't be monitored properly by network -based IDS.

Packets are identified to be of interest if they match a signature. Three primary types of signatures are:

1. *String signatures* — String signatures look for a text string that indicates a possible attack.

2. *Port signatures* — Port signatures watch for connection attempts to well known, frequently attacked ports.

3. *Header condition signatures* — Header signatures watch for dangerous or illogical combinations in packet headers.

IDS Approaches

The most common approaches to ID are statistical anomaly (also known as behavior-based) detection and pattern-matching (also known as knowledge-based or signature-based) detection.

Knowledge-Based ID

Knowledge-based ID systems use a database of previous attacks and known system vulnerabilities to look for current attempts to exploit these vulnerabilities, and they trigger an alarm if an attempt is found. Most IDS today are knowledge-based, and the accuracy of knowledge-based intrusion detection systems is considered good.

The advantages of a knowledge-based ID system are:

✦ System is characterized by low false alarm rates (positives).

✦ Alarms are standardized and are clearly understandable by security personnel.

The disadvantages of knowledge-based ID systems are:

✦ System is resource-intensive. The knowledge database continually needs maintenance and updating with new vulnerabilities and environments to remain accurate.

✦ Since knowledge about attacks is very focused (dependent on the operating system, version, platform, and application), new, unique, or original attacks often go unnoticed.

✦ Detection of insider attacks involving an abuse of privileges is deemed more difficult because no vulnerability is actually exploited by the attacker.

Behavior-Based ID

Behavior-based ID systems dynamically detect deviations from the learned patterns of user behavior and an alarm is triggered when an activity that is considered intrusive (outside of normal system use) occurs. Behavior-based ID systems are less common than knowledge-based ID systems.

Behavior-based ID systems learn the normal or expected behavior of the system or the users and assume that an intrusion can be detected by observing deviations from this norm.

The advantages of behavior-based ID systems are:

✦ They dynamically adapt to new, unique, or original vulnerabilities.

✦ They are not as dependent upon specific operating systems as knowledge-based ID systems.

✦ They help detect abuse-of-privileges types of attacks that do not actually involve exploiting any security vulnerability.

The disadvantages of behavior-based ID systems are:

✦ Characterized by high false alarm rates. High positives are the most common failure of behavior-based ID systems and can create data noise that can make the system unusable or difficult to use.

✦ Activity and behavior of the users while in the networked system might not be static enough to effectively implement a behavior-based ID system.

✦ The network may experience an attack at the same time the intrusion detection system is learning the behavior.

Honey Pots

A honey pot is a system on the network intentionally configured to lure intruders. Honey pots simulate one or more network services, hoping that an attacker will attempt an intrusion. Honey pots are most successful when run on known servers, such as HTTP, mail, or DNS servers, because these systems advertise their services and are often the first point of attack. They are often used to augment the deployment of an IDR system.

A honey pot is configured to interact with potential hackers in such a way as to capture the details of their attacks. These details can be used to identify what the intruders are after, their skill level, and what tools they use.

Honey pots should be physically isolated from the real network and are commonly placed in a DMZ. All traffic to and from the honey pot should also be routed through a dedicated firewall.

A honey pot is usually configured by installing the operating system using defaults, no patches, and the application designed to record the activities of the intruder.

Evidence of an intrusion into a honey pot can be collected through:

✦ The honey pot's firewall logs

✦ The honey pot's system logs

✦ Intrusion detection systems or other monitoring tools

A properly configured honey pot monitors traffic passively, doesn't advertise its presence, and provides a preserved prosecution trail for law enforcement agencies.

Honey Pot Issues

It's important to be aware of legal issues arising out of implementing a honey pot. Some organizations discourage the use of honey pots, citing the legal concerns of luring intruders, and feel that no level of intrusion should be encouraged.

Before the intrusion occurs it's advisable to consult with local law enforcement authorities to determine the type and amount of data they will need in order to prosecute and how to properly preserve the chain of evidence.

Also, as the honey pot must be vigilantly monitored and maintained, some organizations feel it is too resource-intensive for practical use.

Computer Incident Response Team

Response includes notifying the appropriate parties to take action in order to determine the extent of the severity of an incident and to remediate the incident's effects. According to NIST, an organization should address computer security incidents by developing an incident-handling capability. The incident-handling capability should be used to:

✦ Provide the ability to respond quickly and effectively.

✦ Contain and repair the damage from incidents. When left unchecked, malicious software can significantly harm an organization's computing resources, depending on the technology and its connectivity. Containing the incident should include an assessment of whether the incident is part of a targeted attack on the organization or is an isolated incident.

✦ Prevent future damage. An incident-handling capability should assist an organization in preventing (or at least minimizing) damage from future incidents. Incidents can be studied internally to gain a better understanding of the organization's threats and vulnerabilities.

As part of a structured incident-handling program of Intrusion Detection and Response, a Computer Emergency Response Team (CERT) or Computer Incident Response Team (CIRT) is commonly created. Because "CERT" refers specifically to the CERT Coordination Center located at Carnegie Mellon's Software Engineering Institute (SEI), "CIRT" is used more often.

The main tasks of a CIRT are:

✦ Analysis of an event notification

✦ Response to an incident if the analysis warrants it

✦ Escalation path procedures

✦ Resolution, post-incident follow-up, and reporting to the appropriate parties

The prime directive of every CIRT is *Incident Response Management*, which manages a company's response to events that pose a risk to its computing environment. This management often consists of the following:

✦ Coordinating the notification and distribution of information pertaining to the incident to the appropriate parties (those with a need to know) through a pre-defined escalation path

✦ Mitigating risk to the enterprise by minimizing the disruptions to normal business activities and the costs associated with remediating the incident (including public relations)

✦ Assembling teams of technical personnel to investigate the potential vulnerabilities and to resolve specific intrusions

Additional examples of CIRT activities are:

✦ Management of the network logs, including collection, retention, review, and analysis of data

✦ Management of the resolution of an incident, management of the remediation of a vulnerability, and post-event reporting to the appropriate parties

IDS and a Layered Security Approach

Computer security is most effective when multiple layers of security are used within an organization, and ID is best utilized when implemented in a *layered security* approach. This concept implies that multiple steps are taken to secure the data, thereby increasing the workload and time required for an intruder to penetrate the network.

Therefore, while a firewall is an excellent perimeter security device, it is just one element of an effective security strategy. The more elements, or layers, of security that can be added to protect the data, the more secure the infrastructure will remain.

Elements of an effective layered security approach include:

✦ Security policies, procedures, standards, and guidelines, including high-level security policy

✦ Perimeter security, like routers, firewalls, and other edge devices

✦ Hardware and/or software host security products

✦ Auditing, monitoring, intrusion detection, and response

Each of these layers may be implemented independently of the others, yet they are interdependent when functioning. An IDS that alerts to unauthorized access attempts or port scanning is useless without a response plan to react to the problem. Since each layer provides elements of protection, the defeat of any one layer should not lead to a failure of protection.

IDS and Switches

One serious issue with IDS is the proper implementation of IDS sensors in a switched environment. This issue arises from the basic differences between standard hubs and switches. Hubs exclude only the port the packet came in on and echo every packet to every port on the hub. Therefore, in networks employing only hubs, IDS sensors can be placed almost anywhere in the infrastructure.

However, when a packet comes into a switch, a temporary connection in the switch is first made to the destination port, and then the packets are forwarded. This means more care must be exerted when placing IDS sensors in a switched environment to ensure the sensor is able to see all of the network traffic. Figure 3-39 shows an IDS employed on its own subnet.

Some switches permit spanning port configuration, which configures the switch to behave like a hub only for a specific port. The switch can be configured to span the data from a specific port to the IDS port. Unfortunately, some switches cannot be guaranteed to pass all the traffic to the spanned port, and most switches allow only one port to be spanned at a time.

Another partial solution is to place a hub between the monitored connections, say between two switches, a router and switch, or a server and switch. This allows traffic still to flow between the switch and the target but with traffic to be copied off to the IDS. This solution, however, spells the beginning of the end for the switched network and removes the benefits of a switched solution.

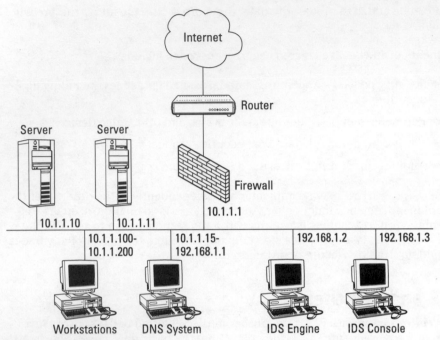

Figure 3-39: IDS on subnet.

IDS Performance

Another issue with the implementation of intrusion detection systems is the performance of the IDS when the network bandwidth begins to reach saturation levels. Obviously, there is a limit to the number of packets that a network intrusion detection sensor can accurately analyze in any given time period. The higher the network traffic level and the more complex the analysis, the more the IDS may experience high error rates, such as the premature discarding of copied network packets.

Network Attacks and Abuses

Attacks against computers, networks, and cryptographic systems have a variety of motivations. Some attacks are aimed at disrupting service, others focus on illegally acquiring sensitive information, and others attempt to deceive or defraud. In general, such attacks target the C.I.A. components of information security. In this section, the most common types of attacks are explored.

The CISSP candidate will need to know in general the various types of attacks on and abuses of networked systems. In current practice, these attacks are constantly evolving. This is probably the most dynamic area of InfoSec today. Large teams and huge amounts of money and resources are dedicated to reacting to the latest twists and turns of intrusions into networked systems, particularly on the Internet. We describe attacks and abuses in almost every chapter; here we focus on those attacks and abuses that commonly apply to networked systems.

Logon Abuse

Logon abuse can refer to legitimate users accessing services of a higher security level that would normally be restricted to them. Unlike network intrusion, this type of abuse focuses primarily on those users who might be legitimate users of a different system or users who have a lower security classification.

Masquerading is the term used when one user pretends to be another user. An attacker socially engineering passwords from an Internet Service Provider (ISP) could be an example of masquerading.

Inappropriate System Use

This style of network abuse refers to the nonbusiness or personal use of a network by otherwise authorized users, such as Internet surfing to inappropriate content sites (travel, pornography, sports, and so forth). As per the (ISC)² Code of Ethics and the Internet Advisory Board (IAB) recommendations, the use of networked services for other than business purposes can be considered abuse of the system. While most employers do not enforce extremely strict Web surfing rules, occasional harassment litigation resulting from employees accessing pornography sites and employees operating private Web businesses using the company's infrastructure can constitute unauthorized use.

Eavesdropping

This type of network attack consists of the unauthorized interception of network traffic. Certain network transmission methods, such as satellite, wireless, mobile, PDA, and so on, are vulnerable to eavesdropping attacks. *Tapping* refers to the physical interception of a transmission medium (like the splicing of a cable or the creation of an induction loop to pick up electromagnetic emanations from copper).

✦ *Passive Eavesdropping* — Covertly monitoring or listening to transmissions that are unauthorized by either the sender or receiver

✦ *Active Eavesdropping* — Tampering with a transmission to create a covert signaling channel, or actively probing the network for infrastructure information

Eavesdropping and probing are often the preliminary steps to session hijacking and other network intrusions. Covert channel eavesdropping refers to using a hidden, unauthorized network connection to communicate unauthorized information. A covert channel is a connection intentionally created to transmit unauthorized information from inside a trusted network to a partner at an outside, untrusted node. Covert channels are described in more detail in Chapter 6, "Operations Security."

War walking (or war driving) refers to scanning for 802.11-based wireless network information by either driving or walking with a laptop, a wireless adapter in promiscuous mode, some type of scanning software such as NetStumbler or AiroPeek, and a Global Positioning System (GPS) (Source: "War Driving by the Bay" by Kevin Poulsen, The Register, April 13, 2001).

Network Intrusion

This type of attack refers to the use of unauthorized access to break into a network primarily from an external source. Unlike a logon abuse attack, the intruders are not considered to be known to the company. Most common conceptions of hacks reside in this category. Also known as a *penetration attack*, it exploits known security vulnerabilities in the security perimeter.

Back doors are very hard to trace, as an intruder will often create several avenues into a network to be exploited later. The only real way to be sure these avenues are closed after an attack is to restore the operating system from the original media, apply the patches, and restore all data and applications.

Piggy-backing in the network domain, refers to an attacker gaining unauthorized access to a system by using a legitimate user's connection. A user leaves a session open or incorrectly logs off, enabling an unauthorized user to resume the session.

Denial of Service (DoS) Attacks

The DoS attack might use some of the following techniques to overwhelm a target's resources:

✦ Filling up a target's hard drive storage space by using huge email attachments or file transfers

✦ Sending a message, which resets a target host's subnet mask, causing a disruption of the target's subnet routing

✦ Using up all of a target's resources to accept network connections, resulting in additional network connections being denied

Specific DoS attacks are discussed in Chapter 2, "Access Control Systems."

Session Hijacking Attacks

Unauthorized access to a system can be achieved by session hijacking. In this type of attack, an attacker hijacks a session between a trusted client and network server. The attacking computer substitutes its IP address for that of the trusted client and the server continues the dialog believing it is communicating with the trusted client.

Some examples of session highjacking attacks are:

IP Spoofing Attacks. Unlike a Smurf attack, where spoofing creates a DoS attack, IP spoofing convinces a system that it is communicating with a known entity, which gives an intruder access. IP spoofing involves an alteration of a packet at the TCP level, which is used to attack Internet-connected systems that provide various TCP/IP services. The attacker sends a packet with an IP source address of a known, trusted host. This target host might accept the packet and act upon it.

C2MYAZZ. C2MYAZZ is a utility that enables server spoofing to implement a session hijacking or man-in-the-middle exploit. It intercepts a client LANMAN authentication logon and obtains the session's logon credentials and password combination, transparently to the user.

TCP Sequence Number Attacks. TCP sequence number attacks exploit the communications session, which was established between the target and the trusted host that initiated the session. The intruder tricks the target into believing it is connected to a trusted host and then hijacks the session by predicting the target's choice of an initial TCP sequence number. This session is then often used to launch various attacks on other hosts.

DNS poisoning. DNS poisoning is also known as *cache poisoning*. It is the process of distributing incorrect IP address information for a specific host with the intent to divert traffic from its true destination.

Fragmentation Attacks

IP fragmentation attacks use varied IP datagram fragmentation to disguise their TCP packets from a target's IP filtering devices. The following are two examples of these types of attacks:

✦ A *tiny fragment attack* occurs when the intruder sends a very small fragment that forces some of the TCP header field into a second fragment. If the target's filtering device does not enforce minimum fragment size, this illegal packet can then be passed on through the target's network.

✦ An *overlapping fragment attack* is another variation on a datagram's zero-offset modification (like the teardrop attack). Subsequent packets overwrite the initial packet's destination address information, and then the second packet is passed by the target's filtering device. This can happen if the target's filtering device does not enforce a minimum fragment offset for fragments with nonzero offsets.

We describe various TCP fragmentation attacks later in the chapter.

Dial-Up Attacks

War dialing. War dialing is a method used to hack into computers by using a software program to automatically call a large pool of telephone numbers to search for those that have a modem attached.

Demon dialing. Demon dialing, similar to war dialing, is a tool used to attack one modem using brute force to guess the password and gain access.

ToneLoc. ToneLoc was one of the first war-dialing tools used by "phone phreakers." (Source: *Hacking Exposed* by Stuart McClure, Joel Scambray, and George Kurtz, Osborne, 1999)

Probing and Scanning

Probing is an active variation of eavesdropping, usually used to give an attacker a road map of the network in preparation for an intrusion or a DoS attack. Attackers use it to discover what ports are open, what services are running, and what system software is being used. Probing enables an attacker to more easily detect and exploit known vulnerabilities within a target machine.

Scanning, or *traffic analysis*, uses a "sniffer" to scan the hosts of various enabled services to document what systems are active on a network and what ports are open.

Both of these can be performed either manually or automatically. Manual vulnerability checks are performed using tools such as Telnet to connect to a remote service to see what is listening. Automated vulnerability scanners are software programs that automatically perform all the probing and scanning steps and report the findings back to the user. Due to its free availability on the Internet, the amount of this type of automated probing has increased.

Vulnerability Scanning

Vulnerability scanning should be implemented by the security professional to help identify weaknesses in a system. It should be conducted on a regular periodic basis to identify compromised or vulnerable systems. The scans directed at a target system can either be internal, originating from within the system, or external, originating from outside the target system.

Because scanning activity is often a prelude to a system attack, monitoring and analysis of the logs and blocking unused and exposed ports should accompany the detection of malicious scans.

Conducting scans inside the enterprise on a regular basis is one way to identify and track several types of potential problems, such as unused ports that respond to network requests. Also, uncontrolled or unauthorized software may be located using these scanning techniques.

A common vulnerability-scanning methodology may employ several steps, including an IP device discovery scan, workstation vulnerability scan, and server vulnerability scan.

Discovery Scanning

The intent of a discovery scan is to collect enough information about each network device to identify what type of device it is (workstation, server, router, firewall, etc.), its operating system, and whether it is running any externally vulnerable services, like Web services, ftp, or email. The discovery scan contains two elements: inventory and classification. The *inventory scan* provides information about the target system's operating system and its available ports. The *classification process* identifies applications running on the target system, which aids in determining the device's function.

Workstation Scanning

A full workstation vulnerability scan of the standard corporate desktop configuration should be implemented regularly. This scan helps ensure that the standard software configuration is current with the latest security patches and software, and it helps locate uncontrolled or unauthorized software.

Server Scanning

A full server vulnerability scan will determine if the server OS has been configured to the corporate standards and whether applications are kept current with the latest security patches and software. All services must be inspected for elements that may compromise security, such as default accounts and weak passwords. Also, unauthorized programs like Trojans may be identified.

Port Scanning

Port scanning describes the process of sending a data packet to a port to gather information about the state of the port. This is also called a *probe*. Port scanning makes it possible to find what TCP and UDP ports are in use. For example, if ports 25, 80 and 110 are open, the device is running the SMTP, HTTP, and POP3 services.

A cracker can use port-scanning software to determine which hosts are active and which are inactive (down) in order to avoid wasting time on inactive hosts. A port scan can gather data about a single host or hosts within a subnet (256 adjacent network addresses).

A scan may first be implemented using the ping utility. Then, after determining which hosts and associated ports are active, the cracker can initiate different types of probes on the active ports.

Examples of probes are:

✦ Gathering information from the Domain Name System (DNS)

✦ Determining the network services that are available, such as email, FTP and remote logon

✦ Determining the type and release of the operating system

TCP/UDP Scanning Types

Many types of TCP/UDP scanning techniques exist. Some are simple and easily detectable by firewalls and intrusion detection systems, whereas some are more complicated and harder to detect.

Stealth Scans

Certain types of scans are called *stealth* scans because they try to evade or minimize their chances of detection. Several of the scans outlined later, such as the TCP SYN or TCP FIN scan, can be described as stealth scans.

Another example of a stealth scan is implemented through fragmenting the IP datagram within the TCP header. This will bypass some packet filtering firewalls because they don't get a complete TCP header to match the filter rules.

Spoofed Scans

Literally, spoofing refers to an attacker deliberately inducing a user (subject) or device (object) into taking an incorrect action by giving it incorrect information. While the term *spoofing* comes up often in any discussion of security, it can also be applied here to conceal the true identity of an attacker. Spoofing allows an attacker to probe the target's ports without revealing the attacker's own IP address. The FTP proxy bounce attack described below is an example of a spoofed scan that compromises a third-party FTP server.

The HPing network analysis tool, also described later, hides the source of its scans by using another host through which to probe the target site. Also, NMap provides spoofing capability by allowing the operator to enter an optional "source" address for the scanning packet.

Let's look at some TCP-based scanning techniques:

> **TCP connect( ).** Connect( ) is the most basic and fastest scanning technique. Connect( ) is able to scan ports quickly simply by attempting to connect to each port in succession. The biggest disadvantage for attackers is that it is the easiest to detect and can be stopped at the firewall.

TCP SYN (half open) scanning. TCP SYN scanning is often referred to as *half-open* scanning because, unlike TCP connect(), a full TCP connection is never opened. The scan works by:

1. Sending a SYN packet to a target port.

2. If a SYN/ACK is received this indicates the port is listening.

3. The scanner then breaks the connection by sending an RST (reset) packet.

4. If an RST is received, this indicates the port is closed.

This is harder to trace because fewer sites log incomplete TCP connections, but some packet-filtering firewalls look for SYNs to restricted ports.

TCP SYN/ACK scan. TCP SYN/ACK is another way to determine if ports are open or closed. The TCP SYN/ACK scan works by:

- Scanner initially sends a SYN/ACK.

- If the port is closed, it assumes the SYN/ACK packet was a mistake and sends an RST.

- If the port was open, the SYN/ACK packet will be ignored and drop the packet.

This is considered a stealth scan since it isn't likely to be logged by the host being scanned, but many intrusion detection systems may catch it.

TCP FIN scanning. TCP FIN is a stealth scan that works like the TCP SYN/ACK scan.

- Scanner sends a FIN packet to a port.

- A closed port replies with an RST.

- An open port ignores the FIN packet.

One issue with this type of scanning is that TCP FIN can be used only to find listening ports on non-Windows machines or to identify Windows machines because Windows ports send an RST regardless of the state of the port.

TCP ftp proxy (bounce attack) scanning. TCP FTP proxy (bounce attack) scanning is a very stealthy scanning technique. It takes advantage of a weakness in proxy ftp connections. It works like this:

- The scanner connects to an FTP server and requests that the server initiate a data transfer process to a third system.

- The scanner uses the PORT FTP command to declare that the data transfer process is listening on the target box at a certain port number.

- It then uses the LIST FTP command to try to list the current directory. The result is sent over the server data transfer process channel.

- If the transfer is successful, the target host is listening on the specified port.

- If the transfer is unsuccessful, a "425 Can't build data connection: Connection refused" message is sent.

Some FTP servers disable the proxy feature to prevent TCP FTP proxy scanning.

IP fragments. Fragmenting IP packets is a variation on the other TCP scanning techniques. Instead of sending a single probe packet, the packet is broken into two or more packets and reassembled at the destination, thus bypassing the packet filters.

ICMP scanning (ping sweep). As ICMP doesn't use ports, this is technically not a port scanning technique, but it should be mentioned. Using ICMP Echo requests, the scanner can perform what is known as a *ping sweep*. Scanned hosts will reply with an ICMP Echo reply indicating that they are alive, whereas no response may mean the target is down or nonexistent.

Determining the OS Type

Determining the type of OS is also an objective of scanning, as this will determine the type of attack to be launched.

Sometimes a target's operating system details can be found very simply by examining its Telnet banners or its File Transfer Protocol (FTP) servers, after connecting to these services.

TCP/IP stack fingerprinting is another technique to identify the particular version of an operating system. Since OS and device vendors implement TCP/IP differently, these differences can help in determining the OS.

Some of these differences include:

- ✦ Time To Live (TTL)
- ✦ Initial Window Size
- ✦ Don't Fragment (DF) bit
- ✦ Type of Service (TOS)

Table 3-11 shows some common Time To Live values. Remember that the TTL will decrement each time the packet passes through a router. This means that the TTL of a router 6 hops away will be 249 (255 − 6).

Another type of OS identification technique is *TCP initial sequence number sampling*. After responding to a connection request, information about the operating system can be inferred from the pattern of the sequence numbers.

Table 3-11 Time To Live (TTL) Values	
Time To Live	**Operating System or Device Type**
255	Many network devices, Unix and Macintosh systems
128	Many Windows systems
60	Hewlett-Packard Jet Direct printers
32	Some versions of Windows 95B/98

Scanning Tools

While many of these tools are used by crackers and intruders, they also help the security administrator detect and stop malicious scans. Used with intrusion detection systems, these tools can provide some level of protection by identifying vulnerable systems, and they can provide data about the level of activity directed against a machine or network. Since scanning is a continuous activity (that is, all networked systems are being scanned all of the time), it's very important that the security professional know what can be compromised. Some common scanning tools are:

✦ *Computer Oracle and Password System (COPS)* — examines a system for a number of known weaknesses and alerts the administrator.

✦ *HPing* — a network analysis tool that sends packets with non-traditional IP stack parameters. It allows the scanner to gather information from the response packets generated.

✦ *Legion* — will scan for and identify shared folders on scanned systems, allowing the scanner to map drives directly.

✦ *Nessus* — a free security-auditing tool for Linux, BSD, and a few other platforms. It requires a back-end server that has to run on a Unix-like platform.

✦ *NMap* — a very common port-scanning package. More information on NMap follows this section.

✦ *Remote Access Perimeter Scanner (RAPS)* — part of the corporate edition of PCAnywhere by Symantec. RAPS will detect most commercial remote control and backdoor packages like NetBus, and it can help lockdown PCAnywhere.

✦ *Security Administrator's Integrated Network Tool (SAINT)* — examines network services, such as finger, NFS, NIS, ftp and tftp, rexd, statd, and others, to report on potential security flaws.

✦ *System Administrator Tool for Analyzing Networks (SATAN)* — is one of the oldest network security analyzers. SATAN scans network systems for well known and often exploited vulnerabilities.

✦ *Tcpview* — will allow identification of what application opened which port on Windows platforms.

✦ *Snort* — is a utility used for network sniffing. Network sniffing is the process of gathering traffic from a network by capturing the data as it passes and storing it to analyze later.

NMap

NMap scans for most ports from 1–1024 and a number of others in the registered and undefined ranges. This helps identify software like PCAnywhere, SubSeven, and BackOrifice. Now that a Windows interface has been written, it no longer has to be run only on a Unix system.

NMap allows scanning of both TCP and UDP ports, with root privilege required for UDP. While NMap doesn't have signature or password cracking capabilities, like L0pht Crack, it will estimate how hard it will be to hijack an open session.

Vulnerable Ports

Although the complete listing of well-known and registered ports is extensive, some ports are attacked more often than others. In Table 3-12, we've listed the ports that are the greatest risk to networked systems.

Table 3-12 **Commonly Attacked Ports**		
Port #	**Service Name**	**Service Description**
21	ftp	File Transfer Protocol
23	telnet	Telnet virtual terminal
25,109,110 143	smtp pop3 imap	Simple Mail Protocol, POP2, POP3 and IMAP Messaging
53	dns	Domain Name Services
80, 8000, 8080	http	Hyper-Text Transfer Protocol and HTTP proxy servers
118	sqlserv	SQL database service
119	nntp	Network News Transfer Protocol
161	snmp	Simple Network Management Protocol
194	irc	Internet Relay Chat
389,636	ldap	Lightweight Directory Access Protocol
2049	nfs	Networking File Systems
5631	PCAnywhere	PCAnywhere Remote Control

How Do We Get Windows NT Passwords?

The NT Security Accounts Manager (SAM) contains the usernames and encrypted passwords of all local (and domain, if the server is a domain controller) users. The SAM uses an older, weaker LanManager hash that can be broken easily by tools like L0phtcrack. Physical access to the NT server and the rdisks must be controlled. The "Sam" file in the repair directory must be deleted after creation of an rdisk. Pwdump and pwdump2 are utilities that allow someone with Administrator rights to target the Local Security Authority Subsystem, isass.exe, from a remote system:

✦ Obtain the backup SAM from the repair directory

✦ Boot the NT server with a floppy containing an alternate operating system

✦ Use pwdump2 to dump the password hashes directly from the registry

Issues with Vulnerability Scanning

Some precautions need to be taken when the security administrator begins a program of vulnerability scanning on his or her own network. Some of these issues could cause a system crash or create unreliable scan data:

False positives. Some legitimate software uses port numbers registered to other software, which can cause false alarms when port scanning. This can lead to blocking legitimate programs that appear to be intrusions.

Heavy traffic. Port scanning can have an adverse effect on WAN links and even effectively disable slow links. Because heavy port scanning generates a lot of traffic, it is usually preferable to perform the scanning outside normal business hours.

False negatives. Port scanning can sometimes exhaust resources on the scanning machine, creating false negatives and not properly identifying vulnerabilities.

System crash. Port scanning has been known to render needed services inoperable or actually crash systems. This may happen when systems have not been currently patched or the scanning process exhausts the targeted system's resources.

Unregistered port numbers. Many port numbers in use are not registered, which complicates the act of identifying what software is using them.

Malicious Code

Malicious code is the name used for any program that adds to, deletes or modifies legitimate software for the purpose of intentionally causing disruption and harm or to circumvent or subvert the existing system's function. Examples of malicious code include viruses, worms, Trojan Horses, and logic bombs. Newer malicious code is based on mobile Active X and Java applets.

Viruses

Viruses are a type of malicious code that attaches to a host program and propagates when an infected program is executed.

A virus infects the operating system in two ways: by completely replacing one or more of the operating system's programs or by attaching itself to existing operating system's programs and altering functionality. Once a virus has changed OS functionality, it can control many OS processes that are running.

To avoid detection, the virus usually creates several hidden files within the OS source code or in "unusable" sectors. Since infections in the OS are difficult to detect, they have deadly consequences on systems relying on the OS for basic functions.

The Virus Lifecycle

There are two main phases in the life cycle of a virus: replication and activation. In the first phase, replication, viruses typically remain hidden and do not interfere with normal system functions. During this time, viruses actively seek out new hosts to infect by attaching themselves to other software programs or by infiltrating the OS, for example.

During the second phase, activation, the beginning of gradual or sudden destruction of the system occurs. Typically, the decision to activate is based on a mathematical formula with criteria such as date, time, number of infected files, and others. The possible damage at this stage could include destroyed data, software or hardware conflicts, space consumption, and abnormal behavior.

Macro Viruses

Macro viruses are the most prevalent computer viruses in the wild, accounting for the vast majority of virus encounters. A macro virus can easily infect many types of applications, such as Microsoft Excel and Word.

To infect the system, macro viruses attach themselves to the application's initialization sequence, and then when the application is executed, the virus's instructions execute before control is given to the application. Then the virus replicates itself, infecting more and more of the system.

These macro viruses move from system to system through email file sharing, demonstrations, data sharing, and disk sharing. Today's widespread sharing of macro-enabled files, primarily through email attachments, is rapidly increasing the macro virus threat.

Common macro viruses are:

+ Executable files infecting the boot sector: Jerusalem, Cascade, Form
+ Word macros: Concept
+ Email enabled Word macros: Melissa
+ Email enabled Visual Basic scripts: I Love You

Polymorphic Viruses

Polymorphic viruses are difficult to detect because they hide themselves from antivirus software by altering their appearance after each infection. Some polymorphic viruses can assume over two billion different identities.

There are three main components of a polymorphic virus: a scrambled virus body, a decryption routine, and a mutation engine. The process of a polymorphic infection is:

1. The decryption routine first gains control of the computer and then decrypts both the virus body and the mutation engine.

2. The decryption routine transfers control of the computer to the virus, which locates a new program to infect.

3. The virus makes a copy of itself and the mutation engine in RAM.

4. The virus invokes the mutation engine, which randomly generates a new decryption routine capable of decrypting the virus yet bearing little or no resemblance to any prior decryption routine.

5. The virus encrypts the new copy of the virus body and mutation engine.

6. The virus appends the new decryption routine, along with the newly encrypted virus and mutation engine, onto a new program.

As a result, not only is the virus body encrypted, but also the virus decryption routine varies from infection to infection. No two infections look alike, confusing the virus scanner searching for the sequence of bytes that identifies a specific decryption routine.

Stealth Viruses

Stealth viruses attempt to hide their presence from both the OS and the antivirus software by:

+ Hiding the change in the file's date and time
+ Hiding the increase in the infected file's size
+ Encrypting themselves

They are similar to polymorphic viruses in that they are very hard to detect.

Trojan Horses

Trojan horses hide malicious code inside a host program that seems to do something useful. Once these programs are executed, the virus, worm, or other type of malicious code hidden in the Trojan horse program is released to attack the workstation, server, or network or to allow unauthorized access to those devices. Trojans are common tools used to create backdoors into the network for later exploitation by crackers.

Trojan horses can be carried via Internet traffic such as FTP downloads or downloadable applets from Web sites, or they can be distributed through email.

Common Trojan horses and ports are:

✦ *Trinoo* — ports 1524, 27444, 27665, 31335
✦ *Back Orifice or BO2K* — port 31337
✦ *NetBus* — port 12345
✦ *SubSeven* — ports 1080, 1234, 2773

Some Trojans are programmed to open specific ports to allow access for exploitation. If a Trojan is installed on a system it often opens a high-numbered port. Then the open Trojan port could be scanned and located, enabling an attacker to compromise the system.

Logic Bombs

Logic bombs are malicious code added to an existing application to be executed at a later date. Every time the infected application is run, the logic bomb checks the date to see whether it is time to run the bomb. If not, control is passed back to the main application and the logic bomb waits. If the date condition is correct, the rest of the logic bomb's code is executed, and it can attack the system.

In addition to the date, there are numerous ways to trigger logic bombs: counter triggers; replication triggers, which activate after a set number of virus reproductions; disk space triggers; and video mode triggers, which activate when video is in a set mode or changes from set modes.

Worms

Instead of attaching themselves to a single host program and then replicating like viruses, worms attack a network by moving from device to device. Worms are constructed to infiltrate legitimate data processing programs and alter or destroy the data.

Malicious Code Prevention

Malicious code prevention is mostly centered on scanning, prevention, and detection products.

Virus Scanners

Most virus scanners use pattern-matching algorithms that can scan for many different signatures at the same time. These algorithms include scanning capabilities that detect known and unknown worms and Trojan horses.

Most antivirus scanning products search hard disks for viruses, detect and remove any that are found, and include an auto-update feature that enables the program to download profiles of new viruses so that it will have the profiles necessary for scanning.

Virus Prevention

Virus infection prevention products are used to prevent malicious code from initially infecting the system and stop the replication process. They either reside in memory and monitor system activity or filter incoming executable programs and specific file types. When an illegal virus accesses a program or boot sector, the system is halted and the user is prompted to remove the particular type of malicious code.

Virus Detection

Virus detection products are designed to detect a malicious code infection after the infection occurs. Two types of virus detection products are commonly implemented: short-term infection detection and long-term infection detection. Short-term infection detection products detect an infection very soon after the infection has occurred. Short-term infection detection products can be implemented through vaccination programs or the snapshot technique.

Long-term infection detection products identify specific malicious code on a system that has already been infected for some time. The two different techniques used by long-term infection detection products are spectral analysis and heuristic analysis. Spectral analysis searches for patterns in the code trails that malicious code leaves. Heuristic analysis analyzes malicious code to figure out its capability.

Web Security

With the transformation of the Internet from a network used primarily by universities and research laboratories to a world-wide communications medium, attacks on the World Wide Web and Internet can have serious consequences. These attacks can involve nuisance attacks, criminal exploits and, in information warfare, incapacitation of a nation's critical infrastructure. Thus, there is a need for protecting nodes on the Internet and for providing for the confidentiality, integrity, and availability of information utilizing these networks.

SSL/TLS

The Secure Sockets Layer (SSL) Protocol was developed by Netscape in 1994 to protect the confidentiality of information transmitted between two applications, to verify the integrity of the communications, and to provide an authentication means in both directions. SSL implements these functions using public and private key encryption and a message authentication code (MAC).

Microsoft has developed a newer version of SSL, Transport Layer Security (TLS). As with SSL, TLS implements confidentiality, integrity, and authentication above the Transport Layer and is application independent. Because SSL and TLS ride on the Transport Layer protocol, they are independent of the application. Thus, SSL and TLS can be used with applications such as Telnet, FTP, HTTP, and email protocols.

Both SSL and TLS use certificates for public key verification that are based on the X.509 standard.

SSL 3.0

The design goals of SSL 3.0 were to provide:

✦ *Cryptographic security*—protection of the confidentiality of transmitted messages.

✦ *Interoperability*—applications should be able to be developed using SSL 3.0 by groups of individuals without knowledge of each other's code.

✦ *Extensibility*—the ability to incorporate different encryption algorithms into SSL 3.0 without major changes to SSL 3.0.

✦ *Relative efficiency*—efficient utilization of computing and network resources.

Session keys generated during SSL private key cryptography transactions are either 40-bits or 128-bits in length. Newer browsers support 128-bit encryption.

The SSL Protocol comprises two layers, the SSL Record Protocol and the SSL Handshake Protocol. The SSL Record Protocol is layered above a transport protocol, such as TCP. This Record Protocol is used for encapsulation of higher-level protocols, such as the SSL Handshake Protocol. The latter protocol is used for client/server mutual authentication, negotiation of a cryptographic algorithm, and exchange of cryptographic keys.

Thus, through these mechanisms, SSL provides:

✦ Mutual authentication using pubic key cryptography based on algorithms such as the Digital Signature Standard (DSS) and RSA

✦ Encryption of messages using private key cryptography based on algorithms such as IDEA, 3DES, and RC4

✦ Integrity verification of the message using a keyed message authentication code (MAC) based on hash functions such as MD5 and SHA.

TLS 1.0

Similar to SSL, the TLS Protocol is comprised of the TLS Record and Handshake Protocols. The TLS Record Protocol is layered on top of a transport protocol such as TCP and provides privacy and reliability to the communications. The privacy is implemented by encryption using symmetric key cryptography such as DES or RC4. The secret key is generated anew for each connection; however, the Record Protocol can be used without encryption. Integrity is provided through the use of a keyed Message Authentication Code (MAC) using hash algorithms such as SHA or MD5.

The TLS Record Protocol is also used to encapsulate a higher-level protocol such as the TLS Handshake Protocol. The server and client use this Handshake Protocol to authenticate each other. The authentication can be accomplished using asymmetric key cryptography such as RSA or DSS. The Handshake Protocol also sets up the encryption algorithm and cryptographic keys to enable the application protocol to transmit and receive information.

Since TLS is based on SSL, they have similar functionality and goals; however, SSL and TLS have enough differences that they cannot interoperate. In order to address this situation, TLS has a built-in mechanism that can be used to make TLS compatible with SSL 3.0.

S-HTTP

Secure HTTP (S-HTTP) is a communications protocol designed to provide secure messaging over HTTP. S-HTTP provides equal and symmetric capabilities to both client and server, but one entity that is S-HTTP-enabled can communicate with another entity that is not S-HTTP capable. In that instance, the security features would not be operable. S-HTTP implements secure, end-to-end transactions.

HTTP/S

Web pages using the SSL Protocol start with HTTPs, denoting the Hypertext Transfer Protocol with SSL.

S-HTTP supports a symmetric key encryption only mode and, therefore, does not require public key encryption for key exchanges. It is flexible, however, and permits the clients and servers to use different forms of transactions related to the signing of messages, encryption of messages, algorithms used, and types of certificates.

In summary, S-HTTP is a protocol that supports:

✦ Option negotiations for defining the type of transactions desired

✦ A variety of key management approaches

✦ Different trust models

✦ Multiple cryptographic algorithms

✦ Multiple operation modes

✦ Different encapsulation formats

Instant Messaging

Instant messaging goes a step beyond email in that it supports the real time exchange of messages between two parties using the Internet. In order to use this service, the user has to have instant messaging client software on his or her computer. The client software then communicates with an instant messaging server. The user provides the server with a contact or "buddy" list of people with which he or she desires to set up instant messaging.

To use instant messaging, the user logs on to the instant messaging server with the user's ID and password. The server authenticates the user. Then, the client sends to the server the user's IP address and the port number on the user's computer that is being used by the instant messaging client. The server stores this information as well as identical information from any other individuals on the user's contact list that are logged in at that time. An important point to note is that once an individual, A, is logged on to the server, the server sends the IP addresses and port numbers of all the others logged on to the server at that time to A's client software. Thus, all people on the contact list who are logged on to the instant messaging server at that time are notified of the online presence and contact information of the others who are also logged on.

A user can send a message to another individual on the contact list who is logged on and that message will instantly appear on the screen of the receiving individual. Because a user's client knows the IP address and port number of the receiving individual, the user's message is sent directly to the intended recipient and does not have to go through the instant messaging server.

With instant messaging, communication takes place between only two individuals. If the situation requires instant conferencing among more than two individuals, a chat room can be set up. A *chat room* is similar to instant messaging, but everyone logged on to the "room" can see a message that is sent by one individual.

When an individual, A, wants to terminate the instant messaging session, A closes his or her message window and exits the instant messaging client. The client then sends a message to the instant messaging server indicating that A has logged off. The server, in turn, sends a message to all the active participants of the contact list that A has exited the session. The members of the contact list still logged on will see the status of A on their windows change from "online" to "offline."

Instant messaging software packages also offer other services, including chat rooms set up, image and sound transmission, voice communication, and streaming content.

 Some of the more popular instant messaging utilities are the freeware ICQ (for "I seek you" at www.icq.com), AIM (America Online's Instant Messenger), Microsoft's instant messaging utility in MSN Explorer, and Yahoo Instant Messenger.

One problem with instant messaging is the lack of interoperability. An individual with an instant messaging utility from one source or vendor may not be able to communicate with a person using a different instant messaging package. In order to address this situation, the Internet Engineering Task Force (IETF) has developed a standard protocol for instant messaging — the Instant Messaging Presence Protocol.

IM Vulnerabilities

Messages sent by means of instant messaging are not inherently secure and safe from prying eyes. The instant messaging server is particularly vulnerable because it contains both the messages and the connection information of the participants. Thus, instant messaging servers should be secure servers located in protected and limited access areas. Additional security features that are provided by some instant messaging software utilities include:

✦ Encryption, integrity, and authentication services using SSL

✦ Authentication against propriety databases, domains, or LDAP

✦ Secure transfer of files

✦ Ability to use any TCP port

✦ Web-based tools for administration of the instant messaging network on the instant messaging server, including tools for user account administration, logging of critical data, and analysis of log information

8.3 Naming Conventions

The Microsoft New Technology File System (NTFS) has the capability to generate file names in the DOS 8.3 naming convention to service 16-bit applications that access files that do not conform DOS 8.3 naming. Windows 2000, Windows NT Server, and Windows NT Workstation support the NTFS file system. Windows 95 and 98 support the earlier File Allocation Table (FAT) file system along with the newer version, FAT 32. The NTFS enhancements over FAT and FAT 32 include optimization of available disk space, fault tolerance, and improved security features.

Web servers that respond to requests for files in their DOS 8.3 file names are vulnerable to attacks that can cause the server to reveal source code. A fix to this problem is to disable DOS 8.3 file name creation on the NTFS server, but this may lead to difficulties in using 16-bit applications.

✦　　✦　　✦

Assessment Questions

You can find the answers to the following questions in Appendix A.

1. Which choice below is NOT an element of a fiber optic cable?

   a. Core

   b. BNC

   c. Jacket

   d. Cladding

2. Which backup method listed below will probably require the backup operator to use the most number of tapes for a complete system restoration if a different tape is used every night in a five-day rotation?

   a. Full

   b. Differential

   c. Incremental

   d. Ad Hoc

3. To what does 10Base-5 refer?

   a. 10 Mbps thinnet coax cabling rated to 185 meters maximum length

   b. 10 Mbps thicknet coax cabling rated to 500 meters maximum length

   c. 10 Mbps baseband optical fiber

   d. 100 Mbps unshielded twisted pair cabling

4. Which LAN transmission method below describes a packet sent from a single source to multiple specific destinations?

   a. Unicast

   b. Multicast

   c. Broadcast

   d. Anycast

5. Which part of the 48-bit, 12-digit hexadecimal number known as the Media Access Control (MAC) address identifies the manufacturer of the network device?

   a. The first three bytes

   b. The first two bytes

   c. The second half of the MAC address

   d. The last three bytes

6. Which choice below BEST describes coaxial cable?

    a. Coax consists of two insulated wires wrapped around each other in a regular spiral pattern.

    b. Coax consists of a hollow outer cylindrical conductor surrounding a single, inner conductor.

    c. Coax does not require the fixed spacing between connections that UTP requires.

    d. Coax carries signals as light waves.

7. Which choice below is NOT one of the legal IP address ranges specified by RFC1976 and reserved by the Internet Assigned Numbers Authority (IANA) for nonroutable private addresses?

    a. 10.0.0.0–10.255.255.255

    b. 127.0.0.0–127.0.255.255

    c. 172.16.0.0–172.31.255.255

    d. 192.168.0.0–192.168.255.255

8. Which statement below about the difference between analog and digital signals is incorrect?

    a. An analog signal produces an infinite waveform.

    b. Analog signals cannot be used for data communications.

    c. An analog signal can be varied by amplification.

    d. A digital signal produces a saw-tooth waveform.

9. Which choice below most accurately describes SSL?

    a. It's a widely used standard of securing email at the Application level.

    b. It gives a user remote access to a command prompt across a secure, encrypted session.

    c. It uses two protocols, the Authentication Header and the Encapsulating Security Payload.

    d. It allows an application to have authenticated, encrypted communications across a network.

10. Which IEEE protocol defines wireless transmission in the 5 GHz band with data rates up to 54 Mbps?

    a. IEEE 802.11a

    b. IEEE 802.11b

    c. IEEE 802.11g

    d. IEEE 802.15

11. Which protocol is used to resolve a known IP address to an unknown MAC address?

    a. ARP

    b. RARP

    c. ICMP

    d. TFTP

12. Which TCP/IP protocol operates at the OSI Network Layer?

    a. FTP

    b. IP

    c. TCP

    d. UDP

13. Which statement accurately describes the difference between 802.11b WLAN ad hoc and infrastructure modes?

    a. The ad hoc mode requires an Access Point to communicate to the wired network.

    b. Wireless nodes can communicate peer-to-peer in the infrastructure mode.

    c. Wireless nodes can communicate peer-to-peer in the ad hoc mode.

    d. Access points are rarely used in 802.11b WLANs.

14. Which answer below is true about the difference between TCP and UDP?

    a. UDP is considered a connectionless protocol and TCP is connection oriented.

    b. TCP is considered a connectionless protocol, and UDP is connection oriented.

    c. UDP acknowledges the receipt of packets, and TCP does not.

    d. TCP is sometimes referred to as an unreliable protocol.

15. Which choice below denotes a packet-switched connectionless wide area network (WAN) technology?

    a. X.25

    b. Frame Relay

    c. SMDS

    d. ATM

16. Which answer below is true about the difference between FTP and TFTP?

   a. FTP does not have a directory-browsing capability, whereas TFTP does.

   b. FTP enables print job spooling, whereas TFTP does not.

   c. TFTP is less secure because session authentication does not occur.

   d. FTP is less secure because session authentication does not occur.

17. Which statement below is correct regarding VLANs?

   a. A VLAN restricts flooding to only those ports included in the VLAN.

   b. A VLAN is a network segmented physically, not logically.

   c. A VLAN is less secure when implemented in conjunction with private port switching.

   d. A closed VLAN configuration is the least secure VLAN configuration.

18. Which statement about a VPN tunnel below is incorrect?

   a. It can be created by implementing only IPSec devices.

   b. It can be created by installing software or hardware agents on the client or network.

   c. It can be created by implementing key and certificate exchange systems.

   d. It can be created by implementing node authentication systems.

19. Which utility below can create a server-spoofing attack?

   a. DNS poisoning

   b. C2MYAZZ

   c. Snort

   d. BO2K

20. What is a server cluster?

   a. A primary server that mirrors its data to a secondary server

   b. A group of independent servers that are managed as a single system

   c. A tape array backup implementation

   d. A group of WORM optical jukeboxes

21. Which attack type below does NOT exploit TCP vulnerabilities?

   a. Sequence Number attack

   b. SYN attack

   c. Ping of Death

   d. land.c attack

22. What is probing used for?

    a. To induce a user into taking an incorrect action

    b. To give an attacker a road map of the network

    c. To use up all of a target's resources

    d. To covertly listen to transmissions

23. Which firewall type below uses a dynamic state table to inspect the content of packets?

    a. A packet-filtering firewall

    b. An application-level firewall

    c. A circuit-level firewall

    d. A stateful-inspection firewall

24. To what does logon abuse refer?

    a. Breaking into a network primarily from an external source

    b. Legitimate users accessing networked services that would normally be restricted to them

    c. Nonbusiness or personal use of the Internet

    d. Intrusions via dial-up or asynchronous external network connections

25. What type of firewall architecture employs two network cards and a single screening router?

    a. A screened-host firewall

    b. A dual-homed host firewall

    c. A screened-subnet firewall

    d. An application-level proxy server

26. To what does covert channel eavesdropping refer?

    a. Using a hidden, unauthorized network connection to communicate unauthorized information

    b. Nonbusiness or personal use of the Internet

    c. Socially engineering passwords from an ISP

    d. The use of two-factor passwords

27. What is one of the most common drawbacks to using a dual-homed host firewall?

    a. The examination of the packet at the Network Layer introduces latency.

    b. The examination of the packet at the Application Layer introduces latency.

    c. The ACLs must be manually maintained on the host.

    d. Internal routing may accidentally become enabled.

28. Which is NOT a property of a bridge?

    a. Forwards the data to all other segments if the destination is not on the local segment

    b. Operates at Layer 2, the Data Link Layer

    c. Operates at Layer 3, the Network Layer

    d. Can create a broadcast storm

29. Which IEEE protocol defines the Spanning Tree protocol?

    a. IEEE 802.5

    b. IEEE 802.3

    c. IEEE 802.11

    d. IEEE 802.1D

30. What does the Data Encapsulation in the OSI model do?

    a. Creates seven distinct layers

    b. Wraps data from one layer around a data packet from an adjoining layer

    c. Provides best-effort delivery of a data packet

    d. Makes the network transmission deterministic

31. Which choice below is NOT an element of IPSec?

    a. Authentication Header

    b. Layer Two Tunneling Protocol

    c. Security Association

    d. Encapsulating Security Payload

32. Which network attack below would NOT be considered a Denial of Service attack?

    a. Ping of Death

    b. SMURF

    c. Brute Force

    d. TCP SYN

33. Which statement is NOT true about the SOCKS protocol?

    a. It is sometimes referred to as an application-level proxy.

    b. It uses an ESP for authentication and encryption.

    c. It operates in the Transport Layer of the OSI model.

    d. Network applications need to be SOCKS-ified to operate.

34. Which choice below is NOT a way to get Windows NT passwords?

    a. Obtain the backup SAM from the repair directory.

    b. Boot the NT server with a floppy containing an alternate operating system.

    c. Obtain root access to the /etc/passwd file.

    d. Use pwdump2 to dump the password hashes directly from the registry.

35. Which type of routing below commonly broadcasts its routing table information to all other routers every minute?

    a. Static

    b. Distance Vector

    c. Link State

    d. Dynamic Control Protocol

36. A back door into a network refers to what?

    a. Socially engineering passwords from a subject

    b. Mechanisms created by hackers to gain network access at a later time

    c. Undocumented instructions used by programmers to debug applications

    d. Monitoring programs implemented on dummy applications to lure intruders

37. What is the protocol that supports sending and receiving email?

   a. SNMP

   b. SMTP

   c. ICMP

   d. RARP

38. Which protocol below does NOT pertain to email?

   a. SMTP

   b. POP

   c. CHAP

   d. IMAP

39. Which choice below does NOT relate to analog dial-up hacking?

   a. War dialing

   b. War walking

   c. Demon dialing

   d. ToneLoc

40. Which level of RAID is commonly referred to as *disk mirroring*?

   a. RAID 0

   b. RAID 1

   c. RAID 3

   d. RAID 5

41. Which choice below is the earliest and the most commonly found Interior Gateway Protocol?

   a. RIP

   b. OSPF

   c. IGRP

   d. EAP

42. What is the Network Layer of the OSI reference model primarily responsible for?

   a. Internetwork packet routing

   b. LAN bridging

   c. SMTP Gateway services

   d. Signal regeneration and repeating

43. Which of the following is NOT a true statement about Network Address Translation (NAT)?

   a. NAT is used when corporations want to use private addressing ranges for internal networks.

   b. NAT is designed to mask the true IP addresses of internal systems.

   c. Private addresses can easily be routed globally.

   d. NAT translates private IP addresses to registered "real" IP addresses.

44. In the DoD reference model, which layer conforms to the OSI Transport Layer?

   a. Process/Application Layer

   b. Host-to-Host Layer

   c. Internet Layer

   d. Network Access Layer

45. The IP address, 178.22.90.1, is considered to be in which class of address?

   a. Class A

   b. Class B

   c. Class C

   d. Class D

46. What does TFTP stand for?

   a. Trivial File Transport Protocol

   b. Transport for TCP/IP

   c. Trivial File Transfer Protocol

   d. Transport File Transfer Protocol

Cryptography

The information system professional should have a fundamental comprehension of the following areas in cryptography:

- ✦ Definitions
- ✦ Background
- ✦ Cryptology fundamentals
- ✦ Symmetric Key Cryptosystem fundamentals
- ✦ Asymmetric Key Cryptosystem fundamentals
- ✦ Key distribution and management issues
- ✦ Public Key Infrastructure (PKI) definitions and concepts

This chapter will address each of these areas to the level required of a practicing information system security professional.

Introduction

The purpose of cryptography is to protect transmitted information from being read and understood by anyone except the intended recipient. In the ideal sense, unauthorized individuals can never read an enciphered message. In practice, reading an enciphered communication can be a function of time; however, the effort and corresponding time that is required for an unauthorized individual to decipher an encrypted message may be so large that it can be impractical. By the time the message is decrypted, the information within the message may be of minimal value.

Definitions

Block Cipher. Obtained by segregating plaintext into blocks of *n* characters or bits and applying the identical encryption algorithm and key, K, to each block. For example, if a plaintext message, M, is divided into blocks M1, M2, . . . Mp, then:

```
E(M, K) = E(M1, K) E(M2, K) . . . E(Mp, K)
```

where the blocks on the right-hand side of the equation are concatenated to form the ciphertext.

Cipher. A cryptographic transformation that operates on characters or bits.

Ciphertext or Cryptogram. An unintelligible message.

 Clustering. A situation in which a plaintext message generates identical ciphertext messages by using the same transformation algorithm but with different cryptovariables or keys.

Codes. A cryptographic transformation that operates at the level of words or phrases.

Cryptanalysis. The act of obtaining the plaintext or key from the ciphertext that is used to obtain valuable information to pass on altered or fake messages in order to deceive the original intended recipient; breaking the ciphertext.

Cryptographic Algorithm. A step-by-step procedure used to encipher plaintext and decipher ciphertext.

Cryptography. The art and science of hiding the meaning of a communication from unintended recipients. The word cryptography comes from the Greek words *kryptos* (hidden) and *graphein* (to write).

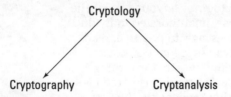

Cryptology. Encompasses cryptography and cryptanalysis.

Cryptosystem. A set of transformations from a message space to a ciphertext space. For example, if M = Plaintext, C = Ciphertext, E = the encryption transformation, and D = the decryption transformation,

```
E(M) = C
D[E(M)] = M
```

To specifically show the dependence of the encipherment and decipherment transformation on the cryptovariable or key, K,

```
E(M, K) = C
D(C, K) = D[E(M, K), K] = M
```

Decipher. To undo the encipherment process and make the message readable.

Encipher. To make the message unintelligible to all but the intended recipients.

End-to-End Encryption. Encrypted information that is sent from the point of origin to the final destination. In symmetric key encryption, this process requires the sender and receiver to have the identical key for the session.

Exclusive Or. Boolean operation that essentially performs binary addition without carry on the input bits, as shown in Table 4-1. For two binary input variables, A and B, the Exclusive Or function produces a binary 1 output when A and B are not equal and a binary 0 when A and B are equal. The symbol ⊗ or the acronym XOR indicates the Exclusive Or operation.

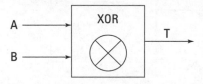

A	Table 4-1 **Exclusive Or (XOR)**	
A	*Inputs B*	*Output T*
0	0	0
0	1	1
1	0	1
1	1	0

The Exclusive Or function is easily implemented in hardware and therefore can be executed at hardware speeds. A valuable property of the Exclusive Or function is that the inverse of the function can be obtained by performing another Exclusive Or on the output. For example, assume that a transformation is performed on a stream cipher by applying the Exclusive Or operation, bit by bit, on the plaintext bits with the bits of a keystream. Then, the decipherment of the enciphered stream is accomplished by applying the Exclusive Or of the keystream, bit by bit, to the enciphered stream. This property is illustrated in Figure 4-1.

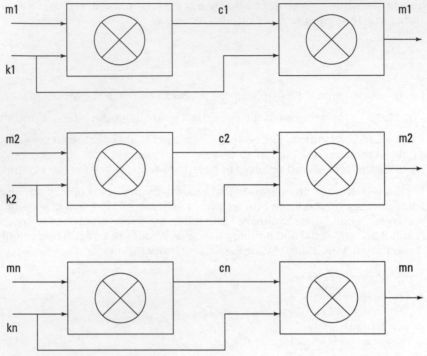

Figure 4-1: Exclusive Or (XOR).

If the bits of the message stream M are m1, m2, . . ., mn, the bits of the keystream K are k1, k2, . . ., kn, and the bits of the cipherstream C are c1, c2, . . ., cn, then

```
E(M,K) = M XOR K = C,  and
D( C) = D[M XOR K] = [M XOR K] XOR K
```

Schematically, the process is illustrated in Figure 4-2.

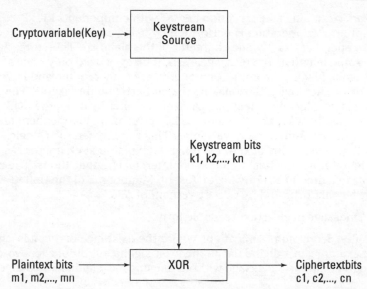

Figure 4-2: Encipherment process using Keystream with an XOR operation.

Key or Cryptovariable. Information or a sequence that controls the enciphering and deciphering of messages.

Link Encryption. Each entity has keys in common with its two neighboring nodes in the transmission chain. Thus, a node receives the encrypted message from its predecessor (the neighboring node), decrypts it, and then re-encrypts it with another key that is common to the successor node. Then, the encrypted message is sent on to the successor node, where the process is repeated until the final destination is reached. Obviously, this mode does not provide protection if the nodes along the transmission path can be compromised. A general representation of link encryption is shown in Figure 4-3.

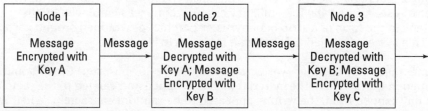

Figure 4-3: Link encryption.

OneTime Pad. Assuming an encryption key, K, with components k1, k2, . . ., kn, the encipherment operation is performed by using each component ki of the key, K, to encipher exactly one character of the plaintext. Therefore, the key has the same length as the message. Also, the key is used only once and is never used again. Ideally, the key's components are truly random and have no periodicity or predictability, thus making the ciphertext unbreakable. The one-time pad is usually implemented as a stream cipher by using the XOR function. The elements k1, k2, . . ., kn of the key stream are independent and are uniformly distributed, random variables. This requirement of a single, independently chosen value of ki to encipher each plaintext character is stringent and might not be practical for most commercial IT applications. The one-time pad was invented in 1917 by Major Joseph Mauborgne of the United States Army Signal Corps and by Gilbert Vernam of AT&T.

Plaintext. A message in cleartext readable form.

Steganography. Secret communications where the existence of the message is hidden. For example, in a digital image the least-significant bit of each word can be used to comprise a message without causing any significant change in the image.

Work Function (Factor). The difficulty in recovering the plaintext from the ciphertext as measured by cost and/or time. A system's security is directly proportional to the value of the work function. The work function needs only to be large enough to suffice for the intended application. If the message to be protected loses its value after a short time period, the work function needs only to be large enough to ensure that the decryption would be highly infeasible in that period of time.

Background

Secret writing can be traced back to 3,000 B.C. when it was used by the Egyptians. They employed hieroglyphics to conceal writings from unintended recipients. *Hieroglyphics* is derived from the Greek word *hieroglyphica*, which means "sacred carvings." Hieroglyphics evolved into *hieratic*, which was a stylized script that was easier to use. Around 400 B.C., military cryptography was employed by the Spartans in the form of a strip of papyrus or parchment wrapped around a wooden rod. This system is called a *Scytale* and is shown in Figure 4-4.

The message to be encoded was written lengthwise down (or up) the rod on the wrapped material. Then, the material was unwrapped and carried to the recipient. In its unwrapped form, the writing appeared to be random characters. When the material was rewound on a rod of the same diameter, *d*, and minimum length, *l*, the message could be read. Thus, as shown in Figure 4-4, the keys to deciphering the message are *d* and *l*.

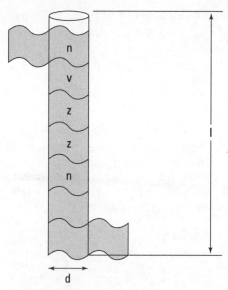

Figure 4-4: A Spartan *Scytale*.

Around 50 B.C., Julius Caesar, the emperor of Rome, used a substitution cipher to transmit messages to Marcus Tullius Cicero. In this cipher, letters of the alphabet are substituted for other letters of the same alphabet. Because only one alphabet was used, this cipher was a monoalphabetic substitution. This particular cipher involved shifting the alphabet by three letters and substituting those letters. This substitution, sometimes known as C3 (for Caesar shifting three places), is shown in Figure 4-5.

Figure 4-5: Caesar C3 substitution cipher.

In general, the Caesar system of ciphers can be written as follows:

```
Zi = Cn (Pi),
```

where the Z_i are ciphertext characters, C_n is a monoalphabetic substitution transformation, n is the number of letters shifted, and the P_i are plaintext characters.

Thus, the message ATTACK AT DAWN would be enciphered using C3 as follows:

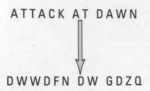

Disks have played an important part in cryptography for the past 500 years. In Italy around 1460, Leon Battista Alberti developed cipher disks for encryption (Figure 4-6). His system consisted of two concentric disks. Each disk had an alphabet around its periphery, and by rotating one disk with respect to the other, a letter in one alphabet could be transformed to a letter in another alphabet.

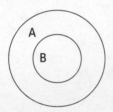

Figure 4-6: Cipher disks.

Cryptographic Technologies

The two principal types of cryptographic technologies are *symmetric key* (secret key or private key) cryptography and *asymmetric key* (public key) cryptography. In symmetric key cryptography, both the receiver and sender share a common secret key. In asymmetric key cryptography, the sender and receiver respectively share a public and private key. The public and private keys are related mathematically, and in an ideal case, they have the characteristic where an individual who has the public key cannot derive the private key.

Because of the amount of computation involved in public key cryptography, private key cryptography is on the order of 1,000 times faster than public key cryptography.

Classical Ciphers

In this section, the basic encipherment operations are discussed in detail in order to provide a basis for understanding the evolution of encryption methods and the corresponding cryptanalysis efforts.

Substitution

The Caesar Cipher, as we discussed earlier in this chapter, is a simple substitution cipher that involves shifting the alphabet three positions to the right. The Caesar Cipher is a subset of the Vigenère polyalphabetic cipher. In the Caesar Cipher, the message's characters and repetitions of the key are added together, modulo 26. In modulo 26 addition, the letters A to Z of the alphabet are given a value of 0 to 25, respectively. Two parameters have to be specified for the key:

> D, the number of repeating letters representing the key
>
> K, the key

In the following example, D = 3 and K = BAD:

The message is: ATTACK AT DAWN

Assigning numerical values to the message yields

```
0 19 19 0 2 10    0 19    3  0  22 13
A  T TA C  K      A  T    D  A  W  N
```

The numerical values of K are

```
1  0  3
B  A  D
```

Now, the repetitive key of 103 is added to the letters of the message as follows:

```
1   0   3   1   0   3   1   0   3   1   0   3     Repeating Key
0   19  19  0   2   10  0   19  3   0   22  13    Message
1   19  22  1   2   13  1   19  6   1   22  16    Ciphertext Numerical
                                                  Equivalents
B   I   W   B   C   N   B   T   G   B   W   Q     Ciphertext
```

Converting the numbers back to their corresponding letters of the alphabet produces the ciphertext as shown.

For the special case of the Caesar Cipher, D is 1 and the Key is D (2).

Taking the same message as an example using the Caesar cipher yields the following:

```
2   2   2   2   2   2   2   2   2   2   2   2     Repeating Key
0   19  19  0   2   10  0   19  3   0   22  13    Message
2   21  21  2   4   12  2   21  5   2   24  15    Ciphertext Numerical
                                                  Equivalents
C   V   V   C   E   M   C   V   F   C   Y   P     Ciphertext
```

Converting the numbers back to their corresponding letters of the alphabet produces the ciphertext, which is the letters of the original message text shifted three positions to the right.

If the sum of any of the additions yields a result greater than or equal to 26, the additions would be modulo 26, in which the final result is the remainder over 26. The following examples illustrate modulo 26 addition:

```
14 12  22  24
12 22   8   5
26 32  30  29    Apparent Sum
0   6   4   3    Result of modulo 26 addition
```

These ciphers can be described by the general equation

```
C = (M + b)mod N
```

where:

>   b is a fixed integer
>
>   N is the size of the alphabet
>
>   M is the Plaintext message in numerical form
>
>   C is the Ciphertext in numerical form

This representation is a special case of an Affine Cryptosystem, which is described in the following equation:

```
C = (aM + b)mod N
```

where:

>   a and b comprise the key

Recall that the following transformation is implemented by the Caesar Cipher:

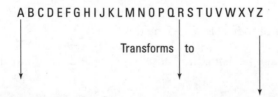

A B C D E F G H I J K L M N O P Q R S T U V W X Y Z

Transforms to

D E F G H I J K L M N O P Q R S T U V W X Y Z A B C

This type of cipher can be attacked by using *frequency analysis*. In frequency analysis, the frequency characteristics shown in the use of the alphabet's letters in a particular language are used. This type of cryptanalysis is possible because the Caesar cipher is a *monoalphabetic* or *simple substitution* cipher where a character of ciphertext is substituted for each character of the plaintext. A *polyalphabetic* cipher is accomplished through the use of multiple substitution ciphers. For example, using the alphabets shown in Figure 4-7, a Caesar cipher with D = 3, and the Key = BAD (103), the plaintext EGGA is enciphered into YGZR. Blaise de Vigenère, a French diplomat born in 1523, consolidated the cryptographic works of Alberti, Trithemius, and Porta to develop the very strong polyalphabetic cipher at that time. Vigenère's cipher used 26 alphabets.

Because multiple alphabets are used, this approach counters frequency analysis. It can, however, be attacked by discovery of the *periods*—when the substitution repeats.

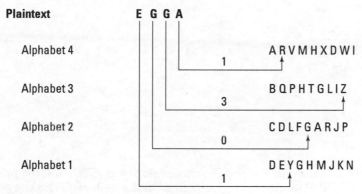

Plaintext E G G A

Alphabet 4   A R V M H X D W I
                        1

Alphabet 3   B Q P H T G L I Z
                      3

Alphabet 2   C D L F G A R J P
                    0

Alphabet 1   D E Y G H M J K N
                  1

Figure 4-7: Polyalphabetic substitution.

Transposition (Permutation)

Another type of cipher is the transposition cipher. In this cipher, the letters of the plaintext are permuted.

For example, the letters of the plaintext A T T A C K A T D A W N could be permuted to D C K A A W N A T A T T.

A columnar transposition cipher is one where the plaintext is written horizontally across the paper and is read vertically, as shown in Figure 4-8.

```
NOWISTHE       Figure 4-8: A columnar transposition cipher.
TIMEFORA
LLGOODME
NTOCOMET
OTHEAIDO
FTHEIRPA
RTY
```

Reading the ciphertext vertically yields: NTLNOFROILTTTTWMGOHHY . . .

The transposition cipher can be attacked through frequency analysis, but it hides the statistical properties of letter pairs and triples, such as IS and TOO.

Vernam Cipher (One-Time Pad)

 The one-time pad or Vernam cipher is implemented through a key that consists of a random set of nonrepeating characters. Each key letter is added modulo 26 to a letter of the plaintext. In the one-time pad, each key letter is used one time for only one message and is never used again. The length of the key character stream is equal to the length of the message. For megabyte and gigabyte messages, the one-time pad is not practical, but it is approximated by shorter random sets of characters with very long periods.

An example of a one-time pad encryption is as follows:

```
Plaintext           HOWAREYOU    7    14    22     0    17     4    24    14    20
One-time pad key    XRAQZTBCN   23    17     0    16    25    19     1     2    13


Apparent sum                    30    31    22    16    42    23    25    16    33
Sum Mod 26                       4     5    22    16    16    23    25    16     7
Ciphertext                       E     F     W     Q     Q     X     Z     Q     H
```

The Vernam machine (shown in Figure 4-9) was developed at AT&T, and the original system performed an XOR of the message bits in a Baudot code with the key bits.

Book or Running Key Cipher

This cipher uses text from a source (say, a book) to encrypt the plaintext. The key, known to the sender and the intended receiver, might be the page and line number of text in the book. This text is matched character for character with the plaintext, and modulo 26 addition is performed to effect the encryption.

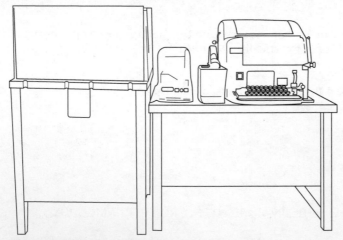

Figure 4-9: A Vernam machine.

The Running Key Cipher eliminates periodicity, but it is attacked by exploiting the redundancy in the key.

Codes

Codes deal with words and phrases and relate these words as phrases to corresponding groups of numbers or letters. For example, the numbers 526 might mean: "Attack at dawn."

Steganography

Steganography is the art of hiding the existence of a message. The word steganography comes from the Greek words steganos, meaning "covered," and graphein, meaning "to write." An example is the microdot, which compresses a message into the size of a period or dot. Steganography can be used to make a digital "watermark" to detect the illegal copying of digital images.

Secret Key Cryptography (Symmetric Key)

Secret key cryptography is the type of encryption that is familiar to most people. In this type of cryptography, the sender and receiver both know a secret key. The sender encrypts the plaintext message with the secret key, and the receiver decrypts the message with the same secret key. Obviously, the challenge is to make the secret key available to both the sender and receiver without compromising it. For increased security, the secret key should be changed at frequent intervals. Ideally, a particular secret key should only be used once.

Figure 4-10 illustrates a secret (symmetric) key cryptographic system.

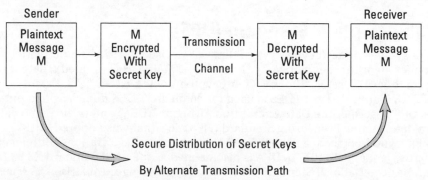

Figure 4-10: A symmetric (secret) key cryptosystem.

A secret key cryptographic system is comprised of information that is public and private. The public information usually consists of the following:

✦ The algorithm for enciphering the plaintext copy of the enciphered message

✦ Possibly, a copy of the plaintext and an associated ciphertext

✦ Possibly, an encipherment of the plaintext that was chosen by an unintended receiver

Private information is:

✦ The key or cryptovariable

✦ One particular cryptographic transformation out of many possible transformations

An important property of any secret key cryptographic system is that the same key can encipher and decipher the message. If large key sizes (> 128 bits) are used, secret key systems are very difficult to break. These systems are also relatively fast and are used to encrypt large volumes of data. There are many symmetric key algorithms available because of this feature. One problem with using a symmetric key system is that because the sender and receiver must share the same secret key, the sender requires a different key for each intended receiver. One commonly used approach is to use public key cryptography to transmit a symmetric session key that can be used for a session between the sender and receiver. Time stamps can be associated with this session key so that it is valid only for a specified period of time. Time stamping is a counter to replay, wherein a session key is somehow intercepted and used at a later time. Symmetric key systems, however, do not provide mechanisms for authentication and non-repudiation. The best-known symmetric key system is probably the Data Encryption Standard (DES). DES evolved from the IBM Lucifer cryptographic system in the early 1970s for commercial use.

Data Encryption Standard (DES)

DES is a symmetric key cryptosystem that was devised in 1972 as a derivation of the Lucifer algorithm developed by Horst Feistel at IBM. He obtained a patent on the technique (H. Feistel, "Block Cipher Cryptographic System," U.S. Patent #3,798,539, March 19, 1974.) DES is used for commercial and non-classified purposes. DES describes the Data Encryption Algorithm (DEA) and is the name of the Federal Information Processing Standard (FIPS) 46-1 that was adopted in 1977 [Data Encryption Standard, FIPS PUB 46-1 (Washington, D.C.: National Bureau of Standards, January 15, 1977)]. DEA is also defined as the ANSI Standard X3.92 [ANSI X3.92 American National Standard for Data Encryption Algorithm, (DEA)," American National Standards Institute, 1981]. The National Institute of Standards and Technology (NIST) recertified DES in 1993. DES will not be recertified again. It will, however, be replaced by the Advanced Encryption Standard (AES).

DEA uses a 64-bit block size and a 56-bit key. It begins with a 64-bit key and strips off eight parity bits. DEA is a 16-round cryptosystem and was originally designed for implementation in hardware. With a 56-bit key, one would have to try 2^{56} or 70 quadrillion possible keys in a brute force attack. Although this number is huge, large numbers of computers cooperating over the Internet could try all possible key combinations. Due to this vulnerability, the U.S. government has not used DES since November 1998. Triple DES — three encryptions using the DEA — has replaced DES and will be used until the AES is adopted.

As previously stated, DES uses 16 rounds of transposition and substitution. It implements the techniques that were suggested by Claude Shannon, the father of Information Theory. Shannon proposed two techniques, *confusion* and *diffusion*, for improving the encryption of plaintext. Confusion conceals the statistical connection between ciphertext and plaintext. It is accomplished in DES through a substitution by means of non-linear substitution S-boxes. An S-box is non-linear because it generates a 4-bit output string from a 6-bit input string.

The purpose of diffusion is to spread the influence of a plaintext character over many ciphertext characters. Diffusion can be implemented by means of a *Product Cipher*. In a Product Cipher, a cryptosystem (E1) is applied to a message (M) to yield ciphertext (C1). Then, another cryptosystem (E2) is applied to ciphertext (C1) to yield ciphertext (C2). Symbolically, this product is generated by E1(M) = C1; E2(C1) = C2. DES implements this product 16 times. Diffusion is performed in DES by permutations in P-Boxes.

DES operates in four modes:

1. Cipher Block Chaining (CBC)

2. Electronic Code Book (ECB)

3. Cipher Feedback (CFB)

4. Output Feedback (OFB)

Cipher Block Chaining

Cipher Block Chaining (CBC) operates with plaintext blocks of 64 bits. A randomly generated 64-bit initialization vector is XORed with the first block of plaintext used to disguise the first part of the message that might be predictable (such as Dear Sir). The result is encrypted by using the DES key. The first ciphertext will then XOR with the next 64-bit plaintext block. This encryption continues until the plaintext is exhausted. Note that in this mode, errors propagate.

A schematic diagram of CBC is shown in Figure 4-11.

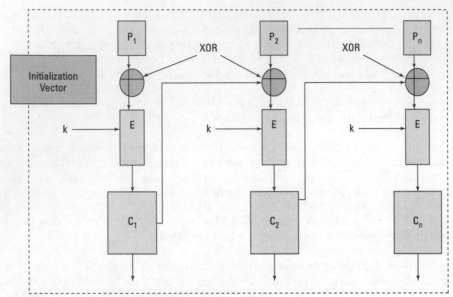

Figure 4-11: Cipher Block Chaining (CBC).

Electronic Code Book (ECB)

Electronic Code Book (ECB) is the "native" mode of DES and is a block cipher. ECB is best suited for use with small amounts of data. It is usually applied to encrypt initialization vectors or encrypting keys. ECB is applied to 64-bit blocks of plaintext, and it produces corresponding 64-bit blocks of ciphertext. ECB operates by dividing the 64-bit input vector into two 32-bit blocks called a Right Block and a Left Block. The bits are then recopied to produce two 48-bit blocks. Then, each of these 48-bit blocks is XORed with a 48-bit encryption key. The nomenclature "code book" is derived from the notion of a codebook in manual encryption, which has pairs of plaintext and the corresponding code. For example, the word "RETREAT" in the codebook might have the corresponding code "5374."

Cipher Feedback (CFB)

The Cipher Feedback (CFB) mode of DES is a stream cipher where the ciphertext is used as feedback into the key generation source to develop the next key stream. The ciphertext generated by performing an XOR of the plaintext with the key stream has the same number of bits as the plaintext. In this mode, errors will propagate. A diagram of the CFB is shown in Figure 4-12.

Output Feedback

The DES Output Feedback (OFB) mode is also a stream cipher that generates the ciphertext key by XORing the plaintext with a key stream. In this mode, errors will not propagate. Feedback is used to generate the key stream; therefore, the key stream varies. An initialization vector is required in OFB. OFB is depicted in Figure 4-13.

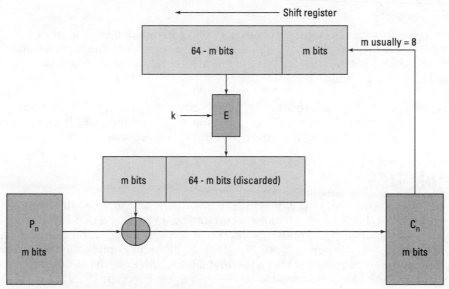

Figure 4-12: DES Cipher Feedback operation.

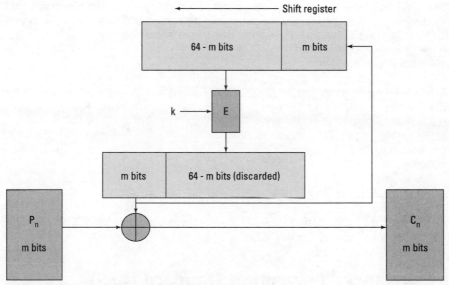

Figure 4-13: DES Output Feedback operation.

DES Security

Due to the increase in computing power that is capable of being incorporated onto Very Large Scale Integration (VLSI) chips and the corresponding decrease in cost, DES has been broken. Through the use of the Internet, a worldwide network of PCs was used to crack DES.

The consensus of the information security community is that DES is vulnerable to attack by an exhaustive research for the 56-bit key. Therefore, DES is being replaced by Triple DES, and then by the Advanced Encryption Standard (AES).

Triple DES

It has been shown that encrypting plaintext with one DES key and then encrypting it with a second DES key is no more secure than using a single DES key. It would seem at first glance that if both keys have n bits, a brute force attack of trying all possible keys would require trying $2^n \times 2^n$ or 2^{2n} different combinations. However, Merkle and Hellman showed that a known plaintext, Meet-in-the-Middle attack could break the double encryption in 2^{n+1} attempts. This type of attack is achieved by encrypting from one end, decrypting from the other, and comparing the results in the middle. Therefore, Triple DES is used to obtain stronger encryption.

Triple DES encrypts a message three times. This encryption can be accomplished in several ways. For example, the message can be encrypted with Key 1, decrypted with Key 2 (essentially another encryption), and encrypted again with Key 1:

`[E{D[E(M,K1)],K2},K1]`

A Triple DES encryption in this manner is denoted as DES–EDE2. If three encryptions are performed using the two keys, it is referred to as DES–EEE2:

`[E{E[E(M,K1)],K2},K1]`

Similarly,

`E{E[E(M,K1)],K2},K3]`

describes a triple encryption DES–EEE3 with three different keys. This encryption is the most secure form of Triple DES.

The Advanced Encryption Standard (AES)

AES is a block cipher that has replaced DES as a Federal standard, but it is anticipated that Triple DES will remain an approved algorithm for U.S. Government use. Triple DES and DES are specified in FIPS 46-3. The AES initiative was announced in January 1997 by NIST, and candidate encryption algorithm submissions were solicited. On August 29, 1998, a group of 15 AES candidates were announced by NIST. In 1999, NIST announced five finalist candidates. These candidates were MARS, RC6, Rijndael, Serpent, and Twofish. NIST closed Round 2 of public analyses of these algorithms on May 15, 2000.

On October 2, 2000, NIST announced the selection of the Rijndael Block Cipher, developed by the Belgian cryptographers Dr. Joan Daemen and Dr. Vincent Rijmen, as the proposed AES algorithm. Rijndael was formalized as the Advanced Encryption Standard (AES) on November 26, 2001, as Federal Information Processing Standard Publication (FIPS PUB 197). FIPS PUB 197 states that, "This standard may be used by Federal departments and agencies when an agency determines that sensitive (unclassified) information (as defined in P.L. 100-235) requires cryptographic protection. Other FIPS-approved cryptographic algorithms may be used in addition to, or in lieu of, this standard." Depending upon which of the three keys is used, the standard might be referred to as "AES-128," "AES-192," or "AES-256." It is expected that AES will be adopted by other private and public organizations inside and outside the United States.

The Rijndael Block Cipher

The Rijndael algorithm was designed to have the following properties:

✦ Resistance against all known attacks

✦ Design simplicity

✦ Code compactness and speed on a wide variety of platforms

The Rijndael cipher can be categorized as an iterated block cipher with a variable block length and key length that can be independently chosen as 128, 192, or 256 bits.

In decimal terms, there are approximately 3.4×10^{38} possible 128-bit keys, 6.2×10^{57} possible 192-bit keys, and 1.1×10^{77} possible 256-bit keys.

AES specifies three key sizes — 128, 192, and 256 bits — with a fixed block size of 128 bits.

As a measure of the relative strength of the Rijndael encryption algorithm, if a computer could crack the DES encryption by trying 2^{56} keys in one second, the same computer would require 149 trillion (149×10^{12}) years to crack Rijndael. For a comparison, the universe is estimated to be fewer than 20 billion (20×10^{9}) years old.

Rijndael defines an intermediate cipher result as a State upon which the transformations that are defined in the cipher operate.

Instead of a Feistel network that takes a portion of the modified plaintext and transposes it to another position, the Rijndael Cipher employs a round transformation that is comprised of three layers of distinct and invertible transformations. These transformations are also defined as uniform, which means that every bit of the State is treated the same. Each of the layers has the following respective functions:

The non-linear layer. The parallel application of S-boxes that have optimum worst-case non-linearity properties.

The linear mixing layer. Layer that provides a guarantee of a high diffusion of multiple rounds.

The key addition layer. An Exclusive Or of the Round Key to the intermediate State.

Round keys are derived from the Cipher key through a *key schedule*, which consists of a key expansion and Round key selection — defined as follows in the Rijndael Block Cipher AES Proposal (AES Proposal: Rijndael, Joan Daemen and Vincent Rijmen, version 2, 9/8/99) submitted to NIST:

The total number of Round key bits is equal to block length multiplied by the number of rounds plus 1 (e.g., for a block length of 128 bits and 10 rounds, 1408 Round Key bits are needed). The Cipher Key is expanded into an Expanded Key. Round Keys are taken from the Expanded Key.

The number of rounds used in the Rijndael Cipher is a function of the key size as follows:

✦ 256-bit key   14 rounds

✦ 192-bit key   12 rounds

✦ 128-bit key   10 rounds

The Rijndael Block Cipher is suited for the following types of implementations:

✦ High-speed chips with no area restrictions

✦ A compact coprocessor on a smart card

The Twofish Algorithm

Another example of the evolution of cryptographic technology is found in the Twofish algorithm, one of the finalists in the AES competition.

In summary, Twofish is a symmetric block cipher that operates on 128-bit blocks in 16 rounds that works in all standard modes. It can accept key lengths up to 256 bits.

Twofish is a Feistel network in that in each round, one-half of the 128-bit block of plaintext or modified plaintext is fed into an element called the F Function box and then is XORed with the other half of the text in the network. This one-half block is broken into two 32-bit units that are, in turn, broken into four bytes. These four bytes are fed into four different, key-dependent S-boxes and emerge from the S-boxes as four transformed output bytes.

The four output bytes of the S-boxes are combined in a Maximum Distance Separable (MDS) matrix to form two 32-bit units. These two 32-bit units are then combined by using a Pseudo-Hadamard Transform (PHT) and are added to two round subkeys. The PHT is a linear operation of the form:

```
d₁ = (2b₁ + b₂)mod 256
```

where b_1 and b_2 are the inputs, and d_1 is the output.

These results are XORed with the right half of the 64 bits of the plaintext. In addition, 1-bit rotations are performed before and after the XOR. These operations are then repeated for 15 more rounds.

Twofish also employs what is termed as *prewhitening* and *postwhitening*, where additional subkeys are XORed with the plaintext before the first round and after the 16th round. This approach makes cryptanalysis more difficult because the whitening subkeys have to be determined in addition to the algorithm key.

In the Twofish algorithm, the MDS matrix, the PHT, and key additions provide diffusion.

The IDEA Cipher

The International Data Encryption Algorithm (IDEA) cipher is a secure, secret, key-block encryption algorithm that was developed by James Massey and Xuejia Lai (X. Lai, "On the Design and Security of Block Ciphers," *ETH Series on Information Processing*, v. 1, Konstanz: Hartung-Gorre Verlag, 1992). It evolved in 1992 from earlier algorithms called the Proposed Encryption Standard and the Improved Proposed Encryption Standard. IDEA operates on 64-bit Plaintext blocks and uses a 128-bit key. It applies both confusion and diffusion.

The IDEA algorithm performs eight rounds and operates on 16-bit subblocks by using algebraic calculations that are amenable to hardware implementation. These operations are modulo 2^{16} addition, modulo 2^{16} + 1 multiplication, and the Exclusive Or.

With its 128-bit key, an IDEA cipher is much more difficult to crack than DES. IDEA operates in the modes described for DES and is applied in the Pretty Good Privacy (PGP) email encryption system that was developed by Phil Zimmerman.

RC5

RC5 is a family of cryptographic algorithms invented by Ronald Rivest in 1994. It is a block cipher of variable block length and encrypts through integer addition, the application of a bit-wise Exclusive Or, and variable rotations. The key size and number of rounds are also variable. Typical block sizes are 32, 64, or 128 bits. The number of rounds can range from 0 to 255 and the key size can range from 0 to 2,048 bits. RSA Data Security patented RC5 in 1997.

Public (Asymmetric) Key Cryptosystems

Unlike secret key cryptosystems, which make use of a single key that is known to a sender and receiver, public key systems employ two keys: a public key and a private key. The public key is made available to anyone wanting to encrypt and send a message. The private key is used to decrypt the message. Thus, the need to exchange secret keys is eliminated. The following are the important points to note:

✦ The public key cannot decrypt the message that it encrypted.

✦ Ideally, the private key cannot be derived from the public key.

✦ A message that is encrypted by one of the keys can be decrypted with the other key.

✦ The private key is kept private.

When Kp is the public key and Ks is the private key, the process is illustrated as follows:

```
C = Kp(P) and P = Ks(C)
```

where C is the ciphertext and P is the plaintext.

In addition, the reverse is also true:

```
C = Ks(P) and P = Kp(C)
```

One-Way Functions

Public key cryptography is possible through the application of a one-way function. A one-way function is a function that is easy to compute in one direction, yet is difficult to compute in the reverse direction. For such a function, if $y = f(x)$, it would be easy to compute y if given x, yet it would be very difficult to derive x when given y. A simple example would be the telephone directory. It is easy to find a number when given a name, but it is difficult to find the name when given a number. For a one-way function to be useful in the context of public key cryptography, it should have a trap door. A *trap door* is a secret mechanism that enables you to easily accomplish the reverse function in a one-way function. Thus, if you know the trap door, you can easily derive x in the previous example when given y.

In the context of public key cryptography, it is very difficult to calculate the private key from the public key unless you know the trap door.

Public Key Algorithms

A number of public key algorithms have been developed. Some of these algorithms are applicable to digital signatures, encryption, or both. Because there are more calculations associated with public key cryptography, it is 1,000 to 10,000 times slower than secret key cryptography. Thus, hybrid systems have evolved that use public key cryptography to safely distribute the secret keys used in symmetric key cryptography.

Some of the important public key algorithms that have been developed include the Diffie-Hellman key exchange protocol, RSA, El Gamal, Knapsack, and Elliptic Curve.

RSA

RSA is derived from the last names of its inventors, Rivest, Shamir, and Addleman (R. L. Rivest, A. Shamir, and L. M. Addleman, "A Method for Obtaining Digital Signatures and Public-Key Cryptosystems," *Communications of the ACM*, v. 21, n. 2, Feb 1978, pp. 120–126). This algorithm is based on the difficulty of factoring a number, N, which is the product of two large prime numbers. These numbers might be 200 digits each. Thus, the difficulty in obtaining the private key from the public key is a hard, one-way function that is equivalent to the difficulty of finding the prime factors of N.

In RSA, public and private keys are generated as follows:

1. Choose two large prime numbers, p and q, of equal length and compute $p \times q = n$, which is the public modulus.

2. Choose a random public key, e, so that e and $(p – 1)(1q – 1)$ are relatively prime.

3. Compute $e \times d = 1 \bmod (p – 1)(q – 1)$, where d is the private key.

4. Thus, $d = e^{-1} \bmod [(p – 1)(q – 1)]$.

From these calculations, (d, n) is the private key and (e, n) is the public key.

The plaintext, P, is thus encrypted to generate ciphertext C as follows:

```
C = Pe mod n,
```

and is decrypted to recover the plaintext, P, as

```
P = Cᵈ mod n
```

Typically, the plaintext will be broken into equal length blocks, each with fewer digits than n, and each block will be encrypted and decrypted as shown.

RSA can be used for encryption, key exchange, and digital signatures.

Diffie-Hellman Key Exchange

The Diffie-Hellman Key Exchange is a method where subjects exchange secret keys over a nonsecure medium without exposing the keys. Dr. W. Diffie and Dr. M. E. Hellman disclosed the method wasin their seminal 1976 paper entitled "New Directions in Cryptography" (Whitfield Diffie and Martin Hellman, "New Directions in Cryptography," *IEEE Transactions on Information Theory*, Vol. IT-22, November 1976, pp. 644–654).

The method enables two users to exchange a secret key over an insecure medium without an additional session key. It has two system parameters, p and g. Both parameters are public and can be used by all the system's users. Parameter p is a prime number, and parameter g, which is usually called a *generator*, is an integer less than p that has the following property: For every number n between 1 and p − 1 inclusive, there is a power k of g such that g^k = n mod p.

For example, when given the following public parameters:

> p = prime number
>
> g = generator
>
> Generating equation y = g^xmodp

Alice and Bob can securely exchange a common secret key as follows:

> Alice can use her private value "a" to calculate:

```
yᵃ = gᵃmodp
```

Also, Bob can use his private value "b" to calculate the following:

```
yᵇ = gᵇmodp
```

Alice can now send y^a to Bob, and Bob can send y^b to Alice. Knowing her private value, a, Alice can calculate $(y_b)^a$, which yields the following:

```
gᵇᵃmodp
```

Similarly, with his private value, b, Bob can calculate $(y_a)^b$ as such:

$g^{ab} \bmod p$

Because $g^{ba} \bmod p$ is equal to $g^{ab} \bmod p$, Bob and Alice have securely exchanged the secret key.

In their paper, Diffie and Hellman primarily described key exchange, yet they also provided a basis for the further development of public key cryptography.

El Gamal

Dr. T. El Gamal extended the Diffie-Hellman concepts to apply to encryption and digital signatures (T. El Gamal, "A Public-Key Crypto System and a Signature Scheme Based on Discrete Logarithms," *Advances in Cryptography: Proceedings of CRYPTO 84*, Springer-Verlag, 1985, pp. 10–18). The El Gamal system is a nonpatented public-key cryptosystem that is based on the discrete logarithm problem. Encryption with El Gamal is illustrated in the following example:

Given the prime number, p, and the integer, g, Alice uses her private key, a, to compute her public key as $y_a = g^a \bmod p$.

For Bob to send message M to Alice:

> Bob generates random #b < p.
>
> Bob computes $y_b = g^b \bmod p$ and $y_m = M \text{ XOR } y_a^b = M \text{ XOR } g^{ab} \bmod p$.
>
> Bob sends y_b, y_m to Alice, and Alice computes $y_b^a = g^{ab} \bmod p$.
>
> Therefore, $M = y_b^a \text{ XOR } y_m = g^{ab} \bmod p \text{ XOR } M \text{ XOR } g^{ab} \bmod p$.

Merkle-Hellman Knapsack

The Merkle-Hellman Knapsack (R.C. Merkle and M. Hellman, "Hiding Information and Signatures in Trapdoor Knapsacks," *IEEE Transactions on Information Theory*, v. 24, n. 5, Sep. 1978, pp. 525–530) is based on the problem of having a set of items with fixed weights and determining which of these items can be added in order to obtain a given total weight.

This concept can be illustrated by using a *superincreasing* set of weights. Superincreasing means that each succeeding term in the set is greater than the sum of the previous terms. The set [2, 3, 6, 12, 27, 52] has these properties. If we have a knapsack with a total weight of 69 for this example, the problem would be to find the terms whose sum is equal to 69. The solution to this simple example is that terms 52, 12, 3, and 2 would be in the knapsack. Or equivalently, if we represent the terms that are in the knapsack by 1s and those that are not by 0s, the ciphertext representing the "plaintext 69" is 110101.

Elliptic Curve (EC)

Elliptic curves are another approach to public key cryptography. This method was developed independently by Neal Koblitz (N. Koblitz, "Elliptic Curve Cryptosystems," *Mathematics of Computation*, v. 48, n. 177, 1987, pp. 203–209) and V.S. Miller (V.S. Miller, "Use of Elliptic Curves in Cryptography," *Advances in Cryptology — CRYPTO '85 Proceedings*, Springer-Verlag, 1986, pp. 417–426). Elliptic curves are usually defined over finite fields, such as real and rational numbers, and implement an analog to the discreet logarithm problem.

An elliptic curve is defined by the following equation:

$y^2 = x^3 + ax + b$ along with a single point O, the point at infinity.

The space of the elliptic curve has properties where:

✦ Addition is the counterpart of modular multiplication.

✦ Multiplication is the counterpart of modular exponentiation.

Thus, given two points, P and R, on an elliptic curve where P = KR, finding K is the hard problem that is known as the *elliptic curve discreet logarithm problem*.

Because it is more difficult to compute elliptic curve discreet logarithms than conventional discreet logarithms or to factor the product of large prime numbers, smaller key sizes in the elliptic curve implementation can yield higher levels of security. For example, an elliptic curve key of 160 bits is equivalent to a 1024-bit RSA key. This characteristic means fewer computational and memory requirements. Therefore, elliptic curve cryptography is suited to hardware applications such as smart cards and wireless devices. Elliptic curves can be used to implement digital signatures, encryption, and key management capabilities.

Public Key Cryptosystems Algorithm Categories

Public key encryption utilizes hard, one-way functions. The calculations associated with this type of encryption are as follows:

✦ Factoring the product of large prime numbers
  • RSA
✦ Finding the discreet logarithm in a finite field
  • El Gamal
  • Diffie-Hellman

- Schnorr's signature algorithm
- Elliptic curve
- Nybergrueppel's signature algorithm

Asymmetric and Symmetric Key Length Strength Comparisons

A comparison of the approximate equivalent strengths of public and private key cryptosystems is provided in Table 4-2.

Table 4-2 Equivalent Strengths of Asymmetric and Symmetric Keys	
Asymmetric Key Size	*Symmetric Key Size*
512 Bits	64 Bits
1792 Bits	112 Bits
2304 Bits	128 Bits

Digital Signatures

The purpose of digital signatures is to detect unauthorized modifications of data and to authenticate the identity of the signatories and non-repudiation. These functions are accomplished by generating a block of data that is usually smaller than the size of the original data. This smaller block of data is bound to the original data and to the identity of the sender. This binding verifies the integrity of data and provides non-repudiation. To quote the NIST Digital Signature Standard (DSS) [National Institute of Standards and Technology, NIST FIPS PUB 186, "Digital Signature Standard," U.S. Department of Commerce, May 1994]:

> Digital signatures are used to detect unauthorized modifications to data and to authenticate the identity of the signatory. In addition, the recipient of signed data can use a digital signature in proving to a third party that the signature was in fact generated by the signatory.

To generate a digital signature, the digital signal program passes the file to be sent through a one-way hash function. This hash function produces a fixed size output from a variable size input. The output of the hash function is called a *message digest*. The message digest is uniquely derived from the input file, and if the hash algorithm is strong, the message digest has the following characteristics:

✦ The hash function is considered one-way because the original file cannot be created from the message digest.

✦ Two files should not have the same message digest.

✦ Given a file and its corresponding message digest, it should not be feasible to find another file with the same message digest.

✦ The message digest should be calculated by using all of the original file's data.

After the message digest is calculated, it is encrypted with the sender's private key. The encrypted message digest is then attached to the original file and is sent to the receiver. The receiver then decrypts the message digest by using the sender's public key. If this public key opens the message digest and it is the true public key of the sender, verification of the sender is then accomplished. Verification occurs because the sender's public key is the only key that can decrypt the message digest encrypted with the sender's private key. Then, the receiver can compute the message digest of the received file by using the identical hash function as the sender. If this message digest is identical to the message digest that was sent as part of the signature, the message has not been modified.

Digital Signature Standard (DSS) and Secure Hash Standard (SHS)

NIST announced the Digital Signature Standard (DSS) Federal Information Processing Standard (FIPS) 186-1. This standard enables the use of the RSA digital signature algorithm or the Digital Signature Algorithm (DSA). The DSA is based on a modification of the El Gamal digital signature methodology and was developed by Claus Schnorr (C.P. Schnorr, "Efficient Signature Generation for Smart Cards," Advances in Cryptology — CRYPTO '89 Proceedings, Springer-Verlag, 1990, pp. 239–252).

Both of these digital signature algorithms use the Secure Hash Algorithm (SHA-1) as defined in FIPS 180 (NIST, NIST FIPS PUB 180, "Secure Hash Standard," U.S. Department of Commerce, May 1993).

SHA-1 computes a fixed-length message digest from a variable length input message. The DSA then processes this message digest to either generate or verify the signature. Applying this process to the shorter message digest is more efficient than applying it to the longer message.

As previously discussed, any modification to the message being sent to the receiver results in a different message digest being calculated by the receiver. Thus, the signature will not be verified.

SHA-1 produces a message digest of 160 bits when any message less than 264 bits is used as an input.

SHA-1 has the following properties:

✦ It is computationally infeasible to find a message that corresponds to a given message digest.

✦ It is computationally infeasible to find two different messages that produce the same message digest.

For SHA-1, the length of the message is the number of bits in a message. Padding bits are added to the message to make the total length of the message, including padding, a multiple of 512. To quote from the NIST DSS/SHS document:

The SHA-1 sequentially processes blocks of 512 bits when computing a message digest. The following specifies how the padding shall be performed. As a summary, a "1" followed by m "0's" followed by a 64-bit integer are applied to the end of the message to produce a padded message of length 512*n. The 64-bit integer is l, the length of the original message. The padded message is then processed by the SHA-1 as n 512-bit blocks.

MD5

MD5 is a message digest algorithm that was developed by Ronald Rivest in 1991. MD5 takes a message of an arbitrary length and generates a 128-bit message digest. In MD5, the message is processed in 512-bit blocks in four distinct rounds.

Sending a Message with a Digital Signature

In summary, to send a message:

1. A hash algorithm is used to generate the message digest from the message.

2. The message digest is fed into the digital signature algorithm that generates the signature of the message. The signing of the message is accomplished by encrypting the message digest with the sender's private key and attaching the result to the message. Thus, the message is a signed message.

3. The message and the attached message digest are sent to the receiver. The receiver then decrypts the attached message digest with the sender's public key.

The receiver also calculates the message digest of the received message by using the same hash function as the sender. The two message digests should be identical. If they are not identical, the message was modified in transmission. If the two message digests are identical, the message sent is identical to the message received, the sender is verified, and the sender cannot repudiate the message.

Hashed Message Authentication Code (HMAC)

An HMAC is a hash algorithm that uses a key to generate a *Message Authentication Code* (MAC). A MAC is a type of checksum that is a function of the information in the message. The MAC is generated before the message is sent, then appended to the message, and then both are transmitted.

At the receiving end, a MAC is generated from the message alone by using the same algorithm as that used by the sender. This MAC is compared to the MAC sent with the message. If they are not identical, the message was modified en route. Hashing algorithms can be used to generate the MAC and hash algorithms using keys that provide stronger protection than an ordinary MAC generation.

Hash Function Characteristics

As described in the previous section, a hash function (H) is used to condense a message of an arbitrary length into a fixed-length message digest. This message digest should uniquely represent the original message, and it will be used to create a digital signature. Furthermore, it should not be computationally possible to find two messages, M1 and M2, such that $H(M1) = H(M2)$. If this situation were possible, an attacker could substitute another message (M2) for the original message (M1), and the message digest would not change. Because the message digest is the key component of the digital signature authentication and integrity process, a false message could be substituted for the original message without detection. Specifically, it should not be computationally possible to find:

✦ A message (M2) that would hash to a specific message digest generated by a different message (M1)

✦ Two messages that hash to any common message digest

These two items refer to an attack against the hash function known as a *birthday attack*. This attack relates to the paradoxes that are associated with the following questions:

1. If you were in a room with other people, what would be the sample size, n, of individuals in the room to have a better than 50/50 chance of someone having the same birthday as you? (The answer is 253.)

2. If you were in a room with other people, what would be the sample size, n, of individuals in the room to have a better than 50/50 chance of at least two people having a common birthday? (The answer is 23, because with 23 people in a room, there are n(n -1)/2 or 253 pairs of individuals in the room.)

Cryptographic Attacks

 As defined earlier, cryptanalysis is the act of obtaining the plaintext or key from the ciphertext. Cryptanalysis is used to obtain valuable information and to pass on altered or fake messages in order to deceive the original intended recipient. This attempt at cracking the cipher is also known as an *attack*. The following are examples of some common attacks:

Brute force. Trying every possible combination of key patterns; the longer the key length, the more difficult it is to find the key with this method.

Known plaintext. The attacker has a copy of the plaintext corresponding to the ciphertext.

Chosen plaintext. Chosen plaintext is encrypted and the output ciphertext is obtained.

Adaptive chosen plaintext. A form of a chosen plaintext attack where the selection of the plaintext is altered according to the previous results.

Ciphertext only. Only the ciphertext is available.

Chosen ciphertext. Portions of the ciphertext are selected for trial decryption while having access to the corresponding decrypted plaintext.

Adaptive chosen ciphertext. A form of a chosen ciphertext attack where the selection of the portions of ciphertext for the attempted decryption is based on the results of previous attempts.

Birthday attack. Usually applied to the probability of two different messages using the same hash function, which produces a common message digest; or given a message and its corresponding message digest, finding another message that when passed through the same hash function generates the same specific message digest. The term *birthday* comes from the fact that in a room with 23 people, the probability of two or more people having the same birthday is greater than 50 percent.

Meet-in-the-middle. Is applied to double encryption schemes by encrypting known plaintext from one end with each possible key (K) and comparing the results "in the middle" with the decryption of the corresponding ciphertext with each possible K.

Man-in-the-middle. An attacker taking advantage of the store-and-forward nature of most networks by intercepting messages and forwarding modified versions of the original message while between two parties attempting secure communications.

Differential cryptanalysis. Is applied to private key cryptographic systems by looking at ciphertext pairs, which were generated through the encryption of plaintext pairs, with specific differences and analyzing the effect of these differences.

Linear cryptanalysis. Using pairs of known plaintext and corresponding ciphertext to generate a linear approximation of a portion of the key.

Differential linear cryptanalysis. Using both differential and linear approaches.

Factoring. Using a mathematical approach to determine the prime factors of large numbers.

Statistical. Exploiting the lack of randomness in key generation.

Public Key Certification Systems

A source that could compromise a public key cryptographic system is an individual (A) who is posting a public key under the name of another individual (B). In this scenario, the people who are using this public key to encrypt the messages that were intended for individual B will actually be sending messages to individual A. Because individual A has the private key that corresponds to the posted public key, individual A can decrypt the messages that were intended for individual B.

Digital Certificates

To counter this type of attack, a certification process can be used to bind individuals to their public keys. A *Certificate Authority* (CA) acts as notary by verifying a person's identity and issuing a certificate that vouches for a public key of the named individual. This certification agent signs the certificate with its own private key. Therefore, the individual is verified as the sender if that person's public key opens the data. The certificate contains the subject's name, the subject's public key, the name of the certificate authority, and the period in which the certificate is valid. To verify the CA's signature, its public key must be cross-certified with another CA. (The X.509 standard defines the format for public key certificates.) This certificate is then sent to a repository, which holds the certificates and *Certificate Revocation Lists* (CRLs) that denote the revoked certificates. The diagram shown in Figure 4-14 illustrates the use of digital certificates in a transaction between a subscribing entity and a transacting party. Digital certificates will be discussed in more detail in the following sections.

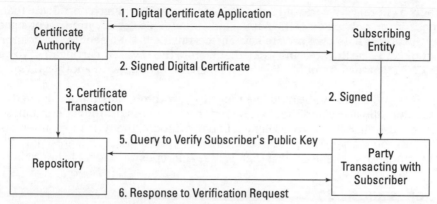

Figure 4-14: A transaction with digital certificates.

Public Key Infrastructure (PKI)

The integration of digital signatures and certificates and the other services required for E-commerce is called the *Public Key Infrastructure* (PKI). These services provide integrity, access control, confidentiality, authentication, and non-repudiation for electronic transactions. The PKI includes the following elements:

✦ Digital certificates

✦ Certificate authority (CA)

✦ Registration authorities

✦ Policies and procedures

✦ Certificate revocation

✦ Non-repudiation support

✦ Timestamping

✦ Lightweight Directory Access Protocol (LDAP)

✦ Security-enabled applications

Digital Certificates

The digital certificate and management of the certificate are major components of PKI. Remember: The purpose of a digital certificate is to verify to all that an individual's public key — posted on a public "key ring" — is actually his. A trusted, third-party CA can verify that the public key is that of the named individual and then issue a certificate attesting to that fact. The CA accomplishes the certification by digitally signing the individual's public key and associated information.

A CA acts as notary by verifying a person's identity and issuing a certificate that vouches for the public key of the named individual. This certification agent signs the certificate with its own private key. The certificate is then sent to a repository, which holds the certificates and CRLs that denote the revoked certificates. To verify the CA's signature, its public key must be cross-certified with another CA's.

Certificates and CRLs can be held in a repository, with responsibilities defined between the repository and the CA. The repository access protocol determines how these responsibilities are assigned. In one protocol, the repository interacts with other repositories, CAs, and users. The CA deposits its certificates and CRLs into the repository. The users can then access the repository for this information.

Directories and X.500

In PKI, a repository is usually referred to as a *directory*. The directory contains entries associated with an object class. An object class can refer to individuals or other computer-related entities. The class defines the attributes of the object. Attributes for PKI are defined in RFC 2587, *Internet X.509 Public Key Infrastructure LDAP v2 Schema* by Boeyen, Howes, and Richard, published in1999. Additional information on attributes can be found in RFC 2079, *Definition of an X.500 Attribute Type and an Object Class to Hold Uniform Resource Identifiers (URLs),* by M. Smith, published in January 1997.

The X.509 certificate standard defines the authentication bases for the X.500 directory. The X.500 directory stores information about individuals and objects in a distributed database residing on network servers. Some of the principal definitions associated with X.500 include the following:

- ✦ *Directory User Agents* (DUAs) — clients
- ✦ *Directory Server Agents* (DSAs) — servers
- ✦ *Directory Service Protocol* (DSP) — enables information exchanges between DSAs
- ✦ *Directory Access Protocol* (DAP) — enables information exchanges from a DUA to a DSA
- ✦ *Directory Information Shadowing Protocol* (DISP) — used by a DSA to duplicate or "shadow" some or all of its contents

DSAs accept requests from anonymous sources as well as authenticated requests. They share information through a *chaining* mechanism.

The Lightweight Directory Access Protocol

The Lightweight Directory Access Protocol (LDAP) was developed as a more efficient version of DAP and has evolved into a second version (Yeong, Y., T. Howes, and S. Killie, *Lightweight Directory Access Protocol*, RFC 1777, 1995). LDAP servers communicate through referrals (that is, a directory receiving a request for information it does not have will query the tables of remote directories). If it finds a directory with the required entry, it sends a referral to the requesting directory. LDAP v2 does not have chaining and shadowing capabilities, but additional protocols can be obtained to provide these functions.

LDAP provides a standard format to access the certificate directories. These directories are stored on network LDAP servers and provide public keys and corresponding X.509 certificates for the enterprise. A directory contains information, such as individuals' names, addresses, phone numbers, and public key certificates. The standards under X.500 define the protocols and information models for computer directory services that are independent of the platforms and other related entities. LDAP servers are subject to attacks that affect availability and integrity. For example, Denial of Service attacks on an LDAP server could prevent access to the CRLs and thus permit the use of a revoked certificate.

The DAP protocol in X.500 was unwieldy and led to most client implementations using LDAP. LDAP version 3 is under development; it will include extensions that provide shadowing and chaining capabilities.

X.509 Certificates

The original X.509 certificate (CCITT, *The Directory—Authentication Framework*, Recommendation X.509, 1988) was developed to provide the authentication foundation for the X.500 directory. Since then, a version 2, version 3, and recently, a version 4 have been developed. Version 2 of the X.509 certificate addresses the reuse of names, version 3 provides for certificate extensions to the core certificate fields, and version 4 provides additional extensions. These extensions can be used as needed by different users and different applications. A version of X.509 that takes into account the requirements of the Internet was published by the IETF (Housley, R., W. Ford, W. Polk, and D. Solo, *Internet X.509 Public Key Infrastructure Certificate and CRL Profile*, RFC 2459, 1999).

The Consultation Committee, International Telephone and Telegraph, International Telecommunications Union (CCITT-ITU)/International Organization for Standardization (ISO) has defined the basic format of an X.509 certificate. This structure is outlined in Figure 4-15.

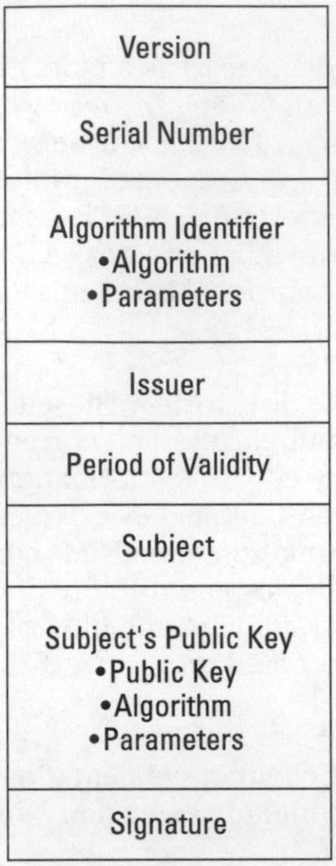

Version
Serial Number
Algorithm Identifier •Algorithm •Parameters
Issuer
Period of Validity
Subject
Subject's Public Key •Public Key •Algorithm •Parameters
Signature

Figure 4-15: The CCITT-ITU/ ISO X.509 certificate format.

If version 3 certificates are used, the optional extensions field can be used. It comes before the signature field components in the certificate. Some typical extensions are the entity's name and supporting identity information, the attributes of the key, certificate policy information, and the type of the subject. The digital signature serves as a tamper-evident envelope.

Some of the different types of certificates that are issued include the following:

CA certificates. Issued to CAs, these certificates contain the public keys used to verify digital signatures on CRLs and certificates.

End entity certificates. Issued to entities that are not CAs, these certificates contain the public keys that are needed by the certificate's user in order to perform key management or verify a digital signature.

Self-issued certificates. These certificates are issued by an entity to itself to establish points of trust and to distribute a new signing public key.

Rollover certificates. These certificates are issued by a CA to transition from an old public key to a new one.

Certificate Revocation Lists

Users check the certificate revocation list (CRL) to determine whether a digital certificate has been revoked. They check for the serial number of the signature. The CA signs the CRL for integrity and authentication purposes. A CRL is shown in Figure 4-16 for an X.509 version 2 certificate.

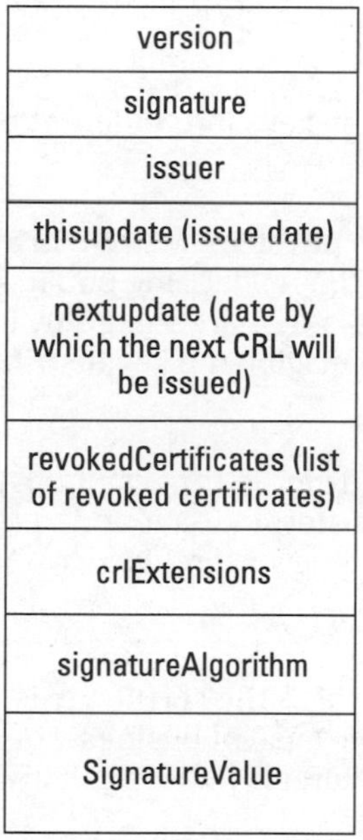

version
signature
issuer
thisupdate (issue date)
nextupdate (date by which the next CRL will be issued)
revokedCertificates (list of revoked certificates)
crlExtensions
signatureAlgorithm
SignatureValue

Figure 4-16: CRL format (version 2).

The CA usually generates the CRLs for its population. If the CA generates the CRLs for its entire population, the CRL is called a *full CRL*.

Key Management

Obviously, when dealing with encryption keys, the same precautions must be used as with physical keys to secure the areas or the combinations to the safes. The components of key management are listed as follows:

Key Distribution

As noted earlier, distributing secret keys in symmetric key encryption poses a problem. Secret keys can be distributed using asymmetric key cryptosystems. Other means of distributing secret keys include face-to-face meetings to exchange keys, sending the keys by secure messenger, or some other secure alternate channel. Another method is to encrypt the secret key with another key, called a *key encryption key*, and send the encrypted secret key to the intended receiver. These key encryption keys can be distributed manually, but they need not be distributed often. The X9.17 Standard (ANSI X9.17 [Revised], "American National Standard for Financial Institution Key Management [Wholesale]," American Bankers Association, 1985) specifies key encryption keys as well as data keys for encrypting the plaintext messages.

Key distribution can also be accomplished by splitting the keys into different parts and sending each part by a different medium.

In large networks, key distribution can become a serious problem because in an N-person network, the total number of key exchanges is N(N-1)/2. Using public key cryptography or the creation and exchange of session keys that are valid only for a particular session and time are useful mechanisms for managing the key distribution problem.

Keys can be *updated* by generating a new key from an old key. If, for example, Alice and Bob share a secret key, they can apply the same transformation function (a hash algorithm) to their common secret key and obtain a new secret key.

Key Revocation

A digital certificate contains a timestamp or period for which the certificate is valid. Also, if a key is compromised or must be made invalid because of business- or personnel-related issues, it must be revoked. The CA maintains a CRL of all invalid certificates. Users should regularly examine this list.

Key Recovery

A system must be put in place to decrypt critical data if the encryption key is lost or forgotten. One method is *key escrow*. In this system, the key is subdivided into different parts, each of which is encrypted and then sent to a different trusted individual in an organization. Keys can also be escrowed onto smart cards.

Key Renewal

Obviously, the longer a secret key is used without changing it, the more it is subject to compromise. The frequency with which you change the key is a direct function of the value of the data being encrypted and transmitted. Also, if the same secret key is used to encrypt valuable data over a relatively long period of time, you risk compromising a larger volume of data when the key is broken. Another important concern if the key is not changed frequently is that an attacker can intercept and change messages and then send different messages to the receiver.

Key encryption keys, because they are not used as often as encryption keys, provide some protection against attacks.

Typically, private keys used for digital signatures are not frequently changed and may be kept for years.

Key Destruction

Keys that have been in use for long periods of time and are replaced by others should be destroyed. If the keys are compromised, older messages sent with those keys can be read.

Keys that are stored on disks or EEPROMS should be overwritten numerous times. One can also destroy the disks by shredding and burning them. However, in some cases, it is possible to recover data from disks that were put into a fire. Any hardware device storing the key, such as an EPROM, should also be physically destroyed.

Older keys stored by the operating system in various locations in memory must also be searched out and destroyed.

Multiple Keys

Usually, an individual has more than one public/private key pair. The keys may be of different sizes for different levels of security. A larger key size may be used for digitally signing documents and a smaller key size may be used for encryption. A person may also have multiple roles or responsibilities wherein they want to sign messages with a different signature. One key pair may be used for business matters, another for personal use, and another for some other activity, such as being a school board member.

Distributed versus Centralized Key Management

A CA is a form of centralized key management. It is a central location that issues certificates and maintains CRLs. An alternative is distributed key management, in which a "chain of trust" or "web of trust" is set up among users who know each other. Because they know each other, they can trust that each one's public key is valid. Some of these users may know other users and can thus verify their public key. The chain spreads outward from the original group. This arrangement results in an informal verification procedure that is based on people knowing and trusting each other.

Approaches to Escrowed Encryption

In some instances, there is a need for law enforcement agencies to have access to information transmitted electronically over computer networks. To have this access, law enforcement agencies need the encryption keys to read the enciphered messages. At the same time, the privacy of citizens must be protected from illegal and unauthorized surveillance of their digital communications. This section describes two approaches to this issue.

The Escrowed Encryption Standard

This standard (National Institute of Standards and Technology, NIST FIPS PUB 185, "Escrowed Encryption Standard," U.S. Department of Commerce, Feb 1994) strives to achieve individual privacy and, at the same time, strives to provide for legal monitoring of the encrypted transmissions. The idea is to divide the key into two parts and then to escrow two portions of the key with two separate trusted organizations. Then law enforcement officials, after obtaining a court order, can retrieve the two pieces of the key from the organizations and decrypt the message. The Escrowed Encryption Standard is embodied in the U.S. Government's *Clipper Chip*, which is implemented in tamper-proof hardware. The Skipjack Secret Key algorithm performs the encryption. Figure 4-17 is a block diagram of the Clipper Chip and the components of a transmitted message.

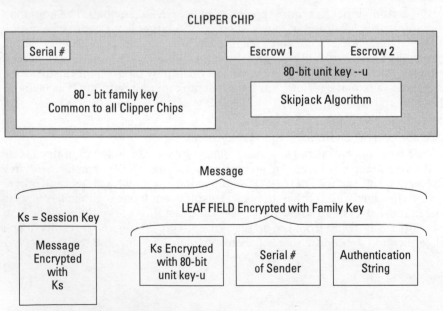

Figure 4-17: A Clipper Chip block diagram.

Each Clipper Chip has a unique serial number and an 80-bit unique unit or secret key. The unit key is divided into two parts and is stored at two separate organizations with the serial number that uniquely identifies that particular Clipper Chip. Initially, two parties that wish to exchange information agree on a session key, Ks. Ks can be exchanged using a Diffie-Hellman or an RSA key exchange. The plaintext message, M, is encrypted with the session key, Ks. Ks is not escrowed. In addition, a Law Enforcement Access Field (LEAF) is transmitted along with the encrypted message, M. The LEAF is encrypted with the family key, which is common to all Clipper Chips, and contains the following:

✦ Ks encrypted with secret key, u

✦ The serial number of sending Clipper Chip

✦ An authentication string

When the intended individual receives the transmitted items, this person decrypts the message with the mutually known session key, Ks.

A law enforcement agency can obtain the session key as follows:

1. Decrypt the LEAF with a family key to obtain the particular Clipper Chip serial number and encrypted session key. Ks is still encrypted with the secret family key, u.

2. Present an authorization court order to the two escrow agencies and obtain the two portions of the key, u.

3. Decrypt Ks with the key, u.

4. Decrypt the message, M, with Ks.

The 80-bit key of the Clipper Chip is weak. Concerns also exist over the escrow agencies' abilities to protect the escrowed keys, and whether these agencies may divulge them in unauthorized ways.

Key Escrow Approaches Using Public Key Cryptography

Another key escrow approach is Fair Cryptosystems. In 1992, Sylvio Micali introduced the concept of Fair Cryptosystems (S. Micali, "Fair Cryptosystems," MIT/LCS/TR-579.b, MIT Laboratory for Computer Science, Nov 1993), where the private key of a public/private key pair is divided into multiple parts and distributed to different trustees. In 1994, Micali obtained patents on this approach that were eventually purchased by Banker's Trust.

One valuable characteristic of Micali's approach is that each portion of the secret key can be verified as correct without having to reconstruct the entire key. This is accomplished by giving each trustee a piece of each public key and private key. Micali also developed calculations that can be used on each trustee's private/public key pieces to verify that they are correct. If authorities have the legal permission to decrypt a message that is encrypted with the secret key, they can obtain all the portions of the private key and read the message. Micali also proposed a threshold approach where some subset of the trustee's set would be sufficient to recover the entire secret key.

Micali's approach can be applied by voluntary trustees in different countries or business areas rather than by a controlled, governmental entity.

Identity-Based Encryption

As noted in the sections on digital certificates and PKI, there is a substantial amount of overhead required to implement and apply these concepts. Some of the issues involved are that users must be online to effect secure communications, certificates must be located and identified for intended message recipients, and certificates must be validated prior to use.

An alternative approach, proposed by Adi Shamir in 1984, is *Identity-Based Encryption* (IBE). The IBE concept proposes that any string can be used as an individual's public key, including his or her email address. Two additional features of IBE are that the sender does not have to go online to obtain the intended recipient's certificate, and mail can be sent to recipients who have not established a public key. IBE, however, was not workable until 2001, when Dr. Daniel Boneh of Stanford University and Dr. Matt Franklin of the University of California at Davis developed a solution (D. Boneh and M. Franklin, "Identity-Based Encryption from the Weil Paring," *Crypto 2001, Lecture Notes in Computer Science, Vol. 2139*, Springer-Verlag, 2001, pp. 213–229.) The solution involves points on an elliptic curve and the mathematical concept of a bi-linear map. Using the *Weil Pairing* form of a bi-linear map, the bi-linear map exhibits the property that Pair $(a \bullet P, b \bullet Q)$ = Pair $(b \bullet P, a \bullet Q)$, where the operation $\bullet$ is multiplication in the elliptic curve space, a and b are integers, and P and Q are points on an elliptic curve. The key to this approach is the one-way function wherein it is easy to perform $a \bullet P$ but virtually impossible to find a, given P and $a \bullet P$.

Using the Weil Pairing, the IBE algorithm can be developed as follows:

1. Parameters x and P are generated as random numbers by a key server. x is a parameter that is to be kept secret.

2. P and $x \bullet P$ are sent to all users.

3. The key server generates a private key for all users based on the users' IDs. For example, if Alice's ID is alice@mymail.com, Alice's private key is $x \bullet$ alice@mymail.com.

4. For Bob to send an encrypted email message to Alice, Bob generates a random number, y, and then generates the key, K, as K = Pair(y•alice@mymail.com, x•P).

5. Bob sends the message M, encrypted with K, to Alice as Ek(M), along with the product y•P.

6. Alice receives the message and now needs the key, K, to decrypt the message.

7. Alice generates the key through the calculation of K = Pair(x•alice@mymail.com, y•P).

8. Because Alice is the only one who has the value x•alice@mymail.com, she is the only person that can decrypt the message.

9. Again, this sequence is possible because under the Weil Pairing, K= Pair(y•alice@mymail.com, x•P) = Pair(x•alice@mymail.com, y•P).

To summarize, the IBE algorithm has four components:

1. *SETUP*—generates the global parameters and a master-key

2. *EXTRACTING*—generates the private key corresponding to an individual's public key string ID using the master-key

3. *ENCRYPTING*—based on the public key ID, encrypts the messages

4. *DECRYPTING*—decrypts the messages with the corresponding private key

Thus, based on the IBE algorithm, for Bob to send an encrypted email to Alice, he does not need to acquire Alice's digital certificate. He encrypts the message using Alice's public key string, `alice@mymail.com`. Upon receipt of the encrypted message, Alice contacts a third party, a Private Key Generation Server. After authenticating Alice, the Server provides Alice with her private key, which she uses to decrypt the email from Bob. With this approach, Bob can send encrypted email to Alice even though she has not yet established her public key certificate.

Quantum Computing

In digital computers, a bit is in either a one or zero state. In a quantum computer, through *linear superposition*, a quantum bit *(qubit)* can be in both states, essentially simultaneously. For example, a qubit can be can be represented by atoms or subatomic particles that exhibit a *spin*. A clockwise spin can be used to represent the digital value of 1 and a counterclockwise spin can represent a 0. In the quantum world, both values can exist simultaneously unless the particle is disturbed by outside influences. Thus, computations consisting of trial evaluations of large binary patterns can, theoretically, take place simultaneously in polynomial time instead of exponential time.

An example of quantum computing applied to cryptography is through the implementation of Shor's algorithm (P.W. Shor, "Polynomial-time Algorithms for Prime Factorization and Discreet Logarithms on a Quantum Computer." *SIAM Journal on Computing 26*, no. 5, 1997, pp. 1484–1509). This algorithm applies Fourier transforms with the linear superposition property of qubits to factor large numbers. As discussed in the RSA public key algorithm description, the strength of that approach is the difficulty of factoring large numbers that are a product of two prime numbers. Thus, if a quantum computer can be physically realized, it will make it possible to defeat cryptographic systems that are now deemed impossible to break. Quantum computing also holds promise in the area of cryptographic transmissions that are impossible to intercept and break because of the property that the state of linear superposition collapses when disturbed by outside influences, such as attempts to intercept the message.

Email Security Issues and Approaches

The main objectives of email security are to ensure the following:

✦ Non-repudiation

✦ Messages are read only by their intended recipients

✦ Integrity of the message

✦ Authentication of the source

✦ Verification of delivery

✦ Labeling of sensitive material

✦ Control of access

The following standards have been developed to address some or all of these issues:

Secure Multi-purpose Internet Mail Extensions (S/MIME)

S/MIME is a specification that adds secure services to email in a MIME format. S/MIME provides for authentication through digital signatures and the confidentiality of encryption. S/MIME follows the Public Key Cryptography Standards (PKCS) and uses the X.509 standard for its digital certificates.

MIME Object Security Services (MOSS)

MOSS provides flexible email security services by supporting different trust models. Introduced in 1995, MOSS provides authenticity, integrity, confidentiality, and non-repudiation to email. It uses MD2/MD5, RSA Public Key, and DES. MOSS also permits user identification outside of the X.509 Standard.

Privacy Enhanced Mail (PEM)

Privacy Enhanced Mail (PEM) is a standard that was proposed by the IETF to be compliant with the Public Key Cryptography Standards (PKCS), which were developed by a consortium that included Microsoft, Novell, and Sun Microsystems. PEM supports the encryption and authentication of Internet email. For message encryption, PEM applies Triple DES-EDE using a pair of symmetric keys. RSA Hash Algorithms MD2 or MD5 are used to generate a message digest, and RSA public key encryption implements digital signatures and secure key distribution. PEM employs certificates that are based on the X.509 standard and are generated by a formal CA.

Pretty Good Privacy (PGP)

In order to bring email security to the "masses," Phil Zimmerman developed the Pretty Good Privacy (PGP) software (Zimmerman, Philip R., *The Official PGP User's Guide*, Cambridge, MA: MIT Press, 1995). Zimmerman derived the PGP name from Ralph's Pretty Good Groceries, which sponsored Garrison Keillor's Prairie Home Companion radio show. PGP uses the symmetric cipher IDEA to encipher the message and RSA for symmetric key exchange and for digital signatures.

Instead of using a CA, PGP uses a Web of Trust. Users can certify each other in a mesh model, which is best applied to smaller groups (as shown in Figure 4-18).

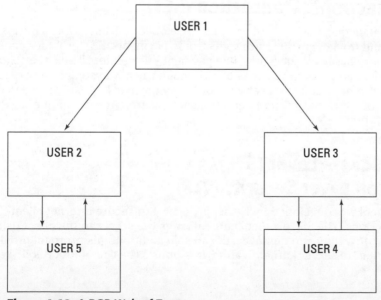

Figure 4-18: A PGP Web of Trust.

Internet Security Applications

With the growing use of the Internet and World Wide Web for commercial transactions, there is a need for providing confidentiality, integrity, and authentication of information. This section describes some of the approaches to obtain secure Internet and World Wide Web e-commerce.

Message Authentication Code (MAC) or the Financial Institution Message Authentication Standard (FIMAS)

In order to protect against fraud in electronic fund transfers, the Message Authentication Code (MAC), ANSI X9.9, was developed. The MAC is a check value derived from the contents of the message itself that is sensitive to the bit changes in a message. It is similar to a Cyclic Redundancy Check (CRC). A MAC is appended to the message before it is transmitted. At the receiving end, a MAC is generated from the received message and is compared to the MAC of an original message. A match indicates that the message was received without any modification occurring while en route.

To strengthen the MAC algorithm, a keyed MAC can be generated using a symmetric key encryption, such as DES. Typically, the Exclusive Or function of the DES key with a message is performed on the sequential, 8-byte blocks of the message to generate the MAC. As with all symmetric key applications, the key must be distributed securely so that sender and receiver have the same key.

Secure Electronic Transaction (SET)

A consortium including MasterCard and Visa developed SET in 1997 as a means of preventing fraud from occurring during electronic payments. SET provides confidentiality for purchases by encrypting the payment information. Thus, the seller cannot read this information. SET uses a DES symmetric key system for encryption of the payment information and uses RSA for the symmetric key exchange and digital signatures. SET covers the end-to-end transactions from the cardholder to the financial institution.

Secure Sockets Layer (SSL)/ Transaction Layer Security (TLS)

The SSL protocol was developed by Netscape in 1994 to secure Internet client-server transactions. The SSL protocol authenticates the server to the client using public key cryptography and digital certificates. In addition, this protocol provides for optional client-to-server authentication. It supports the use of RSA public key algorithms; IDEA, DES, and 3DES private key algorithms; and the MD5 hash function. Web pages using the SSL protocol start with HTTPs. SSL 3.0 and its successor, the Transaction Layer Security (TLS) 1.0 protocol, are de facto standards, but they do not provide the end-to-end capabilities of SET. TLS implements confidentiality, integrity, and authentication above the Transport Layer, and it resides between the application and TCP layer. Thus, TLS, as with SSL, can be used with applications such as Telnet, FTP, HTTP, and email protocols. Both SSL and TLS use certificates for public key verification that are based on the X.509 standard.

Internet Open Trading Protocol (IOTP)

IOTP is an Internet protocol that is aimed at the consumer-to-business transactions. It provides a buyer with the same options as in the ordinary, non–e-commerce marketplace. IOTP is similar to shopping in the real world because it gives buyers the option to choose their method of payment. It supports public and private encryption key algorithms and can use digital certificates. IOTP is designed to be flexible and to accommodate other payment models that may emerge in the future.

MONDEX

The MONDEX International Corporation operates the MONDEX payment system. This system is an example of a cash smart card application. The value of the amount of currency is stored in smart cards and a proprietary encryption algorithm provides security. Because the algorithm is not subject to public scrutiny, its strength and vulnerabilities are not known. The smart card, then, can be used in financial transactions instead of cash. Funds can be transferred among cards using digital signatures. The smart cards are designed to preclude tampering and modifying the stored currency amount. However, if a card is lost, the finder can use it as cash.

IPSec

IPSec is a standard that provides encryption, access control, non-repudiation, and authentication of messages over IP. It is designed to be functionally compatible with IPv6. The two main protocols of IPSec are the *Authentication Header* (AH) and the *Encapsulating Security Payload* (ESP). The AH provides integrity, authentication, and non-repudiation. An ESP primarily provides encryption, but it can also provide limited authentication.

At the heart of IPSec is the *Security Association* (SA). An SA is required for communication between two entities. It provides a one-way (simplex) connection and is comprised of a Security Parameter Index (SPI), destination IP address, and the identity of the security protocol (AH or ESP). The SPI is a 32-bit number that is used to distinguish among various SAs terminating at the receiving station. Because an SA is simplex, two SAs are required for bi-directional communication between entities. Thus, if the AH protocol is used and bi-directional communication is required, two SAs must be established. Similarly, if both the AH and ESP protocols are to be employed bi-directionally, four SAs are needed.

IPSec in a VPN implementation can operate in either the *transport* or *tunnel* modes. In the transport mode, the data in the IP packet is encrypted, but the header is not encrypted. In the tunnel mode, the original IP header is encrypted and a new IP header is added to the beginning of the packet. This additional IP header has the address of the VPN gateway, and the encrypted IP header points to the final destination on the internal network behind the gateway.

The hashing algorithms HMAC-MD5 and HMAC-SHA-1 are used for authentication and integrity, and the IPSEC standard enables the use of a variety of symmetric key systems.

Security Associations (SAs) can be combined into *bundles* to provide authentication, confidentiality, and layered communication. An SA bundle can be developed using *transport adjacency* or *iterated tunneling*. Transport adjacency uses the transport mode for communication, whereas iterated tunneling provides for multiple levels of encapsulation as the protocol stack is being traversed.

In order to set up and manage SAs on the Internet, a standard format called the *Internet Security Association and Key Management Protocol* (ISAKMP) was established. ISAKMP provides for secure key exchange and data authentication. However, ISAKMP is independent of the authentication protocols, security protocols, and encryption algorithms. Strictly speaking, a combination of three protocols is used to define the key management for IPSec. These protocols are ISAKMP, *Secure Key Exchange Mechanism* (SKEME), and *Oakley*. When combined and applied to IPSEC, these protocols are called the *Internet Key Exchange* (IKE) protocol. In general, ISAKMP defines the phases for establishing a secure relationship, SKEME describes a secure exchange mechanism, and Oakley defines the modes of operation needed to establish a secure connection.

An initiative to specify a standard IPSEC implementation for VPNs on the Internet is known as *Secure Wide Area Network* (S/WAN). By defining a common set of IPSEC algorithms and modes of operation, S/WAN promotes the widespread use of VPNs on the Internet.

Secure Hypertext Transfer Protocol (S-HTTP)

S-HTTP is an alternative to SSL for providing security for World Wide Web (WWW) transactions. While SSL is applied to an entire session, S-HTTP can be used to protect individual WWW documents, and it provides authentication, confidentiality, integrity, and non-repudiation. S-HTTP supports a variety of encryption algorithms.

Secure Shell (SSH-2)

Secure Shell (SSH-2) is a set of protocols that are primarily used for remote access over a network by establishing an encrypted tunnel between an SSH client and an SSH server. This protocol can be used to authenticate the client to the server. In addition, it can also provide confidentiality and integrity services. It is comprised of a Transport Layer protocol, a User Authentication protocol, and a Connection protocol.

Wireless Security

With the increasing use and popularity of Personal Digital Assistants (PDAs) and cellular telephones to access the Internet, wireless security is becoming very important. Because information is broadcast like radio transmissions, it is susceptible to interception and can be compromised. As storage and processor technologies improve, *Mobile Commerce* (M-commerce) will be more common. Issues that are associated with wireless security include:

✦ Physical security of wireless devices

✦ Proliferation of many different platforms

✦ Protection of sensitive financial transactions

✦ Limitations of processing power and memory due to space and weight considerations

✦ No standard method for securing wireless transactions

✦ Public Key Infrastructure (PKI)

Wireless Application Protocol (WAP)

The Wireless Application Protocol (WAP) is widely used by mobile devices to access the Internet. Because it is aimed at small displays and systems with limited bandwidth, it is not designed to display large volumes of data. In addition to cellular phones and PDAs, WAP is applied to network browsing through TV and in automotive displays. It has analogies to TCP/IP, IP, and HTML in wired Internet connections and is actually a set of protocols that cover Layer 7 to Layer 3 of the OSI model. Due to the memory and processor limitations on mobile devices, WAP requires less overhead than TCP/IP. The WAP protocol stack contains the following:

✦ Wireless Markup Language (WML) and Script

✦ Wireless Application Environment (WAE)

✦ Wireless Session Protocol (WSP)

✦ Wireless Transaction Protocol (WTP)

✦ Wireless Transport Layer Security Protocol (WTLS)

✦ Wireless Datagram Protocol (WDP)

For wireless security, WAP uses the Wireless Transport Layer Security Protocol (WTLS). WTLS provides the following three classes of security:

1. *Class 1 (Anonymous Authentication).* The client logs on to the server, but in this mode, neither the client nor the server can be certain of the identity of the other.

2. *Class 2 (Server Authentication).* The server is authenticated to the client, but the client is not authenticated to the server.

3. *Class 3 (Two-Way Client and Server Authentication).* The server is authenticated to the client and the client is authenticated to the server.

Authentication and authorization can be performed on the mobile device using smart cards to execute PKI-enabled transactions.

A specific security issue that is associated with WAP is the *WAP GAP*. A WAP GAP results from the requirement to change security protocols at the carrier's WAP gateway from the wireless WTLS to SSL for use over the wired network. At the WAP gateway, the transmission, which is protected by WTLS, is decrypted and then re-encrypted for transmission using SSL. Thus, the data is temporarily in the clear on the gateway and can be compromised if the gateway is not adequately protected. In order to address this issue, the WAP Forum has put forth specifications that will reduce this vulnerability and thus support e-commerce applications. These specifications are defined in WAP 1.2 as *WMLScript Crypto Library* and the *WAP Identity Module* (WIM). The WMLScript Crypto Library supports end-to-end security by providing for cryptographic functions to be initiated on the WAP client from the Internet content server. These functions include digital signatures originating with the WAP client and the encryption and decryption of data. The WIM is a tamper-resistant device, such as a smart card, that cooperates with WTLS and provides cryptographic operations during the handshake phase.

The WAP Forum is also considering another alternative to providing end-to-end encryption for WAP. This alternative, described in WAP specification 1.3, is the use of a client proxy server that communicates authentication and authorization information to the wireless network server.

The *Handheld Device Markup Language* (HDML) is a simpler alternative to WML that actually preceded the Wireless Markup Language (WML). HDML contains minimal security features, however. A direct competitor to WAP is *Compact HTML* (C-HTML).

Used primarily in Japan through NTT DoCoMo's I-mode service, C-HTML is essentially a stripped-down version of HTML. Due to this approach, C-HTML can be displayed on a standard Internet browser.

The Public Key Infrastructure (PKI) for mobile applications provides for the encryption of communications and mutual authentication of the user and application provider. One concern associated with the mobile PKI relates to the possible time lapse between the expiration of a public key certificate and the reissuing of a new valid certificate and associated public key.

This "dead time" may be critical in disasters or in time-sensitive situations. One solution to this problem is to generate one-time keys for use in each transaction.

The IEEE 802.11 Wireless Standard

The IEEE 802.11 is a family of standard specifications that identify an over-the-air interface among a mobile device, wireless client, and base station and between mobile clients. Work on the standard began in 1990, and it has evolved from various draft versions.

The standard comprises five specifications:

✦ 802.11

✦ 802.11a

✦ 802.11b

✦ 802.11g

✦ 802.11e (a draft specification at the time of this writing)

802.11 is the original IEEE wireless LAN standard. The IEEE 802.11 standard places specifications on the parameters of both the *physical* (PHY) and *medium access control* (MAC) layers of the network. The PHY Layer is responsible for the transmission of data among nodes. It can use direct sequence (DS) spread spectrum, frequency-hopping (FH) spread spectrum, or infrared (IR) pulse position modulation. The standard supports data rates of 1 Mbps or 2 Mbps in the 2.4–2.4835 GHz frequency band for spread-spectrum transmission, and 300,000–428,000 GHz for IR transmission. Infrared is generally considered to be more secure against eavesdropping than multi-directional radio transmissions because infrared requires direct line-of-sight paths.

The MAC Layer is a set of protocols responsible for maintaining order in the use of a shared medium. The 802.11 standard specifies a carrier sense multiple access with collision avoidance (CSMA/CA) protocol for LANs, as described in Chapter 3. The MAC Layer provides the following services:

Data transfer. CSMA/CA media access.

Association. Establishment of wireless links between wireless clients and access points in infrastructure networks.

Reassociation. This action takes place in addition to association when a wireless client moves from one Basic Service Set (BSS) to another, such as in roaming.

Authentication. The process of proving a client's identity through the use of the 802.11 option, *Wired Equivalent Privacy* (WEP). In WEP, a shared key is configured into the access point and its wireless clients. Only those devices with a valid shared key will be allowed to be associated to the access point.

Privacy. In the 802.11 standard, data is transferred in the clear by default. If confidentiality is desired, the WEP option encrypts data before it is sent wirelessly. The WEP algorithm of the 802.11 Wireless LAN Standard uses a secret key that is shared between a mobile station (for example, a laptop with a wireless Ethernet card) and a base station access point to protect the confidentiality of information being transmitted on the LAN. The transmitted packets are encrypted with a secret key and an Integrity Check (IC) field comprised of a CRC-32 checksum that is attached to the message. WEP uses the RC4 variable key-size stream cipher encryption algorithm. RC4 was developed in 1987 by Ron Rivest and operates in output feedback mode.

Researchers at the University of California at Berkeley (wep@isaac.cs.berkeley.edu) have found that the security of the WEP algorithm can be compromised, particularly with the following attacks:

✦ Passive attacks to decrypt traffic based on statistical analysis

✦ Active attacks to inject new traffic from unauthorized mobile stations based on known plaintext

✦ Active attacks to decrypt traffic based on tricking the access point

✦ Dictionary-building attacks that, after an analysis of about a day's worth of traffic, allow real-time automated decryption of all traffic

The Berkeley researchers have found that these attacks are effective against both the 40-bit and the so-called 128-bit versions of WEP using inexpensive off-the-shelf equipment. These attacks can also be used against networks that use the 802.11b Standard, which is the extension to 802.11 that supports higher data rates but does not change the WEP algorithm.

The IEEE 802.11i Working Group has addressed the weaknesses in WEP and 802.11. WEP will be upgraded to WEP2 with the following proposed changes:

✦ Modifying the method of creating the initialization vector (IV)

✦ Modifying the method of creating the encryption key

✦ Protecting against replays

✦ Protecting against IV collision attacks

✦ Protecting against forged packets

In the longer term, it is expected that the Advanced Encryption Standard (AES) will replace the RC4 encryption algorithm currently used in WEP.

Two power modes are defined in the IEEE 802.11 standard: an *active* mode used in transmitting and receiving, and *a power save* mode that conserves power but does not enable the user to transmit or receive.

Standard 802.11b is an extension to 802.11. It provides an 11 Mbps data rate but slows down to 5.5, 2, or 1 Mbps, depending upon the strength of the signal. The 802.11b standard operates in the 2.4 GHz band and is referred to as *802.11 high rate* or *WI-FI (wireless fidelity)*. Specification 802.11a was developed as an extension to 802.11b and provides up to 54 Mbps in the 5 GHz band. Specification 802.11g provides 20 Mbps to 54 Mbps transmission rates and operates in the 2.4 GHz band. Draft standard 802.11e focuses on interoperability among home, business, and public environments and provides for quality of service and multimedia services. 802.11e is designed to support video on demand, audio on demand, voice over IP (VOIP), and high speed Internet communications.

✦　　✦　　✦

Assessment Questions

You can find the answers to the following questions in Appendix A.

1. The Secure Hash Algorithm (SHA) is specified in the:

    a. Data Encryption Standard

    b. Digital Signature Standard

    c. Digital Encryption Standard

    d. Advanced Encryption Standard

2. What does Secure Sockets Layer (SSL)/Transaction Security Layer (TSL) do?

    a. Implements confidentiality, authentication, and integrity above the Transport Layer

    b. Implements confidentiality, authentication, and integrity below the Transport Layer

    c. Implements only confidentiality above the Transport Layer

    d. Implements only confidentiality below the Transport Layer

3. What are MD4 and MD5?

    a. Symmetric encryption algorithms

    b. Asymmetric encryption algorithms

    c. Hashing algorithms

    d. Digital certificates

4. Elliptic curves, which are applied to public key cryptography, employ modular exponentiation that characterizes the:

    a. Elliptic curve discrete logarithm problem

    b. Prime factors of very large numbers

    c. Elliptic curve modular addition

    d. Knapsack problem

5. Which algorithm is used in the Clipper Chip?

    a. IDEA

    b. DES

    c. SKIPJACK

    d. 3 DES

6. The hashing algorithm in the Digital Signature Standard (DSS) generates a message digest of:

   a. 120 bits

   b. 160 bits

   c. 56 bits

   d. 130 bits

7. The protocol of the Wireless Application Protocol (WAP), which performs functions similar to SSL in the TCP/IP protocol, is called the:

   a. Wireless Application Environment (WAE)

   b. Wireless Session Protocol (WSP)

   c. Wireless Transaction Protocol (WTP)

   d. Wireless Transport Layer Security Protocol (WTLS)

8. A Security Parameter Index (SPI) and the identity of the security protocol (AH or ESP) are the components of:

   a. SSL

   b. IPSec

   c. S-HTTP

   d. SSH-1

9. When two different keys encrypt a plaintext message into the same cipher-text, this situation is known as:

   a. Public key cryptography

   b. Cryptanalysis

   c. Key clustering

   d. Hashing

10. What is the result of the Exclusive Or operation, 1XOR 0?

   a. 1

   b. 0

   c. Indeterminate

   d. 10

11. A block cipher:

   a. Encrypts by operating on a continuous data stream

   b. Is an asymmetric key algorithm

   c. Converts variable-length plaintext into fixed-length ciphertext

   d. Breaks a message into fixed length units for encryption

12. In most security protocols that support confidentiality, integrity, and authentication:

   a. Public key cryptography is used to create digital signatures.

   b. Private key cryptography is used to create digital signatures.

   c. DES is used to create digital signatures.

   d. Digital signatures are not implemented.

13. Which of the following is an example of a symmetric key algorithm?

   a. Rijndael

   b. RSA

   c. Diffie-Hellman

   d. Knapsack

14. Which of the following is a problem with symmetric key encryption?

   a. It is slower than asymmetric key encryption.

   b. Most algorithms are kept proprietary.

   c. Work factor is not a function of the key size.

   d. It provides secure distribution of the secret key.

15. Which of the following is an example of an asymmetric key algorithm?

   a. IDEA

   b. DES

   c. 3 DES

   d. ELLIPTIC CURVE

16. In public key cryptography:

   a. Only the private key can encrypt, and only the public key can decrypt.

   b. Only the public key can encrypt, and only the private key can decrypt.

   c. The public key is used to encrypt and decrypt.

   d. If the public key encrypts, only the private key can decrypt.

17. In a hybrid cryptographic system, usually:

    a. Public key cryptography is used for the encryption of the message.

    b. Private key cryptography is used for the encryption of the message.

    c. Neither public key nor private key cryptography is used.

    d. Digital certificates cannot be used.

18. What is the block length of the Rijndael Cipher?

    a. 64 bits

    b. 128 bits

    c. Variable

    d. 256 bits

19. A polyalphabetic cipher is also known as:

    a. One-time pad

    b. Vigenère cipher

    c. Steganography

    d. Vernam cipher

20. The classic Caesar cipher is a:

    a. Polyalphabetic cipher

    b. Monoalphabetic cipher

    c. Transposition cipher

    d. Code group

21. In steganography:

    a. Private key algorithms are used.

    b. Public key algorithms are used.

    c. Both public and private key algorithms are used.

    d. The fact that the message exists is not known.

22. What is the key length of the Rijndael Block Cipher?

    a. 56 or 64 bits

    b. 512 bits

    c. 128, 192, or 256 bits

    d. 512 or 1024 bits

23. In a block cipher, diffusion:

    a. Conceals the connection between the ciphertext and plaintext

    b. Spreads the influence of a plaintext character over many ciphertext characters

    c. Is usually implemented by non-linear S-boxes

    d. Cannot be accomplished

24. The NIST Advanced Encryption Standard uses the:

    a. 3 DES algorithm

    b. Rijndael algorithm

    c. DES algorithm

    d. IDEA algorithm

25. The modes of DES do NOT include:

    a. Electronic Code Book

    b. Cipher Block Chaining

    c. Variable Block Feedback

    d. Output Feedback

26. Which of the following is true?

    a. The work factor of triple DES is the same as for double DES.

    b. The work factor of single DES is the same as for triple DES.

    c. The work factor of double DES is the same as for single DES.

    d. No successful attacks have been reported against double DES.

27. The Rijndael Cipher employs a round transformation that is comprised of three layers of distinct, invertible transformations. These transformations are also defined as *uniform*, which means that every bit of the State is treated the same. Which of the following is NOT one of these layers?

    a. The non-linear layer, which is the parallel application of S-boxes that have the optimum worst-case non-linearity properties

    b. The linear mixing layer, which provides a guarantee of the high diffusion of multiple rounds

    c. The key addition layer, which is an Exclusive OR of the Round Key to the intermediate State

    d. The key inversion layer, which provides confusion through the multiple rounds

28. The Escrowed Encryption Standard describes the:

    a. Rijndael Cipher

    b. Clipper Chip

    c. Fair Public Key Cryptosystem

    d. Digital certificates

29. Theoretically, quantum computing offers the possibility of factoring the products of large prime numbers and calculating discreet logarithms in polynomial time. These calculations can be accomplished in such a compressed time frame because:

    a. Information can be transformed into quantum light waves that travel through fiber-optic channels. Computations can be performed on the associated data by passing the light waves through various types of optical filters and solid-state materials with varying indices of refraction, thus drastically increasing the throughput over conventional computations.

    b. A quantum bit in a quantum computer is actually a linear superposition of both the one and zero states and, therefore, can theoretically represent both values in parallel. This phenomenon allows computation that usually takes exponential time to be accomplished in polynomial time because different values of the binary pattern of the solution can be calculated simultaneously.

    c. A quantum computer takes advantage of quantum tunneling in molecular scale transistors. This mode permits ultra high-speed switching to take place, thus exponentially increasing the speed of computations.

    d. A quantum computer exploits the time-space relationship that changes as particles approach the speed of light. At that interface, the resistance of conducting materials effectively is zero and exponential speed computations are possible.

30. Which of the following characteristics does a one-time pad have if used properly?

    a. It can be used more than once.

    b. The key does not have to be random.

    c. It is unbreakable.

    d. The key has to be of greater length than the message to be encrypted.

31. The DES key is:

    a. 128 bits

    b. 64 bits

    c. 56 bits

    d. 512 bits

32. In a digitally-signed message transmission using a hash function:

    a. The message digest is encrypted in the private key of the sender.

    b. The message digest is encrypted in the public key of the sender.

    c. The message is encrypted in the private key of the sender.

    d. The message is encrypted in the public key of the sender.

33. The strength of RSA public key encryption is based on the:

    a. Difficulty in finding logarithms in a finite field

    b. Difficulty of multiplying two large prime numbers

    c. Fact that only one key is used

    d. Difficulty in finding the prime factors of very large numbers

34. Elliptic curve cryptosystems:

    a. Have a higher strength per bit than an RSA

    b. Have a lower strength per bit than an RSA

    c. Cannot be used to implement digital signatures

    d. Cannot be used to implement encryption

35. Which of the following is NOT a fundamental component of Identity-Based Encryption (IBE)?

    a. Bi-linear mapping

    b. Weil Pairing

    c. Multiplication of points on an elliptic curve

    d. A symmetrical session key

Security Architecture and Models

The security architecture of an information system is fundamental to enforcing an organization's information security policy. Therefore, it is important for security professionals to understand the underlying computer architectures, protection mechanisms, distributed environment security issues, and formal models that provide the framework for the security policy. In addition, professionals should have knowledge of the assurance evaluation, certification and accreditation guidelines, and standards. We address the following topics in this chapter:

- ✦ Computer organization
- ✦ Hardware components
- ✦ Software/firmware components
- ✦ Open systems
- ✦ Distributed systems
- ✦ Protection mechanisms
- ✦ Evaluation criteria
- ✦ Certification and accreditation
- ✦ Formal security models
- ✦ Confidentiality models
- ✦ Integrity models
- ✦ Information flow models

Computer Architecture

The term computer architecture refers to the organization of the fundamental elements composing the computer. From another perspective, it refers to the view a programmer has of the computing system when viewed through its instruction set. The main hardware components of a digital computer are the *Central Processing Unit* (CPU), memory, and input/output devices. A basic CPU of a general-purpose digital computer consists of an *Arithmetic Logic Unit* (ALU), control logic, one or more accumulators, multiple general-purpose registers, an instruction register, a program counter, and some on-chip local memory. The ALU performs arithmetic and logical operations on the binary words of the computer.

A group of conductors called a *bus* interconnects these computer elements. The bus runs in a common plane with the different computer elements connected to the bus. A bus can be organized into subunits, such as the *address bus,* the *data bus*, and the *control bus*. A diagram of the organization of a bus is shown in Figure 5-1.

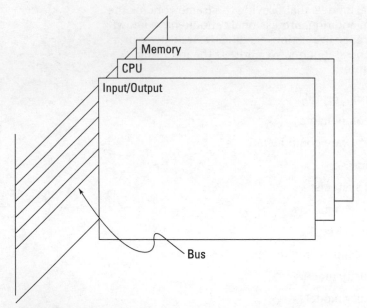

Figure 5-1: A computer bus.

Memory

Several types of memory are used in digital computer systems. The principal types of memory and their definitions are as follows:

Cache memory. A relatively small amount (when compared to primary memory) of very high-speed RAM, which holds the instructions and data from primary memory that have a high probability of being accessed during the currently executing portion of a program. Cache logic attempts to predict which instructions and data in main memory will be used by a currently executing program. It then moves these items to the higher-speed cache in anticipation of the CPU requiring these programs and data. Properly designed caches can significantly reduce the apparent main memory access time and thus increase the speed of program execution.

Random Access Memory (RAM). Memory where locations can be directly addressed and the data that is stored can be altered. RAM is *volatile* due to the fact that the data is lost if power is removed from the system. Dynamic RAM (DRAM) stores the information on parasitic capacitance that decays over time. Therefore, the data on each RAM bit must be periodically refreshed. Refreshing is accomplished by reading and rewriting each bit every few milliseconds. Conversely, Static RAM (SRAM) uses latches to store the bits and does not need to be refreshed. Both types of RAM, however, are volatile.

RDRAM Memory (Rambus DRAM). Based on Rambus Signaling Level (RSL) technology introduced in 1992. RSL RDRAM devices provide systems with 16MB to 2GB of memory capacity at speeds of up to 1066MHz. The RDRAM channel achieves high speeds through the use of separate control and address buses, a highly efficient protocol, low-voltage signaling, and precise clocking to minimize skew between clock and data lines. As of this writing, RSL technology is approaching 1200 MHz speeds.

Programmable Logic Device (PLD). An integrated circuit with connections or internal logic gates that can be changed through a programming process. Examples of a PLD are a *Read Only Memory* (ROM), *a Programmable Array Logic* (PAL) device, the *Complex Programmable Logic Device* (CPLD), and the *Field Programmable Gate Array* (FPGA). Programming of these devices is accomplished by blowing fuse connections on the chip, using an antifuse that makes a connection when a high voltage is applied to the junction, through mask programming when a chip is fabricated, and by using SRAM latches to turn a *Metal Oxide Semiconductor* (MOS) transistor on or off. This last technology is volatile because the power to the chip must be maintained for the chip to operate.

Read Only Memory (ROM). Non-volatile storage where locations can be directly addressed. In a basic ROM implementation, data cannot be altered dynamically. Non-volatile storage retains its information even when it loses power. Some ROMs are implemented with one-way fusible links, and their contents cannot be altered. Other types of ROMs — such as *Erasable, Programmable Read-Only Memories* (EPROMs), *Electrically Alterable Read Only Memories* (EAROMs), *Electrically Erasable Programmable Read Only Memories* (EEPROMs), *Flash memories*, and their derivatives — can be altered by various means, but only at a relatively slow rate when compared to normal computer system reads and writes. ROMs are used to hold programs and data that should normally not be changed or that are changed infrequently. Programs stored on these types of devices are referred to as firmware.

Real or primary memory. The memory directly addressable by the CPU and used for the storage of instructions, and data associated with the program that is being executed. This memory is usually high-speed Random Access Memory (RAM).

Secondary memory. A slower memory (such as magnetic disks) that provides non-volatile storage.

Sequential memory. Memory from which information must be obtained by sequentially searching from the beginning rather than directly accessing the location. A good example of a sequential memory access is reading information from a magnetic tape.

Virtual memory. This type of memory uses secondary memory in conjunction with primary memory to present a CPU with a larger, apparent address space of the real memory locations.

A typical memory hierarchy is shown in Figure 5-2.

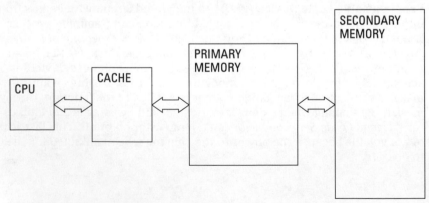

Figure 5-2: A computer memory hierarchy.

There are a number of ways that a CPU can address memory. These options provide flexibility and efficiency when programming different types of applications, such as searching through a table or processing a list of data items. The following are some of the commonly used addressing modes:

Register addressing. Addressing the registers within a CPU, or other special purpose registers that are designated in the primary memory.

Direct addressing. Addressing a portion of primary memory by specifying the actual address of the memory location. The memory addresses are usually limited to the memory page that is being executed or to page zero.

Absolute addressing. Addressing all of the primary memory space.

Indexed addressing. Developing a memory address by adding the contents of the address defined in the program's instruction to that of an index register. The computed, effective address is used to access the desired memory location. Thus, if an index register is incremented or decremented, a range of memory locations can be accessed.

Implied addressing. Used when operations that are internal to the processor must be performed, such as clearing a carry bit that was set as a result of an arithmetic operation. Because the operation is being performed on an internal register that is specified within the instruction itself, there is no need to provide an address.

Indirect addressing. Addressing where the address location that is specified in the program instruction contains the address of the final desired location.

An associated concept is *memory protection*:

Memory protection. Preventing one program from accessing and modifying the memory space contents that belong to another program. Memory protection is implemented by the operating system or by hardware mechanisms.

Instruction Execution Cycle

A basic machine cycle consists of two phases: *fetch* and *execute*. In the fetch phase, the CPU presents the address of the instruction to memory, and it retrieves the instruction located at that address. Then, during the execute phase, the instruction is decoded and executed. This cycle is controlled by and synchronized with the CPU clock signals. Because of the need to refresh dynamic RAM, multiple clock signals known as *multi-phase clock signals* are needed. Static RAM does not require refreshing and uses *single-phase clock signals*. In addition, some instructions might require more than one machine cycle to execute, depending on their complexity. A typical machine cycle showing a single-phase clock is shown in Figure 5-3. Note that in this example, four clock periods are required to execute a single instruction.

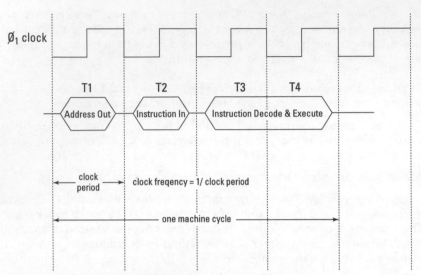

Figure 5-3: A typical machine cycle.

A computer can be in a number of different states during its operation. When a computer is executing instructions, this situation is sometimes called the *run* or *operating state*. When application programs are being executed, the machine is in the *application* or *problem state* because it is hopefully calculating the solution to a problem. For security purposes, users are permitted to access only a subset of the total instruction set that is available on the computer in this state. This subset is known as the *non-privileged* instructions. *Privileged* instructions are executed by the system administrator or by an individual who is authorized to use those instructions. A computer is in a *supervisory state* when it is executing these privileged instructions. The computer can be in a *wait state*, for example, if it is accessing a slow memory relative to the instruction cycle time, which causes it to extend the cycle.

After examining a basic machine cycle, it is obvious that there are opportunities for enhancing the speed of retrieving and executing instructions. Some of these methods include overlapping the fetch and execute cycles, exploiting opportunities for parallelism, anticipating instructions that will be executed later, fetching and decoding instructions in advance, and so on. Modern computer design incorporates these methods, and their key approaches are provided in the following definitions:

Pipelining. Increases the performance of a computer by overlapping the steps of different instructions. For example, if the instruction cycle is divided into three parts — fetch, decode, and execute — instructions can be overlapped (as shown in Figure 5-4) to increase the execution speed of the instructions.

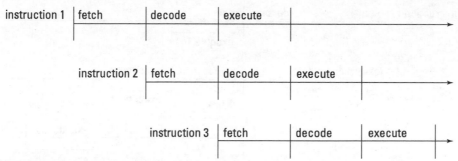

Figure 5-4: Instruction pipelining.

Complex Instruction Set Computer (CISC). Uses instructions that perform many operations per instruction. This concept is based on the fact that in earlier technologies, the instruction fetch was the longest part of the cycle. Therefore, by packing the instructions with several operations, the number of fetches could be reduced.

Reduced Instruction Set Computer (RISC). Uses instructions that are simpler and require fewer clock cycles to execute. This approach was a result of the increase in the speed of memories and other processor components, which enabled the fetch part of the instruction cycle to be no longer than any other portion of the cycle. In fact, performance was limited by the decoding and execution times of the instruction cycle.

Scalar Processor. A processor that executes one instruction at a time.

Superscalar Processor. A processor that enables the concurrent execution of multiple instructions in the same pipeline stage as well as in different pipeline stages.

Very-Long Instruction Word (VLIW) Processor. A processor in which a single instruction specifies more than one concurrent operation. For example, the instruction might specify and concurrently execute two operations in one instruction. VLIW processing is illustrated in Figure 5-5.

Multi-programming. Executes two or more programs simultaneously on a single processor (CPU) by alternating execution among the programs.

Multi-tasking. Executes two or more subprograms or tasks at the same time on a single processor (CPU) by alternating execution among the tasks.

Multi-processing. Executes two or more programs at the same time on multiple processors.

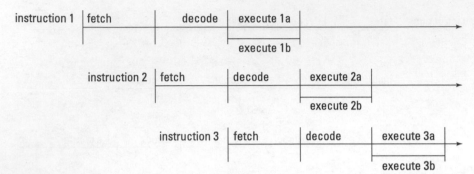

Figure 5-5: Very-Long Instruction Word (VLIW) processing.

Input/Output Structures

A processor communicates with outside devices through interface devices called *input/output (I/O) interface adapters*. In many cases, these adapters are complex devices that provide data buffering and timing and interrupt controls. Adapters have addresses on the computer bus and are selected by the computer instructions. If an adapter is given an address in the memory space and thus takes up a specific memory address, this design is known as *memory-mapped I/O*. The advantage of this approach is that a CPU sees no difference in instructions for the I/O adapter and any other memory location. Therefore, all the computer instructions that are associated with memory can be used for the I/O device. On the other hand, in *isolated I/O* a special signal on the bus indicates that an I/O operation is being executed. This signal distinguishes an address for an I/O device from an address to memory. The signal is generated as a result of the execution of a few selected I/O instructions in the computer instructions' set. The advantage of an isolated I/O is that its addresses do not use up any addresses that could be used for memory. The disadvantage is that the I/O data accesses and manipulations are limited to a small number of specific I/O instructions in the processor's instruction set. Both memory-mapped and isolated I/Os are termed *programmed I/Os*.

In a programmed I/O, data transfers are a function of the speed of the instruction's execution, which manipulates the data that goes through a CPU. A faster alternative is *direct memory access* (DMA). With DMA, data is transferred directly to and from memory without going through a CPU. DMA controllers accomplish this direct transfer in the time interval between the instruction executions. The data transfer rate in DMA is limited primarily by the memory cycle time. The path of the data transfer between memory and a peripheral device is sometimes referred to as a *channel*.

Another alternative to moving data into and out of a computer is through the use of *interrupts*. In *interrupt processing*, an external signal interrupts the normal program flow and requests service. The service might consist of reading data or responding to an emergency situation. Adapters provide the interface for handling the interrupts and the means for establishing priorities among multiple interrupt requests. When a CPU receives an interrupt request, it will save the current state of the information related to the program that is currently running, and it will then jump to another program that services the interrupt. When the interrupt service is completed, the CPU restores the state of the original program and continues processing. Multiple interrupts can be handled concurrently by *nesting* the interrupt service routines. Interrupts can be turned off or *masked* if a CPU is executing high-priority code and does not want to be delayed in its processing.

Software

The CPU of a computer is designed to support the execution of a set of instructions associated with that computer. This set consists of a variety of instructions such as ADD WITH CARRY, ROTATE BITS LEFT, MOVE DATA, and JUMP TO LOCATION X. Each instruction is represented as a binary code that the instruction decoder of the CPU is designed to recognize and execute. These instructions are referred to as *machine language instructions*. The code of each machine language instruction is associated with an English-like mnemonic to make it easier for people to work with the codes. This set of mnemonics for the computer's basic instruction set is called its assembly language, which is specific to that particular computer. Thus, there is a one-to-one correspondence of each assembly language instruction to each machine language instruction. For example, in a simple 8-bit instruction word computer, the binary code for the ADD WITH CARRY machine language instruction might be 10011101, and the corresponding mnemonic could be ADC. A programmer who is writing this code at the machine language level would write the code using mnemonics for each instruction. Then, the mnemonic code would be passed through another program called an assembler that would perform the one-to-one translation of the assembly language code to the machine language code. The code generated by the assembler running on the computer is called the *object code*, and the original assembly code is called the *source code*. The assembler software can be resident on the computer being programmed and thus is called a *resident assembler*. If the assembler is being run on another computer, the assembler is called a *cross assembler*. Cross assemblers can run on various types and models of computers. A *disassembler* reverses the function of an assembler by translating machine language into assembly language.

If a group of assembly language statements is used to perform a specific function, they can be defined to the assembler with a name called a *macro*. Then, instead of writing the list of statements, the *macro* can be called, causing the assembler to insert the appropriate statements.

Because it is desirable to write software in higher-level, English-like statements, *high-level* or *high-order languages* are employed. In these languages, one statement usually requires a number of machine language instructions for its implementation.

Therefore, unlike assembly language, there is a one-to-many relationship of high-level language instructions to machine language instructions. Pascal, FORTRAN, BASIC, and Java are examples of high-level languages. High-level languages are converted to the appropriate machine language instructions through either an *interpreter* or *compiler* programs. An interpreter operates on each high-level language source statement individually and performs the indicated operation by executing a predefined sequence of machine language instructions. Thus, the instructions are executed immediately. Java and BASIC are examples of interpreted languages. In contrast, a compiler translates the entire software program into its corresponding machine language instructions. These instructions are then loaded in the computer's memory and are executed as a program package. FORTRAN is an example of a compiled language. From a security standpoint, a compiled program is less desirable than an interpreted one because malicious code can be resident somewhere in the compiled code, and it is difficult to detect in a very large program.

High-level languages have been grouped into five generations, and they are labeled as a Generation Language (GL). The following is a list of these languages:

✦ 1 GL — A computer's machine language

✦ 2 GL — An assembly language

✦ 3 GL — FORTRAN, BASIC, PL/1, and C languages

✦ 4 GL — NATURAL, FOCUS, and database query languages

✦ 5 GL — Prolog, LISP, and other artificial intelligence languages that process symbols or implement predicate logic

The program (or set of programs) that controls the resources and operations of the computer is called an *operating system* (OS). Operating systems perform process management, memory management, system file management, and I/O management. Windows XP, Windows 2000, Linux, and Unix are some examples of these operating systems.

An OS communicates with I/O systems through a *controller*. A controller is a device that serves as an interface to the peripheral and runs specialized software to manage communications with another device. For example, a disk controller is used to manage the information exchange and operation of a disk drive.

Open and Closed Systems

Open systems are vendor-independent systems that have published specifications and interfaces in order to permit operations with the products of other suppliers. One advantage of an open system is that it is subject to review and evaluation by independent parties. Usually, this scrutiny will reveal any errors or vulnerabilities in that product.

A *closed system* uses vendor-dependent proprietary hardware (and/or software) that is usually not compatible with other systems or components. Closed systems are not subject to independent examination and might have vulnerabilities that are not known or recognized.

Distributed Architecture

The migration of computing from the centralized model to the client-server model has created a new set of issues for information system security professionals. In addition, this situation has been compounded by the proliferation of desktop PCs and workstations. A PC on a user's desktop might contain documents that are sensitive to the business of an organization and that can be compromised. In most operations, a user also functions as the systems administrator, programmer, and operator of the desktop platform. The major concerns in this scenario are as follows:

✦ Desktop systems can contain sensitive information that might be at risk of being exposed.

✦ Users might generally lack security awareness.

✦ A desktop PC or workstation can provide an avenue of access into the critical information systems of an organization.

✦ Modems that are attached to a desktop machine can make the corporate network vulnerable to dial-in attacks.

✦ Downloading data from the Internet increases the risk of infecting corporate systems with a malicious code or an unintentional modification of the databases.

✦ A desktop system and its associated disks might not be protected from physical intrusion or theft.

✦ A lack of proper backup might exist.

Security mechanisms can be put into place to counter the security vulnerabilities that can exist in a distributed environment. Such mechanisms are as follows:

✦ Email and download/upload policies

✦ Robust access control, which includes biometrics to restrict access to desktop systems

✦ Graphical user interface (GUI) mechanisms to restrict access to critical information

✦ File encryption

✦ Separation of the processes that run in privileged or non-privileged processor states

✦ Protection domains

✦ Protection of sensitive disks by locking them in non-movable containers and by physically securing the desktop system or laptop

✦ Distinct labeling of disks and materials according to their classification or an organization's sensitivity

✦ A centralized backup of desktop system files

✦ Regular security awareness training sessions

✦ Control of software installed on desktop systems

✦ Encryption and hash totals for use in sending and storing information

✦ Logging of transactions and transmissions

✦ Application of other appropriate physical, logical, and administrative access controls

✦ Database management systems restricting access to sensitive information

✦ Protection against environmental damage to computers and media

✦ Use of formal methods for software development and application, which includes libraries, change control, and configuration management

✦ Inclusion of desktop systems in disaster recovery and business continuity plans

Protection Mechanisms

In a computational system, multiple processes might be running concurrently. Each process has the capability to access certain memory locations and to execute a subset of the computer's instruction set. The execution and memory space assigned to each process is called a *protection domain*. This domain can be extended to virtual memory, which increases the apparent size of real memory by using disk storage. The purpose of establishing a protection domain is to protect programs from all unauthorized modification or executional interference.

 Security professionals should also know that a *Trusted Computing Base* (TCB) is the total combination of protection mechanisms within a computer system, which includes the hardware, software, and firmware that are trusted to enforce a security policy. The *security perimeter* is the boundary that separates the TCB from the remainder of the system. A *trusted path* must also exist so that a user can access the TCB without being compromised by other processes or users. A *trusted computer system* is one that employs the necessary hardware and software assurance measures to enable its use in processing multiple levels of classified or sensitive information. This system meets the specified requirements for reliability and security.

Resources can also be protected through the principle of *abstraction*. Abstraction involves viewing system components at a high level and ignoring or segregating its specific details. This approach enhances the system's capability to understand complex systems and to focus on critical, high-level issues. In object-oriented programming, for example, methods (programs), and data are *encapsulated* in an object that can be viewed as an abstraction. This concept is called *information hiding* because the object's functioning details are hidden. Communication with this object takes place through messages to which the object responds as defined by its internal method.

Rings

One scheme that supports multiple protection domains is the use of protection rings. These rings are organized with the most privileged domain located in the center of the ring and the least-privileged domain in the outermost ring. This approach is shown in Figure 5-6.

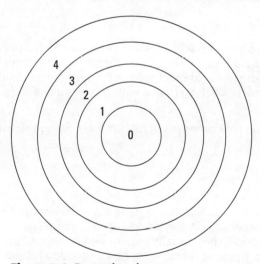

Figure 5-6: Protection rings.

The operating system security kernel is usually located at Ring 0 and has access rights to all domains in that system. A *security kernel* is defined as the hardware, firmware, and software elements of a trusted computing base that implement the reference monitor concept. A *reference monitor* is a system component that enforces access controls on an object. Therefore, the *reference monitor concept* is an abstract machine that mediates all access of subjects to objects. The security kernel must:

✦ Mediate all accesses

✦ Be protected from modification

✦ Be verified as correct

In the ring concept, access rights decrease as the ring number increases. Thus, the most trusted processes reside in the center rings. System components are placed in the appropriate ring according to the principle of least privilege. Therefore, the processes have only the minimum privileges necessary to perform their functions.

 The ring protection mechanism was implemented in MIT's MULTICS time-shared operating system that was enhanced for secure applications by the Honeywell Corporation. MULTICS was initially targeted for use on specific hardware platforms because some of its functions could be implemented through the hardware's customization. It was designed to support 64 rings, but in practice only eight rings were defined.

There are also other related kernel-based approaches to protection:

✦ Using a separate hardware device that validates all references in a system.

✦ Implementing a *virtual machine* monitor, which establishes a number of isolated virtual machines that are running on the actual computer. The virtual machines mimic the architecture of a real machine in addition to establishing a multi-level security environment. Each virtual machine can run at a different security level.

✦ Using a software security kernel that operates in its own hardware protection domain.

Security Labels

A security label is assigned to a resource to denote a type of classification or designation. This label can then indicate special security handling, or it can be used for access control. Once labels are assigned, they usually cannot be altered and are an effective access control mechanism. Because labels must be compared and evaluated in accordance with the security policy, they incur additional processing overhead when used.

Security Modes

An information system operates in different security modes that are determined by an information system's classification level and the clearance of the users. A major distinction in its operation is between the system high mode and the multi-level security mode. In the *system high mode* of operation, a system operates at the highest level of information classification, where all users must have clearances for the highest level. However, not all users may have a need to know for all the data. The *multi-level mode* of operation supports users who have different clearances and data at multiple classification levels. Additional modes of operation are defined as follows:

 Dedicated. All users have a clearance or an authorization and a need to know for all information that is processed by an information system; a system might handle multiple classification levels.

Compartmented. All users have a clearance for the highest level of information classification, but they do not necessarily have the authorization and a need to know for all the data handled by the computer system.

Controlled. This is a type of multi-level security where a limited amount of trust is placed in the system's hardware/software base along with the corresponding restrictions on the classification of the information levels that can be processed.

Limited access. This is a type of system access where the minimum user clearance is not cleared and the maximum data classification is unclassified but sensitive.

Additional Security Considerations

Vulnerabilities in the system security architecture can lead to violations of the system's security policy. Typical vulnerabilities that are architecturally related include the following:

Covert channel. An unintended communication path between two or more subjects sharing a common resource, which supports the transfer of information in such a manner that it violates the system's security policy. The transfer usually takes place through common storage areas or through access to a common path that can use a timing channel for the unintended communication.

Lack of parameter checking. The failure to check the size of input streams specified by parameters. Buffer overflow attacks exploit this vulnerability in certain operating systems and programs.

Maintenance hook. A hardware or software mechanism that was installed to permit system maintenance and to bypass the system's security protections. This vulnerability is sometimes referred to as a trap door.

Time of Check to Time of Use (TOC/TOU) attack. An attack that exploits the difference in the time that security controls were applied and the time the authorized service was used.

Recovery Procedures

Whenever a hardware or software component of a trusted system fails, it is important that the failure does not compromise the security policy requirements of that system. In addition, the recovery procedures should not provide an opportunity for violation of the system's security policy. If a system restart is required, the system must restart in a secure state. Startup should occur in the *maintenance mode* that permits access only by privileged users from privileged terminals. This mode supports the restoring of the system state and the security state.

When a computer or network component fails and the computer or the network continues to function, it is called a *fault-tolerant system*. For fault tolerance to operate, the system must be capable of detecting that a fault has occurred, and the system must then have the capability to correct the fault or operate around it. In a *failsafe system*, program execution is terminated and the system is protected from being compromised when a hardware or software failure occurs and is detected. In a system that is *fail soft* or *resilient*, selected, non-critical processing is terminated when a hardware or software failure occurs and is detected. The computer or network then continues to function in a degraded mode. The term *failover* refers to switching to a duplicate "hot" backup component in real time when a hardware or software failure occurs, which enables the system to continue processing.

A *cold start* occurs in a system when there is a TCB or media failure and the recovery procedures cannot return the system to a known, reliable, secure state. In this case, the TCB and portions of the software and data might be inconsistent and require external intervention. At that time, the maintenance mode of the system usually has to be employed.

Assurance

Assurance is simply defined as the degree of confidence in the satisfaction of security needs. The following sections summarize guidelines and standards that have been developed to evaluate and accept the assurance aspects of a system.

Evaluation Criteria

In 1985, the *Trusted Computer System Evaluation Criteria* (TCSEC) was developed by the National Computer Security Center (NCSC) to provide guidelines for evaluating vendors' products for the specified security criteria. TCSEC provides the following:

✦ A basis for establishing security requirements in the acquisition specifications

✦ A standard of the security services that should be provided by vendors for the different classes of security requirements

✦ A means to measure the trustworthiness of an information system

The TCSEC document, called the Orange Book because of its color, is part of a series of guidelines with covers of different coloring called the Rainbow Series. In the Orange Book, the basic control objectives are security policy, assurance, and accountability. TCSEC addresses confidentiality but does not cover integrity. Also, functionality (security controls applied) and assurance (confidence that security controls are functioning as expected) are not separated in TCSEC as they are in other evaluation criteria developed later. The Orange Book defines the major hierarchical classes of security by the letters D through A as follows:

- ✦ D—Minimal protection
- ✦ C—Discretionary protection (C1 and C2)
- ✦ B—Mandatory protection (B1, B2, and B3)
- ✦ A—Verified protection; formal methods (A1)

The DoD *Trusted Network Interpretation* (TNI) is analogous to the Orange Book. It addresses confidentiality and integrity in trusted computer/communications network systems and is called the Red Book. The Trusted Database Management System Interpretation (TDI) addresses the trusted database management systems.

The *European Information Technology Security Evaluation Criteria* (ITSEC) address C.I.A. issues. The product or system to be evaluated by ITSEC is defined as the *Target of Evaluation* (TOE). The TOE must have a security target, which includes the security enforcing mechanisms and the system's security policy.

ITSEC separately evaluates functionality and assurance, and it includes 10 functionality classes (F), eight assurance levels (Q), seven levels of correctness (E), and eight basic security functions in its criteria. It also defines two kinds of assurance. One assurance measure is the correctness of the security functions' implementation, and the other is the effectiveness of the TOE while in operation.

The ITSEC ratings are in the form F-X,E, where functionality and assurance are listed. The ITSEC ratings that are equivalent to TCSEC ratings are as follows:

F-C1, E1 = C1

F-C2, E2 = C2

F-B1, E3 = B1

F-B2, E4 = B2

F-B3, E5 = B3

F-B3, E6 = A1

The other classes of the ITSEC address high integrity and high availability.

TCSEC, ITSEC, and the *Canadian Trusted Computer Product Evaluation Criteria* (CTCPEC) have evolved into one set of evaluation criteria called the *Common Criteria*. The Common Criteria define a *Protection Profile* (PP), which is an implementation-independent specification of the security requirements and protections of a product that could be built. The Common Criteria terminology for the degree of examination of the product to be tested is the *Evaluation Assurance Level* (EAL). EALs range from EA1 (functional testing) to EA7 (detailed testing and formal design verification). The Common Criteria TOE refers to the product to be tested. A *Security Target* (ST) is a listing of the security claims for a particular IT security product. Also, the Common Criteria describe an intermediate grouping of security requirement components as a *package*. Functionality in the Common Criteria refers to standard and well-understood functional security requirements for IT systems. These functional requirements are organized around TCB entities that include physical and logical controls, startup and recovery, reference mediation, and privileged states.

The essential elements of the Common Criteria are discussed in Appendix D. As with TCSEC and ITSEC, the ratings of the Common Criteria are also hierarchical.

Certification and Accreditation

In many environments, formal methods must be applied to ensure that the appropriate information system security safeguards are in place and that they are functioning per the specifications. In addition, an authority must take responsibility for putting the system into operation. These actions are known as certification and accreditation.

Formally, the definitions are as follows:

> **Certification.** The comprehensive evaluation of the technical and nontechnical security features of an information system and the other safeguards, which are created in support of the accreditation process to establish the extent to which a particular design and implementation meets the set of specified security requirements

> **Accreditation.** A formal declaration by a Designated Approving Authority (DAA) where an information system is approved to operate in a particular security mode by using a prescribed set of safeguards at an acceptable level of risk

The certification and accreditation of a system must be checked after a defined period of time or when changes occur in the system and/or its environment. Then, *recertification* and *re-accreditation* are required.

A detailed discussion of certification and accreditation is given in Chapter 12.

DITSCAP and NIACAP

Two U.S. defense and government certification and accreditation standards have been developed for the evaluation of critical information systems. These standards are the Defense Information Technology Security Certification and Accreditation Process (DITSCAP) and the National Information Assurance Certification and Accreditation Process (NIACAP).

DITSCAP

The DITSCAP establishes a standard process, a set of activities, general task descriptions, and a management structure to certify and accredit the IT systems that will maintain the required security posture. This process is designed to certify that the IT system meets the accreditation requirements and that the system will maintain the accredited security posture throughout its life cycle. These are the four phases of the DITSCAP:

Phase 1, Definition. Phase 1 focuses on understanding the mission, the environment, and the architecture in order to determine the security requirements and level of effort necessary to achieve accreditation.

Phase 2, Verification. Phase 2 verifies the evolving or modified system's compliance with the information agreed on in the System Security Authorization Agreement (SSAA). The objective is to use the SSAA to establish an evolving yet binding agreement on the level of security required before system development begins or changes to a system are made. After accreditation, the SSAA becomes the baseline security configuration document.

Phase 3, Validation. Phase 3 validates the compliance of a fully integrated system with the information stated in the SSAA.

Phase 4, Post Accreditation. Phase 4 includes the activities that are necessary for the continuing operation of an accredited IT system in its computing environment and for addressing the changing threats that a system faces throughout its life cycle.

NIACAP

The NIACAP establishes the minimum national standards for certifying and accrediting national security systems. This process provides a standard set of activities, general tasks, and a management structure to certify and accredit systems that maintain the information assurance and the security posture of a system or site. The NIACAP is designed to certify that the information system meets the documented accreditation requirements and will continue to maintain the accredited security posture throughout the system's life cycle.

There are three types of NIACAP accreditation:

A site accreditation. Evaluates the applications and systems at a specific, self-contained location.

A type accreditation. Evaluates an application or system that is distributed to a number of different locations.

A system accreditation. Evaluates a major application or general support system.

The NIACAP is composed of four phases: Definition, Verification, Validation, and Post Accreditation. These are essentially identical to those of the DITSCAP.

The DITSCAP and NIACAP are presented in greater detail in Chapter 12.

The Systems Security Engineering Capability Maturity Model (SSE-CMM)

The Systems Security Engineering Capability Maturity Model (SSE-CMM; copyright 1999 by the Systems Security Engineering Capability Maturity Model [SSE-CMM] Project) is based on the premise that if you can guarantee the quality of the processes that are used by an organization, then you can guarantee the quality of the products and services generated by those processes. It was developed by a consortium of government and industry experts and is now under the auspices of the International Systems Security Engineering Association (ISSEA) at www.issea.org. The SSE-CMM has the following salient points:

✦ Describes those characteristics of security engineering processes essential to ensure good security engineering

✦ Captures industry's best practices

✦ Accepted way of defining practices and improving capability

✦ Provides measures of growth in capability of applying processes

The SSE-CMM addresses the following areas of security:

✦ Operations Security

✦ Information Security

✦ Network Security

✦ Physical Security

✦ Personnel Security

✦ Administrative Security

- ✦ Communications Security
- ✦ Emanations Security
- ✦ Computer Security

 The SSE-CMM is also reviewed in Chapter 13.

The SSE-CMM methodology and metrics provide a reference for comparing existing systems' security engineering best practices against the essential systems security engineering elements described in the model. It defines two dimensions that are used to measure the capability of an organization to perform specific activities. These dimensions are *domain* and *capability*. The domain dimension consists of all the practices that collectively define security engineering. These practices are called Base Practices (BPs). Related BPs are grouped into Process Areas (PAs). The capability dimension represents practices that indicate process management and institutionalization capability. These practices are called Generic Practices (GPs) because they apply across a wide range of domains. The GPs represent activities that should be performed as part of performing BPs.

For the domain dimension, the SSE-CMM specifies 11 security engineering PAs and 11 organizational and project-related PAs, each consisting of BPs. BPs are mandatory characteristics that must exist within an implemented security engineering process before an organization can claim satisfaction in a given PA. The 22 PAs and their corresponding BPs incorporate the best practices of systems security engineering. The PAs are as follows:

Security Engineering

- ✦ PA01 — Administer Security Controls
- ✦ PA02 — Assess Impact
- ✦ PA03 — Assess Security Risk
- ✦ PA04 — Assess Threat
- ✦ PA05 — Assess Vulnerability
- ✦ PA06 — Build Assurance Argument
- ✦ PA07 — Coordinate Security
- ✦ PA08 — Monitor Security Posture
- ✦ PA09 — Provide Security Input
- ✦ PA10 — Specify Security Needs
- ✦ PA11 — Verify and Validate Security

Project and Organizational Practices

✦ PA12 — Ensure Quality

✦ PA13 — Manage Configuration

✦ PA14 — Manage Project Risk

✦ PA15 — Monitor and Control Technical Effort

✦ PA16 — Plan Technical Effort

✦ PA17 — Define Organization's Systems Engineering Process

✦ PA18 — Improve Organization's Systems Engineering Process

✦ PA19 — Manage Product Line Evolution

✦ PA20 — Manage Systems Engineering Support Environment

✦ PA21 — Provide Ongoing Skills and Knowledge

✦ PA22 — Coordinate with Suppliers

The GPs are ordered in degrees of maturity and are grouped to form and distinguish among five levels of security engineering maturity. The attributes of these five levels are as follows:

✦ Level 1

1.1 BPs Are Performed

✦ Level 2

2.1 Planning Performance

2.2 Disciplined Performance

2.3 Verifying Performance

2.4 Tracking Performance

✦ Level 3

3.1 Defining a Standard Process

3.2 Perform the Defined Process

3.3 Coordinate the Process

✦ Level 4

4.1 Establishing Measurable Quality Goals

4.2 Objectively Managing Performance

✦ Level 5

    5.1 Improving Organizational Capability

    5.2 Improving Process Effectiveness

The corresponding descriptions of the five levels are given as follows:*

✦ Level 1, "Performed Informally," focuses on whether an organization or project performs a process that incorporates the BPs. A statement characterizing this level would be, "You have to do it before you can manage it."

✦ Level 2, "Planned and Tracked," focuses on project-level definition, planning, and performance issues. A statement characterizing this level would be, "Understand what's happening on the project before defining organization-wide processes."

✦ Level 3, "Well Defined," focuses on disciplined tailoring from defined processes at the organization level. A statement characterizing this level would be, "Use the best of what you've learned from your projects to create organization-wide processes."

✦ Level 4, "Quantitatively Controlled," focuses on measurements being tied to the business goals of the organization. Although it is essential to begin collecting and using basic project measures early, measurement and use of data is not expected organization-wide until the higher levels have been achieved. Statements characterizing this level would be, "You can't measure it until you know what 'it' is" and "Managing with measurement is only meaningful when you're measuring the right things."

✦ Level 5, "Continuously Improving," gains leverage from all the management practice improvements seen in the earlier levels and then emphasizes the cultural shifts that will sustain the gains made. A statement characterizing this level would be, "A culture of continuous improvement requires a foundation of sound management practice, defined processes, and measurable goals."

Information Security Models

Models are used in information security to formalize security policies. These models might be abstract or intuitive and will provide a framework for the understanding of fundamental concepts. In this section, three types of models are described: access control models, integrity models, and information flow models.

---

*Source: "The Systems Security Engineering Capability Maturity Model v2.0," 1999.

Access Control Models

Access control philosophies can be organized into models that define the major and different approaches to this issue. These models are the access matrix, the Take-Grant model, the Bell-LaPadula confidentiality model, and the state machine model.

The Access Matrix

The access matrix is a straightforward approach that provides access rights to subjects for objects. *Access rights* are of the type read, write, and execute. A *subject* is an active entity that is seeking rights to a resource or object. A subject can be a person, a program, or a process. An *object* is a passive entity, such as a file or a storage resource. In some cases, an item can be a subject in one context and an object in another. A typical access control matrix is shown in Figure 5-7.

The columns of the access matrix are called *Access Control Lists* (ACLs), and the rows are called *capability lists*. The access matrix model supports discretionary access control because the entries in the matrix are at the discretion of the individual(s) who have the authorization authority over the table. In the access control matrix, a subject's capability can be defined by the *triple* (object, rights, and random #). Thus, the triple defines the rights that a subject has to an object along with a random number used to prevent a replay or spoofing of the triple's source. This triple is similar to the Kerberos tickets previously discussed in Chapter 2.

Subject Object	File Income	File Salaries	Process Deductions	Print Server A
Joe	Read	Read/Write	Execute	Write
Jane	Read/Write	Read	None	Write
Process Check	Read	Read	Execute	None
Program Tax	Read/Write	Read/Write	Call	Write

Figure 5-7: Example of an access matrix.

Take-Grant Model

The Take-Grant model uses a directed graph to specify the rights that a subject can transfer to an object or that a subject can take from another subject. For example, assume that Subject A has a set of rights (S) that includes Grant rights to Object B. This capability is represented in Figure 5-8a. Then, assume that Subject A can transfer Grant rights for Object B to Subject C and that Subject A has another set of rights, (Y), to Object D. In some cases, Object D acts as an object, and in other cases it acts as a subject. Then, as shown by the heavy arrow in Figure 5-8b, Subject C can grant a subset of the Y rights to Subject/Object D because Subject A passed the Grant rights to Subject C.

The Take capability operates in an identical fashion as the Grant illustration.

Bell-LaPadula Model

The Bell-LaPadula Model was developed to formalize the U.S. Department of Defense (DoD) multi-level security policy. The DoD labels materials at different levels of security classification. As previously discussed, these levels are Unclassified, Confidential, Secret, and Top Secret — ordered from least sensitive to most sensitive. An individual who receives a clearance of Confidential, Secret, or Top Secret can access materials at that level of classification or below. An additional stipulation, however, is that the individual must have a need-to-know for that material. Thus, an individual cleared for Secret can access only the Secret-labeled documents that are necessary for that individual to perform an assigned job function. The Bell-LaPadula model deals *only* with the confidentiality of classified material. It does not address integrity or availability.

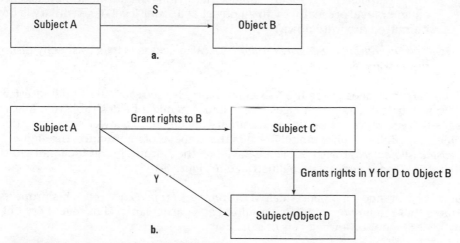

Figure 5-8: Take-Grant model illustration.

The Bell-LaPadula model is built on the *state machine* concept. This concept defines a set of allowable states (A_i) in a system. The transition from one state to another upon receipt of input(s) (X_j) is defined by transition functions (f_k). The objective of this model is to ensure that the initial state is secure and that the transitions always result in a secure state. The transitions between two states are illustrated in Figure 5-9.

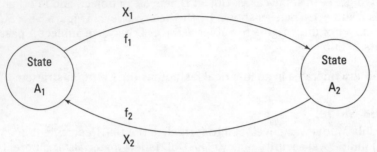

Figure 5-9: State transitions defined by the function f with an input X.

The Bell-LaPadula model defines a *secure state* through three multi-level properties. The first two properties implement mandatory access control, and the third one permits discretionary access control. These properties are defined as follows:

1. *The Simple Security Property (ss Property).* States that reading of information by a subject at a lower sensitivity level from an object at a higher sensitivity level is not permitted (no read up).

2. *The * (star) Security Property.* States that writing of information by a subject at a higher level of sensitivity to an object at a lower level of sensitivity is not permitted (no write-down).

3. *The Discretionary Security Property.* Uses an access matrix to specify discretionary access control.

There are instances where the * (Star) property is too restrictive and it interferes with required document changes. For instance, it might be desirable to move a low-sensitivity paragraph in a higher-sensitivity document to a lower-sensitivity document. The Bell-LaPadula model permits this transfer of information through a *Trusted Subject*. A Trusted Subject can violate the * property, yet it cannot violate its intent. These concepts are illustrated in Figure 5-10.

In some instances, a property called the *Strong * Property* is cited. This property states that reading or writing is permitted at a particular level of sensitivity but not to either higher or lower levels of sensitivity.

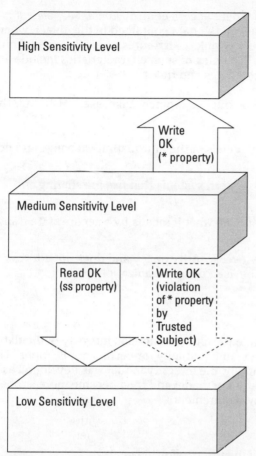

Figure 5-10: The Bell-LaPadula Simple Security and * properties.

This model defines requests (R) to the system. A request is made while the system is in the state v1; a decision (d) is made upon the request, and the system changes to the state v2. (R, d, v1, v2) represents this tuple in the model. Again, the intent of this model is to ensure that there is a transition from one secure state to another secure state.

The discretionary portion of the Bell-LaPadula model is based on the access matrix. The system security policy defines who is authorized to have certain privileges to the system resources. *Authorization* is concerned with how access rights are defined and how they are evaluated. Some discretionary approaches are based on context-dependent and content-dependent access control. *Content-dependent* control makes access decisions based on the data contained in the object, whereas *context-dependent* control uses subject or object attributes or environmental characteristics to make these decisions. Examples of such characteristics include a job role, earlier accesses, and file creation dates and times.

As with any model, the Bell-LaPadula model has some weaknesses. These are the major ones:

✦ The model considers normal channels of the information exchange and does not address covert channels.

✦ The model does not deal with modern systems that use file sharing and servers.

✦ The model does not explicitly define what it means by a secure state transition.

✦ The model is based on a multi-level security policy and does not address other policy types that might be used by an organization.

Integrity Models

In many organizations, both governmental and commercial, integrity of the data is as important or more important than confidentiality for certain applications. Thus, formal integrity models evolved. Initially, the integrity model was developed as an analog to the Bell-LaPadula confidentiality model and then became more sophisticated to address additional integrity requirements.

The Biba Integrity Model

Integrity is usually characterized by the three following goals:

1. The data is protected from modification by unauthorized users.

2. The data is protected from unauthorized modification by authorized users.

3. The data is internally and externally consistent; the data held in a database must balance internally and correspond to the external, real-world situation.

To address the first integrity goal, the Biba model was developed in 1977 as an integrity analog to the Bell-LaPadula confidentiality model. The Biba model is lattice-based and uses the less-than or equal-to relation. A *lattice structure* is defined as a partially ordered set with a *least upper bound* (LUB) and a *greatest lower bound* (GLB). The lattice represents a set of *integrity classes* (ICs) and an ordered relationship among those classes. A lattice can be represented as (IC, ≤, LUB, GUB).

Similar to the Bell-LaPadula model's classification of different sensitivity levels, the Biba model classifies objects into different levels of integrity. The model specifies the three following integrity axioms:

1. *The Simple Integrity Axiom.* States that a subject at one level of integrity is not permitted to observe (read) an object of a lower integrity (no read-down).

2. *The * (star) Integrity Axiom.* States that an object at one level of integrity is not permitted to modify (write to) an object of a higher level of integrity (no write-up).

3. A subject at one level of integrity cannot invoke a subject at a higher level of integrity.

These axioms and their relationships are illustrated in Figure 5-11.

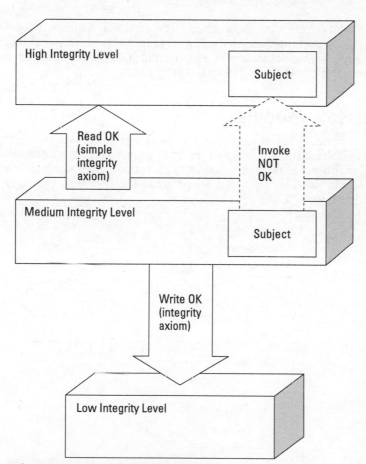

Figure 5-11: The Biba model axioms.

The Clark-Wilson Integrity Model

The approach of the Clark-Wilson model (1987) was to develop a framework for use in the real-world, commercial environment. This model addresses the three integrity goals and defines the following terms:

Constrained data item (CDI). A data item whose integrity is to be preserved.

Integrity verification procedure (IVP). Confirms that all CDIs are in valid states of integrity.

Transformation procedure (TP). Manipulates the CDIs through a well-formed transaction, which transforms a CDI from one valid integrity state to another valid integrity state.

Unconstrained data item. Data items outside the control area of the modeled environment, such as input information

The Clark-Wilson model requires integrity labels to determine the integrity level of a data item and to verify that this integrity was maintained after an application of a TP. This model incorporates mechanisms to enforce internal and external consistency, a separation of duty, and a mandatory integrity policy.

Information Flow Models

An information flow model is based on a state machine, and it consists of objects, state transitions, and lattice (flow policy) states. In this context, objects can also represent users. Each object is assigned a security class and value, and information is constrained to flow in the directions that are permitted by the security policy. An example is shown in Figure 5-12.

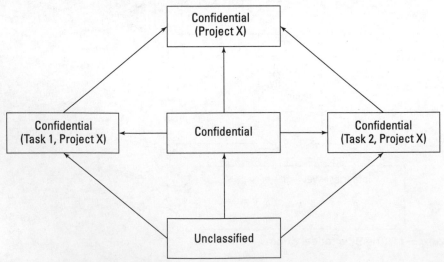

Figure 5-12: An information flow model.

In Figure 5-12, information flows from Unclassified to Confidential in Tasks in Project X and to the combined tasks in Project X. This information can flow in only one direction.

Non-Interference Model

This model is related to the information flow model with restrictions on the information flow. The basic principle of this model is that a group of users (A), who are using the commands (C), do not interfere with the user group (B), who are using commands (D). This concept is written as A, C: | B, D. Restating this rule, the actions of Group A who are using commands C are not seen by users in Group B using commands D.

Composition Theories

In most applications, systems are built by combining smaller systems. An interesting situation to consider is whether the security properties of component systems are maintained when they are combined to form a larger entity.

John McClean studied this issue in 1994 (McLean, J. "A General Theory of Composition for Trace Sets Closed Under Selective Interleaving Functions," *Proceedings of 1994 IEEE Symposium on Research in Security and Privacy*, IEEE Press, 1994).

He defined two compositional constructions: external and internal. The following are the types of external constructs:

Cascading. One system's input is obtained from the output of another system.

Feedback. One system provides the input to a second system, which in turn feeds back to the input of the first system.

Hookup. A system that communicates with another system as well as with external entities

The internal composition constructs are intersection, union, and difference.

The general conclusion of this study was that the security properties of the small systems were maintained under composition (in most instances) in the cascading construct, yet are also subject to other system variables for the other constructs.

✦　　✦　　✦

Assessment Questions

You can find the answers to the following questions in Appendix A.

1. What does the Bell-LaPadula model NOT allow?

    a. Subjects to read from a higher level of security relative to their level of security

    b. Subjects to read from a lower level of security relative to their level of security

    c. Subjects to write to a higher level of security relative to their level of security

    d. Subjects to read at their same level of security

2. In the * (star) property of the Bell-LaPadula model:

    a. Subjects cannot read from a higher level of security relative to their level of security.

    b. Subjects cannot read from a lower level of security relative to their level of security.

    c. Subjects cannot write to a lower level of security relative to their level of security.

    d. Subjects cannot read from their same level of security.

3. The Clark-Wilson model focuses on data's:

    a. Integrity

    b. Confidentiality

    c. Availability

    d. Format

4. The * (star) property of the Biba model states that:

    a. Subjects cannot write to a lower level of integrity relative to their level of integrity.

    b. Subjects cannot write to a higher level of integrity relative to their level of integrity.

    c. Subjects cannot read from a lower level of integrity relative to their level of integrity.

    d. Subjects cannot read from a higher level of integrity relative to their level of integrity.

5. Which of the following does the Clark-Wilson model NOT involve?

    a. Constrained data items

    b. Transformational procedures

    c. Confidentiality items

    d. Well-formed transactions

6. The Take-Grant model:

    a. Focuses on confidentiality

    b. Specifies the rights that a subject can transfer to an object

    c. Specifies the levels of integrity

    d. Specifies the levels of availability

7. The Biba model addresses:

    a. Data disclosure

    b. Transformation procedures

    c. Constrained data items

    d. Unauthorized modification of data

8. Mandatory access controls first appear in the Trusted Computer System Evaluation Criteria (TCSEC) at the rating of:

    a. D

    b. C

    c. B

    d. A

9. In the access control matrix, the rows are:

    a. Access Control Lists (ACLs)

    b. Tuples

    c. Domains

    d. Capability lists

10. What information security model formalizes the U.S. Department of Defense multi-level security policy?

   a. Clark-Wilson

   b. Stark-Wilson

   c. Biba

   d. Bell-LaPadula

11. A Trusted Computing Base (TCB) is defined as:

   a. The total combination of protection mechanisms within a computer system that is trusted to enforce a security policy.

   b. The boundary separating the trusted mechanisms from the remainder of the system.

   c. A trusted path that permits a user to access resources.

   d. A system that employs the necessary hardware and software assurance measures to enable the processing of multiple levels of classified or sensitive information to occur.

12. Memory space insulated from other running processes in a multi-processing system is part of a:

   a. Protection domain

   b. Security perimeter

   c. Least upper bound

   d. Constrained data item

13. The boundary separating the TCB from the remainder of the system is called the:

   a. Star property

   b. Simple security property

   c. Discretionary control boundary

   d. Security perimeter

14. The system component that enforces access controls on an object is the:

   a. Security perimeter

   b. Trusted domain

   c. Reference monitor

   d. Access control matrix

15. Which one the following is NOT one of the three major parts of the Common Criteria (CC)?

    a. Introduction and General Model

    b. Security Evaluation Requirements

    c. Security Functional Requirements

    d. Security Assurance Requirements

16. A computer system that employs the necessary hardware and software assurance measures to enable it to process multiple levels of classified or sensitive information is called a:

    a. Closed system

    b. Open system

    c. Trusted system

    d. Safe system

17. For fault-tolerance to operate, a system must be:

    a. Capable of detecting and correcting the fault

    b. Capable only of detecting the fault

    c. Capable of terminating operations in a safe mode

    d. Capable of a cold start

18. Which of the following choices describes the four phases of the National Information Assurance Certification and Accreditation Process (NIACAP)?

    a. Definition, Verification, Validation, and Confirmation

    b. Definition, Verification, Validation, and Post Accreditation

    c. Verification, Validation, Authentication, and Post Accreditation

    d. Definition, Authentication, Verification, and Post Accreditation

19. In the Common Criteria, an implementation-independent statement of security needs for a set of IT security products that could be built is called a:

    a. Security Target (ST)

    b. Package

    c. Protection Profile (PP)

    d. Target of Evaluation (TOE)

20. The termination of selected, non-critical processing when a hardware or software failure occurs and is detected is referred to as:

   a. Fail safe

   b. Fault tolerant

   c. Fail soft

   d. An exception

21. Which one of the following is NOT a component of a CC Protection Profile?

   a. Target of Evaluation (TOE) description

   b. Threats against the product that must be addressed

   c. Product-specific security requirements

   d. Security objectives

22. Content-dependent control makes access decisions based on:

   a. The object's data

   b. The object's environment

   c. The object's owner

   d. The object's view

23. The term *failover* refers to:

   a. Switching to a duplicate, "hot" backup component

   b. Terminating processing in a controlled fashion

   c. Resiliency

   d. A fail-soft system

24. Primary storage is the:

   a. Memory directly addressable by the CPU, which is for storage of instructions and data that are associated with the program being executed

   b. Memory, such as magnetic disks, that provides non-volatile storage

   c. Memory used in conjunction with real memory to present a CPU with a larger, apparent address space

   d. Memory where information must be obtained by sequentially searching from the beginning of the memory space

25. In the Common Criteria, a Protection Profile:

   a. Specifies the mandatory protection in the product to be evaluated

   b. Is also known as the Target of Evaluation (TOE)

   c. Is also known as the Orange Book

   d. Specifies the security requirements and protections of the products to be evaluated

26. Context-dependent control uses which of the following to make decisions?

   a. Subject or object attributes or environmental characteristics

   b. Data

   c. Formal models

   d. Operating system characteristics

27. The secure path between a user and the Trusted Computing Base (TCB) is called:

   a. Trusted distribution

   b. Trusted path

   c. Trusted facility management

   d. The security perimeter

28. In a ring protection system, where is the security kernel usually located?

   a. Highest ring number

   b. Arbitrarily placed

   c. Lowest ring number

   d. Middle ring number

29. Increasing performance in a computer by overlapping the steps of different instructions is called:

   a. A reduced instruction set computer

   b. A complex instruction set computer

   c. Vector processing

   d. Pipelining

30. Random access memory is:

    a. Non-volatile

    b. Sequentially addressable

    c. Programmed by using fusible links

    d. Volatile

31. In the National Information Assurance Certification and Accreditation Process (NIACAP), a type accreditation performs which one of the following functions?

    a. Evaluates a major application or general support system

    b. Verifies the evolving or modified system's compliance with the information agreed on in the System Security Authorization Agreement (SSAA)

    c. Evaluates an application or system that is distributed to a number of different locations

    d. Evaluates the applications and systems at a specific, self-contained location

32. Processes are placed in a ring structure according to:

    a. Least privilege

    b. Separation of duty

    c. Owner classification

    d. First in, first out

33. The MULTICS operating system is a classic example of:

    a. An open system

    b. Object orientation

    c. Database security

    d. Ring protection system

34. What are the hardware, firmware, and software elements of a Trusted Computing Base (TCB) that implement the reference monitor concept called?

    a. The trusted path

    b. A security kernel

    c. An Operating System (OS)

    d. A trusted computing system

Operations Security

The Operations Security domain of Information Systems Security contains many elements that are important for a CISSP candidate to remember. In this domain, we will describe the controls that a computing operating environment needs to ensure the three pillars of information security: Confidentiality, Integrity, and Availability (C.I.A.). Examples of these elements are controlling the separation of job functions, controlling the hardware and media that are used, and controlling the exploitation of common I/O errors.

Operations Security can be described as the controls over the hardware in a computing facility, over the data media used in a facility, and over the operators using these resources in a facility.

We will approach this material from the three following directions:

1. *Controls and Protections*. We will describe the categories of operational controls needed to ensure C.I.A.

2. *Monitoring and Auditing*. We will describe the need for monitoring and auditing these controls.

3. *Threats and Vulnerabilities*. We will discuss threats and violations that are applicable to the Operations domain.

Domain Definition

Operations Security refers to the act of understanding the threats to and vulnerabilities of computer operations in order to routinely support operational activities that enable computer systems to function correctly. It also refers to the implementation of security controls for normal transaction processing, system administration tasks, and critical external support operations. These controls can include resolving software or hardware problems along with the proper maintenance of auditing and monitoring processes.

Triples

Like the other domains, the Operations Security domain is concerned with triples: threats, vulnerabilities, and assets. We will now look at what constitutes a triple in the Operations Security domain:

Threat. A threat in the Operations Security domain can be defined as the presence of any potential event that could cause harm by violating security. An example of an operations threat is an operator's abuse of privileges that violates confidentiality.

Vulnerability. A vulnerability is defined as a weakness in a system that enables security to be violated. An example of an operations vulnerability is a weak implementation of the separation of duties.

Asset. An asset is considered anything that is a computing resource or ability, such as hardware, software, data, and personnel.

C.I.A.

The following are the effects of operations controls on C.I.A.:

Confidentiality. Operations controls affect the sensitivity and secrecy of the information.

Integrity. How well the operations controls are implemented directly affects the data's accuracy and authenticity.

Availability. Like the Physical Security domain, these controls affect the organization's level of fault tolerance and its capability to recover from failure.

Controls and Protections

The Operations Security domain is concerned with the controls that are used to protect hardware, software, and media resources from the following:

✦ Threats in an operating environment

✦ Internal or external intruders

✦ Operators who are inappropriately accessing resources

A CISSP candidate should know the resources to protect, how privileges should be restricted, and the controls to implement.

In addition, we will also discuss the following two critical aspects of operations controls:

1. Resource protection, which includes hardware control

2. Privileged-entity control

Categories of Controls

The following are the major categories of operations security controls:

Preventative Controls. In the Operations Security domain, preventative controls are designed to achieve two things: to lower the amount and impact of unintentional errors that are entering the system and to prevent unauthorized intruders from internally or externally accessing the system. An example of these controls might be prenumbered forms or a data validation and review procedure to prevent duplications.

Detective Controls. Detective controls are used to detect an error once it has occurred. Unlike preventative controls, these controls operate after the fact and can be used to track an unauthorized transaction for prosecution, or to lessen an error's impact on the system by identifying it quickly. An example of this type of control is an audit trail.

Corrective (or Recovery) Controls. Corrective controls are implemented to help mitigate the impact of a loss event through data recovery procedures. They can be used to recover after damage, such as restoring data that was inadvertently erased from floppy diskettes.

The following are additional control categories:

Deterrent Controls. Deterrent controls are used to encourage compliance with external controls, such as regulatory compliance. These controls are meant to complement other controls, such as preventative and detective controls. Deterrent controls are also known as *directive controls*.

Application Controls. Application controls are the controls that are designed into a software application to minimize and detect the software's operational irregularities. In addition, the following controls are also examples of the various types of application controls.

Transaction Controls. Transaction controls are used to provide control over the various stages of a transaction — from initiation to output through testing and change control. There are several types of transaction controls:

- *Input Controls* — Input controls are used to ensure that transactions are properly input into the system only once. Elements of input controls might include counting the data and timestamping it with the date it was entered or edited.

- *Processing Controls* — Processing controls are used to guarantee that transactions are valid and accurate and that wrong entries are reprocessed correctly and promptly.

- *Output Controls* — Output controls are used for two things: for protecting the confidentiality of an output and for verifying the integrity of an output by comparing the input transaction with the output data. Elements of proper output controls involve ensuring that the output reaches the proper users, restricting access to the printed output storage areas, printing heading and trailing banners, requiring signed receipts before releasing sensitive output, and printing "no output" banners when a report is empty.

- *Change Controls* — Change controls are implemented to preserve data integrity in a system while changes are made to the configuration. Procedures and standards have been created to manage these changes and modifications to the system and its configuration. Change control and configuration management control are thoroughly described later in this chapter.

- *Test Controls* — Test controls are put into place during the testing of a system to prevent violations of confidentiality and to ensure a transaction's integrity. An example of this type of control is the proper use of sanitized test data. Test controls are often part of the change control process.

Orange Book Controls

The Orange Book is one of the books of the Rainbow Series, which is six-foot-tall stack of books on evaluating "Trusted Computer Systems", from the National Security Agency. The term *Rainbow Series* comes from the fact that each book is a different color. The main book (upon which all others expound) is the Orange Book, which defines the Trusted Computer System Evaluation Criteria (TCSEC). Much of the Rainbow Series has been superseded by the Common Criteria Evaluation and Validation Scheme (CCEVS). This information can be found at http://niap.nist.gov/cc-scheme/index.html. Other books in the Rainbow Series can be found at www.fas.org/irp/nsa/rainbow.htm.

The TCSEC defines major hierarchical classes of security by the letters D (least secure) through A (most secure):

D — Minimal protection

C — Discretionary protection (C1&C2)

B — Mandatory protection (B1, B2, B3)

A — Verified protection; formal methods (A1)

Table 6-1 shows these TCSEC Security Evaluation Categories.

Table 6-1
TCSEC Security Evaluation Categories

Class	Description
D:	Minimal Protection
C:	Discretionary Protection
C1:	Discretionary Security Protection
C2:	Controlled Access Protection
B:	Mandatory Protection
B1:	Labeled Security Protection
B2:	Structured Protection
B3:	Security Domains
A1:	Verified Protection

The Orange Book defines assurance requirements for secure computer operations. Assurance is a level of confidence that ensures that a trusted computing base's (TCB) security policy has been correctly implemented and that the system's security features have accurately implemented that policy.

The Orange Book defines two types of assurance — operational assurance and life cycle assurance. Operational assurance focuses on the basic features and architecture of a system while life cycle assurance focuses on the controls and standards that are necessary for building and maintaining a system. An example of an operational assurance is a feature that separates a security-sensitive code from a user code in a system's memory.

The operational assurance requirements specified in the Orange Book are as follows:

✦ System architecture

✦ System integrity

✦ Covert channel analysis

✦ Trusted facility management

✦ Trusted recovery

Life cycle assurance ensures that a TCB is designed, developed, and maintained with formally controlled standards that enforce protection at each stage in the system's life cycle. Configuration management, which carefully monitors and protects all changes to a system's resources, is a type of life cycle assurance.

The life cycle assurance requirements specified in the Orange Book are as follows:

✦ Security testing

✦ Design specification and testing

✦ Configuration management

✦ Trusted distribution

In the Operations Security domain, the operations assurance areas of covert channel analysis, trusted facility management and trusted recovery, and the life cycle assurance area of configuration management are covered.

Covert Channel Analysis

An information transfer path within a system is a generic definition of a *channel*. A channel may also refer to the mechanism by which the path is effected. A *covert channel* is a communication channel that allows a process to transfer information in a manner that violates the system's security policy. A covert channel is an information path that is not normally used for communication within a system; therefore, it is not protected by the system's normal security mechanisms. Covert channels are a secret way to convey information to another person or program.* There are two common types of covert channels: covert storage channels and covert timing channels.

Covert Storage Channel

Covert storage channels convey information by changing a system's stored data. For example, a program can convey information to a less secure program by changing the amount or the patterns of free space on a hard disk. Changing the characteristics of a file is another example of creating a covert channel. A covert storage channel typically involves a finite resource (e.g., sectors on a disk) that is shared by two subjects at different security levels.

Covert Timing Channel

A covert timing channel is a covert channel in which one process signals information to another by modulating its own use of system resources (e.g., CPU time) in such a way that this manipulation affects the real response time observed by the second process. A covert timing channel employs a process that manipulates observable system resources in a way that affects response time.

---

*Sources: DoD 5200.28-STD, Department of Defense Trusted Computer System Evaluation Criteria; and NCSC-TG-030, A Guide To Understanding Covert Channel Analysis of Trusted Systems (Light Pink Book)

Trusted Computing Base (TCB)

The trusted computing base (TCB) refers to the totality of protection mechanisms within a computer system, including hardware, firmware, and software, the combination of which is responsible for enforcing a security policy. A TCB consists of one or more components that together enforce a unified security policy over a product or system. The ability of a trusted computing base to correctly enforce a security policy depends solely on the mechanisms within the TCB and on the correct input by system administrative personnel of parameters (e.g., a user's clearance) related to the security policy.

Covert timing channels convey information by altering the performance of or modifying the timing of a system resource in some measurable way. Timing channels often work by taking advantage of some kind of system clock or timing device in a system. Information is conveyed by using elements such as the elapsed time required to perform an operation, the amount of CPU time expended, or the time occurring between two events.

Covert timing channels operate in real time—that is, the information transmitted from the sender must be sensed by the receiver immediately or it will be lost—whereas covert storage channels do not. For example, a full disk error code may be exploited to create a storage channel that could remain for an indefinite amount of time.

Noise and traffic generation are often ways to combat the use of covert channels. Table 6-2 describes the primary covert channel classes.

Table 6-2
Covert Channel Classes

Class	Description
B2	The system must protect against covert storage channels. It must perform a covert channel analysis for all covert storage channels.
B3 and A1	The system must protect against both covert storage and covert timing channels. It must perform a covert channel analysis for both types.

Trusted Facility Management

Trusted facility management is defined as the assignment of a specific individual to administer the security-related functions of a system. Trusted facility management has two different requirements, one for B2 systems and another for B3 systems. The B2 requirements require that the TCB shall support separate operator and administrator functions.

The B3 requirements require that the functions performed in the role of a security administrator shall be identified. System administrative personnel shall only be able to perform security administrator functions after taking a distinct auditable action to assume the security administrator role on the system. Non-security functions that can be performed in the security administration role shall be limited strictly to those essential to performing the security role effectively.

Although trusted facility management is an assurance requirement only for highly secure systems, many systems evaluated at lower security levels are structured to try to meet this requirement (see Table 6-3).

<table>
<tr><td colspan="2">Table 6-3
Trusted Facility Management Classes</td></tr>
<tr><td>*Class*</td><td>*Requirements*</td></tr>
<tr><td>B2</td><td>Systems must support separate operator and system administrator roles.</td></tr>
<tr><td>B3 and A1</td><td>Systems must clearly identify the functions of the security administrator to perform the security-related functions.</td></tr>
</table>

Trusted facility management uses the concept of *least privilege* (discussed later in this chapter), and it is also related to the administrative concepts of *separation of duties* and *need to know*.

Separation of Duties

Separation of duties (also called segregation of duties) assigns parts of tasks to different personnel. Thus, if no single person has total control of the system's security mechanisms, the theory is that no single person can completely compromise the system.

In many systems, a system administrator has total control of the system's administration and security functions. This consolidation of privilege should not be allowed in a secure system because security tasks and functions should not automatically be assigned to the role of the system administrator. In highly secure systems, three distinct administrative roles might be required: a system administrator, a security administrator who is usually an information system security officer (ISSO), and an enhanced operator function.

The security administrator, system administrator, and operator might not necessarily bedifferent personnel. However, whenever a system administrator assumes the role of the security administrator, this role change must be controlled and audited. Because the security administrator's job is to perform security functions, the performance of non-security tasks must be strictly limited. This separation of duties reduces the likelihood of loss that results from users abusing their authority by taking actions outside of their assigned functional responsibilities. While it might be cumbersome for the person to switch from one role to another, the roles are functionally different and must be executed as such.

In the concept of two-man control, two operators review and approve the work of each other. The purpose of two-man control is to provide accountability and to minimize fraud in highly sensitive or high-risk transactions. The concept of dual control means that both operators are needed to complete a sensitive task.

Typical system administrator or enhanced operator functions can include the following:

✦ Installing system software

✦ Starting up (booting) and shutting down a system

✦ Adding and removing system users

✦ Performing back-ups and recovery

✦ Handling printers and managing print queues

Typical security administrator functions might include the following:

✦ Setting user clearances, initial passwords, and other security characteristics for new users

✦ Changing security profiles for existing users

✦ Setting or changing file sensitivity labels

✦ Setting the security characteristics of devices and communications channels

✦ Reviewing audit data

An operator might perform some system administrator roles, such as backups. This may happen in facilities where personnel resources are constrained.

For proper separation of duties, the function of user account establishment and maintenance should be separated from the function of initiating and authorizing the creation of the account. User account management focuses on identification, authentication, and access authorizations. This is augmented by the process of auditing and otherwise periodically verifying the legitimacy of current accounts and access authorizations. It also involves the timely modification or removal of access and associated issues for employees who are reassigned, promoted, or terminated, or who retire.

Rotation of Duties

Another variation on the separation of duties is called *rotation of duties*, which is defined as the process of limiting the amount of time that an operator is assigned to perform a security-related task before being moved to a different task with a different security classification. This control lessens the opportunity for collusion between operators for fraudulent purposes. Like a separation of duties, a rotation of duties might be difficult to implement in small organizations but can be an effective security control procedure.

The System Administrator's Many Hats

It is not just small organizations anymore that require a system administrator to function as a security administrator. The LAN/Internet Network administrator role creates security risks due to the inherent lack of the separation of duties. With the current pullback in the Internet economy, a network administrator has to wear many hats — and performing security-related tasks is almost always one of them (along with various operator functions). The sometimes cumbersome yet very important concept of separation of duties is vital to preserve operations controls.

Trusted Recovery

Trusted recovery ensures that security is not breached when a system crash or other system failure (sometimes called a *discontinuity*) occurs. It must ensure that the system is restarted without compromising its required protection scheme and that it can recover and roll back without being compromised after the failure. Trusted recovery is required only for B3- and A1-level systems. A system failure represents a serious security risk because the security controls might be bypassed when the system is not functioning normally.

For example, if a system crashes while sensitive data is being written to a disk (where it would normally be protected by controls), the data might be left unprotected in memory and might be accessible by unauthorized personnel. Trusted recovery has two primary activities: preparing for a system failure and recovering the system.

Failure Preparation

Under trusted recovery, preparing for a system failure consists of backing up all critical files on a regular basis. This preparation must enable the data recovery in a protected and orderly manner while ensuring the continued security of the system. These procedures might also be required if a system problem, such as a missing resource, an inconsistent database, or any kind of compromise, is detected, or if the system needs to be halted and rebooted.

System Recovery

While specific, trusted recovery procedures depend upon a system's requirements, general, secure system recovery procedures include the following:

✦ Rebooting the system into a single-user mode — an operating system loaded without the security front end activated — so that no other user access is enabled at this time

✦ Recovering all file systems that were active at the time of the system failure

✦ Restoring any missing or damaged files and databases from the most recent backups

✦ Recovering the required security characteristics, such as file security labels

✦ Checking security-critical files, such as the system password file

After all of these steps have been performed and the system's data cannot be compromised, operators can then access the system.

In addition, the Common Criteria also describes three hierarchical recovery types:

1. *Manual Recovery.* System administrator intervention is required to return the system to a secure state after a crash.

2. *Automated Recovery.* Recovery to a secure state is automatic (without system administrator intervention) when resolving a single failure; however, manual intervention is required to resolve any additional failures.

3. *Automated Recovery without Undue Loss.* Similar to automated recovery, this type of recovery is considered a higher level of recovery defining prevention against the undue loss of protected objects.

Modes of Operation

The *mode of operation* is a description of the conditions under which an AIS functions, based on the sensitivity of data processed and the clearance levels and authorizations of the users. Four modes of operation are defined:

Dedicated Mode. An AIS is operating in the dedicated mode when each user with direct or indirect individual access to the AIS, its peripherals, remote terminals, or remote hosts has all of the following:

a. A valid personnel clearance for all information on the system

b. Formal access approval for, and has signed nondisclosure agreements for all the information stored and/or processed (including all compartments, subcompartments, and/or special access programs)

c. A valid need to know for all information contained within the system

System-High Mode. An AIS is operating in the system-high mode when each user with direct or indirect access to the AIS, its peripherals, remote terminals, or remote hosts has all of the following:

a. A valid personnel clearance for all information on the AIS

b. Formal access approval for, and has signed nondisclosure agreements for, all the information stored and/or processed (including all compartments, subcompartments, and/or special access programs)

c. A valid need to know for some of the information contained within the AIS

Compartmented Mode. An AIS is operating in the compartmented mode when each user with direct or indirect access to the AIS, its peripherals, remote terminals, or remote hosts has all of the following:

a. A valid personnel clearance for the most restricted information processed in the AIS

b. Formal access approval for, and has signed nondisclosure agreements for, that information to which he/she is to have access

c. A valid need to know for that information to which he/she is to have access

Multilevel Mode. An AIS is operating in the multilevel mode when all the following statements are satisfied concerning the users with direct or indirect access to the AIS, its peripherals, remote terminals, or remote hosts:

a. Some do not have a valid personnel clearance for all the information processed in the AIS.

b. All have the proper clearance and have the appropriate formal access approval for that information to which he/she is to have access.

c. All have a valid need to know for that information to which they are to have access.

Configuration Management and Change Control

Change control is the management of security features and a level of assurance provided through the control of the changes made to the system's hardware, software, and firmware configurations throughout the development and operational life cycle.

Change control manages the process of tracking and approving changes to a system. It involves identifying, controlling, and auditing all changes made to the system. It can address hardware and software changes, networking changes, or any other change affecting security. Change control can also be used to protect a trusted system while it is being designed and developed.

The primary security goal of change control is to ensure that changes to the system do not unintentionally diminish security. For example, change control might prevent an older version of a system from being activated as the production system. Proper change control may also make it possible to accurately roll back to a previous version of a system in case a new system is found to be faulty. Another goal of change control is to ensure that system changes are reflected in current documentation to help mitigate the impact that a change might have on the security of other systems, while either in the production or planning stages.

The following are the primary functions of change control:

✦ To ensure that the change is implemented in an orderly manner through formalized testing

✦ To ensure that the user base is informed of the impending change

✦ To analyze the effect of the change on the system after implementation

✦ To reduce the negative impact that the change might have on the computing services and resources

Multilevel Device

A multilevel device is a device that is used in a manner that permits it to process data of two or more security levels simultaneously without risk of compromise. To accomplish this, sensitivity labels are normally stored on the same physical medium and in the same form (i.e., machine readable or human readable) as the data being processed.

Five generally accepted procedures exist to implement and support the change control process:

1. *Applying to introduce a change.* Requests presented to an individual or group responsible for approving and administering changes.

2. *Approval of the change.* Demonstrating trade-off analysis of the change and justifying it.

2. *Cataloging the intended change.* Documenting and updating the change in a change control log.

3. *Testing the change.* Formal testing of the change.

4. *Scheduling and implementing the change.* Scheduling the change and implementing the change.

5. *Reporting the change to the appropriate parties.* Submitting a full report summarizing the change to management.

Configuration management is the more formalized, higher-level process of managing changes to a complicated system, and it is required for formal, trusted systems. Change control is contained in configuration management. The purpose of configuration management is to ensure that changes made to verification systems take place in an identifiable and controlled environment. Configuration managers take responsibility that additions, deletions, or changes made to the verification system do not jeopardize its ability to satisfy trusted requirements. Therefore, configuration management is vital to maintaining the endorsement of a verification system.

Although configuration management is a requirement only for B2, B3, and A1 systems, it is recommended for systems that are evaluated at lower levels. Most developers use some type of configuration management because it is common sense.

Configuration management is a discipline applying technical and administrative direction to do the following:

✦ Identify and document the functional and physical characteristics of each configuration item for the system

✦ Manage all changes to these characteristics

✦ Record and report the status of change processing and implementation

Configuration management involves process monitoring, version control, information capture, quality control, bookkeeping, and an organizational framework to support these activities. The configuration being managed is the verification system plus all tools and documentation related to the configuration process.

The four major aspects of configuration management are*:

✦ Configuration identification

✦ Configuration control

✦ Configuration status accounting

✦ Configuration auditing

Configuration Identification

Configuration management entails decomposing the verification system into identifiable, understandable, manageable, trackable units known as configuration items (CIs). A CI is a uniquely identifiable subset of the system that represents the smallest portion to be subject to independent configuration control procedures. The decomposition process of a verification system into CIs is called configuration identification.

CIs can vary widely in size, type, and complexity. Although there are no hard-and-fast rules for decomposition, the granularity of CIs can have great practical importance. A favorable strategy is to designate relatively large CIs for elements that are not expected to change over the life of the system and small CIs for elements likely to change more frequently.

Configuration Control

Configuration control is a means of ensuring that system changes are approved before being implemented, that only the proposed and approved changes are implemented, and that the implementation is complete and accurate. This involves strict procedures for proposing, monitoring, and approving system changes and their implementation. Configuration control entails central direction of the change process by personnel who coordinate analytical tasks, approve system changes, review the implementation of changes, and supervise other tasks such as documentation.

Configuration Accounting

Configuration accounting documents the status of configuration control activities and in general provides the information needed to manage a configuration effectively. It allows managers to trace system changes and establish the history of any developmental problems and associated fixes.

---

*Sources: National Computer Security Center publication NCSC-TG-006, "A Guide To Understanding Configuration Management In Trusted Systems"; NCSC-TG-014, "Guidelines for Formal Verification Systems."

Configuration accounting also tracks the status of current changes as they move through the configuration control process. Configuration accounting establishes the granularity of recorded information and thus shapes the accuracy and usefulness of the audit function.

The accounting function must be able to locate all possible versions of a CI and all of the incremental changes involved, thereby deriving the status of that CI at any specific time. The associated records must include commentary about the reason for each change and its major implications for the verification system.

Configuration Audit

Configuration audit is the quality assurance component of configuration management. It involves periodic checks to determine the consistency and completeness of accounting information and to verify that all configuration management policies are being followed. A vendor's configuration management program must be able to sustain a complete configuration audit by an NCSC review team.

Configuration Management Plan

Strict adherence to a comprehensive configuration management plan is one of the most important requirements for successful configuration management. The configuration management plan is the vendor's document tailored to the company's practices and personnel. The plan accurately describes what the vendor is doing to the system at each moment and what evidence is being recorded.

Configuration Control Board (CCB)

All analytical and design tasks are conducted under the direction of the vendor's corporate entity called the Configuration Control Board (CCB). The CCB is headed by a chairperson who is responsible for assuring that changes made do not jeopardize the soundness of the verification system and ensures that the changes made are approved, tested, documented, and implemented correctly.

The members of the CCB should interact periodically, either through formal meetings or other available means, to discuss configuration management topics such as proposed changes, configuration status accounting reports, and other topics that may be of interest to the different areas of the system development. These interactions should be held to keep the entire system team updated on all advancements or alterations in the verification system.

Table 6-4 shows the two primary configuration management classes.

	Table 6-4 **Configuration Management Classes**	
Class	*Requirement*
B2 and B3	Configuration management procedures must be enforced during development and maintenance of a system.
A1	Configuration management procedures must be enforced during the entire system's life cycle.

Administrative Controls

Administrative controls can be defined as the controls that are installed and maintained by administrative management to help reduce the threat or impact of violations on computer security. We separate them from the operations controls because these controls have more to do with human resources personnel administration and policy than they do with hardware or software controls.

The following are some examples of administrative controls:

Personnel Security. These controls are administrative human resources controls that are used to support the guarantees of the quality levels of the personnel performing the computer operations. These are also explained in the Physical Security domain. Elements of these include the following:

- *Employment screening or background checks.* Pre-employment screening for sensitive positions should be implemented. For less sensitive positions, post-employment background checks might be suitable.

- *Mandatory taking of vacation in one-week increments.* This practice is common in financial institutions or other organizations where an operator has access to sensitive financial transactions. Some institutions require a two-week vacation, during which the operator's accounts, processes, and procedures are audited carefully to uncover any evidence of fraud.

- *Job action warnings or termination.* These are the actions taken when employees violate the published computer behavior standards.

Separation of Duties and Responsibilities. Separation (or Segregation) of duties and responsibilities is the concept of assigning parts of security-sensitive tasks to several individuals. We described this concept earlier in this chapter.

Least Privilege. *Least privilege* requires that each subject be granted the most restricted set of privileges needed for the performance of their task. We describe this concept later in more detail.

Need to Know. Need to know refers to the access to, knowledge of, or possession of specific information that is required to carry out a job function. It requires that the subject is given only the amount of information required to perform an assigned task. We also describe this concept later in more detail. In addition to whatever specific object or role rights a user may have on the system, the user has also the minimum amount of information necessary to perform his job function.

Change Control. The function of change control is to protect a system from problems and errors that might result from improperly executed or tested changes to a system. We described this concept earlier in this chapter.

Record Retention and Documentation Control. The administration of security controls on documentation and the procedures implemented for record retention have an impact on operational security. We describe these concepts later in more detail.

Least Privilege

The *least privilege* principle requires that each subject in a system be granted the most restrictive set of privileges (or lowest clearance) needed for the performance of authorized tasks. The application of this principle limits the damage that can result from accident, error, or unauthorized use of system resources.

It might be necessary to separate the levels of access based on the operator's job function. A very effective approach is least privilege. An example of least privilege is the concept of computer operators who are not allowed access to computer resources at a level beyond what is absolutely needed for their specific job tasks. Operators are organized into privilege-level groups. Each group is then assigned the most restrictive level that is applicable.

The three basic levels of privilege are defined as follows:

Read Only. This level is the lowest level of privilege and the one to which most operators should be assigned. Operators are allowed to view data but are not allowed to add, delete, or make changes to the original or copies of the data.

Read/Write. The next higher privilege level is read/write access. This level enables operators to read, add to, or write over any data for which they have authority. Operators usually have read/write access only to data copied from an original location; they cannot access the original data.

Access Change. The third and highest level is access change. This level gives operators the right to modify data directly in its original location, in addition to data copied from the original location. Operators might also have the right to change file and operator access permissions in the system (a supervisor right).

These privilege levels are commonly much more granular than we have stated here, and privilege levels in a large organization can, in fact, be very complicated.

Operations Job Function Overview

In a large shop, job functions and duties might be divided among a very large base of IT personnel. In many IT departments, the following roles are combined into fewer positions. The following listing, however, gives a nice overview of the various task components of the operational functions.

> **Computer Operator.** Responsible for backups, running the system console, mounting and unmounting reel tapes and cartridges, recording and reporting operational problems with hardware devices and software products, and maintaining environmental controls
>
> **Operations Analyst.** Responsible for working with application software developers, maintenance programmers, and computer operators
>
> **Job Control Analyst.** Responsible for the overall quality of the production job control language and conformance to standards
>
> **Production Scheduler.** Responsible for planning, creating, and coordinating computer processing schedules for all production and job streams in conjunction with the established processing periods and calendars
>
> **Production Control Analyst.** Responsible for the printing and distribution of computer reports and microfiche/microfilm records
>
> **Tape Librarian.** Responsible for collecting input tapes and scratch tapes, sending tapes to and receiving returns from offsite storage and third parties, and for maintaining tapes

Record Retention

Record retention refers to how long transactions and other types of records (legal, audit trails, email, and so forth) should be retained according to management, legal, audit, or tax compliance requirements. In the Operations Security domain, record retention deals with retaining computer files, directories, and libraries. The retention of data media (tapes, diskettes, and backup media) can be based on one or more criteria, such as the number of days elapsed, number of days since creation, hold time, or other factors. An example of record retention issues could be the mandated retention periods for trial documentation or financial records.

Data Remanence

Data remanence refers to the data left on the media after the media has been erased. After erasure, there might be some physical traces left, which could enable the data to be reconstructed that could contain sensitive material. Object reuse mechanisms ensure that system resources are allocated and reassigned among authorized users in a way that prevents the leak of sensitive information, and they ensure that the authorized user of the system does not obtain residual information from system resources.

Object reuse is defined as "The reassignment to some subject of a storage medium (e.g., page frame, disk sector, magnetic tape) that contained one or more objects.

To be securely reassigned, no residual data can be available to the new subject through standard system mechanisms."* The object reuse requirement of the TCSEC is intended to ensure that system resources, in particular storage media, are allocated and reassigned among system users in a manner that prevents the disclosure of sensitive information.

Systems administrators and security administrators should be informed of the risks involving the issues of object reuse, declassification, destruction, and disposition of storage media. Data remanence, object reuse, and the proper disposal of data media are also discussed in Chapter 10.

Due Care and Due Diligence

The concepts of due care and due diligence require that an organization engage in good business practices relative to the organization's industry. Training employees in security awareness could be an example of due care, unlike simply creating a policy with no implementation plan or follow-up. Mandating statements from the employees that they have read and understood appropriate computer behavior is also an example of due care.

Due diligence might be mandated by various legal requirements in the organization's industry or through compliance with governmental regulatory standards. Due care and due diligence are described in more detail in Chapter 9.

Due care and due diligence are becoming serious issues in computer operations today. In fact, the legal system has begun to hold major partners liable for the lack of due care in the event of a major security breach. Violations of security and privacy are hot-button issues that are confronting the Internet community, and standards covering the best practices of due care are necessary for an organization's protection.

Documentation Control

A security system needs documentation controls. Documentation can include several things: security plans, contingency plans, risk analyses, and security policies and procedures. Most of this documentation must be protected from unauthorized disclosure; for example, printer output must be in a secure location. Disaster recovery documentation must also be readily available in the event of a disaster.

Operations Controls

Operations controls embody the day-to-day procedures used to protect computer operations. A CISSP candidate must understand the concepts of resource protection, hardware/software control, and privileged entity.

---

*Source: NCSC-TG-018, "A Guide to Understanding Object Reuse in Trusted Systems" (Light Blue Book)

The following are the most important aspects of operations controls:

✦ Resource protection

✦ Hardware controls

✦ Software controls

✦ Privileged-entity controls

✦ Media controls

✦ Physical access controls

Resource Protection

Resource protection is just what it sounds like—the concept of protecting an organization's computing resources and assets from loss or compromise. Computing resources are defined as any hardware, software, or data that is owned and used by the organization. Resource protection is designed to help reduce the possibility of damage that can result from the unauthorized disclosure and/or alteration of data by limiting the opportunities for its misuse.

Various examples of resources that require protection are:

Hardware Resources

- Communications, including routers, firewalls, gateways, switches, modems, and access servers

- Storage media, including floppies, removable drives, external hard drives, tapes, and cartridges

- Processing systems, including file servers, mail servers, Internet servers, backup servers, and tape drives

- Standalone computers, including workstations, modems, disks, and tapes

- Printers and fax machines

Software Resources

- Program libraries and source code

- Vendor software or proprietary packages

- Operating system software and systems utilities

Data Resources

- Backup data

- User data files

- Password files

- Operating Data Directories
- System logs and audit trails

Hardware Controls

Hardware Maintenance. System maintenance requires physical or logical access to a system by support and operations staff, vendors, or service providers. Maintenance might be performed on-site, or it might be transported to a repair site. It might also be remotely performed. Furthermore, background investigations of the service personnel might be necessary. Supervising and escorting the maintenance personnel when they are on-site is also necessary.

Maintenance Accounts. Many computer systems provide maintenance accounts. These supervisor-level accounts are created at the factory with preset and widely known passwords. It is critical to change these passwords or at least disable the accounts until these accounts are needed. If an account is used remotely, authentication of the maintenance provider can be performed by using callback or encryption.

Diagnostic Port Control. Many systems have diagnostic ports through which troubleshooters can directly access the hardware. These ports should be used only by authorized personnel and should not enable either internal or external unauthorized access. *Diagnostic port attacks* is the term that describes this type of abuse.

Hardware Physical Control. Many data processing areas that contain hardware might require locks and alarms. The following are some examples:

- Sensitive operator terminals and keyboards
- Media storage cabinets or rooms
- Server or communications equipment data centers
- Modem pools or telecommunication circuit rooms

Locks and alarms are described in more detail in Chapter 10.

Software Controls

An important element of operations controls is software support — controlling what software is used in a system. Elements of controls on software are as follows:

Anti-Virus Management. If personnel can load or execute any software on a system, the system is more vulnerable to viruses, unexpected software interactions, and to the subversion of security controls.

Software Testing. A rigid and formal software-testing process is required to determine compatibility with custom applications or to identify other unforeseen interactions. This procedure should also apply to software upgrades.

Software Utilities. Powerful systems utilities can compromise the integrity of operations systems and logical access controls. Their use must be controlled by security policy.

Safe Software Storage. A combination of logical and physical access controls should be implemented to ensure that the software and copies of backups have not been modified without proper authorization.

Backup Controls. Not only do support and operations personnel back up software and data, but in a distributed environment users may also back up their own data. It is very important to routinely test the restore accuracy of a backup system. A backup should also be stored securely to protect from theft, damage, or environmental problems. A description of the types of backups is in Chapter 3.

Privileged Entity Controls

Privileged entity access, which is also known as privileged operations functions, is defined as an extended or special access to computing resources given to operators and system administrators. Many job duties and functions require privileged access.

Privileged entity access is most often divided into classes. Operators should be assigned to a class based on their job title.

The following are some examples of privileged entity operator functions:

✦ Special access to system commands

✦ Access to special parameters

✦ Access to the system control program

Media Resource Protection

Media resource protection can be classified into two areas: media security controls and media viability controls. Media security controls are implemented to prevent any threat to C.I.A. by the intentional or unintentional exposure of sensitive data. Media viability controls are implemented to preserve the proper working state of the media, particularly to facilitate the timely and accurate restoration of the system after a failure.

Transparency of Controls

One important aspect of controls is the need for their transparency. Operators need to feel that security protections are reasonably flexible and that the security protections do not get in the way of doing their jobs. Ideally, the controls should not require users to perform extra steps, although realistically this result is hard to achieve. Transparency also aids in preventing users from learning too much about the security controls.

Restricting Hardware Instructions

A system control program restricts the execution of certain computing functions and permits them only when a processor is in a particular functional state, known as privileged or supervisor state. Applications can run in different states, during which different commands are permitted. To be authorized to execute privileged instructions, a program should be running in a restrictive state that enables these commands.

Media Security Controls

Media security controls should be designed to prevent the loss of sensitive information when the media is stored outside the system.

A CISSP candidate needs to know several of the following elements of media security controls:

> **Logging.** Logging the use of data media provides accountability. Logging also assists in physical inventory control by preventing tapes from "walking away" and by facilitating their recovery process.

> **Access Control.** Physical access control to the media is used to prevent unauthorized personnel from accessing the media. This procedure is also a part of physical inventory control.

> **Proper Disposal.** Proper disposal of the media after use is required to prevent data remanence. The process of removing information from used data media is called *sanitization*. Three techniques are commonly used for sanitization: overwriting, degaussing, and destruction. These are also described in Chapter 10.

Overwriting

Simply re-copying new data to the media is not recommended because the application may not completely overwrite the old data properly, and strict configuration controls must be in place on both the operating system and the software itself. Also, bad sectors on the media may not permit the software to overwrite old data properly.

To purge the media, the DoD requires overwriting with a pattern, then its complement, and finally with another pattern; for example, overwriting first with 0011 0101, followed by 1100 1010, then 1001 0111. To satisfy the DoD clearing requirement, it is required to write a character to all data locations in the disk. The number of times an overwrite must be accomplished depends on the storage media, sometimes on its sensitivity, and sometimes on differing DoD component requirements, but seven times is most commonly recommended.

Degaussing

Degaussing is often recommended as the best method for purging most magnetic media. Degaussing is a process whereby the magnetic media is erased, that is, returned to its initial virgin state. Erasure via degaussing may be accomplished in two ways:

✦ In AC erasure, the media is degaussed by applying an alternating field that is reduced in amplitude over time from an initial high value (i.e., AC-powered)

✦ In DC erasure, the media is saturated by applying a unidirectional field (i.e., DC-powered or by employing a permanent magnet)

Another point about degaussing: Degaussed magnetic hard drives will generally require restoration of factory-installed timing tracks, so data purging is recommended.

Destruction

Paper reports and diskettes need to be physically destroyed before disposal. Also, physical destruction of optical media (CD-ROM or WORM disks) is necessary.

Destruction techniques can include shredding or burning documentation, physically breaking CD-ROMS and diskettes, and destroying with acid. Paper reports should be shredded by personnel with the proper level of security clearance. Some shredders cut in straight lines or strips; others cross-cut or disintegrate the material into pulp. Care must be taken to limit access to the reports prior to disposal and those stored for long periods. Reports should never be disposed of without shredding, such as when they are placed in a dumpster intact. Burning is also sometimes used to destroy paper reports, especially in the DoD.

In some cases, acid is used to destroy disk pack surfaces. Applying a concentration of hydriodic acid (55% to 58% solution) to the gamma ferric oxide disk surface is a rarely used method of media destruction, and acid solutions should be used in a well-ventilated area only by qualified personnel.

Media Viability Controls

Many physical controls should be used to protect the viability of the data storage media. The goal is to protect the media from damage during handling and transportation or during short-term or long-term storage. Proper marking and labeling of the media is required in the event of a system recovery process.

Marking. All data storage media should be accurately marked or labeled. The labels can be used to identify media with special handling instructions or to log serial numbers or bar codes for retrieval during a system recovery.

There is a difference between this kind of physical storage media marking for inventory control and the logical data labeling of sensitivity classification for mandatory access control, which we described in other chapters, so please do not get them confused.

Handling. Proper handling of the media is important. Some issues with the handling of media include cleanliness of the media and the protection from physical damage to the media during transportation to the archive sites.

Storage. Storage of the media is very important for both security and environmental reasons. A proper heat- and humidity-free, clean storage environment should be provided for the media. Data media is sensitive to temperature, liquids, magnetism, smoke, and dust.

Physical Access Controls

The control of physical access to the resources is the major tenet of the Physical Security domain. Obviously, the Operations Security domain requires physical access control, and the following list contains examples of some of the elements of the operations resources that need physical access control.

Hardware

✦ Control of communications and the computing equipment

✦ Control of the storage media

✦ Control of the printed logs and reports

Software

✦ Control of the backup files

✦ Control of the system logs

✦ Control of the production applications

✦ Control of the sensitive/critical data

Obviously, all personnel require some sort of control and accountability when accessing physical resources, yet some personnel will require special physical access to perform their job functions. The following are examples of this type of personnel:

✦ IT department personnel

✦ Cleaning staff

✦ Heating ventilation and air conditioning (HVAC) maintenance personnel

✦ Third-party service contract personnel

✦ Consultants, contractors, and temporary staff

Special arrangements for supervision must be made when external support providers are entering a data center.

Physical piggybacking describes an unauthorized person going through a door behind an authorized person. The concept of a *man trap* (described in Chapter 10) is designed to prevent physical piggybacking.

Media Librarian

It is the job of a media librarian to control access to the media library and to regulate the media library environment. All media must be labeled in a human- and machine-readable form that should contain information such as the date and who created the media, the retention period, a volume name and version, and security classification.

Monitoring and Auditing

Operational assurance requires the process of reviewing an operational system to see that security controls, both automated and manual, are functioning correctly and effectively. Operational assurance addresses whether the system's technical features are being bypassed or have vulnerabilities and whether required procedures are being followed. To maintain operational assurance, organizations use two basic methods: system audits and monitoring. A system audit is a one-time or periodic event to evaluate security; monitoring refers to an ongoing activity that examines either the system or the users.

Problem identification and problem resolution are the primary goals of monitoring. The concept of monitoring is integral to almost all of the domains of information security. In Chapter 3 we described some technical aspects of monitoring and intrusion detection. Chapter 10 will also describe intrusion detection and monitoring from a physical access perspective. In this chapter, we are more concerned with monitoring the controls implemented in an operational facility in order to identify abnormal computer usage, such as inappropriate use or intentional fraud. Failure recognition and response, which includes reporting mechanisms, is an important part of monitoring.

Monitoring

Monitoring contains the mechanisms, tools, and techniques that permit the identification of security events that could impact the operation of a computer facility. It also includes the actions to identify the important elements of an event and to report that information appropriately.

The concept of monitoring includes monitoring for illegal software installation, monitoring the hardware for faults and error states, and monitoring operational events for anomalies.

Monitoring Techniques

To perform this type of monitoring, an information security professional has several tools at his or her disposal:

✦ Intrusion detection

✦ Penetration testing

✦ Violation processing using clipping levels

Intrusion Detection (ID)

Intrusion Detection (ID) is a useful tool that can assist in the detective analysis of intrusion attempts. ID can be used not only for the identification of intruders, but also to create a sampling of traffic patterns. By analyzing the activities occurring outside of normal clipping levels, a security practitioner can find evidence of events such as in-band signaling or other system abuses.

Penetration Testing

Penetration testing is the process of testing a network's defenses by attempting to access the system from the outside, using the same techniques that an external intruder (for example, a cracker) would use. This testing gives a security professional a better snapshot of the organization's security posture.

Among the techniques used to perform a penetration test are:

> **Scanning and Probing.** Various scanners, such as a port scanner, can reveal information about a network's infrastructure and enable an intruder to access the network's unsecured ports.

> **Demon Dialing.** Demon (or "war") dialers automatically test every phone line in an exchange to try to locate modems that are attached to the network. Information about these modems can then be used to attempt external unauthorized access.

> **Sniffing.** A protocol analyzer can be used to capture data packets that are later decoded to collect information such as passwords or infrastructure configurations.

Other techniques that are not solely technology-based can be used to complement the penetration test. The following are examples of such techniques:

> **Dumpster Diving.** Searching paper disposal areas for unshredded or otherwise improperly disposed of reports.

> **Social Engineering.** The most commonly used technique of all: getting information (like passwords) just by asking for them.

Violation Analysis

One of the most-used techniques to track anomalies in user activity is violation tracking, processing, and analysis. To make violation tracking effective, clipping levels must be established. A *clipping level* is a baseline of user activity that is considered a routine level of user errors. A clipping level enables a system to ignore normal user errors. When the clipping level is exceeded, a violation record is then produced. Clipping levels are also used for variance detection.

Independent Testing

It is important to note that in most cases, external penetration testing should be performed by a reputable, experienced firm that is independent of an organization's IT or Audit departments. This independence guarantees an objective, nonpolitical report on the state of the company's defenses. The firm must be fully vetted, however, and full legal nondisclosure issues must be resolved to the organization's satisfaction before work begins. For this reason, "Black Hat" testers — that is, ex-crackers now working for security firms — are often not recommended.

Using clipping levels and profile-based anomaly detection, the following are the types of violations that should be tracked, processed, and analyzed:

✦ Repetitive mistakes that exceed the clipping level number

✦ Individuals who exceed their authority

✦ Too many people with unrestricted access

✦ Patterns indicating serious intrusion attempts

Profile-based anomaly detection uses profiles to look for abnormalities in user behavior. A profile is a pattern that characterizes the behavior of users. Patterns of usage are established according to the various types of activities the users engage in, such as processing exceptions, resource utilization, and patterns in actions performed, for example. The ways in which the various types of activity are recorded in the profile are referred to as profile metrics.

Benefits of Incident-Handling Capability

The primary benefits of employing an incident-handling capability are containing and repairing damage from incidents and preventing future damage. Additional benefits related to establishing an incident-handling capability are*:

Enhancement of the risk assessment process. An incident-handling capability will allow organizations to collect threat data that may be useful in their risk assessment and safeguard selection processes (e.g, in designing new systems). Statistics on the numbers and types of incidents in the organization can be used in the risk-assessment process as an indication of vulnerabilities and threats.

Enhancement of internal communications and the readiness of the organization to respond to any type of incident, not just computer security incidents. Internal communications will be improved; management will be better organized to receive communications; and contacts within public affairs, legal staff, law enforcement, and other groups will have been pre-established.

---

*Source: National Institute of Standards and Technology Special Publication 800-12, *An Introduction to Computer Security: The NIST Handbook.*

Security training personnel will have a better understanding of users' knowledge of security issues. Trainers can use actual incidents to vividly illustrate the importance of computer security. Training that is based on current threats and controls recommended by incident-handling staff provides users with information more specifically directed to their current needs, thereby reducing the risks to the organization from incidents.

Auditing

The implementation of regular system audits is the foundation of operational security controls monitoring. In addition to enabling internal and external compliance checking, regular auditing of audit (transaction) trails and logs can assist the monitoring function by helping to recognize patterns of abnormal user behavior.

Security Auditing

Information Technology (IT) auditors are often divided into two types: internal and external. Internal auditors typically work for a given organization while external auditors do not. External auditors are often Certified Public Accountants (CPAs) or other audit professionals who are hired to perform an independent audit of an organization's financial statements. Internal auditors, on the other hand, usually have a much broader mandate: checking for compliance and standards of due care, auditing operational cost efficiencies, and recommending the appropriate controls.

IT auditors typically audit the following functions:

✦ Backup controls

✦ System and transaction controls

✦ Data library procedures

✦ Systems development standards

✦ Data center security

✦ Contingency plans

In addition, IT auditors might recommend improvements to controls, and they often participate in a system's development process to help an organization avoid costly re-engineering after the system's implementation.

User Account Review

It is necessary to regularly review user accounts on a system. Such reviews may examine the levels of access each individual has, conformity with the concept of least privilege, whether all accounts are still active, whether management authorizations are up-to-date, or whether required training has been completed, for example. These reviews can be conducted on at least two levels: on an application-by-application basis or on a systemwide basis. Both kinds of reviews can be conducted by, among others, in-house systems personnel (a self-audit), the organization's internal audit staff, or external auditors

Audit Trails

An audit trail is a set of records that collectively provide documentary evidence of processing used to aid in tracing from original transactions forward to related records and reports, and/or backward from records and reports to their component source transactions. Audit trails may be limited to specific events, or they may encompass all of the activities on a system.

An audit (or transaction) trail enables a security practitioner to trace a transaction's history. This transaction trail provides information about additions, deletions, or modifications to the data within a system. Audit trails enable the enforcement of individual accountability by creating a reconstruction of events. Like monitoring, one purpose of an audit trail is to assist in a problem's identification that leads to a problem's resolution. An effectively implemented audit trail also enables an auditor to retrieve and easily certify the data. Any unusual activity or variation from the established procedures should be identified and investigated.

The audit logs should record the following:

✦ The transaction's date and time

✦ Who processed the transaction

✦ At which terminal the transaction was processed

✦ Various security events relating to the transaction

In addition, an auditor should examine the audit logs for the following:

✦ Amendments to production jobs

✦ Production job reruns

✦ Computer operator practices

User audit trails can usually log:

✦ All commands directly initiated by the user

✦ All identification and authentication attempts

✦ Files and resources accessed

It is most useful if options and parameters are also recorded from commands. It is much more useful to know that a user tried to delete a log file (e.g., to hide unauthorized actions) than to know the user merely issued the delete command, possibly for a personal data file.

The audit mechanism of a computer system has five important security goals*:

1. The audit mechanism must "allow the review of patterns of access to individual objects, access histories of specific processes and individuals, and the use of the various protection mechanisms supported by the system and their effectiveness."

2. Allow discovery of both users' and outsiders' repeated attempts to bypass the protection mechanisms.

3. Allow discovery of any use of privileges that may occur when a user assumes a functionality with privileges greater than his or her own, i.e., programmer to administrator. In this case, there may be no bypass of security controls, but nevertheless, a violation is made possible.

4. Act as a deterrent against perpetrators' habitual attempts to bypass the system protection mechanisms. However, to act as a deterrent, the perpetrator must be aware of the audit mechanism's existence and its active use to detect any attempts to bypass system protection mechanisms.

5. Supply "an additional form of user assurance that attempts to bypass the protection mechanisms that are recorded and discovered."** Even if the attempt to bypass the protection mechanism is successful, the audit trail will still provide assurance by its ability to aid in assessing the damage done by the violation, thus improving the system's ability to control the damage.

Other important security issues regarding the use of audit logs are:

✦ Retention and protection of the audit media and reports when their storage is offsite

✦ Protection against the alteration of audit or transaction logs

✦ Protection against the unavailability of an audit media during an event

---

*Source: National Institute of Standards and Technology Special Publication 800-12, *An Introduction to Computer Security: The NIST Handbook*.

**Sources: NCSC-TG-001, A Guide to Understanding Audit in Trusted Systems [Tan Book]; Guidelines for Trusted Facility Management and Audit, by Virgil D. Gligor, University of Maryland, 1985.

Problem Management Concepts

Effective auditing embraces the concepts of problem management. Problem management is a way to control the process of problem isolation and problem resolution. An auditor might use problem management to resolve the issues arising from an IT security audit, for example.

The goal of problem management is threefold:

1. To reduce failures to a manageable level
2. To prevent the occurrence or reoccurrence of a problem
3. To mitigate the negative impact of problems on computing services and resources

The first step in implementing problem management is to define the potential problem areas and the abnormal events that should be investigated. Some examples of potential problem areas are:

✦ The performance and availability of computing resources and services

✦ The system and networking infrastructure

✦ Procedures and transactions

✦ The safety and security of personnel

Some examples of abnormal events that could be discovered during an audit are as follows:

✦ Degraded hardware or software resource availability

✦ Deviations from the standard transaction procedures

✦ Unexplained occurrences in a processing chain

Of course, the final objective of problem management is resolution of the problem.

Electronic Audit Trails

Maintaining a proper audit trail is more difficult now because fewer transactions are recorded to paper media and will thus always stay in an electronic form. In the old paper system, a physical purchase order might be prepared with multiple copies, initiating a physical, permanent paper trail. An auditor's job is now more complicated because digital media is more transient and a paper trail might not exist.

Threats and Vulnerabilities

A threat is simply any event that, if realized, can cause damage to a system and create a loss of confidentiality, availability, or integrity. Threats can be malicious, such as the intentional modification of sensitive information, or they can be accidental — such as an error in a transaction calculation or the accidental deletion of a file.

A vulnerability is a weakness in a system that can be exploited by a threat. Reducing the vulnerable aspects of a system can reduce the risk and impact of threats on the system. For example, a password-generation tool, which helps users choose robust passwords, reduces the chance that users will select poor passwords (the vulnerability) and makes the password more difficult to crack (the threat of external attack).

Threats and vulnerabilities are discussed in several of the 10 domains; for example, many examples of attacks are given in Chapter 2.

Threats

We have grouped the threats into several categories, and we will describe some of the elements of each category.

Accidental Loss

Accidental loss is a loss that is incurred unintentionally, either through the lack of operator training or proficiency or by the malfunctioning of an application's processing procedure. The following are some examples of the types of accidental loss:

> **Operator input errors and omissions.** Manual input transaction errors, entry or data deletion, and faulty data modification.

> **Transaction processing errors.** Errors that are introduced into the data through faulty application programming or processing procedures.

Inappropriate Activities

Inappropriate activity is computer behavior that, while not rising to the level of criminal activity, might be grounds for job action or dismissal.

> **Inappropriate Content.** Using the company systems to store pornography, entertainment, political, or violent content.

> **Waste of Corporate Resources.** Personal use of hardware or software, such as conducting a private business with a company's computer system.

> **Sexual or Racial Harassment.** Using email or other computer resources to distribute inappropriate material.

> **Abuse of Privileges or Rights.** Using unauthorized access levels to violate the confidentiality of sensitive company information.

Illegal Computer Operations and Intentional Attacks

Under this heading, we have grouped the areas of computer activities that are considered as intentional and illegal computer activity for personal financial gain for destruction:

Eavesdropping. Data scavenging, traffic or trend analysis, social engineering, economic or political espionage, sniffing, dumpster diving, keystroke monitoring, and shoulder surfing are all types of eavesdropping to gain information or to create a foundation for a later attack. Eavesdropping is a primary cause of the failure of confidentiality.

Fraud. Examples of the types of fraud are collusion, falsified transactions, data manipulation, and other altering of data integrity for gain.

Theft. Examples of the types of theft are the theft of information or trade secrets for profit or unauthorized disclosure, and physical theft of hardware or software.

Sabotage. Sabotage includes denial of service (DoS), production delays, and data integrity sabotage.

External Attack. Examples of external attacks are malicious cracking, scanning, and probing to gain infrastructure information, demon dialing to locate an unsecured modem line, and the insertion of a malicious code or virus.

Vulnerabilities and Attacks

Traffic/Trend Analysis. Traffic analysis, which is sometimes called trend analysis, is a technique employed by an intruder that involves analyzing data characteristics (message length, message frequency, and so forth) and the patterns of transmissions (rather than any knowledge of the actual information transmitted) to infer information that might be useful to an intruder.

Countermeasures to traffic analysis are similar to the countermeasures to crypto-attacks:

- *Padding messages*. Creating all messages to be a uniform data size by filling empty space in the data

- *Sending noise*. Transmitting non-informational data elements mixed in with real information to disguise the real message

- *Covert channel analysis.* Previously described in the "Orange Book Controls" section of this chapter

Maintenance Accounts. It is a method used to break into computer systems by using maintenance accounts that still have factory-set or easily guessed passwords. Physical access to the hardware by maintenance personnel can also constitute a security violation. (See the "Hardware Controls" section earlier in this chapter.)

Data-Scavenging Attacks. Data scavenging is the technique of piecing together information from found bits of data. There are two common types of data-scavenging attacks:

1. *Keyboard Attacks.* Data scavenging through the resources that are available to normal system users who are sitting at the keyboard and using normal utilities and tools to glean information.

2. *Laboratory Attacks.* Data scavenging by using very precise electronic equipment; these are planned, orchestrated attacks.

IPL Vulnerabilities. The start of a system, the initial program load (IPL), presents very specific system vulnerabilities, whether the system is a centralized mainframe type or a distributed LAN type. During the IPL, the operator brings up the facility's system. This operator has the ability to put a system into a single-user mode, without full security features, which is a very powerful ability. In this state, an operator could load unauthorized programs or data, reset passwords, rename various resources, or reset the system's time and date. The operator could also reassign the data ports or communications lines to transmit information to a confederate outside the data center. In a LAN, a system administrator could start the boot sequence from a tape, CD-ROM, or floppy disk—bypassing the operating system's security on the hard drive.

Social Engineering. This attack uses social skills to obtain information. Common techniques used by an intruder to gain either physical access or system access are*:

• *Asserting authority or pulling rank.* Professing to have the authority, perhaps supported with altered identification, to enter the facility or system

• *Intimidating or threatening.* Browbeating the access control subjects with harsh language or threatening behavior to permit access or release information

• *Praising, flattering, or sympathizing.* Using positive reinforcement to coerce the subjects into giving access or information for system access

Network Address Hijacking. It might be possible for an intruder to reroute data traffic from a server or network device to a personal machine, either by device address modification or by network address "hijacking." This diversion enables the intruder to capture traffic to and from the devices for data analysis or modification or to steal the password file from the server and gain access to user accounts. By rerouting the data output, the intruder can obtain supervisory terminal functions and bypass the system logs.

---

*Source: *Fighting Computer Crime* by Donn B. Parker, Wiley, 1998.

✦   ✦   ✦

Assessment Questions

You can find the answers to the following questions in Appendix A.

1. Place the four systems security modes of operation in order, from the most secure to the least:

   a. System High Mode, Dedicated Mode, Compartmented Mode, and Multilevel Mode

   b. Dedicated Mode, System High Mode, Compartmented Mode, and Multilevel Mode

   c. Dedicated Mode, System High Mode, Multilevel Mode, and Compartmented Mode

   d. System High Mode, Compartmented Mode, Dedicated Mode, and Multilevel Mode

2. Why is security an issue when a system is booted into "single-user mode"?

   a. The operating system is started without the security front-end loaded.

   b. The users cannot log in to the system, and they will complain.

   c. Proper forensics cannot be executed while in single-user mode.

   d. Backup tapes cannot be restored while in single-user mode.

3. An audit trail is an example of what type of control?

   a. Deterrent control

   b. Preventative control

   c. Detective control

   d. Application control

4. Which media control below is the BEST choice to prevent data remanence on magnetic tapes or floppy disks?

   a. Overwriting the media with new application data

   b. Degaussing the media

   c. Applying a concentration of hydriodic acid (55% to 58% solution) to the gamma ferric oxide disk surface

   d. Making sure the disk is recirculated as quickly as possible to prevent object reuse

5. Which choice below is NOT a security goal of an audit mechanism?

    a. Deter perpetrators' attempts to bypass the system protection mechanisms

    b. Review employee production output records

    c. Review patterns of access to individual objects

    d. Discover when a user assumes a functionality with privileges greater than his own

6. Which task below would normally be a function of the security administrator, not the system administrator?

    a. Installing system software

    b. Adding and removing system users

    c. Reviewing audit data

    d. Managing print queues

7. Which of the following is a reason to institute output controls?

    a. To preserve the integrity of the data in the system while changes are being made to the configuration

    b. To protect the output's confidentiality

    c. To detect irregularities in the software's operation

    d. To recover damage after an identified system failure

8. Which statement below is NOT correct about reviewing user accounts?

    a. User account reviews cannot be conducted by outside auditors.

    b. User account reviews can examine conformity with the concept of least privilege.

    c. User account reviews may be conducted on a systemwide basis.

    d. User account reviews may be conducted on an application-by-application basis.

9. Which term below MOST accurately describes the trusted computing base (TCB)?

    a. A computer that controls all access to objects by subjects

    b. A piece of information that represents the security level of an object

    c. Formal proofs used to demonstrate the consistency between a system's specification and a security model

    d. The totality of protection mechanisms within a computer system

10. Which statement below is accurate about the concept of object reuse?

   a. Object reuse protects against physical attacks on the storage medium.

   b. Object reuse ensures that users do not obtain residual information from system resources.

   c. Object reuse applies to removable media only.

   d. Object reuse controls the granting of access rights to objects.

11. Using prenumbered forms to initiate a transaction is an example of what type of control?

   a. Deterrent control

   b. Preventative control

   c. Detective control

   d. Application control

12. Which choice below is the BEST description of operational assurance?

   a. Operational assurance is the process of examining audit logs to reveal usage that identifies misuse.

   b. Operational assurance has the benefit of containing and repairing damage from incidents.

   c. Operational assurance is the process of reviewing an operational system to see that security controls are functioning correctly.

   d. Operational assurance is the process of performing pre-employment background screening.

13. Which of the following is NOT a proper media control?

   a. The data media should be logged to provide a physical inventory control.

   b. All data storage media should be accurately marked.

   c. A proper storage environment should be provided for the media.

   d. The media that is reused in a sensitive environment does not need sanitization.

14. Which choice below is considered the HIGHEST level of operator privilege?

   a. Read/Write

   b. Read Only

   c. Access Change

   d. Write Only

15. Which choice below MOST accurately describes a covert storage channel?

  a. A process that manipulates observable system resources in a way that affects response time

  b. An information transfer path within a system

  c. A communication channel that allows a process to transfer information in a manner that violates the system's security policy

  d. An information transfer that involves the direct or indirect writing of a storage location by one process and the direct or indirect reading of the storage location by another process

16. Which choice below would NOT be a common element of a transaction trail?

  a. The date and time of the transaction

  b. Who processed the transaction

  c. Why the transaction was processed

  d. At which terminal the transaction was processed

17. Which choice below would NOT be considered a benefit of employing incident-handling capability?

  a. An individual acting alone would not be able to subvert a security process or control.

  b. It enhances internal communications and the readiness of the organization to respond to incidents.

  c. It assists an organization in preventing damage from future incidents.

  d. Security training personnel would have a better understanding of users' knowledge of security issues.

18. Which choice below is the BEST description of an audit trail?

  a. Audit trails are used to detect penetration of a computer system and to reveal usage that identifies misuse.

  b. An audit trail is a device that permits simultaneous data processing of two or more security levels without risk of compromise.

  c. An audit trail mediates all access to objects within the network by subjects within the network.

  d. Audit trails are used to prevent access to sensitive systems by unauthorized personnel.

19. Which choice below best describes the function of change control?

    a. To ensure that system changes are implemented in an orderly manner

    b. To guarantee that an operator is given only the privileges needed for the task

    c. To guarantee that transaction records are retained IAW compliance requirements

    d. To assign parts of security-sensitive tasks to more than one individual

20. Which choice below is NOT an example of intentionally inappropriate operator activity?

    a. Making errors when manually inputting transactions

    b. Using the company's system to store pornography

    c. Conducting private business on the company system

    d. Using unauthorized access levels to violate information confidentiality

21. Which book of the Rainbow Series addresses the Trusted Computer System Evaluation Criteria (TCSEC)?

    a. Red Book

    b. Orange Book

    c. Green Book

    d. Purple Book

22. Which term below BEST describes the concept of "least privilege"?

    a. Each user is granted the lowest clearance required for his or her tasks.

    b. A formal separation of command, program, and interface functions.

    c. A combination of classification and categories that represents the sensitivity of information.

    d. Active monitoring of facility entry access points.

23. Which choice below BEST describes a threat as defined in the Operations Security domain?

    a. A potential incident that could cause harm

    b. A weakness in a system that could be exploited

    c. A company resource that could be lost due to an incident

    d. The minimization of loss associated with an incident

24. Which choice below is NOT a common element of user account administration?

    a. Periodically verifying the legitimacy of current accounts and access authorizations

    b. Authorizing the request for a user's system account

    c. Tracking users and their respective access authorizations

    d. Establishing, issuing, and closing user accounts

25. Which choice below is NOT an example of using a social engineering technique to gain physical access to a secure facility?

    a. Asserting authority or pulling rank

    b. Intimidating or threatening

    c. Praising or flattering

    d. Employing the salami fraud

26. Which statement about covert channel analysis is NOT true?

    a. It is an operational assurance requirement that is specified in the Orange Book.

    b. It is required for B2 class systems in order to protect against covert storage channels.

    c. It is required for B2 class systems to protect against covert timing channels.

    d. It is required for B3 class systems to protect against both covert storage and covert timing channels.

27. "Separation of duties" embodies what principle?

    a. An operator does not know more about the system than the minimum required to do the job.

    b. Two operators are required to work in tandem to perform a task.

    c. The operators' duties are frequently rotated.

    d. The operators have different duties to prevent one person from compromising the system.

28. Convert Channel Analysis, Trusted Facility Management, and Trusted Recovery are parts of which book in the TCSEC Rainbow Series?

    a. Red Book

    b. Orange Book

    c. Green Book

    d. Dark Green Book

29. How do covert timing channels convey information?

    a. By changing a system's stored data characteristics

    b. By generating noise and traffic with the data

    c. By performing a covert channel analysis

    d. By modifying the timing of a system resource in some measurable way

30. Which of the following would be the BEST description of clipping levels?

    a. A baseline of user errors above which violations will be recorded

    b. A listing of every error made by users to initiate violation processing

    c. Variance detection of too many people with unrestricted access

    d. Changes a system's stored data characteristics

Applications and Systems Development

There are information system security issues associated with applications software, whether the software is developed internally or acquired from an external source. This chapter addresses these security issues from the viewpoint of the developer, user, and information system security specialist. Thus, a CISSP professional should understand the following areas:

✦ Systems engineering

✦ The software life cycle development process

✦ The software process capability maturity model

✦ Object-oriented systems

✦ Artificial intelligence systems

✦ Database systems

  • Database security issues

  • Data warehousing

  • Data mining

  • Data dictionaries

✦ Application controls

Systems Engineering

Systems engineering is discussed in detail in Chapter 11, but is summarized at the beginning of this section to provide a perspective on the application software life cycle process.

A common definition of *systems engineering* states that it is the branch of engineering concerned with the development of large and complex systems, where a *system* is understood to be an assembly or combination of interrelated elements or parts working together toward a common objective.

The International Council on Systems Engineering (INCOSE), www.incose.org, states, "systems engineering integrates all the disciplines and specialty groups into a team effort forming a structured development process that proceeds from concept to production to operation. Systems engineering considers both the business and the technical needs of all customers with the goal of providing a quality product that meets the user needs."

Chapter 3 of the Information Assurance Technical Forum (www.iatf.net) document 3.1, detailed in Chapter 11, defines a generic systems engineering process that comprises the following components:

✦ Discover needs

✦ Define system requirements

✦ Design system architecture

✦ Develop detailed design

✦ Implement system

✦ Assess effectiveness

The System Life Cycle or System Development Life Cycle (SDLC)

 The System Life Cycle, or System Development Life Cycle (SDLC), as it is sometimes known, is also covered in extensive detail in Chapter 11. The principal elements of the SDLC are given in *Generally Accepted Principles and Practices for Securing Information Technology Systems* (SP 800-14, National Institute of Standards and Technology, September 1996) and *Security Considerations in the Information System Development Life Cycle* (SP 800-64, National Institute of Standards and Technology, September, October 2003). The phases of the System Life Cycle as given in NIST SP 800-14 are:

✦ *Initiation* — The need for the system and its purpose are documented. A *sensitivity assessment* is conducted as part of this phase. A sensitivity assessment evaluates the sensitivity of the IT system and the information to be processed.

✦ *Development/Acquisition* — Comprises the system acquisition and development cycles. In this phase, the system is designed, developed, programmed, and acquired.

✦ *Implementation* — Installation, testing, security testing, and accreditation are conducted.

✦ *Operation/Maintenance* — The system performs its designed functions. This phase includes security operations, modification/addition of hardware and/or software, administration, operational assurance, monitoring, and audits.

✦ *Disposal* — Disposition of system components and products, such as hardware, software, and information; disk sanitization; archiving files; and moving equipment.

The Software Life Cycle Development Process

Software engineering can be defined as the science and art of specifying, designing, implementing, and evolving programs, documentation, and operating procedures so that computers can be made useful to man. This definition is a combination of popular definitions of engineering and software. One definition of engineering is the application of science and mathematics to the design and construction of artifacts that are useful to man. A definition of software is that it consists of the programs, documentation, and operating procedures by which computers can be made useful to man.

In software engineering, the term *verification* is defined as the process of establishing the truth of correspondence between a software product and its specification. *Validation* establishes the fitness or worth of a software product for its operational mission. *Requirements*, as defined in the Waterfall model (W.W. Royce, "Managing the Development of Large Software Systems: Concepts and Techniques," *Proceedings*, WESCON, August 1970), are a complete, validated specification of the required functions, interfaces, and performance for the software product. *Product design* is a complete, verified specification of the overall hardware-software architecture, control structure, and data structure for the product.

Quality software is difficult to obtain without a development process. As with any project, two principal goals of software development are to produce a quality product that meets the customer's requirements and to stay within the budget and time schedule. A succession of models has emerged over time, incorporating improvements in the development process. An early model defined succeeding stages, taking into account the different staffing and planning that was required for each stage. The model was simplistic in that it assumed that each step could be completed and finalized without any effect from the later stages that might require rework. This model is shown in Figure 7-1.

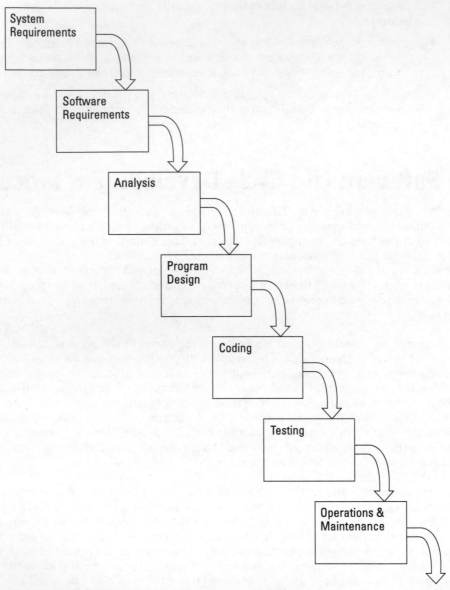

Figure 7-1: A simplistic software development model.

The Waterfall Model

Because subsequent stages, such as design, coding, and testing, in the development process might require modifying earlier stages in the model, the Waterfall model emerged. Under this model, software development can be managed if the developers are limited to going back only one stage to rework. If this limitation is not imposed (particularly on a large project with several team members), then any developer can be working on any phase at any time and the required rework might be accomplished several times. Obviously, this approach results in a lack of project control, and it is difficult to manage. The Waterfall model is shown in Figure 7-2.

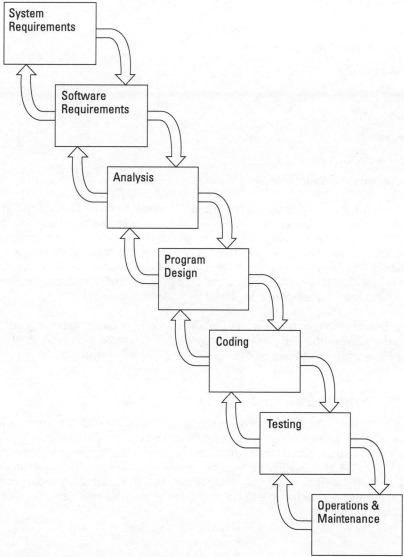

Figure 7-2: The Waterfall model.

One fundamental problem with these models is that they assume that a phase or stage ends at a specific time; however, this is not usually the case in real-world applications. If an ending phase is forcibly tied to a project milestone, the situation can be improved. If rework is required in this mode, the phase is not officially pronounced as ending. The rework must then be accomplished and the project milestone met before the phase is officially recognized as completed. In summary, the steps of the Waterfall model are:

✦ System feasibility

✦ Software plans and requirements

✦ Product design

✦ Detailed design

✦ Code

✦ Integration

✦ Implementation

✦ Operations and maintenance

In 1976, Barry Boehm reinterpreted the Waterfall model to have phases end at project milestones and to have the backward arrows represent back references for *verification and validation* (V&V) against defined baselines. Verification evaluates the product during development against the specification, and validation refers to the work product satisfying the real-world requirements and concepts. In simpler terms, Barry Boehm states, "Verification is doing the job right, and validation is doing the right job." These concepts are illustrated in Figure 7-3.

In this modified version of the Waterfall model, the end of each phase is a point in time for which no iteration of phases is provided. Rework can be accomplished within a phase when the phase end review shows that it is required.

The Spiral Model

In 1988 at TRW, Barry Boehm developed the *Spiral model*, which is actually a meta-model that incorporates a number of the software development models. This model depicts a spiral that incorporates the various phases of software development. As shown in Figure 7-4, the angular dimension represents the progress made in completing the phases, and the radial dimension represents cumulative project cost. The model states that each cycle of the spiral involves the same series of steps for each part of the project.

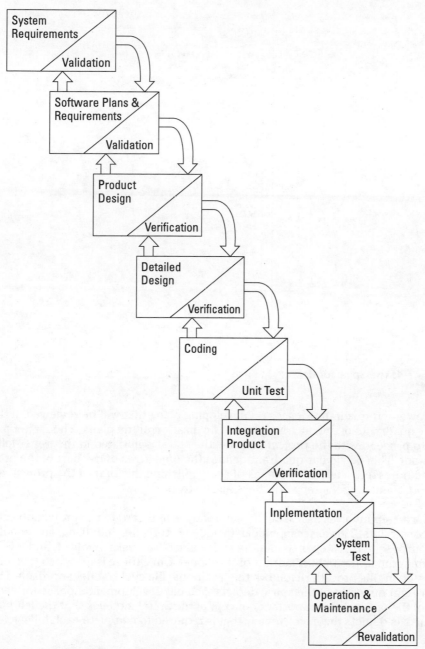

Figure 7-3: A modified Waterfall model incorporating V&V.

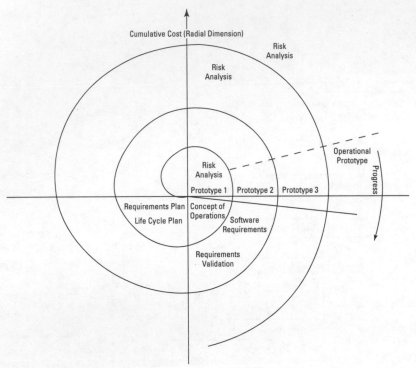

Figure 7-4: The Spiral model.

The lower-left quadrant focuses on developing plans that will be reviewed in the upper quadrants of the diagram prior to finalization of the plans. Then, after a decision to proceed with the project is made, the spiral is initiated in the upper-left quadrant. This particular quadrant defines the objectives of the part of the project being addressed, alternative means of accomplishing this part of the project, and the constraints associated with these alternatives.

The next step involves assessing the alternatives in regard to the project objectives and constraints. This assessment can include prototyping, modeling, and simulation. The purpose of this step is to identify and evaluate the risks involved, and it is shown in the upper-right quadrant of the model. Once these issues are resolved, the next step in this procedure follows the traditional life cycle model approach. The lower-right quadrant of the spiral depicts the final developmental phase for each part of the product. An important concept of the Spiral model is that the left horizontal axis depicts the major review that is required to complete each full cycle.

Cost Estimation Models

An early model for estimating the cost of software development projects was the *Basic COCOMO Model* proposed by Barry Boehm (B.W. Boehm, *Software Engineering Economics*, Prentice-Hall, Englewood Cliffs, New Jersey, 1981). This model estimates software development effort and cost as a function of the size of the software product in source instructions. It develops the following equations:

✦ "The number of man-months (MM) required to develop the most common type of software product, in terms of the number of thousands of delivered source instructions (KDSI) in the software product"

$$MM = 2.4 \ (KDSI)^{1.05}$$

✦ "The development schedule (TDEV) in months"

$$TDEV = 2.5(MM)^{0.38}$$

In addition, Boehm has developed an *Intermediate COCOMO Model* that takes into account hardware constraints, personnel quality, use of modern tools, and other attributes and their aggregate impact on overall project costs. A *Detailed COCOMO Model* by Boehm accounts for the effects of the additional factors used in the intermediate model on the costs of individual project phases.

Another model, the *function point measurement model*, does not require the user to estimate the number of delivered source instructions. The software development effort is determined by using the following five user functions:

✦ External input types

✦ External output types

✦ Logical internal file types

✦ External interface file types

✦ External inquiry types

These functions are tallied and weighted according to complexity and used to determine the software development effort.

A third type of model applies the Rayleigh curve to software development cost and effort estimation. A prominent model using this approach is the *Software Life Cycle Model* (SLIM) estimating method. In this method, estimates based on the number of lines of source code are modified by the following two factors:

✦ The *manpower buildup index* (MBI), which estimates the rate of buildup of staff on the project

✦ A *productivity factor* (PF), which is based on the technology used

Information Security and the Life Cycle Model

As is the case with most engineering and software development practices, the earlier in the process a component is introduced, the better chance there is for success, lower development costs, and reduced rework. Information security is no exception. The conception, development, implementation, testing, and maintenance of information security controls should be conducted concurrently with the system software life cycle phases. This approach is conceptually shown in Figure 7-5.

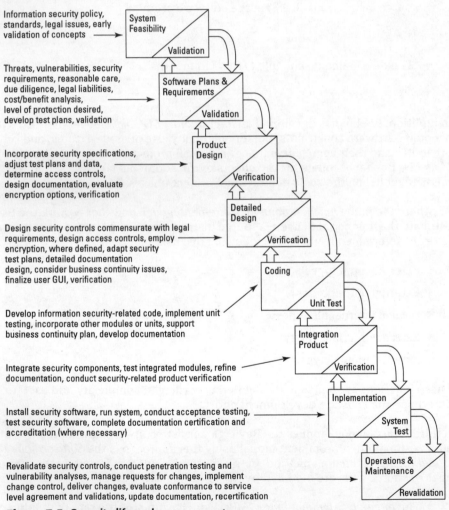

Figure 7-5: Security life cycle components.

Testing Issues

Testing of the software modules or unit testing should be addressed when the modules are being designed. Personnel separate from the programmers should conduct this testing. The test data is part of the specifications. Testing should not only check the modules using normal and valid input data, but it should also check for incorrect types, out-of-range values, and other bounds and/or conditions. Live or actual field data is not recommended for use in the testing procedures because both data types might not cover out-of-range situations and the correct outputs of the test are unknown. Special test suites of data that exercise all paths of the software to the fullest extent possible and whose correct resulting outputs are known beforehand should be used.

The Software Maintenance Phase and the Change Control Process

In the life cycle models we have presented, the maintenance phase is listed at the end of the cycle with operations. One way of looking at the maintenance phase is to divide it into the following three subphases:

1. Request control
2. Change control
3. Release control

The request control activity manages the users' requests for changes to the software product and gathers information that can be used for managing this activity. The following steps are included in this activity:

✦ Establishing the priorities of requests

✦ Estimating the cost of the changes requested

✦ Determining the interface that is presented to the user

The change control process is the principal step in the maintenance phase. Issues that are addressed by change control include the following:

✦ Recreating and analyzing the problem

✦ Developing the changes and corresponding tests

✦ Performing quality control

In addition, there are also other considerations such as the following:

✦ The tool types to be used in implementing the changes

✦ The documentation of the changes

✦ The restriction of the changes' effects on other parts of the code

✦ Recertification and accreditation, if necessary

Release control is associated with issuing the latest release of the software. This step involves deciding which requests will be included in the new release, archiving of the release, configuration management, quality control, distribution, and acceptance testing.

Configuration Management

In order to manage evolving changes to software products and to formally track and issue new versions of software products, configuration management is employed. According to the British Standards Institution (British Standards Institute, U.K., "Information Security Management, British Standard 7799," 1998), *configuration management* is "the discipline of identifying the components of a continually evolving system for the purposes of controlling changes to those components and maintaining integrity and traceability throughout the life cycle." The following definitions are associated with configuration management:

Configuration item. A component whose state is to be recorded and against which changes are to be progressed.

Version. A recorded state of the configuration item.

Configuration. A collection of component configuration items that comprise a configuration item in some stage of its evolution (recursive).

Building. The process of assembling a version of a configuration item from versions of its component configuration items.

Build list. The set of the versions of the component configuration items that is used to build a version of a configuration item.

Software library. A controlled area that is accessible only to approved users who are restricted to the use of approved procedures.

The following procedures are associated with configuration management:

1. Identify and document the functional and physical characteristics of each configuration item (*configuration identification*).

2. Control changes to the configuration items and issue versions of configuration items from the software library (*configuration control*).

3. Record the processing of changes (*configuration status accounting*).

4. Control the quality of the configuration management procedures (*configuration audit*).

The Software Capability Maturity Model (CMM)

The Software CMM is based on the premise that the quality of a software product is a direct function of the quality of its associated software development and maintenance processes. A process is defined by the Carnegie Mellon University Software Engineering Institute (SEI) as "a set of activities, methods, practices, and transformations that people use to develop and maintain systems and associated products" (SEI, "The Capability Maturity Model: Guidelines for Improving the Software Process," Addison Wesley, 1995).

The Software CMM was first developed by the SEI in 1986 with support from the Mitre Corporation. The SEI defines five maturity levels that serve as a foundation for conducting continuous process improvement and as an ordinal scale for measuring the maturity of the organization involved in the software processes. The following are the five maturity levels and their corresponding focuses and characteristics:

Level 1: Initiating. Competent people and heroics; processes are informal and ad hoc.

Level 2: Repeatable. Project management processes; project management practices are institutionalized.

Level 3: Defined. Engineering processes and organizational support; technical practices are integrated with management practices.

Level 4: Managed. Product and process improvement; product and process are quantitatively controlled.

Level 5: Optimizing. Continuous process improvement; process improvement is institutionalized.

In the CMM for software, *software process capability* "describes the range of expected results that can be achieved by following a software process." Software process capability is a means of predicting the outcome of the next software project conducted by an organization. *Software process performance* is the result achieved by following a software process. Thus, software capability is aimed at expected results while software performance is focused on results that have been achieved.

Software process maturity, then, provides for the potential for growth in capability of an organization. An immature organization develops software in a crisis mode, usually exceeds budgets and time schedules, and software processes are developed in an ad hoc fashion during the project. In a mature organization, the software process is effectively communicated to staff, the required processes are documented and consistent, software quality is evaluated, and roles and responsibilities are understood for the project.

The Software CMM is a component that supports the concept of continuous process improvement. This concept is embodied in the SEI Process Improvement IDEAL Model and is shown in Figure 7-6.

Phase 1 of the IDEAL Model is the initiation phase in which management support is obtained for process improvement, the objectives and constraints of the process improvement effort are defined, and the resources and plans for the next phase are obtained.

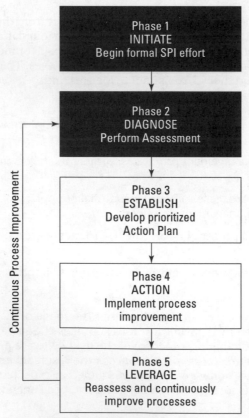

Figure 7-6: The IDEAL model.

Phase 2 identifies the appropriate appraisal method (such as CMM-based), identifies the project(s) to be appraised, trains the appraisal team, conducts the appraisal, and briefs management and the organization on the appraisal results.

In Phase 3, an action plan is developed based on the results of Phase 2, management is briefed on the action plan, and the resources and group(s) are coordinated to implement the action plan.

Phase 4 is the action phase where resources are recruited for implementation of the action plan, the action plan is implemented, the improvement effort is measured, and the plan and implementation are modified based on measurements and feedback.

Phase 5 is the review phase, which ensures that all success criteria have been achieved, all feedback is evaluated, the lessons learned are analyzed, the business plan and process improvement are compared for the desired outcome, and the next stage of the process improvement effort is planned.

The benefits of a long-term, formal software process improvement plan are as follows:

✦ Improved software quality
✦ Reduced life cycle time
✦ More accurate scheduling and meeting of milestones
✦ Management visibility
✦ Proactive planning and tracking

An evolution of the CMM methodology has resulted in the development of the *Capability Maturity Model Integration (CMMI)* by the SEI. As defined by the SEI, the CMMI "consists of best practices that address the development and maintenance of products and services covering the product life cycle from conception through delivery and maintenance." The CMMI integrates the best practices and knowledge from the disciplines of software engineering, acquisition, and systems engineering.

Object-Oriented Systems

An object-oriented system has the potential characteristics of being more reliable and less prone to propagating of program change errors than conventional programming methods. In addition, it is effective in modeling of the "real world." An object-oriented system can be thought of as a group of independent objects that can be requested to perform certain operations or exhibit specific behaviors. These objects cooperate to provide the system's required functionality. The objects have an *identity* and can be created as the program executes (*dynamic lifetime*). To provide the desired characteristics of object-oriented systems, the objects are *encapsulated*; they can be accessed only through messages sent to them to request performance of their defined operations. The object can be viewed as a black box whose internal details are hidden from outside observation and cannot normally be modified. Grady Booch defines encapsulation as "The process of compartmentalizing the elements of an abstraction that constitute its structure and behavior; . . . [it] serves to separate the contractual interface of an abstraction and its implementation." Objects also exhibit the *substitution* property, which means that objects providing compatible operations can be substituted for each other. According to Booch, "An object has a state, behavior, and identity" (Grady Booch, "Object-Oriented Development," *IEEE Transactions on Software Engineering*, Vol. SE-12, No. 2, February 1986, pp. 211–221).

The following definitions are fundamental to object-oriented systems:

Message. A message is the communication to an object to carry out some operation.

Method. A method is the code that defines the actions an object performs in response to a message.

Behavior. Behavior refers to the results exhibited by an object upon receipt of a message.

Class. A class is a collection of the common methods of a set of objects that defines the behavior of those objects. Booch defines a class as "a set of objects that share a common structure and a common behavior."

Instance. Objects are instances of classes that contain their methods.

Inheritance. Methods from a class are inherited by another subclass. Thus, the subclass inherits the behavior of the larger class, or *superclass*, as it is sometimes called.

Multiple inheritance. Multiple inheritance is the situation where a class inherits the behavioral characteristics of more than one parent class.

Delegation. Delegation is the forwarding of a request by an object to another object or *delegate*. This forwarding is necessitated by the fact that the object receiving the request does not have a method to service the request.

Polymorphism. According to Booch, "A name may denote objects of many different classes that are related by some common superclass; thus, any object denoted by this name is able to respond to some common set of operations in a different way."

Polyinstantiation. Polyinstantiation is the development of a detailed version of an object from another object using different values in the new object. In database information security, this term is concerned with the same primary key for different relations at different classification levels being stored in the same database. For example, in a relational database, the name of a military unit may be classified Secret in the database and may have an identification number as the primary key. If another user at a lower classification level attempts to create a confidential entry for another military unit using the same identification number as a primary key, a rejection of this attempt would imply to the lower level user that the same identification number existed at a higher level of classification. To avoid this inference channel of information, the lower level user would be issued the same identification number for their unit and the database management system would manage this situation where the same primary key was used for two different units.

Relative to the software development life cycle phases, object orientation is applied in different phases as follows:

1. *Object-Oriented Requirements Analysis (OORA)*. Defines classes of objects and their interactions.

2. *Object-Oriented Analysis (OOA)*. In terms of object-oriented concepts, understanding and modeling a particular problem within a problem domain.

3. *Domain Analysis (DA)*. According to Booch, "Whereas OOA typically focuses upon one specific problem at a time, domain analysis seeks to identify the classes and objects that are common to all applications within a given domain."

4. *Object-Oriented Design (OOD)*. Object is the basic unit of modularity; objects are instantiations of a class.

5. *Object-Oriented Programming (OOP)*. Emphasizes the employment of objects and methods rather than types or transformations, as in other programming approaches.

A simple example of a class is the class Airplane. From this class, the object called fighter plane can be created. Other objects called passenger plane, cargo plane, and trainer can also be defined as objects in the class Airplane. The method associated with this class would be carried out when the object received a message. The messages to the object could be Climb, Roll, or Descend.

By reusing tested and reliable objects, applications can be developed in less time and at less cost. These objects can be controlled through an object program library that controls and manages the deposit and issuance of tested objects to users. To provide protection from disclosure and violations of the integrity of objects, security controls must be implemented for the program library. In addition, objects can be made available to users through *Object Request Brokers* (ORBs). The purpose of the ORB is to support the interaction of objects in heterogeneous, distributed environments. The objects might be on different types of computing platforms. Therefore, ORBs act as the locators and distributors of objects across networks. ORBs are considered *middleware* because they reside between two other entities. ORBs can also provide security features, or the objects can call security services. An ORB is a component of the *Object Request Architecture* (ORA), which is a high-level framework for a distributed environment. The other components of the ORA are as follows:

✦ Object services

✦ Application objects

✦ Common facilities

The ORA is a product of the Object Management Group (OMG), a nonprofit consortium in Framingham, Massachusetts, which was put together in 1989 to promote the use of object technology in distributed computing systems (www.omg.org). *Object Services* support the ORB in creating and tracking objects as well as performing access control functions. *Application Objects* and Common Facilities support the end user and use the system services to perform their functions.

The OMG has also developed a *Common Object Request Broker Architecture* (CORBA), which defines an industry standard that enables programs written in different languages and using different platforms and operating systems to interface and communicate. To implement this compatible interchange, a user develops a small amount of initial code and an *Interface Definition Language* (IDL) file. The IDL file then identifies the methods, classes, and objects that are the interface targets. For example, CORBA can enable a Java code to access and use code written in C++.

Another standard, the *Common Object Model* (COM), supports the exchange of objects among programs. This capability was formerly known as *Object Linking and Embedding* (OLE). As in the object-oriented paradigm, COM works with encapsulated objects. Communications with a COM object are through an interface contract between an object and its clients that defines the functions that are available in the object and the behavior of the object when the functions are called. The *Distributed Common Object Model* (DCOM) defines the standard for sharing objects in a networked environment.

Some examples of object-oriented systems are Simula 67, C++, and Smalltalk. Simula 67 was the first system to support object-oriented programming, but it was not widely adopted. However, its constructs influenced other object-oriented languages, including C++. C++ supports classes, multiple inheritance, strict type checking, and user-controlled management of storage. Smalltalk was developed at the Xerox Palo Alto Research Center (PARC) as a complete system. It supports incremental development of programs and run-time type checking.

Object orientation, thus, provides an improved paradigm that represents application domains through basic component definition and interfacing. It supports the reuse of software (objects), reduces the development risks for complex systems, and is natural in its representation of real world entities.

Artificial Intelligence Systems

An alternative approach for using software and/or hardware to solve problems is through the use of artificial intelligence systems. These systems attempt to mimic the workings of the human mind. Two types of artificial intelligence systems are covered in this section:

✦ Expert systems

✦ Neural networks

Expert Systems

An expert system exhibits reasoning similar to that of a human expert to solve a problem. It accomplishes this reasoning by building a knowledge base of the domain to be addressed in the form of rules and an inferencing mechanism to determine whether the rules have been satisfied by the system input.

Computer programs are usually defined as:

algorithm + data structures = program

In an expert system, the relationship is

inference engine + knowledge base = expert system

The knowledge base contains facts and the rules concerning the domain of the problem in the form of *if-then statements*. The inference engine compares information it has acquired in memory to the *if* portion of the rules in the knowledge base to see whether there is a match. If there is a match, the rule is ready to "fire" and is placed in a list for execution. Certain rules may have a higher priority or *salience*, and the system will fire these rules before others that have a lower salience.

The expert system operates in either a forward-chaining or backward-chaining mode. In a *forward-chaining* mode, the expert system acquires information and comes to a conclusion based on that information. Forward-chaining is the reasoning approach that can be used when there are a small number of solutions relative to the number of inputs. In a backward-chaining mode, the expert system backtracks to determine if a given hypothesis is valid. *Backward-chaining* is generally used when there are a large number of possible solutions relative to the number of inputs.

Another type of expert system is the blackboard. A *blackboard* is an expert system–reasoning methodology in which a solution is generated by the use of a virtual "blackboard," wherein information or potential solutions are placed on the blackboard by a plurality of individuals or expert knowledge sources. As more information is placed on the blackboard in an iterative process, a solution is generated.

As with human reasoning, there is a degree of uncertainty in the conclusions of the expert system. This uncertainty can be handled through a number of approaches, such as Bayesian networks, certainty factors, or fuzzy logic.

Bayesian networks are based on Bayes' theorem:

$$P(H|E) = P\{E|H\}*P(H)/ P(E)$$

that gives the probability of an event (H) given that an event (E) has occurred.

Certainty factors are easy to develop and use. These factors are the probability that a belief is true. For example, a probability of 85 percent can be assigned to Object A occurring under certain conditions.

Fuzzy logic is used to address situations where there are degrees of uncertainty concerning whether something is true or false. This situation is often the case in real world situations. A *fuzzy expert system* incorporates fuzzy functions to develop conclusions. The inference engine steps in fuzzy logic are as follows:

Fuzzification. The membership functions defined on the input variables are applied to their actual values to determine the degree of truth for each rule premise.

Inference. The truth-value for the premise of each rule is computed and applied to the conclusion part of each rule. This results in one fuzzy subset to be assigned to each output variable for each rule.

Composition. All of the fuzzy subsets assigned to each output variable are combined together to form a single fuzzy subset for each output variable.

Defuzzification. Used when it is useful to convert the fuzzy output set to a quantitative number. One approach to defuzzification is the CENTROID method. With this method, a value of the output variable is computed by finding the variable value of the center of gravity of the membership function for the fuzzy output value.

The Spiral model can be used to build an expert system. The following are the common steps when building a Spiral model:

✦ Analysis

✦ Specification

✦ Development

✦ Deployment

A key element in this process is the acquisition of knowledge. This activity involves interviewing experts in the domain field and obtaining data from other expert sources. Knowledge acquisition begins in the specification phase and runs into the development phase.

Verification and validation of an expert system are concerned with inconsistencies inherent in conflicting rules, redundant rules, circular chains of rules, and unreferenced values along with incompleteness resulting from unreferenced or unallowable data values.

Neural Networks

A neural network is based on the functioning of biological neurons. In biological neurons, signals are exchanged among neurons through electrical pulses traveling along an *axon*. The electrical pulses arrive at a neuron at points called *synapses*. When a pulse arrives at the synapse, it causes the release of a chemical neurotransmitter that travels across the synaptic cleft to the post-synaptic receptor sites on the dendrite side of the synapse. The neurotransmitter then causes a change in the dendrite membrane's post-synaptic-potential (PSP). These PSPs are integrated by the neuron over time. If the integrated PSPs exceed a threshold, the neuron fires and generates an electrical pulse that travels to other neurons.

An analog of the biological neuron system is provided in Figure 7-7. Inputs I_i to the neuron are modified by weights, W_i, and then summed in unit Σ. If the weighted sum exceeds a threshold, unit Σ will produce an output, Z. The functioning of this artificial neural network is shown in the following equation:

$$Z = W_1 I_1 .. + W_2 I_2 + ... + W_n I_n$$

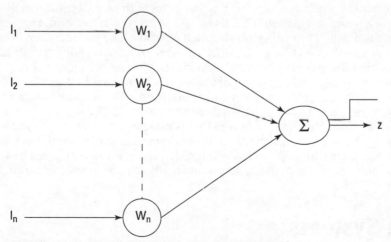

Figure 7-7: A single-layer artificial neural network.

If the sum of the weighted inputs then exceeds the threshold, the neuron will "fire" and there will be an output from that neuron. An alternative approach would be to have the output of the neuron be a linear function of the sum of the artificial neuron inputs.

Because there is only one summing node in Figure 7-7, this network is called a *single-layer network*. Networks with more than one level of summing nodes are called *multi-layer networks*. The value of a neural network is its ability to dynamically adjust its weights in order to associate the given input vectors with corresponding output vectors. A "training" period for the neural network has the input vectors repeatedly presented and the weights dynamically adjusted according to the learning paradigm. The delta rule is an example of a learning rule. In the delta rule, the change in weight, $\Delta_{ij} = R * I_i * (T_j - Z_j)$ where R is the learning rate, I_i is the input vector, T_j is the target output vector, and Z_j is the actual output of node Σ. For example, if a specific output vector were required for a specific input where the relationship between input and output was non-linear, the neural network would be trained by applying a set of input vectors. Using the delta rule, the neural network would repetitively adjust the weights until it produced the correct output vector for each given input vector. The neural network would then be said to have learned to provide the correct response for each input vector.

Genetic Algorithms

Another type of artificial intelligence technology involves *genetic algorithms*. These algorithms are part of the general class known as *evolutionary computing*. Evolutionary computing uses the Darwinian principles of survival of the fittest, mutation, and the adaptation of successive generations of populations to their environment. The genetic algorithm implements this process through iteration of generations of a constant-size population of items or individuals. Each individual is characterized by a finite string of symbols called *genomes*. The genomes are used to represent possible solutions to a problem in a fixed search space. For example, if the fixed population of the first generation of individuals consists of random binary numbers and the problem is to find the minimum binary number that can be represented by an individual, each binary number is assigned a *fitness value* based on the individual's binary number value. The smaller the binary number represented by a *parent* individual, the higher level of fitness that is assigned to it. Through crossbreeding among the numbers (known as *crossover*), mutations of the numbers, and pairing of the numbers with high fitness ratings, the smallest value that can be represented by the number of bits in the binary number will emerge in later generations.

Database Systems

A database system can be used as a general mechanism for defining, storing, and manipulating data without writing specific programs to perform these functions. A

Database Management System (DBMS) provides high-level commands to operate on the data in the database. Some of the different types of databases are as follows:

✦ Hierarchical

✦ Mesh

✦ Object-oriented

✦ Relational

Much research on information security has been done with relational databases. The information security applications of relational databases are discussed in Chapter 2.

Database Security Issues

In a relational database, security can be provided through the use of views. A *view* is a virtual relation that combines information from other relations. A view can be used to restrict the data made available to users based on their privileges and need to know. A database information security vulnerability can be exploited through the DBMS. Designed to facilitate queries to the database, the DBMS can be a possible source of data compromise by circumventing the normal security controls. The *granularity* of the access to objects in a database refers to the fineness in which this access can be controlled or limited. Other database security issues are *aggregation* and *inference*. Aggregation is the act of obtaining information of a higher sensitivity by combining information from lower levels of sensitivity. Inference is the ability of users to infer or deduce information about data at sensitivity levels for which they do not have access privileges. A link that enables inference to occur is called an *inference channel*.

Open Database Connectivity (ODBC) is a Microsoft-developed standard for supporting access to databases through different applications. This access must be controlled to avoid compromising the database.

Data Warehouse and Data Mining

A data warehouse is a repository of information from heterogeneous databases that is available to users for making queries. A more formal definition of a data warehouse is given by Bill Inmon, a pioneer in the field. He defines a *data warehouse* as a "subject-oriented, integrated, time-variant, non-volatile collection of data in support of management's decision-making process."

To create a data warehouse, data is taken from an operational database, redundancies are removed, and the data is "cleaned up" in general. This activity is referred to as *normalizing* the data. Then the data is placed into a relational database and can be analyzed by using *On-Line Analytical Processing* (OLAP) and statistical modeling tools. The data warehouse can be used as a Decision Support System (DSS), for example, by performing a time series analysis of the data. The data in the data warehouse must be maintained to ensure that it is timely and valid. The term *data scrubbing* refers to maintenance of the data warehouse by deleting information that is unreliable or no longer relevant.

A *data mart* is a database that is comprised of data or relations that have been extracted from the data warehouse. Information in the data mart is usually of interest to a particular group of people. For example, a data mart can be developed for all health care–related data. Searching among the data in the warehouse for data correlations and relationships that were unknown up until now is called *data mining*. The correlations or "data about data" are referred to as *metadata*. The information obtained from the metadata should, however, be sent back for incorporation into the data warehouse to be available for future queries and metadata analyses. Data mining can be applied to information system security as an intrusion detection tool to discover abnormal system characteristics in order to determine whether there are aggregation or inference problems and for analyzing audit information.

Data Dictionaries

A data dictionary is a database for system developers. It records all the data structures used by an application. Advanced data dictionaries incorporate application generators that use the data stored in the dictionary to automate some of the program production tasks. The data dictionary interacts with the DBMS, the program library, applications, and the information security system. In some instances, the data dictionary system is organized into a primary data dictionary and one or more secondary data dictionaries. The primary data dictionary provides a baseline of data definitions and central control, while the secondary data dictionaries are assigned to separate development projects to provide backup to the primary dictionary and to serve as a partition between the development and test databases.

Application Controls

The goal of application controls is to enforce the organization's security policy and procedures and to maintain the confidentiality, integrity, and availability of the computer-based information. Application security involves the input to the system, the data being processed, and the output of the system. The controls can be classified into preventive, detective, and corrective measures that apply to different security categories. These controls and categories are listed in Table 7-1.

Table 7-1
Application Control Types

Application Control Type	Accuracy	Security	Consistency
Preventive	Data checks, forms, custom screens, validity checks, contingency planning, and backups.	Firewalls, reference monitors, sensitivity labels, traffic padding, encryption, data classification, one-time passwords, contingency planning, separation of development, application and test environments.	Data dictionary, programming standards, and database.
Detective	Cyclic redundancy checks, structured walk-throughs, hash totals, and reasonableness checks.	Intrusion detection systems and audit trails.	Comparison controls, relationship tests, and reconciliation controls.
Corrective	Backups, control reports, before/after imaging reporting, and checkpoint restarts.	Emergency response and reference monitor.	Program comments and database controls.

Users running applications require the availability of the system. A *service level agreement* (SLA) guarantees the quality of a service to a subscriber by a network service provider. Defined service levels provide a basis for measuring the delivered services and are useful in anticipating, identifying, and correcting problems. Some of the metrics in service-level agreements are as follows:

✦ Turnaround times

✦ Average response times

✦ Number of online users

✦ System utilization rates

✦ System up times

✦ Volume of transactions

✦ Production problems

Distributed Systems

Distributed systems are commonplace and pose special challenges to information systems security implementation. Security in distributed systems should include access control mechanisms, identification, authentication, some type of intrusion detection capability, emergency response plans, logs, and audit trails.

The client/server model implements a type of distributed system. In this model, the client requests services and the server provides the requested service. The client provides the interface to the user, supports the entry of information, and provides the reports. The server provides access to data, holds the databases, provides data to the client, performs backups, and provides security services.

Distributed environments support agents. An *agent* is a surrogate program or process performing services in one environment on behalf of a principal in another environment. This behavior differs from that of a *proxy* in that a proxy acts on behalf of a principal, but it may hide the characteristics of that principal. Similarly, *applets* are small applications that may be written in various languages, which include C++ and Java. Both of these languages are object-oriented. C++ was developed at Bell Laboratories and is an extension of C. Java is a multi-threaded, interpreted language that was developed at Sun Microsystems. A *thread* is considered a lightweight process and has a lower overhead for maintaining state and switching contexts. *Multiple threads* run in the protection domain of a task or process, and they share a single address space. An *interpreted language* executes each instruction in real-time. This action is referred to as *run-time binding*. A *compiled language* has all the high-level instructions translated into *machine code* (*object code*) by a *compiler*. Then the computer executes the code. With a compiler, the binding occurs at compile time. Compiled code poses more of a security risk than interpreted code because malicious code can be embedded in the compiled code and can be difficult to detect.

Applets can be accessed and downloaded from the World Wide Web (WWW) into a Web browser such as Netscape. This applet can execute in the network browser and may contain malicious code. These types of downloadable programs are also known as *mobile code*. For protection of the system, Java code is designed to run in a constrained space in the client Web browser called a *sandbox*. A sandbox is an access control–based protection mechanism and is usually interpreted by a *virtual machine* such as the Java Virtual Machine (JVM). The Microsoft ActiveX environment also supports the downloading of mobile code written in languages such as Visual BASIC or C++ to Web browsers and thus has the potential for causing harm to a system. ActiveX, however, establishes a trust relationship between the client and the server through the use of digital certificates, guaranteeing that the server is trusted. Some security controls that can be applied to mitigate the effects of malicious mobile code are as follows:

  ✦ Configure firewalls to screen applets.
  ✦ Configure Web browsers to restrict or prevent the downloading of applets.

✦ Configure Web browsers to permit the receipt of applets only from trusted servers.

✦ Provide training to users to make them aware of mobile code threats.

A client/server implementation approach in which any platform can act as a client or server or both is called *peer-to-peer*.

Centralized Architecture

A centralized system architecture is less difficult to protect than a distributed system architecture because, in the latter, the components are interconnected through a network. Centralized systems provide for implementation of the local security and application system controls, whereas distributed systems have to deal with geographically separate entities communicating via a network or through many networks.

Real-Time Systems

Another system classification that is based on temporal considerations rather than on architectural characteristics is real-time systems. Real-time systems operate by acquiring data from transducers or sensors in real time and then making computations and control decisions in a fixed time window. An example of such a system would be a "fly by wire" control of supersonic aircraft, where adjustment of the planes' control surfaces is time-critical. Availability of such systems is crucial and, as such, can be addressed through *Redundant Array of Independent Disks* (RAID) technology, disk mirroring, disk duplexing, fault-tolerant systems, and recovery mechanisms to cope with system failures. In *disk mirroring*, a duplicate of the disk is used, and in *disk duplexing*, the disk controller is backed up with a redundant controller. A *fault-tolerant system* has to detect a fault and then take action to recover from that fault.

✦　　✦　　✦

Assessment Questions

You can find the answers to the following questions in Appendix A.

1. What is a data warehouse?

   a. A remote facility used for storing backup tapes

   b. A repository of information from heterogeneous databases

   c. A table in a relational database system

   d. A hot backup building

2. What does normalizing data in a data warehouse mean?

   a. Redundant data is removed.

   b. Numerical data is divided by a common factor.

   c. Data is converted to a symbolic representation.

   d. Data is restricted to a range of values.

3. What is a neural network?

   a. A hardware or software system that emulates the reasoning of a human expert

   b. A collection of computers that are focused on medical applications

   c. A series of networked PCs performing artificial intelligence tasks

   d. A hardware or software system that emulates the functioning of biological neurons

4. A neural network learns by using various algorithms to:

   a. Adjust the weights applied to the data

   b. Fire the rules in the knowledge base

   c. Emulate an inference engine

   d. Emulate the thinking of an expert

5. The SEI Software Capability Maturity Model is based on the premise that:

   a. Good software development is a function of the number of expert programmers in the organization.

   b. The maturity of an organization's software processes cannot be measured.

   c. The quality of a software product is a direct function of the quality of its associated software development and maintenance processes.

   d. Software development is an art that cannot be measured by conventional means.

6. In configuration management, a configuration item is:

   a. The version of the operating system that is operating on the workstation that provides information security services

   b. A component whose state is to be recorded and against which changes are to be progressed

   c. The network architecture used by the organization

   d. A series of files that contain sensitive information

7. In an object-oriented system, polymorphism denotes:

   a. Objects of many different classes that are related by some common superclass; thus, any object denoted by this name can respond to some common set of operations in a different way.

   b. Objects of many different classes that are related by some common superclass; thus, all objects denoted by this name can respond to some common set of operations in identical fashion.

   c. Objects of the same class; thus, any object denoted by this name can respond to some common set of operations in the same way.

   d. Objects of many different classes that are unrelated but respond to some common set of operations in the same way.

8. The simplistic model of software life cycle development assumes that:

   a. Iteration will be required among the steps in the process.

   b. Each step can be completed and finalized without any effect from the later stages that might require rework.

   c. Each phase is identical to a completed milestone.

   d. Software development requires reworking and repeating some of the phases.

9. What is a method in an object-oriented system?

   a. The means of communication among objects

   b. A guide to the programming of objects

   c. The code defining the actions that the object performs in response to a message

   d. The situation where a class inherits the behavioral characteristics of more than one parent class

10. What does the Spiral model depict?

    a. A spiral that incorporates various phases of software development

    b. A spiral that models the behavior of biological neurons

    c. The operation of expert systems

    d. Information security checklists

11. In the software life cycle, verification:

    a. Evaluates the product in development against real-world requirements

    b. Evaluates the product in development against similar products

    c. Evaluates the product in development against general baselines

    d. Evaluates the product in development against the specification

12. In the software life cycle, validation:

    a. Refers to the work product satisfying the real-world requirements and concepts.

    b. Refers to the work product satisfying derived specifications.

    c. Refers to the work product satisfying software maturity levels.

    d. Refers to the work product satisfying generally accepted principles.

13. In the modified Waterfall model:

    a. Unlimited backward iteration is permitted.

    b. The model was reinterpreted to have phases end at project milestones.

    c. The model was reinterpreted to have phases begin at project milestones.

    d. Product verification and validation are not included.

14. Cyclic redundancy checks, structured walk-throughs, and hash totals are examples of what type of application controls?

    a. Preventive security controls

    b. Preventive consistency controls

    c. Detective accuracy controls

    d. Corrective consistency controls

15. In a system life cycle, information security controls should be:

    a. Designed during the product implementation phase

    b. Implemented prior to validation

    c. Part of the feasibility phase

    d. Specified after the coding phase

16. The software maintenance phase controls consist of:

    a. Request control, change control, and release control

    b. Request control, configuration control, and change control

    c. Change control, security control, and access control

    d. Request control, release control, and access control

17. In configuration management, what is a software library?

    a. A set of versions of the component configuration items

    b. A controlled area accessible only to approved users who are restricted to the use of an approved procedure

    c. A repository of backup tapes

    d. A collection of software build lists

18. What is configuration control?

    a. Identifying and documenting the functional and physical characteristics of each configuration item

    b. Controlling changes to the configuration items and issuing versions of configuration items from the software library

    c. Recording the processing of changes

    d. Controlling the quality of the configuration management procedures

19. What is searching for data correlations in the data warehouse called?

    a. Data warehousing

    b. Data mining

    c. A data dictionary

    d. Configuration management

20. The security term that is concerned with the same primary key existing at different classification levels in the same database is:

    a. Polymorphism

    b. Normalization

    c. Inheritance

    d. Polyinstantiation

21. What is a data dictionary?

    a. A database for system developers

    b. A database of security terms

    c. A library of objects

    d. A validation reference source

22. Which of the following is an example of mobile code?

    a. Embedded code in control systems

    b. Embedded code in PCs

    c. Java and ActiveX code downloaded into a Web browser from the World Wide Web (WWW)

    d. Code derived following the Spiral model

23. Which of the following is NOT true regarding software unit testing?

    a. The test data is part of the specifications.

    b. Correct test output results should be developed and known beforehand.

    c. Live or actual field data is recommended for use in the testing procedures.

    d. Testing should check for out-of-range values and other bounds conditions.

24. The definition "the science and art of specifying, designing, implementing, and evolving programs, documentation, and operating procedures whereby computers can be made useful to man" is that of:

    a. Structured analysis/structured design (SA/SD)

    b. Software engineering

    c. An object-oriented system

    d. Functional programming

25. In software engineering, the term *verification* is defined as:

    a. To establish the truth of correspondence between a software product and its specification

    b. A complete, validated specification of the required functions, interfaces, and performance for the software product

    c. To establish the fitness or worth of a software product for its operational mission

    d. A complete, verified specification of the overall hardware-software architecture, control structure, and data structure for the product

26. The discipline of identifying the components of a continually evolving system for the purposes of controlling changes to those components and maintaining integrity and traceability throughout the life cycle is called:

    a. Change control

    b. Request control

    c. Release control

    d. Configuration management

27. The basic version of the Construction Cost Model (COCOMO), which proposes quantitative life cycle relationships, performs what function?

    a. Estimates software development effort based on user function categories

    b. Estimates software development effort and cost as a function of the size of the software product in source instructions

    c. Estimates software development effort and cost as a function of the size of the software product in source instructions modified by manpower buildup and productivity factors

    d. Estimates software development effort and cost as a function of the size of the software product in source instructions modified by hardware and input functions

28. A refinement to the basic Waterfall model that states that software should be developed in increments of functional capability is called:

    a. Functional refinement

    b. Functional development

    c. Incremental refinement

    d. Incremental development

29. The Spiral model of the software development process (B.W. Boehm, "A Spiral Model of Software Development and Enhancement," *IEEE Computer*, May 1988) uses the following metric relative to the spiral:

    a. The radial dimension represents the cost of each phase.

    b. The radial dimension represents progress made in completing each cycle.

    c. The angular dimension represents cumulative cost.

    d. The radial dimension represents cumulative cost.

30. In the Capability Maturity Model (CMM) for software, the definition "describes the range of expected results that can be achieved by following a software process" is that of:

   a. Structured analysis/structured design (SA/SD)

   b. Software process capability

   c. Software process performance

   d. Software process maturity

Business Continuity Planning and Disaster Recovery Planning

The Business Continuity Planning (BCP) and Disaster Recovery Planning (DRP) domain is all about business. We're not talking about infringements of security policy or unauthorized access; rather, this is about making contingency plans for a business-threatening emergency and continuing the business in the event of a disaster. While the other domains are concerned with preventing risks and protecting the infrastructure against attack, this domain assumes that the worst has happened.

The CISSP candidate should know the following:

+ The basic difference between BCP and DRP

+ The difference between natural and manmade disasters

+ The four prime elements of BCP

+ The reasons for and steps in conducting a Business Impact Assessment (BIA)

+ The steps in creating a disaster recovery plan

+ The five types of disaster recovery plan tests

+ The various types of backup services

Domain Definition

The BCP and DRP domains address the preservation of business in the face of major disruptions to normal operations.

Business Continuity Planning and Disaster Recovery Planning involve the preparation, testing, and updating of the actions required to protect critical business processes from the effects of major system and network failures. The CISSP candidate must have an understanding of the preparation of specific actions required to preserve the business in the event of a major disruption to normal business operations.

The BCP process includes the following:

✦ Scope and plan initiation

✦ Business Impact Assessment (BIA)

✦ Business continuity plan development

The DRP process includes the following:

✦ Disaster Recovery Planning (DRP) processes

✦ Testing the disaster recovery plan

✦ Disaster recovery procedures

Business Continuity Planning

Simply put, business continuity plans are created to prevent interruptions to normal business activity. They are designed to protect critical business processes from natural or manmade failures or disasters and the resultant loss of capital due to the unavailability of normal business processes. Business continuity planning is a strategy to minimize the effect of disturbances and to allow for the resumption of business processes.

A disruptive event is any intentional or unintentional security violation that suspends normal operations. The aim of BCP is to minimize the effects of a disruptive event on a company. The primary purpose of business continuity plans is to reduce the risk of financial loss and enhance a company's capability to recover promptly from a disruptive event. The business continuity plan should also help minimize the cost associated with the disruptive event and mitigate the risk associated with it.

Business continuity plans should look at all critical information processing areas of the company, including but not limited to the following:

✦ LANs, WANs, and servers

✦ Telecommunications and data communication links

✦ Workstations and workspaces

✦ Applications, software, and data

✦ Media and records storage

✦ Staff duties and production processes

Disaster Definition

The disaster, emergency management, and business continuity community consists of many different types of entities, such as governmental (federal, state, and local), non-governmental (business and industry), and individuals. Each entity has its own focus and its own definition of a disaster. A very common definition of a disaster is "a suddenly occurring or unstoppable developing event that":

✦ Causes loss of life, suffering, loss of valuables, or damage to the environment

✦ Overwhelms local resources or efforts

✦ Has a long-term impact on social or natural life that is always negative in the beginning

Life safety, or protecting the health and safety of everyone in the facility, is the first priority in an emergency or disaster. While we talk about the preservation of capital, resumption of normal business processing activities, and other business continuity issues, the main overriding concern of all plans is to get the personnel out of harm's way. Evacuation routes, assembly areas, and accounting for personnel (head counts and last-known locations) are the most important elements of emergency procedures. If at any time there's a conflict between preserving hardware or data and the threat of physical danger to personnel, the protection of the people always comes first. Personnel evacuation and safety must be the first element of a disaster response plan. Providing restoration and recovery and implementing alternative production methods come later.

Continuity Disruptive Events

The events that can affect business continuity and require disaster recovery are well documented in the Physical Security domain. Here, we are concerned with those events, either natural or manmade, that are of such a substantial nature as to pose a threat to the continuing existence of the organization. All of the plans and processes in this section are "after the fact"; that is, no preventative controls similar to the controls discussed in the Operations Security domain will be demonstrated here. Business continuity plans are designed to minimize the damage done by the event and facilitate rapid restoration of the organization to its full operational capability.

We can make a simple list of these events, categorized as to whether their origination was natural or human. Examples of natural events that can affect business continuity are as follows:

✦ Fires, explosions, or hazardous material spills of environmental toxins

✦ Earthquakes, storms, floods, and fires due to acts of nature

✦ Power outages or other utility failures

Asset Loss

The loss of assets entails more than just the hard costs of replacing destroyed systems. Other examples of business assets that could be lost or damaged during a disaster are:

✦ Revenues lost during the incident

✦ Ongoing recovery costs

✦ Fines and penalties incurred by the event.

✦ Competitive advantage, credibility, or good will damaged by the incident

Examples of manmade events that can affect business continuity are:

✦ Bombings, sabotage, or other intentional attacks

✦ Strikes and job actions

✦ Employee or operator unavailability due to emergency evacuation or other issues (these could be either manmade or naturally caused)

✦ Communications infrastructure failures or testing-related outages (including a massive failure of configuration management controls)

The Four Prime Elements of BCP

There are four major elements of the BCP process:

Scope and Plan Initiation. This phase marks the beginning of the BCP process. It entails creating the scope and the other elements needed to define the parameters of the plan.

Business Impact Assessment. A BIA is a process used to help business units understand the impact of a disruptive event. This phase includes the execution of a vulnerability assessment.

Business Continuity Plan Development. This term refers to using the information collected in the BIA to develop the actual business continuity plan. This process includes the areas of plan implementation, plan testing, and ongoing plan maintenance.

Plan Approval and Implementation. This process involves getting the final senior management signoff, creating enterprise-wide awareness of the plan, and implementing a maintenance procedure for updating the plan as needed.

Scope and Plan Initiation

The Scope and Plan Initiation phase is the first step toward creating a business continuity plan. This phase marks the beginning of the BCP process. It entails creating the scope for the plan and the other elements needed to define the parameters of the plan. This phase embodies an examination of the company's operations and support services. Scope activities could include: creating a detailed account of the work required, listing the resources to be used, and defining the management practices to be employed.

With the advent of the personal computer in the workplace, distributed processing introduces special problems into the BCP process. It's important that the centralized planning effort encompass all distributed processes and systems.

Roles and Responsibilities

The BCP process involves many personnel from various parts of the enterprise. Creation of a BCP committee will represent the first enterprise-wide involvement of the major critical functional business units. All other business units will be involved in some way later, especially during the implementation and awareness phases.

> **The BCP committee.** A BCP committee should be formed and given the responsibility to create, implement, and test the plan. The committee is made up of representatives from senior management, all functional business units, information systems, and security administration. The committee initially defines the scope of the plan, which should deal with how to recover promptly from a disruptive event and mitigate the financial and resource loss due to a disruptive event.
>
> **Senior Management's Role.** Senior management has the ultimate responsibility for all phases of the plan, which includes not only initiation of the plan process but also monitoring and management of the plan during testing and supervision and execution of the plan during a disruptive event. This support is essential, and without management being willing to commit adequate tangible and intangible resources, the plan will not be successful.

The business resumption, or business continuity plan, must have total, highly visible senior management support. Senior management must agree on the scope of the project, delegate resources for the success of the project, and support the timeline and training efforts.

Contingency Planners

Contingency planners have many roles and responsibilities when planning business continuity, disaster recovery, emergency management, or business resumption processes. Some of these roles and responsibilities can include:

✦ Providing direction to senior management and ensuring executive management compliance with the contingency plan program

✦ Integrating the planning process across business units

✦ Providing periodic management reports and status

✦ Ensuring the identification of all critical business functions

✦ Coordinating and integrating the activation of emergency response organizations

Also, many elements of the BCP will address senior management, such as the statement of importance and priorities, the statement of organizational responsibility, and the statement of urgency and timing. Table 8-1 shows the roles and responsibilities in the BCP process.

Some organizations with mature business resumption plans (BRPs) employ a tiered structure that mirrors the organization's hierarchy. Senior management is always the highest level of decision-makers in the BRP process, although the policy group also consists of upper-level executives. The policy group approves emergency management decisions involving expenditures, liabilities, and service impacts. The next group, the disaster management team, often consists of department and business unit representatives and makes decisions regarding life safety and disaster recovery efforts. The next group, the emergency response team, supplies tactical response to the disaster, and may consist of members of data processing, user support, or persons with first aid and evacuation responsibilities.*

Because of the concept of due diligence, stockholders may hold senior managers as well as the board of directors personally responsible if a disruptive event causes losses that adherence to base industry standards of due care could have prevented. For this reason and others, it is in the senior managers' best interest to be fully involved in the BCP process.

Table 8-1 BCP Department Involvement	
Who	**Does What**
Executive management staff	Initiates the project, gives final approval, and gives ongoing support
Senior business unit management	Identifies and prioritizes time-critical systems
BCP committee	Directs the planning, implementation, and test processes
Functional business units	Participate in implementation and testing

Senior corporate executives are increasingly being held liable for failure of due care in disasters. They may also face civil suits from shareholders and clients for compensatory damages. The definition of due care is being updated to include computer functionality outages as more and more people around the world depend upon data information to do their jobs.

---

*Source: *Contingency Planning and Management,* "Business Contingency Planning 201," by Paul H. Rosenthal, May 2000.

The FCPA

The Foreign Corrupt Practices Act of 1977 imposes civil and criminal penalties if publicly held organizations fail to maintain adequate controls over their information systems. Organizations must take reasonable steps to ensure not only the integrity of their data, but also the system controls the organization put in place.

Business Impact Assessment

The purpose of a BIA is to create a document to be used to help understand what impact a disruptive event would have on the business. The impact might be financial (quantitative) or operational (qualitative, such as the inability to respond to customer complaints). A vulnerability assessment is often part of the BIA process.

BIA has three primary goals:

Criticality Prioritization. Every critical business unit process must be identified and prioritized, and the impact of a disruptive event must be evaluated. Obviously, non–time-critical business processes will require a lower priority rating for recovery than time-critical business processes.

Downtime Estimation. The BIA is used to help estimate the *Maximum Tolerable Downtime* (MTD) that the business can tolerate and still remain a viable company; that is, what is the longest period of time a critical process can remain interrupted before the company can never recover? It is often found during the BIA process that this time period is much shorter than expected; that is, the company can tolerate only a much briefer period of interruption than was previously thought.

Resource Requirements. The resource requirements for the critical processes are also identified at this time, with the most time-sensitive processes receiving the most resource allocation.

A BIA generally takes the form of these four steps:

1. Gathering the needed assessment materials
2. Performing the vulnerability assessment
3. Analyzing the information compiled
4. Documenting the results and presenting recommendations

Gathering Assessment Materials

The initial step of the BIA is identifying which business units are critical to continuing an acceptable level of operations. Often, the starting point is a simple organizational chart that shows the business units' relationships to each other. Other documents might also be collected at this stage in an effort to define the functional interrelationships of the organization.

As the materials are collected and the functional operations of the business are identified, the BIA will examine these business function interdependencies with an eye toward several factors, such as determining the business success factors involved, establishing a set of priorities between the units, and deciding what alternate processing procedures can be utilized.

The Vulnerability Assessment

The vulnerability assessment is often part of a BIA. It is similar to a Risk Assessment in that there is a quantitative (financial) section and a qualitative (operational) section. It differs in that it is smaller than a full risk assessment and is focused on providing information that is used solely for the business continuity plan or disaster recovery plan.

A function of a vulnerability assessment is to conduct a loss impact analysis. Because there will be two parts to the assessment, a financial assessment and an operational assessment, it will be necessary to define loss criteria both quantitatively and qualitatively.

Quantitative loss criteria can be defined as follows:

✦ Incurring financial losses from loss of revenue, capital expenditure, or personal liability resolution

✦ The additional operational expenses incurred due to the disruptive event

✦ Incurring financial loss from resolution of violation of contract agreements

✦ Incurring financial loss from resolution of violation of regulatory or compliance requirements

Qualitative loss criteria can consist of the following:

✦ The loss of competitive advantage or market share

✦ The loss of public confidence or credibility, or incurring public embarrassment

During the vulnerability assessment, critical support areas must be defined in order to assess the impact of a disruptive event. A critical support area is defined as a business unit or function that must be present to sustain continuity of the business processes, maintain life safety, or avoid public relations embarrassment.

Critical support areas could include the following:

✦ Telecommunications, data communications, or information technology areas

✦ Physical infrastructure or plant facilities, transportation services

✦ Accounting, payroll, transaction processing, customer service, purchasing

The *granular elements* of these critical support areas will also need to be identified. By granular elements we mean the personnel, resources, and services the critical support areas need to maintain business continuity.

Common steps to performing a vulnerability assessment could be*:

1. List potential emergencies, both internally to your facility and externally to the community. Natural, manmade, technological, and human errors are all categories of potential emergencies and errors.

2. Estimate the likelihood that each emergency could occur, in a subjective analysis.

3. Assess the potential impact of the emergency on the organization in the areas of human impact (death or injury), property impact (loss or damage), and business impact (market share or credibility).

4. Assess external and internal resources required to deal with the emergency, and determine whether they are located internally or if external capabilities or procedures are required.

Figure 8-1 shows a sample *vulnerability matrix*. This can be used to create a subjective impact analysis for each type of emergency and its probability. The lower the final number the better, as a high number means a high probability, impact, or lack of remediation resources.

TYPE OF EMERGENCY	Probability	Human Impact	Property Impact	Business Impact	Internal Resources	External Resources	Total
	High 5 ←——→ Low 1	High Impact 5 ←——→ 1 Low Impact			Weak Resources 5 ←——→ 1 Strong Resources		

Figure 8-1: Sample vulnerability assessment matrix.

*Source: "Emergency Management Guide for Business and Industry," Federal Emergency Management Agency, August 1998.

The Criticality Survey

A criticality survey is another term for a standardized questionnaire or survey methodology, such as the *InfoSec Assessment Method* (IAM) promoted by the federal government's National Security Agency (NSA), or it could be a subset of the Security Systems Engineering Capability Maturity Model (SSE-CMM). Its purpose is to help identify the most critical business functions by gathering input from management personnel in the various business units.

Analyzing the Information

During the analysis phase of the BIA, several activities take place, such as documenting required processes, identifying interdependencies, and determining what an acceptable interruption period would be.

The goal of this section is to clearly describe what support the defined critical areas will require to preserve the revenue stream and maintain predefined processes, such as transaction processing levels and customer service levels. Therefore, elements of the analysis will have to come from many areas of the enterprise.

Documentation and Recommendation

The last step of the BIA entails a full documentation of all of the processes, procedures, analyses, and results and the presentation of recommendations to the appropriate senior management.

The report will contain the previously gathered material, list the identified critical support areas, summarize the quantitative and qualitative impact statements, and provide the recommended recovery priorities generated from the analysis.

Business Continuity Plan Development

Business Continuity Plan development refers to using the information collected in the BIA to create the recovery strategy plan to support these critical business functions. Here we take the information gathered from the BIA and begin to map out a strategy for creating a continuity plan.

This phase consists of two main steps:

1. Defining the continuity strategy
2. Documenting the continuity strategy

Defining the Continuity Strategy

To define the BCP strategy, the information collected from the BIA is used to create a continuity strategy for the enterprise. This task is large, and many elements of the enterprise must be included in defining the continuity strategy, such as:

Computing. A strategy needs to be defined to preserve the elements of hardware, software, communication lines, applications, and data.

Facilities. The strategy needs to address the use of the main buildings or campus and any remote facilities.

People. Operators, management, and technical support personnel will have defined roles in implementing the continuity strategy.

Supplies and equipment. Paper, forms, HVAC, or specialized security equipment must be defined as they apply to the continuity plan.

In developing plans, consideration should be given to both short-term and long-term goals and objectives. Short-term goals can include:

✦ Vital personnel, systems, operations, and equipment

✦ Priorities for restoration and mitigation

✦ Acceptable downtime before restoration to a minimum level of operations

✦ Minimum resources needed to accomplish the restoration

Long-term goals and objectives can include*:

✦ The organization's strategic plan

✦ Management and coordination of activities

✦ Funding and fiscal management

✦ Management of volunteer, contractual, and entity resources

The Information Technology Department

The IT department plays a very important role in identifying and protecting the company's internal and external information dependencies. Also, the information technology elements of the BCP should address several vital issues, including:

✦ Ensuring that the organization employs an adequate data backup and restoration process, including off-site media storage

✦ Ensuring that the company employs sufficient physical security mechanisms to preserve vital network and hardware components, including file and print servers

✦ Ensuring that the organization uses sufficient logical security methodologies (authentication, authorization, etc.) for sensitive data

✦ Ensuring that the department implements adequate system administration, including up-to-date inventories of hardware, software, and media storage

*Source: "NFPA 1600 Standard on Disaster/Emergency Management and Business Continuity," National Fire Protection Association, 2000 edition.

Documenting the Continuity Strategy

Documenting the continuity strategy simply refers to the creation of documentation of the results of the continuity strategy definition phase. You will see the word *documentation* a lot in this chapter. Documentation is required in almost all sections, and it is the nature of BCP/DRP to require a lot of paper.

Plan Approval and Implementation

As the last step, the Business continuity plan is implemented. The plan itself must contain a roadmap for implementation. Implementation here doesn't mean executing a disaster scenario and testing the plan, but rather it refers to the following steps:

1. Approval by senior management.

2. Creating an awareness of the plan enterprise-wide.

3. Maintenance of the plan, including updating when needed.

   Senior management approval. As previously mentioned, senior management has the ultimate responsibility for all phases of the plan. Because they have the responsibility for supervision and execution of the plan during a disruptive event, they must have final approval. When a disaster strikes, senior management must be able to make informed decisions quickly during the recovery effort.

   Plan awareness. Enterprise-wide awareness of the plan is important. There are several reasons for this, including the fact that the capability of the organization to recover from an event will most likely depend on the efforts of many individuals. Also, employee awareness of the plan will emphasize the organization's commitment to its employees. Specific training may be required for certain personnel to carry out their tasks, and quality training is perceived as a benefit that increases the interest and the commitment of personnel in the BCP process.

   Plan maintenance. Business continuity plans often get out of date: a major similarity among recovery plans is how quickly they become obsolete, for many different reasons. The company may reorganize and the critical business units may be different than when the plan was first created. Most commonly, the network or computing infrastructure changes, including the hardware, software, and other components. The reasons also might be administrative: cumbersome plans are not easily updated, personnel lose interest or forget, or employee turnover may affect involvement.

   Whatever the reason, plan maintenance techniques must be employed from the outset to ensure that the plan remains fresh and usable. It's important to build maintenance procedures into the organization by using job descriptions that centralize responsibility for updates. Also, create audit procedures that can report regularly on the state of the plan. It's also important to ensure that multiple versions of the plan do not exist because it could create confusion during an emergency. Always replace older versions of the text with updated versions throughout the enterprise when a plan is changed or replaced.

Disaster Recovery Planning (DRP)

A disaster recovery plan is a comprehensive statement of consistent actions to be taken before, during, and after a disruptive event that causes a significant loss of information systems resources. Disaster Recovery Plans are the procedures for responding to an emergency, providing extended backup operations during the interruption, and managing recovery and salvage processes afterwards, should an organization experience a substantial loss of processing capability.

The primary objective of the disaster recovery plan is to provide the capability to implement critical processes at an alternate site and return to the primary site and normal processing within a time frame that minimizes the loss to the organization by executing rapid recovery procedures.

Goals and Objectives of DRP

A major goal of DRP is to provide an organized way to make decisions if a disruptive event occurs. The purpose of the disaster recovery plan is to reduce confusion and enhance the ability of the organization to deal with the crisis.

Obviously, when a disruptive event occurs, the organization will not have the luxury to create and execute a recovery plan on the spot. Therefore, the amount of planning and testing that can be done beforehand will determine the capability of the organization to withstand a disaster.

The objectives of the DRP are multiple, but each is important. They can include the following:

✦ Protecting an organization from major computer services failure

✦ Minimizing the risk to the organization from delays in providing services

✦ Guaranteeing the reliability of standby systems through testing and simulation

✦ Minimizing the decision-making required by personnel during a disaster

In this section, we will examine the following areas of DRP:

✦ The DRP process

✦ Testing the disaster recovery plan

✦ Disaster recovery procedures

The Disaster Recovery Planning Process

This phase involves the development and creation of the recovery plans, which are similar to the BCP process. However, in BCP we were involved in BIA and loss criteria for identifying the critical areas of the enterprise that the business requires to sustain continuity and financial viability; here, we're assuming that those identifications have been made and the rationale has been created. Now we're defining the steps we will need to perform to protect the business in the event of an actual disaster. Table 8-2 shows a common scheme to classify the recovery timeframe needs of each business function.

Table 8-2 Recovery Timeframe Requirements Classification	
Rating Class	*Recovery Timeframe Requirements*
AAA	Immediate recovery needed; no downtime allowed
AA	Full functional recovery required within four hours
A	Same day business recovery required
B	Up to 24 hours downtime acceptable
C	24 to 72 hours downtime acceptable
D	Greater than 72 hours downtime acceptable

The steps in the disaster planning process phase are:

> **Data Processing Continuity Planning.** Planning for the disaster and creating the plans to cope with it.

> **Data Recovery Plan Maintenance.** Keeping the plans up-to-date and relevant.

Data Processing Continuity Planning

The various means of processing backup services are all important elements to the disaster recovery plan. Here we look at the most common alternate processing types:

✦ Mutual aid agreements

✦ Subscription services

✦ Multiple centers

✦ Service bureaus

✦ Other data center backup alternatives

Mutual Aid Agreements

A mutual aid agreement (sometimes called a *reciprocal agreement*) is an arrangement with another company that may have similar computing needs. The other company may have similar hardware or software configurations or may require the same network data communications or Internet access as your organization.

Disaster Recovery Plan Software Tools

There are several vendors that distribute automated tools to create disaster recovery plans. These tools can improve productivity by providing formatted templates customized to the particular organization's needs. Some vendors also offer specialized recovery software focused on a particular type of business or vertical market. A good source of links to various vendors is located at: www.intiss.com/intisslinks.

In this type of agreement, both parties agree to support each other in the case of a disruptive event. This arrangement is made on the assumption that each organization's operations area will have the capacity to support the other's in time of need. This is a big assumption.

There are clear advantages to this type of arrangement. It allows an organization to obtain a disaster-processing site at very little or no cost, thereby creating an alternate processing site even though a company may have very few financial resources to create one. Also, if the companies have very similar processing needs, that is, the same network operating system, the same data communications needs, or the same transaction processing procedures, this type of agreement may be workable.

This type of agreement has serious disadvantages, however, and really should be considered only if the organization has the perfect partner (a subsidiary, perhaps) and has no other alternative to disaster recovery (i.e., a solution would not exist otherwise). One disadvantage is that it is highly unlikely that each organization's infrastructure will have the extra, unused capacity to enable full operational processing during the event. Also, as opposed to a hot or warm site, this type of arrangement severely limits the responsiveness and support available to the organization during an event and can be used only for short-term outage support.

The biggest flaw in this type of plan is obvious if we ask what happens when the disaster is large enough to affect both organizations. A major outage can easily disrupt both companies, thereby canceling any advantage that this agreement might provide. The capacity and logistical elements of this type of plan make it seriously limited.

Subscription Services
Another type of alternate processing scenario is presented by subscription services. In this scenario, third-party commercial services provide alternate backup and processing facilities. Subscription services are probably the most common of the alternate processing site implementations. They have very specific advantages and disadvantages, as we will see.

There are three basic forms of subscription services with some variations:

✦ Hot site

✦ Warm site

✦ Cold site

Hot Site

This is the Cadillac of disaster recovery alternate backup sites. A hot site is a fully configured computer facility with electrical power, heating, ventilation, and air conditioning (HVAC) and functioning file/print servers and workstations. The applications that are needed to sustain remote transaction processing are installed on the servers and workstations and are kept up-to-date to mirror the production system. Theoretically, personnel and/or operators should be able to walk in and, with a data restoration of modified files from the last backup, begin full operations in a very short time. If the site participates in *remote journaling*, that is, mirroring transaction processing with a high-speed data line to the hot site, even the backup time may be reduced or eliminated.

This type of site requires constant maintenance of the hardware, software, data, and applications to ensure that the site accurately mirrors the state of the production site. This adds administrative overhead and can be a strain on resources, especially if a dedicated disaster recovery maintenance team does not exist.

The advantages to a hot site are numerous. The primary advantage is that 24/7 availability and exclusivity of use are assured. The site is available immediately (or within the allowable time tolerances) after the disruptive event occurs. The site can support an outage for a short time as well as a long-term outage.

Some of the drawbacks of a hot site are as follows:

✦ It is seriously the most expensive of any alternative. Full redundancy of all processing components (e.g., hardware, software, communications lines, and applications) is expensive, and the services provided to support this function will not be cheap.

✦ It is common for the service provider to oversell its processing capabilities, betting that not all of its clients will need the facilities simultaneously. This situation could create serious contention for the site's resources if a disaster were large enough to affect a major geographic region.

✦ There also exists a security issue at the hot site, as the applications may contain mirrored copies of live production data. Therefore, all of the security controls and mechanisms that are required at the primary site must be duplicated at the hot site. Access must be controlled and the organization must be aware of the security methodology implemented by the service organization.

✦ Also, a hot site might be administratively resource-intensive because controls must be implemented to keep the data up-to-date and the software patched.

Warm Site

A warm site could best be described as a cross between a hot site and cold site. Like a hot site, the warm site is a computer facility readily available with electrical power, HVAC, and computers, but the applications may not be installed or configured. It might have file/print servers, but not a full complement of workstations. External communication links and other data elements that commonly take a long time to order and install will be present, however.

To enable remote processing at this type of site, workstations will have to be delivered quickly and applications and their data will need to be restored from backup media.

The advantages to this type of site, as opposed to the hot site, are primarily as follows:

Cost. This type of configuration will be considerably less expensive than a hot site.

Location. Because this type of site requires less extensive control and configuration, more flexibility exists in the choice of site.

Resources. Administrative resource drain is lower than with the maintenance of a hot site.

The primary disadvantage of a warm site, compared to a hot site, is the difference in the amount of time and effort it will take to start production processing at the new site. If extremely urgent critical transaction processing is not needed, this may be an acceptable alternative.

Cold Site

A cold site is the least ready of any of the three choices, but it is probably the most common of the three. A cold site differs from the other two in that it is ready for equipment to be brought in during an emergency, but no computer hardware (servers or workstations) resides at the site. The cold site is a room with electrical power and HVAC, but computers must be brought on-site if needed, and communications links may be ready or not. File and print servers have to be brought in, as well as all workstations, and applications will need to be installed and current data restored from backups.

A cold site is not considered an adequate resource for disaster recovery because of the length of time required to get it going and all of the variables that will not be resolved before the disruptive event. In reality, using a cold site will most likely make effective recovery impossible. It will be next to impossible to perform an in-depth disaster recovery test or to do parallel transaction processing, making it very hard to predict the success of a disaster recovery effort.

There are some advantages to a cold site, however, the primary one being cost. If an organization has very little budget for an alternative backup-processing site, the cold site might be better than nothing. Also, resource contention with other organizations will not be a problem, and neither will geographic location likely be an issue.

The big problem with this type of site is that having the cold site could engender a false sense of security. But until a disaster strikes, there's really no way to tell whether it works or not, and by then it will be too late.

Multiple Centers

A variation on the previously listed alternative sites is called multiple centers, or *dual sites*. In a multiple-center concept, the processing is spread over several operations centers, creating a distributed approach to redundancy and sharing of available resources. These multiple centers could be owned and managed by the same organization (in-house sites) or used in conjunction with some sort of reciprocal agreement.

The advantages are primarily financial because the cost is contained. Also, this type of site will often allow for resource and support sharing among the multiple sites. The main disadvantage is the same as for mutual aid: a major disaster could easily overtake the processing capability of the sites. Also, multiple configurations could be difficult to administer.

Service Bureaus

In rare cases, an organization may contract with a service bureau to fully provide all alternate backup-processing services. The big advantage to this type of arrangement is the quick response and availability of the service bureau, testing is possible, and the service bureau may be available for more than backup. The disadvantages of this type of setup are primarily the expense and resource contention during a large emergency.

Other Data Center Backup Alternatives

There are a few other alternatives to the ones we have previously mentioned. Quite often an organization may use some combination of these alternatives in addition to one of the preceding scenarios.

> **Rolling/mobile backup sites.** Contracting with a vendor to provide mobile backup services. This may take the form of mobile homes or flatbed trucks with power and HVAC sufficient to stage the alternate processing required. This is considered a cold site variation.

> **In-house or external supply of hardware replacements.** Vendor re-supply of needed hardware, or internal stockpiling of critical components inventory. The organization may have a subscription service with a vendor to send identified critical components overnight. May be acceptable for a warm site but is not acceptable for a hot site.

Prefabricated buildings. It's not unusual for a company to employ a service organization to construct prefabricated buildings to house the alternate processing functions if a disaster should occur. Not too different from a mobile backup site—a very cold site.

Transaction Redundancy Implementations

The CISSP candidate should understand the three concepts used to create a level of fault tolerance and redundancy in transaction processing. While these processes are not used solely for disaster recovery, they are often elements of a larger disaster recovery plan. If one or more of these processes are employed, the ability of a company to get back on-line is greatly enhanced.

Electronic vaulting. Electronic vaulting refers to the transfer of backup data to an off-site location. This is primarily a batch process of dumping the data through communications lines to a server at an alternate location.

Remote journaling. Remote journaling refers to the parallel processing of transactions to an alternate site, as opposed to a batch dump process like electronic vaulting. A communications line is used to transmit live data as it occurs. This feature enables the alternate site to be fully operational at all times and introduces a very high level of fault tolerance.

Database shadowing. Database shadowing uses the live processing of remote journaling, but it creates even more redundancy by duplicating the database sets to multiple servers. See "Server Redundancy" in Chapter 3.

Disaster Recovery Plan Maintenance

Disaster recovery plans often get out of date. A similarity common to all recovery plans is how quickly they become obsolete, for many different reasons. The company may reorganize and the critical business units may be different than when the plan was first created. Most commonly, changes in the network or computing infrastructure may change the location or configuration of hardware, software, and other components. The reasons might be administrative: complex disaster recovery plans are not easily updated, personnel lose interest in the process, or employee turnover might affect involvement.

Whatever the reason, plan maintenance techniques must be employed from the outset to ensure that the plan remains fresh and usable. It's important to build maintenance procedures into the organization by using job descriptions that centralize responsibility for updates. Also, create audit procedures that can report regularly on the state of the plan. It's also important to ensure that multiple versions of the plan do not exist because it could create confusion during an emergency. Always replace older versions of the text with updated versions throughout the enterprise when a plan is changed or replaced.

Emergency management plans, business continuity plans, and disaster recovery plans should be regularly reviewed, evaluated, modified, and updated. At a minimum, the plan should be reviewed at an annual audit. The plan should also be re-evaluated:

✦ After tests or training exercises, to adjust any discrepancies between the test results and the plan

✦ After a disaster response or an emergency recovery, as this is an excellent time to amend the parts of the plan that were not effective

✦ When personnel, their responsibilities, their resources, or organizational structures change, to familiarize new or reorganized personnel with procedures

✦ When polices, procedures, or infrastructures change

Testing the Disaster Recovery Plan

Testing the disaster recovery plan is very important (a tape backup system cannot be considered working until full restoration tests have been conducted); a disaster recovery plan has many elements that are only theoretical until they have actually been tested and certified. The test plan must be created, and testing must be carried out in an orderly, standardized fashion and be executed on a regular basis.

Also, there are five specific disaster recovery plan–testing types that the CISSP candidate must know (see "The Five Disaster Recovery Plan Test Types" later in this chapter). Regular disaster recovery drills and tests are a cornerstone of any disaster recovery plan. No demonstrated recovery capability exists until the plan is tested. The tests must exercise every component of the plan for confidence to exist in the plan's ability to minimize the impact of a disruptive event.

Reasons for Testing

In addition to the general reasons for testing we have previously mentioned, there are several specific reasons to test, primarily to inform management of the recovery capabilities of the enterprise. Other specific reasons are as follows:

✦ Testing verifies the accuracy of the recovery procedures and identifies deficiencies.

✦ Testing prepares and trains the personnel to execute their emergency duties.

✦ Testing verifies the processing capability of the alternate backup site.

Creating the Test Document

To get the maximum benefit and coordination from the test, a document outlining the test scenario must be produced, containing the reasons for the test, the objectives of the test, and the type of test to be conducted (see the five following types).

Also, this document should include granular details of what will happen during the test, including the following:

✦ The testing schedule and timing

✦ The duration of the test

✦ The specific test steps

✦ Who will be the participants in the test

✦ The task assignments of the test personnel

✦ The resources and services required (supplies, hardware, software, documentation, and so forth)

Certain fundamental concepts will apply to the testing procedure. Primarily, the test must not disrupt normal business functions. Also, the test should start with the easy testing types (see the following section) and gradually work up to major simulations after the recovery team has acquired testing skills.

It's important to remember that the reason for the test is to find weaknesses in the plan. If no weaknesses were found, it was probably not an accurate test. The test is not a graded contest on how well the recovery plan or personnel executing the plan performed. Mistakes will be made, and this is the time to make them. Document the problems encountered during the test and update the plan as needed, then test again.

The Five Disaster Recovery Plan Test Types

Disaster recovery/emergency management plan testing scenarios have several levels and can be called different things, but there are generally five types of disaster recovery plan tests. The listing here is prioritized, from the simplest to the most complete testing type. As the organization progresses through the tests, each test is progressively more involved and more accurately depicts the actual responsiveness of the company. Some of the testing types, for example, the last two, require major investments of time, resources, and coordination to implement. The CISSP candidate should know all of these and what they entail.

The following are the testing types:

Checklist review. During a checklist type of disaster recovery plan, copies of the plan are distributed to each business unit's management. The plan is then reviewed to ensure the plan addresses all procedures and critical areas of the organization. This is considered a preliminary step to a real test and is not a satisfactory test in itself.

Table-top exercise or structured walk-through test. In this type of test, members of the emergency management group and business unit management representatives meet in a conference room setting to discuss their responsibilities and how they would react to emergency scenarios by stepping through the plan. The goal is to ensure that the plan accurately reflects the organization's ability to recover successfully, at least on paper. Each step of the plan is walked-through in the meeting and marked as performed. Major glaring faults with the plan should be apparent during the walk-through.

Walk-through drill or simulation test. The emergency management group and response teams actually perform their emergency response functions by walking through the test, without actually initiating recovery procedures. During a simulation test, all of the operational and support personnel expected to perform during an actual emergency meet in a practice session. The goal here is to test the ability of the personnel to respond to a simulated disaster. The simulation goes to the point of relocating to the alternate backup site or enacting recovery procedures, but it does not perform any actual recovery process or alternate processing.

Functional drill or parallel test. Tests specific functions such as medical response, emergency notifications, warning and communications procedures, and equipment, although not necessarily all at once. Also includes evacuation drills, where personnel walk the evacuation route to a designated area where procedures for accounting for the personnel are tested. A parallel test is a full test of the recovery plan, utilizing all personnel. The goal of this type of test is to ensure that critical systems will actually run at the alternate processing backup site. Systems are relocated to the alternate site, parallel processing is initiated, and the results of the transactions and other elements are compared.

Full-interruption or full-scale exercise. A real-life emergency situation is simulated as closely as possible. Involves all of the participants that would be responding to the real emergency, including community and external organizations. The test may involve ceasing some real production processing. The plan is totally implemented as if it were a real disaster, to the point of involving emergency services (although for a major test, local authorities might be informed and help coordinate).

Table 8-3 lists the five disaster recovery plan testing types in priority.

Plan Viability

Remember: The functionality of the recovery plan will directly determine the survivability of the organization. The plan shouldn't be a document gathering dust in the CIO's bookcase. It has to reflect the actual capability of the organization to recover from a disaster, and therefore needs to be tested regularly.

Table 8-3
Disaster Recovery Plan Testing Types

Level	Type	Description
1	Checklist	Copies of plan are distributed to management for review.
2	Table-top Exercise	Management meets to step through the plan.
3	Simulation	All support personnel meet in a practice execution session.
4	Functional Drill	All systems are functionally tested and drills executed.
5	Full-Scale Exercise	Real-life emergency situation is simulated.

Disaster Recovery Procedures

This part of the plan details what roles various personnel will take on, what tasks must be implemented to recover and salvage the site, how the company interfaces with external groups, and what financial considerations will arise. Senior management must resist the temptation to participate hands-on in the recovery effort, as these efforts should be delegated. Senior management has many very important roles in the process of disaster recovery, including:

✦ Remaining visible to employees and stakeholders

✦ Directing, managing, and monitoring the recovery

✦ Rationally amending business plans and projections

✦ Clearly communicating new roles and responsibilities

Information or technology management has more tactical roles to play, such as:

✦ Identifying and prioritizing mission-critical applications

✦ Continuously reassessing the recovery site's stability

✦ Recovering and constructing all critical data

Monitoring employee morale and guarding against employee burnout during a disaster recovery event is the proper role of human resources. Other emergency recovery tasks associated with human resources could include:

✦ Providing appropriate retraining

✦ Monitoring productivity of personnel

✦ Providing employees and family with counseling and support

The financial area is primarily responsible for:

✦ Reestablishing accounting processes, such as payroll, benefits, and accounts payable

✦ Reestablishing transaction controls and approval limits

Isolation of the incident scene should begin as soon as the emergency has been discovered. Authorized personnel should attempt to secure the scene and control access; however, no one should be placed in physical danger to perform these functions. It's important for life safety that access be controlled immediately at the scene, and only by trained personnel directly involved in the disaster response. Additional injury or exposure to recovery personnel after the initial incident must be prevented.

The Recovery Team

A recovery team will be clearly defined with the mandate to implement the recovery procedures at the declaration of the disaster. The recovery team's primary task is to get the predefined critical business functions operating at the alternate backup-processing site.

Among the many tasks the recovery team will have will be the retrieval of needed materials from off-site storage, that is, backup tapes, media, workstations, and so on. When this material has been retrieved, the recovery team will install the necessary equipment and communications. The team will also install the critical systems, applications, and data required for the critical business units to resume working.

The Salvage Team

A salvage team, separate from the recovery team, will be dispatched to return the primary site to normal processing environmental conditions. It's advisable to have a different team because this team will have a different mandate from the recovery team. They are not involved with the same issues the recovery team is concerned with, like creating production processing and determining the criticality of data. The salvage team has the mandate to quickly and, more importantly, safely clean, repair, salvage, and determine the viability of the primary processing infrastructure after the immediate disaster has ended.

Clearly, this cannot begin until all possibility of personal danger has ended. Firefighters or police might control the return to the site. The salvage team must identify sources of expertise, equipment, and supplies that can make the return to the site possible. The salvage team supervises and expedites the cleaning of equipment or storage media that might have suffered from smoke damage, the removal of standing water, and the drying of water-damaged media and reports.

This team is often also given the authority to declare when the site is up and running again; that is, when the resumption of normal duties can begin at the primary site. This responsibility is large because many elements of production must be examined before the green light is given to the recovery team that operations can return.

Normal Operations Resume

This job is normally the task of the recovery team, or another, separate resumption team may be created. The plan must have full procedures on how the company will return production processing from the alternate site to the primary site with the minimum of disruption and risk. It's interesting to note that the steps to resume normal processing operations will be different than the steps in the recovery plan; that is, the least critical work should be brought back first to the primary site.

It's important to note that the emergency is not over until all operations are back in full production mode at the primary site. Reoccupying the site of a disaster or emergency should not be undertaken until a full safety inspection has been done. Ideally the investigation into the cause of the emergency has been completed and all damaged property has been salvaged and restored before returning. During and after an emergency, the safety of personnel must be monitored, any remaining hazards must be assessed, and security must be maintained at the scene. After all safety precautions have been taken, an inventory of damaged and undamaged property must be done to begin salvage and restoration tasks. Also, the site must not be reoccupied until all on-site investigative processes have been completed. Detailed records must be kept of all disaster-related costs and valuations must be made of the effect of the business interruption.*

All elements discussed here involve well-coordinated logistical plans and resources. To manage and dispatch a recovery team, a salvage team, and perhaps a resumption team is a major effort, and the short descriptions we have here should not give the impression that it is not a very serious task.

When Is a Disaster Over?

When is a disaster over? The answer is very important. The disaster is not over until all operations have been returned to their normal location and function. A very large window of vulnerability exists when transaction processing returns from the alternate backup site to the original production site. The disaster can be officially called over only when all areas of the enterprise are back to normal in their original home, and all data has been certified as accurate.

---

*Source: "Emergency Management Guide for Business and Industry," Federal Emergency Management Agency, August 1998.

Other Recovery Issues

Several other issues must be discussed as important elements of a disaster scenario:

- ✦ Interfacing with external groups
- ✦ Employee relations
- ✦ Fraud and crime
- ✦ Financial disbursement
- ✦ Media relations

When an emergency occurs that could potentially have an impact outside the facility, the public must be informed, regardless of whether there is any immediate threat to public safety. The disaster recovery plan should include determinations of the audiences that may be affected by an emergency and procedures to communicate with them. Information the public will want to know could include public safety or health concerns, the nature of the incident, the remediation effort, and future prevention steps. Common audiences for information could include:

- ✦ The media
- ✦ Unions and contractors
- ✦ Shareholders
- ✦ Neighbors
- ✦ Employees' families and retirees

Since the media is such an important link to the public, disaster plans and tests must contain procedures for addressing the media and communicating important information. A trained spokesperson should be designated, and established communications procedures should be prepared. Accurate and approved information should be released in a timely manner, without speculation, blame, or obfuscation.

Interfacing with External Groups

Quite often the organization might be well equipped to cope with a disaster in relation to its own employees, but it overlooks its relationship with external parties. The external parties could be municipal emergency groups like police, fire, EMS, medical, or hospital staff; they could be civic officials, utility providers, the press, customers, or shareholders. How all personnel, from senior management on down, interact with these groups will impact the success of the disaster recovery effort. The recovery plan must clearly define steps and escalation paths for communications with these external groups.

One of the elements of the plan will be to identify how close the operations site is to emergency facilities: medical (hospital, clinic), police, and fire. The timeliness of the response of emergency groups will have a bearing on implementation of the plan when a disruptive event occurs.

Employee Relations

Another important facet of the disaster recovery plan is how the organization manages its relationship with its employees and their families. In the event of a major life and/or safety-endangering event, the organization has an inherent responsibility to its employees (and families, if the event is serious enough). The organization must make preparations to be able to continue salaries even when business production has stopped. This salary continuance may be for an extended period of time, and the company should be sure its insurance can cover this cost, if needed. Also, the employees and their families may need funds for various types of emergency assistance for relocation or extended living support, as can happen with a major natural event such as an earthquake or flood.

Fraud and Crime

Other problems related to the event may crop up. Beware of those individuals or organizations that might seek to capitalize financially on the disaster by exploiting security concerns or other opportunities for fraud. In a major physical disaster, vandalism and looting are common occurrences. The plan must consider these contingencies.

Financial Disbursement

An often-overlooked facet of the disaster will be expense disbursement. Procedures for storing signed, authorized checks off-site must be considered in order to facilitate financial reimbursement. Also, the possibility that the expenses incurred during the event may exceed the emergency manager's authority must be addressed.

Media Relations

A major part of any disaster recovery scenario involves the media. An important part of the plan must address dealing with the media and with civic officials. It's important for the organization to prepare an established and unified organizational response that will be projected by a credible, trained, informed spokesperson. The company should be accessible to the media so they don't go to other sources; report your own bad news so as to not appear to be covering up. Tell the story quickly, openly, and honestly to avoid suspicion or rumors. Before the disaster, as part of the plan, determine the appropriate clearance and approval processes for the media. It's important to take control of dissemination of the story quickly and early in the course of the event.

✦   ✦   ✦

Assessment Questions

You can find the answers to the following questions in Appendix A.

1. Which choice below is the first priority in an emergency?

    a. Communicating to employees' families the status of the emergency

    b. Notifying external support resources for recovery and restoration

    c. Protecting the health and safety of everyone in the facility

    d. Warning customers and contractors of a potential interruption of service

2. Which choice below is NOT considered an appropriate role for senior management in the business continuity and disaster recovery process?

    a. Delegate recovery roles

    b. Publicly praise successes

    c. Closely control media and analyst communications

    d. Assess the adequacy of information security during the disaster recovery

3. Why is it so important to test disaster recovery plans frequently?

    a. The businesses that provide subscription services might have changed ownership.

    b. A plan is not considered viable until a test has been performed.

    c. Employees might get bored with the planning process.

    d. Natural disasters can change frequently.

4. Which disaster recovery/emergency management plan–testing type below is considered the most cost-effective and efficient way to identify areas of overlap in the plan before conducting more demanding training exercises?

    a. Full-scale exercise

    b. Walk-through drill

    c. Table-top exercise test

    d. Evacuation drill

5. Which type of backup subscription service will allow a business to recover quickest?

    a. A hot site

    b. A mobile or rolling backup service

    c. A cold site

    d. A warm site

6. Which choice below represents the most important first step in creating a business resumption plan?

    a. Performing a risk analysis

    b. Obtaining senior management support

    c. Analyzing the business impact

    d. Planning recovery strategies

7. What could be a major disadvantage to a mutual aid or reciprocal type of backup service agreement?

    a. It is free or at a low cost to the organization.

    b. The use of prefabricated buildings makes recovery easier.

    c. In a major emergency, the site might not have the capacity to handle the operations required.

    d. Annual testing by the Info Tech department is required to maintain the site.

8. In developing an emergency or recovery plan, which choice below would NOT be considered a short-term objective?

    a. Priorities for restoration

    b. Acceptable downtime before restoration

    c. Minimum resources needed to accomplish the restoration

    d. The organization's strategic plan

9. When is the disaster considered to be officially over?

    a. When the danger has passed and the disaster has been contained

    b. When the organization has processing up and running at the alternate site

    c. When all of the elements of the business have returned to normal functioning at the original site

    d. When all employees have been financially reimbursed for their expenses

10. When should the public and media be informed about a disaster?

    a. Whenever site emergencies extend beyond the facility

    b. When any emergency occurs at the facility, internally or externally

    c. When the public's health or safety is in danger

    d. When the disaster has been contained

11. What is the number one priority of disaster response?

   a. Resuming transaction processing

   b. Personnel safety

   c. Protecting the hardware

   d. Protecting the software

12. Which choice below is the BEST description of the criticality prioritization goal of the Business Impact Assessment (BIA) process?

   a. The identification and prioritization of every critical business unit process

   b. The identification of the resource requirements of the critical business unit processes

   c. The estimation of the maximum downtime the business can tolerate

   d. The presentation of the documentation of the results of the BIA

13. Which choice below most accurately describes a business impact analysis (BIA)?

   a. A program that implements the strategic goals of the organization

   b. A management-level analysis that identifies the impact of losing an entity's resources

   c. A prearranged agreement between two or more entities to provide assistance

   d. Activities designed to return an organization to an acceptable operating condition

14. What is considered the major disadvantage to employing a hot site for disaster recovery?

   a. Exclusivity is assured for processing at the site.

   b. Maintaining the site is expensive.

   c. The site is immediately available for recovery.

   d. Annual testing is required to maintain the site.

15. Which choice below is NOT considered an appropriate role for Financial Management in the business continuity and disaster recovery process?

   a. Tracking the recovery costs

   b. Monitoring employee morale and guarding against employee burnout

   c. Formally notifying insurers of claims

   d. Reassessing cash flow projections

16. Which choice below is the MOST accurate description of a warm site?

    a. A backup processing facility with adequate electrical wiring and air conditioning but no hardware or software installed

    b. A backup processing facility with most hardware and software installed, which can be operational within a matter of days

    c. A backup processing facility with all hardware and software installed and 100% compatible with the original site, operational within hours

    d. A mobile trailer with portable generators and air conditioning

17. Which of the following is NOT one of the five disaster recovery plan testing types?

    a. Simulation

    b. Checklist

    c. Mobile

    d. Full Interruption

18. Which choice below is an example of a potential hazard due to a technological event, rather than a human event?

    a. Sabotage

    b. Financial collapse

    c. Mass hysteria

    d. Enemy attack

19. Which of the following is NOT considered an element of a backup alternative?

    a. Electronic vaulting

    b. Remote journaling

    c. Warm site

    d. Checklist

20. Which choice below refers to a business asset?

    a. Events or situations that could cause a financial or operational impact to the organization

    b. Protection devices or procedures in place that reduce the effects of threats

    c. Competitive advantage, credibility, or good will

    d. Personnel compensation and retirement programs

21. Which statement below is NOT correct regarding the role of the recovery team during the disaster?

    a. The recovery team must be the same as the salvage team as they perform the same function.

    b. The recovery team is often separate from the salvage team as they perform different duties.

    c. The recovery team's primary task is to get predefined critical business functions operating at the alternate processing site.

    d. The recovery team will need full access to all backup media.

22. Which choice below is incorrect regarding when a BCP, DRP, or emergency management plan should be evaluated and modified?

    a. Never; once it has been fully tested it should not be changed.

    b. Annually, in a scheduled review.

    c. After training drills, tests, or exercises.

    d. After an emergency or disaster response.

23. When should security isolation of the incident scene start?

    a. Immediately after the emergency is discovered

    b. As soon as the disaster plan is implemented

    c. After all personnel have been evacuated

    d. When hazardous materials have been discovered at the site

24. Which choice below is NOT a recommended step to take when resuming normal operations after an emergency?

    a. Reoccupy the damaged building as soon as possible.

    b. Account for all damage-related costs.

    c. Protect undamaged property.

    d. Conduct an investigation.

25. Which choice below would NOT be a good reason to test the disaster recovery plan?

    a. Testing verifies the processing capability of the alternate backup site.

    b. Testing allows processing to continue at the database shadowing facility.

    c. Testing prepares and trains the personnel to execute their emergency duties.

    d. Testing identifies deficiencies in the recovery procedures.

26. Which statement below is NOT true about the post-disaster salvage team?

    a. The salvage team must return to the site as soon as possible regardless of the residual physical danger.

    b. The salvage team manages the cleaning of equipment after smoke damage.

    c. The salvage team identifies sources of expertise to employ in the recovery of equipment or supplies.

    d. The salvage team may be given the authority to declare when operations can resume at the disaster site.

27. Which statement below is the most accurate about the results of the disaster recovery plan test?

    a. If no deficiencies were found during the test, then the plan is probably perfect.

    b. The results of the test should be kept secret.

    c. If no deficiencies were found during the test, then the test was probably flawed.

    d. The plan should not be changed no matter what the results of the test.

28. Which statement is true regarding the disbursement of funds during and after a disruptive event?

    a. Because access to funds is rarely an issue during a disaster, no special arrangements need to be made.

    b. No one but the finance department should ever disburse funds during or after a disruptive event.

    c. In the event senior-level or financial management is unable to disburse funds normally, the company will need to file for bankruptcy.

    d. Authorized, signed checks should be stored securely off-site for access by lower-level managers in the event senior-level or financial management is unable to disburse funds normally.

29. Which statement is true regarding company/employee relations during and after a disaster?

    a. The organization has a responsibility to continue salaries or other funding to the employees and/or families affected by the disaster.

    b. The organization's responsibility to the employee's families ends when the disaster stops the business from functioning.

    c. Employees should seek any means of obtaining compensation after a disaster, including fraudulent ones.

    d. Senior-level executives are the only employees who should receive continuing salaries during the disruptive event.

30. Which choice below is the correct definition of a Mutual Aid Agreement?

    a. A management-level analysis that identifies the impact of losing an entity's resources

    b. An appraisal or determination of the effects of a disaster on human, physical, economic, and natural resources

    c. A prearranged agreement to render assistance to the parties of the agreement

    d. Activities taken to eliminate or reduce the degree of risk to life and property

31. Which choice below most accurately describes a business continuity program?

    a. Ongoing process to ensure that the necessary steps are taken to identify the impact of potential losses and maintain viable recovery

    b. A program that implements the mission, vision, and strategic goals of the organization

    c. A determination of the effects of a disaster on human, physical, economic, and natural resources

    d. A standard that allows for rapid recovery during system interruption and data loss

32. Which of the following would best describe a cold backup site?

    a. A computer facility with electrical power and HVAC, all needed applications installed and configured on the file/print servers, and enough workstations present to begin processing

    b. A computer facility with electrical power and HVAC but with no workstations or servers on-site prior to the event and no applications installed

    c. A computer facility with no electrical power or HVAC

    d. A computer facility available with electrical power and HVAC and some file/print servers, although the applications are not installed or configured, and all of the needed workstations may not be on site or ready to begin processing

Law, Investigation, and Ethics

Law, as it applies to information systems security, has multiple facets. A security professional is expected to know and understand what laws apply to computer crimes, how to determine whether a crime has occurred, how to preserve evidence, the basics of conducting an investigation, and the liabilities under the law.

In addition to legal obligations, a security practitioner has ethical responsibilities to the employer, the constituency that is being served, and to the profession as a whole. These ethical factors are delineated by a number of professional organizations, including the International Information Systems Security Certification Consortium (ISC)[2], the Internet Activities Board (IAB), and the Computer Ethics Institute.

Types of Computer Crime

Numerous government and private sector surveys show that computer crimes are increasing. It is difficult to estimate the economic impact of these crimes, however, because many are never detected or reported. It is not unreasonable to assume, however, that computer crimes result in billions of dollars in losses to companies in the worldwide economy. In general, computer crimes fall into two categories—crimes committed against the computer and crimes using the computer. The following is a general listing of the most prominent types of computer crimes:

> ◆ *Denial of Service (DoS) and Distributed Denial of Service.* Overloading or "hogging" a system's resources so that it is unable to provide the required services. In the distributed mode, requests for service from a particular resource can be launched from large numbers of hosts where software has been planted to become active at a particular time or upon receiving a particular command.

✦ *Theft of passwords*. Illegally acquiring a password to gain unauthorized access to an information system.

✦ *Network Intrusions*. Unauthorized penetrations into networked computer resources.

✦ *Emanation eavesdropping*. Receipt and display of information, which is resident on computers or terminals, through the interception of Radio Frequency (RF) signals generated by those computers or terminals. The U.S. government has established a program called Tempest that addresses this problem by requiring shielding and other emanation-reducing mechanisms to be employed on computers processing sensitive and classified government information.

✦ *Social engineering*. Using social skills to obtain information, such as passwords or PIN numbers, to be used in an attack against computer-based systems.

✦ *Illegal content of material*. Pornography is an example of this type of crime.

✦ *Fraud*. Using computers or the Internet to perpetrate crimes such as auctioning material that will not be delivered after receipt of payment.

✦ *Software piracy*. Illegal copying and use of software.

✦ *Dumpster diving*. Obtaining sensitive data, such as manuals and trade secrets, by gathering information that has been discarded as garbage in dumpsters or at recycling locations.

✦ *Malicious code*. Programs (such as viruses, Trojan horses, and worms) that, when activated, cause DoS or destruction/modification of the information on computers.

✦ *Spoofing of IP addresses*. Inserting a false IP address into a message to disguise the original location of the message or to impersonate an authorized source.

✦ *Information warfare*. Attacking the information infrastructure of a nation — including military/government networks, communication systems, power grids, and the financial community — to gain military and/or economic advantages.

✦ *Espionage*

✦ *Destruction or the alteration of information*

✦ *Use of readily available attack scripts on the Internet*. Scripts, which have been developed by others and are readily available through the Internet, which can be employed by unskilled individuals to launch attacks on networks and computing resources.

✦ *Masquerading*. Pretending to be someone else usually to gain higher access privileges to information that is resident on networked systems.

✦ *Embezzlement*. Illegally acquiring funds, usually through the manipulation and falsification of financial statements.

✦ *Data-diddling*. The modification of data.

✦ *Terrorism*

Examples of Computer Crime

The following are some specific instances of computer crimes:

✦ The Sapphire or Slammer worm of January 2003 that exploited buffer overflow vulnerabilities on computers running Microsoft SQL Server Desk Engine (MSDE 2000) or Microsoft SQL Server. This worm employs *random scanning* to randomly search for IP addresses to infect. With this approach, it spread at a phenomenal rate, doubling every 8.5 seconds.

✦ Code Red worm attack in July of 2001. Code Red is also a random scanning worm that spread through numerous threads to try random IP addresses. It doubled approximately every 37 minutes.

✦ Klez worm, alias ElKern, Klaz, or Kletz. Klez is a mass-mailer worm that appeared around January 2002 and contains a polymporphic .exe virus called ElKern. In Klez, there is no message text in the body of the email, but the worm portion contains a hidden message aimed at anti-virus researchers. KlezH is a later version of the Klez worm that appeared in April 2002 from Asia. Similar to its predecessor, KlezH sends email messages with randomly named attachments and subject fields.

✦ Distributed DoS attacks against Yahoo!, Amazon.com, and ZDNet in February 2000.

✦ Love Letter (Love Bug) worm released by Onel de Guzman in the Philippines that spread worldwide in May 2000.

✦ Inadvertent transmission of emails containing personal client information to 19 unintended recipients by Kaiser Permanente HMO in August 2000.

✦ Penetration of Microsoft Corporation's network in October 2000 by a cracker who gained access to software under development.

✦ Kevin Mitnick's attacks against telephone systems. Mitnick was convicted in 1989 for computer and access device fraud but eluded police and the FBI for more than two years while he was on probation. On Christmas 1995, he broke into the computers of Tsutomu Shimomura in San Diego, California. Tsutomu tracked down Mitnick after a cross-country electronic pursuit, and he was arrested by the FBI in Raleigh, North Carolina on February 15, 1995.

✦ Teenagers in Wisconsin (area code 414), known as the 414 Gang who, in 1982, launched attacks into the Sloan-Kettering Cancer Hospital's medical records systems.

✦ The Morris Internet Worm that spread through the Internet in November 1988 and resulted in a DoS. The cause of this disruption was a small program written by Robert Tappan Morris, a 23-year-old doctoral student at Cornell University.

✦ Attacks against U.S classified computer systems in 1986 by Germans working for the KGB described in the book *The Cuckoo's Egg* written by Clifford Stoll (Clifford Stoll, *The Cuckoo's Egg*, Doubleday, copyright 1989; ISBN 0-385-24946-2). Stoll uncovered this activity after he noticed a 75-cent error in a computer account at the Lawrence Livermore Laboratories.

Laws have been passed in many countries to address these crimes. Obviously, there are jurisdictional problems associated with the international character of the Internet that make prosecution difficult and sometimes impossible. Some of the international organizations that are addressing computer crime are the United Nations, Interpol, the European Union, and the G8 leading industrial nations.

The rapid development of new technology usually outpaces the law. Thus, law enforcement uses traditional laws against embezzlement, fraud, DoS, and wiretapping to prosecute computer criminals. The issues of digital signatures, e-commerce, and digital currency will certainly have to be addressed by the legal system as these technologies are deployed.

Law

There are many types of legal systems in the world that differ in how they treat evidence, the rights of the accused, and the role of the judiciary. Examples of these different legal systems are Common Law, Islamic and other Religious Law, and Civil Law. The Common Law System is employed in the United States, United Kingdom, Australia, and Canada. Civil Law Systems are used in France, Germany, and Quebec, to name a few.

Example: The United States

Under the Common Law system of the United States, there are three branches of government that make the laws. These branches are the legislative branch, the administrative agencies, and the judicial branch. The legislative branch makes statutory laws, the administrative agencies create administrative laws, and the judicial branch makes the common laws found in court decisions.

Compilation of Statutory Law

Statutory laws are collected as session laws, which are arranged in order of enactment or as statutory codes, which arrange the laws according to subject matter. In the United States at the federal level, the session laws are found in the *Statutes at Large* (Stat.), and the statutory codes are held in the *United States Code* (U.S.C.). The statutory laws for the states are also arranged in these two categories.

Federal statutes are usually cited to the United States Code, and this citation contains the following elements:

- ✦ The Code title number (each title is a grouping of statutes dealing with a particular subject matter)
- ✦ The abbreviation for the code (U.S.C.)
- ✦ The statutory section number within the title
- ✦ The date of the edition or supplement

For example, "18 U.S.C. § 1001 (1992)" refers to Section 1001 in Title 18 of the 1992 edition of the United States Code. Title 18 in the United States Code is Crimes and Criminal Procedures, and many computer crimes are prosecuted under this title. The U.S. Computer Fraud and Abuse Act that addresses the use of federal interest computers to commit fraud can be found as "18 U.S.C. § 1030 (1986)" Other titles are as follows:

Title 12. Banks and Banking

Title 15. Commerce and Trade

Title 26. Internal Revenue Code

Title 49. Transportation

Compilation of Administrative Law

Administrative laws are also arranged either chronologically in administrative registers or by subject matter in administrative codes. At the federal level, these arrangements are respectively called the *Federal Register* (Fed. Reg.) and the *Code of Federal Regulations* (C.F.R.). A citation to the Code of Federal Regulations includes the following:

✦ The number of the C.F.R. title

✦ The abbreviation for the Code (C.F.R.)

✦ The section number

✦ The year of publication

Thus, the reference "12 C.F.R. § 100.4 (1992)" points to Section 100.4 in Title 12 of the 1992 edition of the Code of Federal Regulations.

Compilation of Common Law

Common law is compiled as Case Reporters in chronological fashion and in Case Digests arranged by subject matter.

Common Law System Categories

The main categories of laws under the Common Law system (not to be confused with common law resulting from court decisions) are criminal law, civil (tort) law, and administrative/regulatory law.

Criminal law. Laws about individual conduct that violates government laws enacted for the protection of the public. Punishment can include financial penalties and imprisonment.

Civil law. Laws about a wrong inflicted upon an individual or organization that results in damage or loss. Punishment cannot include imprisonment, but financial awards comprised of punitive, compensatory, or statutory damages can be mandated.

Administrative/regulatory law. Standards of performance and conduct expected by government agencies from industries, organizations, officials, and officers. Violations of these laws can result in financial penalties and/or imprisonment.

Other categories of law under the common law system that relate to information systems are intellectual property and privacy laws.

Intellectual Property Law

The following categories fall under intellectual property law:

Patent. A patent provides the owner of the patent with a legally enforceable *right to exclude* others from practicing the invention covered by the patent for a specified period of time. It is of interest to note that a patent does not necessarily grant the owner the right to make, use, or sell the invention. A patent obtained by an individual might build on other patents, and thus, the individual must obtain permission from the owner(s) of the earlier patent(s) to exploit the new patent.

There are four criteria that an invention must meet in order to be patentable. These criteria are:

The invention must fall into one of the following five classes:

- Processes
- Machines
- Manufactures (objects made by humans or machines)
- Compositions of matter
- New uses of any of the above

The invention must be *useful*. One aspect of this test for utility is that the invention cannot be only a theoretical phenomenon.

The invention must be *novel*; it must be something that no one has developed before.

The invention must be *obvious* to "a person having ordinary skill in the art to which said subject matter pertains."

Patent law protects inventions and processes ("utility" patents), ornamental designs ("design" patents), and new varieties of plants ("plant" patents). In the United States, as of June 8, 1995, utility patents are granted for a period of 20 years from the date the application was filed. For patents in force prior to June 8, 1995 and patents granted on applications pending before that date, the patent term is the greater of 17 years from the date of issue (the term under prior law) or 20 years from the date of filing. Design patents are granted for a period of 14 years and a plant patent has a term of 17 years. Once the patent on an invention or design has expired, anyone is free to make, use, or sell the invention or design.

Copyright. A copyright protects "original works of authorship" and protects the right of the author to control the reproduction, adaptation, public distribution, and performance of these original works. Copyrights can also be applied to software and databases. The copyright law has two provisions that address uses of copyrighted material by educators, researchers, and librarians. These provisions:

- Codify the doctrine of *fair use*, under which limited copying of copyrighted works without the permission of the owner is allowed for certain teaching and research purposes

- Establish special limitations and exemptions for the reproduction of copyrighted works by libraries and archives

The Sonny Bono Copyright Term Extension Act, signed into law on October 27, 1998, amends the provisions concerning duration of copyright protection. The Act states that the terms of copyright are generally extended for an additional 20 years. Two specific example provisions of the Sonny Bono Copyright Term Extension Act are as follows:

- Works originally created on or after January 1, 1978 are protected from the time of their creation and are usually given a term of the author's life plus an additional 70 years after the author's death.

- Works originally created before January 1, 1978, but not published or registered by that date are covered by the statute, also with a duration of the author's life plus an additional 70 years after the author's death. In addition, the statute provides that in no case will the term of copyright for these types of works expire before December 31, 2002. For works published on or before December 31, 2002, the term of copyright will not expire before December 31, 2047.

Materials might fall into other copyright categories depending on the age of the work, if the copyright was renewed, if it was developed as work for hire, and so on. Detailed information can be found in the following publications of the U.S. Copyright Office:

- Circular 15, "Renewal of Copyright"

- Circular 15a, "Duration of Copyright"

- Circular 15t, "Extension of Copyright Terms"

Trade Secret. Secures and maintains the confidentiality of proprietary technical or business-related information that is adequately protected from disclosure by the owner. Corollaries to this definition are that the owner has invested resources to develop this information, it is valuable to the business of the owner, it would be valuable to a competitor, and it is not obvious.

Trademark. Establishes a word, name, symbol, color, sound, product shape, device, or combination of these that will be used to identify goods and to distinguish them from those made or sold by others.

Warranty. A warranty is a contract that commits an organization to stand behind its product. There are two types of warranties, implied and express. An *implied* warranty is an unspoken, unwritten promise created by state law that goes from a manufacturer or merchant to the customer. Under implied warranties, there are two categories — the implied warranty of fitness for a particular purpose and the implied warranty of merchantability. The implied warranty of *fitness for a particular purpose* is a commitment made by the seller when the consumer relies on the advice of the seller that the product is suited for a specific purpose. The implied *warranty of merchantability* is the seller's or manufacturer's promise that the product sold to the consumer is fit to be sold and will perform the functions that it is intended to perform. An *express* warranty is a warranty that is explicitly offered by the manufacturer or seller to the customer at the time of the sales transaction. This type of warranty contains voluntary commitments to remedy defects and malfunctions that some customers may encounter in using the product. An express warranty can be made orally or in writing. If it is in writing, it falls under the Magnuson-Moss Warranty Act.

The *Magnuson-Moss Warranty Act* is the 1975 U.S. federal law that governs warranties on consumer products. The Act requires manufacturers and sellers of consumer products to provide consumers with detailed information concerning warranty coverage. In addition, the FTC adopted three rules under the Act. These rules are the *Rule on Disclosure of Written Consumer Product Warranty Terms and Conditions* (the *Disclosure Rule*), the *Rule on Pre-Sale Availability of Written Warranty Terms* (the *Pre-Sale Availability Rule*), and the *Rule on Informal Dispute Settlement Procedures* (the *Dispute Resolution Rule*.) These Rules and the Act detail three basic requirements that apply to a warrantor or seller. These requirements are:

1. A warrantor must designate, or title, the written warranty as either *full* or *limited*.

2. A warrantor must state certain specified information about the coverage of the warranty in a single, clear, and easy-to-read document.

3. The warrantor or seller must ensure that warranties are available at the site of sale of the warranted consumer products so that consumers can read them before purchasing a product.

Regarding used products, an implied warranty can be disclaimed by if a written warranty is not provided. This disclaimer must be made in a conspicuous manner, preferably in writing, so that the consumer is aware that there is no warranty on the product. Terms such as this product is being sold "with all faults," or "as is" should be used. Some states do not permit disclaiming of the implied warranty.

Information Privacy and Privacy Laws

Privacy is the right of an individual to protection from unauthorized disclosure of the individual's personally identifiable information (PII). For example, the Health Insurance Portability & Accountability Act (HIPAA) lists the following 16 items as a person's individual identifiers:

✦ Names

✦ Postal address information, other than town or city, state, and zip code

✦ Telephone numbers

✦ Fax numbers

✦ Electronic mail addresses

✦ Social security numbers

✦ Medical record numbers

✦ Health plan beneficiary numbers

✦ Account numbers

✦ Certificate/license numbers

✦ Vehicle identifiers and serial numbers, including license plate numbers

✦ Device identifiers and serial numbers

✦ Web Universal Resource Locators (URLs)

✦ Internet Protocol (IP) address numbers

✦ Biometric identifiers, including finger- and voiceprints

✦ Full face photographic images and any comparable images

An individual's right to privacy is embodied in the following fundamental principles of privacy:

✦ *Notice* — regarding collection, use and disclosure of PII

✦ *Choice* — to opt out or opt in regarding disclosure of PII to third parties

✦ *Access* — by consumers to their PII to permit review and correction of information

✦ *Security* — to protect PII from unauthorized disclosure

✦ *Enforcement* — of applicable privacy policies and obligations

Privacy Policy

Organizations develop and publish privacy policies that describe their approach to handling PII. Web sites of organizations usually have their privacy policies available to read online and these policies usually cover the following areas:

✦ Statement of the organization's commitment to privacy

✦ The type of information collected, such as names, addresses, credit card numbers, phone numbers, and so on

✦ Retaining and using email correspondence

✦ Information gathered through cookies and Web server logs and how that information is used

✦ How information is shared with affiliates and strategic partners

✦ Mechanisms to secure information transmissions, such as encryption and digital signatures

✦ Mechanisms to protect PII stored by the organization

✦ Procedures for review of the organization's compliance with the privacy policy

✦ Evaluation of information protection practices

✦ Means for the user to access and correct PII held by the organization

✦ Rules for disclosing PII to outside parties

✦ Providing PII that is legally required

Privacy-Related Legislation and Guidelines

The following list summarizes some important legislation and recommended guidelines for privacy:

✦ *The Cable Communications Policy Act* provides for discretionary use of PII by cable operators internally but imposes restrictions on disclosures to third parties

✦ *The Children's Online Privacy Protection Act* (COPPA) is aimed at providing protection to children under the age of 13

✦ *Customer Proprietary Network Information Rules* apply to telephone companies and restrict their use of customer information both internally and to third parties

✦ *The Financial Services Modernization Act (Gramm-Leach-Bliley)* requires financial institutions to provide customers with clear descriptions of the institution's polices and procedures for protecting the PII of customers

✦ *Telephone Consumer Protection Act* restricts communications between companies and consumers, such as in telemarketing

✦ *The 1973 U.S. Code of Fair Information Practices* states that:

   1. There must not be personal data record–keeping systems whose very existence is secret.

   2. There must be a way for a person to find out what information about them is in a record and how it is used.

3. There must be a way for a person to prevent information about them, which was obtained for one purpose, from being used or made available for another purposes without their consent.

4. Any organization creating, maintaining, using, or disseminating records of identifiable personal data must ensure the reliability of the data for their intended use and must take precautions to prevent misuses of that data.

✦ *The Health Insurance Portability and Accountability Act* (HIPAA), Administrative Simplification Title, includes Privacy and Security Rules and standards for electronic transactions and code sets.

European Union (EU) Principles

The protection of information on private individuals from intentional or unintentional disclosure or misuse is the goal of the information privacy laws. The intent and scope of these laws widely varies from country to country. The European Union (EU) has defined privacy principles that in general are more protective of individual privacy than those applied in the United States. Therefore, the transfer of personal information from the EU to the United States, when equivalent personal protections are not in place in the United States, is prohibited. The EU principles include the following:

✦ Data should be collected in accordance with the law.

✦ Information collected about an individual cannot be disclosed to other organizations or individuals unless authorized by law or by consent of the individual.

✦ Records kept on an individual should be accurate and up to date.

✦ Individuals have the right to correct errors contained in their personal data.

✦ Data should be used only for the purposes for which it was collected, and it should be used only for a reasonable period of time.

✦ Individuals are entitled to receive a report on the information that is held about them.

✦ Transmission of personal information to locations where equivalent personal data protection cannot be assured is prohibited.

Health Care-Related Privacy Issues

An excellent example of the requirements and application of individual privacy principles is in the area of health care. The protection from disclosure and misuse of a private individual's medical information is a prime example of a privacy law. Some of the common health care security issues are as follows:

✦ Access controls of most health care information systems do not provide sufficient granularity to implement the principle of least privilege among users.

✦ Most off-the-shelf applications do not incorporate adequate information security controls.

✦ Systems must be accessible to outside partners, members, and some vendors.

✦ Providing users with the necessary access to the Internet creates the potential for enabling violations of the privacy and integrity of information.

✦ Criminal and civil penalties can be imposed for the improper disclosure of medical information.

✦ A large organization's misuse of medical information can cause the public to change its perception of the organization.

✦ Health care organizations should adhere to the following information privacy principles (based on European Union principles):

- An individual should have the means to monitor the database of stored information about themselves and should have the ability to change or correct that information.

- Information obtained for one purpose should not be used for another purpose.

- Organizations collecting information about individuals should ensure that the information is provided only for its intended use and should provide safeguards against the misuse of this information.

- The existence of databases containing personal information should not be kept secret.

The U.S. *Kennedy-Kassebaum Health Insurance Portability and Accountability Act* (HIPAA-Public Law 104–191), effective August 21, 1996, addresses the issues of health care privacy and plan portability in the United States. With respect to privacy, this Act stated, "Not later than the date that is 12 months after the date of the enactment of this Act, the Secretary of Health and Human Services shall submit . . . detailed recommendations on standards with respect to the privacy of individually identifiable health information." This Act further stated "the recommendations . . . shall address at least the following:

✦ The rights that an individual who is a subject of individually identifiable health information should have:

- The procedures that should be established for the exercise of such rights

- The uses and disclosures of such information that should be authorized or required"

The Privacy regulations were reopened for public comment for an additional period that closed on March 30, 2001. In March 2002, HHS proposed changes to the HIPAA Privacy Rule in response to input from health-care related organizations as well as the private sector. The changes were put into effect in August 2002. The Final Privacy Rule refers to security issues as illustrated in the following statements:

"(1) Standard: safeguards. A covered entity must have in place appropriate administrative, technical, and physical safeguards to protect the privacy of protected health information.

(2) Implementation specification: safeguards. A covered entity must reasonably safeguard protected health information from any intentional or unintentional use or disclosure that is in violation of the standards, implementation specifications or other requirements of this subpart."

The Platform for Privacy Preferences (P3P)

The Platform for Privacy Preferences was developed by the World Wide Web Consortium (W3C) to implement privacy practices on Web sites. The W3C P3P Specification states "P3P enables Web sites to express their privacy practices in a standard format that can be retrieved automatically and interpreted easily by user agents. P3P user agents will allow users to be informed of site practices (in both machine- and human-readable formats) and to automate decision-making based on these practices when appropriate. Thus users need not read the privacy policies at every site they visit."

The W3C P3P document can be found at www.w3.org/TR. With P3P, an organization can post its privacy policy in machine-readable form (XML) on its Web site. This policy statement should include:

✦ Who has access to collected information

✦ The type of information collected

✦ How the information is used

✦ The legal entity making the privacy statement

The P3P specification contains the following items:

✦ A standard vocabulary for describing a Web site's data practices

✦ A set of data elements that Web sites can refer to in their P3P privacy policies

✦ A standard schema for data a Web site may wish to collect, known as the "P3P base data schema"

✦ A standard set of uses, recipients, data categories, and other privacy disclosures

✦ An XML format for expressing a privacy policy

✦ A means of associating privacy policies with Web pages or sites and cookies

✦ A mechanism for transporting P3P policies over HTTP

A useful consequence of implementing P3P on a Web site is that Web site owners are required to answer multiple-choice questions about their privacy practices. This activity will cause the organization sponsoring the Web site to think about and evaluate their privacy policy and practices in the event that they have not already done so. After answering the necessary P3P privacy questions, an organization can then proceed to develop their policy. A number of sources provide free policy editors and assistance in writing privacy policies. Some of these resources can be found at www.w3.org/P3P/ and http://p3ptoolbox.org/.

P3P also supports user agents that allow a user to configure a P3P-enabled Web browser with the user's privacy preferences. Then, when the user attempts to access a Web site, the user agent compares the user's stated preferences with the privacy policy in machine-readable form at the Web site. Access will be granted if the preferences match the policy. Otherwise, either access to the Web site will be blocked or a pop-up window will appear notifying the user that he or she must change the privacy preferences. Microsoft's Internet Explorer 6 (IE6) Web browser supports P3P and can be used to generate and display a report describing a particular Web site's P3P-implemented privacy policy.

Another P3P implementation is provided by AT&T's Privacy Bird software that is an add-on to a browser and inserts an icon of a bird in the top right corner of a user's Web browser. The AT&T software reads the XML privacy policy statements from a Web site and causes the bird to chirp and change color to inform the user if the user's listed privacy preference settings are satisfied by the Web site's P3P policy statements. Clicking on the bird provides more detailed information concerning mismatches between the Web site's policy practices and the user's provided preferences.

Electronic Monitoring

Additional personal security issues involve keystroke monitoring, email monitoring, surveillance cameras, badges, and magnetic entry cards. Key issues in electronic monitoring are that the monitoring is conducted in a lawful manner and that it is applied in a consistent fashion. With email, for example, an organization monitoring employee email should:

✦ Inform all that email is being monitored by means of a prominent logon banner or some other frequent notification

  • This banner should state that by logging on to the system, the individual consents to electronic monitoring and is subject to a predefined punishment if the system is used for unlawful activities or if the user violates the organization's information security policy. It should also state that unauthorized access and use of the system is prohibited and subject to punishment.

✦ Ensure that monitoring is uniformly applied to all employees

✦ Explain what is considered acceptable use of the email system

✦ Explain who can read the email and how long it is backed up

✦ Not provide a guarantee of email privacy

In this context, it is useful to examine the difference between *enticement* and *entrapment*. Enticement occurs after an individual has gained unauthorized access to a system. The intruder is then lured to an attractive area or honey pot in order to provide time to determine the origin of the intrusion and eventually the identity of the intruder. For example, a student breaking into a professor's computer might be lured to a file entitled "Final Examination Questions." Entrapment, on the other hand, encourages the commission of a crime that the individual initially had no intention of committing.

Recent legislation has given the U.S. government additional license to monitor electronic communications and computer files. See the discussion on the Patriot Act in the section on "Computer Security, Privacy, and Crime Laws."

Computer Security, Privacy, and Crime Laws

The following is a summary of laws, regulations, and directives that lists requirements pertaining to the protection of computer-related information:

1970 U.S. Fair Credit Reporting Act. Covers consumer reporting agencies.

1970 U.S. Racketeer Influenced and Corrupt Organization (RICO) Act. Addresses both criminal and civil crimes involving racketeers influencing the operation of legitimate businesses; crimes cited in this act include mail fraud, securities fraud, and the use of a computer to perpetrate fraud.

1973 U.S. Code of Fair Information Practices. Applies to personal record keeping.

 1974 U.S. Privacy Act. Applies to federal agencies; provides for the protection of information about private individuals that is held in federal databases, and grants access by the individual to these databases. The law imposes civil and criminal penalties for violations of the provisions of the Act. The Act assigns the U.S. Treasury Department the responsibilities of implementing physical security practices, information management practices, and computer and network controls.

1978 Foreign Intelligence Surveillance Act (FISA). FISA can be used to conduct electronic surveillance and physical searches under a court order and without a warrant in cases of international terrorism, spying, or sabotage activities that are conducted by a foreign power or its agent. FISA is not intended for use in prosecuting U.S. citizens.

1980 Organization for Economic Cooperation and Development (OECD) Guidelines. Provides for data collection limitations, the quality of the data, specifications of the purpose for data collection, limitations on data use, information security safeguards, openness, participation by the individual on whom the data is being collected, and accountability of the data controller

1984 U.S. Medical Computer Crime Act. Addresses illegal access or alteration of computerized medical records through phone or data networks

1984 (strengthened in 1986 and 1994) First U.S. Federal Computer Crime Law Passed. Covers classified defense or foreign relations information, records of financial institutions or credit reporting agencies, and government computers. Unauthorized access or access in excess of authorization became a felony for classified information and a misdemeanor for financial information. This law made it a misdemeanor to knowingly access a U.S. Government computer without or beyond authorization if the U.S government's use of the computer would be affected.

1986 (amended in 1996) U.S. Computer Fraud and Abuse Act. Clarified the 1984 law and added three new crimes:

1. When use of a federal interest computer furthers an intended fraud

2. When altering, damaging, or destroying information in a federal interest computer or preventing the use of the computer or information that causes a loss of $1,000 or more or could impair medical treatment

3. Trafficking in computer passwords if it affects interstate or foreign commerce or permits unauthorized access to government computers

1986 U.S. Electronic Communications Privacy Act. Prohibits eavesdropping or the interception of message contents without distinguishing between private or public systems. This law updated the Federal privacy clause in the Omnibus Crime Control and Safe Streets Act of 1968 to include digitized voice, data, or video, whether transmitted over wire, microwave, or fiber optics. Court warrants are required to intercept wire or oral communications, except for phone companies, the FCC, and police officers that are party to a call with the consent of one of the parties.

1987 U.S. Computer Security Act. Places requirements on federal government agencies to conduct security-related training, to identify sensitive systems, and to develop a security plan for those sensitive systems. A category of sensitive information called *Sensitive But Unclassified* (SBU) has to be considered. This category, formerly called Sensitive Unclassified Information (SUI), pertains to information below the government's classified level that is important enough to protect, such as medical information, financial information, and research and development knowledge. This act also partitioned the government's responsibility for security between the National Institute of Standards and Technology (NIST) and the National Security Agency (NSA). NIST was given responsibility for information security in general, primarily for the commercial and SBU arenas, and NSA retained the responsibility for cryptography for classified government and military applications.

The Computer Security Act established the *National Computer System Security and Privacy Advisory Board* (CSSPAB), which is a twelve-member advisory group of experts in computer and telecommunications systems security.

1990 United Kingdom Computer Misuse Act. Defines computer-related criminal offenses

1991 U.S. Federal Sentencing Guidelines. Provides punishment guidelines for those found guilty of breaking federal law. These guidelines are as follows:

1. Treat the unauthorized possession of information without the intent to profit from the information as a crime.

2. Address both individuals and organizations.

3. Make the degree of punishment a function of the extent to which the organization has demonstrated due diligence (due care or reasonable care) in establishing a prevention and detection program.

4. Invoke the prudent man rule that requires senior officials to perform their duties with the care that ordinary, prudent people would exercise under similar circumstances.

5. Place responsibility on senior organizational management for the prevention and detection programs with fines of up to $290 million for nonperformance.

1992 OECD Guidelines to Serve as a Total Security Framework. The Framework includes laws, policies, technical and administrative measures, and education.

1994 U.S. Communications Assistance for Law Enforcement Act. Requires all communications carriers to make wiretaps possible.

1994 U.S. Computer Abuse Amendments Act. This act accomplished the following:

1. Changed the federal interest computer to a computer used in interstate commerce or communications

2. Covers viruses and worms

3. Included intentional damage as well as damage done with "reckless disregard of substantial and unjustifiable risk"

4. Limited imprisonment for the unintentional damage to one year

5. Provides for civil action to obtain compensatory damages or other relief

Paperwork Reduction Acts of 1980, 1995. The 1980 act amended in 1995 provides Information Resources Management (IRM) directives for the U.S. Government. This law established the Office of Information and Regulatory Affairs (OIRA) in the Office of Management and Budget (OMB). One result of the Act is to require government agencies to apply information technology systems to increase productivity, improve delivery of services, and minimize waste.

The OMB was assigned the responsibility for improving government efficiency through the application of new technologies and was also made responsible for developing guidance on information security for government agencies. Under the Paperwork Reduction Act, agencies must:

• Manage information resources to improve integrity, quality, and utility of information to all users

• Manage information resources to protect privacy and security

• Designate a senior official, reporting directly to the Secretary of the Treasury, to ensure that the responsibilities assigned by the Act are accomplished

> •Identify and afford security protections in conformance with the Computer Security Act of 1987 commensurate with the magnitude of harm and risk that might result from the misuse, loss, or unauthorized access relative to information collected by an agency or maintained on behalf of an agency
>
> • Implement and enforce applicable policies, procedures, standards, and guidelines on privacy, confidentiality, security, disclosures, and sharing of information collected or maintained by or for the agency

1995 Council Directive (Law) on Data Protection for the European Union (EU). Declares that each EU nation is to enact protections similar to those of the OECD Guidelines.

1996 U.S. Economic and Protection of Proprietary Information Act. Addresses industrial and corporate espionage and extends the definition of property to include proprietary economic information in order to cover the theft of this information

1996 U.S. Kennedy-Kassebaum Health Insurance and Portability Accountability Act (HIPAA). With additional requirements added in December 2000. Addresses the issues of personal health care information privacy, security, transactions and code sets, unique identifiers, and health plan portability in the United States.

1996 U.S. National Information Infrastructure Protection Act. Enacted in October 1996 as part of Public Law 104-294, it amended the Computer Fraud and Abuse Act, which is codified at 18 U.S.C. § 1030. The amended Computer Fraud and Abuse Act is patterned after the OECD Guidelines for the Security of Information Systems and addresses the protection of the confidentiality, integrity, and availability of data and systems. This path is intended to encourage other countries to adopt a similar framework, thus creating a more uniform approach to addressing computer crime in the existing global information infrastructure.

1996 Information Technology Management Reform Act (ITMRA) of 1996, National Defense Authorization Act for Fiscal Year 1996 (Clinger-Cohen Act). ITMRA is also known as the Clinger-Cohen Act. This legislation relieves the General Services Administration of responsibility for procurement of automated systems and contract appeals. OMB is charged with providing guidance, policy, and control for information technology procurement. With the Paperwork Reduction Act, as amended, this Act delineates OMB's responsibilities for overseeing agency practices regarding information privacy and security.

1996, Title I, Economic Espionage Act. The Economic Espionage Act address the numerous acts concerned with economic espionage and the national security aspects of the crime. The theft of trade secrets is also defined in the Act as a federal crime.

1998 U.S. Digital Millennium Copyright Act (DMCA). The DMCA prohibits trading, manufacturing, or selling in any way that is intended to bypass copyright protection mechanisms. It also addresses ISPs that unknowingly support the posting of copyrighted material by subscribers. If the ISP is notified that the material is copyrighted, the ISP must remove the material. Additionally, if the posting party proves that the removed material was of "lawful use," the ISP must restore the material and notify the copyright owner within 14 business days.

Two important rulings regarding the DMCA were made in 2001. The rulings involved DeCSS, which is a program that bypasses the Content Scrambling System (CSS) software used to prevent the viewing of DVD movie disks on unlicensed platforms. In a trade secrecy case (*DVD-CCA v. Banner*), the California appellate court overturned a lower court ruling that an individual who posted DeCSS on the Internet had revealed the trade secret of CSS. The appeals court has reversed an injunction on the posting of DeCSS, stating that the code is speech protected by the First Amendment.

The second case (*Universal City v. Reimerdes*) was the first constitutional challenge to DMCA anticircumvention rules. The case involved Eric Corley, the publisher of the hacker magazine *2600 Magazine*. Corley was covering the DeCSS situation, and as part of that coverage he posted DeCSS on his publication's Web site. The trial and appellate courts both ruled that the posting violated the DMCA and was, therefore, illegal. This ruling upheld the DMCA. It appears that there will be more challenges to DMCA in the future.

1999 U.S. Uniform Computers Information Transactions Act (UCITA). The National Commissioners on Uniform State Laws (NCCUSL) voted to approve the Uniform Computers Information Transactions Act (UCITA) on July 29, 1999. This legislation, which will have to be enacted state-by-state, will greatly affect libraries' access to and use of software packages. It also will keep in place the current licensing practices of software vendors. At present, shrink-wrap or click-wrap licenses limit rights that are normally granted under copyright law. Under Section 109 of the U.S. 1976 Copyright Act, the first sale provision permits "the owner of a particular copy without the authority of the copyright owner, to sell or otherwise dispose of the possession of that copy." The software manufacturers use the term "license" in their transactions, however. As opposed to the word "sale," the term "license" denotes that the software manufacturers are permitting users to use a copy of their software. Thus, the software vendor still owns the software. Until each state enacts the legislation, it is not clear whether shrink-wrap licenses that restrict users' rights under copyright law are legally enforceable. For clarification, shrink-wrap licenses physically accompany a disk while click-on and active click-wrap licenses are usually transmitted electronically. Sometimes, the term shrink-wrap is interpreted to mean both physical and electronic licenses to use software. The focus of the UCITA legislation is not on the physical media but on the information contained on the media.

2000 U.S. Congress Electronic Signatures in Global and National Commerce Act ("ESIGN"). Facilitates the use of electronic records and signatures in interstate and foreign commerce by ensuring the validity and legal effect of contracts entered into electronically. An important provision of the act requires that businesses obtain electronic consent or confirmation from consumers to receive information electronically that a law normally requires to be in writing.

The legislation is intent on preserving the consumers' rights under consumer protection laws and went to extraordinary measures to meet this goal. Thus, a business must receive confirmation from the consumer in electronic format that the consumer consents to receiving information electronically that used to be in written form. This provision ensures that the consumer has access to the Internet and is familiar with the basics of electronic communications.

2001 USA Provide Appropriate Tools Required to Intercept and Obstruct Terrorism (PATRIOT) Act. This act permits the:

- Subpoena of electronic records

- Monitoring of Internet communications

- Search and seizure of information on live systems (including routers and servers), backups, and archives

This act gives the U.S. government new powers to subpoena electronic records and to monitor Internet traffic. In monitoring information, the government can require the assistance of ISPs and network operators. This monitoring can extend even into individual organizations. In the Patriot Act, Congress permits investigators to gather information about email without having to show probable cause that the person to be monitored has committed a crime or was intending to commit a crime. Routers, servers, backups, and so on now fall under existing search and seizure laws. A new twist is delayed notification of a search warrant. Under the Patriot Act, if it is suspected that notification of a search warrant would cause a suspect to flee, a search can be conducted before notification of a search warrant is given.

Generally Accepted Systems Security Principles (GASSP). These items are not laws but are accepted principles that have a foundation in the OECD Guidelines:

1. Computer security supports the mission of the organization.

2. Computer security is an integral element of sound management.

3. Computer security should be cost-effective.

4. Systems owners have security responsibilities outside their organizations.

5. Computer security responsibilities and accountability should be made explicit.

6. Computer security requires a comprehensive and integrated approach.

7. Computer security should be periodically reassessed.

8. Computer security is constrained by societal factors.

2002 E-Government Act. Title III, the Federal Information Security Management Act (FISMA). This Act was written to:

1. "Provide a comprehensive framework for ensuring the effectiveness of information security controls over information resources that support Federal operations and assets

2. Recognize the highly networked nature of the current Federal computing environment and provide effective government-wide management and oversight of the related information security risks, including coordination of information security efforts throughout the civilian, national security, and law enforcement communities

3. Provide for development and maintenance of minimum controls required to protect Federal information and information systems

4. Provide a mechanism for improved oversight of Federal agency information security programs"

Additional information on FISMA is given in Chapter 14.

Investigation

The field of investigating computer crime is also known as *computer forensics*. Specifically, computer forensics is the collecting of information from and about computer systems that is admissible in a court of law.

Computer Investigation Issues

Because of the nature of information that is stored on the computer, investigating and prosecuting computer criminal cases have unique issues, such as the following:

✦ Investigators and prosecutors have a compressed time frame for the investigation.

✦ The information is intangible.

✦ The investigation might interfere with the normal conduct of the business of an organization.

✦ There might be difficulty in gathering the evidence.

✦ Data associated with the criminal investigation might be located on the same computer as data needed for the normal conduct of business (co-mingling of data).

✦ In many instances, an expert or specialist is required.

✦ Locations involved in the crime might be geographically separated by long distances in different jurisdictions. This separation might result in differences in laws, attitudes toward computer crimes, definitions of computer crimes, as well as difficulty in obtaining search warrants, lack of cooperation, and so forth.

✦ Many jurisdictions have expanded the definition of property to include electronic information.

Evidence

The gathering, control, storage, and preservation of evidence are extremely critical in any legal investigation. Because the evidence involved in a computer crime might be intangible and subject to easy modification without a trace, evidence must be carefully handled and controlled throughout its entire life cycle. Specifically, there is a *chain of evidence* that one must follow and protect. The following are the major components of this chain of evidence:

✦ Location of evidence when obtained

✦ Time evidence was obtained

✦ Identification of individual(s) who discovered evidence

✦ Identification of individual(s) who secured evidence

✦ Identification of individual(s) who controlled evidence and/or who maintained possession of that evidence

The *evidence life cycle* covers the evidence gathering and application process. This life cycle has the following components:

✦ Discovery and recognition

✦ Protection

✦ Recording

✦ Collection:

  • Collect all relevant storage media.

  • Make an image of the hard disk before removing power.

  • Print out the screen.

  • Avoid degaussing equipment.

✦ Identification (tagging and marking)

✦ Preservation:

  • Protect magnetic media from erasure.

  • Store in a proper environment.

✦ Transportation

✦ Presentation in a court of law

✦ Return of evidence to owner

Evidence Admissibility

To be admissible in a court of law, evidence must meet certain stringent requirements. The evidence must be *relevant*, *legally permissible*, *reliable*, *properly identified*, and *properly preserved*. The main points of these requirements are as follows:

Relevant. The evidence is related to the crime in that it shows that the crime
has been committed, can provide information describing the crime, can provide information as to the perpetrator's motives, can verify what has
occurred, and can fix the crime's time of occurrence.

Legally permissible. The evidence was obtained in a lawful manner.

Reliability. The evidence has not been tampered with or modified.

Identification. The evidence is properly identified without changing or damaging the evidence. In computer forensics, this process includes the following:

- Labeling printouts with permanent markers

- Identifying the operating system used, the hardware types, and so on

- Recording serial numbers

- Marking evidence without damaging it or by placing it in sealed containers that are marked

Preservation. The evidence is not subject to damage or destruction. The
following are the recommended procedures for preservation:

- Do not prematurely remove power.

- Back up the hard disk image by using disk imaging hardware or software.

- Avoid placing magnetic media in the proximity of sources of magnetic
fields.

- Store media in a dust- and smoke-free environment at a proper temperature and humidity.

- Write-protect media.

- Authenticate the file system by creating a digital signature based on the
contents of a file or disk sector. One-way hash algorithms, such as the
Secure Hash Algorithm (SHA) described in Chapter 4, can be used.

Types of Evidence

Legal evidence can be classified into the following types:

Best evidence. Original or primary evidence rather than a copy or duplicate
of the evidence

Secondary evidence. A copy of evidence or oral description of its contents; not as reliable as best evidence

Direct evidence. Proves or disproves a specific act through oral testimony based on information gathered through the witness's five senses

Conclusive evidence. Incontrovertible; overrides all other evidence

Opinions. The following are the two types of opinions:

- *Expert*—Can offer an opinion based on personal expertise and facts
- *Nonexpert*—Can testify only as to facts

Circumstantial evidence. Inference of information from other, intermediate, relevant facts

Hearsay evidence (third party). Evidence that is not based on personal, first-hand knowledge of the witness but that was obtained from another source. Under the U.S. Federal Rules of Evidence (803), hearsay evidence is generally not admissible in court. Computer-generated records and other business records fall under the category of hearsay evidence because these records cannot be proven accurate and reliable. This inadmissibility is known as the *hearsay rule*. However, there are certain exceptions to the hearsay rule for records that are:

- Made during the regular conduct of business and authenticated by witnesses familiar with their use
- Relied upon in the regular course of business
- Made by a person with knowledge of the records
- Made by a person with information transmitted by a person with knowledge
- Made at or near the time of occurrence of the act being investigated
- In the custody of the witness on a regular basis

Searching and Seizing Computers

The U.S. Department of Justice (DOJ) Computer Crime and Intellectual Property Section (CCIPS) has issued the publication *Searching and Seizing Computers and Obtaining Evidence in Criminal Investigations* (January 2001). The document introduction states, "This publication provides a comprehensive guide to the legal issues that arise when federal law enforcement agents search and seize computers and obtain electronic evidence in criminal investigations. The topics covered include the application of the Fourth Amendment to computers and the Internet, the Electronic Communications and Privacy Act, workplace privacy, the law of electronic surveillance and evidentiary information system security uses." The document also cites the following U.S. Codes relating to searching and seizing computers:

18 U.S.C. § 12510 — Definitions

18 U.S.C. § 2511 — Interception and disclosure of wire, oral, or electronic communications prohibited

18 U.S.C. § 2701 — Unlawful access to stored communications

18 U.S.C. § 2702 — Disclosure of contents

18 U.S.C. § 2703 — Requirements for governmental access

18 U.S.C. § 2705 — Delayed notice

18 U.S.C. § 2711 — Definitions

18 U.S.C. § 2000aa — Searches and seizures by government officers and employees in connection with the investigation or prosecution of criminal offenses

The headings of these codes illustrate the areas covered and, in general, the increased concern for the privacy of the individual.

Export Issues and Technology

In July 2000, the U.S. announced a relaxation of its encryption export policy to certain countries. To quote the President's Chief of Staff, John D. Podesta, "Under our new policy, American companies can export any encryption product to any end user in the European Union and eight other trading partners. We're also speeding up the time to market by eliminating the thirty-day waiting period when exporting encryption goods to these countries."

Podesta also pointed out the effect that advancing technology has had on the *Electronic Communications and Privacy Act* (ECPA). He pointed out, "ECPA, like its predecessors, has, in many ways, become outdated by the new advances in computer technology and electronic communication. Since its passage in 1986, we've seen a communications revolution with the explosion of the cell phone and the development and use of the World Wide Web. Today, there more than 95 million cell phone users, and more than 50 million households on line in the United States. More than 1.4 billion e-mails [sic] change hands every day . . . ECPA was not devised to address many of the issues related to these newer, faster means of electronic communication. It doesn't extend the stringent Title III protections to the capture of email that you send to your friends or business partners." Podesta cited legislation, which is being proposed to amend existing statutes and outmoded language, which applies primarily to wiretapping and to define protections for hardware and software systems in general.

Conducting the Investigation

There are many issues involved in the conduct of an investigation of suspected computer crime. For example, in a corporate environment, an investigation should involve management, corporate security, human resources, the legal department, and other appropriate staff members. The act of investigating may also affect critical operations. For example, it may prompt a suspect to commit retaliatory acts that may compromise data or result in a DoS, generate negative publicity, or open individual privacy issues. Thus, it is important to prepare a plan beforehand on how to handle reports of suspected computer crimes. A committee of appropriate personnel should be set up beforehand to address the following issues:

✦ Establishing a prior liaison with law enforcement

✦ Deciding when and whether to bring in law enforcement (in the United States, the FBI and Secret Service have jurisdiction over computer crimes)

✦ Setting up means of reporting computer crimes

✦ Establishing procedures for handling and processing reports of computer crime

✦ Planning for and conducting investigations

✦ Involving senior management and the appropriate departments, such as legal, internal audit, information systems, and human resources

✦ Ensuring the proper collection of evidence, which includes identification and protection of the various storage media

If a computer crime is suspected, it is important not to alert the suspect. A preliminary investigation should be conducted to determine whether a crime has been committed by examining the audit records and system logs, interviewing witnesses, and assessing the damage incurred. It is critical to determine whether disclosure to legal authorities is required by law or regulation. U.S. Federal Sentencing Guidelines require organizations to report criminal acts. There are a number of pertinent issues to consider relative to outside disclosure. Negative publicity resulting in a lack of confidence in the business of the organization is an obvious concern. Once an outside entity such as law enforcement is involved, information dissemination is out of the hands of the organization. Law enforcement involvement necessarily involves support from the organization in terms of personnel time.

The timing of requesting outside assistance from law enforcement is another major issue. In the United States, law enforcement personnel are bound by the Fourth Amendment to the U.S. Constitution and must obtain a warrant to search for evidence. This amendment protects individuals from unlawful search and seizure. Search warrants are issued when there is probable cause for the search and provide legal authorization to search a location for specific evidence. Private citizens are not held to this strict requirement, and thus, in some cases, a private individual can conduct a search for possible evidence without a warrant. However, if a private individual were asked by a law enforcement officer to search for evidence, a warrant would be required because the private individual would be *acting as an agent of law enforcement*.

An exception to the search warrant requirement for law enforcement officers is the *Exigent Circumstances Doctrine*. Under this doctrine, if probable cause is present and destruction of the evidence is deemed imminent, the search can be conducted without the delay of having the warrant in-hand.

Thus, if law enforcement is called in too early when a computer crime is suspected, the law enforcement investigators will be held to a stricter standard than the organization's employees in regard to searching for and gathering evidence. However, there is a higher probability that any evidence acquired will be admissible in court because law enforcement personnel are trained in preserving the chain of evidence. As stated previously, the dissemination of information and the corresponding publicity will also be out of the organization's control when the investigation is turned over to law enforcement. Conversely, if law enforcement is called in too late to investigate a possible computer crime, improper handling of the investigation and evidence by untrained organization employees may reduce or eliminate the chances of a successful prosecution.

Good sources of evidence include telephone records, video cameras, audit trails, system logs, system backups, witnesses, results of surveillance, and emails.

A standard discriminator used to determine whether a subject may be the perpetrator of a crime is to evaluate whether the individual had a *Motive*, the *Opportunity*, and the *Means* to commit the crime. This test is known as MOM.

If the investigation is undertaken internally, the suspect should be interviewed to acquire information and to determine who committed the offense. This interrogation should be planned in advance, and expert help should be obtained in the conduct of the interview. Obviously, the suspect is alerted when he or she is scheduled for interrogation, and a common mistake in setting up and conducting the interview is providing the suspect with too much information. With this information, the suspect may try to alter additional evidence, leave the premises, or warn other coconspirators. In the conduct of the interrogation, the pertinent information relative to the crime should be obtained and the questions should be scripted beforehand. Original documents should not be used in the conduct of the interview to avoid the possible destruction of critical information by the suspect.

Liability

In 1997, the Federal Sentencing Guidelines were extended to apply to computer crime. Recall that under these guidelines, senior corporate officers can be personally subject to up to $290 million in fines if their organizations do not comply with the law. These guidelines also treat the possession of illegally acquired material without intent to resell as a crime.

Management has the obligation to protect the organization from losses due to natural disasters, malicious code, compromise of proprietary information, damage to reputation, violation of the law, employee privacy suits, and stockholder suits. Management must follow the *prudent man rule* that "requires officers to perform duties with diligence and care that ordinary, prudent people would exercise under similar circumstances." The officers must exercise *due care* or *reasonable care* to carry out their responsibilities to the organization. In exercising due care, corporate officers must institute the following protections:

✦ Means to prevent the organization's computer resources from being used as a source of attack on another organization's computer system (such as in Distributed DoS attacks)

  • Relates to the principle of *proximate causation* in which an action that was taken or not taken was part of a chain that resulted in negative consequences

✦ Backups

✦ Scans for malicious code

✦ Business continuity/disaster recovery plans

✦ Local and remote access control

✦ Elimination of unauthorized and unsecured modems

✦ Organizational security policies, procedures, and guidelines

✦ Personnel screening procedures:

  • Ensuring the confidentiality, integrity, and availability of organizational databases

  • Addressing the organization's responsibilities to other entities such as customers and prime contractors

✦ Establishing an organizational incident-handling capability

The criteria for evaluating the legal requirements for implementing safeguards is to evaluate the cost (C) of instituting the protection versus the estimated loss (L) resulting from exploitation of the corresponding vulnerability. If C < L, then a legal liability exists.

Incident handling, noted in the prevention list, is an important part of contingency planning that addresses the handling of malicious attacks, usually by technical means. Incident handling or an emergency response should be planned for prior to the occurrence of any incidents and should address the following questions:

✦ What is considered an incident?

✦ How should an incident be reported?

✦ To whom should the incident be reported?

✦ When should management be informed of the incident?

✦ What action should be taken if an incident is detected?

✦ Who should handle the response to the incident?

✦ How much damage was caused by the incident?

✦ What information was damaged or compromised by the incident?

✦ Are recovery procedures required to remediate damages caused by the incident?

✦ What type of follow-up and review should be conducted after the incident is handled?

✦ Should additional safeguards be instituted as a result of the incident?

Incident handling can be considered as the portion of contingency planning that responds to malicious technical threats and can be addressed by establishing a *Computer Incident Response Team* (CIRT). A proper incident response is important to limit the resulting damage, to provide information for prevention of future incidents, and to serve as a means of increasing employee awareness. The majority of incidents do not occur from outside sources, such as crackers and malicious code. Many incidents are the result of incompetent employees, malicious employees, other insiders, accidental actions, and natural disasters. The Carnegie Mellon University Computer Emergency Response Team Coordination Center (CERT®/CC) is an excellent source of information for establishing and maintaining organizational CIRTs.

Ethics

Ethical computing is a phrase that is often used but difficult to define. Certified professionals are morally and legally held to a higher standard of ethical conduct. In order to instill proper computing behavior, ethics should be incorporated into an organizational policy and further developed into an organizational ethical computing policy. A number of organizations have addressed the issue of ethical computing and have generated guidelines for ethical behavior. A few of these ethical codes are presented to provide a familiarization with the items addressed in such codes. Some of these lists are under revision. However, the versions illustrate the general areas that are important in ethical computing behavior.

(ISC)² Code of Ethics

Certified Information Systems Security Professionals (CISSPs) shall:

1. Conduct themselves in accordance with the highest standards of moral, ethical, and legal behavior

2. Not commit or be a party to any unlawful or unethical act that may negatively affect their professional reputation or the reputation of their profession

3. Appropriately report activity related to the profession that they believe to be unlawful and shall cooperate with resulting investigations

4. Support efforts to promote understanding and acceptance of prudent information security measures throughout the public, private, and academic sectors of our global information society

5. Provide competent service to their employers and clients, and shall avoid any conflicts of interest

6. Execute responsibilities in a manner consistent with the highest standards of their profession

7. Not misuse the information with which they come into contact during the course of their duties, and they shall maintain the confidentiality of all information in their possession that is so identified

The Computer Ethics Institute's Ten Commandments of Computer Ethics

In 1992, the Coalition for Computer Ethics incorporated as the Computer Ethics Institute (CEI) to focus on the interface of advances in information technologies, ethics, and corporate and public policy. The CEI addresses industrial, academic, and public policy organizations. The Institute's founding organizations are the Brookings Institution, IBM, the Washington Consulting Group, and the Washington Theological Consortium. The Institute is concerned with the ethical issues associated with the advancement of information technologies in society and has generated the following ten commandments of computer ethics:

1. Thou shalt not use a computer to harm other people.

2. Thou shalt not interfere with other people's computer work.

3. Thou shalt not snoop around in other people's computer files.

4. Thou shalt not use a computer to steal.

5. Thou shalt not use a computer to bear false witness.

6. Thou shalt not copy or use proprietary software for which you have not paid.

7. Thou shalt not use other people's computer resources without authorization or the proper compensation.

8. Thou shalt not appropriate other people's intellectual output.

9. Thou shalt think about the social consequences of the program you are writing for the system you are designing.

10. Thou shalt use a computer in ways that ensure consideration and respect for your fellow humans.

The Internet Activities Board (IAB) Ethics and the Internet (RFC 1087)

"Access to and use of the Internet is a privilege and should be treated as such by all users of the system."

Any activity is defined as unacceptable and unethical that purposely:

1. Seeks to gain unauthorized access to the resources of the Internet

2. Destroys the integrity of computer-based information

3. Disrupts the intended use of the Internet

4. Wastes resources such as people, capacity, and computers through such actions

5. Compromises the privacy of users

6. Involves negligence in the conduct of Internet-wide experiments

The U.S. Department of Health, Education, and Welfare Code of Fair Information Practices

The United States Department of Health, Education, and Welfare has developed the following list of fair information practices that focuses on the privacy of individually identifiable personal information:

1. There must not be personal data record-keeping systems whose very existence is secret.

2. There must be a way for a person to find out what information about them is in a record and how it is used.

3. There must be a way for a person to prevent information about them, which was obtained for one purpose, from being used or made available for other purposes without their consent.

4. Any organization creating, maintaining, using, or disseminating records of identifiable personal data must ensure the reliability of the data for their intended use and must take precautions to prevent misuses of that data.

Individual ethical behavior widely varies because a person's perception of ethics is a function of many variables in that person's background. Because one is not stealing physical property, the "borrowing" or "viewing" of information on an organization's computers is perceived by many as innocent behavior. Some crackers (malicious hackers) feel that any information available for access or subject to access by virtue of inadequate control measures is fair game. Others are of the opinion that hacking into an organization's information systems is performing a service by alerting the organization to weaknesses in their system safeguards. These naïve and incorrect perspectives trample on the rights of individual privacy and compromise critical and organizational proprietary information.

These breaches of security can result in million-dollar losses to an organization through the destruction or unavailability of critical data and resources or through stock devaluation. From the national perspective, destructive cracker behavior could seriously affect a nation's critical infrastructure, economic health, and national security. Clearly, these types of malicious hacking results cannot be explained away by claims of freedom of speech and freedom of expression rights.

The Organization for Economic Cooperation and Development (OECD)

The Organization for Economic Cooperation and Development (OECD) (www.oecd.org) has issued guidelines that are summarized as follows:

✦ Collection Limitation Principle:

1. There should be limits to the collection of personal data, and any such data should be obtained by lawful and fair means and, where appropriate, with the knowledge or consent of the data subject.

✦ Data Quality Principle:

2. Personal data should be relevant to the purposes for which they are to be used, and to the extent necessary for those purposes, should be accurate, complete and kept up-to-date.

✦ Purpose Specification Principle:

3. The purposes for which personal data are collected should be specified not later than at the time of data collection and the subsequent use limited to the fulfillment of those purposes or such others as are not incompatible with those purposes and as are specified on each occasion of change of purpose.

✦ Use Limitation Principle:

4. Personal data should not be disclosed, made available, or otherwise used for purposes other than those specified in accordance with Paragraph 9 except:

    a) With the consent of the data subject

    b) By the authority of law

✦ Security Safeguards Principle:

5. Personal data should be protected by reasonable security safeguards against such risks as loss or unauthorized access, destruction, use, modification, or disclosure of data.

✦ Openness Principle:

6. There should be a general policy of openness about developments, practices, and policies with respect to personal data. Means should be readily available of establishing the existence and nature of personal data and the main purposes of their use, as well as the identity and usual residence of the data controller.

✦ Individual Participation Principle:

7. An individual should have the right:

a) To obtain from a data controller, or otherwise, confirmation of whether or not the data controller has data relating to him

b) To have communicated to him data relating to him within a reasonable time at a charge, if any, that is not excessive

In a reasonable manner

In a form that is readily intelligible to him

c) To be given reasons if a request made under subparagraphs (a) and (b) is denied, and to be able to challenge such denial

d) To challenge data relating to him and, if the challenge is successful to have the data erased, rectified, completed or amended

✦ Accountability Principle:

8. A data controller should be accountable for complying with measures that give effect to the principles stated above.

✦ Transborder Issues:

9. A Member country should refrain from restricting transborder flows of personal data between itself and another Member country except where the latter does not yet substantially observe these Guidelines or where the re-export of such data would circumvent its domestic privacy legislation.

10. A Member country can also impose restrictions in respect of certain categories of personal data for which its domestic privacy legislation includes specific regulations in view of the nature of those data and for which the other Member country provides no equivalent protection.

✦ ✦ ✦

Assessment Questions

You can find the answers to the following questions in Appendix A.

1. According to the Internet Activities Board (IAB), an activity that causes which of the following is considered a violation of ethical behavior on the Internet?

   a. Wasting resources

   b. Appropriating other people's intellectual output

   c. Using a computer to steal

   d. Using a computer to bear false witness

2. Which of the following best defines social engineering?

   a. Illegal copying of software

   b. Gathering information from discarded manuals and printouts

   c. Using people skills to obtain proprietary information

   d. Destruction or alteration of data

3. Because the development of new technology usually outpaces the law, law enforcement uses which traditional laws to prosecute computer criminals?

   a. Malicious mischief

   b. Embezzlement, fraud, and wiretapping

   c. Immigration

   d. Conspiracy and elimination of competition

4. Which of the following is NOT a category of law under the Common Law System?

   a. Criminal law

   b. Civil law

   c. Administrative/Regulatory law

   d. Derived law

5. A trade secret:

   a. Provides the owner with a legally enforceable right to exclude others from practicing the art covered for a specified time period

   b. Protects original works of authorship

   c. Secures and maintains the confidentiality of proprietary technical or business-related information that is adequately protected from disclosure by the owner

   d. Is a word, name, symbol, color, sound, product shape, or device used to identify goods and to distinguish them from those made or sold by others

6. Which of the following is NOT a European Union (EU) principle?

    a. Data should be collected in accordance with the law.

    b. Transmission of personal information to locations where equivalent personal data protection cannot be assured is permissible.

    c. Data should be used only for the purposes for which it was collected and should be used only for a reasonable period of time.

    d. Information collected about an individual cannot be disclosed to other organizations or individuals unless authorized by law or by consent of the individual.

7. The Federal Sentencing Guidelines:

    a. Hold senior corporate officers personally liable if their organizations do not comply with the law

    b. Prohibit altering, damaging, or destroying information in a federal interest computer

    c. Prohibit eavesdropping or the interception of message contents

    d. Established a category of sensitive information called Sensitive But Unclassified (SBU)

8. What does the prudent man rule require?

    a. Senior officials to post performance bonds for their actions

    b. Senior officials to perform their duties with the care that ordinary, prudent people would exercise under similar circumstances

    c. Senior officials to guarantee that all precautions have been taken and that no breaches of security can occur

    d. Senior officials to follow specified government standards

9. Information Warfare is:

    a. Attacking the information infrastructure of a nation to gain military and/or economic advantages

    b. Developing weapons systems based on artificial intelligence technology

    c. Generating and disseminating propaganda material

    d. Signal intelligence

10. The chain of evidence relates to:

    a. Securing laptops to desks during an investigation

    b. DNA testing

    c. Handling and controlling evidence

    d. Making a disk image

11. The Kennedy-Kassebaum Act is also known as:

   a. RICO

   b. OECD

   c. HIPAA

   d. EU Directive

12. Which of the following refers to a U.S. government program that reduces or eliminates emanations from electronic equipment?

   a. CLIPPER

   b. ECHELON

   c. ECHO

   d. TEMPEST

13. Imprisonment is a possible sentence under:

   a. Civil (tort) law

   b. Criminal law

   c. Both civil and criminal law

   d. Neither civil nor criminal law

14. Which one of the following conditions must be met if legal electronic monitoring of employees is conducted by an organization?

   a. Employees must be unaware of the monitoring activity.

   b. All employees must agree with the monitoring policy.

   c. Results of the monitoring cannot be used against the employee.

   d. The organization must have a policy stating that all employees are regularly notified that monitoring is being conducted.

15. Which of the following is a key principle in the evolution of computer crime laws in many countries?

   a. All members of the United Nations have agreed to uniformly define and prosecute computer crime.

   b. Existing laws against embezzlement, fraud, and wiretapping cannot be applied to computer crime.

   c. The definition of property was extended to include electronic information.

   d. Unauthorized acquisition of computer-based information without the intent to resell is not a crime.

16. The concept of *due care* states that senior organizational management must ensure that:

    a. All risks to an information system are eliminated.

    b. Certain requirements must be fulfilled in carrying out their responsibilities to the organization.

    c. Other management personnel are delegated the responsibility for information system security.

    d. The cost of implementing safeguards is greater than the potential resultant losses resulting from information security breaches.

17. Liability of senior organizational officials relative to the protection of the organization's information systems is prosecutable under:

    a. Criminal law

    b. Civil law

    c. International law

    d. Financial law

18. Responsibility for handling computer crimes in the United States is assigned to:

    a. The Federal Bureau of Investigation (FBI) and the Secret Service

    b. The FBI only

    c. The National Security Agency (NSA)

    d. The Central Intelligence Agency (CIA)

19. In general, computer-based evidence is considered:

    a. Conclusive

    b. Circumstantial

    c. Secondary

    d. Hearsay

20. Investigating and prosecuting computer crimes is made more difficult because:

    a. Backups may be difficult to find.

    b. Evidence is mostly intangible.

    c. Evidence cannot be preserved.

    d. Evidence is hearsay and can never be introduced into a court of law.

21. Which of the following criteria are used to evaluate suspects in the commission of a crime?

    a. Motive, Intent, and Ability

    b. Means, Object, and Motive

    c. Means, Intent, and Motive

    d. Motive, Means, and Opportunity

22. Which one of the following U.S. government entities was assigned the responsibility for improving government efficiency through the application of new technologies and for developing guidance on information security for government agencies by the Paperwork Reduction Act of 1980,1995?

    a. The National Institute for Standards and Technology (NIST)

    b. The General Services Administration (GSA)

    c. The Office of Management and Budget (OMB)

    d. The National Security Agency (NSA)

23. What is enticement?

    a. Encouraging the commission of a crime when there was initially no intent to commit a crime

    b. Assisting in the commission of a crime

    c. Luring the perpetrator to an attractive area or presenting the perpetrator with a lucrative target after the crime has already been initiated

    d. Encouraging the commission of one crime over another

24. Which of the following is NOT a computer investigation issue?

    a. Evidence is easy to obtain.

    b. The time frame for investigation is compressed.

    c. An expert may be required to assist.

    d. The information is intangible.

25. Conducting a search without the delay of obtaining a warrant if destruction of evidence seems imminent is possible under:

    a. Federal Sentencing Guidelines

    b. Proximate Causation

    c. Exigent Circumstances

    d. Prudent Man Rule

26. Which one of the following items is NOT TRUE concerning the Platform for Privacy Preferences (P3P) developed by the World Wide Web Consortium (W3C)?

  a. It allows Web sites to express their privacy practices in a standard format that can be retrieved automatically and interpreted easily by user agents.

  b. It allows users to be informed of site practices in human-readable format.

  c. It does not provide the site privacy practices to users in machine-readable format.

  d. It automates decision-making based on the site's privacy practices when appropriate.

27. The 1996 Information Technology Management Reform Act (ITMRA), or Clinger-Cohen Act, did which one of the following?

  a. Relieved the General Services Administration of responsibility for procurement of automated systems and contract appeals and charged the Office of Management and Budget with providing guidance on information technology procurement

  b. Relieved the General Services Administration of responsibility for procurement of automated systems and contract appeals and charged the National Institute for Standards and Technology with providing guidance on information technology procurement

  c. Relieved the Office of Management and Budget of responsibility for procurement of automated systems and contract appeals and charged the General Services Administration with providing guidance on information technology procurement

  d. Relieved the General Services Administration of responsibility for procurement of automated systems and contract appeals and charged the National Security Agency with providing guidance on information technology procurement

28. Which one of the following U.S. Acts prohibits trading, manufacturing, or selling in any way that is intended to bypass copyright protection mechanisms?

  a. The 1999 Uniform Information Transactions Act (UCITA)

  b. The 1998 Digital Millennium Copyright Act (DMCA)

  c. The 1998 Sonny Bono Copyright Term Extension Act

  d. The 1987 U.S. Computer Security Act

29. Which of the following actions by the U.S. government is NOT permitted or required by the U.S. Patriot Act, signed into law on October 26, 2001?

    a. Subpoena of electronic records

    b. Monitoring of Internet communications

    c. Search and seizure of information on live systems (including routers and servers), backups, and archives

    d. Reporting of cash and wire transfers of $5,000 or more

30. Which Act required U.S. government agencies to do the following?

    • Manage information resources to protect privacy and security

    • Designate a senior official, reporting directly to the Secretary of the Treasury, to ensure that the responsibilities assigned by the Act are accomplished

    • Identify and afford security protections in conformance with the Computer Security Act of 1987 commensurate with the magnitude of harm and risk that might result from the misuse, loss, or unauthorized access relative to information collected by an agency or maintained on behalf of an agency

    • Implement and enforce applicable policies, procedures, standards, and guidelines on privacy, confidentiality, security, disclosures, and sharing of information collected or maintained by or for the agency

    a. 1994 U.S. Computer Abuse Amendments Act

    b. 1996, Title I, Economic Espionage Act

    c. 1987 U.S. Computer Security Act

    d. Paperwork Reduction Act of 1980,1995

Physical Security

CHAPTER

10

◆　◆　◆　◆

The Physical Security domain examines those elements of the surrounding physical environment and supporting infrastructure that affect the confidentiality, integrity, and availability (C.I.A.) of information systems. We are not talking about logical controls here, but you will notice that some of the physical controls described are duplicated in some of the other domains, such as biometrics in the Operations and Access Control domain. Natural disasters are an example of physical threats to security. Facility controls to unauthorized entry or theft are elements of physical security. The area known as Industrial Security contains many of these concepts, such as closed-circuit television (CCTV), guards, fencing, lighting, and so forth. To most engineers or security professionals, this domain is probably the least sexy of the 10 domains. Who cares how high perimeter fencing should be to protect critical buildings? But you need to know this stuff because 1) some of this information will be on the test, and 2) the best-configured firewall in the world will not stand up to a well-placed brick.

A security practitioner needs to be aware of the elements that threaten the physical security of an enterprise and those controls that can mitigate the risk incurred from those threats. In this chapter, we will examine threats to physical security and controls for physical security.

Domain Definition

The Physical Security domain addresses the threats, vulnerabilities, and countermeasures that can be utilized to physically protect an enterprise's resources and sensitive information. These resources include personnel, the facility in which they work, and the data, equipment, support systems, and media with which they work. Physical security often refers to the measures taken to protect systems, buildings, and the related supporting infrastructure against threats that are associated with the physical environment.

Physical computer security can also be defined as the process used to control personnel, the physical plant, equipment, and data involved in information processing. A CISSP candidate will be expected to understand the threats and controls that are related to physically protecting the enterprise's sensitive information assets.

A CISSP professional should fully understand:

✦ The elements involved in choosing a secure site and its design and configuration

✦ The methods for securing a facility against unauthorized access

✦ The methods for securing the equipment against theft of either the equipment or its contained information

✦ The environmental and safety measures needed to protect personnel, the facility, and its resources

Threats to Physical Security

Before we can begin an investigation into the various ways an enterprise can implement proper physical security, we obviously need to know what aspects of our environment constitute a threat to our computing infrastructure. When a risk analysis or business impact assessment is performed, a list of all possible threats must be compiled. It does not matter whether the likelihood of any specific vulnerability is low or nonexistent (a tsunami in Ohio, for example); all possible threats must be compiled and examined. Many assessment methods (SSE-CMM or IAM) have the practitioner compile these complete lists before making a determination as to their likelihood.

The triad of confidentiality, integrity, and availability is at risk in the physical environment and must be protected. Examples of risks to C.I.A. include the following:

✦ Interruptions in providing computer services (Availability)

✦ Physical damage (Availability)

✦ Unauthorized disclosure of information (Confidentiality)

✦ Loss of control over system (Integrity)

✦ Physical theft (Confidentiality, Integrity, and Availability)

Examples of threats to physical security are as follows:

✦ Emergencies

  • Fire and smoke contaminants

  • Building collapse or explosion

- Utility loss (electrical power, air conditioning, heating)
- Water damage (pipe breakage)
- Toxic materials release

✦ Natural disasters

- Earth movement (such as earthquakes and mudslides)
- Storm damage (such as snow, ice, and floods)

✦ Human intervention

- Sabotage
- Vandalism
- War
- Strikes

Donn B. Parker (Parker, Donn B., *Fighting Computer Crime*, John Wiley and Sons, 1998) has compiled a very comprehensive list that he calls the seven major sources of physical loss with examples provided for each:

1. *Temperature.* Extreme variations of heat or cold, such as sunlight, fire, freezing, and heat.

2. *Gases.* War gases, commercial vapors, humidity, dry air, and suspended particles are included. Examples of these would be Sarin nerve gas, PCP from exploding transformers, air conditioning failures, smoke, smog, cleaning fluid, fuel vapors, and paper particles from printers.

3. *Liquids.* Water and chemicals are included. Examples of these are floods, plumbing failures, precipitation, fuel leaks, spilled drinks, acid and base chemicals used for cleaning, and computer printer fluids.

4. *Organisms.* Viruses, bacteria, people, animals, and insects are included. Examples of these are sickness of key workers, molds, contamination from skin oils and hair, contamination and electrical shorting from defecation and release of body fluids, consumption of information media such as paper or cable insulation, and shorting of microcircuits from cobwebs.

5. *Projectiles.* Tangible objects in motion and powered objects are included. Examples of these are meteorites, falling objects, cars and trucks, bullets and rockets, explosions, and wind.

6. *Movement.* Collapse, shearing, shaking, vibration, liquefaction, flows, waves, separation, and slides are included. Examples of these are dropping or shaking of fragile equipment, earthquakes, mudslides, lava flows, sea waves, and adhesive failures.

7. *Energy anomalies.* Types of electric anomalies are electric surges or failure, magnetism, static electricity, aging circuitry, radiation, sound, light, and radio, microwave, electromagnetic, and atomic waves. Examples of these include electric utility failures, proximity of magnets and electromagnets, carpet static, decomposition of circuit materials, decomposition of paper and magnetic disks, Electro-Magnetic Pulse (EMP) from nuclear explosions, lasers, loudspeakers, high-energy radio frequency (HERF) guns, radar systems, cosmic radiation, and explosions.

Controls for Physical Security

Under the heading of Physical Security Controls, there are several areas. In general, these controls should match up with the listed threats. In this chapter, we have grouped the controls into two areas: Administrative Controls and Physical and Technical Controls.

Administrative Controls

Administrative controls, as opposed to physical or technical controls, can be thought of as the area of physical security protection that benefits from the proper administrative steps. These steps encompass proper emergency procedures, personnel control (in the area of Human Resources), planning, and policy implementation.

We will look at the following various elements of Administrative Controls:

✦ Facility Requirements Planning

✦ Facility Security Management

✦ Administrative Personnel Controls

Facility Requirements Planning

Facility Requirements Planning describes the need for planning for physical security controls in the early stages of the construction of a data facility. There might be an occasion when security professionals are able to provide input at the construction phase of a building or data center. Some of the physical security elements involved at the construction stage include choosing and designing a secure site.

Choosing a Secure Site

The environmental placement of the facility is also a concern during initial planning. Security professionals need to consider such questions as:

Visibility. What kind of neighbors will the proposed site have? Will the site have any external markings that will identify it as a sensitive processing area? Low visibility is the rule here.

Local considerations. Is the proposed site near possible hazards (for example, a waste dump)? What is the local rate of crime (such as forced entry and burglary)?

Natural disasters. Is it likely this location will have more natural disasters than other locations? Natural disasters can include weather-related problems (wind, snow, flooding, and so forth) and the existence of an earthquake fault.

Transportation. Does the site have a problem due to excessive air, highway, or road traffic?

Joint tenancy. Are access to environmental and HVAC controls complicated by a shared responsibility? A data center might not have full access to the systems when an emergency occurs.

External services. Do you know the relative proximity of the local emergency services, such as police, fire, and hospitals or medical facilities?

Designing a Secure Site

Information Security processing areas are the main focus of physical control. Examples of areas that require attention during the construction planning stage are:

Walls. Entire walls, from the floor to the ceiling, must have an acceptable fire rating. Closets or rooms that store media must have a high fire rating.

Ceilings. Issues of concern regarding ceilings are the weight-bearing rating and the fire rating.

Floors. The following are the concerns about flooring:

- *Slab* — If the floor is a concrete slab, the concerns are the physical weight it can bear (known as loading, which is commonly 150 pounds per square foot) and its fire rating.

- *Raised* — The fire rating, its electrical conductivity (grounding against static buildup), and that it employs a non-conducting surface material are concerns of raised flooring in the data center. Electrical cables must be enclosed in metal conduit, and data cables must be enclosed in raceways, with all abandoned cable removed. Openings in the raised floor must be smooth and nonabrasive, and they should be protected to minimize the entrance of debris or other combustibles.

Windows. Windows are normally not acceptable in the data center. If they do exist, however, they must be translucent and shatterproof.

Doors. Doors in the data center must resist forcible entry and have a fire rating equal to the walls. Emergency exits must be clearly marked and monitored or alarmed. Electric door locks on emergency exits should revert to a disabled state if power outages occur to enable safe evacuation. While this may be considered a security issue, personnel safety always takes precedence, and these doors should be manned in an emergency.

Sprinkler system and fire resistance. The location and type of fire suppression system must be known. The fire-resistant rating of construction materials is a major factor in determining the fire safety of a computer operations room. The term *fire-resistant* refers to materials or construction that has a fire resistance rating of not less than the specified standard. For example, the computer room must be separated from other occupancy areas by construction with a fire-resistant rating of not less than one hour.

Liquid or gas lines. Security professionals should know where the shutoff valves are to water, steam, or gas pipes entering the building. Also, water drains should be "positive;" that is, they should flow outward, away from the building, so they do not carry contaminants into the facility.

Air conditioning. AC units should have dedicated power circuits. Security professionals should know where the Emergency Power Off (EPO) switch is. As with water drains, the AC system should provide outward, positive air pressure and have protected intake vents to prevent air-carried toxins from entering the facility.

Electrical requirements. The facility should have established backup and alternate power sources. Dedicated feeders and circuits are required in the data center. Security professionals should check for access controls to the electrical distribution panels and circuit breakers.

Facility Security Management

Under the grouping of Facility Security Management, we list audit trails and emergency procedures. These are elements of the Administrative Security Controls that are not related to the initial planning of the secure site but are required to be implemented on an ongoing basis.

Audit Trails

An audit trail (or *access log*) is a record of events. A computer system might have several audit trails, each focused on a particular type of activity, such as detecting security violations, performance problems, and design and programming flaws in applications. In the domain of Physical Security, audit trails and access control logs are vital because management needs to know where access attempts occurred and who attempted them.

The audit trails or access logs must record the following:

✦ The date and time of the access attempt

✦ Whether the attempt was successful or not

✦ Where the access was granted (which door, for example)

✦ Who attempted the access

✦ Who modified the access privileges at the supervisor level

Some audit trail systems can also send alarms or alerts to personnel whether multiple access failure attempts have been made.

Remember that audit trails and access logs are detective, rather than preventative. They do not stop an intrusion, although knowing that an audit trail of the entry attempt is being compiled may influence the intruder to not attempt entry. Audit trails do help an administrator reconstruct the details of an intrusion post-event, however.

Emergency Procedures

The implementation of emergency procedures and the employee training and knowledge of these procedures is an important part of administrative physical controls. These procedures should be clearly documented, readily accessible (including copies stored off-site in the event of a disaster), and updated periodically.

Elements of emergency procedure administration should include the following:

✦ Emergency system shutdown procedures

✦ Evacuation procedures

✦ Employee training, awareness programs, and periodic drills

✦ Periodic equipment and systems tests

Administrative Personnel Controls

Administrative Personnel Controls encompass those administrative processes that commonly are implemented by the Human Resources department during employee hiring and firing. Examples of personnel controls implemented by HR often include the following:

✦ Preemployment screening:

  • Employment, references, or educational history checks

  • Background investigation or credit rating checks for sensitive positions

✦ Ongoing employee checks:

  • Security clearances — generated only if the employee is to have access to classified documents

  • Ongoing employee ratings or reviews by their supervisor

✦ Post-employment procedures:

  • Exit interview

  • Removal of network access and change of passwords

  • Return of computer inventory or laptops

Environmental and Life Safety Controls

Environmental and Life Safety Controls are considered to be those elements of physical security controls that are required to sustain either the computer's operating environment or the personnel's operating environment. The following are the three main areas of environmental control:

1. Electrical power
2. Fire detection and suppression
3. Heating, Ventilation, and Air Conditioning (HVAC)

Electrical Power

Electrical systems are the lifeblood of computer operations. The continued supply of clean, steady power is required to maintain the proper personnel environment as well as to sustain data operations. Many elements can threaten power systems, the most common being noise, brownouts, and humidity.

Noise

Noise in power systems refers to the presence of electrical radiation in the system that is unintentional and interferes with the transmission of clean power. There are several types of noise, the most common being electromagnetic interference (EMI) and radio frequency interference (RFI). EMI and RFI are terms used to describe disruption or noise generated by electromagnetic waves. RFI refers to noise generated from radio waves, and EMI is the general term for all electromagnetic interference, including radio waves. EMI and RFI are often generated naturally, for example from solar sunspots or the earth's magnetic field. Manmade sources of EMI and RFI pose the largest threat to electronic equipment from sources like cell phones, laptops, and other computers.

EMI is noise that is caused by the generation of radiation due to the charge difference between the three electrical wires — the hot, neutral, and ground wires.

Two common types of EMI generated by electrical systems are:

Common-mode noise. Noise from the radiation generated by the charge difference between the hot and ground wires

Traverse-mode noise. Noise from the radiation generated by the charge difference between the hot and neutral wires

RFI is generated by the components of an electrical system, such as radiating electrical cables, fluorescent lighting, and electric space heaters. RFI can be so serious that it not only interferes with computer operations but also can permanently damage sensitive components.

Guidelines to prevent EMI and RFI interference in the computer room should be adopted, such as limiting the use and placement of magnets or cell phones around sensitive equipment. The United States government created the TEMPEST (Transient ElectroMagnetic Pulse Emanations Standard) standard to prevent EMI eavesdropping by employing heavy metal shielding.

Several protective measures for noise exist. Some of the ones that need to be noted are:

✦ Power line conditioning

✦ Proper grounding of the system to the earth

✦ Cable shielding

✦ Limiting exposure to magnets, fluorescent lights, electric motors, and space heaters

Table 10-1 lists various electrical power terms and descriptions.

Table 10-1 Electrical Power Definitions	
Element	**Description**
Fault	Momentary power loss
Blackout	Complete loss of power
Sag	Momentary low voltage
Brownout	Prolonged low voltage
Spike	Momentary high voltage
Surge	Prolonged high voltage
Inrush	Initial surge of power at the beginning
Noise	Steady interfering disturbance
Transient	Short duration of line noise disturbances
Clean	Non-fluctuating pure power
Ground	One wire in an electrical circuit must be grounded

Brownouts

Unlike a sag, a brownout is a prolonged drop in supplied usable voltage that can do serious physical damage to delicate electronic components. The American National Standards Institute (ANSI) standards permit an 8 percent drop between the power source and the building's meter and permit a 3.5 percent drop between the meter and the wall. In New York City, 15 percent fluctuations are common, and a prolonged brownout can lower the supplied voltage more than 10 percent.

In addition, surges and spikes occurring when the power comes back up from either a brownout or an outage can be damaging to the components. All computer equipment should be protected by surge suppressors, and critical equipment will need an uninterruptible power supply (UPS).

Humidity

The ideal operating humidity range is defined as 40 percent to 60 percent. High humidity, which is defined as greater than 60 percent, can produce a problem by creating condensation on computer parts. High humidity also creates problems with the corrosion of electrical connections. A process similar to electroplating occurs, causing the silver particles to migrate from the connectors onto the copper circuits, thus impeding the electrical efficiency of the components.

Low humidity of less than 40 percent increases the static electricity damage potential. A static charge of 4,000 volts is possible under normal humidity conditions on a hardwood or vinyl floor, and charges up to 20,000 volts or more are possible under conditions of very low humidity with non–static-free carpeting. Although you cannot control the weather, you certainly can control your relative humidity level in the computer room through your HVAC systems.

Some precautions you can take to reduce static electricity damage are:

✦ Use anti-static sprays where possible.

✦ Operations or computer centers should have anti-static flooring.

✦ Building and computer rooms should be grounded properly.

✦ Anti-static table or floor mats can be used.

✦ HVAC should maintain the proper level of relative humidity in computer rooms.

Check Your Carpets

A major New York City legal client once brought me into an emergency situation. They were scheduled for a cut over to a major new computer system the next weekend and were having problems keeping their system online. They had been operating it successfully in parallel for a few weeks in the lab, but once the system was moved to the operations center, it would frequently abort and reset for no apparent reason. After examining every conceivable parameter of the configuration and scratching my head for a bit, I noticed that I could cause a very small static discharge when I touched the case, thereby resetting the unit. Evidently the building contractor had run out of static-free carpet in the operations center and had finished the job with regular carpeting. Once we relocated the system, everything ran fine.

Fire Detection and Suppression

The successful detection and suppression of fire is an absolute necessity for the safe, continued operation of information systems. A CISSP candidate will need to know the classes, combustibles, detectors, and suppression methods of fire safety.

The National Fire Protection Association (NFPA) defines risk factors to consider when designing fire and safety protection for computing environments.* The factors to be used when assessing the impact of damage and interruption resulting from a fire, in priority order, are:

✦ The life safety aspects of the function, such as air traffic controls or safety processing controls

✦ The fire threat of the installation to the occupants or property of the computing area

✦ The economic loss incurred from the loss of computing function or loss of stored records

✦ The economic loss incurred from the loss of the value of the equipment

As in all evaluations of risk, not only fire risk, life safety is always the number one priority.

Fire Classes and Combustibles

Fire combustibles are rated as either Class A, B, C, or D based upon their material composition, thus determining which type of extinguishing system or agent is used. Table 10-2 lists the three main types of fires, what type of combustible gives the fire its class rating, and the recommended extinguishing agent.

Table 10-2
Fire Suppression Mediums

Class	Description	Suppression Medium
A	Common combustibles	Water or soda acid
B	Liquid	CO_2, soda acid, or Halon
C	Electrical	CO_2 or Halon

*Source: NFPA 75 "Standard for the Protection of Electronic Computer/Data Processing Equipment," National Fire Protection Association, 1999 Edition.

For rapid oxidation (a fire) to occur, three elements must be present: oxygen, heat, and fuel. Each suppression medium affects a different element and is therefore better suited for different types of fires.

Water. Suppresses the temperature required to sustain the fire.

Soda Acid. Suppresses the fuel supply of the fire.

CO_2. Suppresses the oxygen supply required to sustain the fire.

Halon. A little different, it suppresses combustion through a chemical reaction that kills the fire.

Anyone who has had the misfortune to throw water on a grease fire in a skillet and has suffered the resultant explosion will never need to be reminded that certain combustibles require very specific suppression methods.

The NFPA recommends that only the absolute minimum essential records, paper stock, inks, unused recording media, or other combustibles be housed in the computer room. Because of the threat of fire, these combustibles, including old, unused cabling, should not be stored in the computer room or under raised flooring. Under floor abandoned cables can interfere with airflow and extinguishing systems. Cables that are not intended to be used should be removed from the room. It also recommends that tape libraries and record storage rooms be protected by an extinguishing system and separated from the computer room by wall construction fire-resistant rated for not less than one hour.

Table 10-3 shows the NFPA fire class ratings for various combustible materials.

Table 10-3
Combustible Materials Fire Class Ratings

Fire Class	Combustible Materials
A	Wood, cloth, paper, rubber, most plastics, ordinary combustibles
B	Flammable liquids and gases, oils, greases, tars, oil-base paints and lacquers
C	Energized electrical equipment
D	Flammable chemicals such as magnesium and sodium

Fire Detectors

Fire detectors respond to heat, flame, or smoke to detect thermal combustion or its by-products. Different types of detectors have various properties and use the different properties of a fire to raise an alarm.

Heat-sensing. Heat-actuated sensing devices usually detect one of two conditions: 1) the temperature reaches a predetermined level, or 2) the temperature rises quickly regardless of the initial temperature. The first type, the fixed temperature device, has a much lower rate of false positives (false alarms) than the second, the rate-of-rise detector.

Flame-actuated. Flame-actuated sensing devices are fairly expensive, as they sense either the infrared energy of a flame or the pulsation of the flame and have a very fast response time. They are usually used in specialized applications for the protection of valuable equipment.

Smoke-actuated. Smoke-actuated fire sensing devices are used primarily in ventilation systems where an early-warning device would be useful. Photoelectric devices are triggered by the variation in the light hitting the photoelectric cell as a result of the smoke condition. Another type of smoke detector, the radioactive smoke detection device, generates an alarm when the ionization current created by its radioactive material is disturbed by the smoke.

Automatic dial-up fire alarm. This is a type of signal response mechanism that dials the local fire and/or police stations and plays a prerecorded message when a fire is detected. This alarm system is often used in conjunction with the previous fire detectors. These units are inexpensive but can easily be intentionally subverted.

Fire Extinguishing Systems

Fire extinguishing systems come in two flavors: water sprinkler systems and gas discharge systems.

Water sprinkler systems come in four variations:

Wet pipe. Wet pipe sprinkler systems always contain water and are also called a *closed head system*. In the most common implementation, the fusible link in the nozzle melts in the event of a heat rise to 165° F, causing a gate valve to open and allowing water to flow. This is considered the most reliable sprinkler system; however, its main drawbacks are that nozzle or pipe failure can cause a water flood, and the pipe can freeze if exposed to cold weather.

Dry pipe. In a dry pipe system, there is no water standing in the pipe; it is being held back by a clapper valve. Upon the previously described fire conditions arising, the valve opens, the air is blown out of the pipe, and the water flows. While this system is considered less efficient, it is commonly preferred over wet pipe systems for computer installations because a time delay may enable the computer systems to power down before the dry pipe system activates.

Deluge. A deluge system is a type of dry pipe, but the volume of water discharged is much larger. Unlike a sprinkler head, a deluge system is designed to deliver a large amount of water to an area quickly. It is not considered appropriate for computer equipment, however, due to the time required to get back on-line after an incident.

Preaction. This is currently the most recommended water system for a computer room. It combines both the dry and wet pipe systems by first releasing the water into the pipes when heat is detected (dry pipe) and then releasing the water flow when the link in the nozzle melts (wet pipe). This feature enables manual intervention before a full discharge of water on the equipment occurs.

Gas discharge systems employ a pressurized inert gas and are usually installed under the computer room raised floor. The fire detection system typically activates the gas discharge system to quickly smother the fire either under the floor in the cable areas or throughout the room. Typical agents of a gas discharge system are carbon dioxide (CO_2) or Halon. Halon 1211 does not require the sophisticated pressurization system of Halon 1301 and is used in self-pressurized portable extinguishers. Of the various replacements for Halon, FM-200 is now the most common.

Suppression Mediums

Carbon Dioxide (CO_2). CO_2 is a colorless and odorless gas commonly used in gas discharge fire suppression systems. It is very effective in fire suppression due to the fact that it quickly removes any oxygen that can be used to sustain the fire. This oxygen removal also makes it very dangerous for personnel, and it is potentially lethal. It is primarily recommended for use in unmanned computer facilities. If used in manned operations centers, the fire detection and alarm system must enable personnel ample time to either exit the facility or to cancel the release of the CO_2.

Portable fire extinguishers commonly contain CO_2 or Soda Acid and should be:

- Commonly located at exits
- Clearly marked with their fire types
- Checked regularly by licensed personnel

Halon. At one time, Halon was considered the perfect fire suppression method in computer operations centers due to the fact that it is not harmful to the equipment, mixes thoroughly with the air, and spreads extremely fast. The benefits of using Halons are that they do not leave liquid or solid residues when discharged. Therefore, they are preferred for sensitive areas, such as computer rooms and data storage areas.

Several issues arose with its deployment, however. For example, it cannot be breathed safely in concentrations greater than 10 percent, and when deployed on fires with temperatures greater than 900 degrees, it degrades into seriously toxic chemicals — hydrogen fluoride, hydrogen bromide, and bromine. Implementation of halogenated extinguishing agents in computer rooms must be extremely well designed to enable personnel to evacuate immediately when deployed, whether Halon is released under the flooring or overhead in the raised ceiling.

At the Montreal Protocol of 1987, Halon was designated an ozone-depleting substance due to its use of chlorofluorocarbon compounds (CFCs). Halon has an extremely high ozone-depleting potential (three to ten times more than CFCs), and its intended use results in its release into the environment.

No new Halon 1301 installations are allowed, and existing installations are encouraged to replace Halon with a non-toxic substitute, like the ones in the following list. Current federal regulations prohibit the production of Halons and the import and export of recovered Halons except by permit. There are federal controls on the uses, releases, and mandatory removal of Halon prior to decommissioning equipment, and reporting Halon releases, accidental or not, is mandatory.

There are alternatives to Halon. Many large users of Halon are taking steps to remove Halon-containing equipment from all but the most critical areas. Most Halon 1211 in commercial and industrial applications is being replaced and recovered. Halon 1301 is being banked for future use.

The two types of Halon used are:

- *Halon 1211* — A liquid steaming agent that is used in portable extinguishers
- *Halon 1301* — A gaseous agent that is used in fixed total flooding systems

Some common EPA-acceptable Halon replacements are:

- FM-200 (HFC-227ea)
- CEA-410 or CEA-308
- NAF-S-III (HCFC Blend A)
- FE-13 (HFC-23)
- Argon (IG55) or Argonite (IG01)
- Inergen (IG541)
- Low-pressure water mists

Either halocarbon agents or inert gas agents can be replacements for Halon 1301 and Halon 1211 in gas-discharge fire extinguishing systems. Halocarbon agents contain one or more organic compounds as primary components, such as the elements fluorine, chlorine, bromine, or iodine. Inert gas agents contain as primary components one or more of the gases helium, neon, argon, or nitrogen. Some inert gas agents also contain carbon dioxide as a secondary component. Halocarbon agents are hydrofluorocarbons (HFCs), hydrochlo-roflurocarbons (HCFCs), perfluorocarbons (PFCs or FCs), or fluoroiodocar-bons (FICs). Common inert gas agents for fire extinguishing systems are IG-01, IG-100, IG -55, and IG-541.

Because Halon was banned for use in fire suppression systems, many different chemical agents have been used. Some of these agents are called *clean agents* because they do not leave a residue on electronic parts after evaporation. CO_2, carbon dioxide, does leave a corrosive residue, and it is therefore not recommended for computer facility fire suppression systems. A clean agent is defined as an electrically nonconducting, nonvolatile fire extinguishant that does not leave a residue upon evaporation. IG-55 and IG-01 are inert gas agents that do not decompose measurably or leave corrosive decomposition products and are, therefore, considered clean agents.

Contamination

Environmental contamination resulting from the fire (or its suppression) can cause damage to the computer systems by depositing conductive particles on the components.

The following are some examples of fire contaminants:

✦ Smoke

✦ Heat

✦ Water

✦ Suppression medium contamination (Halon or CO_2)

Immediate smoke exposure to electronic equipment does little damage. However, the particulate residue left after the smoke has dissipated contains active by-products that corrode metal contact surfaces in the presence of moisture and oxygen. Removal of the contaminant from the electrical contacts, such as printed circuit boards and backplanes, should be implemented as soon as possible as much of the damage is done during this corrosion period. Also, power should be immediately disconnected to the affected equipment as continuing voltage can plate the contaminants into the circuitry permanently.

The order of steps to be taken after electronic equipment or media has been exposed to smoke contaminants are:

1. Turn off power to equipment.

2. Move equipment into an air-conditioned and humidity-controlled environment.

3. Spray connectors, backplanes, and printed circuit boards with Freon or Freon-alcohol solvents.

4. Spray corrosion-inhibiting aerosol to stabilize metal contact surfaces.

Water Damage

Water-based emergencies could include pipe breakage or damage to sensitive electronic equipment due to the proper use of water fire sprinklers. The first order of business is shutting down the power to the effected equipment to prevent shock hazards, shorting, or further damage. Any visible standing water should be removed and allowed to drain from around and the inside the unit. As the room may still be extremely humid, move the equipment, if possible, to a humidity-controlled environment, and then wipe the parts and use water displacement sprays. If corrective action is initiated immediately, the damage done to the computer equipment can be greatly reduced and the chances of recovering the data are increased.

The proper order of steps to be taken after electronic equipment or media has been exposed to water are:

1. Turn off all electrical power to the equipment.

2. Open cabinet doors and remove panels and covers to allow water to run out.

3. Place all affected equipment or media in an air-conditioned area, if portable.

4. Wipe with alcohol or Freon-alcohol solutions or spray with water-displacement aerosol sprays.

Table 10-4 lists the temperatures required to damage various computer parts.

Table 10-4 Heat Damage Temperatures	
Item	*Temperature*
Computer hardware	175° F
Magnetic storage	100° F
Paper products	350° F

Heating, Ventilation, and Air Conditioning

HVAC is sometimes referred to as *HVACR* for the addition of refrigeration. HVAC systems can be quite complex in modern high-rise buildings, and they are the focal point for environmental controls. An IT manager needs to know who is responsible for HVAC, and clear escalation steps need to be defined well in advance of an environment-threatening incident. The same department is often responsible for fire, water, and other disaster response, all of which impact the availability of the computer systems.

Underfloor ventilation, as is true of all computer room ventilation, should not vent to any other office or area. HVAC air ducts serving other rooms should not pass through the computer room unless an automatic damping system is provided. A damper is activated by fire and smoke detectors and prevents the spread of computer room smoke or toxins through the building HVAC.

Physical and Technical Controls

Under this general grouping, we discuss those elements of physical security that are not considered specifically administrative solutions, although they obviously have administrative aspects. Here we have the areas of environmental controls, fire protection, electrical power, guards, and locks.

We will discuss the elements of control as they relate to the areas of:

✦ Facility control requirements

✦ Facility access control devices

✦ Intrusion detection and alarms

✦ Computer inventory control

✦ Media storage requirements

Facility Control Requirements

Several elements are required to maintain physical site security for facility control:

Guards

Guards are the oldest form of security surveillance. Guards still have a very important and primary function in the physical security process, particularly in perimeter control. A guard can make determinations that hardware or other automated security devices cannot make due to his ability to adjust to rapidly changing conditions, to learn and alter recognizable patterns, and to respond to various conditions in the environment. Guards provide deterrent, response, and control capabilities, in addition to receptionist and escort functions. Guards are also the best resource during periods of personnel safety risks (they maintain order, crowd control, and evacuation) and are better at making value decisions at times of incidents. They are appropriate whenever immediate, discriminating judgment is required by the security entity.

Guards have several drawbacks, however, such as the following:

Availability. They cannot exist in environments that do not support human intervention.

Reliability. The preemployment screening and bonding of guards is not foolproof.

Training. Guards can be socially engineered or may not always have up-to-date lists of access authorization.

Cost. Maintaining a guard function either internally or through an external service is expensive.

Dogs

Using guard dogs is almost as old a concept as using people to guard something. Dogs are loyal, reliable (they rarely have substance abuse issues), and have a keen sense of smell and hearing. However, a guard dog is primarily acceptable for perimeter physical control and is not as useful as a human guard for making judgment calls. Some additional drawbacks include cost, maintenance, and insurance/liability issues.

Fencing

Fencing is the primary means of perimeter/boundary facility access control. The category of fencing includes fences, gates, turnstiles, and mantraps.

Fencing and other barriers provide crowd control and help deter casual trespassing by controlling access to entrances. Drawbacks to fencing include its cost, its appearance (it might be ugly), and its inability to stop a determined intruder. Table 10-5 is a very important table; a CISSP candidate should know these heights.

Table 10-5 Fencing Height Requirements	
Height	*Protection*
3' to 4' high	Deters casual trespassers
6' to 7' high	Too hard to climb easily
8' high with 3 strands of barbed wire	Deters most intruders

Mantrap

A mantrap is a physical access control method where the entrance to a facility or area is routed through a set of double doors. One door must be closed for the next door to open. It may or may not be monitored by a guard.

Piggybacking describes an unauthorized person entering a facility through a carded or controlled door by following an authorized person who has opened the door. A mantrap is intended to control physical personnel entrance to the facility by piggybacking. Of course, the best protection from this type of intrusion is through security awareness training to prevent employees from holding the door open or allowing unauthorized intruders to enter.

Lighting

Lighting is also one of the most common forms of perimeter or boundary protection. Extensive outside protective lighting of entrances or parking areas can discourage prowlers or casual intruders. Critical protected buildings should be illuminated up to 8 feet high with 2 feet candlepower. Common types of lighting include floodlights, streetlights, Fresnel lights, and searchlights.

Locks

After the use of guards, locks are probably one of the oldest access control methods ever used. Locks can be divided into two types: preset and programmable.

Preset locks. These are your typical door locks. The combinations to enter cannot be changed except by physically removing them and replacing the internal mechanisms. There are various types of preset locks, including key-in-knob, mortise, and rim locks. These all consist of variations of latches, cylinders, and dead bolts.

Programmable locks. These locks can be either mechanically or electronically based. A mechanical programmable lock is often a typical dial combination lock, like the kind you would use on your gym locker. Another type of mechanical programmable lock is the common five-key pushbutton lock that requires the user to enter a combination of numbers. This is a very popular lock for IT operations centers. An electronic programmable lock requires the user to enter a pattern of digits on a numerical-style keypad, and it may display the digits in random order each time to prevent shoulder surfing for input patterns. It is also known as a cipher lock or keypad access control.

Closed-Circuit Television (CCTV)

Visual surveillance or recording devices such as closed circuit television are used in conjunction with guards in order to enhance their surveillance ability and to record events for future analysis or prosecution. These devices can be either photographic in nature (as in still or movie film cameras) or electronic in nature (the closed-circuit TV camera). CCTV can be used to monitor live events occurring in an area remote to the guard, or they can be used in conjunction with a VCR for a cost-effective method of recording these events.

Facility Access Control Devices

This access includes personnel access control to the facility and general operations centers, in addition to specific data center access control.

Security Access Cards

Security access cards are a common method of physical access control. There are two common card types — photo-image and digitally encoded cards. These two groups are also described as *dumb* and *smart* cards. Dumb cards require a guard to make a decision as to its validity, whereas smart cards make the entry decision electronically:

Photo-image cards. Photo-image cards are simple identification cards with the photo of the bearer for identification. These are your standard photo ID cards, like a drivers license or employee ID badge. These cards are referred to as dumb cards because they have no intelligence imbedded in them, and they require an active decision to be made by the entry personnel as to their authenticity.

Digital-coded cards. Digitally encoded cards contain chips or magnetically encoded strips (possibly in addition to a photo of the bearer). The card reader may be programmed to accept or deny an entry based upon an online access control computer that can also provide information about the date and time of entry. These cards may also be able to create multi-level access groupings. There are two common forms of digitally encoded cards, which are referred to as *smart* and *smarter* cards.

Smart entry cards can have either a magnetic stripe or a small integrated circuit (IC) chip imbedded in them. This card may require knowledge of a password or personal identification number (PIN) to enable entry. A bank ATM card is an example of this card type. These cards may contain a processor encoded with the host system's authentication protocol, read-only memory storage of programs and data, and even some kind of user interface.

Wireless proximity readers. A proximity reader does not require the user to physically insert the access card. This card may also be referred to as a wireless security card. The card reader senses the card in possession of a user in the general area (proximity) and enables access. There are two general types of proximity readers — *user activated* and *system sensing*:

- A user-activated proximity card transmits a sequence of keystrokes to a wireless keypad on the reader. The keypad on the reader contains either a fixed preset code or a programmable unique key pattern.

- A system-sensing proximity card recognizes the presence of the coded device in the reader's general area. The following are the three common types of system-sensing cards, which are based upon the way the power is generated for these devices:

  1. *Passive devices*. These cards contain no battery or power on the card but sense the electromagnetic field transmitted by the reader and transmit at different frequencies using the power field of the reader.

  2. *Field-powered devices*. They contain active electronics, a radio frequency transmitter, and a power supply circuit on the card.

  3. *Transponders*. Both the card and reader contain a receiver, transmitter, active electronics, and a battery. The reader transmits an interrogating signal to the card, which in turn causes it to transmit an access code. These systems are often used as portable devices for dynamically assigning access control.

A smart card or access token could be part of a complete Enterprise Identity Management system, used to track the location of employees and manage secure access. A smart card can be coupled with an authentication token that generates a one-time or challenge-response password or PIN. While two-actor (or dual-factor) authentication is most often used for logical access to network services, it can be combined with an intelligent card reader to provide extremely strong facility access control.

Table 10-6 lists the various types of security access cards.

Table 10-6 Dumb, Smart, and Smarter Cards	
Type of Card	*Description*
Photo ID	Facial photograph
Optical-coded	Laser-burned lattice of digital dots
Electric circuit	Printed IC on the card
Magnetic stripe	Stripe of magnetic material
Magnetic strip	Rows of copper strips
Passive electronic	Electrically tuned circuitry read by RF
Active electronic	Badge transmitting encoded electronics

Biometric Devices

Biometric access control devices and techniques, such as fingerprinting or retinal scanning, are discussed thoroughly in Chapter 2. Keep in mind that because they constitute a physical security control, biometric devices are also considered a physical access security control device.

Intrusion Detectors and Alarms

Intrusion detection refers to the process of identifying attempts to penetrate a system or building to gain unauthorized access. While Chapter 3 details ID systems that detect logical breaches of the network infrastructure, here we are talking about devices that detect physical breaches of perimeter security, such as a burglar alarm.

Perimeter Intrusion Detectors

The two most common types of physical perimeter detectors are based either on photoelectric sensors or dry contact switches.

What Are Those Three Things Again?

What are the three elements, which we learned, that are commonly used for authentication? 1) something you have (like a token card), 2) something you know (like your PIN or password), and 3) something you are (biometrics).

Photoelectric sensors. Photoelectric sensors receive a beam of light from a light-emitting device, creating a grid of either visible white light, or invisible infrared light. An alarm is activated when the beams are broken. The beams can be physically avoided if seen; therefore, invisible infrared light is often used. Also, employing a substitute light system can defeat the sensor.

Dry contact switches. Dry contact switches and tape are probably the most common types of perimeter detection. This can consist of metallic foil tape on windows, or metal contact switches on doorframes. This type of physical intrusion detection is the cheapest and easiest to maintain, and it is very commonly used for shop front protection.

Motion Detectors

In addition to the two types of intrusion detectors previously mentioned, motion detectors are used to sense unusual movement within a predefined interior security area. They can be grouped into three categories: wave pattern motion detectors, capacitance detectors, and audio amplification devices.

Wave pattern. Wave pattern motion detectors generate a frequency wave pattern and send an alarm if the pattern is disturbed as it is reflected back to its receiver. These frequencies can either be in the low (sonic), ultrasonic, or microwave range. Table 10-7 shows the relative frequency of each of these detectors.

Capacitance. Capacitance detectors monitor an electrical field surrounding the object being monitored. They are used for spot protection within a few inches of the object, rather than for overall room security monitoring used by wave detectors. Penetration of this field changes the electrical capacitance of the field enough to generate an alarm.

Audio detectors. Audio detectors are passive in that they do not generate any fields or patterns like the previous two methods. Audio detectors simply monitor a room for any abnormal sound wave generation and trigger an alarm. This type of detection device generates a higher number of false alarms than the other two methods and should be used only in areas that have controlled ambient sound.

Table 10-7
Motion Detection System Frequencies

Detector Type	Frequency
Sonic	1500–2000 hertz
Ultrasonic	19,000–20,000 hertz
Microwave	400–10,000 megahertz

Alarm Systems

The detection devices previously listed monitor and report on a specific change in the environment. These detectors can be grouped together to create alarm systems. There are four general types of alarm systems:

Local alarm systems. A local alarm system rings an audible alarm on the local premises that it protects. This alarm must be protected from tampering and must be audible for at least 400 feet. It also requires guards to respond locally to the intrusion.

Central station systems. Private security firms operate these systems, which are monitored around the clock. The central stations are signaled by detectors over leased lines. These stations typically offer many additional features, such as CCTV monitoring and printed reports, and the customers' premises are commonly less than 10 minutes travel time away from the central monitoring office.

Proprietary systems. These systems are similar to the central station systems, except that the monitoring system is owned and operated by the customer. They are like local alarms, except that a sophisticated computer system provides many of the features in-house that a third-party firm would provide with a central station system.

Auxiliary station systems. Any of the previous three systems may have auxiliary alarms that ring at the local fire or police stations. Most central station systems include this feature, which requires permission from the local authorities before implementation.

Two other terms related to alarms are:

Line supervision. Line supervision is a process where an alarm-signaling transmission medium is monitored to detect any line tampering to subvert its effectiveness. The Underwriters Laboratory (UL) standard 611-1968 states, "the connecting line between the central station and the protection shall be supervised so as to automatically detect a compromise attempt by methods of resistance substitution, potential substitution, or any single compromise attempt." Secure detection and alarm systems require line supervision.

Power supplies. Alarm systems require separate circuitry and backup power with 24 hours minimum discharge time. These alarms help reduce the probability of an alarm system's failure due to a power failure.

Computer Inventory Control

Computer Inventory Control is the control of computers and computer equipment from physical theft and protection from damage. The two main areas of concern are computer physical control and laptop control.

PC Physical Control

Due to the proliferation of distributed computing and the proliferation of laptops, inventory control at the microcomputer level is a major headache. Some groups estimate that 40 percent of computer inventory shrinkage is due to microcomputer parts walking out the door. Several physical controls must be taken to minimize this loss:

Cable locks. A cable lock consists of a vinyl-covered steel cable anchoring the PC or peripherals to the desk. They often consist of screw kits, slot locks, and cable traps.

Port controls. Port controls are devices that secure data ports (such as a floppy drive or a serial or parallel port) and prevent their use.

Switch controls. A switch control is a cover for the on/off switch, which prevents a user from switching off the file server's power.

Peripheral switch controls. These types of controls are lockable switches that prevent a keyboard from being used.

Electronic security boards. These boards are inserted into an expansion slot in the PC and force a user to enter a password when the unit is booted. This is also a standard part of the Basic Input Output System (BIOS) of many off-the-shelf PCs. They might also be called cryptographic locks.

Laptop Control

The proliferation of laptops and portables is the next evolution of distributed computing and constitutes a challenge to security practitioners. Now the computing resources can be strewn all over the globe, and physical inventory control is nearly impossible for an organization without a substantive dedication of IT resources. A laptop theft is a very serious issue because it creates a failure of all three elements of C.I.A.: confidentiality, as the data can now be read by someone outside of a monitored environment; availability, as the user has lost the unit's computing ability; and integrity, as the data residing on the unit and any telecommunications from it are now suspect.

Media Storage Requirements

The ongoing storage of data media and the proper disposal of unneeded media and reports is a serious concern to security practitioners. Sometimes an organization will devote a large amount of resources to perimeter protection and network security, and then will dispose of reports improperly. Or they will reuse laptops or diskettes without fully and appropriately wiping the data.

Because laptop theft is rampant, encryption of any sensitive data on a portable is also an absolute necessity. An associate of mine was recently lent a laptop while working at a top brokerage firm, only to discover that the hard drive had not been reformatted and contained dozens of sensitive emails pertaining to the 1996 presidential election (the previous owner had worked as an advisor to the GOP Bob Dole campaign).

The following types of media commonly require storage, destruction, or reuse:

✦ Data backup tapes

✦ CDs

✦ Diskettes

✦ Hard drives

✦ Paper printouts and reports

The common storage areas for such media are:

On-site. Areas within the facility, such as operations centers, offices, desks, storage closets, cabinets, safes, and so on.

Off-site. Areas outside of the facility, such as data backup vault services, partners and vendors, and disposal systems. Transportation to or from an external data vault services vendor is a security concern, and it should be examined for problems relating to theft, copying, alteration, or destruction of data.

We have the following resources and elements in our control to protect the media:

✦ Physical access control to the storage areas

✦ Environmental controls, such as fire and water protections

✦ Diskette inventory controls and monitoring

✦ Audits of media use

Data Destruction and Reuse

Data that is no longer needed or used must be destroyed. Information on magnetic media is typically destroyed by degaussing or overwriting. Formatting a disk once does not completely destroy all data, so the entire media must be overwritten or formatted seven times to conform to standards for object reuse.

Diskette Storage Tips

A few basic controls should be put in place to protect diskettes (or other magnetic media) from damage or loss, such as

1. Keep the disks in locked cases.

2. Don't bend the diskettes.

3. Maintain the proper temperature and humidity.

4. Avoid external magnetic fields (such as TVs or radios).

5. Don't write directly on the jacket or sleeve.

The Joy of Dumpster Diving

New York is the capital of ticker-tape parades. New Yorkers never seem to tire of trying to find some reason to throw large volumes of paper out of high story office windows. Sometimes, however, the enthusiasm for the moment overrides the immediate availability of shredded reports, and some office workers will begin to toss out unshredded, full-page printed pages. Local reporters have begun to collect these reports before they are swept up by sanitation and have reported that the information contained is considerable (especially due to the fact that the parades are often down Broadway, past Wall Street). These pages often contain credit card account numbers, bank account numbers and balances, credit rating details, and so forth.

Personnel with the proper level of security clearance should shred paper reports . Some shredders cut in straight lines or strips, whereas others crosscut or disintegrate the material into pulp. Care must be taken to limit access to the reports prior to disposal and to those stored for long periods. Reports should never be disposed of without shredding, such as when they are placed in a dumpster intact. Burning is also sometimes used to destroy paper reports, especially in the Department of Defense and military.

Object Reuse and Data Remanence

Object reuse is the concept of reusing data storage media after its initial use. Data remanence is the problem of residual information remaining on the media after erasure, which may be subject to restoration by another user, thereby resulting in a loss of confidentiality. Diskettes, hard drives, tapes, and any magnetic or writable media are susceptible to data remanence. Retrieving the bits and pieces of data that have not been thoroughly removed from storage media is a common method of computer forensics, and law enforcement personnel often use it to preserve evidence and to construct a trail of misuse. Anytime a storage medium is reused (and also when it is discarded), there is the potential for the media's information to be retrieved. Methods must be employed to properly destroy the existing data to ensure that no residual data is available to new users. The Orange Book standard recommends that magnetic media be formatted seven times before discard or reuse.

Terminology relative to the various stages of data erasure is:

Clearing. This term refers to the overwriting of data media (primarily magnetic) intended to be reused in the same organization or monitored environment.

Purging. This term refers to degaussing or overwriting media intended to be removed from a monitored environment, such as during resale (laptops) or donations to charity.

Destruction. This term refers to completely destroying the media, and therefore the residual data. Paper reports, diskettes, and optical media (CD-ROMs) need to be physically destroyed before disposal.

The following are the common problems with magnetic media erasure that may cause data remanence:

1. Erasing the data through an operating system does not remove the data; it just changes the File Allocation Table and renames the first character of the file. This is the most common way computer forensics investigators can restore files.

2. Damaged sectors of the disk may not be overwritten by the format utility. Degaussing may need to be used. Formatting seven times is also recommended.

3. Rewriting files on top of the old files may not overwrite all data areas on the disk because the new file may not be as long as the older file, and data may be retrieved past the file end control character.

4. Degausser equipment failure or operator error may result in an inadequate erasure.

5. There may be an inadequate number of formats. Magnetic media containing sensitive information should be formatted seven times or more.

Walk-Through Security List

The simplest way to get a handle on your office's state of physical security is to do a minimal "walk-about." This consists of an after-hours walk-through of your site, checking for these specific things:

1. Sensitive company information is not lying open on desks or in traffic areas.

2. Workstations are logged out and turned off.

3. Offices are locked and secured.

4. Stairwell exits are not propped open. (I have seen them propped open with fire extinguishers, so folks wouldn't have to use the elevators!)

5. Files, cabinets, and desks are locked and secured.

6. Diskettes and data tapes are put away and secured.

✦   ✦   ✦

Assessment Questions

You can find the answers to the following questions in Appendix A.

1. Which choice below is NOT a type of motion-detection system?

    a. Ultrasonic-detection system

    b. Microwave-detection system

    c. Host-based intrusion-detection system

    d. Sonic-detection system

2. Which type of personnel control below helps prevent piggybacking?

    a. Mantraps

    b. Back doors

    c. Brute force

    d. Maintenance hooks

3. Which choice below most accurately describes the prime benefit of using guards?

    a. Human guards are less expensive than guard dogs.

    b. Guards can exercise discretionary judgment in a way that automated systems can't.

    c. Automated systems have a greater reliability rate than guards.

    d. Guard dogs cannot discern an intruder's intent.

4. The recommended optimal relative humidity range for computer operations is:

    a. 10%–30%

    b. 30%–40%

    c. 40%–60%

    d. 60%–80%

5. How many times should a diskette be formatted to comply with TCSEC Orange Book object reuse recommendations?

    a. Three

    b. Five

    c. Seven

    d. Nine

6. Which of the following more closely describes the combustibles in a Class B-rated fire?

   a. Paper

   b. Gas

   c. Liquid

   d. Electrical

7. Which of the following is NOT the proper suppression medium for a Class B fire?

   a. CO_2

   b. Soda Acid

   c. Halon

   d. Water

8. What does an audit trail or access log usually NOT record?

   a. How often a diskette was formatted

   b. Who attempted access

   c. The date and time of the access attempt

   d. Whether the attempt was successful

9. A brownout can be defined as a:

   a. Prolonged power loss

   b. Momentary low voltage

   c. Prolonged low voltage

   d. Momentary high voltage

10. Which statement below is NOT accurate about smoke damage to electronic equipment?

   a. Smoke exposure during a fire for a relatively short period does little immediate damage.

   b. Continuing power to the smoke-exposed equipment can increase the damage.

   c. Moisture and oxygen corrosion constitute the main damage to the equipment.

   d. The primary damage done by smoke exposure is immediate.

11. A surge can be defined as a(n):

    a. Prolonged high voltage

    b. Initial surge of power at start

    c. Momentary power loss

    d. Steady interfering disturbance

12. Which is NOT a type of a fire detector?

    a. Heat-sensing

    b. Gas-discharge

    c. Flame-actuated

    d. Smoke-actuated

13. Which of the following is NOT considered an acceptable replacement for Halon discharge systems?

    a. FA200

    b. Inergen (IG541)

    c. Halon 1301

    d. Argon (IG55)

14. Which type of fire extinguishing method contains standing water in the pipe and therefore generally does not enable a manual shutdown of systems before discharge?

    a. Dry pipe

    b. Wet pipe

    c. Preaction

    d. Deluge

15. Which type of control below is NOT an example of a physical security access control?

    a. Retinal scanner

    b. Guard dog

    c. Five-key programmable lock

    d. Audit trail

16. Which is NOT a recommended way to dispose of unwanted used data media?

    a. Destroying CD-ROMs

    b. Formatting diskettes seven or more times

    c. Shredding paper reports by cleared personnel

    d. Copying new data over existing data on diskettes

17. According to the NFPA, which choice below is NOT a recommended risk factor to consider when determining the need for protecting the computing environment from fire?

    a. Life safety aspects of the computing function or process

    b. Fire threat of the installation to occupants or exposed property

    c. Distance of the computing facility from a fire station

    d. Economic loss of the equipment's value

18. Which choice below is NOT an example of a Halocarbon Agent?

    a. HFC-23

    b. FC-3-1-10

    c. IG-541

    d. HCFC-22

19. Which statement below most accurately describes a dry pipe sprinkler system?

    a. Dry pipe is the most commonly used sprinkler system.

    b. Dry pipe contains air pressure.

    c. Dry pipe sounds an alarm and delays water release.

    d. Dry pipe may contain carbon dioxide.

20. The theft of a laptop poses a threat to which tenet of the C.I.A. triad?

    a. Confidentiality

    b. Integrity

    c. Availability

    d. All of the above

21. Which is a benefit of a guard over an automated control?

    a. Guards can use discriminating judgment.

    b. Guards are cheaper.

    c. Guards do not need training.

    d. Guards do not need preemployment screening.

22. Which is NOT considered a preventative security measure?

   a. Fences

   b. Guards

   c. Audit trails

   d. Preset locks

23. Which is NOT a PC security control device?

   a. A cable lock

   b. A switch control

   c. A port control

   d. A file cabinet lock

24. Which choice below is NOT an example of a clean fire-extinguishing agent?

   a. CO_2

   b. IG-55

   c. IG-01

   d. HCFC-22

25. What is the recommended height of perimeter fencing to keep out casual trespassers?

   a. 1' to 2' high

   b. 3' to 4' high

   c. 6' to 7' high

   d. 8' to 12' high

26. Why should extensive exterior perimeter lighting of entrances or parking areas be installed?

   a. To enable programmable locks to be used

   b. To create two-factor authentication

   c. To discourage prowlers or casual intruders

   d. To prevent data remanence

27. Which of the following is NOT a form of data erasure?

   a. Clearing

   b. Remanence

   c. Purging

   d. Destruction

28. Which is NOT considered a physical intrusion detection method?

  a. Audio motion detector

  b. Photoelectric sensor

  c. Wave pattern motion detector

  d. Line supervision

29. Which choice below represents the BEST reason to control the humidity in computer operations areas?

  a. Computer operators do not perform at their peak if the humidity is too high.

  b. Electrostatic discharges can harm electronic equipment.

  c. Static electricity destroys the electrical efficiency of the circuits.

  d. If the air is too dry, electroplating of conductors may occur.

30. Which term below refers to a standard used in determining the fire safety of a computer room?

  a. Noncombustible

  b. Fire-resistant

  c. Fire retardant

  d. Nonflammable

The Information Systems Security Engineering Professional (ISSEP) Concentration

♦ ♦ ♦ ♦

Systems Security Engineering

The Systems Security Engineering domain of the ISSEP concentration is designed to enable the candidate to use the processes defined in the Information Assurance Technical Framework (IATF). These processes, described in the IATF document, Release 3.1, provide guidance for the protection of information systems. The IATF is result of the activities of the Information Assurance Technical Framework Forum (IATFF).

The Information Assurance Technical Framework Forum

The IATF document, Release 3.1, is a product of the IATFF. The IATFF, sponsored by the National Security Agency (NSA), encourages and supports technical interchanges on the topic of information assurance among U.S. industry, U.S. academic institutions, and U.S. government agencies.

The forum meets every six months and works toward the following goals:

1. Achieving consensus on a framework for information assurance solutions that will satisfy the needs of users

2. Supporting the development and application of solutions that are compatible with the framework

Information on the IATFF can be found at its Web site, www.iatf.net.

The Information Assurance Technical Framework

The IATF document 3.1 provides a technical process for developing systems with inherent information assurance, emphasizing the criticality of the *people* involved, the *operations* required, and the *technology* needed to meet the organization's mission. It also defines the information security requirements of the system hardware and software. Applying the process of document 3.1 results in a layered protection scheme known as Defense in Depth for critical information system components. The Defense in Depth strategy comprises the following areas:

✦ Defending the network and infrastructure

✦ Defending the enclave boundary

✦ Defending the computing environment

✦ Supporting Infrastructures

These topics will be discussed in detail later in this chapter.

The IATF is divided into the following four groups, as illustrated in Figure 11-1:

✦ Chapters 1-4, **Main Body**

✦ Chapters 5-10 & Appendices A-E, H-J, **Technical Sections**

✦ Appendix F, **Executive Summaries**

✦ Appendix G, **Protection Profiles**

Organization of IATF Document, Release 3.1

The *Main Body* of the IATF document offers general guidelines on information assurance for information security engineers, information system users, and security architects.

The *Technical Sections* of the document cover the requirements and solutions for the Defense in Depth layers.

The *Executive Summaries* appendix provides a reference guide of sample situations in typical environments that the user can examine to see whether these solutions might apply to a specific environment. These summaries delineate threats and recommended solutions that might be valuable to the user.

The *Protection Profiles* appendix provides assurance requirements and functionality for a system or product based on the Common Criteria (ISO standard 15408).

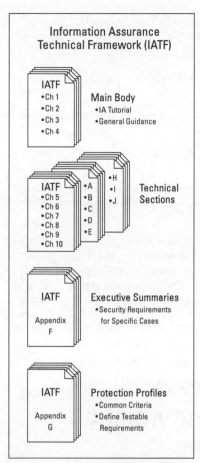

Figure 11-1: Organization of the IATF (from IATF document, Release 3.1, September 2002).

Specific Requirements of the ISSEP Candidate

The Systems Security Engineering domain of the ISSEP Concentration area is divided into the following five components:

1. Discover information protection needs

2. Define system security requirements

3. Design system security architecture

4. Develop detailed security design

5. Implement system security

These areas will be covered in detail in this chapter. As stated in the ISSEP Study Guide, the ISSEP candidate is expected to be able to do the following after completing this chapter:

1. Describe the Information Systems Security Engineering (ISSE) process as documented in the IATF

2. Describe systems engineering processes in general and infer how security engineering integrates with these processes

3. Explain the applicability of evaluated products and the various types of evaluation and evaluation processes

4. Construct network architectures according to the principles of Defense- n Depth

5. Construct proper documentation for each phase of the ISSE process

In addition, the candidate should understand the fundamental concepts of risk assessment and the system life cycle, or, as it is sometimes called, the system development life cycle (SDLC). These areas are covered in NIST Special Publication 800-30, "Risk Management Guide for Information Technology Systems"; NIST Special Publication 800-14, "Generally Accepted Principles and Practices for Securing Information Technology Systems"; and NIST Special Publication 800-27, "Engineering Principles for Information Technology Security (A Baseline for Achieving Security.)"

Systems Engineering Processes and Their Relationship to Information System Security Engineering

Information system security engineering should be conducted in parallel with and according to the proven principles of systems engineering (SE). Even though the terms ISSE and SE are commonly used, it is important to formally define these two concepts so that there is no misunderstanding of their meaning. In Chapter 3 of IATF document 3.1, ISSE is defined as "the art and science of discovering users' information protection needs and then designing and making information systems, with economy and elegance, so that they can safely resist the forces to which they may be subjected."

Systems engineering has been defined in numerous ways. Six such definitions are:

✦ The branch of engineering concerned with the development of large and complex systems, where a system is understood to be an assembly or combination of interrelated elements or parts working together toward a common objective. (This is a commonly accepted definition of systems engineering.)

✦ The branch of engineering, based on systems analysis and information theory, concerned with the design of integrated systems. (From the *Collins English Dictionary*, Harper Collins Publishers, 2000.)

✦ The selective application of scientific and engineering efforts to:

- Transform an operational need into a description of the system configuration which best satisfies the operational need according to the measures of effectiveness

- Integrate related technical parameters and ensure compatibility of all physical, functional, and technical program interfaces in a manner which optimizes the total system definition and design

- Integrate the efforts of all engineering disciplines and specialties into the total engineering effort

(This definition is from the "Systems Engineering Capability Model" [SE-CMM-95-0I] document, version 1.1, from the Carnegie Mellon Software Engineering Institute [SEI]. The definition in the SE-CMM was taken from the U.S. Army Field Manual, 770-78.)

✦ The interdisciplinary approach and means to enable the realization of successful systems. It focuses on defining customer needs and required functionality early in the development cycle, documenting requirements, then proceeding with design synthesis and system validation while considering the complete problem:

- Operations

- Performance

- Test

- Manufacturing

- Cost & Schedule

- Training & Support

- Disposal

Systems Engineering integrates all the disciplines and specialty groups into a team effort forming a structured development process that proceeds from concept to production to operation. Systems Engineering considers both the business and the technical needs of all customers with the goal of providing a quality product that meets the user needs. (This definition is from The International Council on Systems Engineering [INCOSE], www.incose.org.)

✦ An interdisciplinary approach to evolve and verify an integrated and life cycle balanced set of system product and process solutions that satisfy customer needs. Systems engineering: (a) encompasses the scientific and engineering efforts related to the development, manufacturing, verification, deployment, operations, support, and disposal of system products and processes, (b) develops needed user training equipments, procedures, and data, (c) establishes and maintains configuration management of the system, (d) develops work breakdown structures and statements of work, and (e) provides information for management decision making. (This definition is from MIL-STD-499B. This standard was never officially released, but a coordination copy was issued on May 6, 1992, and was to be the first military standard that addressed systems engineering as a whole. The May 1992 release, however, has been widely used, and it provided the basis for the IEEE 1220 and EIA/IS 632 system engineering standards. Newer standards that have since evolved are EIA 632 and ISO/IEC 15288.)

✦ A process that will:

- Transform approved operational needs and requirements into an integrated system design solution through concurrent consideration of all life cycle needs (that is, development, manufacturing, testing and evaluation, deployment, operations, support, training, and disposal).

- Ensure the interoperability and integration of all operational, functional, and physical interfaces. Ensure that system definition and design reflect the requirements for all system elements: hardware, software, facilities, people, and data.

- Characterize and manage technical risks.

- Apply scientific and engineering principles, using the system security engineering process, to identify security vulnerabilities and minimize or contain information assurance and force protection risks associated with these vulnerabilities.

(This definition of systems engineering is taken from DoD regulation 5000.2-R, April 5, 2002. The regulation establishes mandatory procedures for Major Defense Acquisition Programs [MDAPs] and Major Automated Information System [MAIS] acquisition programs).

The Systems Engineering Process

To begin this section, four systems engineering processes will be outlined to provide perspective on such processes. These processes are from MIL-STD-499B, DoD 5000.2-R, IEEE STD 1220-198, and IATF document 3.1.

MIL-STD-499B defines the following nine phases of the SE process:

✦ Mission requirements analysis

✦ Functional analysis

✦ Allocation

✦ Synthesis

✦ Logistic engineering, including

- logistics support analysis

- maintenance engineering analysis

- repair level analysis

- logistic support modeling

- ✦ Life cycle cost analysis
- ✦ Optimization, including
  - • trade-off studies
  - • system/cost effectiveness analysis
  - • effectiveness analysis modeling
- ✦ Production engineering analysis
- ✦ Generation of specifications

In DoD 5000.2-R, the systems engineering process comprises:

- ✦ Requirements Analysis
- ✦ Functional Analysis/Allocation
- ✦ Synthesis

This process is detailed in Figure 11-2.

IEEE STD 1220-1998 defines the following systems engineering process:

- ✦ Requirements Analysis
- ✦ Requirements Verification
- ✦ Functional Analysis
- ✦ Functional Verification
- ✦ Synthesis
- ✦ Design Verification

The IEEE STD 1220-1998 process is given in Figure 11-3.

The fourth systems engineering process is taken from Chapter 3 of the IATF document 3.1. This generic SE process *will be used as the basis for integration with the ISSE process in this chapter* and comprises the following components:

- ✦ Discover needs
- ✦ Define system requirements
- ✦ Design system architecture
- ✦ Develop detailed design
- ✦ Implement system
- ✦ Assess effectiveness

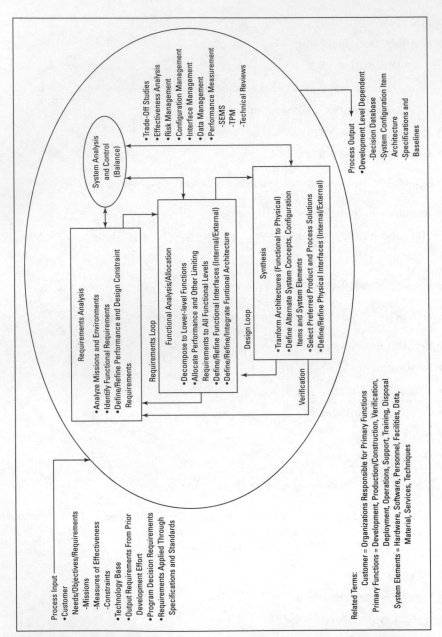

Figure 11-2: The DoD 5000.2-R systems engineering process (from IATF document, Release 3.1, September 2002).

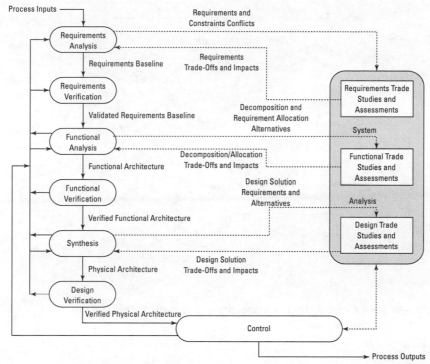

Figure 11-3: The IEEE STD 1220-1998 systems engineering process (from IATF document, Release 3.1, September 2002).

An important characteristic of this process is that it emphasizes the application of SE over the entire development life cycle. Figure 11-4 illustrates the IATF generic SE process; the arrows show the information flow among activities in the process. The notation of USERS/USERS' REPRESENTATIVES in Figure 11-4 is included to emphasize the interaction among the users and the systems engineer throughout the SE process.

A good systems or information systems security engineer will always keep the problem to be solved in perspective. Some rules of thumb are to remember that the purpose of a project is to meet the customer's needs in his or her environment, the problem and solution spaces should be kept separate, and the solution space must be determined by the problem space. This approach relates to the simple but elegant definitions of verification and validation stated by Barry Boehm. He offered that "verification is doing the job right and validation is doing the right job."

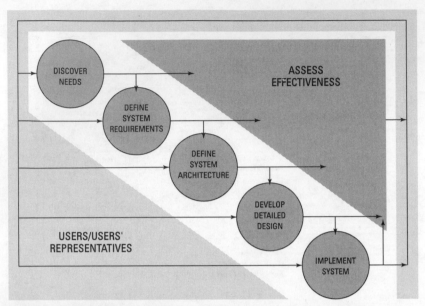

Figure 11-4: The generic systems engineering process (from IATF document, Release 3.1, September 2002).

The Information Systems Security Engineering Process

The ISSE process mirrors the generic SE process of IATF document 3.1. The ISSE process elements and the associated SE process elements, respectively, are:

✦ Discover Information Protection Needs — Discover Needs

✦ Define System Security Requirements — Define System Requirements

✦ Design System Security Architecture — Design System Architecture

✦ Develop Detailed Security Design — Develop Detailed Design

✦ Implement System Security — Implement System

✦ Assess Information Protection Effectiveness — Assess Effectiveness

Each of the six ISSE process activities will be explained in detail in the following sections.

Discover Information Protection Needs

The information systems security engineer can obtain a portion of the information required for this activity from the SE process. The objectives of this activity are to understand and document the customer's needs and to develop solutions that will meet these needs. This approach is illustrated in Figure 11-5.

Figure 11-5: Discover Information Protection Needs activity (from IATF document, Release 3.1, September 2002).

The information systems security engineer should use any reliable sources of information to learn about the customer's mission and business operations, including areas such as human resources, finance, command and control, engineering, logistics, and research and development. This knowledge can be used to generate a *concept of operations* (CONOPS) document or *a mission needs statement* (MNS). Then, with this information in hand, an *information management model* (IMM) should be developed that ultimately defines a number of *information domains*. Information management is defined as:

✦ Creating information

✦ Acquiring information

✦ Processing information

✦ Storing and retrieving information

✦ Transferring information

✦ Deleting information

Information domains identify the members of a particular domain; the applicable privileges, roles, rules, and responsibilities of the users in the domain; and a list of the information entities that are under control in the domain. The information management model should take into account:

✦ The information being processed

✦ Processes being used

✦ Information generators

✦ Information consumers

✦ User roles

✦ Information management policy requirements

✦ Regulations

✦ Agreements or contracts

The principle of *least privilege* should be used in developing the model by permitting users to access only the information required for them to accomplish their assigned tasks.

The IMM is illustrated in Figure 11-6.

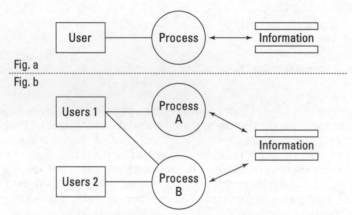

Figure 11-6: Graphic of the information management model (from IATF document, Release 3.1, Appendix H, September 2002).

A short example of an IMM is given in Table 11-1.

	Table 11-1 Information Management Model		
Users	*Rules*	*Process*	*Information*
President	Read/Write	Corporate Finance	Policy
Treasurer	Read/Write	Corporate Finance	Policy
Senior V.P.	Read	Corporate Finance	Policy

A similar example of the output domains of the IMM is given in Table 11-2.

Domain	Users	Rules	Process	Information
Table 11-2 **IMM Information Domain Example**				
Human Resources	Director	Read/Write	Corporate Finance	Financial Reports, Salaries
Human Resources	Benefits Staff	Read	Corporate Finance	Financial Reports, Salaries

After the IMM has been developed, the information systems security engineer can use the information in the model to determine the appropriate controls, regulations, directives, laws, and policies to use for each of the customer's domains. For example, the model might indicate that material must be classified at a certain level or that Certification and Accreditation (C&A) are required. Another advantage of identifying the information domains is the ability of the information systems security engineer to evaluate the types of potential threats to a domain and the impact of a threat realized upon a domain. As part of the Discover Information Protection Needs activity, metrics are assigned to threats, or *potentially harmful events* (PHE), and to the level of *harm to informa*tion (HTI) for each domain. The information system security principles of confidentiality, integrity, and availability (C.I.A.) are applied to estimate the HTI. This process is illustrated in Figure 11-7.

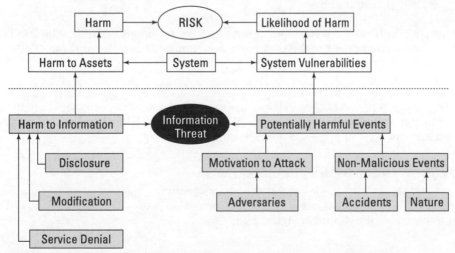

Figure 11-7: The PHE and HTI process (from IATF document, Release 3.1, Appendix H, September 2002).

For example, the metrics could be numbers ranging from 0 to 3 for the PHE and HTI, and they could be displayed as shown in Figure 11-8.

		PHE			
	Measures	None	Low	Medium	High
HTI	Serious	0	2	3	3
	Significant	0	1	2	3
	Mild	0	1	1	2
	None	0	0	0	0

Figure 11-8: A PHE-HTI combination matrix (from IATF document, Release 3.1, Appendix H, September 2002).

In the Discover Information Protection Needs activity of the ISSE process, the information systems security engineer must document all elements of the activity. These elements include:

✦ Roles

✦ Responsibilities

✦ Threats

✦ Strengths

✦ Security services

✦ Priorities

✦ Design constraints

These items form the basis of an *Information Protection Policy* (IPP), which in turn becomes a component of the *customer's Information Management Policy* (IMP), as shown in Figure 11.5.

The information systems security engineer must also support the certification and accreditation (C&A) of the system. For example, the security engineer can identify the Designated Approving Authority (DAA) and the Certification Authority (CA). A detailed discussion of C&A is given in Chapter 12.

Define System Security Requirements

In this ISSE activity, the information systems security engineer identifies one or more solution sets that can satisfy the information protection needs of the IPP. This subprocess is illustrated in Figure 11-9.

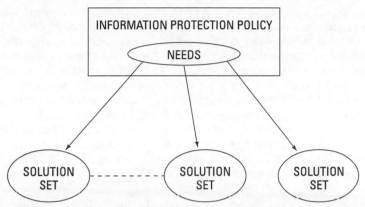

Figure 11-9: Mapping of solution sets to information protection needs.

In selecting a solution set, the information systems security engineer must also consider the needs of external systems such as Public Key Infrastructure (PKI) or other cryptographic-related systems, as shown in Figure 11-10.

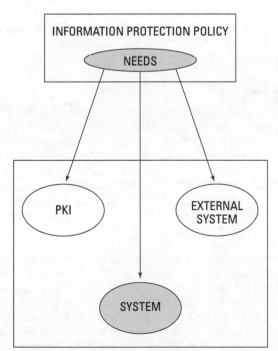

Figure 11-10: Mapping of needs to solution set components.

A solution set consists of a *preliminary security CONOPS*, the *system context*, and the *system requirements*. In close cooperation with the customer and based on the IPP, the information systems security engineer selects the best solution among the solution sets. The information protection functions and the information management functions are delineated in the preliminary security CONOPS, and the dependencies among the organization's mission and the services provided by other entities are identified. In developing the system context, the information systems security engineer uses systems engineering techniques to identify the boundaries of the system to be protected and allocates security functions to this system as well as to external systems. The information systems security engineer accomplishes this allocation by analyzing the flow of data among the system to be protected and the external systems and by using the information compiled in the IPP and IMM.

The third component of the solution set — the system security requirements — is generated by the information systems security engineer in collaboration with the systems engineers. Requirements should be unambiguous, comprehensive, and concise, and they should be obtained through the process of requirements analysis. The functional requirements and constraints on the design of the information security components include regulations, the operating environment, targeting internal as well as external threats, and customer needs.

At the end of this process, the information systems security engineer reviews the security CONOPS, the security context, and the system security requirements with the customer to ensure that they meet the needs of the customer and are accepted by the customer. As with all activities in the ISSE process, documentation is very important and should be generated in accordance with the C&A requirements.

Design System Security Architecture

The requirements generated in the Define System Security Requirements activity of the ISSE process are necessarily stated in functional terms, indicating what is needed, but not how to accomplish what is needed. In Design System Security Architecture, the information systems security engineer performs a *functional decomposition* of the requirements that can be used to select the components required to implement the designated functions. Some aids that are used to implement the functional decomposition are timeline analyses, flow block diagrams, and a requirements allocation sheet. The result of the functional decomposition is the *functional architecture* of the information security systems, shown schematically in Figure 11-11.

In the decomposition process, the performance requirements at the higher level are mapped onto the lower level functions to ensure that the resulting system performs as required. Also as part of this activity, the information systems security engineer determines, at a functional level, the security services that should be assigned to the system to be protected as well as to external systems. Such services include encryption, key management, and digital signatures. Because implementations are not specified in this activity, a complete risk analysis is not possible. General risk analysis, however, can be done by estimating the vulnerabilities in the classes of components that are likely to be used.

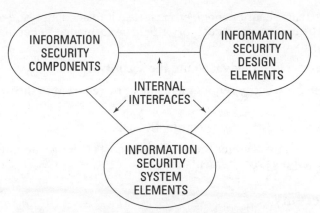

Figure 11-11: Design system security architecture.

As always, documentation in accordance with requirements of the C&A process should be performed.

Develop Detailed Security Design

The information protection design is achieved through continuous assessments of risks and the comparison of these risks with the information system security requirements by the ISSE personnel. The design activity is iterative, and it involves both the SE and ISSE professionals. The design documentation should meet the requirements of the C&A process. It should be noted that this activity specifies the system and components but does not specify products or vendors.

The tasks performed by the information systems security engineer include:

✦ Mapping security mechanisms to system security design elements

✦ Cataloging candidate commercial off-the-shelf (COTS) products

✦ Cataloging candidate government off-the-shelf (GOTS) products

✦ Cataloging custom security products

✦ Qualifying external and internal element and system interfaces

✦ Developing specifications such as Common Criteria protection profiles

Some characteristics of this effort are:

✦ The design documents should be under configuration control.

✦ The design must meet the customer's design constraints.

✦ The components in the design must address both technical and nontechnical information security mechanisms.

✦ The interdependency and interaction among security mechanisms must be included in the risk analysis process.

✦ The information systems security engineer must take into account trade-offs that might have to be made among cost, priorities, performance, schedule, and remaining security risks.

✦ The security requirements should map onto the security design.

✦ Any failures to meet the security requirements must be reported to the C&A authorities.

✦ The design should produce a revised security CONOPS.

✦ The design should take into account the effects and costs of long-lead-time items and life cycle support requirements.

Implement System Security

This activity moves the system from the design phase to the operational phase. The steps in this process are shown in Figure 11-12.

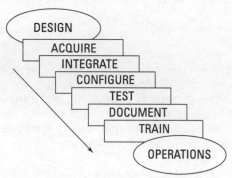

Figure 11-12: The path from design to operations in the Implement System Security activity.

The Implement System Security activity concludes with a system effectiveness assessment that produces evidence that the system meets the requirements and needs of the mission. Security accreditation usually follows this assessment.

The assessment is accomplished through the following actions of the information systems security engineer:

✦ Verifying that the implemented system does address and protect against the threats itemized in the original threat assessment

✦ Providing inputs to the C&A process

✦ Application of information protection assurance mechanisms related to system implementation and testing

✦ Providing inputs to and reviewing the evolving system life cycle support plans

✦ Providing inputs to and reviewing the operational procedures

✦ Providing inputs to and reviewing the maintenance training materials

✦ Taking part in multidisciplinary examinations of all system issues and concerns

An important part of the Implement System Security activity is the determination of the specific components of the information system security solution. Some of the factors that have to be considered in selecting the components include:

✦ Availability now and in the future

✦ Cost

✦ Form factor

✦ Reliability

✦ Risk to system caused by substandard performance

✦ Conformance to design specifications

✦ Compatibility with existing components

✦ Meeting or exceeding evaluation criteria (Typical evaluation criteria include the Commercial COMSEC Evaluation Program [CCEP], National Information Assurance Partnership [NIAP], Federal Information Processing Standards [FIPS], NSA criteria, and NIST criteria.)

In some cases, components might have to be built and customized to meet the requirements if no suitable components are available for purchase or lease. The information systems security engineer is responsible for configuring the security components to provide the specified security controls and services.

Additional tasks related to the Implement System Security activity conducted by the systems and design engineers in cooperation with the information systems security engineer include:

✦ Conducting unit testing of components

✦ Developing test procedures to ensure that the designed system performs as required; these procedures should incorporate:

  • Test planning, to include facilities, schedule, personnel, tools, and required resources

  • Integration testing

  • Functional testing to ensure that systems and subsystems operate properly

  • Generation of test reports

  • Tests of all interfaces, as feasible

✦ Developing documentation and placing documentation under version control; the documentation should include:

- Installation procedures
- Operational procedures
- Support procedures
- Maintenance procedures
- Defects discovered in the procedures

✦ Using documentation for training of administrators and users

The information systems security engineer will perform the following information security–related tasks as part of the ISSE process:

✦ Developing test plans and procedures, to include:

- Tools
- Hardware
- Test cases
- Required software

✦ Taking part in the testing of information protection mechanisms and operations

✦ Coordinating the application of information protection assurance mechanisms with their counterparts in the systems implementation and testing effort

✦ Continuation of the risk management effort

✦ Contributing to life cycle security planning, including:

- Training
- Logistics
- Maintenance

✦ Monitoring of the systems security-related issues associated with the integration, configuration, documentation, and interfacing tasks

✦ Providing results of tests to the design engineers in the event that design modifications are required

✦ Providing support to the C&A process, including ensuring that the necessary documentation required for C&A is provided

✦ Ensuring that the security design is properly implemented

✦ Ensuring that proper and adequate material is available for the conduct of training

Assess Information Protection Effectiveness

In order to assess the effectiveness of the information protection mechanisms and services effectively, this activity must be conducted as part of all the activities of the complete ISSE and SE process. Table 11-3, with information taken from the IATF document, Release 3.1, September 2002, lists the tasks of the Assess Information Protection activity that correspond to the other activities of the ISSE process.

Table 11-3 — Assess Information Protection Effectiveness Tasks and Corresponding ISSE Activities	
ISSE Activity Effectiveness Tasks	**Assess Information Protection**
Discover Information Protection Needs	Present the process overview
	Summarize the information model
	Describe threats to the mission or business through information attacks
	Establish security services to counter those threats and identify their relative importance to the customer
	Obtain customer agreement on the conclusions of this activity as a basis for determining the system security effectiveness
Define System Security Requirements	Ensure that the selected solution set meets the mission or business security needs
	Coordinate the system boundaries
	Present security context, security CONOPS, and system security requirements to the customer and gain customer concurrence
	Ensure that the projected security risks are acceptable to the customer
Design System Security Architecture	Begin the formal risk analysis process to ensure that the selected security mechanisms provide the required security services and explain to the customer how the security architecture meets the security requirements
Develop Detailed Security Design	Review how well the selected security services and mechanisms counter the threats by performing an interdependency analysis to compare desired to effective security service strengths
	Once completed, the risk assessment results, particularly any mitigation needs and residual risk, will be documented and shared with the customer to obtain their concurrence
Implement System Security	The risk analysis will be conducted/updated
	Strategies will be developed for the mitigation of identified risks
	Identify possible mission impacts and advise the customer and the customer's Certifiers and Accreditors

Summary Showing the Correspondence of the SE and ISSE Activities

As discussed in the descriptions of the SE and ISSE processes, there is a one-to-correspondence of activities in the ISSE process to those in the SE process. Table 11-4, taken from IATF document, Release 3.1, September 2002, summarizes those activities in the ISSE process that correspond to activities in the SE process.

Table 11-4 Corresponding SE and ISSE Activities	
SE Activities	*ISSE Activities*
Discover Needs	**Discover Information Protection Needs**
The systems engineer helps the customer understand and document the information management needs that support the business or mission. Statements about information needs may be captured in an information management model (IMM).	The information systems security engineer helps the customer understand the information protection needs that support the mission or business. Statements about information protection needs may be captured in an Information Protection Policy (IPP).
Define System Requirements	**Define System Security Requirements**
The systems engineer allocates identified needs to systems. A system context is developed to identify the system environment and to show the allocation of system functions to that environment. A preliminary system concept of operations (CONOPS) is written to describe operational aspects of the candidate system (or systems). Baseline requirements are established.	The information systems security engineer allocates information protection needs to systems. A system security context, a preliminary system security CONOPS, and baseline security requirements are developed.
Design System Architecture	**Design System Security Architecture**
The systems engineer performs functional analysis and allocation by analyzing ` candidate architectures, allocating requirements, and selecting mechanisms. The systems engineer identifies components, or elements, allocates functions to those elements, and describes the relationships between the elements.	The information systems security engineer works with the systems engineer in the areas of functional analysis and allocation by analyzing candidate architectures, allocating security services, and selecting security mechanisms. The information systems security engineer identifies components, or elements, allocates security functions to those elements, and describes the relationships between the elements.

SE Activities	ISSE Activities
Develop Detailed Design	**Develop Detailed Security Design**
The systems engineer analyzes design constraints, analyzes trade-offs, does detailed system design, and considers life cycle support. The systems engineer traces all of the system requirements to the elements until all are addressed. The final detailed design results in component and interface specifications that provide sufficient information for acquisition when the system is implemented.	The information systems security engineer analyzes design constraints, analyzes trade-offs, does detailed system and security design, and considers life cycle support. The information systems security engineer traces all of the system security requirements to the elements until all are addressed. The final detailed security design results in component and interface specifications that provide sufficient information for acquisition when the system is implemented.
Implement System	**Implement System Security**
The systems engineer moves the system from specifications to the tangible. The main activities are acquisition, integration, configuration, testing, documentation, and training. Components are tested and evaluated to ensure that they meet the specifications. After successful testing, the individual components—hardware, software, and firmware—are integrated, properly configured, and tested as a system.	The information systems security engineer participates in a multidisciplinary examination of all system issues and provides inputs to C&A process activities, such as verification that the system as implemented protects against the threats identified in the original threat assessment; tracking of information protection assurance mechanisms related to system implementation and testing practices; and providing inputs to system life cycle support plans, operational procedures, and maintenance training materials.
Assess Effectiveness	**Assess Information Protection Effectiveness**
The results of each activity are evaluated to ensure that the system will meet the users' needs by performing the required functions to the required quality standard in the intended environment. The systems engineer examines how well the system meets the needs of the mission.	The information systems security engineer focuses on the effectiveness of the information protection—whether the system can provide the confidentiality, integrity, availability, authentication and nonrepudiation for the information it is processing that is required for mission success.

ISSE and Its Relationship to C&A Processes

The ISSE process provides input to the C&A process in the form of evidence and documentation. Thus, the information systems security engineer has to consider the requirements of the DAA. The Defense Information Technology Security Certification and Accreditation Process (DITSCAP) certifies that the information system meets the defined system security requirements and the system assurance requirements. It is not a design process. Details of DITSCAP are presented in Chapter 12 of this text. The SE/ISSE process also benefits by receiving information back from the C&A process that might result in modifications to the SE/ISSE process activities. Figure 11-13 illustrates the relationship of the SE/ISSE process to the C&A process.

In summary, the outputs of the SE/ISSE process are the implementation of the system and the corresponding system documentation. The outputs of the C&A process are Certification documentation, Certification recommendations, and an Accreditation decision.

Another means of specifying information system assurance requirements are through Common Criteria protection profiles. Protection profiles, which are independent of implementation, comprise:

✦ Security-related functional requirements

✦ Security objectives

✦ Information assurance requirements

✦ Assumptions

✦ Rationale

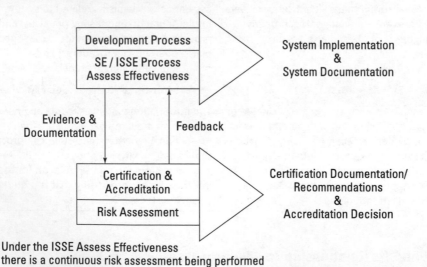

Under the ISSE Assess Effectiveness
there is a continuous risk assessment being performed

Figure 11-13: Relationship of the SE/ISSE process to the C&A process (from IATF document, Release 3.1, September 2002).

Many protection profiles are available on the IATF Web site at www.iatf.net/ protection_profiles/. Protection profiles that are provided include:

✦ Firewalls

✦ Switches and routers

✦ Mobile code

✦ Biometrics

✦ Certificate management

Principles of Defense in Depth

The strategy of Defense in Depth is aimed at protecting U.S. federal and defense information systems and networks from the various types and classes of attacks. The technology focus areas of the Defense in Depth strategy are:

✦ Defending the network and infrastructure

✦ Defending the enclave boundary

✦ Defending the computing environment

✦ Defending the supporting infrastructures

The second item in this list refers to an *enclave*. In DoD Directive 8500.1, "Information Assurance (IA)," October 24, 2002, an enclave is defined as a "collection of computing environments connected by one or more internal networks under the control of a single authority and security policy, including personnel and physical security. Enclaves always assume the highest mission assurance category and security classification of the Automated Information System (AIS) applications or outsourced IT-based processes they support, and derive their security needs from those systems. They provide standard IA capabilities such as boundary defense, incident detection and response, and key management, and also deliver common applications such as office automation and electronic mail. Enclaves are analogous to general support systems as defined in OMB A-130. Enclaves may be specific to an organization or a mission, and the computing environments may be organized by physical proximity or by function independent of location. Examples of enclaves include local area networks and the applications they host, backbone networks, and data processing centers."

The Defense in Depth strategy promotes application of the following information assurance principles:

✦ *Defense in multiple places* — deployment of information protection mechanisms at multiple locations to protect against internal and external threats.

✦ *Layered defenses* — deployment of multiple information protection and detection mechanisms so that an adversary or threat will have to negotiate multiple barriers to gain access to critical information.

✦ *Security robustness* — based on the value of the information system component to be protected and the anticipated threats, estimation of the robustness of each information assurance components. Robustness is measured in terms of assurance and strength of the information assurance component.

✦ *Deploy KMI/PKI* — deployment of robust key management infrastructures (KMI) and public key infrastructures.

✦ *Deploy intrusion detection systems* — deployment of intrusion detection mechanisms to detect intrusions, evaluate information, examine results, and, if necessary, to take action.

Types and Classes of Attack

IATF document 3.1 lists the following types of attacks:

✦ Passive

✦ Active

✦ Close-in

✦ Insider

✦ Distribution

These attacks and their characteristics, taken from IATF document 3.1, September 2002, are given in Table 11-5.

Table 11-5
Classes of Attack

Attack	Description
Passive	Passive attacks include traffic analysis, monitoring of unprotected communications, decrypting weakly encrypted traffic, and capture of authentication information (such as passwords). Passive intercept of network operations can give adversaries indications and warnings of impending actions. Passive attacks can result in disclosure of information or data files to an attacker without the consent or knowledge of the user. Examples include the disclosure of personal information such as credit card numbers and medical files.
Active	Active attacks include attempts to circumvent or break protection features, introduce malicious code, or steal or modify information. These attacks may be mounted against a network backbone, exploit information in transit, electronically penetrate an enclave, or attack an authorized remote user during an attempt to connect to an enclave. Active attacks can result in the disclosure or dissemination of data files, denial of service, or modification of data.

Attack	Description
Close-In	Close-in attack consists of individuals attaining close physical proximity to networks, systems, or facilities for the purpose of modifying, gathering, or denying access to information. Close physical proximity is achieved through surreptitious entry, open access, or both.
Insider	Insider attacks can be malicious or nonmalicious. Malicious insiders intentionally eavesdrop, steal, or damage information; use information in a fraudulent manner; or deny access to other authorized users. Nonmalicious attacks typically result from carelessness, lack of knowledge, or intentional circumvention of security for such reasons as "getting the job done."
Distribution	Distribution attacks focus on the malicious modification of hardware or software at the factory or during distribution. These attacks can introduce malicious code into a product, such as a back door to gain unauthorized access to information or a system function at a later date.

The enclaves in the U.S. federal and defense computing environments can be categorized as:

✦ Classified

✦ Private

✦ Public

The attacks categorized in Table 11-5 are the types that can be perpetrated on the computing environment enclaves. The relationships of the classes of attacks to computing environment enclaves are depicted in Figure 11-14.

The Defense in Depth Strategy

The Defense in Depth strategy is built upon three critical elements: *people*, *technology*, and *operations*.

People

To implement effective information assurance in an organization, there must be a high-level commitment from management to the process. This commitment is manifested through the following items and activities:

✦ Development of information assurance policies and procedures

✦ Assignment of roles and responsibilities

✦ Training of critical personnel

✦ Enforcement of personal accountability

✦ Commitment of resources

✦ Establishment of physical security controls

✦ Establishment of personnel security controls

✦ Penalties associated with unauthorized behavior

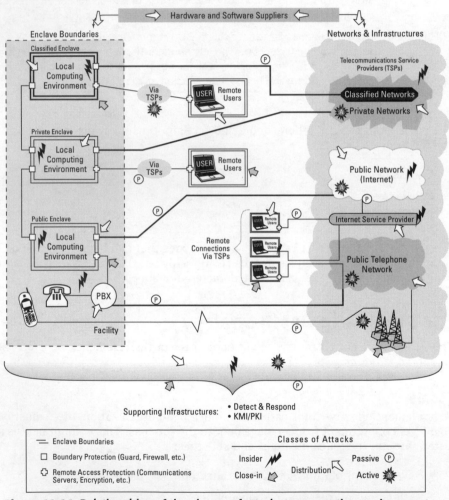

Figure 11-14: Relationships of the classes of attacks to computing environment enclaves (from IATF document, Release 3.1, September 2002).

Technology

An organization has to ensure that the proper technologies are acquired and deployed to implement the required information protection services. These objectives are accomplished through processes and policies for the acquisition of technology. The processes and policies should include the following items:

✦ A security policy

✦ System level information assurance architectures

✦ System level information assurance standards

✦ Information assurance principles

✦ Specification criteria for the required information assurance products

✦ Acquisition of reliable, third-party, validated products

✦ Configuration recommendations

✦ Risk assessment processes for the integrated systems

Operations

Operations emphasize the activities and items that are necessary to maintain an organization's effective security posture on a day-to-day basis. These activities and items include:

✦ A visible and up-to-date security policy

✦ Enforcement of the information security policy

✦ Certification and accreditation

✦ Information security posture management

✦ Key management services

✦ Readiness assessments

✦ Protection of the infrastructure

✦ Performing systems security assessments

✦ Monitoring and reacting to threats

✦ Attack sensing, warning, and response (ASW&R)

✦ Recovery and reconstitution

The Defense in Depth approach has become widely accepted and has been incorporated into a number of federal and DoD policies and guidelines. One example is the DoD *Global Information Grid (GIG) Information Assurance Policy and Implementation Guidance* (www.c3i.osd.mil/org/cio/doc/gigia061600.pdf). Figure 11-15 illustrates the embodiment of the Defense in Depth strategy as shown in the GIG *Policy and Implementation Guidance*.

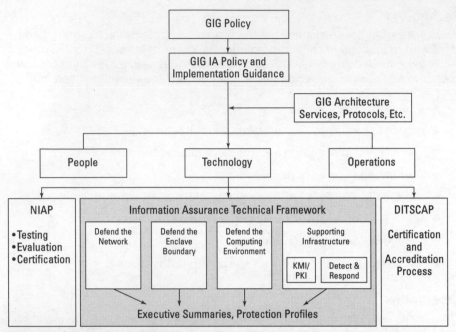

Figure 11-15: Defense in Depth as applied in the GIG *Information Assurance Policy and Implementation Guidance* (from IATF document, Release 3.1, September 2002).

The Approach to Implementing the Defense in Depth Strategy

From the previous discussion of the Defense in Depth strategy, it is clear that large investments of time and resources are required for an effective strategy implementation. In order to maximize the productivity of the resources available and minimize the various costs associated with the implementation of the Defense in Depth strategy, the following guidelines are offered by the IATF document 3.1, Chapter 2:

✦ Make information assurance decisions based on risk analysis and keyed to the organization's operational objectives.

✦ Use a composite approach, based on balancing protection capability against cost, performance, operational impact, and changes to the operation itself considering both today's and tomorrow's operations and environments.

✦ Draw from all three facets of Defense in Depth — people, operations, and technology. Technical mitigations are of no value without trained people to use them and operational procedures to guide their application.

✦ Establish a comprehensive program of education, training, practical experience, and awareness. Professionalization and certification licensing provide a validated and recognized expert cadre of system administrators.

✦ Exploit available commercial off-the-shelf (COTS) products and rely on in-house development for those items not otherwise available.

✦ Plan and follow a continuous migration approach to take advantage of evolving information processing and network capabilities, both functional and security related, and ensure adaptability to changing organizational needs and operating environments.

✦ Periodically assess the IA posture of the information infrastructure. Technology tools, such as automated scanners for networks, can assist in vulnerability assessments.

✦ Take into account not only the actions of those with hostile intent, but also inadvertent or unwitting actions that may have ill effects and natural events that may affect the system.

✦ Adhere to the principles of commonality, standardization, and procedures, to interoperability, and to policies.

✦ Judiciously use emerging technologies, balancing enhanced capability with increased risk.

✦ Employ multiple means of threat mitigation, overlapping protection approaches to counter anticipated events so that loss or failure of a single barrier does not compromise the overall information infrastructure.

✦ Implement and hold to a robust IA posture, that is, one that can cope with the unexpected.

✦ Ensure that only trustworthy personnel have physical access to the system. Methods of providing such assurance include appropriate background investigations, security clearances, credentials, and badges.

✦ Monitor vulnerability listings and implementation of fixes, ensuring that security mechanisms are interoperable, keeping constant watch over the security situation and mechanisms, properly employing and upgrading tools and techniques, and dealing rapidly and effectively with issues.

✦ Use established procedures to report incident information provided by intrusion detection mechanisms to authorities and specialized analysis and response centers.

Sample U.S. Government User Environments

The target systems of a Defense in Depth strategy can be put in perspective by examining two U.S. government computing environments — the Department of Energy (DoE) and Department of Defense information systems.

The DoE interconnects its laboratories and other facilities through wide area networks (WANs), including the Energy Science Network (ESN). ESN supports classified and unclassified DoE networking for research and mission-critical applications. The DoE computing environment is shown in Figure 11-16.

The DoD Defense Information Infrastructure (DII) provides networking and information services to more than 2 million primary users and 2 million extension users. The DII enclaves typically comprise more than 20,000 local networks and 300,000 secure telephone users. The DII also includes worldwide networks such as the Joint Worldwide Intelligence Communications System (JWICS), the Secret Internet Protocol Router Network (SIPRNet), and the Non-Secure Internet Protocol Router Network (NIPRNet). An example DII site is shown in Figure 11-17.

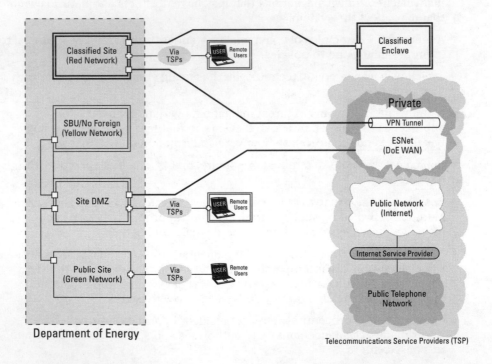

☐ Boundary Protection (Guard, Firewall, etc.) ⬦ Remote Access Protection (Communications Server, Encryptor, etc.)
TSP - Telecommunications Service Provider

Figure 11-16: The DoE computing environment (from IATF document, Release 3.1, September 2002).

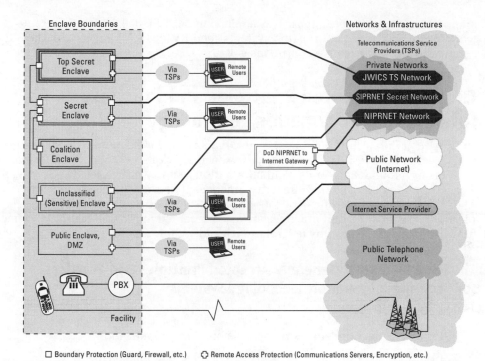

Figure 11-17: A typical DII site (from IATF document, Release 3.1, September 2002).

Implementing Information Assurance in the System Life Cycle

The documents providing the basis for material in this section are *Generally Accepted Principles and Practices for Securing Information Technology Systems,* SP 800-14, National Institute of Standards and Technology, September 1996; *Engineering Principles for Information Technology Security (A Baseline for Achieving Security),* SP 800-27, National Institute of Standards and Technology, June 2001; and *Security Considerations in the Information System Development Life Cycle,* SP 800-64, National Institute of Standards and Technology, September–October 2003. In some publications, the System Life Cycle is also referred to as the System Development Life Cycle (SDLC).

Document SP 800-14 defines eight system security principles and 14 practices. Publication 800-27 develops another set of 33 engineering principles for information technology security (EP-ITS) that provide a system-level perspective of information system security. These 33 principles incorporate the concepts developed in the eight principles and 14 practices detailed in SP 800-14. With this foundation, the five system life cycle phases are then defined and each of the 33 EP-ITS principles are mapped onto the life cycle phases, as applicable. NIST SP 800-64 details a framework for incorporating information systems security into all the phases of the SDLC activity, using cost-effective control measures.

Generally Accepted Principles and Practices for Securing Information Technology

NIST Special Publication 800-14 used the Organization for Economic Cooperation and Development (OECD) guidelines (www.oecd.org) for the security of information systems as a foundation for its eight information security principles. In addition, SP 800-14 provides 14 common IT security practices that are in general use today. These practices are specific applications of the eight information security principles. These principles and practices are also presented in NIST SP 800-14 in a checklist form that can be used by federal agencies for self-evaluation.

The NIST SP 800-14 Generally Accepted Principles and Practices for Securing Information Technology Systems

The eight principles are:

1. Computer security supports the mission of the organization.

2. Computer security is an integral element of sound management.

3. Computer security should be cost-effective.

4. Systems owners have security responsibilities outside their own organizations.

5. Computer security responsibilities and accountability should be made explicit.

6. Computer security requires a comprehensive and integrated approach.

7. Computer security should be periodically reassessed.

8. Computer security is constrained by societal factors.

Common IT Security Practices

The 14 security practices listed in SP 800-14 are:

1. *Policy* — Have in place the following three types of policies:

   • A *Program policy* to create and define a computer security program

   • An *Issue Specific policy* to address specific areas and issues

   • A *System Specific policy* to focus on decisions made by management

   These policies are sometimes referred to as plans, procedures, or directives.

2. *Program Management*—Management of computer security at appropriate multiple levels with centralized enforcement and oversight.

3. *Risk Management*—The process of assessing risk, taking steps to reduce risk to an acceptable level, and maintaining that level of risk.

4. *Life Cycle Planning*—Managing security by planning throughout the system life cycle. A security plan should be developed prior to initiation of the life cycle activities so that it can be followed during the life cycle process. The IT system life cycle as defined in SP 800-14 is comprised of the following five phases:

   • Initiation

   • Development/Acquisition

   • Implementation

   • Operation/Maintenance

   • Disposal

These five phases will be discussed later in this chapter.

5. *Personnel/User Issues*—These issues relate to managers, users, and implementers and their authorizations and access to IT computing resources.

6. *Preparing for Contingencies and Disasters*—Planning to ensure that the organization can continue operations in the event of disasters and disruptions.

7. *Computer Security Incident Handling*—Reacting quickly and effectively in response to malicious code and internal or external unauthorized intrusions.

8. *Awareness and Training*—Providing computer security awareness training to all personnel interacting with the IT systems.

9. *Security Considerations in Computer Support and Operations*—Applying information system security principles to the tasks performed by system administrators and to external system support activities.

10. *Physical and Environmental Security*—Implementing environmental and physical security controls.

11. *Identification and Authentication*—Implementing the access control measures of identification and authentication to ensure that unauthorized personnel do not have privileges to access the resources of an IT system.

12. *Logical Access Control*—Technical means of enforcing the information system security policy to limit access to IT resources to authorized personnel.

13. *Audit Trails* — Recording system activity and providing the capability to accomplish individual accountability, detection of intrusions, reconstruction of past events, and identification of problems.

14. *Cryptography* — Providing security services, including protecting the confidentiality and integrity of information and implementing electronic signatures.

NIST 800-27 Engineering Principles for Information Technology Security

The EP-ITS system-level information security principles are:

1. Establish a sound security policy as the "foundation" for design.

2. Treat security as an integral part of the overall system design.

3. Clearly delineate the physical and logical security boundaries governed by associated security policies.

4. Reduce risk to an acceptable level.

5. Assume that external systems are insecure.

6. Identify potential trade-offs between reducing risk and increased costs and decrease in other aspects of operational effectiveness.

7. Implement layered security (ensure no single point of vulnerability).

8. Implement tailored system security measures to meet organizational security goals.

9. Strive for simplicity.

10. Design and operate an IT system to limit vulnerability and to be resilient in response.

11. Minimize the system elements to be trusted.

12. Implement security through a combination of measures distributed physically and logically.

13. Provide assurance that the system is, and continues to be, resilient in the face of unexpected threats.

14. Limit or contain vulnerabilities.

15. Formulate security measures to address multiple overlapping information domains.

16. Isolate public access systems from mission-critical resources (for example, data, processes).

17. Use boundary mechanisms to separate computing systems and network infrastructures.

18. Where possible, base security on open standards for portability and interoperability.

19. Use common language in developing security requirements.

20. Design and implement audit mechanisms to detect unauthorized use and to support incident investigations.

21. Design security to allow for regular adoption of new technology, including a secure and logical technology upgrade process.

22. Authenticate users and processes to ensure appropriate access control decisions both within and across domains.

23. Use unique identities to ensure accountability.

24. Implement least privilege.

25. Do not implement unnecessary security mechanisms.

26. Protect information while it is being processed, in transit, and in storage.

27. Strive for operational ease of use.

28. Develop and exercise contingency or disaster recovery procedures to ensure appropriate availability.

29. Consider custom products to achieve adequate security.

30. Ensure proper security in the shutdown or disposal of a system.

31. Protect against all likely classes of attacks.

32. Identify and prevent common errors and vulnerabilities.

33. Ensure that developers are trained in how to develop secure software.

The System Life Cycle Phases

NIST SP 800-14 defines the system life cycle phases as follows:

✦ *Initiation* — The need for the system and its purpose are documented. A sensitivity assessment is conducted as part of this phase. A sensitivity assessment evaluates the sensitivity of the IT system and the information to be processed.

✦ *Development/Acquisition* — Comprises the system acquisition and development cycles. In this phase, the system is designed, developed, programmed, and acquired.

✦ *Implementation* — Installation, testing, security testing, and accreditation are conducted.

✦ *Operation/Maintenance* — The system performs its designed functions. This phase includes security operations, modification/addition of hardware and/or software, administration, operational assurance, monitoring, and audits.

✦ *Disposal* — Disposition of system components and products, such as hardware, software, and information; disk sanitization; archiving files; and moving equipment.

Application of EP-ITS Principles to the Phases of the System Life Cycle

The EP-ITS principles can be applied during each phase of the system life cycle. Some principles are critical to certain phases, whereas others can be considered optional or not necessary. Table 11-6, taken from NIST SP 800-27, indicates which principles should be used for a specified life cycle phase. In Table 11-6, a single check, ✔, indicates that the principle can be applied to a particular life cycle phase, and two checks, ✔✔, indicate that the principle *must* be applied to successfully complete the life cycle phase.

Table 11-6
Application of EP-ITS Principles to System Life Cycle Phases

	Life Cycle Applicability				
Principle	Initiation	Deve/Acquis	Implement	Oper/Maint	Disposal
1	✔✔	✔	✔	✔	✔
2	✔✔	✔✔	✔✔	✔✔	✔
3	✔✔	✔✔	✔	✔	
4	✔✔	✔✔	✔✔	✔✔	✔✔
5	✔✔	✔✔	✔✔	✔✔	✔
6	✔✔	✔✔		✔✔	
7	✔	✔✔	✔	✔✔	✔
8	✔	✔✔	✔	✔✔	✔
9	✔	✔✔	✔	✔✔	
10	✔	✔✔		✔✔	
11	✔	✔✔	✔	✔✔	
12		✔✔	✔	✔	✔

Principle	Initiation	Deve/Acquis	Implement	Oper/Maint	Disposal
13	✔	✔✔	✔	✔✔	✔
14		✔✔	✔	✔	
15	✔	✔✔	✔	✔	
16	✔	✔✔	✔	✔	
17		✔✔	✔	✔✔	
18	✔	✔✔	✔		
19	✔✔	✔✔		✔✔	
20	✔	✔✔	✔✔	✔	
21		✔✔	✔	✔✔	
22	✔	✔	✔	✔✔	
23	✔	✔	✔	✔✔	
24	✔	✔	✔	✔✔	
25	✔	✔✔	✔✔	✔	✔
26	✔	✔✔	✔	✔✔	✔
27	✔	✔✔	✔	✔✔	
28	✔	✔	✔	✔✔	
29	✔	✔✔	✔	✔	
30		✔		✔	✔✔
31	✔	✔✔	✔✔	✔	✔
32		✔✔	✔✔		
33	✔✔	✔✔	✔		

NIST SP 800-64 Security Considerations in the Information System Development Cycle

Publication 800-64 complements NIST Special Publications 800-14 and 800-27 and expands on the SDLC concepts presented in these two publications. Table 11-7, taken from SP 800-64, illustrates information systems security as applied in the SDLC.

Table 11-7
Information Systems Security in the SDLC

	Initiation	Acquisition/ Development	Implementation	Operations/ Maintenance	Disposition
SDLC	Needs Determination: * Perception of a Need * Linkage of Need to Mission and Performance Objectives * Assessment of Alternatives to Capital Assets * Preparing for investment review and budgeting	Functional Statement of Need Market Research Feasibility Study Requirements Analysis Alternatives Analysis Cost-Benefit Analysis Software Conversion Study Cost Analysis Risk Management Plan Acquisition Planning	Installation Inspection Acceptance Testing Initial User Training Documentation	Performance Measurement Contract Modifications Operations Maintenance	Appropriateness of Disposal Exchange and Sale Internal Organization Screening Transfer and Donation Contract Closeout Secutiry Considerations
	Security Categorization Preliminary Risk Assessment	Risk Assessment Security Functional Requirements Analysis Security Assurance Requirements Analysis Cost Considerations and Reporting Security Planning Security Control Development Developmental Security Test and Evaluation Other Planning Components	Inspection and Acceptance Security Control Integration Security Certification Security Accreditation	Configuration Management and Control Continuous Monitoring	Information Preservation Media Sanitization Hardware and Software Disposal

A detailed description of these steps is provided in NIST SP 800-64 as follows:

> An organization will either use the general SDLC described in this document or will have developed a tailored SDLC that meets its specific needs. In either case, NIST recommends that organizations incorporate the associated IT security steps of this general SDLC into their development process:

✦ **Initiation Phase**:

- *Security Categorization* — defines three levels (low, moderate, or high) of potential impact on organizations or individuals should there be a breach of security (a loss of confidentiality, integrity, or availability). Security categorization standards assist organizations in making the appropriate selection of security controls for their information systems.

- *Preliminary Risk Assessment* — results in an initial description of the basic security needs of the system. A preliminary risk assessment should define the threat environment in which the system will operate.

✦ **Acquisition/Development Phase**:

- *Risk Assessment* — analysis that identifies the protection requirements for the system through a formal risk assessment process. This analysis builds on the initial risk assessment performed during the Initiation phase, but will be more in-depth and specific.

- *Security Functional Requirements Analysis* — analysis of requirements that may include the following components: (1) system security environment (that is, enterprise information security policy and enterprise security architecture) and (2) security functional requirements.

- *Assurance Requirements Analysis Security* — analysis of requirements that address the developmental activities required and assurance evidence needed to produce the desired level of confidence that the information security will work correctly and effectively. The analysis, based on legal and functional security requirements, will be used as the basis for determining how much and what kinds of assurance are required.

- *Cost Considerations and Reporting* — determines how much of the development cost can be attributed to information security over the life cycle of the system. These costs include hardware, software, personnel, and training.

- *Security Planning* — ensures that agreed-upon security controls, planned or in place, are fully documented. The security plan also provides a complete characterization or description of the information system as well as attachments or references to key documents supporting the agency's information security program (e.g., configuration management plan, contingency plan, incident response plan, security awareness and training plan, rules of behavior, risk assessment, security test and evaluation results, system interconnection agreements, security authorizations/accreditations, and plan of action and milestones).

- *Security Control Development*—ensures that security controls described in the respective security plans are designed, developed, and implemented. For information systems currently in operation, the security plans for those systems may call for the development of additional security controls to supplement the controls already in place or the modification of selected controls that are deemed to be less than effective.

- *Developmental Security Test and Evaluation* — ensures that security controls developed for a new information system are working properly and are effective. Some types of security controls (primarily those controls of a non-technical nature) cannot be tested and evaluated until the information system is deployed—these controls are typically management and operational controls.

- *Other Planning Components* — ensures that all necessary components of the development process are considered when incorporating security into the life cycle. These components include selection of the appropriate contract type, participation by all necessary functional groups within an organization, participation by the certifier and accreditor, and development and execution of necessary contracting plans and processes.

✦ **Implementation Phase**:

- *Inspection and Acceptance*—ensures that the organization validates and verifies that the functionality described in the specification is included in the deliverables.

- *Security Control Integration*—ensures that security controls are integrated at the operational site where the information system is to be deployed for operation. Security control settings and switches are enabled in accordance with vendor instructions and available security implementation guidance.

- *Security Certification* — ensures that the controls are effectively implemented through established verification techniques and procedures and gives organization officials confidence that the appropriate safeguards and countermeasures are in place to protect the organization's information system. Security certification also uncovers and describes the known vulnerabilities in the information system.

- *Security Accreditation*—provides the necessary security authorization of an information system to process, store, or transmit information that is required. This authorization is granted by a senior organization official and is based on the verified effectiveness of security controls to some agreed-upon level of assurance and an identified residual risk to agency assets or operations.

✦ **Operations/Maintenance Phase**:

- *Configuration Management and Control*—ensures adequate consideration of the potential security impacts due to specific changes to an information system or its surrounding environment. Configuration management and configuration control procedures are critical to establishing an initial baseline of hardware, software, and firmware components for the information system and subsequently controlling and maintaining an accurate inventory of any changes to the system.

- *Continuous Monitoring*—ensures that controls continue to be effective in their application through periodic testing and evaluation. Security control monitoring (that is, verifying the continued effectiveness of those controls over time) and reporting the security status of the information system to appropriate agency officials is an essential activity of a comprehensive information security program.

✦ **Disposition Phase**:

- *Information Preservation*—ensures that information is retained, as necessary, to conform to current legal requirements and to accommodate future technology changes that may render the retrieval method obsolete.

- *Media Sanitization*—ensures that data is deleted, erased, and written over as necessary.

- *Hardware and Software Disposal*—ensures that hardware and software is disposed of as directed by the information system security officer. After discussing these phases and the information security steps in detail, the guide provides specifications, tasks, and clauses that can be used in an RFP to acquire information security features, procedures, and assurances.

The ISSEP candidate should also understand the relationship between the SDLC phases and the acquisition process for the corresponding information system. This relationship is illustrated in Table 11-8, also taken from NIST SP 800-64.

Table 11-8
Relationship between Information Systems Acquisition Cycle Phases and the SDLC

Acquisition Cycle Phases				
Mission and Business Planning	Acquisition Planning	Acquisition	Contract Performance	Disposal and Contract Close-Out
Initiation	Acquisition/ Development	Implementation	Operation/ Maintenance	Disposition
SDLC Phases				

NIST SP 800-64 also defines the following acquisition-related terms:

✦ *Acquisition* includes all stages of the process of acquiring property or services, beginning with the process for determining the need for the property or services and ending with contract completion and closeout.

✦ The *acquisition initiator* is the key person who represents the program office in formulating information technology requirements and managing presolicitation activities.

✦ The *acquisition technical evaluation* is a component of the selection process and is defined as the examination of proposals to determine technical acceptability and merit.

An additional, valuable tool in the acquisition process is the *spiral model of the acquisition management process*. This approach is known as an evolutionary acquisition strategy. This model depicts the acquisition management process as a set of phases and decision points in a circular representation. The model illustrates the concept that a mission need is defined and translated into a solution that undergoes a continuous circle of improvement and evolution until it is no longer required.

NIST SP 800-64 also lists the key personnel associated with system acquisition and development as follows:

✦ *Chief information officer (CIO)* — The CIO is responsible for the organization's information system planning, budgeting, investment, performance and acquisition. As such, the CIO provides advice and assistance to senior organization personnel in acquiring the most efficient and effective information system to fit the organization's enterprise architecture.

✦ *Contracting officer* — The contracting officer is the person who has the authority to enter into, administer, or terminate contracts and make related determinations and findings.

✦ *Contracting officer's technical representative (COTR)* — The COTR is a qualified employee appointed by the contracting officer to act as his or her technical representative in managing the technical aspects of a particular contract.

✦ *Information Technology Investment Board (or equivalent)* — The Information Technology (IT) Investment Board, or its equivalent, is responsible for managing the capital planning and investment control process defined by the Clinger-Cohen Act of 1996 (Section 5).

✦ *Information security program manager* — The information security program manager is responsible for developing enterprise standards for information security. This individual plays a leading role in introducing an appropriate, structured methodology to help identify, evaluate, and minimize information security risks to the organization. Information security program managers coordinate and perform system risk analyses, analyze risk mitigation alternatives, and build the business case for the acquisition of appropriate security solutions that help ensure mission accomplishment in the face of real-world threats. They also support senior management in ensuring that security management activities are conducted as required to meet the organization's needs.

✦ *Information system security officer* — The information system security officer is responsible for ensuring the security of an information system throughout its life cycle.

✦ *Program manager (owner of data)/acquisition initiator/program official* — This person represents programmatic interests during the acquisition process. The program manager, who has been involved in strategic planning initiatives of the acquisition, plays an essential role in security and is, ideally, intimately aware of functional system requirements.

✦ *Privacy officer* — The privacy officer is responsible for ensuring that the services or system being procured meet existing privacy policies regarding protection, dissemination (information sharing and exchange), and information disclosure.

✦ *Legal advisor/contract attorney* — This individual is responsible for advising the team on legal issues during the acquisition process.

ISSEP candidates who are interested in additional information contained in NIST SP 800-64 can obtain the document from the NIST Web site: http://csrc.nist.gov/publications/nistpubs/.

Risk Management and the System Development Life Cycle

The risk management process minimizes the impact of threats realized and provides a foundation for effective management decision making. Thus, it is very important that risk management be a part of the system development life cycle. As defined in NIST SP 800-30, risk management is comprised of three processes:

✦ Risk assessment

✦ Risk mitigation

✦ Evaluation and assessment

These processes should be performed during each of the five phases of the SDLC. Table 11-9, taken from NIST SP 800-30, details the risk management activities that should be performed for each SDLC phase.

Table 11-9
Risk Management in the SDLC Cycle

SDLC	Phase	Risk Management Activities
Phase 1 — Initiation	The need for an IT system is expressed and the purpose and scope of the IT system is documented	Identified risks are used to support the development of the system requirements, including security requirements, and a security concept of operations (strategy)
Phase 2 — Development or Acquisition	The IT system is designed, purchased, programmed, developed, or otherwise constructed	The risks identified during this phase can be used to support the security analyses of the IT system that may lead to architecture and design tradeoffs during system development
Phase 3 — Implementation	The system security features should be configured, enabled, tested, and verified	The risk management process supports the assessment of the system implementation against its requirements and within its modeled operational environment. Decisions regarding risks identified must be made prior to system operation
Phase 4 — Operation or Maintenance	The system performs its functions. Typically the system is being modified on an ongoing basis through the addition of hardward and software and by changes to organizational processes, policies, and procedures	Risk management activities are performed for periodic system reauthorization (or reaccreditation) or whenever major changes are made to an IT system in its operational, production environment (e.g., new system interfaces)
Phase 5 — Disposal	This phase may involved the disposition of information, hardware, and software. Activities may include moving, archiving, discarding, or destroying information and sanitizing the hardware and software	Risk management activities are performed for system components that will be disposed of or replaced to ensure that the hardware and software are properly disposed of, that residual data is appropriately handled, and that system migration is conducted in a secure and systematic manner

Roles of Key Personnel in the Risk Management Process

To be effective, risk management must be supported by management and information system security practitioners. Some of the key personnel that should actively participate in the risk management activities are:

✦ *Senior management* — Provide the required resources and meet responsibilities under the principle of due care

✦ *Chief information officer (CIO)* — Considers risk management in IT planning, budgeting, and meeting system performance requirements

✦ *System and information owners* — Ensure that controls and services are implemented to address information system confidentiality, integrity, and availability

✦ *Business and functional managers* — Make trade-off decisions regarding business operations and IT procurement that affect information security

✦ *Information system security officer (ISSO)* — Participates in applying methodologies to identify, evaluate, and reduce risks to the mission-critical IT systems

✦ *IT security practitioners* — Ensure the correct implementation of IT system information system security requirements

✦ *Security awareness trainers* — Incorporate risk assessment in training programs for the organization's personnel

The Risk Assessment Process

As defined in NIST SP 800-30, "Risk is a function of the likelihood of a given threat-source's exercising a particular potential vulnerability, and the resulting impact of that adverse event on the organization." Risk assessment comprises the following steps:

1. System characterization
2. Threat identification
3. Vulnerability identification
4. Control analysis
5. Likelihood determination
6. Impact analysis
7. Risk determination

8. Control recommendations

9. Results documentation

Each of these steps will be summarized in the following sections.

System Characterization

This step characterizes and defines the scope of the risk assessment process. During this step, information about the system has to be gathered. This information includes:

✦ Software

✦ Hardware

✦ Data

✦ Information

✦ System interfaces

✦ IT system users

✦ IT system support personnel

✦ System mission

✦ Criticality of the system and data

✦ System and data sensitivity

✦ Functional system requirements

✦ System security policies

✦ System security architecture

✦ Network topology

✦ Information storage protection

✦ System information flow

✦ Technical security controls

✦ Physical security environment

✦ Environmental security

This information can be gathered using *questionnaires, on-site interviews, review of documents,* and *automated scanning tools.* The outputs from this step are:

✦ Characterization of the assessed IT system

✦ Comprehension of the IT system environment

✦ Delineation of the system boundary

Threat Identification

This step identifies potential threat-sources and compiles a statement of the threat-sources that relate to the IT system under evaluation. A *threat* is defined in NIST SP 800-30 as "the potential for a threat-source to exercise (accidentally trigger or intentionally exploit) a specific vulnerability. A *threat-source* is defined in the same document as "either (1) intent and method targeted at the intentional exploitation of a vulnerability or (2) a situation and method that may accidentally trigger a vulnerability." Common threat-sources include *natural threats* such as storms and floods, *human threats* such as malicious attacks and unintentional acts, and *environmental threats* such as power failure and liquid leakage. A *vulnerability* is defined as "a flaw or weakness in system security procedures, design, implementation, or internal controls that could be exercised (accidentally triggered or intentionally exploited) and result in a security breach or a violation of the system's security policy."

Sources of threat information include the Federal Computer Incident Response Center (FedCIRC), intelligence agencies, mass media, and Web-based resources. The output from this step is a statement that provides a list of threat-sources that could exploit the system's vulnerabilities.

Vulnerability Identification

This activity results in a list of system vulnerabilities that might be exploited by potential threat-sources. Vulnerabilities can be identified through vulnerability analyses, including information from previous information assessments; audit reports; the NIST vulnerability database (http://icat.nist.gov/icat.cfm); FedCIRC and DoE security bulletins; vendor data; commercial computer incident response teams; and system software security analyses. Testing of the IT system will also yield important results. This testing can be accomplished using penetration-testing techniques, automated vulnerability scanning tools, and security test and evaluation (ST&E) procedures.

This phase also involves determining whether the security requirements identified during system characterization are being met. Usually, the security requirements are listed in a table with a corresponding statement about how the requirement is or is not being met. The checklist addresses management, operational, and technical information system security areas. The result of this effort is a *security requirements checklist*. Some useful references for this activity are the Computer Security Act of 1987, the Privacy Act of 1974, the organization's security policies, industry best practices, and NIST SP 800-26, *Security Self-Assessment Guide for Information Technology Systems*.

The output from this step is a list of system vulnerabilities/observations that could be exploited by the potential threat-sources.

Control Analysis

The control analysis step analyzes the controls that are in place or in the planning stage to minimize or eliminate the probability that a threat will exploit vulnerability in the system.

Controls can be implemented through technical means such as computer hardware or software, encryption, intrusion detection mechanisms, and identification and authentication subsystems. Other controls such as security policies, administrative actions, physical and environmental mechanisms are considered nontechnical controls. Both technical and nontechnical controls can further be classified as preventive or detective controls. As the names imply, preventive controls attempt to anticipate and stop attacks. Examples of preventive, technical controls are encryption and authentication devices. Detective controls are used to discover attacks or events through such means as audit trails and intrusion detection systems.

Changes in the control mechanisms should be reflected in the security requirement checklist.

The output of this step is a list of current and planned control mechanisms for the IT system to reduce the likelihood that a vulnerability will be exercised and to reduce the impact of an attack or event.

Likelihood Determination

This activity develops a rating that provides an indication of the probability that a potential vulnerability might be exploited based on the defined threat environment. This rating takes into account the type of vulnerability, the capability and motivation of the threat-source, and the existence and effectiveness of information system security controls. The likelihood levels are given as high, medium, and low, as illustrated in Table 11-10.

Table 11-10 Definitions of Likelihood	
Level of Likelihood	Definition of Likelihood
High	A highly motivated and capable threat-source and ineffective controls to prevent exploitation of the associated vulnerability
Medium	A highly motivated and capable threat-source and controls that might impede exploitation of the associated vulnerability
Low	Lack of motivation or capability in the threat-source or controls in place to prevent or significantly impede the exploitation of the associated vulnerability

The output of this step is a likelihood rating of high, medium, or low.

Impact Analysis

If a threat does exploit a vulnerability in an IT system, it is critical to know the negative impact that would result to the system. Three important factors should be considered in calculating the negative impact:

✦ The mission of the system, including the processes implemented by the system

✦ The criticality of the system, determined by its value and the value of the data to the organization

✦ The sensitivity of the system and its data

The information necessary to conduct an impact analysis can be obtained from existing organizational documentation, including a business impact analysis (BIA), or mission impact analysis report as it is sometimes called. This document uses either quantitative or qualitative means to determine the impacts caused by compromise or harm to the organization's information assets. An attack or adverse event can result in compromise or loss of information system confidentiality, integrity, and availability. As with the likelihood determination, the impact on the system can be qualitatively assessed as high, medium, or low, as shown in Table 11-11.

Table 11-11
Definitions of Likelihood

Impact Magnitude	Definition of Impact
High	Possibility of costly loss of major tangible assets or resources; might cause significant harm or impedance to the mission of an organization; might cause significant harm to an organization's reputation or interest; might result in human death or injury
Medium	Possibility of costly loss of tangible assets or resources; might cause harm or impedance to the mission of an organization; might cause harm to an organization's reputation or interest; might result in human injury
Low	Possibility of loss of some tangible assets or resources; might affect noticeably an organization's mission; might affect noticeably an organization's reputation or interest

Qualitative analysis is more easily accomplished and provides identifiable areas for immediate improvement. However, it does not provide specific measures of magnitudes of measures and thus makes a cost-benefit analysis difficult. Quantitative analysis does provide magnitudes of measurements but may take more time. It is sometimes very difficult or impossible to place quantitative values on abstract items such as reputation.

Other items that should be included in the impact analysis are the estimated frequency of the threat-source's exploitation of a vulnerability on annual basis, the approximate cost of each of these occurrences, and a weight factor based on the relative impact of a specific threat exploiting a specific vulnerability.

The output of this step is the magnitude of impact: high, medium, or low.

Risk Determination

This step, the seventh step in the risk assessment process, determines the level of risk to the IT system. The risk is assigned for a threat/vulnerability pair and is a function of the following characteristics:

✦ The likelihood that a particular threat-source will exploit an existing IT system vulnerability

✦ The magnitude of the resulting impact of a threat-source successfully exploiting the IT system vulnerability

✦ The adequacy of the existing or planned information system security controls for eliminating or reducing the risk

Mission risk is calculated by multiplying the threat likelihood ratings (the probability that a threat will occur) by the impact of the threat realized. A useful tool for estimating risk in this manner is the risk-level matrix. An example risk-level matrix is shown in Table 11-12. In the table, a high likelihood that the threat will occur is given a value of 1.0; a medium likelihood is assigned a value of 0.5; and a low likelihood of occurrence is given a rating of 0.1. Similarly, a high impact level is assigned a value of 100, a medium impact level 50, and a low impact level 10.

Table 11-12		
A Risk-Level Matrix Example		
Likelihood of Threat	*Low Impact (10)*	*Medium Impact (50)*	*High Impact (100)*
High (1.0)	Low $10 \times 1.0 = 10$	Medium $50 \times 1.0 = 50$	High $100 \times 1.0 = 100$
Medium (0.5)	Low $10 \times 0.5 = 5$	Medium $50 \times 0.5 = 25$	High $100 \times 0.5 = 50$
Low (0.1)	Low $10 \times 0.1 = 1$	Medium $50 \times 0.1 = 5$	High $100 \times 0.1 = 10$

Using the risk level as a basis, the next step is to determine the actions that senior management and other responsible individuals must take to mitigate estimated risk. General guidelines for each level of risk are:

✦ *High risk level* — At this level, there is a high level of concern and a strong need for a plan for corrective measures to be developed as soon as possible.

✦ *Medium risk level* — For medium risk, there is concern and a need for a plan for corrective measures to be developed within a reasonable period of time.

✦ *Low risk level* — For low risk, the DAA of the system must decide whether to accept the risk or implement corrective actions.

The output of the risk determination step is risk level of high, medium, or low.

Control Recommendations

With the risks identified and general guidelines provided for risk mitigation in the previous step, this step specifies the controls to be applied for risk mitigation. In order to specify appropriate controls, issues such as cost-benefit, operational impact, and feasibility have to be considered. In addition, other factors, including applicable legislative regulations, organizational policy, safety, reliability, and the overall effectiveness of the recommended controls should be taken into account.

The output of this step is a recommendation of controls and any alternative solutions to mitigate risk.

Results Documentation

The last step in the risk assessment process is the development of a risk assessment report. This report is directed at management and should contain information to support appropriate decisions on budget, policies, procedures, management, and operational issues.

The output of this step is a risk assessment report that descries threats and vulnerabilities, risk measurements, and recommendations for implementation of controls.

Risk Mitigation

Risk mitigation prioritizes, evaluates, and implements the controls that are an output of the risk assessment process. Risk mitigation is the second component of the risk management process.

Because risk can never be completely eliminated and control implementation must make sense under a cost-benefit analysis, a least-cost approach with minimal adverse impact on the IT system is usually taken.

Risk Mitigation Options

Risk mitigation can be classified into the following options:

✦ *Risk assumption* — accept the risk and keep operating

✦ *Risk avoidance* — forgo some functions

✦ *Risk limitation* — implement controls to minimize the adverse impact of threats realized

✦ *Risk planning* — develop a risk mitigation plan to prioritize, implement, and maintain controls

✦ *Research and development* — researching control types and options

✦ *Risk transference* — transfer risk to other sources, such as purchasing insurance

A flow diagram of a risk mitigation strategy, taken from SP 800-30, appears in Figure 11-18.

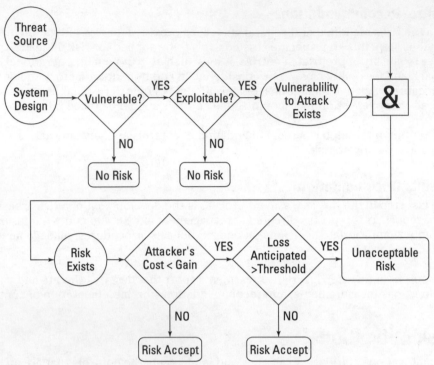

Figure 11-18: A risk mitigation strategy (from NIST SP 800-30).

SP 800-30 emphasizes the following guidance on implementing controls:

> Address the greatest risks and strive for sufficient risk mitigation at the lowest cost, with minimal impact on other mission capabilities.

The control implementation approach from the risk mitigation methodology recommended by SP 800-30 is given in Figure 11-19.

Categories of Controls

Controls to mitigate risks can be broken into the following categories:

✦ Technical

✦ Management

✦ Operational

✦ A combination of the above

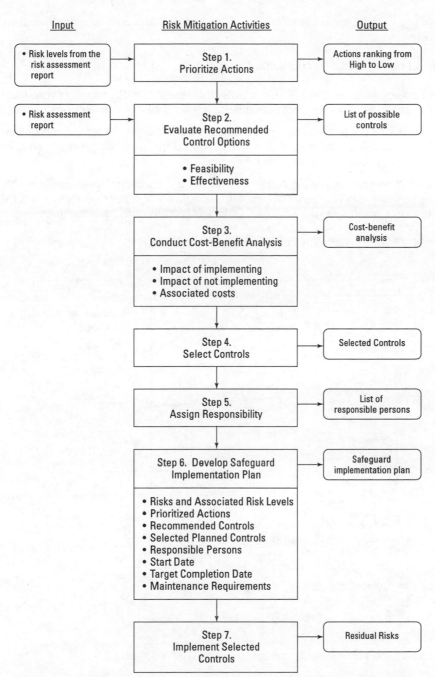

Figure 11-19: A control implementation approach (from NIST SP 800-30).

Each of the categories of controls can be further decomposed into additional sub-categories.

Technical controls can be subdivided into:

✦ *Supporting controls* — These controls implement identification, cryptographic key management, security administration, and system protections.

✦ *Preventive controls* — Preventive technical controls include authentication, authorization, access control enforcement, nonrepudiation, protected communications, and transaction privacy.

✦ *Detection and recovering controls* — These technical controls include audit, intrusion detection and containment, proof of wholeness (system integrity), restoration to a secure state, and virus detection and eradication.

Figure 11-20 summarizes the technical security controls.

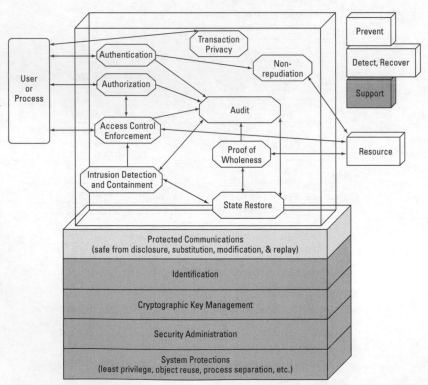

Figure 11-20: Technical security controls (from NIST SP 800-30).

Management controls comprise:

- ✦ *Preventive controls* — Preventive management controls include assigning responsibility for security, developing and maintaining security plans, personnel security controls, and security awareness and technical training.

- ✦ *Detection controls* — Detection controls involve background checks, personnel clearance, periodic review of security controls, periodic system audits, risk management, and authorization of IT systems to address and accept residual risk.

- ✦ *Recovery controls* — These controls provide continuity of support to develop, test, and maintain the continuity of the operations plan and establish an incident response capability.

Operational security controls are divided into preventive and detection types. Their functions are listed as follows:

- ✦ *Preventive controls* — These operational controls comprise control of media access and disposal, limiting external data distribution, control of software viruses, securing wiring closest, providing backup capability, protecting laptops and personal computers, protecting IT assets from fire damage, providing an emergency power source, and control of humidity and temperature.

- ✦ *Detection controls* — Detection operation controls include providing physical security through the use of items such as cameras and motion detectors and ensuring environmental security by using smoke detectors, sensors, and alarms.

Determination of Residual Risk

The risk that remains after the implementation of controls is called the *residual risk*. All systems will have residual risk because it is virtually impossible to completely eliminate risk to an IT system. An organization's senior management or the DAA is responsible for authorizing/accrediting the IT system to begin or continue to operate. The authorization/accreditation must take place every three years in federal agencies or whenever major changes are made to the system. The DAA signs a statement accepting the residual risk when accrediting the IT system for operation. If the DAA determines that the residual risk is at an unacceptable level, the risk management cycle must be redone with the objective of lowering the residual risk to an acceptable level.

Figure 11-21 shows the relationship between residual risk and the implementation of controls.

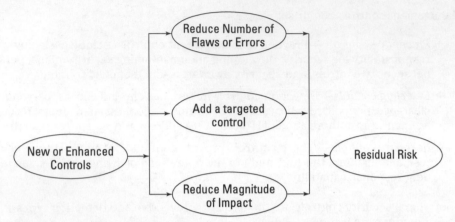

Figure 11-21: The relationship between residual risk and implementation of controls (from NIST SP 800-30).

Risk Management Summary

As stated in SP 800-30, "A successful risk management program will rely on (1) senior management's commitment; (2) the full support and participation of the IT; (3) the competence of the risk assessment team, which must have the expertise to apply the risk assessment methodology to a specific site and system, identify mission risks, and provide cost-effective safeguards that meet the needs of the organization; (4) the awareness and cooperation of members of the user community, who must follow procedures and comply with the implemented controls to safeguard the mission of their organization; and (5) an ongoing evaluation and assessment of the IT-related mission risks."

✦   ✦   ✦

Assessment Questions

You can find the answers to the following questions in Appendix A.

1. Which one of the following is NOT one of the five system life cycle planning phases as defined in NIST SP 800-14?

   a. Initiation phase

   b. Requirements phase

   c. Implementation phase

   d. Disposal phase

2. Which one of the following sets of activities BEST describes a subset of the Acquisition Cycle phases as given in NIST SP 800-64, *Security Considerations in the Information System Development Life Cycle*?

   a. Mission and business planning, acquisition planning, contract performance, disposal and contract closeout

   b. Initiation, mission and business planning, acquisition planning, contract performance

   c. Initiation, acquisition/development, contract performance, disposal and contract closeout

   d. Mission and business planning, acquisition/development, contract performance, disposal and contract closeout

3. The IATF document 3.1 stresses that information assurance relies on three critical components. Which one of the following answers correctly lists these components?

   a. People, documentation, technology

   b. People, Defense in Depth, technology

   c. People, evaluation, certification

   d. People, operations, technology

4. In the 14 Common IT Security Practices listed in NIST SP 800-14, one of the practices addresses having three types of policies in place. Which one of the following items is NOT one of these types of policies?

   a. A program policy

   b. An issue specific policy

   c. A system specific policy

   d. An enclave specific policy

5. Risk management, as defined in NIST SP 800-30, comprises which three processes?

   a. Risk assessment, risk mitigation, and evaluation and assessment

   b. Risk identification, risk mitigation, and evaluation and assessment

   c. Risk assessment, risk impacts, and risk mitigation

   d. Risk assessment, risk mitigation, and risk identification.

6. In the system development life cycle, SDLC, or system life cycle as it is sometimes called, in which one of the of the five phases are the system security features configured, enabled, tested, and verified?

   a. Operation/maintenance

   b. Development/acquisition

   c. Implementation

   d. Initiation

7. Which one of the following activities is performed in the Development/Acquisition phase of the SDLC?

   a. The scope of the IT system is documented.

   b. The IT system is developed, programmed, or otherwise constructed.

   c. The system performs its function.

   d. Disposition of information, hardware, or software.

8. In NIST SP 800-30, risk is defined as a function of which set of the following items?

   a. Threat likelihood, vulnerabilities, and impact

   b. Threat likelihood, mission, and impact

   c. Vulnerabilities, mission and impact

   d. Threat likelihood, sensitivity, and impact

9. The risk assessment methodology described in NIST SP 800-30 comprises nine primary steps. Which one of the following is NOT one of these steps?

   a. System characterization

   b. Control analysis

   c. Impact analysis

   d. Accreditation boundaries

10. The engineering principles for information technology security (EP-ITS), described in NIST SP 800-27, are which one of the following?

   a. A list of 33 system-level security principles to be considered in the design, development, and operation of an information system

   b. A list of eight principles and 14 practices derived from OECD guidelines

   c. Part of the Common Criteria (CC)

   d. Component of the Defense in Depth strategy

11. Which one of the following items is NOT one of the activities of the generic systems engineering (SE) process?

   a. Discover needs

   b. Define system requirements

   c. Obtain accreditation

   d. Assess effectiveness

12. The elements of Discover information protection needs, Develop detailed security design, and Assess information protection effectiveness are part of what process?

   a. The systems engineering (SE) process

   b. The information systems security engineering process (ISSE)

   c. The system development life cycle (SDLC)

   d. The risk management process

13. In the ISSE process, information domains are defined under the Discover Information Protection Needs process. Which one of the following tasks is NOT associated the information domain?

   a. Identify the members of the domain

   b. List the information entities that are under control in the domain

   c. Identify the applicable privileges, roles, rules, and responsibilities of the users in the domain

   d. Map security mechanisms to security design elements in the domain.

14. In the Discover Information Protection Needs activity of the ISSE process, the information systems security engineer must document the elements of this activity, including roles, responsibilities, threats, strengths, security services, and priorities. These items form the basis of which one of the following:

   a. Threat matrix

   b. Functional analysis

   c. Synthesis

   d. Information protection policy (IPP)

15. As part of the Define System Security Requirements activity of the ISSE process, the information systems security engineer identifies and selects a solution set that can satisfy the requirements of the IPP. Which one of the following elements is NOT a component of the solution set?

    a. Functional decomposition

    b. Preliminary security concept of operations (CONOPS)

    c. System context

    d. System requirements

16. The information systems security engineer's tasks of cataloging candidate commercial off-the-shelf (COTS) products, government off-the-shelf (GOTS) products, and custom security products are performed in which one of the following ISSE process activities?

    a. Define System Security Requirements

    b. Develop Detailed Security Design

    c. Implement System Security

    d. Design System Security Architecture

17. Which ISSE activity includes conducting unit testing of components, integration testing, and developing installation and operational procedures?

    a. Assess Information Protection Effectiveness

    b. Develop Detailed Security Design

    c. Implement System Security

    d. Design System Security Architecture

18. Security certification is performed in which phase of the SDLC?

    a. Implementation phase

    b. Validation phase

    c. Development/Acquisition phase

    d. Operations/Maintenance phase

19. The certification and accreditation process receives inputs from the ISSE process. These inputs are which one of the following items?

    a. Certification documentation

    b. Certification recommendations

    c. Accreditation decision

    d. Evidence and documentation

20. Which one of the following items is NOT part of an implementation-independent protection profile (PP) of the Common Criteria (CC)?

   a. Security objectives

   b. Information assurance requirements

   c. Security-related functional requirements

   d. Defense of the enclave boundary

21. Which one of the following is NOT one of the technology focus areas of the Defense in Depth strategy?

   a. Defend the certificate management

   b. Defend the network and infrastructure

   c. Defend the computing environment

   d. Defend the supporting infrastructure

22. Security categorization is part of which phase of the SDLC?

   a. Initiation

   b. Acquisition/Development

   c. Implementation

   d. Requirements

23. The Defense in Depth strategy identifies five types of attacks on information systems as listed in IATF document 3.1. Which one of the following types of attacks is NOT one of these five types?

   a. Passive

   b. Active

   c. Close-in

   d. Outsider

24. Which one of the following items is NOT an activity under the Acquisition/ Development phase of the SDLC?

   a. Preliminary risk assessment

   b. Security functional requirements analysis

   c. Cost considerations and reporting

   d. Developmental security evaluation

25. Which one of the following types of enclaves is NOT one of those categorized in the U.S. federal and defense computing environments?

   a. Private

   b. Public

   c. Classified

   d. Secure

26. According to NIST SP 800-64, which phase of the SDLC includes the activities of functional statement of need, market research, cost-benefit analysis, and a cost analysis?

    a. Initiation

    b. Acquisition/Development

    c. Implementation

    d. Operations/Maintenance

27. Which one of the following models is an evolutionary model used to represent the acquisition management process?

    a. The acquisition process model

    b. The Spiral model

    c. The Waterfall model

    d. The acquisition/development model

28. In NIST SP 800-30, a threat is defined as which one of the following items?

    a. Intent and method targeted at the intentional exploit of a vulnerability

    b. The likelihood that a given threat-source will exercise a particular potential vulnerability, and the resulting impact of that adverse event on the organization

    c. The potential for a threat-source to exercise a specific vulnerability

    d. A flaw or weakness in system security procedures, design, implementation, or internal controls that could be exercised and result in a security breach or a violation of the system's security policy

29. Questionnaires, on-site interviews, review of documents, and automated scanning tools are primarily used to gather information for which one of the following steps of the risk assessment process?

    a. System characterization

    b. Risk determination

    c. Vulnerability identification

    d. Control analysis

30. In performing an impact analysis as part of the risk assessment process, three important factors should be considered in calculating the negative impact. Which one of the following items is NOT one of these factors?

    a. The sensitivity of the system and its data

    b. The management of the system

    c. The mission of the system

    d. The criticality of the system, determined by its value and the value of the data to the organization

Certification and Accreditation (C&A)

In many environments, formal methods must be applied to ensure that the appropriate information system security safeguards are in place and that they are functioning per the specifications. In addition, an authority must take responsibility for putting the system into operation. These actions are known as *Certification* and *Accreditation* (C&A), respectively.

What Is C&A?

Certification is the comprehensive evaluation of the technical and nontechnical security features of an information system and the other safeguards, which are created in support of the accreditation process, to establish the extent in which a particular design and implementation meets the set of specified security requirements.

Accreditation is the formal declaration by a *Designated Approving Authority* (DAA) that an information system is approved to operate in a particular security mode by using a prescribed set of safeguards at an acceptable level of risk. *Recertification* and re-*accreditation* are required when changes occur in the system and/or its environment, or after a defined period of time after accreditation.

Two U.S. defense and government certification and accreditation standards have been developed for the evaluation of critical information systems. These standards are the *National Information Assurance Certification and Accreditation Process* (NIACAP) and the *Defense Information Technology Security Certification and Accreditation Process* (DITSCAP).

The National Information Assurance Certification and Accreditation Process (NIACAP)

The National Security Telecommunications and Information Systems Security Instruction (NSTISSI) No. 1000 defines the National Information Assurance Certification and Accreditation Process (NIACAP). The NIACAP establishes the minimum national standards for certifying and accrediting national security systems. This process provides a standard set of activities, general tasks, and a management structure to certify and accredit systems that maintain the information assurance and the security posture of a system or site. The NIACAP is designed to certify that the information system meets the documented accreditation requirements and will continue to maintain the accredited security posture throughout the system's life cycle.

Under Executive Order (E.O.) 13231 of October 16, 2001, *Critical Infrastructure Protection in the Information Age*, the National Security Telecommunications and Information Systems Security Committee (NSTISSC) as been redesignated the Committee on National Security Systems (CNSS). The Department of Defense continues to chair the committee under the authorities established by NSD-42 (www.nstissc.gov/).

The process is started when the concept design of a new information system or modification to an existing system is begun in response to an identified business case, operational requirement, or mission need. Any security-relevant changes should initiate the NIACAP for any existing or legacy IS.

NIACAP Roles

The four minimum roles needed to perform a NIACAP security assessment are the:

1. IS program manager
2. Designated Approving Authority (DAA), also referred to as the accreditor
3. Certification agent (certifier)
4. User representative

NIACAP and NSTISSP # 6

The NIACAP provides guidance on how to implement the NSTISSP No. 6 policy, which establishes the requirement for federal departments and agencies to implement a C&A process for national security systems. The requirements of the NSTISSI No. 6 apply to all U.S. government executive branch departments, agencies, and their contractors and consultants.

The individuals in these roles tailor and scope the C&A efforts to the particular mission, environment, system architecture, threats, funding, and schedule of the system. These individuals resolve critical schedule, budget, security, functionality, and performance issues. We'll examine these roles in more detail later in the chapter.

Additional roles may be added to increase the integrity and objectivity of C&A decisions. For example, the Information Systems Security Officer (ISSO) usually performs a key role in the maintenance of the security posture after the accreditation and may also play a key role in the C&A of the system.

Program Manager

The program manager represents the interests of the system in areas such as:

✦ Acquisition

✦ Life cycle schedules

✦ Funding responsibility

✦ System operation

✦ System performance

✦ Maintenance

Which organization the program manager represents is determined by the phase in the life cycle of the system. The program manager coordinates all aspects of the system from initial concept, through development, to implementation and system maintenance. The DAA, certifier, and user representative give advice, information, and guidance to the program manager throughout the NIACAP.

The program manager:

✦ Is responsible for the IS throughout the life cycle (cost, schedule, and performance of the system development)

✦ Ensures that the security requirements are integrated in a way that will result in an acceptable level of risk to the operational infrastructure as documented in the System Security Authorization Agreement (SSAA)

✦ Keeps all NIACAP participants informed of life cycle actions, security requirements, and documented user needs

Additionally, the program manager provides details of the system and its life cycle management to the DAA, certifier, and user representative during Phase 2. The program manager must verify that the implementation of the system is consistent with the system security characteristics reflected in the SSAA. As additional system details become available, the program manager ensures the SSAA is updated. At the end of Phase 2, the program manager ensures that a configuration management procedure is in place and that the system is properly controlled during the certification process.

The PM also ensures that the certification-ready system is under configuration management during Phase 3. The DAA, certifier, and user representative validate that the operational environment and system configuration are consistent with the security characteristics reflected in the SSAA.

Designated Approving Authority (DAA)

The DAA is the primary government official responsible for implementing system security. The DAA is an executive with the authority and ability to balance the needs of the system with the security risks. He/she determines the acceptable level of residual risk for a system and must have the authority to oversee the budget and IS business operations of systems under his/her purview.

Based on the information available in the SSAA, the DAA can grant the accreditation, an Interim Approval to Operate (IATO), or may determine that the system's risks are not at an acceptable level and it is not ready to be operational. In reaching these decisions, the DAA is supported by all the documentation provided in the SSAA.

Certification Agent

The certifier (or certification team) provides the technical expertise to conduct the certification throughout the system's life cycle based on the security requirements documented in the SSAA. The certifier determines the existing level of residual risk and makes an accreditation recommendation to the DAA. The certifier is the technical expert that documents tradeoffs among security requirements, cost, availability, and schedule to manage security risk.

The certifier determines whether a system is ready for certification and conducts the certification process — a comprehensive evaluation of the technical and non-technical security features of the system. At the completion of the certification effort, the certifier reports the status of certification and recommends to the DAA whether to accredit the system based on documented residual risk.

To avoid conflicts of interest, the certifier should be independent from the organization responsible for the system development or operation. Organizational independence of the certifier ensures the most objective information for the DAA to make accreditation decisions.

User Representative

The operational interests of system users are vested in the user representative. In the NIACAP process, the user representative is concerned with system availability, access, integrity, functionality, performance, and confidentiality as they relate to the mission environment.

Users and their representatives are found at all levels of an agency. As noted in the SSAA, the user representative:

+ Is responsible for the identification of operational requirements

+ Is responsible for the secure operation of a certified and accredited IS

+ Represents the user community

+ Assists in the C&A process

+ Functions as the liaison for the user community throughout the life cycle of the system

+ Defines the system's operations and functional requirements

+ Is responsible for ensuring that the user's operational interests are maintained throughout system development, modification, integration, acquisition, and deployment

System Security Authorization Agreement (SSAA)

An important element in the NIACAP is the agreement among the program manager, DAA, certifier, and user representative. The NIACAP agreements are documented in the System Security Authorization Agreement (SSAA). The SSAA is a formal agreement among the DAA(s), certifier, user representative, and program manager. The objective of the SSAA is to establish an evolving yet binding agreement on the level of security required before the system development begins or changes to a system are made.

The SSAA is used throughout the entire NIACAP to guide actions, document decisions, specify IA requirements, document certification tailoring and level of effort, identify possible solutions, and maintain operational systems security. After accreditation, the SSAA becomes the baseline security configuration document.

The SSAA:

+ Describes the operating environment and threat

+ Describes the system security architecture

+ Establishes the C&A boundary of the system to be accredited

+ Documents the formal agreement among the DAA(s), certifier, program manager, and user representative

+ Documents all requirements necessary for accreditation

+ Minimizes documentation requirements by consolidating applicable information into the SSAA (security policy, concept of operations, architecture description, test procedures, and so on)

✦ Documents the NIACAP plan

✦ Documents test plans and procedures, certification results, and residual risk

✦ Forms the baseline security configuration document

Accreditation Types

There are three types of NIACAP accreditation depending on what is being certified. They are:

1. *Site accreditation* — Evaluates the applications and systems at a specific, self-contained location

2. *Type accreditation* — Evaluates an application or system that is distributed to a number of different locations

3. *System accreditation* — Evaluates a major application or general support system

The NIACAP applies to each of these accreditation types and can be tailored to meet the specific needs of the organization and IS.

NIACAP Phases

The NIACAP is composed of four phases:

1. *Definition* — Phase 1, Definition, is focused on understanding the IS business case, environment, and architecture to determine the security requirements and level of effort necessary to achieve certification and accreditation. The objective of Phase 1 is to agree on the security requirements, C&A boundary, schedule, level of effort, and resources required.

2. *Verification* — Phase 2, Verification, confirms the evolving or modified system's compliance with the information in the SSAA. The objective of Phase 2 is to ensure the fully integrated system will be ready for certification testing.

3. *Validation* — Phase 3, Validation, confirms compliance of the fully integrated system with the security policy and requirements stated in the SSAA. The objective of Phase 3 is to produce the required evidence to support the DAA in making an informed decision to grant approval to operate the system (accreditation or *Interim Approval to Operate* [IATO]).

4. *Post Accreditation* — Phase 4, Post Accreditation, starts after the system has been certified and accredited for operations. Phase 4 includes those activities necessary for the continuing operation of the accredited IS in its computing environment and to address the changing threats and small-scale changes a system faces through its life cycle. The objective of Phase 4 is to ensure secure system management, operation, and maintenance to preserve an acceptable level of residual risk.

Each phase consists of defined activities with specific tasks and procedures.

Phase 1, Definition

Phase 1 begins with a review of the system and related documents and ends by producing the SSAA. The goals of Phase1 are to define the C&A level of effort, identify the principle C&A roles and responsibilities, and create an agreement on the method for implementing the security requirements that will be documented in the SSAA.

Phase 1 (see Figure 12-1) contains three activities:

✦ Preparation

✦ Registration

✦ Negotiation

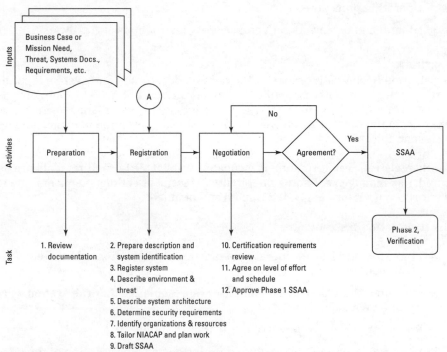

Figure 12-1: NIACAP Phase 1 — Definition.

Preparation

Information and documentation are collected about the system during preparation, including capabilities and functions the system will perform, desired interfaces and data flows associated with those interfaces, information to be processed, operational organizations supported, intended operational environment, and operational threat.

This information comes from many sources. Examples of the types of documentation and information collected and reviewed during the preparation phase includes:

✦ Business case

✦ Mission need statement

✦ System specifications

✦ Architecture and design documents

✦ Network diagrams

✦ Configuration management documents

✦ Threat analysis

✦ User manuals

✦ Operating procedures

✦ Federal and organization IA and security instructions and policies

Registration

Registration begins with preparing the mission description and system identification and concludes with preparing an initial draft of the SSAA. The main purpose of the registration activity during Phase 1 is to initiate the risk management agreement process among the four principals: the DAA, certifier, program manager, and user representative.

During registration, information is evaluated, applicable IA requirements are determined, risk management and vulnerability assessment actions begin, and the level of effort required for C&A is determined and planned.

The registration tasks include:

✦ Preparing business or operational functional description and system identification.

✦ Informing the DAA, certifier, and user representative that the system will require C&A support.

✦ Preparing the environment and threat description.

✦ Preparing a system architecture description and a description of the C&A boundary.

✦ Determining system security requirements.

✦ Tailoring NIACAP tasks, determining the C&A level-of-effort, and preparing a NIACAP plan.

✦ Identifying organizations that will be involved in the C&A identifying resources required.

✦ Developing the first draft of the SSAA.

A very important registration task is the preparation of a description of the C&A boundary. The accreditation boundary should include all IS facilities and equipment under the control of the DAA to be addressed in the C&A. The relationship of the accreditation boundary to any existing external interfaces or other equipment or systems also must be determined. Any facility or equipment that is not under the control of the DAA is considered an external interface.

When registration activities are concluded, the draft SSAA is submitted to the DAA, certifier, program manager, and user representative. The draft SSAA is then used as the basis for discussions during the negotiation phase. The program manager normally drafts the SSAA, but the certifier (or certification team) may also draft it.

Negotiation

During negotiation, all participants involved in the IS's development, acquisition, operation, security certification, and accreditation agree on the implementation strategy to be used to satisfy the security requirements identified during system registration. The purpose of negotiation is to ensure that the SSAA properly and clearly defines the approach and level of effort.

The primary negotiation tasks are:

1. Conduct the Certification Requirement Review (CRR).
2. Agree on the security requirements, level of effort, and schedule.
3. Approve final Phase 1 SSAA.

All participants will develop an understanding of their roles and responsibilities during negotiation. They review the proposed certification efforts and resource requirements to determine that the appropriate assurance is being applied.

Each role has a defined task during negotiation:

✦ The DAA conducts a complete review of the draft SSAA to determine that all appropriate IA and security requirements are included.

✦ The certifier conducts a comprehensive evaluation of the technical and non-technical security features of the IS.

✦ The program manager reviews the SSAA for accuracy, completeness, costs, and schedule considerations.

✦ The user representative reviews the SSAA to determine whether the system will support the user's mission and that appropriate security operating procedures will be available at system delivery.

Negotiation ends when the responsible organizations adopt the SSAA and concur that those objectives have been reached. The Certification Requirement Review (CRR) must result in an agreement regarding the level of effort and the approach that will be taken to implement the security requirements. The CRR must include the information documented in the SSAA (mission and system information, operational and security functionality, operational environment, security policy, system security requirements, known security problems or deficiencies, and other relevant security information).

Phase 2, Verification

Phase 2 activities occur between the signing of the initial version of the SSAA and the formal C&A of the system. These activities are intended to verify the evolving system's compliance with the risk management requirements in the SSAA. They verify security requirements during system development or modification by certification analysis and assessment of the certification results.

As shown in Figure 12-2, Phase 2 contains three major activities:

1. Refine the SSAA

2. System Development and Integration

3. Initial Certification Analysis

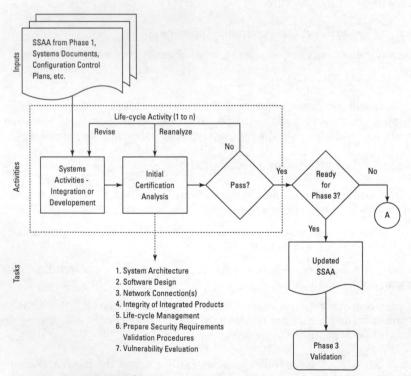

Figure 12-2: NIACAP Phase 2 — Verification.

Refine the SSAA

At each stage of development or modification, details are added to the SSAA. Throughout Phase 2 the SSAA is reviewed and updated to include changes made during system development and the results of the certification analysis.

Any changes in the system that affect its security posture must be submitted to the DAA, certifier, program manager, and user representative for approval and inclusion in the revised SSAA.

System Development and Integration

System development and integration activities are those activities required for development or integration of the information system components as defined in the system's functional and security requirements. The specific activities will vary depending on the overall program strategy, the life cycle management process, and the position of the information system in the life cycle.

System development and integration tasks include:

✦ Preparing the system architecture

✦ Preparing high level and detailed design documents

✦ Integrating commercial-off-the-shelf (COTS) products

✦ Conducting system integration testing

Initial Certification Analysis

The initial certification analysis determines whether the IS is ready to be evaluated and tested under Phase 3. It verifies by analysis, investigation, and comparison methodologies that the IS design implements the SSAA requirements and that the IS components critical to security function properly. This verifies that the development, modification, and integration efforts will result in a higher probability of success for an accreditable IS before Phase 3 begins.

When the Phase 2 initial certification analysis is completed, the system should have a documented security specification, comprehensive test procedures, and written assurance that all network and other interconnection requirements have been implemented.

Initial certification analysis tasks include:

> **System architecture analysis.** Verifies that the system architecture complies with the architecture description in the SSAA. The interfaces between this and other systems must be identified and evaluated to assess their effectiveness in maintaining the security posture of the infrastructure.

Software, hardware, and firmware design analysis. Evaluates how well the software, hardware and firmware reflect the security requirements of the SSAA and the security architecture of the system.

Network connection rule compliance analysis. This task evaluates the intended connections to other systems and networks to ensure the system design will enforce specific network security policies and protect the IS from adverse confidentiality, integrity, availability, and accountability impacts.

Integrity analysis of integrated products. Evaluates the integration of COTS or GOTS software, hardware, and firmware to ensure that their integration into the system design complies with the system security architecture. The product security functionality should be verified by the certification team to confirm that the needed security functions are present and properly integrated into the system.

Life cycle management analysis. Verifies that change control and configuration management practices are in place, or will be, and are sufficient to preserve the integrity of the security-relevant software and hardware.

Security requirements validation procedure preparation. Defines the procedures to be used to verify compliance with all the defined security requirements. The security requirements document must identify the type of review required to validate each requirement. If test procedures are prepared, they should be added to the SSAA.

Vulnerability assessment. The initial certification analysis tasks conclude with a vulnerability assessment to identify the residual risk. A vulnerability assessment evaluates security vulnerabilities with regard to confidentiality, integrity, availability, and accountability and recommends applicable countermeasures. It uses techniques such as static penetration, flaw hypothesis, and threat-vulnerability pairing to determine the ability to exploit the vulnerabilities.

Assess Analysis Results

At the conclusion of each development or integration milestone, the certification analysis results are reviewed for SSAA compliance. If the results indicate significant deviation from the SSAA, the NIACAP should return to Phase 1 to resolve the problems. If the risk exceeds the maximum acceptable risk, the system must return to Phase 1 for reconsideration of the IS business functions, operating environment, and IS architecture. If the results are acceptable, the NIACAP proceeds to Phase 3.

Phase 3, Validation

This phase consists of activities that culminate in the accreditation of the IS (for systems in development, this phase occurs after system integration). Phase 3 activities validate that the preceding work has produced an IS that operates in a specified computing environment with an acceptable level of residual risk.

As shown in Figure 12-3, Phase 3 activities include:

1. Continue to review and refine the SSAA
2. Perform certification evaluation of the integrated system
3. Develop recommendation to the DAA
4. Certification and accreditation decision

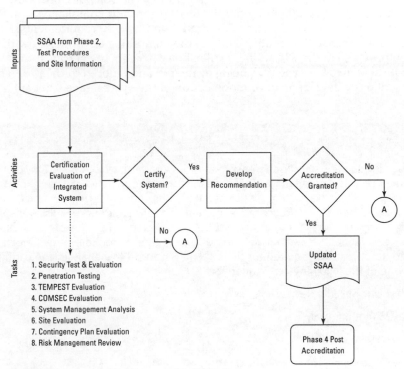

Figure 12-3: NIACAP Phase 3 — Validation.

Refine the SSAA

Phase 3 begins with a review of the SSAA to ensure that its requirements and agreements still apply. That review continues throughout Phase 3. At each stage of the validation process, details are added to the document, reflecting the current state of the system and refining the SSAA. Required changes must be submitted to the DAA, certifier, program manager, and user representative so that the revised agreement may be approved and implemented.

Certification Evaluation of the Integrated System

This activity certifies that the fully integrated and operational system complies with the requirements stated in the SSAA and that the system operates with an acceptable level of residual risk. During this activity, certification tasks are performed to ensure that the IS is functionally ready for operational deployment. The certification tasks and their extent will depend on the level of certification analysis in the SSAA.

Phase 3 certification tasks must include certification of the software, firmware, and hardware and inspections of operational sites to ensure their compliance with the physical security, procedural security, TEMPEST, and COMSEC requirements. Phase 3 includes tasks to certify the compatibility of the computing environment with the description provided in the SSAA. NIACAP flexibility permits the certification actions to be scaled to the type of IS being evaluated and tailored to the program strategy used in the development or modification of the system (see sidebar).

NIACAP Levels of Certification

NIACAP has four levels of certification to ensure that the appropriate C&A is performed for varying schedule and budget limitations. To determine the appropriate level of certification, the certifier must analyze the system's business functions; national, departmental, and agency security requirements; criticality of the system to the organizational mission; software products; computer infrastructure; types of data processed; and types of users. After analyzing this information, the certifier determines the degree of confidentiality, integrity, availability, and accountability required for the system. Based on this analysis, the certifier recommends one of the following certification levels:

✦ **Level 1** — Basic Security Review

✦ **Level 2** — Minimum Analysis

✦ **Level 3** — Detailed Analysis

✦ **Level 4** — Comprehensive Analysis The certification tasks include:

> **Security Test and Evaluation (ST&E).** Validates the correct implementation of identification and authentication, audit capabilities, access controls, object reuse, trusted recovery, and network connection rule compliance. Assesses the technical implementation of the security design, and ascertains that security software, hardware, and firmware features have been implemented as documented in the SSAA.

> **Penetration Testing.** Assesses the system's ability to withstand intentional attempts to circumvent system security features by exploiting technical security vulnerabilities. It may include internal and external penetration attempts based on common vulnerabilities for the technology being used.

> **TEMPEST and RED-BLACK Verification.** May be required to validate that the equipment and site meet TEMPEST and RED-BLACK verification security requirements.

Validation of Communication Security (COMSEC) Compliance. Validates that NSA-approved COMSEC is in use and that approved COMSEC key management procedures are used. Evaluates how well the COMSEC materials and procedures meet the requirements defined in the SSAA.

System Management Analysis. Examines the system management infrastructure to determine whether it adequately supports the maintenance of the environment, mission, and architecture described in the SSAA. It also provides an indication of the effectiveness of the security personnel.

Site Evaluation. Validates that the site operation of the information system is accomplished as documented in the SSAA. It analyzes the operational procedures for the IS, environment, personnel security, and physical security to determine whether they pose any unacceptable risks to the information being processed.

Contingency Plan Evaluation. Analyzes the contingency, back-up, and continuity of service plans to ensure the plans are consistent with the requirements identified in the SSAA. The plans should consider natural disasters, enemy actions, or malicious actions.

Risk Management Review. Assesses the operation of the system to determine whether the risk to confidentiality, integrity, availability, and accountability is being maintained at an acceptable level. This is the final review before developing the recommendation to the DAA.

Develop Recommendation to the DAA

This begins after completion of all certification tasks. Its purpose is to consolidate the findings developed during certification of the integrated system and submit the certifier's report to the DAA.

Based on the certifiers' findings, one of three activities will occur:

1. If the certifier concludes that the integrated IS satisfies the SSAA security requirements, the certifier issues a system certification statement. This certifies that the IS has complied with the documented security requirements. Supplemental recommendations also might be made to improve the system's security posture. Such recommendations should provide input to future system enhancements and change management decisions.

2. In some cases, the certifier may uncover security deficiencies but continue to believe that the short-term system operation is within the bounds of acceptable risk. The certifier may recommend an IATO, with the understanding that deficiencies will be corrected in a time period specified by the DAA.

3. If the certifier determines that the system does not satisfy the security requirements and that short-term risks place the system operation or information in jeopardy, the certifier must recommend that the IS not be accredited.

The Certification and Accreditation Decision

After receipt of the certifier's recommendation, the DAA reviews the SSAA and makes an accreditation determination. The final SSAA accreditation package includes the certifier's recommendation, the DAA authorization to operate, and supporting documentation.

If the decision is to accredit, the decision must include the security parameters under which the information system is authorized to operate. When a decision is made to accredit the system, the NIACAP begins Phase 4.

If the system does not meet the requirements stated in the SSAA but mission criticality mandates that the system become operational, an IATO may be issued. The DAA, certifier, program manager, and user representative must agree to the proposed solutions, schedule, security actions, milestones, and maximum length of time for the IATO validity.

If the decision is made to not authorize the system to operate, the NIACAP process reverts to Phase 1 and the DAA, certifier, program manager, and user representative must agree to the proposed solutions necessary to meet an acceptable level of risk. The decision must state the specific reasons for denial and, if possible, provide suggested solutions.

Phase 4, Post Accreditation

Phase 4 begins after the system has been accredited in Phase 3. This phase contains the activities required to continue to operate and manage the system, ensuring it will maintain an acceptable level of residual risk.

The primary post-accreditation activities (see Figure 12-4) include:

1. System operations and security operations
2. Maintenance of the SSAA
3. Change management
4. Compliance validation

Phase 4 continues until either:

✦ The information system is removed from service. In this case the NIACAP responsibilities of the acquisition organization shift to the system manager or a designated maintenance organization.

✦ A major change is planned for the system. In this case the NIACAP reverts to Phase 1.

✦ A periodic compliance validation is required. In this case the NIACAP also reverts to Phase 1.

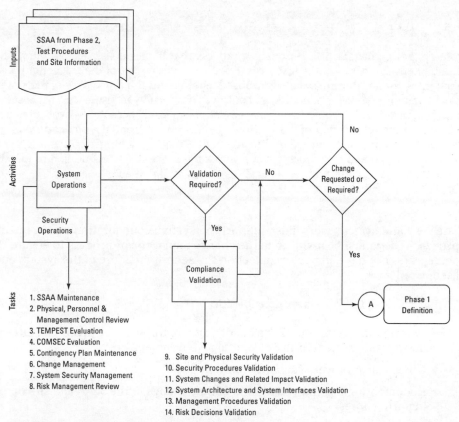

Figure 12-4: NIACAP Phase 4 — Post Accreditation.

System and Security Operations

The system operation activity concerns the secure operation of the IS and the associated computing environment. System maintenance tasks ensure that the IS continues to operate within the stated parameters of the accreditation. Site operations staff and the ISSO are responsible for maintaining an acceptable level of residual risk.

SSAA Maintenance

Phase 4 involves ongoing review of the SSAA to ensure it remains current. The user representative, DAA, certifier, and program manager must approve revisions to the SSAA. On approval, the necessary changes to the mission, environment, and architecture are documented in the SSAA.

Change Management

After an IS is approved for operation, changes to the IS must be controlled. Change management is required to maintain an acceptable level of residual risk, as changes may adversely affect the overall security posture of the infrastructure and the IS.

Secure System Management

Secure system management is an ongoing process that manages risk against the IS, the computing environment, and its resources. Effective management of the risk continuously evaluates the threats that the system is exposed to, evaluates the capabilities of the system and environment to minimize the risk, and balances the security measures against cost and system performance. Secure system management preserves an acceptable level of residual risk based on the relationship of the mission, the environment, and the architecture of the information system and its computing environment. Secure system management is a continuous review and approval process that involves the users, ISSOs, acquisition or maintenance organizations, configuration management officials, and the DAA.

The ISSO and system users must support the system configuration management process. They must be involved in the change management process to ensure that changes do not have an adverse affect on the security posture of the system and its associated IS.

During Phase 4, the ISSO is responsible for:

✦ Determining the extent that a change affects the security posture of either the information system or the computing environment

✦ Obtaining approval of security-relevant changes

✦ Documenting the implementation of that change in the SSAA and site operating procedures

✦ Forwarding changes that significantly affect the system security posture to the DAA, certifier, user representative, and program manager

Users are responsible for operating the system under the security guidelines established in the SSAA.

Compliance Validation

Compliance validation consists of a periodic review of the operational system and its computing environment occurring at predefined intervals. This ensures the continued compliance with the security requirements, current threat assessment, and concept of operations as stated and documented in the SSAA. During compliance validation the following minimum tasks should be completed:

✦ Site and Physical Security Validation

✦ Security Procedures Validation

✦ System Changes and Related Impact Validation

✦ System Architecture and System Interfaces Validation

✦ Management Procedures Validation

✦ Risk Decisions Validation

DoD Information Technology Security Certification and Accreditation Process (DITSCAP)

The Office of Assistant Secretary of Defense directed the Defense Wide Information Systems Security Program (DISSP) to create standardized requirements and processes for accreditation of computers, systems, and networks in its August 19, 1992, memorandum, "The Defense Information Systems Security Program." A security process improvement working group was formed to develop this standard process. Their task was to develop a standard C&A process that would meet the policies defined in DoD Directive 5200.28, Public Law (P. L.) 100-235 (1988), Office of Management and Budget (OMB) Circular A-130, Appendix III, Director of Central Intelligence (DCID) 1/16, and DoD Directive 5220.22.

The result, DoD Directive 5200.40 "DoD Information Technology Security Certification and Accreditation Process (DITSCAP)," established the DITSCAP as the standard C&A process for the Department of Defense. DITSCAP establishes a standard process, a set of activities, general task descriptions, and a management structure to certify and accredit the IT systems that will maintain the required security posture. This process is designed to certify that the IT system meets the accreditation requirements and that the system will maintain the accredited security posture throughout its life cycle.

The objective of the DITSCAP is to establish a DoD standard, infrastructure-centric approach that protects and secures the entities comprising the Defense Information Infrastructure (DII). The set of activities presented in the DITSCAP standardizes the C&A process for single IT entities and leads to more secure system operations and a more secure DII. The process considers the system mission, environment, and architecture while assessing the impact of operation of that system on the DII.

As shown in Figure 12-5, DITSCAP, like NIACAP, is designed to be adaptable to any type of IT system and any computing environment and mission. It may be adapted to include existing system certifications and evaluated products, use new security technology or programs, and adjust to applicable standards. The DITSCAP may be mapped to any system life-cycle process but is independent of the life-cycle strategy. The DITSCAP is designed to adjust to the development, modification, and operation of life-cycle phases.

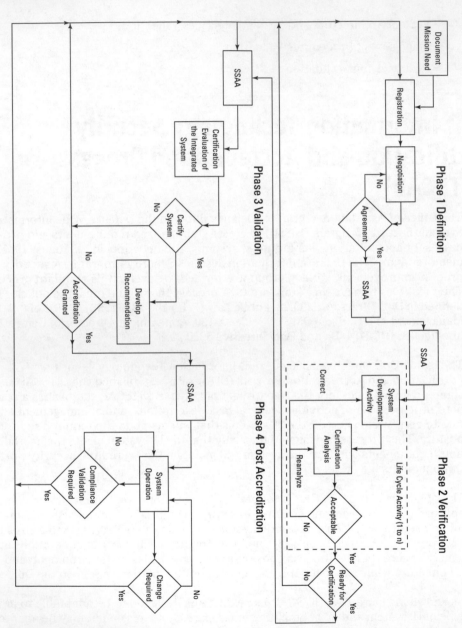

Figure 12-5: DITSCAP overview.

The primary elements of DITSCAP are that it:

✦ Implements policies, assigns responsibilities, and prescribes procedures under reference (a) for Certification and Accreditation (C&A) of information technology (IT), including automated information systems, networks, and sites in the Department of Defense.

✦ Creates the DoD IT Security Certification and Accreditation Process (DITSCAP) for security C&A of unclassified and classified IT to implement references (a) through (d).

✦ Stresses the importance of a life-cycle management approach to the C&A and reaccreditations of DoD IT.

DITSCAP applies to the Office of the Secretary of Defense (OSD), the Military Departments, the Chairman of the Joint Chiefs of Staff, the Combatant Commands, the Inspector General of the Department of Defense (IG, DoD), the Defense Agencies, and the DoD Field Activities (hereafter referred to collectively as "the DoD Components"), their contractors, and agents. It also applies to the acquisition, operation and sustainment of any DoD system that collects, stores, transmits, or processes unclassified or classified information. It applies to any IT or information system life cycle, including the development of new IT systems, the incorporation of IT systems into an infrastructure, the incorporation of IT systems outside the infrastructure, the development of prototype IT systems, the reconfiguration or upgrade of existing systems, and legacy systems.

DITSCAP Phases

The DITSCAP is composed of four phases: Definition, Verification, Validation, and Post Accreditation. These are essentially identical to those of the NIACAP:

Phase 1, Definition. Phase 1 focuses on understanding the mission, the environment, and the architecture in order to determine the security requirements and level of effort necessary to achieve accreditation.

Phase 2, Verification. Phase 2 verifies the evolving or modified system's compliance with the information agreed on in the System Security Authorization Agreement (SSAA).

Phase 3, Validation. Phase 3 validates the compliance of a fully integrated system with the information stated in the SSAA.

Phase 4, Post Accreditation. Phase 4 includes the activities that are necessary for the continuing operation of an accredited IT system in its computing environment and for addressing the changing threats that a system faces throughout its life cycle.

Because the phases function similarly to the NICAP phases, let's briefly review those phases.

DITSCAP Phase 1, Definition

Similarly to NIACAP, the DITSCAP Phase 1 starts with the input of the mission need statement (or other justification for the system) and ends by producing the SSAA.

Phase 1, shown in Figure 12-6, contains three process activities:

✦ Document mission need

✦ Registration

✦ Negotiation

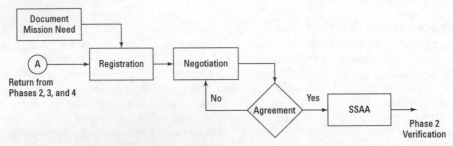

Figure 12-6: DITSCAP Phase 1 activities.

SSAA

As in the NIACAP, the product of the DITSCAP Phase 1 is the final SSAA. It should:

✦ Document the formal agreement among the DAA(s), the CA, the user representative, and the program manager

✦ Document all requirements necessary for accreditation

✦ Document all security criteria for use throughout the IT system life cycle

✦ Minimize documentation requirements by consolidating applicable information into the SSAA (security policy, concept of operations (CONOPS), plans, architecture description, and so on)

✦ Document the DITSCAP plan

DITSCAP Phase 2, Verification

The process activities of phase 2 verify the evolving system's compliance with the requirements agreed on in the SSAA. This phase consists of those process activities that occur between the signing of the initial version of the SSAA and the formal C&A of the system. As shown in Figure 12-7, Phase 2 process activities include:

✦ Continuing refinement of the SSAA

✦ System development or modification

✦ Certification analysis

✦ Analysis of the certification results

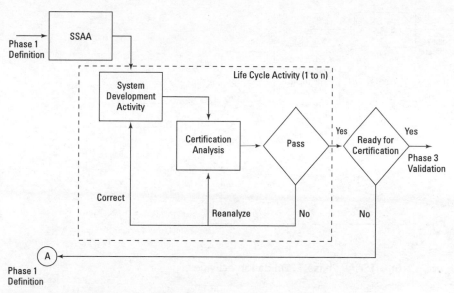

Figure 12-7: DITSCAP Life-cycle management documentation.

DITSCAP Phase 3, Validation

Phase 3 process activities, shown in Figure 12-8, validate that the preceding work has produced an information system that operates in a specified computing environment with an acceptable level of residual risk. This phase consists of process activities that occur after the system is integrated and culminates in the accreditation of the IT system. Phase 3 includes:

✦ Review of the SSAA

✦ Evaluation of the integrated IT system

✦ Certification, and accreditation

DITSCAP Phase 4, Post Accreditation

Phase 4 contains process activities necessary to continue to operate and manage the system so that it will maintain an acceptable level of residual risk (see Figure 12-9). Post-accreditation process activities include:

✦ Ongoing maintenance of the SSAA

✦ System operations

✦ Change management

✦ Compliance validation

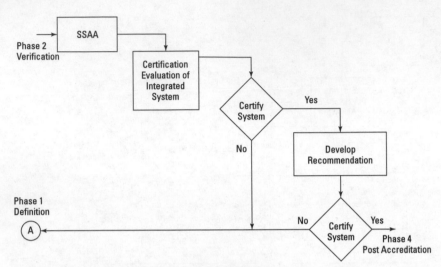

Figure 12-8: DITSCAP Phase 3, Validation activities.

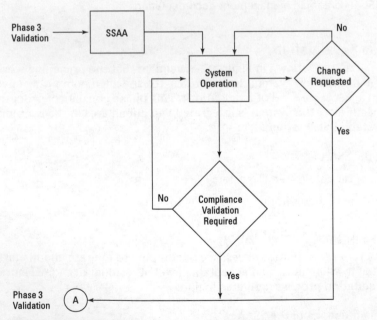

Figure 12-9: DITSCAP Phase 4, Post Accreditation.

DITSCAP Roles

The four key roles in the DITSCAP are essentially the same as in the NIACAP:

System program manager. The program manager represents the interests either of the system acquisition or maintenance organization, with engineering, scheduling, and funding responsibility; or of the system operations organization, with responsibility for daily operations, performance, and maintenance. The organization the program manager represents is usually determined by the phase in the life cycle of the system.

DAA. The DAA is usually a senior operational commander with the authority and ability to evaluate the operational needs for the system in view of the security risks. The DAA must have the authority to oversee the operations and use of systems under his/her purview. The DAA represents the interests of mission need, controls the operating environment, and defines the system level security requirements.

Certification agent (CA). The CA provides the technical expertise to conduct the certification. The CA, security teams, and so forth are the technical experts that support the C&A process.

User representative. The interests of the systems users are vested in the user representative. In the DITSCAP process, the user representative, at minimum, is concerned with system availability, access, integrity, functionality, and performance.

As with NIACAP, these individuals reach agreement during phase 1, Negotiation, and approve the SSAA. During phases 2, 3, and 4, the four key individuals return to phase 1 negotiation and subsequent revision of the SSAA if the system is changed or any of the agreements delineated in the SSAA are modified.

Other Assessment Methodologies

In addition to the NIACAP and DITSCAP methodologies, the ISSEP candidate should be aware of other C&A methodologies. The primary methodologies are the Federal Information Processing Standard (FIPS) 102, the INFOSEC assessment methodology (IAM), the Operationally Critical Threat, Asset, and Vulnerability Evaluation (OCTAVE), and the Federal Information Technology Security Assessment Framework.

Federal Information Processing Standard (FIPS) 102

Federal Information Processing Standard (FIPS) 102, the *Guideline for Computer Security Certification and Accreditation*, was published on September 27, 1983. FIPS 102 is a comprehensive guide explaining how to establish a C&A program and execute a complete C&A.

FIPS 102 details a 6-step approach:

1. Planning
2. Data collection
3. Basic evaluation
4. Detailed evaluation
5. Report of findings
6. Accreditation

FIPS 102 has four roles: the accreditor, the program manager, the certification manager and the evaluator. The roles are a little different from NIACAP, in that the NIACAP program manager is responsible for system acquisition and development, while the FIPS program manager is responsible for the defining and managing the security program within an agency. Also, both the FIPS 102 certifier and evaluator provide the independent security technical evaluation. That function is solely the responsibility of the certifier in NIACAP.

Federal Information Processing Standards are now mandatory. With the passage of the Federal Information Security Management Act (FISMA) of 2002, there is no longer a statutory provision to allow for agencies to waive mandatory Federal Information Processing Standards. The waiver provision had been included in the Computer Security Act of 1987; however, FISMA supercedes that Act. Therefore, the references to the "waiver process" contained in many FIPS are no longer relevant.

INFOSEC Assessment Methodology (IAM)

The INFOSEC Assessment Methodology (IAM) is a detailed and systematic way of examining cyber vulnerabilities that was developed by National Security Agency (NSA) Information Security (INFOSEC) assessors in conjunction with Presidential Decision Directive #63, forming the National Infrastructure Protection Center. The NSA has attempted to use the IAM to assist both INFOSEC assessment suppliers and consumers requiring assessments. The NSA has developed specialized knowledge with regard to information systems security assessments through its completion of INFOSEC assessments for its U.S. Government customers over the past fifteen years.

The IAM examines the mission, organization, security policies and programs, information systems, and the threat to these systems. The goal is to determine the vulnerabilities of information systems and recommend effective low cost countermeasures.

The IAM Process

The IAM process is a Level I assessment, a non-intrusive standardized baseline analysis of the InfoSec posture of an automated system. A Level II assessment commonly defines a more hands-on evaluation of the security systems (both Level I and Level II are considered "cooperative"). A Level III evaluation is a "red team" assessment, possibly noncooperative, and may include external penetration testing. The IAM process will also provide recommendations for the elimination or mitigation of the vulnerability.

The IAM is conducted in three phases:

1. *Pre-assessment phase* — The assessment team defines the customer's needs and begins to identify the system, its boundaries, and the criticality of the information. The team then begins to write the assessment plan. This phase normally takes about two to four weeks.

2. *On-site phase* — Explore and confirm the conclusions made during phase I, gather data and documentation, conduct interviews, and provide an initial analysis. This phase takes about one to two weeks.

3. *Post-assessment phase* — Finalize the analysis; prepare and distribute the report and recommendations. This phase can take anywhere from two to eight weeks.

The heart of the IAM is the creation of the Organizational Criticality Matrix (see Table 12-1). In this chart, all relevant automated systems are assigned impact attributes (high, medium, or low) based upon their estimated effect on Confidentiality, Integrity, and Availability and their criticality to the organization. Other elements may be added to the matrix, such as non-repudiation, or authentication, but the three basic tenets of InfoSec are required.

Table 12-1
Sample IAM Organizational Criticality Matrix

System	Confidentiality	Integrity	Availability
Criminal Records	M	H	M
Informants	H	M	M
Investigations	M	M	M
Warrants	L	H	M

Operationally Critical Threat, Asset, and Vulnerability Evaluation (OCTAVE)

Carnegie Mellon University's Software Engineering Institute (SEI) has created the Operationally Critical Threat, Asset, and Vulnerability Evaluation (OCTAVE). OCTAVE is a self-guided assessment implemented in a series of short workshops focusing on key organizational areas.

It is conducted in three phases:

1. Identify critical assets and the threats to those assets

2. Identify the vulnerabilities that expose those threats

3. Develop an appropriate protection strategy for the organization's mission and priorities

Each phase activity consists of catalogs of practices, surveys, and templates designed to capture information during focused discussions and problem-solving sessions.

Federal Information Technology Security Assessment Framework (FITSAF)

On December 8, 2000, the Chief Information Officers (CIO) Council released the first version of the Federal Information Technology Security Assessment Framework. It was prepared for its Security, Privacy, and Critical Infrastructure Committee by the National Institute of Standards and Technology (NIST), Computer Security Division Systems and Network Security Group.

The Federal Information Technology (IT) Security Assessment Framework provides a method for agency officials to determine the current status of their security programs relative to existing policy and to establish a target for improvement. The framework does not create new security requirements but provides a vehicle to consistently and effectively apply existing policy and guidance.

Also, FITSAF may be used to assess the status of security controls for a given asset or collection of assets. These assets include information, individual systems (e.g., major applications, general support systems, and mission critical systems), or a logically related grouping of systems that support operational programs, or the operational programs themselves (e.g., air traffic control, Medicare, student aid). Assessing all asset security controls and all interconnected systems that the asset depends on produces a picture of both the security condition of an agency component and of the entire agency.

FITSAF is divided into five levels (see Figure 12-10), based on SEI's Capability Maturity Model (CMM). Each level represents a more complete and effective security program:

✦ Level 1 reflects that an asset has documented a security policy.

✦ Level 2 shows that the asset has documented procedures and controls to implement the policy.

✦ Level 3 indicates that these procedures and controls have been implemented.

✦ Level 4 shows that the procedures and controls are tested and reviewed.

✦ Level 5 shows that the asset has procedures and controls fully integrated into a comprehensive program.

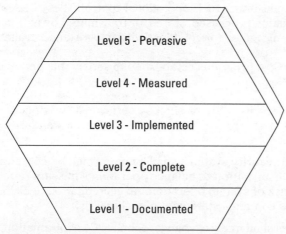

Figure 12-10: FITSAF security assessment framework levels.

The security status is measured by determining whether specific security controls are documented, implemented, tested, reviewed, and incorporated into a cyclical review/improvement program, as well as whether unacceptable risks are identified and mitigated. Agencies are expected to bring all assets to level 4 and ultimately level 5. When an individual system does not achieve level 4, agencies should determine whether that system meets the criteria found in OMB Memorandum M00-07 (February 28, 2000) "Incorporating and Funding Security in Information Systems Investments."

C&A – Government Agency Applicability

C&A is required for all federal government departments and agencies, as determined by the National Policy on Certification and Accreditation of National Security Telecommunications And Information Systems, issued April 8, 1994. The policy is intended to provide the national security community with standard methodologies for C&A processes, assign authority and responsibilities, and lay a basis for mutual recognition of certification results in order to ensure the security of national security systems. Its goals are the development of cost-effective policies, procedures, and methodologies for the certification and accreditation (C&A) of national telecommunications and information systems.

NSTISSP No. 6 determines that all federal government departments and agencies establish and implement programs mandating the certification and accreditation (C&A) of national security systems under their operational control. These C&A programs must ensure that information processed, stored, or transmitted by national security systems is adequately protected for confidentiality, integrity, and availability.

It specifically determines that C&A programs established to satisfy this policy be based on the following principles:

✦ Certification of national security systems shall be performed and documented by competent personnel in accordance with specified criteria, standards, and guidelines.

✦ Accreditation of national security systems shall be performed by competent management personnel in a position to balance operational mission requirements and the residual risk of system operation. All accreditation decisions shall be documented and contain a statement of residual risk.

✦ Departments and agencies shall freely exchange technical C&A information, coordinate programs, and participate in cooperative projects wherever possible.

✦ To promote cost-effective security across the federal government, department and agency programs for the C&A of national security systems shall be developed in concert with similar programs that address security of sensitive information pursuant to the Computer Security Act of 1987 (Public Law 100-235).

✦ As cornerstones of a continuous process of effective security management, activities in support of certification and accreditation shall be performed at appropriate points throughout the total system life cycle.

It defines responsibilities at a high level by stating that heads of U.S. Government departments and agencies shall:

✦ Ensure that C&A programs consistent with the policy and principles set forth in this NSTISSP are established and implemented.

✦ Ensure that a DAA is identified for each system under their operational control, and that DAAS have the ability to influence the application of resources to achieve an acceptable level of security.

OMB A-130

Office of Management and Budget (OMB) Circular A-130, *Management of Federal Information Resources*, Appendix III, "Security of Federal Automated Information Resources," requires accreditation for an information system to operate based on an assessment of management, operational, and technical controls. The security plan documents the security controls that are in place and are planned for future implementation.

Other C&A-related governmental policies and guidance documents are:

✦ Clinger-Cohen Act of 1996

✦ Paperwork Reduction Act of 1995

✦ Computer Security Act of 1987

✦ GAO/AIMD-12.19.6, FISCAM

✦ NIST Special Publication 800-14, GSSP

✦ OMB Memorandum 99-18 "Privacy Policies on Federal Web Sites"

✦   ✦   ✦

Assessment Questions

You can find the answers to the following questions in Appendix A.

1. Which statement is NOT true about the NIACAP SSAA?

   a. The SSAA is used throughout the entire NIACAP process.

   b. The SSAA is a formal agreement among the DAA(s), certifier, user representative, and program manager.

   c. The SSAA is used only through Phase 3, Validation.

   d. The SSAA documents the conditions of the C&A for an IS.

2. Which choice BEST describes NIACAP Phase 1, Definition?

   a. The objective of Phase 1 is to ensure the fully integrated system will be ready for certification testing.

   b. The objective of Phase 1 is to produce the required evidence to support the DAA in making an informed decision to grant approval to operate the system (accreditation or Interim Approval to Operate [IATO]).

   c. The objective of Phase 1 is to agree on the security requirements, C&A boundary, schedule, level of effort, and resources required.

   d. The objective of Phase 1 is to ensure secure system management, operation, and maintenance to preserve an acceptable level of residual risk.

3. Which choice BEST describes NIACAP Phase 3, Accreditation?

   a. The objective of Phase 3 is to ensure the fully integrated system will be ready for certification testing.

   b. The objective of Phase 3 is to agree on the security requirements, C&A boundary, schedule, level of effort, and resources required.

   c. The objective of Phase 3 is to ensure secure system management, operation, and maintenance to preserve an acceptable level of residual risk.

   d. The objective of Phase 3 is to produce the required evidence to support the DAA in making an informed decision to grant approval to operate the system (accreditation or Interim Approval to Operate [IATO]).

4. Which NIACAP role is also referred to as the accreditor?

   a. IS program manager

   b. Designated Approving Authority (DAA)

   c. Certification agent

   d. User representative

5. Which is NOT a NIACAP role?

   a. IS program manager

   b. Certifier

   c. Vendor representative

   d. User representative

6. Which is NOT a NIACAP accreditation type?

   a. Site accreditation

   b. Process accreditation

   c. Type accreditation

   d. System accreditation

7. Which statement is NOT true about the Designated Approving Authority (DAA)?

   a. The DAA determines the existing level of residual risk and makes an accreditation recommendation.

   b. The DAA is the primary government official responsible for implementing system security.

   c. The DAA is an executive with the authority and ability to balance the needs of the system with the security risks.

   d. The DAA can grant an accreditation or an Interim Approval to Operate (IATO), or may determine that the system's risks are not at an acceptable level and it is not ready to be operational.

8. Which statement is NOT true about the certification agent?

   a. The certifier provides the technical expertise to conduct the certification throughout the system's life cycle based on the security requirements documented in the SSAA.

   b. The certifier determines the acceptable level of residual risk for a system.

   c. The certifier determines whether a system is ready for certification and conducts the certification process.

   d. The certifier should be independent from the organization responsible for the system development or operation.

9. What is the task of the certifier at the completion of the certification effort?

    a. Recommends to the DAA whether or not to accredit the system based on documented residual risk.

    b. Provides details of the system and its life cycle management to the DAA.

    c. Ensures that the security requirements are integrated in a way that will result in an acceptable level of risk.

    d. Keeps all NIACAP participants informed of life cycle actions, security requirements, and documented user needs.

10. Why does NIACAP have a user representative?

    a. The user representative is an executive with the authority and ability to balance the needs of the system with the security risks.

    b. The user representative is concerned with system availability, access, integrity, functionality, performance, and confidentiality as they relate to the mission environment.

    c. The user representative determines the acceptable level of residual risk for a system.

    d. The user representative is the primary government official responsible for implementing system security.

11. Which is NOT a responsibility of the NIACAP user representative?

    a. The user representative is responsible for the secure operation of a certified and accredited IS.

    b. The user representative represents the user community.

    c. The user representative determines whether a system is ready for certification and conducts the certification process.

    d. The user representative functions as the liaison for the user community throughout the life cycle of the system.

12. Which is NOT an activity in NIACAP Phase 2?

    a. System Development and Integration

    b. Initial Certification Analysis

    c. Refine the SSAA

    d. Negotiation

13. Which statement about certification and accreditation (C&A) is NOT correct?

   a. Certification is the comprehensive evaluation of the technical and non-technical security features of an information system.

   b. C&A is optional for most federal agencies' security systems.

   c. Accreditation is the formal declaration by a DAA approving an information system to operate.

   d. C&A consists of formal methods applied to ensure that the appropriate information system security safeguards are in place and that they are functioning per the specifications.

14. Which is NOT an activity in NIACAP Phase 1?

   a. Preparation

   b. Initial Certification Analysis

   c. Registration

   d. Negotiation

15. During which NIACAP phase does the Security Test and Evaluation (ST&E) occur?

   a. Phase 1

   b. Phase 2

   c. Phase 3

   d. Phase 4

16. Which choice below BEST describes the objective of the Security Test and Evaluation (ST&E)?

   a. The objective of the ST&E is to update the SSAA to include changes made during system development and the results of the certification analysis.

   b. The objective of the ST&E is to evaluate the integration of COTS software, hardware, and firmware.

   c. The objective of the ST&E is to verify that change control and configuration management practices are in place.

   d. The objective of the ST&E is to assess the technical implementation of the security design.

17. Penetration Testing is part of which NIACAP phase?

    a. Phase 1

    b. Phase 2

    c. Phase 3

    d. Phase 4

18. The DAA accreditation decision is made at the last step of which phase?

    a. Phase 1

    b. Phase 2

    c. Phase 3

    d. Phase 4

19. If the DAA does not accredit the system, what happens?

    a. The NIACAP process reverts to Phase 1.

    b. The NIACAP process moves on to Phase 4.

    c. The NIACAP project is ended.

    d. The NIACAP stays in Phase 3 until the system is accredited.

20. What is the main purpose of the post-accreditation phase?

    a. To initiate the risk management agreement process among the four principals: the DAA, certifier, program manager, and user representative

    b. To continue to operate and manage the system so that it will maintain an acceptable level of residual risk

    c. To ensure that the SSAA properly and clearly defines the approach and level of effort

    d. To collect Information and documentation about the system, such as capabilities and functions the system will perform

21. How long does Phase 4 last?

    a. Until the initial certification analysis determines whether the IS is ready to be evaluated and tested

    b. Until the DAA reviews the SSAA and makes an accreditation determination

    c. Until the information system is removed from service, a major change is planned for the system, or a periodic compliance validation is required

    d. Until the responsible organizations adopt the SSAA and concur that those objectives have been reached

22. SSAA maintenance continues under which phase?

    a. Phase 1

    b. Phase 2

    c. Phase 3

    d. Phase 4

23. Change management is initiated under which phase?

    a. Phase 1

    b. Phase 2

    c. Phase 3

    d. Phase 4

24. How many levels of certification does NIACAP specify to ensure that the appropriate C&A is performed for varying schedule and budget limitations?

    a. Two

    b. Three

    c. Four

    d. Five

25. What happens to the SSAA after the NIACAP accreditation?

    a. The SSAA becomes the baseline security configuration document.

    b. The SSAA is discarded as the project is finished.

    c. The SSAA cannot be reviewed or changed.

    d. The ISSO can revise the SSAA independently.

26. Which policy document determines that all federal government departments and agencies establish and implement programs mandating the certification and accreditation (C&A) of national security systems under their operational control?

    a. DoD 8510.1-M, "Department of Defense Information Technology Security Certification and Accreditation Process (DITSCAP) Application Manual," July 31, 2000

    b. FIPS PUB102, "Guidelines for Computer Security Certification and Accreditation," September 27, 1983

    c. NSTISS Instruction (NSTISSI) No. 1000, "National Information Assurance Certification and Accreditation Process (NIACAP)," April 2000

    d. NSTISS Policy (NSTISSP) No. 6, "National Policy on Certification and Accreditation of National Security Telecommunications and Information Systems," 8 April 1994

27. Which assessment methodology below is a self-guided assessment implemented in a series of short workshops focusing on key organizational areas and conducted in three phases?

   a. Federal Information Technology Security Assessment Framework (FITSAF)

   b. Operationally Critical Threat, Asset, and Vulnerability Evaluation (OCTAVE)

   c. Office of Management and Budget (OMB) Circular A-130

   d. INFOSEC Assessment Methodology (IAM)

28. Which assessment methodology below is a 6-step comprehensive C&A guide?

   a. Federal Information Processing Standard (FIPS) 102

   b. Operationally Critical Threat, Asset, and Vulnerability Evaluation (OCTAVE)

   c. Federal Information Technology Security Assessment Framework (FITSAF)

   d. INFOSEC Assessment Methodology (IAM)

29. Which assessment methodology below was developed by the National Security Agency to assist both assessment suppliers and consumers?

   a. Operationally Critical Threat, Asset, and Vulnerability Evaluation (OCTAVE)

   b. Federal Information Processing Standard (FIPS) 102

   c. Federal Information Technology Security Assessment Framework (FITSAF)

   d. INFOSEC Assessment Methodology (IAM)

30. What is the order of phases in a DITSCAP assessment?

   a. Verification, Definition, Validation, and Post Accreditation

   b. Definition, Verification, Validation, and Post Accreditation

   c. Definition, Validation, Verification, and Post Accreditation

   d. Validation, Definition, Verification, and Post Accreditation

Technical Management

To meet the challenges of successful security project management, a combination of technical and management skills are required. Understanding just the technical process is not enough; the proper program management environment must also be created. Many mature methods and tools are used to ensure successful project management, and each should be implemented as early in the SDLC as possible. This chapter will examine the processes and tools the program manager uses, as well as the responsibilities of the program manager to satisfy the needs of the project.

It should be noted that Chapter 1 has a lot of material that is relevant to the ISSEP examination, particularly the section on Trade-Off Analysis. Also, the assessment questions in Chapter 1 are useful to the ISSEP candidate.

Capability Maturity Models (CMMs)

In 1986, in collaboration with Mitre Corporation, the Carnegie Mellon Software Engineering Institute (SEI) developed a methodology for measuring the maturity of software development processes. This methodology was formalized into the Capability Maturity Model (CMM) of Software. A CMM describes the stages through which processes progress as they are defined, implemented, and improved. *Process capability* is defined as the quantifiable range of expected results that can be achieved by following a process. To quote from the Systems Security Engineering Capability Maturity Model (SSE-CMM):

"The model provides a guide for selecting process improvement strategies by determining the current capabilities of specific processes and identifying the issues most critical to quality and process improvement within a particular domain. A CMM may take the form of a reference model to be used as a guide for developing and improving a mature and defined process."

The CMM has been applied to many environments as the framework for implementing process improvement. Table 13-1 contrasts the SSE-CMM with other related efforts. Note that the SSE-CMM is the only approach that is focused on information system security engineering.

Table 13-1
The SSE-CMM and Related Efforts

Effort	Goal	Approach	Scope
SSE-CMM	Define, improve, and assess security engineering capability	Continuous security engineering maturity model and appraisal method	Security engineering organizations
SE-CMM	Improve system or product engineering process	Continuous maturity model of systems-engineering practices and appraisal method	Systems engineering organizations
SEI CMM for Software	Improve the management of software development	Staged maturity model of software engineering and management practices	Software engineering organizations
Trusted CMM	Improve the process of high-integrity software development and its environment	Staged maturity model of software engineering and management practices, including security	High integrity software organizations
CMMI	Combine existing process-improvement models into a single architectural framework	Sort, combine, and arrange process-improvement building blocks to form tailored models	Engineering organizations
Systems Engineering CM (EIA731)	Define, improve, and assess systems engineering capability	Continuous systems engineering maturity model and appraisal method	Systems engineering organizations
Common Criteria	Improve security by enabling reusable protection profiles for classes of technology	Set of functional and assurance requirements for security, along with an evaluation process	Information technology
CISSP	Make security professional a recognized discipline	Security body of knowledge and certification tests for security profession	Security practitioners

Effort	Goal	Approach	Scope
Assurance Frameworks	Improve security assurance by enabling a broad range of evidence	Structured approach for creating assurance arguments and efficiently producing evidence	Security engineering organizations
ISO 9001	Improve organizational quality management	Specific requirements for quality management practices	Service organizations
ISO 15504	Software process improvement and assessment	Software process improvement model and appraisal methodology	Software engineering organizations
ISO 13335	Improvement of information technology security management	Guidance on process used to achieve and maintain appropriate levels of security for information and services	Security engineering organizations

Systems Engineering CMM (SE-CMM)

The SSE-CMM is based on the Systems Engineering CMM (SE-CMM). The 11 project and organizational PAs of the SSE-CMM come directly from the SE-CMM. These process areas are:

✦ **PA12** — Ensure Quality

✦ **PA13** — Manage Configuration

✦ **PA14** — Manage Project Risk

✦ **PA15** — Monitor and Control Technical Effort

✦ **PA16** — Plan Technical Effort

✦ **PA17** — Define Organization's Systems Engineering Process

✦ **PA18** — Improve Organization's Systems Engineering Process

✦ **PA19** — Manage Product Line Evolution

✦ **PA20** — Manage Systems Engineering Support Environment

✦ **PA21** — Provide Ongoing Skills and Knowledge

✦ **PA22** — Coordinate with Suppliers

The SE-CMM describes the essential elements of an organization's systems engineering process that must exist in order to ensure good systems engineering. It also provides a reference to compare existing systems engineering practices against the essential systems engineering elements described in the model. The definition of systems engineering on which the SE-CMM is based is defined as the selective application of scientific and engineering efforts to:

✦ Transform an operational need into a description of the system configuration that best satisfies the operational need according to the measures of effectiveness

✦ Integrate related technical parameters and ensure the compatibility of all physical, functional, and technical program interfaces in a manner that optimizes the total system definition and design

✦ Integrate the efforts of all engineering disciplines and specialties into the total engineering effort

Similarly, a system is defined as:

✦ An integrated composite of people, products, and processes that provides a capability to satisfy a need or objective

✦ An assembly of things or parts forming a complex or unitary whole; a collection of components organized to accomplish a specific function or set of functions

✦ An interacting combination of elements that are viewed in relation to function

Systems Security Engineering Capability Maturity Model (SSE-CMM)

The SSE-CMM takes a process-based approach to information systems security and is based on the SE-CMM. The methodology and metrics of the SE-CMM are duplicated in the SSE-CMM in that they provide a reference for comparing the existing best systems security engineering practices against the essential systems security engineering elements described in the model.

The SSE-CMM defines two dimensions that are used to measure the capability of an organization to perform specific activities: *domain* and *capability*. The domain dimension consists of all of the practices that collectively define security engineering. These practices are called *Base Practices* (BPs).

The capability dimension represents practices that indicate process management and institutionalization capability. These practices are called *Generic Practices* (GPs) because they apply across a wide range of domains. The GPs represent activities that should be performed as part of performing BPs. The relationship between BPs and GPs is given in Figure 13-1, illustrating the evaluation of allocating resources in order to support the BP with identifying system security vulnerabilities.

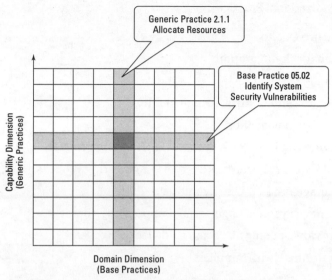

Figure 13-1: The capability and domain dimensions of the SSE-CMM.

For the domain dimension, the SSE-CMM specifies 11 security engineering *Process Areas* (PAs) and 11 organizational and project-related PAs, each of which are comprised of BPs. BPs are mandatory characteristics that must exist within an implemented security engineering process before an organization can claim satisfaction in a given PA. The 22 PAs and their corresponding BPs incorporate the best practices of systems security engineering. The 22 PAs are:

Technical Practices:

- **PA01** — Administer Security Controls
- **PA02** — Assess Impact
- **PA03** — Assess Security Risk
- **PA04** — Assess Threat
- **PA05** — Assess Vulnerability
- **PA06** — Build Assurance Argument
- **PA07** — Coordinate Security
- **PA08** — Monitor Security Posture
- **PA09** — Provide Security Input
- **PA10** — Specify Security Needs
- **PA11** — Verify and Validate Security

Project and Organizational Practices:

- **PA12** — Ensure Quality
- **PA13** — Manage Configuration
- **PA14** — Manage Project Risk
- **PA15** — Monitor and Control Technical Effort
- **PA16** — Plan Technical Effort
- **PA17** — Define Organization's Systems Engineering Process
- **PA18** — Improve Organization's Systems Engineering Process
- **PA19** — Manage Product Line Evolution
- **PA20** — Manage Systems Engineering Support Environment
- **PA21** — Provide Ongoing Skills and Knowledge
- **PA22** — Coordinate with Suppliers

The GPs are ordered in degrees of maturity and are grouped to form and distinguish among five levels of security engineering maturity.

The five levels are:

1. *Level 1, "Performed Informally"* — Focuses on whether an organization or project performs a process that incorporates the BPs. A statement characterizing this level would be, "You have to do it before you can manage it." The attributes of this level simply require that the BPs are performed.

2. *Level 2, "Planned and Tracked"* — Focuses on project-level definition, planning, and performance issues. A statement characterizing this level would be, "Understand what's happening with the project before defining organization-wide processes." The attributes of this level are:

    - **2.1** — Planning Performance
    - **2.2** — Disciplined Performance
    - **2.3** — Verifying Performance
    - **2.4** — Tracking Performance

3. *Level 3, "Well Defined"* — Focuses on disciplined tailoring from defined processes at the organization level. A statement characterizing this level would be, "Use the best of what you've learned from your projects to create organization-wide processes." The attributes of this level are:

    - **3.1** — Defining a Standard Process
    - **3.2** — Perform the Defined Process
    - **3.3** — Coordinate the Process

4. *Level 4, "Quantitatively Controlled"* — Focuses on measurements being tied to the business goals of the organization. Although it is essential to begin collecting and using basic project measures early, the measurement and use of data is not expected organization-wide until the higher levels have been achieved. Statements characterizing this level would be, "You can't measure it until you know what 'it' is" and "Managing with measurement is only meaningful when you're measuring the right things." The attributes of this level are:

- **4.1** — Establishing Measurable Quality Goals
- **4.2** — Objectively Managing Performance

5. *Level 5, "Continuously Improving"* — Gains leverage from all of the management practice improvements seen in the earlier levels, then emphasizes the cultural shifts that will sustain the gains made. A statement characterizing this level would be, "A culture of continuous improvement requires a foundation of sound management practice, defined processes, and measurable goals." The attributes of this level are:

- **5.1** — Improving Organizational Capability
- **5.2** — Improving Process Effectiveness

Let's look at the 22 Process Areas from the SSE-CMM v2.0 in more detail.

SSE-CMM Technical PAs

The first 11 PAs are the technical practice process areas.

PA01 Administer Security Controls

The goal of this process area and the related best practices are:

- ✦ **Goal 1** — Security controls are properly configured and used.
- ✦ **BP.01.01** — Establish responsibilities and accountability for security controls and communicate them to everyone in the organization.
- ✦ **BP.01.02** — Manage the configuration of system security controls.
- ✦ **BP.01.03** — Manage security awareness, training, and education programs for all users and administrators.
- ✦ **BP.01.04** — Manage periodic maintenance and administration of security services and control mechanisms.

PA02 Assess Impact

The goal of this process area and the related best practices are:

- ✦ **Goal 1** — The security impacts of risks to the system are identified and characterized.
- ✦ **BP.02.01** — Identify, analyze, and prioritize operational, business, or mission capabilities leveraged by the system.

✦ **BP.02.02**—Identify and characterize the system assets that support the key operational capabilities or the security objectives of the system.

✦ **BP.02.03**—Select the impact metric to be used for this assessment.

✦ **BP.02.04**—Identify the relationship between the selected metrics for this assessment and metric conversion factors if required.

✦ **BP.02.05**—Identify and characterize impacts.

✦ **BP.02.06**—Monitor ongoing changes in the impacts.

PA03 Assess Security Risk

The goals of this process area and the related best practices are:

✦ **Goal 1**—An understanding of the security risk associated with operating the system within a defined environment is achieved.

✦ **Goal 2**—Risks are prioritized according to a defined methodology.

✦ **BP.03.01**—Select the methods, techniques, and criteria by which security risks for the system in a defined environment are analyzed, assessed, and compared.

✦ **BP.03.02**—Identify threat/vulnerability/impact triples (exposures).

✦ **BP.03.03**—Assess the risk associated with the occurrence of an exposure.

✦ **BP.03.04**—Assess the total uncertainty associated with the risk for the exposure.

✦ **BP.03.05**—Order the risks by priority.

✦ **BP.03.06**—Monitor ongoing changes in the risk spectrum and changes to their characteristics.

PA04 Assess Threat

The goal of this process area and the related best practices are:

✦ **Goal 1**—Threats to the security of the system are identified and characterized.

✦ **BP.04.01**—Identify applicable threats arising from a natural source.

✦ **BP.04.02**—Identify applicable threats arising from man-made sources, either accidental or deliberate.

✦ **BP.04.03**—Identify appropriate units of measure, and applicable ranges, in a specified environment.

✦ **BP.04.04**—Assess capability and motivation of threat agent for threats arising from manmade sources.

✦ **BP.04.05**—Assess the likelihood of an occurrence of a threat event.

✦ **BP.04.06**—Monitor ongoing changes in the threat spectrum and changes to their characteristics.

PA05 Assess Vulnerability

The goal of this process area and the related best practices are:

✦ **Goal 1** — An understanding of system security vulnerabilities within a defined environment is achieved.

✦ **BP.05.01** — Select the methods, techniques, and criteria by which security system vulnerabilities in a defined environment are identified and characterized.

✦ **BP.05.02** — Identify system security vulnerabilities.

✦ **BP.05.03** — Gather data related to the properties of the vulnerabilities.

✦ **BP.05.04** — Assess the system vulnerability and aggregate vulnerabilities that result from specific vulnerabilities and combinations of specific vulnerabilities.

✦ **BP.05.05** — Monitor changes in applicable vulnerabilities and to their characteristics.

PA06 Build Assurance Agreement

The goal of this process area and the related best practices are:

✦ **Goal 1** — The work products and processes clearly provide the evidence that the customer's security needs have been met.

✦ **BP.06.01** — Identify the security assurance objectives.

✦ **BP.06.02** — Define a security assurance strategy to address all assurance objectives.

✦ **BP.06.03** — Identify and control security assurance evidence.

✦ **BP.06.04** — Perform analysis of security assurance evidence.

✦ **BP.06.05** — Provide a security assurance argument that demonstrates the customer's security needs are met.

PA07 Coordinate Security

The goals of this process area and the related best practices are:

✦ **Goal 1** — All members of the project team are aware of and involved with security engineering activities to the extent necessary to perform their functions.

✦ **Goal 2** — Decisions and recommendations related to security are communicated and coordinated.

✦ **BP.07.01** — Define security engineering coordination objectives and relationships.

✦ **BP.07.02** — Identify coordination mechanisms for security engineering.

✦ **BP.07.03** — Facilitate security engineering coordination.

✦ **BP.07.04** — Use the identified mechanisms to coordinate decisions and recommendations related to security.

PA08 Monitor Security Posture

The goals of this process area and the related best practices are:

✦ **Goal 1** — Both internal and external security-related events are detected and tracked.

✦ **Goal 2** — Incidents are responded to in accordance with policy.

✦ **Goal 3** — Changes to the operational security posture are identified and handled in accordance with the security objectives.

✦ **BP.08.01** — Analyze event records to determine the cause of an event, how it proceeded, and likely future events.

✦ **BP.08.02** — Monitor changes in threats, vulnerabilities, impacts, risks, and environments.

✦ **BP.08.03** — Identify security-relevant incidents.

✦ **BP.08.04** — Monitor the performance and functional effectiveness of security safeguards.

✦ **BP.08.05** — Review the security posture of the system to identify necessary changes.

✦ **BP.08.06** — Manage the response to security-relevant incidents.

✦ **BP.08.07** — Ensure that the artifacts related to security monitoring are suitably protected.

PA09 Provide Security Input

The goals of this process area and the related best practices are:

✦ **Goal 1** — All system issues are reviewed for security implications and are resolved in accordance with security goals.

✦ **Goal 2** — All members of the project team have an understanding of security so they can perform their functions.

✦ **Goal 3** — The solution reflects the security input provided.

✦ **BP.09.01** — Work with designers, developers, and users to ensure that appropriate parties have a common understanding of security input needs.

✦ **BP.09.02** — Determine the security constraints and considerations needed to make informed engineering choices.

✦ **BP.09.03** — Identify alternative solutions to security-related engineering problems.

✦ **BP.09.04** — Analyze and prioritize engineering alternatives using security constraints and considerations.

✦ **BP.09.05** — Provide security-related guidance to the other engineering groups.

✦ **BP.09.06** — Provide security-related guidance to operational system users and administrators.

PA10 Specific Security Needs

The goal of this process area and the related best practices are:

✦ **Goal 1** — A common understanding of security needs is reached between all parties, including the customer.

✦ **BP.10.01** — Gain an understanding of the customer's security needs.

✦ **BP.10.02** — Identify the laws, policies, standards, external influences, and constraints that govern the system.

✦ **BP.10.03** — Identify the purpose of the system in order to determine the security context.

✦ **BP.10.04** — Capture a high-level security-oriented view of the system operation.

✦ **BP.10.05** — Capture high-level goals that define the security of the system.

✦ **BP.10.06** — Define a consistent set of statements that define the protection to be implemented in the system.

✦ **BP.10.07** — Obtain agreement that the specified security meets the customer's needs.

PA11 Verify and Validate Security

The goals of this process area and the related best practices are:

✦ **Goal 1** — Solutions meet security requirements.

✦ **Goal 2** — Solutions meet the customer's operational security needs.

✦ **BP.11.01** — Identify the solution to be verified and validated.

✦ **BP.11.02** — Define the approach and level of rigor for verifying and validating each solution.

✦ **BP.11.03** — Verify that the solution implements the requirements associated with the previous level of abstraction.

✦ **BP.11.04** — Validate the solution by showing that it satisfies the needs associated with the previous level of abstraction, ultimately meeting the customer's operational security needs.

✦ **BP.11.05** — Capture the verification and validation results for the other engineering groups.

SSE-CMM Project and Organizational PAs

The project and organizational PA category groups together those PAs that are primarily concerned with improving project and organizational capability.

PA12 Ensure Quality

The goals of this process area and the related best practices are:

- ✦ **Goal 1** — Process quality is defined and measured.
- ✦ **Goal 2** — Expected work product quality is achieved.
- ✦ **BP.12.01** — Monitor conformance to the defined process.
- ✦ **BP.12.02** — Measure work product quality.
- ✦ **BP.12.03** — Measure quality of the process.
- ✦ **BP.12.04** — Analyze quality measurements.
- ✦ **BP.12.05** — Obtain participation.
- ✦ **BP.12.06** — Initiate quality improvement activities.
- ✦ **BP.12.07** — Detect need for corrective actions.

PA13 Manage Configurations

The goal of this process area and the related best practices are:

- ✦ **Goal 1** — Control over work product configurations is maintained.
- ✦ **BP.13.01** — Establish configuration management methodology.
- ✦ **BP.13.02** — Identify configuration units.
- ✦ **BP.13.03** — Maintain work product baselines.
- ✦ **BP.13.04** — Control changes.
- ✦ **BP.13.05** — Communicate configuration status.

PA14 Manage Project Risk

The goal of this process area and the related best practices are:

- ✦ **Goal 1** — Risks to the program are identified, understood, and mitigated.
- ✦ **BP.14.01** — Develop a risk-management approach.
- ✦ **BP.14.02** — Identify risks.
- ✦ **BP.14.03** — Assess risks.
- ✦ **BP.14.04** — Review your risk assessment.
- ✦ **BP.14.05** — Execute risk mitigation.
- ✦ **BP.14.06** — Track risk mitigation.

PA15 Monitor and Control Technical Effort
The goal of this process area and the related best practices are:

✦ **Goal 1** — The technical effort is monitored and controlled.

✦ **BP.15.01** — Direct the technical effort.

✦ **BP.15.02** — Track project resources.

✦ **BP.15.03** — Track technical parameters.

✦ **BP.15.04** — Review project performance.

✦ **BP.15.05** — Analyze project issues.

✦ **BP.15.06** — Take corrective action.

PA17 Define Organization's Security Engineering Process
The goal of this process area and the related best practices are:

✦ **Goal 1** — A standard systems engineering process is defined for the organization.

✦ **BP.17.01** — Establish process goals.

✦ **BP.17.02** — Collect process assets.

✦ **BP.17.03** — Develop the organization's security engineering process.

✦ **BP.17.04** — Define tailoring guidelines.

PA21 Provide Ongoing Skills and Knowledge
The goal of this process area and the related best practices are:

✦ **Goal 1** — The organization has the skills necessary to achieve project and organizational objectives.

✦ **BP.21.01** — Identify training needs.

✦ **BP.21.02** — Select mode of knowledge or skill acquisition.

✦ **BP.21.03** — Assure availability of skill and knowledge.

✦ **BP.21.04** — Prepare training materials.

✦ **BP.21.05** — Train personnel.

✦ **BP.21.06** — Assess training effectiveness.

✦ **BP.21.07** — Maintain training records.

✦ **BP.21.08** — Maintain training materials.

PA22 Coordinate with Suppliers

The goal of this process area and the related best practices are:

✦ **Goal 1** — Effective suppliers are selected and used.

✦ **BP.22.01** — Identify systems components or services.

✦ **BP.22.02** — Identify competent suppliers or vendors.

✦ **BP.22.03** — Choose suppliers or vendors.

✦ **BP.22.04** — Provide expectations.

✦ **BP.22.05** — Maintain communications.

The IDEAL Model

In addition to the SSE-CMM, the ISSEP candidate should be aware of the Carnegie Mellon Software Engineering Institute's *IDEAL* model. (IDEAL stands for Initiating, Diagnosing, Establishing, Acting, and Learning.) Security engineering process improvement is a fundamental component of managing and maintaining the security program.

Process Improvement

The basic premise of process improvement is that the quality of services produced is a direct function of the quality of the associated development and maintenance processes.

Knowledge of the basic principles of process change is required to implement a successful security engineering process improvement activity. The principles are:

✦ Major changes must be sponsored by senior management.

✦ Focus on fixing the process, not assigning blame.

✦ Understand the current process first.

✦ Change is continuous.

✦ Improvement requires investment.

✦ Retaining improvement requires periodic reinforcement.

The goal is to establish a continuous cycle of evaluating the current status of your organization, making improvements, and repeating this cycle.

The IDEAL model is shown in Table 13-2.

Phase	Description	Activity
	Table 13-2	
	The IDEAL Model	
I	Initiating	Laying the groundwork for a successful improvement effort
D	Diagnosing	Determining where you are relative to where you want to be
E	Establishing	Planning the specifics of how you will reach your destination
A	Acting	Doing the work according to the plan
L	Learning	Learning from the experience and improving your ability

Each of the five phases of the IDEAL approach is made up of several activities.

The Initiating Phase

Embarking upon a security engineering process improvement effort should be handled in the same manner in which all new projects within an organization are approached. One must become familiar with the project's objectives and the means for their accomplishment, develop a business case for the implementation, gain the approval and confidence of management, and develop a method for the project's implementation.

Effective and continuous support of the effort throughout its lifetime is essential for successful process improvement. Sponsorship involves not only making available the financial resources necessary to continue the process but also requires personal attention from management to the project.

After the relationship between the proposed effort and business goals has been established and key sponsors have given their commitment, a mechanism for the project's implementation must be established.

The Diagnosing Phase

In order to perform process development/improvement activities, it is imperative that an understanding of the organization's current and desired future state of process maturity be established. These parameters form the basis of the organization's process improvement action plan.

Performing a gap analysis emphasizes the differences between the current and desired states of the organization's processes and reveals additional information or findings about the organization. Grouped according to area of interest, these findings form the basis of the recommendations for how to improve the organization.

The Establishing Phase

In this phase, a detailed plan of action based on the goals of the effort and the recommendations made during the diagnosing phase is developed. In addition, the plan must take into consideration any possible constraints, such as resource limitations, which might limit the scope of the improvement effort. Priorities, along with specific outputs and responsibilities, are also put forth in the plan.

Time constraints, available resources, organizational priorities, and other factors might not allow for all of the goals to be realized or recommendations implemented during a single instance of the process improvement life cycle. Therefore, the organization must establish priorities for its improvement effort.

As a result of established priorities and the organization characterization defined in the diagnosing phase, the scope of the process improvement effort might be different from that developed in the initiating phase. The develop-approach step requires that the redefined objectives and recommendations be mapped to potential strategies for accomplishing the desired outcomes.

At this point, all of the data, approaches, recommendations, and priorities are brought together in the form of a detailed action plan. Included in the plan are the allocation of responsibilities, resources, and specific tasks; tracking tools to be used; and established deadlines and milestones. The plan should also include contingency plans and coping strategies for any unforeseen problems.

The Acting Phase

This phase is the implementation phase and requires the greatest level of effort of all the phases both in terms of resources and time. Achieving the goals of the organization might require multiple parallel cycles within the acting phase in order to address all of the desired improvements and priorities.

Solutions, or improvement steps, for each problem area are developed based on available information on the issue and on the resources for implementation. At this stage, the solutions are the best-guess efforts of a technical working group.

The first step in designing processes that will meet the business needs of an enterprise is to understand the business, product, and organizational context that will be present when the process is being implemented. Some questions that need to be answered before process design include the following:

✦ How is security engineering practiced within the organization?

✦ What life cycle will be used as a framework for this process?

✦ How is the organization structured to support projects?

✦ How are support functions handled (for example, by the project or by the organization)?

✦ What are the management and practitioner roles used in this organization?

✦ How critical are these processes to organizational success?

Because first attempts at generating solutions rarely succeed, all solutions must be tested before they are implemented across an organization. How an organization chooses to test its solutions is dependent upon the nature of the area of interest, the proposed solution, and the resources of the organization.

Using information collected during testing, potential solutions should be modified to reflect new knowledge about the solution. The importance of the processes under focus as well as the complexity of the proposed improvements will dictate the degree of testing and refinement proposed solutions must undergo before being considered acceptable for implementation throughout the organization.

Once a proposed improved process has been accepted, it must be implemented beyond the test group. Depending upon the nature and degree to which a process is being improved, the implementation stage might require significant time and resources. Implementation can occur in a variety of ways, depending upon the organization's goals.

The Learning Phase

The learning phase is both the final stage of the initial process improvement cycle and the initial phase of the next process improvement effort. Here the entire process improvement effort is evaluated in terms of goal realization and how future improvements can be instituted more efficiently. This phase is only as constructive as the detail of records kept throughout the process and the ability of participants to make recommendations.

Determining the success of process improvement requires analyzing the final results in light of the established goals and objectives. It also requires evaluating the efficiency of the effort and determining where further enhancements to the process are required. These lessons learned are then collected, summarized, and documented.

Based on the analysis of the improvement effort itself, the lessons learned are translated into recommendations for improving subsequent efforts. These recommendations should be promulgated outside those guiding the improvement effort for incorporation in this and other efforts.

Planning and Managing the Technical Effort

The key to the successful implementation of any security engineering effort is early planning. Planning for security system engineering activities is initiated with the definition of program requirements and the development of a Program Management Plan (PMP). This leads to the identification of system security engineering requirements and the preparation of a detailed Systems Engineering Management Plan (SEMP).

Program Manager Responsibilities

The program manager is the lead for all activities involving cost, schedule, and performance responsibilities. For example, the program manager's function in the DITSCAP is to ensure security requirements are integrated into the IT architecture in a way that will result in an acceptable level of risk to the operational infrastructure. As we saw in Chapter 12, the DITSCAP PM works directly with the development integration, maintenance, configuration management, quality assurance, test verification, and validation organizations. The PM drafts or supports the drafting of the SSAA and coordinates security requirements with the DAA, the CA, and the user representative. The PM continuously keeps all DITSCAP participants informed of acquisition and development action, security requirements, and user needs. Figure 13-2 shows the PM security management relationship in the DITSCAP.

Figure 13-2: DITSCAP program manager security management relationships.

Program Management Plan (PMP)

Usually there is one overall planning document for every program or project, which covers all requirements at a high level and leads to a variety of lower-level plans that address specific areas of activity. Although the specific nomenclature may vary from one program to the next, the title Program Management Plan (PMP) is most often selected to represent this high-level plan. Two major components of the PMP are the Systems Engineering Management Plan (SEMP) and the Work Breakdown Structure (WBS).

Systems Engineering Management Plan (SEMP)

All of the key participants in the system development process must know not only their own responsibilities but also how to interface with one another. This interaction of responsibilities and authority within the project must be defined and controlled, and it is accomplished through the preparation and dissemination of a System Engineering Management Plan (SEMP). An important function of the SEMP is to ensure that all of the participants know their responsibilities to one another.

The SEMP also serves as a reference for the procedures that are to be followed in carrying out the numerous systems security engineering tasks. Often the contractor is required to prepare a SEMP as part of the concept definition effort. The place of the SEMP in the program management plan is shown in Figure 13-3.

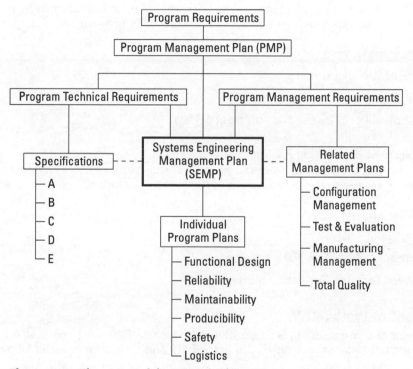

Figure 13-3: Placement of the SEMP in the program management plan.
(Source: A. Kossiakoff and W. N. Sweet, Systems Engineering: Principles and Practice, Wiley Publishing, Inc., 2003. Used by permission.)

The SEMP is intended to be a dynamic document. It starts as an outline and is updated as the security system development process goes on. The SEMP covers all management functions associated with the performance of security systems engineering activities for a given program. The responsibility for the SEMP must be clearly defined and supported by the program manager.

SEMP Elements

The SEMP contains detailed statements of how the systems security engineering functions are to be carried out during development. Two major elements of the SEMP are:

✦ Development program planning and control

✦ Security systems engineering process

Development Program Planning and Control

Development program planning and control describes the tasks that must be implemented to manage the development phase of the security program, including:

✦ Statement Of Work (SOW)

✦ Organizational Structure

✦ Scheduling and Cost Estimation

✦ Technical Performance Measurement (TPM)

Security Systems Engineering Process

Security systems engineering process describes the security systems engineering process as it applies to the development of the system, including:

✦ Operational Requirements

✦ Functional Analysis

✦ System Analysis And Trade-Off Strategy

✦ System Test And Evaluation Strategy

Statement of Work (SOW)

The Statement of Work (SOW) is a narrative description of the work required for a given project. It is commonly described in the PMP and should include the following:

✦ Summary statement of the tasks to be accomplished.

✦ Identification of the input requirements from other tasks, including tasks accomplished by the customer and supplier.

✦ References to applicable specifications, standards, procedures, and related documentation.

✦ Description of specific results to be achieved and a proposed schedule of delivery.

Work Breakdown Structure (WBS)

After the generation of the SOW and the identification of the organizational structure, one of the initial steps in program planning is the development of the Work Breakdown Structure (WBS). The WBS is a tree that leads to the identification of the activities, functions, tasks, and subtasks that must be completed.

The WSB is an important technique to ensure that all essential tasks are properly defined, assigned, scheduled, and controlled. It contains a hierarchical structure of the tasks to be accomplished during the project. The WBS may be a contractual requirement in competitive bid system developments.

The WSB structure generally includes three levels of activity:

+ *Level 1*—Identifies the entire program scope of work to be produced and delivered. Level 1 may be used as the basis for the authorization of the program work.

+ *Level 2*—Identifies the various projects, or categories of activity, that must be completed in response to program requirements. Program budgets are usually prepared at this level.

+ *Level 3*—Identifies the activities, functions, major tasks, and/or components of the system that are directly subordinate to the Level 2 items. Program schedules are generally prepared at this level.

The WBS provides many benefits, such as:

+ Provides for the reporting of system technical performance measures (TPMs)

+ The entire security system can be easily defined by the breakdown of its elements into discrete work packages

+ Aids in linking objectives and activities with available resources

+ Facilitates budgeting and cost reporting

+ Responsibility assignments can be readily identified through the assignment of tasks

+ Provides a greater probability that every activity will be accounted for

WBS Components

The use of the WBS as a project-organizing framework generally begins in the concept exploration phase. Later, in the concept definition phase, the WBS is defined in detail as the basis for organizing, costing, and scheduling. The WBS format follows a hierarchical structure designed to ensure a slot for every significant task and activity.

In the example below, the entire security system project is at Level 1 in the hierarchy, and the five components represent the Level 2 categories.

1.1 *Security System Product*—The effort required to develop, produce, and integrate the security system.

1.2 *Security System Support*—The equipment, facilities, and services necessary for the development and operation of the system product.

1.3 *Security System Testing*—Testing begins after the design of the individual components has been validated via component tests. A very significant fraction of the total test effort is usually allocated to system level testing

1.4 *Project Management*—All activities associated with project planning and control, including all management of the WBS, costing, scheduling, performance measurement, project reviews, reports, and associated activities.

1.5 *Security Systems Engineering*—The actions of the security systems engineering staff in guiding the engineering of the system through all its conceptual and engineering phases.

Each of the Level 2 categories will have deeper, associated Level 3, Level 4, and possibly Level 5 categories as each component is further broken down. These lower level categories represent the breakdown of each component into definable products of development, the lowest level defining each step of the component's design, development, and testing. This is vital for establishing cost allocation and controls. The WBS should be structured so that every task is identified at the appropriate place within the WBS hierarchy.

Cost Control and Estimating

Cost control starts with the initial development of cost estimates for the program and continues with the functions of cost monitoring, the collection of cost data, the analysis of the data, and the immediate initiation of corrective action. Cost control requires good overall cost management, including:

✦ Cost estimating

✦ Cost accounting

✦ Cost monitoring

✦ Cost analysis and reporting

✦ Control functions

The cost control process is typically performed in this order:

1. Define the elements of work, as extracted from the SOW

2. Integrate the tasks defined in the WBS

3. Develop the estimated costs for each task

4. Develop a functional cost data collection and reporting capability

5. Develop a procedure for evaluation and quick corrective action

Critical Path Method (CPM)

Critical path analysis is an essential project management tool that traces each major element of the system back through the engineering of its constituent parts. Estimates are made up not only of the size, but also of the duration of effort required for each step. The particular path that is estimated to require the longest time to complete is called the *critical path*. The differences between this time and the times required for other paths are called "slack" for those paths.

For more information about the cost control process, please see Appendix E, "The Cost Analysis Process."

Outsourcing

Outsourcing refers to the identification of, selection of, and contracting with one or more outside suppliers for the procurement and acquisition of materials and services for a given system. The term *suppliers* is defined here as a broad class of external organizations that provide products, components, materials, and/or services to a producer or prime contractor.

The prime activities of the outsourcing process are:

1. Identification of potential suppliers

2. Development of a request for proposal (RFP)

3. Review and evaluation of supplier proposals

4. Selection of suppliers and contract negotiation

5. Supplier monitoring and control

System Design Testing

An important step in the security systems development process is the development of a well-designed test plan for determining whether the security system design is stable. A well-planned test program often requires the following five steps:

1. *Planning* — The test approach must be planned properly to uncover potential design deficiencies and acquire sufficient test data to identify areas needing correction. This includes the activities:

   • Development of a test plan

   • Development of test procedures

   • Development of a test analysis plan

2. *Development or acquisition of test equipment and facilities* — The process in the creation of test equipment and test facilities includes:

   • *Creating the Test Environment* — The design and construction of the test environment and the acquisition of equipment for the realistic generation of all of the input functions and the measurement of the resulting outputs.

   • *Test Software* — The acquisition of the software to be used for testing, tailored to the system at hand.

   • *Test Equipment Validation* — The test equipment itself must be validated to ensure that it is sufficiently accurate and reliable.

3. *Demonstration and validation testing* — The actual conduct of the test to demonstrate and validate the security system design. This is often the most critical period in the development of a new system.

4. *Analysis and evaluation of test results* — The outputs from the component under examination and the results of the test must then be analyzed to disclose all significant discrepancies, in order to identify their source and assess whether correction is required.

5. *Correction of Design Deficiencies* — The final step is a prioritized effort to quickly correct identified design deficiencies.

Test and Evaluation Master Plan (TEMP)

The methods and techniques to be used for measuring and evaluating the system to ensure compliance with security system design requirements must be described early in the SDLC. Individual tests to be performed at each level of the WBS are defined in a series of separate test plans and procedures.

An overall description of test objectives and content and a listing of the individual test to be performed should also be set forth in an integrated test planning and management document, the Test and Evaluation Management Plan (TEMP). The TEMP is developed during the later stages of system design. In DoD parlance, this is parallel to the Security Test and Evaluation (ST&E) plan described in Chapter 12.

Test Analysis Planning

The planning of how the test results are to be analyzed is just as important as planning how the tests are to be conducted. The following steps should be taken:

✦ Determine what data must be collected

✦ Consider the methods by which these data can be obtained; examples include special laboratory tests, simulations, subsystems test, or full-scale systems tests.

✦ Define how all data will be processed, analyzed, and presented.

Initial test planning is included in the TEMP, which commonly consists of:

✦ Requirements for testing and evaluation

✦ Categories of tests

✦ Procedures for accomplishing testing

✦ Resources required

✦ Associated planning information, such as tasks, schedules, organizational responsibilities, and costs

Other methods used to determine compliance with the initial specification of security system design requirements may entail using simulations and related analytical methods, using an engineering model for test and evaluation purposes, testing a production model, evaluating an operational configuration in the consumer's environment, or some combination of these methods.

In the Defense sector, a TEMP is required for most large programs and includes the planning and implementation of procedures for the Development Test and Evaluation (DT&E) and the Operational Test and Evaluation (OT&E). The DT&E basically equates to the Analytical, Type 1, and Type 2 testing (see "Testing and Evaluation Categories" below), and the OT&E is equivalent to Type 3 and Type 4 testing.

Testing and Evaluation Categories

Testing and evaluation processes often involve several stages of testing categories or phases, such as:

1. *Analytical*—Design evaluations conducted early in the system life cycle using computerized techniques such as CAD, CAM, CALS, simulation, rapid prototyping, and other related approaches.

2. *Type 1 testing*—The evaluation of system components in the laboratory using bench test models and service test models, designed to verify performance and physical characteristics.

3. *Type 2 testing*—Testing performed during the latter stages of the detail design and development phase when preproduction prototype equipment and software are available.

4. *Type 3 testing*—Tests conducted after initial system qualification and prior to the completion of the production or construction phase. This is the first time that all elements of the system are operated and evaluated on an integrated basis.

5. *Type 4 testing*—Testing conducted during the system operational use and life cycle support phase, intended to provide further knowledge of the system in the user environment.

Figure 13-4 shows a common security system test and evaluation corrective-action loop.

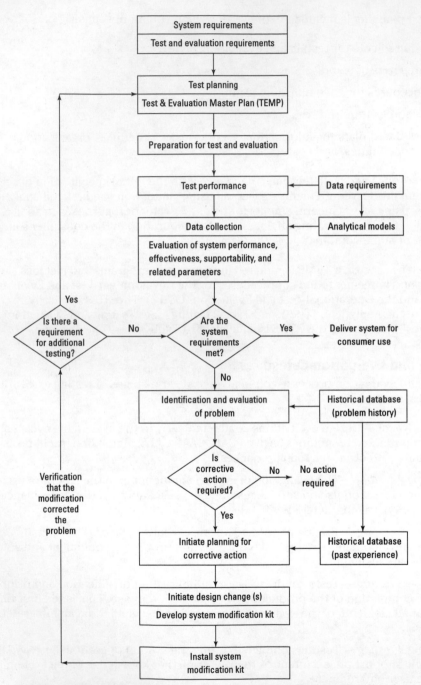

Figure 13-4: Security system test and evaluation corrective-action loop.
(Source: B. Blanchard, Systems Engineering Management, Third Edition, Wiley Publishing, Inc., 2004. Used by permission.)

Testing Resource Trade-Offs

Although the ideal testing configuration would be a replica of the entire system and its environment, such a configuration would be too costly in terms of resources. A more practical solution would be to incorporate the elements to be tested into a prototype subsystem, simulating of the rest of the system and utilizing the relevant part of the operating environment. The choice of a specific test configuration requires a complex balancing of risks, costs, and contingency plans, requiring a high level of judgment.

Technical Performance Measurement (TPM)

As the security system development effort progresses, periodic reviews will need to be conducted. Within the systems specification should be the identification and prioritization of Technical Performance Measurements (TPMs). Checklists may be utilized to aid in the evaluation process, identifying those characteristics that have been incorporated into and directly support the TPM objectives. Design parameters and the applicable TPMs will be measured and tracked.

✦   ✦   ✦

Assessment Questions

You can find the answers to the following questions in Appendix A.

1. Which statement about the SSE-CMM is incorrect?

    a. The SSE-CMM defines two dimensions that are used to measure the capability of an organization to perform specific activities.

    b. The domain dimension consists of all of the practices that collectively define security engineering.

    c. The domain dimension represents practices that indicate process management and institutionalization capability.

    d. The capability dimension represents practices that indicate process management and institutionalization capability.

2. Which description of the SSE-CMM Level 5 Generic Practice is correct?

    a. Planned and Tracked

    b. Continuously Improving

    c. Quantitatively Controlled

    d. Performed Informally

3. Which statement about testing and evaluation is NOT true?

    a. A TEMP is required for most large programs.

    b. A DT&E is equivalent to Analytical, Type 1, and Type 2 testing.

    c. A OT&E is equivalent to Type 5 and Type 6 testing.

    d. A OT&E is equivalent to Type 3 and Type 4 testing.

4. Which attribute about the Level 1 SSE-CMM Generic Practice is correct?

    a. Performed Informally

    b. Planned and Tracked

    c. Well Defined

    d. Continuously Improving

5. Which choice below is NOT a true statement about good cost control?

    a. Cost control starts with the initiation of corrective action.

    b. Cost control requires good overall cost management.

    c. Cost control requires immediate initiation of corrective action.

    d. Cost control starts with the initial development of cost estimates for the program.

6. Which statement about the SE-CMM is NOT correct?

   a. The SE-CMM describes the essential elements of an organization's systems engineering process that must exist in order to ensure good systems engineering.

   b. The SE-CMM provides a reference to compare existing systems engineering practices against the essential systems engineering elements described in the model.

   c. The SE-CMM goal is to improve the system- or product-engineering process.

   d. The SE-CMM was created to define, improve, and assess security-engineering capability.

7. Which statement about system security testing and evaluation (ST&E) categories is correct?

   a. Type 1 testing is performed during the latter stages of the detail design and development phase.

   b. Type 2 testing is design evaluation conducted early in the system life cycle.

   c. Type 3 testing is performed during the latter stages of the detail design and development phase.

   d. Type 4 testing is conducted during the system operational use and life cycle support phase.

8. Which choice is NOT an activity in the cost control process?

   a. Identifying potential suppliers

   b. Developing a functional cost data collection capability

   c. Developing the costs as estimated for each task

   d. Creating a procedure for cost evaluation

9. Which choice does NOT describe a common outsourcing activity?

   a. Review of proposals

   b. Develop a functional cost reporting capability

   c. Contract negotiation

   d. Development of an RFP

10. Which choice is NOT an accurate description of an activity level of the WBS?

    a. Level 1 may be used as the basis for the authorization of the program work.

    b. Program budgets are usually prepared at level 1.

    c. Level 2 identifies the various projects that must be completed.

    d. Program schedules are generally prepared at level 3.

11. Which choice below is NOT a phase in the IDEAL model?

    a. Authorizing

    b. Learning

    c. Diagnosing

    d. Establishing

12. Which choice below best describes systems engineering, as defined in the SSE-CMM?

    a. An integrated composite of people, products, and processes that provides a capability to satisfy a need or objective.

    b. The selective application of scientific and engineering efforts to integrate the efforts of all engineering disciplines and specialties into the total engineering effort

    c. A narrative description of the work required for a given project.

    d. The contracting with one or more outside suppliers for the procurement and acquisition of materials and services.

13. Which choice below is NOT a benefit of the WBS?

    a. The WBS facilitates the initial allocation of budgets.

    b. The WBS facilitates the collection and reporting of costs.

    c. The system can easily be described through the logical breakout of its elements into work packages.

    d. The WBS integrates the efforts of all engineering disciplines and specialties into the total engineering effort.

14. Which choice is NOT an element of the Statement of Work (SOW)?

    a. An identification of the input requirements from other tasks

    b. A description of specific results to be achieved

    c. Management of security awareness, training, and education programs

    d. A proposed schedule for delivery of the product

15. Which statement below best describes the difference between a Type 1 testing and evaluation category and a Type 2 category?

    a. Type 1 testing is the evaluation of system components in the laboratory, designed to verify performance and physical characteristics.

    b. Type 2 testing is the evaluation of system components in the laboratory, designed to verify performance and physical characteristics.

    c. Type 1 testing establishes design evaluations conducted early in the system life cycle.

    d. Type 2 testing is conducted after initial system qualification and prior to the completion of the production or construction phase.

16. Which choice has the outsourcing activities listed in their proper order?

    a. Review and evaluation of supplier proposals, supplier monitoring and control, development of a Request For Proposal (RFP), and selection of suppliers.

    b. Development of a Request For Proposal (RFP), review and evaluation of supplier proposals, supplier monitoring and control, and selection of suppliers.

    c. Development of a Request For Proposal (RFP), review and evaluation of supplier proposals, selection of suppliers, and supplier monitoring and control.

    d. Review and evaluation of supplier proposals, selection of suppliers, development of a Request For Proposal (RFP), and supplier monitoring and control.

17. Which answer BEST describes a Statement of Work (SOW)?

    a. A narrative description of the work required for a given project.

    b. An integrated composite of people, products, and processes that provides a capability to satisfy a need or objective.

    c. The contracting with one or more outside suppliers for the procurement and acquisition of materials and services.

    d. The development of a functional cost reporting capability.

18. Which statement about SSE-CMM Base Practices is correct?

    a. BPs are mandatory characteristics that must exist within an implemented security engineering process before an organization can claim satisfaction in a given PA.

    b. BPs are ordered in degrees of maturity and are grouped to form and distinguish among five levels of security engineering maturity.

    c. BPs are ordered in degrees of maturity and are grouped to form and distinguish among 22 levels of security engineering maturity.

    d. BPs are optional characteristics that must exist within an implemented security engineering process before an organization can claim satisfaction in a given PA.

19. As per the SE-CMM, which statement defining a system is incorrect?

    a. An interacting combination of elements that are viewed in relation to function

    b. A continuous cycle of evaluating the current status of an organization, making improvements, and repeating the cycle

    c. An assembly of things or parts forming a complex or unitary whole

    d. An integrated composite of people, products, and processes that provides a capability to satisfy a need or objective

20. Which choice below best describes the purpose of the Learning phase of the IDEAL model?

    a. The Learning phase is the implementation phase and requires the greatest level of effort of all the phases both in terms of resources and time.

    b. The Learning phase is both the final stage of the initial process improvement cycle and the initial phase of the next process improvement effort.

    c. In the Learning phase, it is imperative that an understanding of the organization's current and desired future state of process maturity be established.

    d. In the Learning phase, a detailed plan of action based on the goals of the effort and the recommendations developed during the Diagnosing phase is developed.

21. Which statement about the System Engineering Management Plan (SEMP) is NOT true?

    a. Development program planning and control is a SEMP element.

    b. The goal of SEMP is to establish a continuous cycle of evaluating the current status of the organization.

    c. The SEMP contains detailed statements of how the systems security engineering functions are to be carried out during development.

    d. The security systems engineering process is a SEMP element.

22. Which choice has the correct order of activities in the IDEAL model?

    a. Learning, Initiating, Diagnosing, Establishing, and Acting

    b. Initiating, Learning, Diagnosing, Establishing, and Acting

    c. Learning, Diagnosing, Initiating, Establishing, and Acting

    d. Initiating, Diagnosing, Establishing, Acting, and Learning

23. Which choice is an incorrect statement regarding the Systems Engineering Management Plan (SEMP)?

    a. The SEMP covers all management functions associated with the performance of security systems engineering activities for a given program.

    b. It starts as an outline and is updated as the security system development process goes on.

    c. It contains detailed statements of how the systems security engineering functions are to be carried out during development.

    d. The SEMP is a static document, intended to remain unchanged.

24. Which choice best describes an outsourced supplier?

    a. A broad class of external organizations that provide products, components, materials, and/or services to a producer or prime contractor.

    b. An interacting combination of elements that are viewed in relation to function.

    c. An integrated composite of people, products, and processes that provides a capability to satisfy a need or objective.

    d. Practices that indicate process management and institutionalization capability.

25. Which statement below best describes the main premise of process improvement?

    a. Major changes must be sponsored by senior management.

    b. The quality of services produced is a direct function of the quality of the associated development and maintenance processes.

    c. Focus on fixing the process, not assigning blame.

    d. All suppliers must be security vetted prior to contracting.

26. What is the main purpose of the Work Breakdown Structure (WBS)?

    a. It creates a hierarchical tree of work packages.

    b. It may be a contractual requirement in competitive bid system developments.

    c. It ensures the authorization for the program work.

    d. It ensures that all essential tasks are properly defined, assigned, scheduled, and controlled.

27. Which choice is not an activity in the Development Program Planning and Control element of the SEMP?

   a. System Test and Evaluation Strategy

   b. Scheduling and Cost Estimation

   c. Technical Performance Measurement

   d. Statement of Work

28. At what point in the project is the Work Breakdown Structure (WBS) usually created?

   a. After the generation of the SOW and the identification of the organizational structure

   b. After the development of a functional cost data collection and reporting capability

   c. After the costs for each task are estimated

   d. After the development of an RFP but before the identification of the organizational structure

29. Which choice accurately lists the five levels of security engineering maturity as defined by the SSE-CMM?

   a. Planned and Tracked, Well Defined, Performed Informally, Quantitatively Controlled, and Continuously Improving

   b. Planned and Tracked, Performed Informally, Well Defined, Quantitatively Controlled, and Continuously Improving

   c. Performed Informally, Planned and Tracked, Well Defined, Quantitatively Controlled, and Continuously Improving

   d. Performed Informally, Planned and Tracked, Quantitatively Controlled, Well Defined, and Continuously Improving

30. Which choice has the correct order of activities in the security system design testing process?

   a. Acquisition, Testing, Analysis, Planning, and Correction

   b. Acquisition, Planning, Testing, Analysis, and Correction

   c. Planning, Analysis, Testing, Acquisition, and Correction

   d. Planning, Acquisition, Testing, Analysis, and Correction

U.S. Government Information Assurance (IA) Regulations

Specific Requirements of the ISSEP Candidate

The U.S. Government Information Assurance Regulations domain of the ISSEP concentration is designed to enable the candidate to identify, understand, and apply the practices as defined by the U.S. Government IA regulations and policies.

Common U.S. Government Information Assurance Terminology

A large amount of U.S. government assurance terminology has, necessarily, been defined and used in the material preceding this chapter. Therefore, it is not necessary to repeat those definitions in this section. However, the definitions of a number of important terms as they are used in the context of U.S. government information assurance will be presented in this section to ensure that the candidate is familiar with them. Also, National Security Telecommunications and Information Systems Security Instruction (NSTISSI) Publication No. 4009, "National Information Systems Security (INFOSEC) Glossary," September, 2000, Appendix F provides a comprehensive list of U.S. government IA terms.

Important Government IA Definitions

The following definitions, taken from NIST Special Publication 800-12, "An Introduction to Computer Security: The NIST Handbook," October 1995, are fundamental to the understanding of U.S. government IA material.

1. *Management controls* — Techniques and concerns that are normally addressed by management in the organization's computer security program.

2. *Operational controls* — Security controls that are usually implemented by people instead of systems.

3. *Technical controls* — Security controls that the computer system executes.

4. *Computer security* — The protection afforded to an automated information system in order to attain the applicable objectives of preserving the integrity, availability and confidentiality of information system resources (includes hardware, software, firmware, information/data, and telecommunications).

5. *Integrity* — In lay usage, information has integrity when it is timely, accurate, complete, and consistent. However, computers are unable to provide or protect all of these qualities. Therefore, in the computer security field, integrity is often discussed more narrowly as having two facets: *data integrity* and *system integrity*. As defined in National Research Council, *Computers at Risk*, National Academy Press, Washington, D.C., 1991, p. 54: "Data integrity is a requirement that information and programs are changed only in a specified and authorized manner." System integrity is defined in National Computer Security Center, Publication NCSC-TG-004-88 as a requirement that a system "performs its intended function in an unimpaired manner, free from deliberate or inadvertent unauthorized manipulation of the system."

6. *Availability* — *Computers at Risk*, p. 54, defines availability as a "requirement intended to assure that systems work promptly and service is not denied to authorized users."

7. *Confidentiality* — A requirement that private or confidential information not be disclosed to unauthorized individuals.

The additional definitions that follow are selectively taken from the (NSTISSI) Publication No. 4009, Glossary. They are listed to provide the candidate with knowledge of terminology that is used in government IA publications. This list gives the definitions of fundamental concepts that are important to the ISSEP certification:

8. *Assurance* — Measure of confidence that the security features, practices, procedures, and architecture of an IS accurately mediates and enforces the security policy.

9. *Authentication* — Security measure designed to establish the validity of a transmission, message, or originator, or a means of verifying an individual's authorization to receive specific categories of information.

10. *Binding*—Process of associating a specific communications terminal with a specific cryptographic key or associating two related elements of information.

11. *BLACK*—Designation applied to information systems and to associated areas, circuits, components, and equipment, in which national security information is encrypted or is not processed.

12. *CCI Assembly*—Device embodying a cryptographic logic or other COMSEC design that NSA has approved as a Controlled Cryptographic Item (CCI). It performs the entire COMSEC function, but depends upon the host equipment to operate.

13. *CCI Component*—Part of a Controlled Cryptographic Item (CCI) that does not perform the entire COMSEC function but depends upon the host equipment, or assembly, to complete and operate the COMSEC function.

14. *Certification Authority Workstation (CAW)*—Commercial-off-the-shelf (COTS) workstation with a trusted operating system and special purpose application software that is used to issue certificates.

15. *Certification Package*—Product of the certification effort documenting the detailed results of the certification activities.

16. *Certification Test and Evaluation (CT&E)*—Software and hardware security tests conducted during development of an IS.

17. *Certified TEMPEST Technical Authority (CTTA)*—An experienced, technically qualified U.S. Government employee who has met established certification requirements in accordance with CNSS (NSTISSC)-approved criteria and has been appointed by a U.S. Government Department or Agency to fulfill CTTA responsibilities.

18. *Ciphony*—Process of enciphering audio information, resulting in encrypted speech.

19. *Classified information*—Information that has been determined pursuant to Executive Order 12958 or any predecessor Order, or by the Atomic Energy Act of 1954, as amended, to require protection against unauthorized disclosure and is marked to indicate its classified status.

20. *Clearance*—Formal security determination by an authorized adjudicative office that an individual is authorized access, on a need to know basis, to a specific level of collateral classified information (TOP SECRET, SECRET, or CONFIDENTIAL).

21. *Commercial COMSEC Evaluation Program (CCEP)*—Relationship between NSA and industry in which NSA provides the COMSEC expertise (i.e., standards, algorithms, evaluations, and guidance) and industry provides design, development, and production capabilities to produce a type 1 or type 2 product. Products developed under the CCEP may include modules, subsystems, equipment, systems, and ancillary devices.

22. *Compartmentalization* — A nonhierarchical grouping of sensitive information used to control access to data more finely than with hierarchical security classification alone.

23. *Compartmented mode* — Mode of operation wherein each user with direct or indirect access to a system, its peripherals, remote terminals, or remote hosts has all of the following: (a) valid security clearance for the most restricted information processed in the system; (b) formal access approval and signed nondisclosure agreements for that information which a user is to have access; and (c) valid need-to-know for information which a user is to have access.

24. *COMSEC boundary* — Definable perimeter encompassing all hardware, firmware, and software components performing critical COMSEC functions, such as key generation and key handling and storage.

25. *Concept of Operations (CONOP)* — Document detailing the method, act, process, or effect of using an IS.

26. *Controlled Cryptographic Item (CCI)* — Secure telecommunications or information-handling equipment, or associated cryptographic component, that is unclassified but governed by a special set of control requirements. Such items are marked "CONTROLLED CRYPTOGRAPHIC ITEM" or, where space is limited, "CCI."

27. *Crypto-ignition key (CIK)* — Device or electronic key used to unlock the secure mode of crypto-equipment.

28. *Dangling threat* — Set of properties about the external environment for which there is no corresponding vulnerability and therefore no implied risk.

29. *Dangling vulnerability* — Set of properties about the internal environment for which there is no corresponding threat and, therefore, no implied risk.

30. *Enclave* — Collection of computing environments connected by one or more internal networks under the control of a single authority and security policy, including personnel and physical security.

31. *Enclave boundary* — Point at which an enclave's internal network service layer connects to an external network's service layer, i.e., to another enclave or to a Wide Area Network (WAN).

32. *Endorsed for Unclassified Cryptographic Item (EUCI)* — Unclassified cryptographic equipment that embodies a U.S. Government classified cryptographic logic and is endorsed by NSA for the protection of national security information. See type 2 product.

33. *Evaluated Products List (EPL)* — Equipment, hardware, software, and/or firmware evaluated by the National Computer Security Center (NCSC) in accordance with DoD TCSEC and found to be technically compliant at a particular level of trust. The EPL is included in the NSA *Information Systems Security Products and Services Catalogue*.

34. *Evaluation Assurance Level (EAL)* — Set of assurance requirements that represents a point on the Common Criteria predefined assurance scale.

35. *Global Information Infrastructure (GII)* — Worldwide interconnections of the information systems of all countries, international and multinational organizations, and international commercial communications.

36. *High Assurance Guard (HAG)* — Device comprised of both hardware and software that is designed to enforce security rules during the transmission of X.400 message and X.500 directory traffic between enclaves of different classification levels (e.g., UNCLASSIFIED and SECRET).

37. *IA architecture* — Framework that assigns and portrays IA roles and behavior among all IT assets and prescribes rules for interaction and interconnection.

38. *Information assurance (IA)* — Measures that protect and defend information and information systems by ensuring their availability, integrity, authentication, confidentiality, and non-repudiation. These measures include providing for restoration of information systems by incorporating protection, detection, and reaction capabilities.

39. *Information systems security (INFOSEC)* — Protection of information systems against unauthorized access to or modification of information, whether in storage, processing, or transit, and against the denial of service to authorized users, including those measures necessary to detect, document, and counter such threats.

40. *Information Systems Security Engineering (ISSE)* — Process that captures and refines information protection requirements and ensures their integration into IT acquisition processes through purposeful security design or configuration.

41. *Key-auto-key (KAK)* — Cryptographic logic using previous key to produce a key.

42. *Multilevel mode* — INFOSEC mode of operation wherein all the following statements are satisfied concerning the users who have direct or indirect access to the system, its peripherals, remote terminals, or remote hosts: a) some users do not have a valid security clearance for all the information processed in the IS; b) all users have the proper security clearance and appropriate formal access approval for that information to which they have access; and c) all users have a valid need-to-know only for information to which they have access.

43. *Multilevel security (MLS)* — Concept of processing information with different classifications and categories that simultaneously permits access by users with different security clearances and denies access to users who lack authorization.

44. *National Information Assurance Partnership (NIAP)* — Joint initiative between NSA and NIST responsible for security testing needs of both IT consumers and producers and promoting the development of technically sound security requirements for IT products and systems and appropriate measures for evaluating those products and systems.

45. *National Information Infrastructure (NII)* — Nationwide interconnection of communications networks, computers, databases, and consumer electronics that make a vast amount of information available to users. It includes both public and private networks, the Internet, the public switched network, and cable, wireless, and satellite communications.

46. *National security information (NSI)* — Information that has been determined, pursuant to Executive Order 12958 or any predecessor order, to require protection against unauthorized disclosure.

47. *No-lone zone* — Area, room, or space that, when staffed, must be occupied by two or more appropriately cleared individuals who remain within sight of each other.

48. *Operations security (OPSEC)* — Systematic and proven process by which potential adversaries can be denied information about capabilities and intentions by identifying, controlling, and protecting generally unclassified evidence of the planning and execution of sensitive activities. The process involves five steps: identification of critical information, analysis of threats, analysis of vulnerabilities, assessment of risks, and application of appropriate countermeasures.

49. *Partitioned security mode* — IS security mode of operation wherein all personnel have the clearance, but not necessarily formal access approval and need-to-know, for all information handled by an IS.

50. *Policy Approving Authority (PAA)* — First level of the PKI Certification Management Authority that approves the security policy of each PCA.

51. *Policy Certification Authority (PCA)* — Second level of the PKI Certification Management Authority that formulates the security policy under which it and its subordinate CAs will issue public key certificates.

52. *QUADRANT* — Short name referring to technology that provides tamper-resistant protection to crypto-equipment.

53. *RED* — Designation applied to an IS and associated areas, circuits, components, and equipment in which unencrypted national security information is being processed.

54. *RED/BLACK concept* — Separation of electrical and electronic circuits, components, equipment, and systems that handle national security information (RED) in electrical form, from those that handle non-national security information (BLACK) in the same form.

55. *Red team* — Independent and focused threat-based effort by an interdisciplinary, simulated adversary to expose and exploit vulnerabilities as a means to improve the security posture of ISs.

56. *RED signal* — Any electronic emission (e.g., plain text, key, key stream, subkey stream, initial fill, or control signal) that would divulge national security information if recovered.

57. *Risk management* — Process of identifying and applying countermeasures commensurate with the value of the assets protected, based on a risk assessment.

58. *Security fault analysis (SFA)* — Assessment, usually performed on IS hardware, to determine the security properties of a device when a hardware fault is encountered.

59. *Security test and evaluation (ST&E)* — Examination and analysis of the safeguards required to protect an IS, as they have been applied in an operational environment, to determine the security posture of that system.

60. *Sensitive Compartmented Information (SCI)* — Classified information concerning or derived from intelligence sources, methods, or analytical processes, which is required to be handled within formal access control systems established by the Director of Central Intelligence.

61. *Sensitive Compartmented Information Facility (SCIF)* — An accredited area, room, or group of rooms, buildings, or installation where SCI may be stored, used, discussed, and/or processed.

62. *Special Access Program (SAP)* — Program established for a specific class of classified information that imposes safeguarding and access requirements that exceed those normally required for information at the same classified level.

63. *Superencryption* — Process of encrypting encrypted information. Occurs when a message, encrypted off-line, is transmitted over a secured, on-line circuit, or when information encrypted by the originator is multiplexed onto a communications trunk, which is then bulk encrypted.

64. *System high* — Highest security level supported by an IS.

65. *System high mode* — IS security mode of operation wherein each user, with direct or indirect access to the IS, its peripherals, remote terminals, or remote hosts, has all of the following: a) valid security clearance for all information within an IS; b) formal access approval and signed nondisclosure agreements for all the information stored and/or processed (including all compartments, subcompartments, and/or special access programs); and c) a valid need-to-know for some of the information contained within the IS.

66. *TEMPEST* — Short name referring to investigation, study, and control of compromising emanations from IS equipment.

67. *TEMPEST zone* — Designated area within a facility where equipment with appropriate TEMPEST characteristics (TEMPEST zone assignment) may be operated.

68. *Tranquility* — Property whereby the security level of an object cannot change while the object is being processed by an IS.

69. *Type 1 product* — Classified or controlled cryptographic item endorsed by the NSA for securing classified and sensitive U.S. Government information, when appropriately keyed. The term refers only to products and not to information, keys, services, or controls. Type 1 products contain approved NSA algorithms. They are available to U.S. Government users, their contractors, and federally sponsored non-U.S. Government activities subject to export restrictions in accordance with International Traffic in Arms Regulation.

70. *Type 2 product* — Unclassified cryptographic equipment, assembly, or component, endorsed by the NSA, for use in national security systems as defined in Title 40 U.S.C. Section 1452.

U.S. National Policies

In the U.S., the Committee on National Security Systems (CNSS) was assigned the responsibility to set national policy for national security systems. CNSS is the result of Executive Order (E.O.) 13231, "Critical Infrastructure Protection in the Information Age," that was issued on October 16, 2001. E.O. 13231 renamed the National Security Telecommunications and Information Systems Security Committee (NSTISSC) as CNSS. CNSS is a standing committee of the President's Critical Infrastructure Board and is chaired by the U.S. DoD.

E.O. 13231directed the following actions:

✦ Protection of information systems for critical infrastructure

✦ Protection of emergency preparedness communications

✦ Protection of supporting physical assets

The E.O. also assigned the following responsibilities to the U.S. Secretary of Defense and the Director of Central Intelligence regarding the security of systems with national security information:

✦ Developing government-wide policies

✦ Overseeing the implementation of government-wide policies, procedures, standards, and guidelines

National security systems are categorized as systems with one or more of the following characteristics:

✦ Contain classified information

✦ Involved with the command and control of military forces

✦ Employ cryptographic activities related to national security

✦ Support intelligence actives

✦ Associated with equipment that is an integral part of weapon or weapons system(s)

✦ Critical to the direct fulfillment of military or intelligence missions but not including routine administrative and business applications

The responsibilities of the CNSS for national security systems outlined in E.O. 13231 include:

✦ Providing a forum for the discussion of policy issues

✦ Setting national policy

✦ Through the CNSS Issuance System, providing operational procedures, direction, and guidance

An index of CNSS Issuances can be found at www.nstissc.gov/Assets/pdf/index.pdf

Agency Policies

In response to the events of September 11, 2001, the U.S. Congress enacted the E-Government Act of 2002 (Public Law 107-347). Title III of the E-Government Act, the Federal Information Security Management Act (FISMA), was written to:

1. "Provide a comprehensive framework for ensuring the effectiveness of information security controls over information resources that support Federal operations and assets

2. Recognize the highly networked nature of the current Federal computing environment and provide effective government-wide management and oversight of the related information security risks, including coordination of information security efforts throughout the civilian, national security, and law enforcement communities

3. Provide for development and maintenance of minimum controls required to protect Federal information and information systems

4. Provide a mechanism for improved oversight of Federal agency information security programs"

Under FISMA, the Director of the Office of Management and Budget has the responsibility of overseeing the security polices and practices of U.S. government agencies. The OMB is charged with:

1. Developing and overseeing the implementation of information security policies

2. Requiring agencies to identify and provide information security protections commensurate with the risk and magnitude of the harm resulting from the unauthorized access, use, disclosure, disruption, modification, or destruction of information or information systems used by or on behalf of an agency (including systems operated by agency contractors)

3. Coordinating the development of standards and guidelines between NIST and the NSA and other agencies with responsibility for national security systems

Standards associated with the national defense establishment remain the responsibility of the DoD and NSA.

NIST Special Publication 800-37, "Guide for the Security Certification and Accreditation of Federal Information Systems," Second Public Draft, June 2003, summarizes the tasks under FISMA that each government agency must perform "to develop, document, and implement an agency-wide information security program." FISMA specifies that the program must include:

1. Periodic assessments of risk, including the magnitude of harm that could result from the unauthorized access, use, disclosure, disruption, modification, or destruction of information and information systems that support the operations and assets of the agency

2. Policies and procedures that are based on risk assessments, cost-effectively reduce information security risks to an acceptable level, and ensure that

information security is addressed throughout the life cycle of each agency information system

3. Subordinate plans for providing adequate information security for networks, facilities, information systems, or groups of information systems, as appropriate

4. Security awareness training to inform personnel (including contractors and other users of information systems that support the operations and assets of the agency) of the information security risks associated with their activities and their responsibilities in complying with agency policies and procedures designed to reduce these risks

5. Periodic testing and evaluation of the effectiveness of information security policies, procedures, practices, and controls to be performed with a frequency depending on risk, but no less than annually

6. A process for planning, implementing, evaluating, and documenting remedial action to address any deficiencies in the information security policies, procedures, and practices of the agency

7. Procedures for detecting, reporting, and responding to security incidents

8. Plans and procedures to ensure continuity of operations for information systems that support the operations and assets of the agency

Standards

FISMA also charged NIST with responsibilities for standards and guidelines. FIPS Publication 199, "Standards for Security Categorization of Federal Information and Information Systems," NIST Pre-Publication Final Draft, December, 2003, summarizes the FISMA standards charter to NIST to develop the following:

1. "Standards to be used by all Federal agencies to categorize all information and information systems collected or maintained by or on behalf of each agency based on the objectives of providing appropriate levels of information security according to a range of risk levels

2. Guidelines recommending the types of information and information systems to be included in each category

3. Minimum information security requirements (i.e., management, operational, and technical controls)"

FIPS Publication 199 accomplishes task 1 in the above list, namely to develop standards for categorizing information and information systems. FIPS PUB 199 cites the following reasons for developing the categorizing standards:

"To provide a common framework and understanding for expressing security that, for the Federal government promotes: (i) effective management and oversight of information security programs, including the coordination of information security efforts throughout the civilian, national security, emergency preparedness, homeland security, and law enforcement communities; and (ii) consistent reporting to the Office of Management and Budget (OMB) and Congress on the adequacy and effectiveness of information security policies, procedures, and practices. Subsequent NIST standards and guidelines will address the second and third tasks cited."

FIPS PUB 199 lists the following areas where the standards shall apply:

✦ "All information within the Federal government other than that in-formation that has been determined pursuant to Executive Order 12958, as amended by Executive Order 13292, or any predecessor order, or by the Atomic Energy Act of 1954, as amended, to require protection against unauthorized disclosure and is marked to indicate its classified status

✦ All Federal information systems other than those information systems designated as national security systems as defined in 44 United States Code Section 3542(b)(2). Agency officials shall use the security categorizations described in FIPS Publication 199 whenever there is a Federal requirement to provide such a categorization of information or information systems."

Prior to discussing the security categories, levels of impact of a threat realized on an information system have to be defined. FIPS Pub 199 lists the three levels of potential impact on organizations or individuals based on the information security objectives of confidentiality, integrity, and availability. The impacts are summarized in Table 14-1, taken from FIPS Pub 199.

A security category can, thus, be defined as function of the potential impact on information or information systems should a threat successfully exploit a vulnerability in the system. A security category can apply to information types and information systems.

The general formula developed in FIPS Pub 199 for defining a security category (SC) of an *information type* is:

$$SC_{\text{information type}} = \{(\text{confidentiality}, \textit{impact}), (\text{integrity}, \textit{impact}), (\text{availability}, \textit{impact})\},$$

where the acceptable values for potential impact are low, moderate, high, or not applicable.

For example, if the human resources department of an organization determines that there is a high potential impact from a loss of confidentiality, a high potential impact from a loss of integrity, and a moderate potential impact from a loss of availability, the security category, SC, of this information type would be:

$$SC_{\text{administrative information}} = \{(\text{confidentiality}, \text{HIGH}), (\text{integrity}, \text{HIGH}), (\text{availability}, \text{MODERATE})\}.$$

Table 14-1
Impact Definitions for Security Objectives

Security Objective	Potential Impact		
	Low	Moderate	High
Confidentiality Preserving authorized restrictions on information access and disclosure, including means for protecting personal privacy and proprietary information. *[44 U.S.C., SEC. 3542]*	The unauthorized disclosure of information could be expected to have a **limited** adverse effect on organizational operations, organizational assets, or individuals.	The unauthorized disclosure of information could be expected to have a **serious** adverse effect on organizational operations, organizational assets, or individuals.	The unauthorized disclosure of information could be expected to have a **severe or catastrophic** adverse effect on organizational operations, organizational assets, or individuals.
Integrity Guarding against improper information modification or destruction, and includes ensuring information non-repudiation and authenticity. *[44 U.S.C., SEC. 3542]*	The unauthorized modification or destruction of information could be expected to have a **limited** adverse effect on organizational operations, organizational assets, or individuals.	The unauthorized modification or destruction of information could be expected to have a **serious** adverse effect on organizational operations, organizational assets, or individuals.	The unauthorized modification or destruction of information could be expected to have a **severe or catastrophic** adverse effect on organizational operations, organizational assets, or individuals.
Availability Ensuring timely and reliable access to and use of information. *[44 U.S.C., SEC. 3542]*	The disruption of access to or use of information or an information system could be expected to have a **limited** adverse effect on organizational operations, organizational assets, or individuals.	The disruption of access to or use of information or an information system could be expected to have a **serious** adverse effect on organizational operations, organizational assets, or individuals.	The disruption of access to or use of information or an information system could be expected to have a **severe or catastrophic** adverse effect on organizational operations, organizational assets, or individuals.

For information systems, the corresponding formula is:

$SC_{\text{information system}}$ = {(confidentiality, *impact*), (integrity, *impact*), (availability, *impact*)},

where the acceptable values for potential impact are LOW, MODERATE, or HIGH. A value on NOT APPLICABLE cannot be applied to an impact level of an information system. To develop a category for an information system, the potential impact values assigned to the security objectives of confidential, integrity, and availability must be the maximum (worst case) values assigned among the security categories that have been assigned to the different types of information residing on the system.

As an example, suppose a federal agency has a database of proposals residing on an acquisition information system that are responses to an RFP issued by the agency. The agency determines that for these proposals, the potential impact from a loss of confidentiality is high, the potential impact from a loss of integrity is high, and the potential impact from a loss of availability is moderate.

The corresponding security category, SC, would be expressed as:

$SC_{\text{proposal information}}$ = {(confidentiality, HIGH), (integrity, HIGH), (availability, MODERATE)}.

Now, assume that the same acquisition information system also supports some of the agency's administrative functions and has the following SC for the administrative information:

$SC_{\text{administrative information}}$ = {(confidentiality, LOW), (integrity, HIGH), (availability, LOW)}.

The security category of the acquisition information system would be comprised of the highest values of the two information categories resident on the system. Thus, the SC would be:

$SC_{\text{acquisition formation system}}$ = {(confidentiality, HIGH), (integrity, HIGH), (availability, MODERATE)}.

Additional Agency Policy Guidance

Additional valuable guidance on polices for federal agencies is provided in OMB Circular A-130, "Management of Federal Information Resources, Transmittal 4," November 30, 2000. This circular addresses information management policy and management of information systems and information technology policy. These policies are summarized in the following two sections.

Information Management Policy

For government agencies, an information management policy should address the following entities:

✦ Conducting information management planning

✦ Establishing guidelines for information collection

✦ Establishing guidelines for electronic information collection

✦ Implementing records management

✦ Providing information to the public

✦ Implementing an information dissemination management system

✦ Avoiding improperly restrictive practices

✦ Disseminating electronic information

✦ Implementing safeguards

Management of Information Systems and Information Technology Policy

A policy for the management of information systems should include the following items:

✦ Use of a process for capital planning and investment control

✦ Documentation and submission of the initial enterprise architecture (EA) to OMB and submission of updates when significant changes to the EA occur. The OMB Circular defines EA as "the explicit description and documentation of the current and desired relationships among business and management processes and information technology."

✦ Ensure security in information systems

✦ Acquisition of information technology

In performing the oversight function, Circular A-130 states "The Director of OMB will use information technology planning reviews, fiscal budget reviews, information collection budget reviews, management reviews, and such other measures as the Director deems necessary to evaluate the adequacy and efficiency of each agency's information resources management and compliance with this Circular."

Department of Defense Policies

The policies and guidance for information assurance in U.S. defense organizations are given in DoD Directive 8500.1, "Information Assurance (IA)," October 4, 2002. Additional support and implementation guidance is also provided by DoD Directive 8500.2, "Information Assurance (IA) Implementation," February 6, 2003; DoD 5025.1-M, "DoD Directives System Procedures," current edition; and DoD Directive 8000.1, "Management of DoD Information Resources and Information Technology,"

February 27, 2002. The principle components of U.S. DoD IA policy as embodied in DoD Directive 8500.1 are summarized in the following section.

DoD Directive 8500.1

DoD Directive 8500.1 "Establishes policy and assigns responsibilities to achieve Department of Defense (DoD) information assurance (IA) through a defense-in-depth approach that integrates the capabilities of personnel, operations, and technology, and supports the evolution to network centric warfare."

There are 26 policy items listed in Directive 8500.1. The main elements of these policy statements taken from the Directive are given as follows:

1. Information assurance requirements shall be identified and included in the design, acquisition, installation, operation, upgrade, or replacement of all DoD information systems in accordance with 10 U.S.C. Section 2224, Office of Management and Budget Circular A-130, DoD Directive 5000.1, this Directive, and other IA-related DoD guidance, as issued.

2. All DoD information systems shall maintain an appropriate level of confidentiality, integrity, authentication, non-repudiation, and availability that reflect a balance among the importance and sensitivity of the information and information assets; documented threats and vulnerabilities; the trustworthiness of users and interconnecting systems; the impact of impairment or destruction to the DoD information system; and cost effectiveness.

3. Information assurance shall be a visible element of all investment portfolios incorporating DoD-owned or -controlled information systems, to include outsourced business processes supported by private sector information systems and outsourced information technologies.

4. Interoperability and integration of IA solutions within or supporting the Department of Defense shall be achieved through adherence to an architecture that will enable the evolution to network-centric warfare by remaining consistent with the Command, Control, Communications, Computers, Intelligence, Surveillance, Reconnaissance Architecture Framework, and a defense-in-depth approach.

5. The Department of Defense shall organize, plan, assess, train for, and conduct the defense of DoD computer networks as integrated computer network defense (CND) operations that are coordinated across multiple disciplines in accordance with DoD Directive O-8530.1.

6. Information assurance readiness shall be monitored, reported, and evaluated as a distinguishable element of mission readiness throughout all the DoD Components, and validated by the DoD CIO.

7. All DoD information systems shall be assigned a mission assurance category that is directly associated with the importance of the information they contain relative to the achievement of DoD goals and objectives, particularly the war fighters' combat mission.

8. Access to all DoD information systems shall be based on a demonstrated need-to-know and granted in accordance with applicable laws and DoD 5200.2-R.

9. In addition to the requirements in item 8, foreign exchange personnel and representatives of foreign nations, coalitions, or international organizations may be authorized access to DoD information systems containing classified or sensitive information only if all of the following conditions are met:

    • Access is authorized only by the DoD Component Head in accordance with the Department of Defense, the Department of State (DoS), and DCI disclosure and interconnection policies, as applicable.

    • Mechanisms are in place to strictly limit access to information that has been cleared for release to the represented foreign nation, coalition, or international organization, (e.g., North Atlantic Treaty Organization) in accordance with DoD directives.

10. Authorized users who are contractors, DoD direct or indirect hire foreign national employees, or foreign representatives as described in item 9, above, shall always have their affiliation displayed as part of their e-mail addresses.

11. Access to DoD-owned, -operated, or -outsourced Web sites shall be strictly controlled by the Web site owner using technical, operational, and procedural measures appropriate to the Web site audience and information classification or sensitivity.

12. DoD information systems shall regulate remote access and access to the Internet by employing positive technical controls such as proxy services and screened subnets, also called demilitarized zones (DMZ), or through systems that are isolated from all other DoD information systems through physical means. This includes remote access for telework.

13. All DoD information systems shall be certified and accredited in accordance with DoD Instruction 5200.40.

14. All interconnections of DoD information systems shall be managed to continuously minimize community risk by ensuring that the assurance of one system is not undermined by vulnerabilities of interconnected systems.

15. All DoD information systems shall comply with DoD ports and protocols guidance and management processes, as established.

16. The conduct of all DoD communications security activities, including the acquisition of COMSEC products, shall be in accordance with DoD Directive C-5200.5.

17. All IA or IA-enabled IT hardware, firmware, and software components for products incorporated into DoD information systems must comply with the evaluation and validation requirements of National Security Telecommunications and Information Systems Security Policy Number 11.

18. All IA and IA-enabled IT products incorporated into DoD information systems shall be configured in accordance with DoD-approved security configuration guidelines.

19. Public domain software products, and other software products with limited or no warranty, such as those commonly known as freeware or shareware, shall only be used in DoD information systems to meet compelling operational requirements. Such products shall be thoroughly assessed for risk and accepted for use by the responsible DAA.

20. DoD information systems shall be monitored based on the assigned mission assurance category and assessed risk in order to detect, isolate, and react to intrusions, disruption of services, or other incidents that threaten the IA of DoD operations or IT resources, including internal misuse. DoD information systems also shall be subject to active penetrations and other forms of testing used to complement monitoring activities in accordance with DoD and Component policy and restrictions.

21. Identified DoD information system vulnerabilities shall be evaluated for DoD impact, and tracked and mitigated in accordance with DoD-directed solutions, e.g., Information Assurance Vulnerability Alerts (IAVAs).

22. All personnel authorized access to DoD information systems shall be adequately trained in accordance with DoD and Component policies and requirements and certified as required in order to perform the tasks associated with their IA responsibilities.

23. Individuals shall be notified of their privacy rights and security responsibilities in accordance with DoD Component General Counsel–approved processes when attempting access to DoD information systems.

24. Mobile code technologies shall be categorized and controlled to reduce their threat to DoD information systems in accordance with DoD and Component policy and guidance.

25. A DAA shall be appointed for each DoD information system operating within or on behalf of the Department of Defense, to include outsourced business processes supported by private sector information systems and outsourced information technologies. The DAA shall be a U.S. citizen, a DoD employee, and have a level of authority commensurate with accepting, in writing, the risk of operating DoD information systems under his or her purview.

26. All military voice radio systems, to include cellular and commercial services, shall be protected consistent with the classification or sensitivity of the information transmitted on the system.

✦   ✦   ✦

Assessment Questions

You can find the answers to the following questions in Appendix A.

1. Techniques and concerns that are normally addressed by management in the organization's computer security program are defined in NIST SP 800-12 as:

   a. Administrative controls

   b. Management controls

   c. Operational controls

   d. Technical controls

2. The National Research Council publication, *Computers at Risk*, defines an element of computer security as a "requirement intended to assure that systems work properly and service is not denied to authorized users." Which one of the following elements best fits this definition?

   a. Availability

   b. Assurance

   c. Integrity

   d. Authentication

3. NSTISSI Publication No. 4009, "National Information Systems Security (INFOSEC) Glossary," defines the term *assurance* as:

   a. Requirement that information and programs are changed only in a specified and authorized manner

   b. Measure designed to establish the validity of a transmission, message, or originator, or a means of verifying an individual's authorization to receive specific categories of information

   c. Measure of confidence that the security features, practices, procedures, and architecture of an IS accurately mediate and enforce the security policy

   d. Requirement that private or confidential information not be disclosed to unauthorized individuals

4. The "National Information Systems Security (INFOSEC) Glossary," defines an information system security term as a "formal determination by an authorized adjudicative office that an individual is authorized access, on a need to know basis, to a specific level of collateral classified information." This definition refers to which one of the following terms?

   a. Sensitivity of information

   b. Classification of information

   c. Clearance

   d. Compartmentalization

5. In NSTISSI Publication No. 4009, what term is defined as a "document detailing the method, act, process, or effect of using an information system (IS)"?

   a. QUADRANT

   b. Concept of Operations (CONOPS)

   c. Evaluation Assurance Level (EAL)

   d. Information Assurance (IA) architecture

6. Which one of the following definitions best describes the National Information Assurance Partnership (NIAP) according to NSTISSI Publication No. 4009?

   a. Nationwide interconnection of communications networks, computers, databases, and consumer electronics that makes vast amounts of information available to users.

   b. Worldwide interconnections of the information systems of all countries, international and multinational organizations, and international commercial communications

   c. Joint initiative between NSA and NIST responsible for security testing needs of both IT consumers and producers, promoting the development of technically sound security requirements for IT products

   d. First level of the PKI Certification Management Authority that approves the security policy of each Policy Certification Authority (PCA)

7. TEMPEST refers to which one of the following definitions?

   a. Property whereby the security level of an object cannot change while the object is being processed by an IS

   b. Investigation, study, and control of compromising emanations from IS equipment

   c. Program established for a specific class of classified information that imposes safeguarding and access requirements that exceed those normally required for information at the same classified level

   d. Unclassified cryptographic equipment

8. Executive Order (E.O.) 13231, issued on October 16, 2001, renamed the National Security Telecommunications and Information Systems Security Committee (NSTISSC) as which one of the following committees?

   a. Committee for Information Systems Security (CISS)

   b. Committee on National Security Systems (CNSS)

   c. Committee on National Infrastructure Protection (CNIP)

   d. Committee for the Protection of National Information Systems (CPNIS)

9. In addressing the *security of systems with national security information*, E.O. 3231 assigned the responsibilities of developing government-wide policies and overseeing the implementation of government-wide policies, procedures, standards, and guidelines to the:

   a. U.S. Secretary of Defense and the Director of the FBI

   b. FBI and the Director of Central Intelligence

   c. NIST and the U.S. Secretary of Defense

   d. U.S. Secretary of Defense and the Director of Central Intelligence

10. Which one of the following characteristics is NOT associated with the definition of a national security system?

    a. Contains classified information

    b. Involved in industrial commerce

    c. Supports intelligence activities

    d. Involved with the command and control of military forces

11. In 2002, the U.S. Congress enacted the E-Government Act (Public Law 107-347). Title III of the E-Government Act was written to provide for a number of protections of Federal information systems, including to "provide a comprehensive framework for ensuring the effectiveness of information security controls over information resources that support Federal operations and assets." Title III of the E-Government Act is also known as the:

    a. Computer Security Act (CSA)

    b. Computer Fraud and Abuse Act (CFAA)

    c. Federal Information Security Management Act (FISMA)

    d. Cyber Security Enhancement Act

12. FISMA assigned which one of the following entities the responsibility of overseeing the security policies and practices of U.S. government agencies?

    a. The FBI

    b. The U.S. Secretary of Defense

    c. The Director of the Office of Management and Budget (OMB)

    d. The Director of Central Intelligence

13. Which information system security–related Act requires government agencies to perform periodic assessments of risk, develop policies and procedures that are based on risk assessments, conduct security awareness training, perform

periodic testing and evaluation of the effectiveness of information security policies, and implement procedures for detecting, reporting, and responding to security incidents?

    a. Computer Security Act (CSA)

    b. Federal Information Security Management Act (FISMA)

    c. Computer Fraud and Abuse Act (CFAA)

    d. Cyber Security Enhancement Act

14. FISMA charged which one of the following entities to develop information system security standards and guidelines for federal agencies?

    a. FBI

    b. DoD

    c. NSA

    d. NIST

15. The general formula for categorization of an *information type* developed in FIPS Publication 199, "Standards for Security Categorization of Federal Information and Information Systems," is which one of the following?

    a. $SC_{\text{information type}}$ = {(**confidentiality**, *risk*), (**integrity**, *risk*), (**availability**, *risk*)}

    b. $SC_{\text{information type}}$ = {(**confidentiality**, *impact*), (**integrity**, *impact*), (**availability**, *impact*)}

    c. $SC_{\text{information type}}$ = {(**assurance**, *impact*), (**integrity**, *impact*), (**authentication**, *impact*)}

    d. $SC_{\text{information type}}$ = {(**confidentiality**, *controls*), (**integrity**, *controls*), (**availability**, *controls*)}

16. Circular A-130 directs that an oversight function should be performed consisting of the use of information technology planning reviews, fiscal budget reviews, information collection budget reviews, management reviews, and such other measures as deemed necessary to evaluate the adequacy and efficiency of each agency's information resources management and compliance with the Circular. Which one of the following individuals does the Circular designate as being responsible for this oversight function?

    a. The Secretary of Commerce

    b. The Director of the Office of Management and Budget

    c. The U.S. Secretary of Defense

    d. The Director of NSA

17. The National Computer Security Center Publication NCSC-TG-004-88 includes a definition that refers to the characteristic of a system that "performs its intended function in an unimpaired manner, free from deliberate, inadvertent, or unauthorized manipulation of the system." This characteristic defines which one of the following terms?

    a. Data integrity

    b. System integrity

    c. Enterprise integrity

    d. Risk integrity

18. Which one of the following terms best describes a secure telecommunications or associated cryptographic component that is unclassified but governed by a special set of control requirements, as defined in NSTISSI Publication 4009?

    a. Controlled cryptographic item (CCI) assembly

    b. Controlled cryptographic item (CCI) component

    c. Controlled cryptographic item (CCI)

    d. Crypto-ignition key (CIK)

19. What is a definable perimeter encompassing all hardware, firmware, and software components performing critical COMSEC functions, such as key generation and key handling and storage?

    a. COMSEC area

    b. COMSEC compartment

    c. COMSEC partition

    d. COMSEC boundary

20. What process involves the five steps of identification of critical information, analysis of threats, analysis of vulnerabilities, assessment of risks, and application of appropriate countermeasures?

    a. Operations security

    b. Application security

    c. Administrative security

    d. Management security

21. Information that has been determined pursuant to Executive Order 12958 or any predecessor order to require protection against unauthorized disclosures is known as:

    a. Protected information (PI)

    b. National security information (NSI)

    c. Personally identifiable information (PII)

    d. Secure information (SI)

22. An area that, when staffed, must be occupied by two or more appropriately cleared individuals who remain within sight of each other is referred to as which one of the following terms?

    a. No-lone zone

    b. Restricted area

    c. Protected occupancy zone

    d. Cleared area

23. According to NSTISSI Publication 4009, the process of identifying and applying countermeasures commensurate with the value of the assets protected based on a risk assessment is called a:

    a. Vulnerability assessment

    b. Continuity planning

    c. Risk management

    d. Risk control

24. In the context of information systems security, the abbreviation ST&E stands for which one of the following terms?

    a. Security training and evaluation

    b. Security test and evaluation

    c. Security test and engineering

    d. Sensitivity test and evaluation

25. Which one of the following designations refers to a product that is a classified or controlled cryptographic item endorsed by the NSA for securing classified and sensitive U.S. government information when appropriately keyed?

    a. Cleared product

    b. Type 3 product

    c. Type 1 product

    d. Type 2 product

26. Which one of the following items is NOT one of the responsibilities of the Committee on National Security Systems (CNSS) for the security of national security systems?

    a. Providing a forum for the discussion of policy issues

    b. Setting national policy

    c. Providing operational procedures, direction, and guidance.

    d. Requiring agencies to identify and provide information security protections commensurate with the risk and magnitude of the harm to information or information systems of government agencies

27. FISMA, Title III of the E-Government Act of 2002, reserves the responsibility for standards associated with the national defense establishment to which of the following entities?

    a. DoD and NSA

    b. DoD and CIA

    c. CIA and NSA

    d. CIA and NIST

28. FIPS Publication 199, "Standards for Security Characterization of Federal Information and Information Systems, NIST Pre-Publication Final Draft," December 2003, characterizes 3 levels of potential impact on organizations or individuals based on the objectives of confidentiality, integrity, and availability. What is the level of impact specified in Publication 199 for the following description of integrity: "The unauthorized modification or destruction of information could be expected to have a *serious* adverse effect on organizational operations, organizational assets, or individuals."?

    a. High

    b. Moderate

    c. Low

    d. Severe

29. Referring to question 28, the following impact description refers to which one of the three security objectives and which corresponding level of impact: "The disruption of access to or use of information or an information system could be expected to have a *limited* adverse effect on organizational operations, organizational assets, or individuals."?

    a. Confidentiality—Low

    b. Availability—Moderate

    c. Availability—Low

    d. Availability—High

30. DoD Directive 8500.1, "Information Assurance (IA)," October 4, 2002, specifies a defense-in-depth approach that integrates the capabilities of which set of the following entities?

    a. Personnel, operations, and technology

    b. Personnel, research and development, and technology

    c. Operations, resources, and technology

    d. Personnel, operations, and resources

Appendices

Answers to Assessment Questions

Chapter 1

1. Which choice below is an incorrect description of a control?

    a. Detective controls discover attacks and trigger preventative or corrective controls.

    b. Corrective controls reduce the likelihood of a deliberate attack.

    c. Corrective controls reduce the effect of an attack.

    d. Controls are the countermeasures for vulnerabilities.

Answer: b

The other three answers are correct descriptions of controls.

2. Which statement below is accurate about the reasons to implement a layered security architecture?

    a. A layered security approach is not necessary when using COTS products.

    b. A good packet-filtering router will eliminate the need to implement a layered security architecture.

    c. A layered security approach is intended to increase the work-factor for an attacker.

    d. A layered approach doesn't really improve the security posture of the organization.

Answer: c

Security designs should consider a layered approach to increase the work-factor an attacker must expend to successfully attack the system.

3. Which choice below represents an application or system demonstrating a need for a high level of confidentiality protection and controls?

    a. Unavailability of the system could result in inability to meet payroll obligations and could cause work stoppage and failure of user organizations to meet critical mission requirements. The system requires 24-hour access.

    b. The application contains proprietary business information and other financial information, which if disclosed to unauthorized sources, could cause an unfair advantage for vendors, contractors, or individuals and could result in financial loss or adverse legal action to user organizations.

    c. Destruction of the information would require significant expenditures of time and effort to replace. Although corrupted information would present an inconvenience to the staff, most information, and all vital information, is backed up by either paper documentation or on disk.

    d. The mission of this system is to produce local weather forecast information that is made available to the news media forecasters and the general public at all times. None of the information requires protection against disclosure.

Answer: b

Although elements of all of the systems described could require specific controls for confidentiality, given the descriptions above, system b fits the definition most closely of a system requiring a very high level of confidentiality. Answer a is an example of a system requiring high availability. Answer c is an example of a system that requires medium integrity controls. Answer d is a system that requires only a low level of confidentiality.

4. Which choice below is NOT a concern of policy development at the high level?

    a. Identifying the key business resources

    b. Identifying the type of firewalls to be used for perimeter security

    c. Defining roles in the organization

    d. Determining the capability and functionality of each role

Answer: b

Answers a, c, and d are elements of policy development at the highest level. Key business resources would have been identified during the risk assessment process. The various roles are then defined to determine the various levels of access to those resources. Answer d is the final step in the policy creation process and combines steps a and c. It determines which group gets access to each resource and what access privileges its members are assigned. Access to resources should be based on roles, not on individual identity.

5. Which choice below is NOT an accurate statement about the visibility of IT security policy?

    a. The IT security policy should not be afforded high visibility.

    b. The IT security policy could be visible through panel discussions with guest speakers.

    c. The IT security policy should be afforded high visibility.

    d. The IT security policy should be included as a regular topic at staff meetings at all levels of the organization.

    Answer: a

    The other three answers are correct statements about the visibility of IT security policy.

6. Which question below is NOT accurate regarding the process of risk assessment?

    a. The likelihood of a threat must be determined as an element of the risk assessment.

    b. The level of impact of a threat must be determined as an element of the risk assessment.

    c. Risk assessment is the first process in the risk management methodology

    d. Risk assessment is the final result of the risk management methodology.

    Answer: d

    Risk assessment is the first process in the risk management methodology.

7. Which choice below would NOT be considered an element of proper user account management?

    a. Users should never be rotated out of their current duties.

    b. The users' accounts should be reviewed periodically.

    c. A process for tracking access authorizations should be implemented.

    d. Periodically re-screen personnel in sensitive positions.

    Answer: a

    The other answers are elements of proper user account management.

8. Which choice below is NOT one of NIST's 33 IT security principles?

    a. Implement least privilege.

    b. Assume that external systems are insecure.

    c. Totally eliminate any level of risk.

    d. Minimize the system elements to be trusted.

Answer: c

Risk can never be totally eliminated. NIST IT security principle #4 states: "Reduce risk to an acceptable level."

9. How often should an independent review of the security controls be performed, according to OMB Circular A-130?

    a. Every year

    b. Every three years

    c. Every five years

    d. Never

Answer: b

OMB Circular A-130 requires that a review of the security controls for each major government application be performed at least every three years.

10. Which choice below BEST describes the difference between the System Owner and the Information Owner?

    a. There is a one-to-one relationship between system owners and information owners.

    b. One system could have multiple information owners.

    c. The Information Owner is responsible for defining the system's operating parameters.

    d. The System Owner is responsible for establishing the rules for appropriate use of the information.

Answer: b

A single system may utilize information from multiple Information Owners.

11. Which choice below is NOT a generally accepted benefit of security aware- ness, training, and education?

   a. A security awareness program can help operators understand the value of the information.

   b. A security education program can help system administrators recognize unauthorized intrusion attempts.

   c. A security awareness and training program will help prevent natural dis- asters from occurring.

   d. A security awareness and training program can help an organization reduce the number and severity of errors and omissions.

Answer: c

The other answers are generally accepted benefits of security awareness, training, and education.

12. Who has the final responsibility for the preservation of the organization's information?

   a. Technology providers

   b. Senior management

   c. Users

   d. Application owners

Answer: b

Senior management has the final responsibility through due care and due dili- gence to preserve the capital of the organization and further its business model through the implementation of a security program. Although senior management does not have the functional role of managing security proce- dures, it has the ultimate responsibility to see that business continuity is preserved.

13. Which choice below is NOT an example of an issue-specific policy?

   a. Email privacy policy

   b. Virus-checking disk policy

   c. Defined router ACLs

   d. Unfriendly employee termination policy

Answer: c

Answer c is an example of a system-specific policy — in this case the router's access control lists. The other three answers are examples of issue-specific policy, as defined by NIST.

14. Which statement below is NOT true about security awareness, training, and educational programs?

    a. Awareness and training help users become more accountable for their actions.

    b. Security education assists management in determining who should be promoted.

    c. Security improves the users' awareness of the need to protect information resources.

    d. Security education assists management in developing the in-house expertise to manage security programs.

Answer: b

The other answers are correct statements about security awareness, training, and educational programs.

15. Which choice below is an accurate statement about standards?

    a. Standards are the high-level statements made by senior management in support of information systems security.

    b. Standards are the first element created in an effective security policy program.

    c. Standards are used to describe how policies will be implemented within an organization.

    d. Standards are senior management's directives to create a computer security program.

Answer: c

Answers a, b, and d describe policies. Procedures, standards, and guidelines are used to describe how these policies will be implemented within an organization.

16. Which choice below is a role of the Information Systems Security Officer?

    a. The ISO establishes the overall goals of the organization's computer security program.

    b. The ISO is responsible for day-to-day security administration.

    c. The ISO is responsible for examining systems to see whether they are meeting stated security requirements.

    d. The ISO is responsible for following security procedures and reporting security problems.

Answer: b

Answer a is a responsibility of senior management. Answer c is a description of the role of auditing. Answer d is the role of the user, or consumer, of security in an organization.

17. Which statement below is NOT correct about safeguard selection in the risk analysis process?

    a. Maintenance costs need to be included in determining the total cost of the safeguard.

    b. The best possible safeguard should always be implemented, regardless of cost.

    c. The most commonly considered criteria is the cost effectiveness of the safeguard.

    d. Many elements need to be considered in determining the total cost of the safeguard.

Answer: b

Performing a cost-benefit analysis of the proposed safeguard before implementation is vital. The level of security afforded could easily outweigh the value of a proposed safeguard. Other factors need to be considered in the safeguard selection process, such as accountability, auditability, and the level of manual operations needed to maintain or operate the safeguard.

18. Which choice below is usually the number-one-used criterion to determine the classification of an information object?

    a. Value

    b. Useful life

    c. Age

    d. Personal association

Answer: a

Value of the information asset to the organization is usually the first and foremost criteria used in determining its classification.

19. What are high-level policies?

    a. They are recommendations for procedural controls.

    b. They are the instructions on how to perform a Quantitative Risk Analysis.

    c. They are statements that indicate a senior management's intention to support InfoSec.

    d. They are step-by-step procedures to implement a safeguard.

Answer: c.

High-level policies are senior management statements of recognition of the importance of security controls to the mission of the organization.

20. Which policy type is MOST likely to contain mandatory or compulsory standards?

    a. Guidelines

    b. Advisory

    c. Regulatory

    d. Informative

Answer: c

Answer b, advisory policies, might specify penalties for noncompliance, but regulatory policies are required to be followed by the organization. Answers a and d are informational or recommended policies only.

21. What does an Exposure Factor (EF) describe?

    a. A dollar figure that is assigned to a single event

    b. A number that represents the estimated frequency of the occurrence of an expected threat

    c. The percentage of loss that a realized threat event would have on a specific asset

    d. The annual expected financial loss to an organization from a threat

Answer: c

Answer a is an SLE, b is an ARO, and d is an ALE.

22. What is the MOST accurate definition of a safeguard?

    a. A guideline for policy recommendations

    b. A step-by-step instructional procedure

    c. A control designed to counteract a threat

    d. A control designed to counteract an asset

Answer: c

Answer a is a guideline, b is a procedure, and d is a distracter.

23. Which choice MOST accurately describes the differences between standards, guidelines, and procedures?

    a. Standards are recommended policies, whereas guidelines are mandatory policies.

    b. Procedures are step-by-step recommendations for complying with mandatory guidelines.

    c. Procedures are the general recommendations for compliance with mandatory guidelines.

    d. Procedures are step-by-step instructions for compliance with mandatory standards.

Answer: d

The other answers are incorrect.

24. What are the detailed instructions on how to perform or implement a control called?

    a. Procedures

    b. Policies

    c. Guidelines

    d. Standards

Answer: a

25. How is an SLE derived?

    a. (Cost – benefit) × (% of Asset Value)

    b. AV × EF

    c. ARO × EF

    d. % of AV – implementation cost

Answer: b.

A Single Loss Expectancy is derived by multiplying the Asset Value with its Exposure Factor. The other answers do not exist.

26. What is a noncompulsory recommendation on how to achieve compliance with published standards called?

    a. Procedures

    b. Policies

    c. Guidelines

    d. Standards

Answer: c

27. Which group represents the MOST likely source of an asset loss through inappropriate computer use?

    a. Crackers

    b. Hackers

    c. Employees

    d. Saboteurs

Answer: c

Internal personnel far and away constitute the largest amount of dollar loss due to unauthorized or inappropriate computer use.

28. Which choice MOST accurately describes the difference between the role of a data owner versus the role of a data custodian?

    a. The custodian implements the information classification scheme after the initial assignment by the owner.

    b. The data owner implements the information classification scheme after the initial assignment by the custodian.

    c. The custodian makes the initial information classification assignments, whereas the operations manager implements the scheme.

    d. The custodian implements the information classification scheme after the initial assignment by the operations manager.

Answer: a

29. What is an ARO?

    a. A dollar figure assigned to a single event

    b. The annual expected financial loss to an organization from a threat

    c. A number that represents the estimated frequency of an occurrence of an expected threat

    d. The percentage of loss that a realized threat event would have on a specific asset

Answer: c

Answer a is the definition of SLE, b is an ALE, and d is an EF.

30. Which formula accurately represents an Annualized Loss Expectancy (ALE) calculation?

   a. SLE × ARO

   b. Asset Value (AV) × EF

   c. ARO × EF − SLE

   d. % of ARO × AV

Answer: a

Answer b is the formula for an SLE, and answers c and d are nonsense.

Chapter 2

1. The goals of integrity do NOT include:

   a. Accountability of responsible individuals

   b. Prevention of the modification of information by unauthorized users

   c. Prevention of the unauthorized or unintentional modification of information by authorized users

   d. Preservation of internal and external consistency

Answer: a

The correct answer is a. Accountability is holding individuals responsible for their actions. Answers b, c, and d are the three goals of integrity.

2. Kerberos is an authentication scheme that can be used to implement:

   a. Public key cryptography

   b. Digital signatures

   c. Hash functions

   d. Single Sign-On (SSO)

Answer: d

The correct answer is d. Kerberos is a third-party authentication protocol that can be used to implement SSO. Answer a is incorrect because public key cryptography is not used in the basic Kerberos protocol. Answer b is a public key-based capability, and answer c is a one-way transformation used to disguise passwords or to implement digital signatures.

3. The fundamental entity in a relational database is the:

    a. Domain

    b. Relation

    c. Pointer

    d. Cost

Answer: b

The correct answer is b. The fundamental entity in a relational database is the relation in the form of a table. Answer a is the set of allowable attribute values, and answers c and d are distracters.

4. In a relational database, security is provided to the access of data through:

    a. Candidate keys

    b. Views

    c. Joins

    d. Attributes

Answer: b

The correct answer is b. Candidate keys, (answer a) are the set of unique keys from which the primary key is selected. Answer c, joins, indicates operations that can be performed on the database, and the attributes (d) denote the columns in the relational table.

5. In biometrics, a one-to-one search to verify an individual's claim of an identity is called:

    a. Audit trail review

    b. Authentication

    c. Accountability

    d. Aggregation

Answer: b

The correct answer is b. Answer a is a review of audit system data, usually done after the fact. Answer c is holding individuals responsible for their actions, and answer d is obtaining higher-sensitivity information from a number of pieces of information of lower sensitivity.

6. Biometrics is used for identification in the physical controls and for authentication in the:

    a. Detective controls

    b. Preventive controls

    c. Logical controls

    d. Corrective controls

Answer: c

The correct answer is c. The other answers are different categories of controls where preventive controls attempt to eliminate or reduce vulnerabilities before an attack occurs; detective controls attempt to determine that an attack is taking place or has taken place; and corrective controls involve taking action to restore the system to normal operation after a successful attack.

7. Referential integrity requires that for any foreign key attribute, the referenced relation must have:

    a. A tuple with the same value for its primary key

    b. A tuple with the same value for its secondary key

    c. An attribute with the same value for its secondary key

    d. An attribute with the same value for its other foreign key

Answer: a

The correct answer is a. Answers b and c are incorrect because a secondary key is not a valid term. Answer d is a distracter because referential integrity has a foreign key referring to a primary key in another relation.

8. A password that is the same for each logon is called a:

    a. Dynamic password

    b. Static password

    c. Passphrase

    d. One-time pad

Answer: b

The correct answer is b. In answer a, the password changes at each logon. For answer c, a passphrase is a long word or phrase that is converted by the system to a password. In answer d, a one-time pad refers to a using a random key only once when sending a cryptographic message.

9. Which one of the following is NOT an access attack?

   a. Spoofing

   b. Back door

   c. Dictionary

   d. Penetration test

Answer: d

The correct answer is d, a distracter. A penetration test is conducted to obtain a high level evaluation of a system's defense or to perform a detailed analysis of the information system's weaknesses. A penetration test can determine how a system reacts to an attack, whether or not a system's defenses can be breached, and what information can be acquired from the system. It is performed with the approval of the target organization.

10. An attack that uses a detailed listing of common passwords and words in general to gain unauthorized access to an information system is BEST described as:

   a. Password guessing

   b. Software exploitation

   c. Dictionary attack

   d. Spoofing

Answer: c

The correct answer is c. In a dictionary attack, a dictionary of common words and passwords are applied to attempt to gain unauthorized access to an information system. In answer a, password guessing, the attacker guesses passwords derived from sources such as notes on the user's desk, the user's birthday, a pet's name, applying social engineering techniques, and so on. Answer b refers to exploiting software vulnerabilities and answer d, spoofing, is a method used by an attacker to convince an information system that it is communicating with a known, trusted entity.

11. A statistical anomaly–based intrusion detection system:

   a. Acquires data to establish a normal system operating profile

   b. Refers to a database of known attack signatures

   c. Will detect an attack that does not significantly change the system's operating characteristics

   d. Does not report an event that caused a momentary anomaly in the system

Answer: a

The correct answer is a. A statistical anomaly–based intrusion detection system acquires data to establish a normal system operating profile. Answer b is incorrect because it is used in signature-based intrusion detection. Answer c is incorrect because a statistical anomaly–based intrusion detection system will not detect an attack that does not significantly change the system operating characteristics. Similarly, answer d is incorrect because the statistical anomaly–based IDS is susceptible to reporting an event that caused a momentary anomaly in the system.

12. Which one of the following definitions BEST describes system scanning?

    a. An attack that uses dial-up modems or asynchronous external connections to an information system in order to bypass information security control mechanisms.

    b. An attack that is perpetrated by intercepting and saving old messages and then sending them later, impersonating one of the communicating parties.

    c. Acquisition of information that is discarded by an individual or organization

    d. A process used to collect information about a device or network to facilitate an attack on an information system

    Answer: d

    The correct answer is d. Answer a describes a back door attack, answer b is a replay attack, and answer c refers to dumpster diving.

13. In which type of penetration test does the testing team have access to internal system code?

    a. Closed box

    b. Transparent box

    c. Open box

    d. Coding box

    Answer: c

    The correct answer is c, open box testing. In answer a, closed box testing, the testing team does not have access to internal system code. The other answers are distracters.

14. A standard data manipulation and relational database definition language is:

    a. OOD

    b. SQL

    c. SLL

    d. Script

    Answer: b

    The correct answer is b. All other answers do not apply.

15. An attack that can be perpetrated against a remote user's callback access control is:

   a. Call forwarding

   b. A Trojan horse

   c. A maintenance hook

   d. Redialing

Answer: a

The correct answer is a. A cracker can have a person's call forwarded to another number to foil the callback system. Answer b is incorrect because it is an example of malicious code embedded in useful code. Answer c is incorrect because it might enable bypassing controls of a system through a means used for debugging or maintenance. Answer d is incorrect because it is a distracter.

16. The definition of CHAP is:

   a. Confidential Hash Authentication Protocol

   b. Challenge Handshake Authentication Protocol

   c. Challenge Handshake Approval Protocol

   d. Confidential Handshake Approval Protocol

Answer: b

17. Using symmetric key cryptography, Kerberos authenticates clients to other entities on a network and facilitates communications through the assignment of:

   a. Public keys

   b. Session keys

   c. Passwords

   d. Tokens

Answer: b

The correct answer is b. Session keys are temporary keys assigned by the KDC and used for an allotted period of time as the secret key between two entities. Answer a is incorrect because it refers to asymmetric encryption that is not used in the basic Kerberos protocol. Answer c is incorrect because it is not a key, and answer d is incorrect because a token generates dynamic passwords.

18. Three things that must be considered for the planning and implementation of access control mechanisms are:

    a. Threats, assets, and objectives

    b. Threats, vulnerabilities, and risks

    c. Vulnerabilities, secret keys, and exposures

    d. Exposures, threats, and countermeasures

Answer: b

The correct answer is b. Threats define the possible source of security policy violations; vulnerabilities describe weaknesses in the system that might be exploited by the threats; and the risk determines the probability of threats being realized. All three items must be present to meaningfully apply access control. Therefore, the other answers are incorrect.

19. In mandatory access control, the authorization of a subject to have access to an object is dependent upon:

    a. Labels

    b. Roles

    c. Tasks

    d. Identity

Answer: a

The correct answer is a. Mandatory access controls use labels to determine whether subjects can have access to objects, depending on the subjects' clearances. Answer b, roles, is applied in nondiscretionary access control, as is answer c, tasks. Answer d, identity, is used in discretionary access control.

20. The type of access control that is used in local, dynamic situations where subjects have the ability to specify what resources certain users can access is called:

    a. Mandatory access control

    b. Rule-based access control

    c. Sensitivity-based access control

    d. Discretionary access control

Answer: d

The correct answer is d. Answers a and b require strict adherence to labels and clearances. Answer c is a made-up distracter.

21. Role-based access control is useful when:

   a. Access must be determined by the labels on the data.

   b. There are frequent personnel changes in an organization.

   c. Rules are needed to determine clearances.

   d. Security clearances must be used.

   Answer: b

   The correct answer is b. Role-based access control is part of nondiscretionary access control. Answers a, c, and d relate to mandatory access control.

22. Clipping levels are used to:

   a. Limit the number of letters in a password.

   b. Set thresholds for voltage variations.

   c. Reduce the amount of data to be evaluated in audit logs.

   d. Limit errors in callback systems.

   Answer: c

   The correct answer is c—reducing the amount of data to be evaluated by definition. Answer a is incorrect because clipping levels do not relate to letters in a password. Answer b is incorrect because clipping levels in this context have nothing to do with controlling voltage levels. Answer d is incorrect because they are not used to limit callback errors.

23. Identification is:

   a. A user being authenticated by the system

   b. A user providing a password to the system

   c. A user providing a shared secret to the system

   d. A user professing an identity to the system

   Answer: d

   The correct answer is d. A user presents an ID to the system as identification. Answer a is incorrect because presenting an ID is not an authentication act. Answer b is incorrect because a password is an authentication mechanism. Answer c is incorrect because it refers to cryptography or authentication.

24. Authentication is:

   a. The verification that the claimed identity is valid

   b. The presentation of a user's ID to the system

c. Not accomplished through the use of a password

d. Applied only to remote users

Answer: a

The correct answer is a. Answer b is incorrect because it is an identification act. Answer c is incorrect because authentication can be accomplished through the use of a password. Answer d is incorrect because authentication is applied to local and remote users.

25. An example of two-factor authentication is:

   a. A password and an ID

   b. An ID and a PIN

   c. A PIN and an ATM card

   d. A fingerprint

Answer: c

The correct answer is c. These items are something you know and something you have. Answer a is incorrect because essentially, only one factor is being used — something you know (password). Answer b is incorrect for the same reason. Answer d is incorrect because only one biometric factor is being used.

26. In biometrics, a good measure of the performance of a system is the:

   a. False detection

   b. Crossover Error Rate (CER)

   c. Positive acceptance rate

   d. Sensitivity

Answer: b

The correct answer is b. The other items are made-up distracters.

27. In finger scan technology:

   a. The full fingerprint is stored.

   b. Features extracted from the fingerprint are stored.

   c. More storage is required than in fingerprint technology.

   d. The technology is applicable to large, one-to-many database searches.

Answer: b

The correct answer is b. The features extracted from the fingerprint are stored. Answer a is incorrect because the equivalent of the full fingerprint is not stored in finger scan technology. Answers c and d are incorrect because the opposite is true of finger scan technology.

28. An acceptable biometric throughput rate is:

    a. One subject per two minutes

    b. Two subjects per minute

    c. Ten subjects per minute

    d. Five subjects per minute

Answer: c

29. Which one of the following is NOT a type of penetration test?

    a. Sparse knowledge test

    b. Full knowledge test

    c. Partial knowledge test

    d. Zero knowledge test

Answer: a

The correct answer is a, a distracter.

30. Object-Oriented Database (OODB) systems:

    a. Are ideally suited for text-only information

    b. Require minimal learning time for programmers

    c. Are useful in storing and manipulating complex data, such as images and graphics

    d. Consume minimal system resources

Answer: c

The correct answer is c. The other answers are false because for answer a, relational databases are ideally suited to text-only information. For b and d, OODB systems have a steep learning curve and consume a large amount of system resources.

Chapter 3

1. Which choice below is NOT an element of a fiber optic cable?

    a. Core

    b. BNC

    c. Jacket

    d. Cladding

Answer: b

A BNC refers to a Bayonet Neil Concelman RG58 connector for 10Base2. Fiber-optic cable has three basic physical elements: the core, the cladding, and the jacket. The core is the innermost transmission medium, which can be glass or plastic. The next outer layer, the cladding, is also made of glass or plastic, but it has different properties and helps to reflect the light back into the core. The outermost layer, the jacket, provides protection from heat, moisture, and other environmental elements.

2. Which backup method listed below will probably require the backup operator to use the most number of tapes for a complete system restoration if a different tape is used every night in a five-day rotation?

    a. Full

    b. Differential

    c. Incremental

    d. Ad Hoc

Answer: c

Most backup methods use the Archive file attribute to determine whether the file should be backed up. The backup software determines which files need to be backed up by checking to see whether the Archive file attribute has been set and then resets the Archive bit value to null after the backup procedure. The Incremental backup method backs up only files that have been created or modified since the last backup was made because the Archive file attribute is reset. This can result in the backup operator needing several tapes to do a complete restoration, as every tape with changed files as well as the last full backup tape will need to be restored.

Answer a, a Full or Complete backup, backs up all files in all directories stored on the server regardless of when the last backup was made and whether the files have already been backed up. The Archive file attribute is changed to mark that the files have been backed up, and the tape or tapes will have all data and applications on it. It's an incorrect answer for this question, however, as it's assumed answers b and c will additionally require differential or incremental tapes.

Answer b, the Differential backup method, backs up only files that have been created or modified since the last backup was made, like an incremental backup. However, the difference between an incremental backup and a differential backup is that the Archive file attribute is not reset after the differential backup is completed; therefore the changed file is backed up every time the differential backup is run. The backup set grows in size until the next full backup as these files continue to be backed up during each subsequent differential backup. The advantage of this backup method is that the backup operator should need only the full backup and the one differential backup to restore the system.

Answer d is a distracter.

3. To what does 10Base-5 refer?

    a. 10 Mbps thinnet coax cabling rated to 185 meters maximum length

    b. 10 Mbps thicknet coax cabling rated to 500 meters maximum length

    c. 10 Mbps baseband optical fiber

    d. 100 Mbps unshielded twisted pair cabling

Answer: b

Answer a refers to 10Base-2; answer c refers to 10Base-F; and answer d refers to 100Base-T.

4. Which LAN transmission method below describes a packet sent from a single source to multiple specific destinations?

    a. Unicast

    b. Multicast

    c. Broadcast

    d. Anycast

Answer: b

Unicast describes a packet sent from a single source to a single destination. Answer c, broadcast, describes a packet sent to all nodes on the network segment. Answer d, anycast, refers to communication between any sender and the nearest of a group of receivers in a network.

5. Which part of the 48-bit, 12-digit hexadecimal number known as the Media Access Control (MAC) address identifies the manufacturer of the network device?

    a. The first three bytes

    b. The first two bytes

    c. The second half of the MAC address

    d. The last three bytes

Answer: a

The first three bytes (or first half) of the six-byte MAC address is the manufacturer's identifier. This can be a good troubleshooting aid if a network device is acting up, as it will isolate the brand of the failing device. The other answers are distracters.

6. Which choice below BEST describes coaxial cable?

    a. Coax consists of two insulated wires wrapped around each other in a regular spiral pattern.

    b. Coax consists of a hollow outer cylindrical conductor surrounding a single, inner conductor.

    c. Coax does not require the fixed spacing between connections that UTP requires.

    d. Coax carries signals as light waves.

Answer: b

Coax consists of a hollow outer cylindrical conductor surrounding a single, inner wire conductor. Answer a describes UTP. Coax requires fixed spacing between connections, and answer d describes fiber-optic cable.

7. Which choice below is NOT one of the legal IP address ranges specified by RFC1976 and reserved by the Internet Assigned Numbers Authority (IANA) for nonroutable private addresses?

    a. 10.0.0.0–10.255.255.255

    b. 127.0.0.0–127.0.255.255

    c. 172.16.0.0–172.31.255.255

    d. 192.168.0.0–192.168.255.255

Answer: b

The other three address ranges can be used for Network Address Translation (NAT). While NAT is, in itself, not a very effective security measure, a large network can benefit from using NAT with Dynamic Host Configuration Protocol (DHCP) to help prevent certain internal routing information from being exposed. The address 127.0.0.1 is called the *loopback* address.

8. Which statement below about the difference between analog and digital signals is incorrect?

    a. An analog signal produces an infinite waveform.

    b. Analog signals cannot be used for data communications.

    c. An analog signal can be varied by amplification.

    d. A digital signal produces a saw-tooth waveform.

Answer: b.

The other answers are all properties of analog or digital signals.

9. Which choice below most accurately describes SSL?

    a. It's a widely used standard of securing email at the Application level.

    b. It gives a user remote access to a command prompt across a secure, encrypted session.

    c. It uses two protocols, the Authentication Header and the Encapsulating Security Payload.

    d. It allows an application to have authenticated, encrypted communications across a network.

Answer: d

The Secure Socket Layer (SSL) sits between higher-level application functions and the TCP/IP stack and provides security to applications. It includes a variety of encryption algorithms to secure transmitted data, but the functionality must be integrated into the application. Answer a refers to the Secure/Multipurpose Internet Mail Extension (S/MIME). Most major email clients support S/MIME today. Answer b describes Secure Shell (SSH). Answer c refers to IPSec. IPSec enables security to be built directly into the TCP/IP stack, without requiring application modification.

10. Which IEEE protocol defines wireless transmission in the 5 GHz band with data rates up to 54 Mbps?

    a. IEEE 802.11a

    b. IEEE 802.11b

    c. IEEE 802.11g

    d. IEEE 802.15

Answer: a

IEEE 802.11a specifies high-speed wireless connectivity in the 5 GHz band using Orthogonal Frequency Division Multiplexing with data rates up to 54 Mbps. Answer b, IEEE 802.11b, specifies high-speed wireless connectivity in the 2.4 GHz ISM band up to 11 Mbps. Answer c, IEEE 802.11g, is a proposed standard that offers wireless transmission over relatively short distances at speeds from 20 Mbps up to 54 Mbps and operates in the 2.4 GHz range (and is therefore expected to be backward-compatible with existing 802.11b-based networks). Answer d, IEEE 802.15, defines Wireless Personal Area Networks (WPAN), such as Bluetooth, in the 2.4-2.5 GHz band.

11. Which protocol is used to resolve a known IP address to an unknown MAC address?

    a. ARP

    b. RARP

    c. ICMP

    d. TFTP

Answer: a

The Address Resolution Protocol (ARP) sends a broadcast asking for the host with a specified IP address to reply with its MAC, or hardware address. This information is kept in the ARP Cache. Answer b, the Reverse Address Resolution Protocol (RARP) is commonly used on diskless machines when the MAC is known, but not the IP address. It asks a RARP server to provide a valid IP address, which is somewhat the reverse of ARP. Answer c, the Internet Control Message Protocol (ICMP) is a management protocol for IP. Answer d, the Trivial File Transfer Protocol (TFTP), is a stripped-down version of the File Transfer Protocol (FTP).

12. Which TCP/IP protocol operates at the OSI Network Layer?

    a. FTP

    b. IP

    c. TCP

    d. UDP

Answer: b

IP operates at the Network Layer of the OSI model and at the Internet layer of the TCP/IP model. FTP operates at the Application layer of the TCP/IP model, which is roughly similar to the top three layers of the OSI model: the Application, Presentation, and Session Layers. TCP and UDP both operate at the OSI Transport Layer, which is similar to the TCP/IP host-to-host layer.

13. Which statement accurately describes the difference between 802.11b WLAN ad hoc and infrastructure modes?

    a. The ad hoc mode requires an Access Point to communicate to the wired network.

    b. Wireless nodes can communicate peer-to-peer in the infrastructure mode.

    c. Wireless nodes can communicate peer-to-peer in the ad hoc mode.

    d. Access points are rarely used in 802.11b WLANs.

Answer: c

Nodes on an IEEE 802.11b wireless LANs can communicate in one of two modes: ad hoc or infrastructure. In ad hoc mode, the wireless nodes communicate directly with each other, without establishing a connection to an access point on a wired LAN. In infrastructure mode, the wireless nodes communicate to an access point, which operates similarly to a bridge or router and manages traffic between the wireless network and the wired network.

14. Which answer below is true about the difference between TCP and UDP?

    a. UDP is considered a connectionless protocol and TCP is connection-oriented.

    b. TCP is considered a connectionless protocol, and UDP is connection-oriented.

    c. UDP acknowledges the receipt of packets, and TCP does not.

    d. TCP is sometimes referred to as an unreliable protocol.

Answer: a

As opposed to the Transmission Control Protocol (TCP), the User Datagram Protocol (UDP) is a connectionless protocol. It does not sequence the packets or acknowledge the receipt of packets and is referred to as an unreliable protocol.

15. Which choice below denotes a packet-switched connectionless wide area network (WAN) technology?

    a. X.25

    b. Frame Relay

    c. SMDS

    d. ATM

Answer: c

Switched Multimegabit Data Service (SMDS) is a high-speed, connectionless, packet-switching public network service that extends LAN-like performance to a metropolitan area network (MAN) or a wide area network (WAN). It's generally delivered over a SONET ring with a maximum effective service radius of around 30 miles. Answer a, X.25, defines an interface to the first commercially successful connection-oriented packet-switching network, in which the packets travel over virtual circuits. Answer b, Frame Relay, was a successor to X.25 and offers a connection-oriented packet-switching network. Answer d, Asynchronous Transfer Mode (ATM), was developed from an outgrowth of ISDN standards and is fast-packet, connection-oriented, cell-switching technology.

16. Which answer below is true about the difference between FTP and TFTP?

    a. FTP does not have a directory-browsing capability, whereas TFTP does.

    b. FTP enables print job spooling, whereas TFTP does not.

    c. TFTP is less secure because session authentication does not occur.

    d. FTP is less secure because session authentication does not occur.

Answer: c

The Trivial File Transfer Protocol (TFTP) is considered less secure than the File Transfer Protocol (FTP) because authentication does not occur during session establishment.

17. Which statement below is correct regarding VLANs?

    a. A VLAN restricts flooding to only those ports included in the VLAN.

    b. A VLAN is a network segmented physically, not logically.

    c. A VLAN is less secure when implemented in conjunction with private port switching.

    d. A closed VLAN configuration is the least secure VLAN configuration.

Answer: a

A virtual local area network (VLAN) allows ports on the same or different switches to be grouped so that traffic is confined to members of that group only, and it restricts broadcast, unicast, and multicast traffic. Answer b is incorrect because a VLAN is segmented logically, rather than physically. Answer c is incorrect. When a VLAN is implemented with private port, or single-user, switching, it provides fairly stringent security because broadcast vulnerabilities are minimized. Answer d is incorrect, as a closed VLAN authenticates a user to an access control list on a central authentication server, where they are assigned authorization parameters to determine their level of network access.

18. Which statement about a VPN tunnel below is incorrect?

    a. It can be created by implementing only IPSec devices.

    b. It can be created by installing software or hardware agents on the client or network.

    c. It can be created by implementing key and certificate exchange systems.

    d. It can be created by implementing node authentication systems.

Answer: a

IPSec-compatible and non-IPSec compatible devices are used to create VPNs. The other three answers are all ways in which VPNs can be created.

19. Which utility below can create a server-spoofing attack?

    a. DNS poisoning

    b. C2MYAZZ

    c. Snort

    d. BO2K

Answer: b

C2MYAZZ is a utility that enables server spoofing to implement a session hijacking or man-in-the-middle exploit. It intercepts a client LANMAN authentication logon and obtains the session's logon credentials and password combination transparently to the user. Answer a, DNS poisoning, is also known as cache poisoning. It is the process of distributing incorrect IP address information for a specific host with the intent to divert traffic from its true destination. Answer c, Snort, is a utility used for network sniffing. Network sniffing is the process of gathering traffic from a network by capturing the data as it passes and storing it to analyze later. Answer d, Back Orifice 2000 (BO2K), is an application-level Trojan Horse used to give an attacker backdoor network access.

20. What is a server cluster?

   a. A primary server that mirrors its data to a secondary server

   b. A group of independent servers that are managed as a single system

   c. A tape array backup implementation

   d. A group of WORM optical jukeboxes

Answer: b

A server cluster is a group of servers that appears to be a single server to the user. Answer a refers to redundant servers.

21. Which attack type below does NOT exploit TCP vulnerabilities?

   a. Sequence Number attack

   b. SYN attack

   c. Ping of Death

   d. land.c attack

Answer: c

The Ping of Death exploits the fragmentation vulnerability of large ICMP ECHO request packets by sending an illegal packet with more than 65K of data, creating a buffer overflow. Answer a is a TCP sequence number attack, which exploits the nonrandom predictable pattern of TCP connection sequence numbers to spoof a session. Answer b, a TCP SYN attack, is a DoS attack that exploits the TCP three-way handshake. The attacker rapidly generates randomly sourced SYN packets filling the target's connection queue before the connection can timeout. Answer d, land.c attack, is also a DoS attack that exploits TCP SYN packets. The attacker sends a packet that gives both the source and destination as the target's address and uses the same source and destination port.

22. What is probing used for?

   a. To induce a user into taking an incorrect action

   b. To give an attacker a road map of the network

   c. To use up all of a target's resources

   d. To covertly listen to transmissions

Answer: b

Probing is a procedure whereby the intruder runs programs that scan the network to create a network map for later intrusion. Answer a is spoofing, answer c is the objective of a DoS attack, and answer d describes passive eavesdropping.

23. Which firewall type below uses a dynamic state table to inspect the content of packets?

   a. A packet-filtering firewall

   b. An application-level firewall

   c. A circuit-level firewall

   d. A stateful-inspection firewall

Answer: d

A stateful-inspection firewall intercepts incoming packets at the Network level, and then uses an Inspection Engine to extract state-related information from upper layers. It maintains the information in a dynamic state table and evaluates subsequent connection attempts. Answer a, packet-filtering firewall, is the simplest type of firewall commonly implemented on routers. It operates at the Network layer and offers good performance but is the least secure. Answer b, application-level firewall or application-layer gateway, is more secure because it examines the packet at the Application layer but at the expense of performance. Answer c, circuit-level firewall, is similar to the application-level firewall in that it functions as a proxy server, but it differs in that special proxy application software is not needed.

24. To what does logon abuse refer?

   a. Breaking into a network primarily from an external source

   b. Legitimate users accessing networked services that would normally be restricted to them

   c. Nonbusiness or personal use of the Internet

   d. Intrusions via dial-up or asynchronous external network connections

Answer: b

Logon abuse entails an otherwise proper user attempting to access areas of the network that are deemed off-limits. Answer a is called network intrusion, and d refers to back-door remote access.

25. What type of firewall architecture employs two network cards and a single screening router?

   a. A screened-host firewall

   b. A dual-homed host firewall

   c. A screened-subnet firewall

   d. An application-level proxy server

Answer: a

Like a dual-homed host, a screened-host firewall uses two network cards to connect to the trusted and untrusted networks, but it adds a screening router between the host and the untrusted network. Answer b, dual-homed host, has two NICs but not necessarily a screening router. Answer c, screened-subnet firewall, also uses two NICs but has two screening routers with the host acting as a proxy server on its own network segment. One screening router controls traffic local to the network while the second monitors and controls incoming and outgoing Internet traffic. Answer d, application-level proxy, is unrelated to this question.

26. To what does covert channel eavesdropping refer?

   a. Using a hidden, unauthorized network connection to communicate unauthorized information

   b. Nonbusiness or personal use of the Internet

   c. Socially engineering passwords from an ISP

   d. The use of two-factor passwords

Answer: a

A covert channel is a connection intentionally created to transmit unauthorized information from inside a trusted network to a partner at an outside, untrusted node. Answer c is called masquerading.

27. What is one of the most common drawbacks to using a dual-homed host firewall?

   a. The examination of the packet at the Network Layer introduces latency.

   b. The examination of the packet at the Application Layer introduces latency.

   c. The ACLs must be manually maintained on the host.

   d. Internal routing may accidentally become enabled.

Answer: d

A dual-homed host uses two NICs to attach to two separate networks, commonly a trusted network and an untrusted network. It's important that the internal routing function of the host be disabled to create an Application-layer chokepoint and filter packets. Many systems come with routing enabled by default, such as IP forwarding, which makes the firewall useless. The other answers are distracters.

28. Which is NOT a property of a bridge?

    a. Forwards the data to all other segments if the destination is not on the local segment

    b. Operates at Layer 2, the Data Link Layer

    c. Operates at Layer 3, the Network Layer

    d. Can create a broadcast storm

Answer: c

A bridge operates at Layer 2 and therefore does not use IP addressing to make routing decisions.

29. Which IEEE protocol defines the Spanning Tree protocol?

    a. IEEE 802.5

    b. IEEE 802.3

    c. IEEE 802.11

    d. IEEE 802.1D

Answer: d

The 802.1D spanning tree protocol is an Ethernet link-management protocol that provides link redundancy while preventing routing loops. Because only one active path can exist for an Ethernet network to route properly, the STP algorithm calculates and manages the best loop-free path through the network. Answer a, IEEE 802.5, specifies a token-passing ring access method for LANs. Answer b, IEEE 802.3, specifies an Ethernet bus topology using Carrier Sense Multiple Access Control/Carrier Detect (CSMA/CD). Answer c, IEEE 802.11, is the IEEE standard that specifies 1 Mbps and 2 Mbps wireless connectivity in the 2.4 MHz ISM (Industrial, Scientific, Medical) band.

30. What does the Data Encapsulation in the OSI model do?

    a. Creates seven distinct layers

    b. Wraps data from one layer around a data packet from an adjoining layer

    c. Provides best-effort delivery of a data packet

    d. Makes the network transmission deterministic

Answer: b

Data Encapsulation attaches information from one layer to the packet as it travels from an adjoining layer. The OSI-layered architecture model creates seven layers. The TCP/IP protocol UDP provides best effort packet delivery, and a token-passing transmission scheme creates a deterministic network because it is possible to compute the maximum predictable delay.

31. Which choice below is NOT an element of IPSec?

    a. Authentication Header

    b. Layer Two Tunneling Protocol

    c. Security Association

    d. Encapsulating Security Payload

Answer: b

The Layer Two Tunneling Protocol (L2TP) is a layer two tunneling protocol that allows a host to establish a virtual connection. Although L2TP, an enhancement to Layer Two Forwarding Protocol (L2F) that supports some features of the Point to Point Tunneling Protocol (PPTP), may coexist with IPSec, it is not natively an IPSec component. Answer a, the Authentication Header (AH), is an authenticating protocol that uses a hash signature in the packet header to validate the integrity of the packet data and the authenticity of the sender. Answer c, the Security Association (SA), is a component of the IPSec architecture that contains the information the IPSec device needs to process incoming and outbound IPSec packets. IPSec devices embed a value called the Security Parameter Index (SPI) in the header to associate a datagram with its SA and to store SAs in a Security Association Database (SAD). Answer d, the Encapsulating Security Payload (ESP), is an authenticating and encrypting protocol that provides integrity, source authentication, and confidentiality services.

32. Which network attack below would NOT be considered a Denial of Service attack?

    a. Ping of Death

    b. SMURF

    c. Brute Force

    d. TCP SYN

Answer: c

A brute force attack is an attempt to use all combinations of key patterns to decipher a message. The other three attacks are commonly used to create a Denial of Service (DoS). Answer a, Ping of Death, exploits ICMP by sending an illegal ECHO packet of >65K octets of data, which can cause an overflow of system variables and lead to a system crash. Answer b, SMURF, is a type of attack using spoofed ICMP ECHO requests to broadcast addresses, which the routers attempt to propagate, congesting the network. Three participants are required for a SMURF attack: the attacker, the amplifying network, and the victim. Answer d, a TCP SYN flood attack, generates phony TCP SYN packets from random IP addresses at a rapid rate to fill up the connection queue and stop the system from accepting legitimate users.

33. Which statement is NOT true about the SOCKS protocol?

    a. It is sometimes referred to as an application-level proxy.

    b. It uses an ESP for authentication and encryption.

    c. It operates in the Transport Layer of the OSI model.

    d. Network applications need to be SOCKS-ified to operate.

Answer: b

The Encapsulating Security Payload (ESP) is a component of IPSec. Socket Security (SOCKS) is a Transport layer, secure networking proxy protocol. SOCKS replaces the standard network systems calls with its own calls. These calls open connections to a SOCKS proxy server for client authentication, transparently to the user. Common network utilities, like TELNET or FTP, need to be SOCKS-ified or have their network calls altered to recognize SOCKS proxy calls.

34. Which choice below is NOT a way to get Windows NT passwords?

    a. Obtain the backup SAM from the repair directory.

    b. Boot the NT server with a floppy containing an alternate operating system.

    c. Obtain root access to the /etc/passwd file.

    d. Use pwdump2 to dump the password hashes directly from the registry.

Answer: c

The /etc/passwd file is a Unix system file. The NT Security Accounts Manager, SAM, contains the usernames and encrypted passwords of all local (and domain, if the server is a domain controller) users. The SAM uses an older, weaker LanManager hash that can be broken easily by tools like L0phtcrack. Physical access to the NT server and the rdisks must be controlled. The "Sam._" file in the repair directory must be deleted after creation of an rdisk. Pwdump and pwdump2 are utilities that allow someone with Administrator rights to target the Local Security Authority Subsystem, isass.exe, from a remote system.

35. Which type of routing below commonly broadcasts its routing table information to all other routers every minute?

    a. Static

    b. Distance Vector

    c. Link State

    d. Dynamic Control Protocol

Answer: b

Distance vector routing uses the routing information protocol (RIP) to maintain a dynamic table of routing information that is updated regularly. It is the oldest and most common type of dynamic routing. Answer a, static routing, defines a specific route in a configuration file on the router and does not require the routers to exchange route information dynamically. Answer c, link state routers, functions like distance vector routers, but it uses first-hand information when building routing tables only by maintaining a copy of every other router's Link State Protocol (LSP) frame. This helps to eliminate routing errors and considerably lessens convergence time. Answer d is a distracter.

36. A *back door* into a network refers to what?

   a. Socially engineering passwords from a subject

   b. Mechanisms created by hackers to gain network access at a later time

   c. Undocumented instructions used by programmers to debug applications

   d. Monitoring programs implemented on dummy applications to lure intruders

Answer: b

Back doors are very hard to trace, as an intruder will often create several avenues into a network to be exploited later. The only real way to be sure these avenues are closed after an attack is to restore the operating system from the original media, apply the patches, and restore all data and applications. Answer a, social engineering, is a technique used to manipulate users into revealing information like passwords. Answer c refers to a *trap door*, which is an undocumented hook into an application to assist programmers with debugging. Although intended innocently, these can be exploited by intruders. Answer d is a "honey pot" or "padded cell." A honey pot uses a dummy server with bogus applications as a decoy for intruders.

37. What is the protocol that supports sending and receiving email?

   a. SNMP

   b. SMTP

   c. ICMP

   d. RARP

Answer: b

Simple Mail Transport Protocol (SMTP) queues and transfers email. SNMP stands for Simple Network Management Protocol. ICMP stands for Internet Control Message Protocol. RARP stands for Reverse Address Resolution Protocol.

38. Which protocol below does NOT pertain to email?

    a. SMTP

    b. POP

    c. CHAP

    d. IMAP

Answer: c

The Challenge Handshake Authentication Protocol (CHAP) is used at the startup of a remote link to verify the identity of a remote node. Answer a, the Simple Mail Transfer Protocol (RFCs 821 and 1869), is used by a server to deliver email over the Internet. Answer b, the Post Office Protocol (RFC 1939), enables users to read their email by downloading it from a remote server on to their local computer. Answer d, the Internet Message Access Protocol (RFC 2060), allows users to read their email on a remote server without download-ing the mail locally.

39. Which choice below does NOT relate to analog dial-up hacking?

    a. War dialing

    b. War walking

    c. Demon dialing

    d. ToneLoc

Answer: b

War walking (or war driving) refers to scanning for 802.11-based wireless net-work information by either driving or walking with a laptop, a wireless adapter in promiscuous mode, some type of scanning software such as NetStumbler or AiroPeek, and a Global Positioning System (GPS). Answer a, war dialing, is a method used to hack into computers by using a software pro-gram to automatically call a large pool of telephone numbers to search for those that have a modem attached. Answer c, demon dialing, similar to war dialing, is a tool used to attack one modem using brute force to guess the password and gain access. Answer d, ToneLoc, was one of the first war-dialing tools used by phone phreakers.

40. Which level of RAID is commonly referred to as *disk mirroring*?

    a. RAID 0

    b. RAID 1

    c. RAID 3

    d. RAID 5

Answer: b

Redundant Array of Inexpensive Disks (RAID) is a method of enhancing hard disk fault tolerance, which can improve performance (see Table A.8). RAID 1 maintains a complete copy of all data by duplicating each hard drive. Performance can suffer in some implementations of RAID 1, and twice as many drives are required. Novell developed a type of disk mirroring called disk duplexing, which uses multiple disk controller cards, increasing both performance and reliability. Answer a, RAID 0, gives some performance gains by striping the data across multiple drives but reduces fault tolerance, as the failure of any single drive disables the whole volume. Answer c, RAID 3, uses a dedicated error-correction disk called a parity drive, and it stripes the data across the other data drives. Answer RAID 5, uses all disks in the array for both data and error correction, increasing both storage capacity and performance.

41. Which choice below is the earliest and the most commonly found Interior Gateway Protocol?

    a. RIP

    b. OSPF

    c. IGRP

    d. EAP

Answer: a

The Routing Information Protocol (RIP) bases its routing path on the distance (number of hops) to the destination. RIP maintains optimum routing paths by sending out routing update messages if the network topology changes. For example, if a router finds that a particular link is faulty, it will update its routing table and then send a copy of the modified table to each of its neighbors. Answer b, the Open Shortest Path First (OSPF), is a link-state hierarchical routing algorithm intended as a successor to RIP. It features least-cost routing, multipath routing, and load balancing. Answer c, the Internet Gateway Routing Protocol (IGRP), is a Cisco protocol that uses a composite metric as its routing metric, including bandwidth, delay, reliability, loading, and maximum transmission unit. Answer d, the Extensible Authentication Protocol (EAP), is a general protocol for PPP authentication that supports multiple remote authentication mechanisms.

42. What is the Network Layer of the OSI reference model primarily responsible for?

    a. Internetwork packet routing

    b. LAN bridging

    c. SMTP Gateway services

    d. Signal regeneration and repeating

Answer: a

Although many routers can perform most of the functions above, the OSI Network Layer is primarily responsible for routing. Answer b, bridging, is a Data Link Layer function. Answer c, gateways, most commonly function at the higher layers. Answer d, signal regeneration and repeating, is primarily a Physical Layer function.

43. Which of the following is NOT a true statement about Network Address Translation (NAT)?

   a. NAT is used when corporations want to use private addressing ranges for internal networks.

   b. NAT is designed to mask the true IP addresses of internal systems.

   c. Private addresses can easily be routed globally.

   d. NAT translates private IP addresses to registered "real" IP addresses.

Answer: c

Private addresses are not easily routable.

44. In the DoD reference model, which layer conforms to the OSI Transport Layer?

   a. Process/Application Layer

   b. Host-to-Host Layer

   c. Internet Layer

   d. Network Access Layer

Answer: b

In the DoD reference model, the Host-to-Host layer parallels the function of the OSI's Transport Layer. This layer contains the Transmission Control Protocol (TCP), and the User Datagram Protocol (UDP). Answer a, the DoD Process/Application layer, corresponds to the OSI's top three layers, the Application, Presentation, and Session Layers. Answer c, the DoD Internet layer, corresponds to the OSI's Network Layer, and answer d, the DoD Network Access layer, is the equivalent of the Data Link and Physical Layers of the OSI model.

45. The IP address, 178.22.90.1, is considered to be in which class of address?

   a. Class A

   b. Class B

   c. Class C

   d. Class D

Answer: b

The class A address range is 1.0.0.0 to 126.255.255.255. The class B address range is 128.0.0.0 to 191.255.255.255. The class C address range is from 192.0.0.0 to 223.255.255.255. The class D address range is 244.0.0.0 to 239.255.255.255 and is used for multicast packets.

46. What does TFTP stand for?

    a. Trivial File Transport Protocol

    b. Transport for TCP/IP

    c. Trivial File Transfer Protocol

    d. Transport File Transfer Protocol

Answer: c

The other acronyms do not exist.

Chapter 4

1. The Secure Hash Algorithm (SHA) is specified in the:

    a. Data Encryption Standard

    b. Digital Signature Standard

    c. Digital Encryption Standard

    d. Advanced Encryption Standard

Answer: b

The correct answer is b. Answer a refers to DES, a symmetric encryption algorithm; answer c is a distracter — there is no such term; answer d is the Advanced Encryption Standard, which has replaced DES and is now the Rijndael algorithm.

2. What does Secure Sockets Layer (SSL)/Transaction Security Layer (TSL) do?

    a. Implements confidentiality, authentication, and integrity above the Transport Layer

    b. Implements confidentiality, authentication, and integrity below the Transport Layer

    c. Implements only confidentiality above the Transport Layer

    d. Implements only confidentiality below the Transport Layer

Answer: a

The correct answer is a by definition. Answer b is incorrect because SSL/TLS operates above the Transport Layer; answer c is incorrect because authentication and integrity are provided also, and answer d is incorrect because it cites only confidentiality and SSL/TLS operates above the Transport Layer.

3. What are MD4 and MD5?

    a. Symmetric encryption algorithms

    b. Asymmetric encryption algorithms

    c. Hashing algorithms

    d. Digital certificates

Answer: c

The correct answer is c. Answers a and b are incorrect because they are general types of encryption systems, and answer d is incorrect because hashing algorithms are not digital certificates.

4. Elliptic curves, which are applied to public key cryptography, employ modular exponentiation that characterizes the:

    a. Elliptic curve discrete logarithm problem

    b. Prime factors of very large numbers

    c. Elliptic curve modular addition

    d. Knapsack problem

Answer: a

The correct answer is a. Modular exponentiation in elliptic curves is the analog of the modular discreet logarithm problem. Answer b is incorrect because prime factors are involved with RSA public key systems; answer c is incorrect because modular addition in elliptic curves is the analog of modular multiplication; and answer d is incorrect because the knapsack problem is not an elliptic curve problem.

5. Which algorithm is used in the Clipper Chip?

    a. IDEA

    b. DES

    c. SKIPJACK

    d. 3 DES

Answer: c

The correct answer is c. Answers a, b, and d are other symmetric key algorithms.

6. The hashing algorithm in the Digital Signature Standard (DSS) generates a message digest of:

    a. 120 bits

    b. 160 bits

    c. 56 bits

    d. 130 bits

Answer: b

7. The protocol of the Wireless Application Protocol (WAP), which performs functions similar to SSL in the TCP/IP protocol, is called the:

    a. Wireless Application Environment (WAE)

    b. Wireless Session Protocol (WSP)

    c. Wireless Transaction Protocol (WTP)

    d. Wireless Transport Layer Security Protocol (WTLS)

Answer: d

The correct answer is d. SSL performs security functions in TCP/IP. The other answers refer to protocols in the WAP protocol stack also, but their primary functions are not security.

8. A Security Parameter Index (SPI) and the identity of the security protocol (AH or ESP) are the components of:

    a. SSL

    b. IPSec

    c. S-HTTP

    d. SSH-1

Answer: b

The correct answer is b. The SPI, AH and/or ESP and the destination IP address are components of an IPSec Security Association (SA.) The other answers describe protocols other than IPSec.

9. When two different keys encrypt a plaintext message into the same cipher-text, this situation is known as:

    a. Public key cryptography

    b. Cryptanalysis

    c. Key clustering

    d. Hashing

Answer: c

The correct answer is c. Answer a describes a type of cryptographic system using a public and a private key; answer b is the art/science of breaking ciphers; answer d is the conversion of a message of variable length into a fixed-length message digest.

10. What is the result of the Exclusive Or operation, 1XOR 0?

    a. 1

    b. 0

    c. Indeterminate

    d. 10

Answer: a

The correct answer is a. An XOR operation results in a 0 if the two input bits are identical and a 1 if one of the bits is a 1 and the other is a 0.

11. A block cipher:

    a. Encrypts by operating on a continuous data stream

    b. Is an asymmetric key algorithm

    c. Converts variable-length plaintext into fixed-length ciphertext

    d. Breaks a message into fixed length units for encryption

Answer: d

The correct answer is d. Answer a describes a stream cipher; answer b is incorrect because a block cipher applies to symmetric key algorithms; and answer c describes a hashing operation.

12. In most security protocols that support confidentiality, integrity, and authentication:

    a. Public key cryptography is used to create digital signatures.

    b. Private key cryptography is used to create digital signatures.

    c. DES is used to create digital signatures.

    d. Digital signatures are not implemented.

Answer: a

The correct answer is a. Answer b is incorrect because private key cryptography does not create digital signatures; answer c is incorrect because DES is a private key system and, therefore, follows the same logic as in b; and answer d is incorrect because digital signatures are implemented to obtain authentication and integrity.

13. Which of the following is an example of a symmetric key algorithm?

     a. Rijndael

     b. RSA

     c. Diffie-Hellman

     d. Knapsack

Answer: a

The correct answer is a. The other answers are examples of asymmetric key systems.

14. Which of the following is a problem with symmetric key encryption?

     a. It is slower than asymmetric key encryption.

     b. Most algorithms are kept proprietary.

     c. Work factor is not a function of the key size.

     d. It provides secure distribution of the secret key.

Answer: d

The correct answer is d. Answer a is incorrect because the opposite is true; answer b is incorrect because most symmetric key algorithms are published; and answer c is incorrect because work factor is a function of key size. The larger the key is, the larger the work factor.

15. Which of the following is an example of an asymmetric key algorithm?

     a. IDEA

     b. DES

     c. 3 DES

     d. ELLIPTIC CURVE

Answer: d

The correct answer is d. All the other answers refer to symmetric key algorithms.

16. In public key cryptography:

     a. Only the private key can encrypt, and only the public key can decrypt.

     b. Only the public key can encrypt, and only the private key can decrypt.

     c. The public key is used to encrypt and decrypt.

     d. If the public key encrypts, only the private key can decrypt.

Answer: d

The correct answer is d. Answers a and b are incorrect because if one key encrypts, the other can decrypt. Answer c is incorrect because if the public key encrypts, it cannot decrypt.

17. In a hybrid cryptographic system, usually:

   a. Public key cryptography is used for the encryption of the message.

   b. Private key cryptography is used for the encryption of the message.

   c. Neither public key nor private key cryptography is used.

   d. Digital certificates cannot be used.

Answer: b

The correct answer is b. Answer a is incorrect because public key cryptography is usually used for the encryption and transmission of the secret session key. Answer c is incorrect because both public and private key encryption are used, and answer d is incorrect because digital certificates can be used (and normally are used).

18. What is the block length of the Rijndael Cipher?

   a. 64 bits

   b. 128 bits

   c. Variable

   d. 256 bits

Answer: c

The correct answer is c. The other answers with fixed numbers are incorrect.

19. A polyalphabetic cipher is also known as:

   a. One-time pad

   b. Vigenère cipher

   c. Steganography

   d. Vernam cipher

Answer: b

The correct answer is b. Answer a is incorrect because a one-time pad uses a random key with a length equal to the plaintext message and is used only once. Answer c is the process of sending a message with no indication that a message even exists. Answer d is incorrect because it applies to stream ciphers that are XORed with a random key string.

20. The classic Caesar cipher is a:

    a. Polyalphabetic cipher

    b. Monoalphabetic cipher

    c. Transposition cipher

    d. Code group

Answer: b

The correct answer is b. It uses one alphabet shifted three places. Answers a and c are incorrect because in answer a, multiple alphabets are used, and in answer c, the letters of the message are transposed. Answer d is incorrect because code groups deal with words and phrases and ciphers deal with bits or letters.

21. In steganography:

    a. Private key algorithms are used.

    b. Public key algorithms are used.

    c. Both public and private key algorithms are used.

    d. The fact that the message exists is not known.

Answer: d

The correct answer is d. The other answers are incorrect because neither algorithm is used.

22. What is the key length of the Rijndael Block Cipher?

    a. 56 or 64 bits

    b. 512 bits

    c. 128, 192, or 256 bits

    d. 512 or 1024 bits

Answer: c

23. In a block cipher, diffusion:

    a. Conceals the connection between the ciphertext and plaintext

    b. Spreads the influence of a plaintext character over many ciphertext characters

    c. Is usually implemented by non-linear S-boxes

    d. Cannot be accomplished

Answer: b

The correct answer is b. Answer a defines confusion; answer c defines how confusion is accomplished; and answer d is incorrect because it can be accomplished.

24. The NIST Advanced Encryption Standard uses the:

   a. 3 DES algorithm

   b. Rijndael algorithm

   c. DES algorithm

   d. IDEA algorithm

Answer: b

The correct answer is b. By definition, the others are incorrect.

25. The modes of DES do NOT include:

   a. Electronic Code Book

   b. Cipher Block Chaining

   c. Variable Block Feedback

   d. Output Feedback

Answer: c

The correct answer is c. There is no such encipherment mode.

26. Which of the following is true?

   a. The work factor of triple DES is the same as for double DES.

   b. The work factor of single DES is the same as for triple DES.

   c. The work factor of double DES is the same as for single DES.

   d. No successful attacks have been reported against double DES.

Answer: c

The correct answer is c. The Meet-in-the-Middle attack has been successfully applied to double DES, and the work factor is equivalent to that of single DES. Thus, answer d is incorrect. Answer a is false because the work factor of triple DES is greater than that for double DES. In triple DES, three levels of encryption and/or decryption are applied to the message. The work factor of double DES is equivalent to the work factor of single DES. Answer b is false because the work factor of single DES is less than for triple DES.

27. The Rijndael Cipher employs a round transformation that is comprised of three layers of distinct, invertible transformations. These transformations are also defined as *uniform*, which means that every bit of the State is treated the same. Which of the following is NOT one of these layers?

    a. The non-linear layer, which is the parallel application of S-boxes that have the optimum worst-case non-linearity properties

    b. The linear mixing layer, which provides a guarantee of the high diffusion of multiple rounds

    c. The key addition layer, which is an Exclusive OR of the Round Key to the intermediate State

    d. The key inversion layer, which provides confusion through the multiple rounds

Answer: d

The correct answer is d. This answer is a distracter and does not exist.

28. The Escrowed Encryption Standard describes the:

    a. Rijndael Cipher

    b. Clipper Chip

    c. Fair Public Key Cryptosystem

    d. Digital certificates

Answer: b

29. Theoretically, quantum computing offers the possibility of factoring the products of large prime numbers and calculating discreet logarithms in polynomial time. These calculations can be accomplished in such a compressed time frame because:

    a. Information can be transformed into quantum light waves that travel through fiber-optic channels. Computations can be performed on the associated data by passing the light waves through various types of optical filters and solid-state materials with varying indices of refraction, thus drastically increasing the throughput over conventional computations.

    b. A quantum bit in a quantum computer is actually a linear superposition of both the one and zero states and, therefore, can theoretically represent both values in parallel. This phenomenon allows computation that usually takes exponential time to be accomplished in polynomial time because different values of the binary pattern of the solution can be calculated simultaneously.

    c. A quantum computer takes advantage of quantum tunneling in molecular scale transistors. This mode permits ultra high-speed switching to take place, thus exponentially increasing the speed of computations.

    d. A quantum computer exploits the time-space relationship that changes as particles approach the speed of light. At that interface, the resistance of conducting materials effectively is zero and exponential speed computations are possible.

Answer: b

In digital computers, a bit is in either a one or zero state. In a quantum computer, through linear superposition, a quantum bit can be in both states, essentially simultaneously. Thus, computations consisting of trail evaluations of binary patterns can take place simultaneously in exponential time. The probability of obtaining a correct result is increased through a phenomenon called constructive interference of light, while the probability of obtaining an incorrect result is decreased through destructive interference. Answer a describes optical computing that is effective in applying Fourier and other transformations to data to perform high-speed computations. Light representing large volumes of data passing through properly shaped physical objects can be subjected to mathematical transformations and recombined to provide the appropriate results. However, this mode of computation is not defined as quantum computing. Answers c and d are diversionary answers that do not describe quantum computing.

30. Which of the following characteristics does a one-time pad have if used properly?

    a. It can be used more than once.

    b. The key does not have to be random.

    c. It is unbreakable.

    d. The key has to be of greater length than the message to be encrypted.

Answer: c

The correct answer is c. If the one-time-pad is used only once and its corresponding key is truly random and does not have repeating characters, it is unbreakable. Answer a is incorrect because if used properly, the one-time-pad should be used only once. Answer b is incorrect because the key should be random. Answer d is incorrect because the key has to be of the same length as the message.

31. The DES key is:

  a. 128 bits

  b. 64 bits

  c. 56 bits

  d. 512 bits

Answer: c

32. In a digitally-signed message transmission using a hash function:

  a. The message digest is encrypted in the private key of the sender.

  b. The message digest is encrypted in the public key of the sender.

  c. The message is encrypted in the private key of the sender.

  d. The message is encrypted in the public key of the sender.

Answer: a

The correct answer is a. The hash function generates a message digest. The message digest is encrypted with the private key of the sender. Thus, if the message can be opened with the sender's public key that is known to all, the message must have come from the sender. The message is not encrypted with the public key because the message is usually longer than the message digest and would take more computing resources to encrypt and decrypt. Because the message digest uniquely characterizes the message, it can be used to verify the identity of the sender.

Answers b and d will not work because a message encrypted in the public key of the sender can be read only by using the private key of the sender. Because the sender is the only one who knows this key, no one else can read the message. Answer c is incorrect because the message is not encrypted; the message digest is encrypted.

33. The strength of RSA public key encryption is based on the:

  a. Difficulty in finding logarithms in a finite field

  b. Difficulty of multiplying two large prime numbers

  c. Fact that only one key is used

  d. Difficulty in finding the prime factors of very large numbers

Answer: d

The correct answer is d. Answer a applies to public key algorithms such as Diffie-Hellman and Elliptic Curve. Answer b is incorrect because it is easy to multiply two large prime numbers. Answer c refers to symmetric key encryption.

34. Elliptic curve cryptosystems:

    a. Have a higher strength per bit than an RSA

    b. Have a lower strength per bit than an RSA

    c. Cannot be used to implement digital signatures

    d. Cannot be used to implement encryption

Answer: a

The correct answer is a. It is more difficult to compute elliptic curve discreet logarithms than conventional discreet logarithms or factoring. Smaller key sizes in the elliptic curve implementation can yield higher levels of security. Therefore, answer b is incorrect. Answers c and d are incorrect because elliptic curve cryptosystems can be used for digital signatures and encryption.

35. Which of the following is NOT a fundamental component of Identity-Based Encryption (IBE)?

    a. Bi-linear mapping

    b. Weil Pairing

    c. Multiplication of points on an elliptic curve

    d. A symmetrical session key

Answer: d

IBE is based on using an arbitrary string as an individual's public key. It is based on public key cryptography; therefore, a symmetric key is not involved in the process.

Chapter 5

1. What does the Bell-LaPadula model NOT allow?

    a. Subjects to read from a higher level of security relative to their level of security

    b. Subjects to read from a lower level of security relative to their level of security

    c. Subjects to write to a higher level of security relative to their level of security

    d. Subjects to read at their same level of security

Answer: a

The correct answer is a. The other options are not prohibited by the model.

2. In the * (star) property of the Bell-LaPadula model:

   a. Subjects cannot read from a higher level of security relative to their level of security.

   b. Subjects cannot read from a lower level of security relative to their level of security.

   c. Subjects cannot write to a lower level of security relative to their level of security.

   d. Subjects cannot read from their same level of security.

   Answer: c

   The correct answer is c by definition of the star property.

3. The Clark-Wilson model focuses on data's:

   a. Integrity

   b. Confidentiality

   c. Availability

   d. Format

   Answer: a

   The correct answer is a. The Clark-Wilson model is an integrity model.

4. The * (star) property of the Biba model states that:

   a. Subjects cannot write to a lower level of integrity relative to their level of integrity.

   b. Subjects cannot write to a higher level of integrity relative to their level of integrity.

   c. Subjects cannot read from a lower level of integrity relative to their level of integrity.

   d. Subjects cannot read from a higher level of integrity relative to their level of integrity.

   Answer: b

5. Which of the following does the Clark-Wilson model NOT involve?

   a. Constrained data items

   b. Transformational procedures

   c. Confidentiality items

   d. Well-formed transactions

   Answer: c

   The correct answer is c. Answers a, b, and d are parts of the Clark-Wilson model.

6. The Take-Grant model:

    a. Focuses on confidentiality

    b. Specifies the rights that a subject can transfer to an object

    c. Specifies the levels of integrity

    d. Specifies the levels of availability

Answer: b

7. The Biba model addresses:

    a. Data disclosure

    b. Transformation procedures

    c. Constrained data items

    d. Unauthorized modification of data

Answer: d

The correct answer is d. The Biba model is an integrity model. Answer a is associated with confidentiality. Answers b and c are specific to the Clark-Wilson model.

8. Mandatory access controls first appear in the Trusted Computer System Evaluation Criteria (TCSEC) at the rating of:

    a. D

    b. C

    c. B

    d. A

Answer: c

9. In the access control matrix, the rows are:

    a. Access Control Lists (ACLs)

    b. Tuples

    c. Domains

    d. Capability lists

Answer: d

The correct answer is d. Answer a is incorrect because the access control list is not a row in the access control matrix. Answer b is incorrect because a tuple is a row in the table of a relational database. Answer c is incorrect because a domain is the set of allowable values a column or attribute can take in a relational database.

10. What information security model formalizes the U.S. Department of Defense multi-level security policy?

   a. Clark-Wilson

   b. Stark-Wilson

   c. Biba

   d. Bell-LaPadula

Answer: d

The correct answer is d. The Bell-LaPadula model addresses the confidentiality of classified material. Answers a and c are integrity models, and answer b is a distracter.

11. A Trusted Computing Base (TCB) is defined as:

   a. The total combination of protection mechanisms within a computer system that is trusted to enforce a security policy.

   b. The boundary separating the trusted mechanisms from the remainder of the system.

   c. A trusted path that permits a user to access resources.

   d. A system that employs the necessary hardware and software assurance measures to enable the processing of multiple levels of classified or sensitive information to occur.

Answer: a

The correct answer is a. Answer b is the security perimeter. Answer c is the definition of a trusted path. Answer d is the definition of a trusted computer system.

12. Memory space insulated from other running processes in a multi-processing system is part of a:

   a. Protection domain

   b. Security perimeter

   c. Least upper bound

   d. Constrained data item

Answer: a

13. The boundary separating the TCB from the remainder of the system is called the:

    a. Star property

    b. Simple security property

    c. Discretionary control boundary

    d. Security perimeter

Answer: d

The correct answer is d. Answers a and b deal with security models, and answer c is a distracter.

14. The system component that enforces access controls on an object is the:

    a. Security perimeter

    b. Trusted domain

    c. Reference monitor

    d. Access control matrix

Answer: c

15. Which one the following is NOT one of the three major parts of the Common Criteria (CC)?

    a. Introduction and General Model

    b. Security Evaluation Requirements

    c. Security Functional Requirements

    d. Security Assurance Requirements

Answer: b

The correct answer is b, a distracter. Answer a is Part 1 of the CC. It defines general concepts and principles of information security and defines the contents of the Protection Profile (PP), Security Target (ST), and the Package. The Security Functional Requirements, answer c, are Part 2 of the CC, which contains a catalog of well-defined standard means of expressing security requirements of IT products and systems. Answer d is Part 3 of the CC and comprises a catalog of a set of standard assurance components.

16. A computer system that employs the necessary hardware and software assurance measures to enable it to process multiple levels of classified or sensitive information is called a:

    a. Closed system

    b. Open system

    c. Trusted system

    d. Safe system

Answer: c

The correct answer is c, by definition of a trusted system. Answers a and b refer to open, standard information on a product as opposed to a closed or proprietary product. Answer d is a distracter.

17. For fault-tolerance to operate, a system must be:

    a. Capable of detecting and correcting the fault

    b. Capable only of detecting the fault

    c. Capable of terminating operations in a safe mode

    d. Capable of a cold start

Answer: a

The correct answer is a, the two conditions required for a fault-tolerant system. Answer b is a distracter. Answer c is the definition of fail safe, and answer d refers to starting after a system shutdown.

18. Which of the following choices describes the four phases of the National Information Assurance Certification and Accreditation Process (NIACAP)?

    a. Definition, Verification, Validation, and Confirmation

    b. Definition, Verification, Validation, and Post Accreditation

    c. Verification, Validation, Authentication, and Post Accreditation

    d. Definition, Authentication, Verification, and Post Accreditation

Answer: b

19. In the Common Criteria, an implementation-independent statement of security needs for a set of IT security products that could be built is called a:

    a. Security Target (ST)

    b. Package

    c. Protection Profile (PP)

    d. Target of Evaluation (TOE)

Answer: c

The correct answer is c. Answer a, ST, is a statement of security claims for a particular IT product or system. A Package, answer b, is defined in the CC as "an intermediate combination of security requirement components." A TOE, answer d, is "an IT product or system to be evaluated."

20. The termination of selected, non-critical processing when a hardware or software failure occurs and is detected is referred to as:

   a. Fail safe

   b. Fault tolerant

   c. Fail soft

   d. An exception

Answer: c

21. Which one of the following is NOT a component of a CC Protection Profile?

   a. Target of Evaluation (TOE) description

   b. Threats against the product that must be addressed

   c. Product-specific security requirements

   d. Security objectives

Answer: c

The correct answer is c. Product-specific security requirements for the product or system are contained in the Security Target (ST). Additional items in the PP are:

   • TOE security environment description

   • Assumptions about the security aspects of the product's expected use

   • Organizational security policies or rules

   • Application notes

   • Rationale

22. Content-dependent control makes access decisions based on:

   a. The object's data

   b. The object's environment

   c. The object's owner

   d. The object's view

Answer: a

The correct answer is a. Answer b is context-dependent control. Answers c and d are distracters.

23. The term *failover* refers to:

  a. Switching to a duplicate, "hot" backup component

  b. Terminating processing in a controlled fashion

  c. Resiliency

  d. A fail-soft system

Answer: a

The correct answer is a. Failover means switching to a "hot" backup system that maintains duplicate states with the primary system. Answer b refers to fail safe, and answers c and d refer to fail soft.

24. Primary storage is the:

  a. Memory directly addressable by the CPU, which is for storage of instructions and data that are associated with the program being executed

  b. Memory, such as magnetic disks, that provides non-volatile storage

  c. Memory used in conjunction with real memory to present a CPU with a larger, apparent address space

  d. Memory where information must be obtained by sequentially searching from the beginning of the memory space

Answer: a

The correct answer is a. Answer b refers to secondary storage. Answer c refers to virtual memory, and answer d refers to sequential memory.

25. In the Common Criteria, a Protection Profile:

  a. Specifies the mandatory protection in the product to be evaluated

  b. Is also known as the Target of Evaluation (TOE)

  c. Is also known as the Orange Book

  d. Specifies the security requirements and protections of the products to be evaluated

Answer: d

The correct answer is d. Answer a is a distracter. Answer b is the product to be evaluated. Answer c refers to TCSEC.

26. Context-dependent control uses which of the following to make decisions?

  a. Subject or object attributes or environmental characteristics

  b. Data

c. Formal models

d. Operating system characteristics

Answer: a

The correct answer is a. Answer b refers to content-dependent characteristics, and answers c and d are distracters.

27. The secure path between a user and the Trusted Computing Base (TCB) is called:

a. Trusted distribution

b. Trusted path

c. Trusted facility management

d. The security perimeter

Answer: b

Answer a, *trusted distribution*, ensures that valid and secure versions of software have been received correctly. *Trusted facility management*, answer c, is concerned with the proper operation of trusted facilities as well as system administration and configuration. Answer d, the *security perimeter*, is the boundary that separates the TCB from the remainder of the system. Recall that the TCB is the totality of protection mechanisms within a computer system that are trusted to enforce a security policy.

28. In a ring protection system, where is the security kernel usually located?

a. Highest ring number

b. Arbitrarily placed

c. Lowest ring number

d. Middle ring number

Answer: c

29. Increasing performance in a computer by overlapping the steps of different instructions is called:

a. A reduced instruction set computer

b. A complex instruction set computer

c. Vector processing

d. Pipelining

Answer: d

30. Random access memory is:

  a. Non-volatile

  b. Sequentially addressable

  c. Programmed by using fusible links

  d. Volatile

Answer: d

The correct answer is d. RAM is volatile. The other answers are incorrect because RAM is volatile, randomly accessible, and not programmed by fusible links.

31. In the National Information Assurance Certification and Accreditation Process (NIACAP), a type accreditation performs which one of the following functions?

  a. Evaluates a major application or general support system

  b. Verifies the evolving or modified system's compliance with the information agreed on in the System Security Authorization Agreement (SSAA)

  c. Evaluates an application or system that is distributed to a number of different locations

  d. Evaluates the applications and systems at a specific, self-contained location

Answer: c

Answer a is the NIACAP *system accreditation*. Answer b is the Phase 2 or *Verification phase* of the Defense Information Technology Security Certification and Accreditation Process (DITSCAP). The objective is to use the SSAA to establish an evolving yet binding agreement on the level of security required before the system development begins or changes to a system are made. After accreditation, the SSAA becomes the baseline security configuration document. Answer d is the NIACAP *site accreditation*.

32. Processes are placed in a ring structure according to:

  a. Least privilege

  b. Separation of duty

  c. Owner classification

  d. First in, first out

Answer: a

The correct answer is a. A process is placed in the ring that gives it the minimum privileges necessary to perform its functions.

33. The MULTICS operating system is a classic example of:

  a. An open system

  b. Object orientation

  c. Database security

  d. Ring protection system

Answer: d

The correct answer is d. Multics is based on the ring protection architecture.

34. What are the hardware, firmware, and software elements of a Trusted Computing Base (TCB) that implement the reference monitor concept called?

  a. The trusted path

  b. A security kernel

  c. An Operating System (OS)

  d. A trusted computing system

Answer: b

The correct answer is b.

Chapter 6

1. Place the four systems security modes of operation in order, from the most secure to the least:

  a. System High Mode, Dedicated Mode, Compartmented Mode, and Multilevel Mode

  b. Dedicated Mode, System High Mode, Compartmented Mode, and Multilevel Mode

  c. Dedicated Mode, System High Mode, Multilevel Mode, and Compartmented Mode

  d. System High Mode, Compartmented Mode, Dedicated Mode, and Multilevel Mode

Answer: b

Dedicated Mode, System High Mode, Compartmented Mode, and Multilevel Mode

2. Why is security an issue when a system is booted into single-user mode?

   a. The operating system is started without the security front-end loaded.

   b. The users cannot log in to the system, and they will complain.

   c. Proper forensics cannot be executed while in single-user mode.

   d. Backup tapes cannot be restored while in single-user mode.

Answer: a

When the operator boots the system in single-user mode, the user front-end security controls are not loaded. This mode should be used only for recovery and maintenance procedures, and all operations should be logged and audited.

3. An audit trail is an example of what type of control?

   a. Deterrent control

   b. Preventative control

   c. Detective control

   d. Application control

Answer: c

An audit trail is a record of events to piece together what has happened and allow enforcement of individual accountability by creating a reconstruction of events. They can be used to assist in the proper implementation of the other controls, however.

4. Which media control below is the BEST choice to prevent data remanence on magnetic tapes or floppy disks?

   a. Overwriting the media with new application data

   b. Degaussing the media

   c. Applying a concentration of hydriodic acid (55% to 58% solution) to the gamma ferric oxide disk surface

   d. Making sure the disk is recirculated as quickly as possible to prevent object reuse

Answer: b

Degaussing is recommended as the best method for purging most magnetic media. Answer a is not recommended because the application may not completely overwrite the old data properly. Answer c is a rarely used method of media destruction, and acid solutions should be used in a well-ventilated area only by qualified personnel. Answer d is wrong.

5. Which choice below is NOT a security goal of an audit mechanism?

    a. Deter perpetrators' attempts to bypass the system protection mechanisms

    b. Review employee production output records

    c. Review patterns of access to individual objects

    d. Discover when a user assumes a functionality with privileges greater than his own

Answer: b

Answer b is a distracter; the other answers reflect proper security goals of an audit mechanism.

6. Which task below would normally be a function of the security administrator, not the system administrator?

    a. Installing system software

    b. Adding and removing system users

    c. Reviewing audit data

    d. Managing print queues

Answer: c

Reviewing audit data should be a function separate from the day-to-day administration of the system.

7. Which of the following is a reason to institute output controls?

    a. To preserve the integrity of the data in the system while changes are being made to the configuration

    b. To protect the output's confidentiality

    c. To detect irregularities in the software's operation

    d. To recover damage after an identified system failure

Answer: b

In addition to being used as a transaction control verification mechanism, output controls are used to ensure that output, such as printed reports, is distributed securely. Answer a is an example of change control, c is an example of application controls, and d is an example of recovery controls.

8. Which statement below is NOT correct about reviewing user accounts?

   a. User account reviews cannot be conducted by outside auditors.

   b. User account reviews can examine conformity with the concept of least privilege.

   c. User account reviews may be conducted on a systemwide basis.

   d. User account reviews may be conducted on an application-by-application basis.

Answer: a

Reviews can be conducted by, among others, in-house systems personnel (a self-audit), the organization's internal audit staff, or external auditors.

9. Which term below MOST accurately describes the trusted computing base (TCB)?

   a. A computer that controls all access to objects by subjects

   b. A piece of information that represents the security level of an object

   c. Formal proofs used to demonstrate the consistency between a system's specification and a security model

   d. The totality of protection mechanisms within a computer system

Answer: d

The Trusted Computing Base (TCB) represents totality of protection mechanisms within a computer system, including hardware, firmware, and software, the combination of which is responsible for enforcing a security policy. Answer a describes the reference monitor concept, answer b refers to a sensitivity label, and answer c describes formal verification.

10. Which statement below is accurate about the concept of Object Reuse?

   a. Object reuse protects against physical attacks on the storage medium.

   b. Object reuse ensures that users do not obtain residual information from system resources.

   c. Object reuse applies to removable media only.

   d. Object reuse controls the granting of access rights to objects.

Answer: b

Object reuse mechanisms ensure system resources are allocated and assigned among authorized users in a way that prevents the leak of sensitive information, and they ensure that the authorized user of the system does not obtain residual information from system resources. Answer a is incorrect, answer c is incorrect, and answer d refers to authorization, the granting of access rights to a user, program, or process.

11. Using prenumbered forms to initiate a transaction is an example of what type of control?

    a. Deterrent control

    b. Preventative control

    c. Detective control

    d. Application control

Answer: b

Prenumbered forms are an example of preventative controls. They can also be considered a transaction control and input control.

12. Which choice below is the BEST description of operational assurance?

    a. Operational assurance is the process of examining audit logs to reveal usage that identifies misuse.

    b. Operational assurance has the benefit of containing and repairing damage from incidents.

    c. Operational assurance is the process of reviewing an operational system to see that security controls are functioning correctly.

    d. Operational assurance is the process of performing pre-employment background screening.

Answer: c

Operational assurance is the process of reviewing an operational system to see that security controls, both automated and manual, are functioning correctly and effectively. Operational assurance addresses whether the system's technical features are being bypassed or have vulnerabilities and whether required procedures are being followed. Answer a is a description of an audit trail review, answer b is a description of a benefit of incident handling, and answer d describes a personnel control.

13. Which of the following is NOT a proper media control?

    a. The data media should be logged to provide a physical inventory control.

    b. All data storage media should be accurately marked.

    c. A proper storage environment should be provided for the media.

    d. The media that is reused in a sensitive environment does not need sanitization.

Answer: d

Sanitization is the process of removing information from used data media to prevent data remanence. Different media require different types of sanitation. All the others are examples of proper media controls.

14. Which choice below is considered the HIGHEST level of operator privilege?

   a. Read/Write

   b. Read Only

   c. Access Change

   d. Write Only

Answer: c

The three common levels of operator privileges, based on the concept of "least privilege," are:

   • *Read Only*—Lowest level, view data only

   • *Read/Write*—View and modify data

   • *Access Change*—Highest level, right to change data/operator permissions

Answer d is a distracter.

15. Which choice below MOST accurately describes a covert storage channel?

   a. A process that manipulates observable system resources in a way that affects response time

   b. An information transfer path within a system

   c. A communication channel that allows a process to transfer information in a manner that violates the system's security policy

   d. An information transfer that involves the direct or indirect writing of a storage location by one process and the direct or indirect reading of the storage location by another process

Answer: d

A covert storage channel typically involves a finite resource (e.g., sectors on a disk) that is shared by two subjects at different security levels. Answer a is a partial description of a covert timing channel, and answer b is a generic definition of a channel. A channel may also refer to the mechanism by which the path is effected. Answer c is a higher-level definition of a covert channel. While a covert storage channel fits this definition generically, answer d is the proper specific definition.

16. Which choice below would NOT be a common element of a transaction trail?

   a. The date and time of the transaction

   b. Who processed the transaction

   c. Why the transaction was processed

   d. At which terminal the transaction was processed

Answer: c

Why the transaction was processed is not initially a concern of the audit log, but we will investigate it later. The other three elements are all important information that the audit log of the transaction should record.

17. Which choice below would NOT be considered a benefit of employing incident-handling capability?

   a. An individual acting alone would not be able to subvert a security process or control.

   b. It enhances internal communications and the readiness of the organization to respond to incidents.

   c. It assists an organization in preventing damage from future incidents.

   d. Security training personnel would have a better understanding of users' knowledge of security issues.

Answer: a

The primary benefits of employing an incident-handling capability are containing and repairing damage from incidents and preventing future damage. Answer a is a benefit of employing "separation of duties" controls.

18. Which choice below is the BEST description of an audit trail?

   a. Audit trails are used to detect penetration of a computer system and to reveal usage that identifies misuse.

   b. An audit trail is a device that permits simultaneous data processing of two or more security levels without risk of compromise.

   c. An audit trail mediates all access to objects within the network by subjects within the network.

   d. Audit trails are used to prevent access to sensitive systems by unauthorized personnel.

Answer: a

An audit trail is a set of records that collectively provide documentary evidence of processing used to aid in tracing from original transactions forward to related records and reports and/or backward from records and reports to their component source transactions. Answer b is a description of a multilevel device, and answer c refers to a network reference monitor. Answer d is incorrect because audit trails are detective, and answer d describes a preventative process — access control.

19. Which choice below best describes the function of change control?

    a. To ensure that system changes are implemented in an orderly manner

    b. To guarantee that an operator is given only the privileges needed for the task

    c. To guarantee that transaction records are retained IAW compliance requirements

    d. To assign parts of security-sensitive tasks to more than one individual

Answer: a

Answer b describes least privilege, answer c describes record retention, and answer d describes separation on duties.

20. Which choice below is NOT an example of intentionally inappropriate operator activity?

    a. Making errors when manually inputting transactions

    b. Using the company's system to store pornography

    c. Conducting private business on the company system

    d. Using unauthorized access levels to violate information confidentiality

Answer: a

While choice a is most certainly an example of a threat to a system's integrity, it is considered unintentional loss, not an intentional activity.

21. Which book of the Rainbow Series addresses the Trusted Computer System Evaluation Criteria (TCSEC)?

    a. Red Book

    b. Orange Book

    c. Green Book

    d. Purple Book

Answer: b

22. Which term below BEST describes the concept of least privilege?

    a. Each user is granted the lowest clearance required for his or her tasks.

    b. A formal separation of command, program, and interface functions.

    c. A combination of classification and categories that represents the sensitivity of information.

    d. Active monitoring of facility entry access points.

Answer: a

The least privilege principle requires that each subject in a system be granted the most restrictive set of privileges (or lowest clearance) needed for the performance of authorized tasks. Answer b describes separation of privilege, answer c describes a security level, and answer d is a distracter.

23. Which choice below BEST describes a threat as defined in the Operations Security domain?

    a. A potential incident that could cause harm

    b. A weakness in a system that could be exploited

    c. A company resource that could be lost due to an incident

    d. The minimization of loss associated with an incident

Answer: a

Answer b describes a vulnerability, answer c describes an asset, and answer d describes risk management.

24. Which choice below is NOT a common element of user account administration?

    a. Periodically verifying the legitimacy of current accounts and access authorizations

    b. Authorizing the request for a user's system account

    c. Tracking users and their respective access authorizations

    d. Establishing, issuing, and closing user accounts

Answer: b

For proper separation of duties, the function of user account establishment and maintenance should be separated from the function of initiating and authorizing the creation of the account. User account management focuses on identification, authentication, and access authorizations.

25. Which choice below is NOT an example of using a social engineering technique to gain physical access to a secure facility?

    a. Asserting authority or pulling rank

    b. Intimidating or threatening

    c. Praising or flattering

    d. Employing the salami fraud

Answer: d

The salami fraud is an automated fraud technique. In the salami fraud, a programmer will create or alter a program to move small amounts of money into his personal bank account. The amounts are intended to be so small as to be unnoticed, such as rounding in foreign currency exchange transactions. Hence the reference to slicing a salami. The other three choices are common techniques used by an intruder to gain either physical access or system access.

26. Which statement about Covert Channel Analysis is NOT true?

    a. It is an operational assurance requirement that is specified in the Orange Book.

    b. It is required for B2 class systems in order to protect against covert storage channels.

    c. It is required for B2 class systems to protect against covert timing channels.

    d. It is required for B3 class systems to protect against both covert storage and covert timing channels.

Answer: c

Orange Book B2 class systems do not need to be protected from covert timing channels. Covert channel analysis must be performed for B2-level class systems to protect against only covert storage channels. B3 class systems need to be protected from both covert storage channels and covert timing channels.

27. "Separation of duties" embodies what principle?

    a. An operator does not know more about the system than the minimum required to do the job.

    b. Two operators are required to work in tandem to perform a task.

    c. The operators' duties are frequently rotated.

    d. The operators have different duties to prevent one person from compromising the system.

Answer: d

Separation of duties means that the operators are prevented from generating and verifying transactions alone, for example. A task might be divided into different smaller tasks to accomplish this, or in the case of an operator with multiple duties, the operator makes a logical, functional job change when performing such conflicting duties. Answer a is need-to-know, answer b is dual-control, and c is job rotation.

28. Convert Channel Analysis, Trusted Facility Management, and Trusted Recovery are parts of which book in the TCSEC Rainbow Series?

    a. Red Book

    b. Orange Book

    c. Green Book

    d. Dark Green Book

Answer: b

Answer a, the Red Book, is the Trusted Network Interpretation (TNI) summary of network requirements (described in the Telecommunications and Network Security domain); c, the Green Book, is the Department of Defense (DoD) Password Management Guideline; and d, the Dark Green Book, is *The Guide to Understanding Data Remanence in Automated Information Systems.*

29. How do covert timing channels convey information?

    a. By changing a system's stored data characteristics

    b. By generating noise and traffic with the data

    c. By performing a covert channel analysis

    d. By modifying the timing of a system resource in some measurable way

Answer: d

A covert timing channel alters the timing of parts of the system to enable it to be used to communicate information covertly (outside the normal security function). Answer a is the description of the use of a covert storage channel, b is a technique to combat the use of covert channels, and c is the Orange Book requirement for B3, B2, and A1 evaluated systems.

30. Which of the following would be the BEST description of clipping levels?

    a. A baseline of user errors above which violations will be recorded

    b. A listing of every error made by users to initiate violation processing

    c. Variance detection of too many people with unrestricted access

    d. Changes a system's stored data characteristics

Answer: a

This description of a clipping level is the best. It is not b because one reason to create clipping levels is to prevent auditors from having to examine every error. The answer c is a common use for clipping levels but is not a definition. Answer d is a distracter.

Chapter 7

1. What is a data warehouse?

    a. A remote facility used for storing backup tapes

    b. A repository of information from heterogeneous databases

    c. A table in a relational database system

    d. A hot backup building

Answer: b

The correct answer is b, a repository of information from heterogeneous databases. Answers a and d describe physical facilities for backup and recovery of information systems, and answer c describes a relation in a relational database.

2. What does normalizing data in a data warehouse mean?

    a. Redundant data is removed.

    b. Numerical data is divided by a common factor.

    c. Data is converted to a symbolic representation.

    d. Data is restricted to a range of values.

Answer: a

The correct answer is a, removing redundant data.

3. What is a neural network?

    a. A hardware or software system that emulates the reasoning of a human expert

    b. A collection of computers that are focused on medical applications

    c. A series of networked PCs performing artificial intelligence tasks

    d. A hardware or software system that emulates the functioning of biological neurons

Answer: d

The correct answer is d. A neural network is a hardware or software system that emulates the functioning of biological neurons. Answer a refers to an expert system, and answers b and c are distracters.

4. A neural network learns by using various algorithms to:

    a. Adjust the weights applied to the data

    b. Fire the rules in the knowledge base

    c. Emulate an inference engine

    d. Emulate the thinking of an expert

Answer: a

The correct answer is "A neural network learns by using various algorithms to adjust the weights applied to the data." Answers b, c, and d are terminology referenced in expert systems.

5. The SEI Software Capability Maturity Model is based on the premise that:

  a. Good software development is a function of the number of expert programmers in the organization.

  b. The maturity of an organization's software processes cannot be measured.

  c. The quality of a software product is a direct function of the quality of its associated software development and maintenance processes.

  d. Software development is an art that cannot be measured by conventional means.

Answer: c

The correct answer is c. The quality of a software product is a direct function of the quality of its associated software development and maintenance processes. Answer a is false because the SEI Software CMM relates the production of good software to having the proper processes in place in an organization and not to expert programs or heroes. Answer b is false because the Software CMM provides means to measure the maturity of an organization's software processes. Answer d is false for the same reason as answer b.

6. In configuration management, a configuration item is:

  a. The version of the operating system that is operating on the workstation that provides information security services

  b. A component whose state is to be recorded and against which changes are to be progressed

  c. The network architecture used by the organization

  d. A series of files that contain sensitive information

Answer: b

The correct answer is b, a component whose state is to be recorded and against which changes are to be progressed. Answers a, c, and d are incorrect by the definition of a configuration item.

7. In an object-oriented system, polymorphism denotes:

  a. Objects of many different classes that are related by some common superclass; thus, any object denoted by this name can respond to some common set of operations in a different way.

  b. Objects of many different classes that are related by some common superclass; thus, all objects denoted by this name can respond to some common set of operations in identical fashion.

  c. Objects of the same class; thus, any object denoted by this name can respond to some common set of operations in the same way.

  d. Objects of many different classes that are unrelated but respond to some common set of operations in the same way.

Answer: a

The correct answer is a, objects of many different classes that are related by some common superclass that are able to respond to some common set of operations in a different way. Answers b, c, and d are incorrect by the definition of polymorphism.

8. The simplistic model of software life cycle development assumes that:

   a. Iteration will be required among the steps in the process.

   b. Each step can be completed and finalized without any effect from the later stages that might require rework.

   c. Each phase is identical to a completed milestone.

   d. Software development requires reworking and repeating some of the phases.

Answer: b

The correct answer is b. Each step can be completed and finalized without any effect from the later stages that might require rework. Answer a is incorrect because no iteration is allowed for in the model. Answer c is incorrect because it applies to the modified Waterfall model. Answer d is incorrect because no iteration or reworking is considered in the model.

9. What is a method in an object-oriented system?

   a. The means of communication among objects

   b. A guide to the programming of objects

   c. The code defining the actions that the object performs in response to a message

   d. The situation where a class inherits the behavioral characteristics of more that one parent class

Answer: c

The correct answer is c. A method in an object-oriented system is the code that defines the actions that the object performs in response to a message. Answer a is incorrect because it defines a message. Answer b is a distracter, and answer d refers to multiple inheritance.

10. What does the Spiral model depict?

   a. A spiral that incorporates various phases of software development

   b. A spiral that models the behavior of biological neurons

   c. The operation of expert systems

   d. Information security checklists

Answer: a

The correct answer is a — a spiral that incorporates various phases of software development. The other answers are distracters.

11. In the software life cycle, verification:

    a. Evaluates the product in development against real-world requirements

    b. Evaluates the product in development against similar products

    c. Evaluates the product in development against general baselines

    d. Evaluates the product in development against the specification

Answer: d

The correct answer is d. In the software life cycle, verification evaluates the product in development against the specification. Answer a defines validation. Answers b and c are distracters.

12. In the software life cycle, validation:

    a. Refers to the work product satisfying the real-world requirements and concepts.

    b. Refers to the work product satisfying derived specifications.

    c. Refers to the work product satisfying software maturity levels.

    d. Refers to the work product satisfying generally accepted principles.

Answer: a

The correct answer is a. In the software life cycle, validation is the work product satisfying the real-world requirements and concepts. The other answers are distracters.

13. In the modified Waterfall model:

    a. Unlimited backward iteration is permitted.

    b. The model was reinterpreted to have phases end at project milestones.

    c. The model was reinterpreted to have phases begin at project milestones.

    d. Product verification and validation are not included.

Answer: b

The correct answer is b. The modified Waterfall model was reinterpreted to have phases end at project milestones. Answer a is false because unlimited backward iteration is not permitted in the modified Waterfall model. Answer c is a distracter, and answer d is false because verification and validation are included.

14. Cyclic redundancy checks, structured walk-throughs, and hash totals are examples of what type of application controls?

    a. Preventive security controls

    b. Preventive consistency controls

    c. Detective accuracy controls

    d. Corrective consistency controls

Answer: c

The correct answer is c. Cyclic redundancy checks, structured walkthroughs, and hash totals are examples of detective accuracy controls. The other answers do not apply by the definition of the types of controls.

15. In a system life cycle, information security controls should be:

    a. Designed during the product implementation phase

    b. Implemented prior to validation

    c. Part of the feasibility phase

    d. Specified after the coding phase

Answer: c

The correct answer is c. In the system life cycle, information security controls should be part of the feasibility phase. The other answers are incorrect because the basic premise of information system security is that controls should be included in the earliest phases of the software life cycle and not added later in the cycle or as an afterthought.

16. The software maintenance phase controls consist of:

    a. Request control, change control, and release control

    b. Request control, configuration control, and change control

    c. Change control, security control, and access control

    d. Request control, release control, and access control

Answer: a

The correct answer is a. The software maintenance phase controls consist of request control, change control, and release control by definition. The other answers are, therefore, incorrect.

17. In configuration management, what is a software library?

    a. A set of versions of the component configuration items

    b. A controlled area accessible only to approved users who are restricted to the use of an approved procedure

    c. A repository of backup tapes

    d. A collection of software build lists

Answer: b

The correct answer is b. In configuration management, a software library is a controlled area accessible only to approved users who are restricted to the use of approved procedure. Answer a is incorrect because it defines a build list. Answer c is incorrect because it defines a backup storage facility. Answer d is a distracter.

18. What is configuration control?

    a. Identifying and documenting the functional and physical characteristics of each configuration item

    b. Controlling changes to the configuration items and issuing versions of configuration items from the software library

    c. Recording the processing of changes

    d. Controlling the quality of the configuration management procedures

Answer: b

The correct answer is b. Configuration control is controlling changes to the configuration items and issuing versions of configuration items from the software library. Answer a is the definition of configuration identification. Answer c is the definition of configuration status accounting, and answer d is the definition of configuration audit.

19. What is searching for data correlations in the data warehouse called?

    a. Data warehousing

    b. Data mining

    c. A data dictionary

    d. Configuration management

Answer: b

The correct answer is b. Searching for data correlations in the data warehouse is called data mining. Answer a is incorrect because data warehousing is creating a repository of information from heterogeneous databases that is available to users for making queries. Answer c is incorrect because a data dictionary is a database for system developers. Answer d is incorrect because configuration management is the discipline of identifying the components of a continually evolving system for the purposes of controlling changes to those components and maintaining integrity and traceability throughout the life cycle.

20. The security term that is concerned with the same primary key existing at different classification levels in the same database is:

 a. Polymorphism

 b. Normalization

 c. Inheritance

 d. Polyinstantiation

Answer: d

The correct answer is d. The security term that is concerned with the same primary key existing at different classification levels in the same database is polyinstantiation. Answer a is incorrect because polymorphism is defined as objects of many different classes that are related by some common superclass; thus, any object denoted by this name is able to respond to some common set of operations in a different way. Answer b is incorrect because normalization refers to removing redundant or incorrect data from a database. Answer c is incorrect because inheritance refers to methods from a class inherited by another subclass.

21. What is a data dictionary?

 a. A database for system developers

 b. A database of security terms

 c. A library of objects

 d. A validation reference source

Answer: a

The correct answer is a. A data dictionary is a database for system developers. Answers b, c, and d are distracters.

22. Which of the following is an example of mobile code?

 a. Embedded code in control systems

 b. Embedded code in PCs

 c. Java and ActiveX code downloaded into a Web browser from the World Wide Web (WWW)

 d. Code derived following the Spiral model

Answer: c

The correct answer is c. An example of mobile code is Java and ActiveX code downloaded into a Web browser from the World Wide Web. Answers a, b, and d are incorrect because they are types of code that are not related to mobile code.

23. Which of the following is NOT true regarding software unit testing?

   a. The test data is part of the specifications.

   b. Correct test output results should be developed and known beforehand.

   c. Live or actual field data is recommended for use in the testing procedures.

   d. Testing should check for out-of-range values and other bounds conditions.

Answer: c

The correct answer is c. Live or actual field data are NOT recommended for use in testing because they do not thoroughly test all normal and abnormal situations and the test results are not known beforehand. Answers a, b, and d are true of testing.

24. The definition "the science and art of specifying, designing, implementing, and evolving programs, documentation, and operating procedures whereby computers can be made useful to man" is that of:

   a. Structured analysis/structured design (SA/SD)

   b. Software engineering

   c. An object-oriented system

   d. Functional programming

Answer: b

This definition of software engineering is a combination of popular definitions of engineering and software. One definition of engineering is "the application of science and mathematics to the design and construction of artifacts which are useful to man." A definition of software is that it "consists of the programs, documentation and operating procedures by which computers can be made useful to man." Answer a, SA/SD, deals with developing specifications that are abstractions of the problem to be solved and are not tied to any specific programming languages. Thus, SA/SD, through data flow diagrams (DFDs), shows the main processing entities and the data flow between them without any connection to a specific programming language implementation.

An object-oriented system, answer c, is a group of independent objects that can be requested to perform certain operations or exhibit specific behaviors. These objects cooperate to provide the system's required functionality. The objects have an identity and can be created as the program executes (dynamic lifetime). To provide the desired characteristics of object-oriented systems, the objects are encapsulated, i.e., they can be accessed only through messages sent to them to request performance of their defined operations. The object can be viewed as a black box whose internal details are hidden from outside observation and cannot normally be modified. Objects also exhibit the substitution property, which means that objects providing compatible operations can be substituted for each other. In summary, an object-oriented system contains objects that exhibit the following properties:

- *Identity* — Each object has a name that is used to designate that object.

- *Encapsulation* — An object can be accessed only through messages to perform its defined operations.

- *Substitution* — Objects that perform compatible operations can be substituted for each other.

- *Dynamic lifetimes* — Objects can be created as the program executes.

Answer d, functional programming, uses only mathematical functions to perform computations and solve problems. This approach is based on the assumption that any algorithm can be described as a mathematical function. Functional languages have the characteristics that:

- They support functions and allow them to be manipulated by being passed as arguments and stored in data structures.

- Functional abstraction is the only method of procedural abstraction.

25. In software engineering, the term *verification* is defined as:

   a. To establish the truth of correspondence between a software product and its specification

   b. A complete, validated specification of the required functions, interfaces, and performance for the software product

   c. To establish the fitness or worth of a software product for its operational mission

   d. A complete, verified specification of the overall hardware-software architecture, control structure, and data structure for the product

Answer: a

In the Waterfall model (W.W. Royce, "Managing the Development of Large Software Systems: Concepts and Techniques," *Proceedings, WESCON*, August 1970), answer b defines the term *requirements*. Similarly, answer c, defines the term *validation*, and answer d is the definition of *product design*. In summary, the steps of the Waterfall model are:

- System feasibility

- Software plans and requirements

- Product design

- Detailed design
- Code
- Integration
- Implementation
- Operations and maintenance

In this model, each phase finishes with a verification and validation (V&V) task that is designed to eliminate as many problems as possible in the results of that phase.

26. The discipline of identifying the components of a continually evolving system for the purposes of controlling changes to those components and maintaining integrity and traceability throughout the life cycle is called:

   a. Change control

   b. Request control

   c. Release control

   d. Configuration management

Answer: d

This is demonstrated in *Configuration management of computer-based systems*, British Standards Institution, 1984. Answers a, b, and c are components of the maintenance activity of software life cycle models. In general, one can look at the maintenance phase as the progression from request control, through change control, to release control. Answer b, *request control*, is involved with the users' requests for changes to the software. *Change control*, answer a, involves the analysis and understanding of the existing code, the design of changes, and the corresponding test procedures. Answer c, *release control*, involves deciding which requests are to be implemented in the new release, performing the changes, and conducting testing.

27. The basic version of the Construction Cost Model (COCOMO), which proposes quantitative life cycle relationships, performs what function?

   a. Estimates software development effort based on user function categories

   b. Estimates software development effort and cost as a function of the size of the software product in source instructions

   c. Estimates software development effort and cost as a function of the size of the software product in source instructions modified by manpower buildup and productivity factors

   d. Estimates software development effort and cost as a function of the size of the software product in source instructions modified by hardware and input functions

Answer: b

The Basic COCOMO Model (B.W. Boehm, *Software Engineering Economics*, Prentice-Hall, Englewood Cliffs, New Jersey, 1981) proposes the following equations:

> "The number of man-months (MM) required to develop the most common type of software product, in terms of the number of thousands of delivered source instructions (KDSI) in the software product"

```
MM = 2.4(KDSI)^1.05
```

> "The development schedule (TDEV) in months"

```
TDEV = 2.5(MM)^0.38
```

In addition, Boehm has developed an intermediate COCOMO Model that takes into account hardware constraints, personnel quality, use of modern tools, and other attributes and their aggregate impact on overall project costs. A detailed COCOMO Model, by Boehm, accounts for the effects of the additional factors used in the intermediate model on the costs of individual project phases.

Answer b describes a *function point measurement model* that does not require the user to estimate the number of delivered source instructions. The software development effort is determined using the following five user functions:

- External input types
- External output types
- Logical internal file types
- External interface file types
- External inquiry types

These functions are tallied and weighted according to complexity and used to determine the software development effort.

Answer c describes the Rayleigh curve applied to software development cost and effort estimation. A prominent model using this approach is the Software Life Cycle Model (SLIM) estimating method. In this method, estimates based on the number of lines of source code are modified by the following two factors:

- The manpower buildup index (MBI), which estimates the rate of buildup of staff on the project
- A productivity factor (PF), which is based on the technology used

Answer d is a distracter.

28. A refinement to the basic Waterfall model that states that software should be developed in increments of functional capability is called:

    a. Functional refinement

    b. Functional development

    c. Incremental refinement

    d. Incremental development

Answer: d

The advantages of *incremental development* include the ease of testing increments of functional capability and the opportunity to incorporate user experience into a successively refined product. Answers a, b, and c are distracters.

29. The Spiral model of the software development process (B.W. Boehm, "A Spiral Model of Software Development and Enhancement," *IEEE Computer*, May 1988) uses the following metric relative to the spiral:

    a. The radial dimension represents the cost of each phase.

    b. The radial dimension represents progress made in completing each cycle.

    c. The angular dimension represents cumulative cost.

    d. The radial dimension represents cumulative cost.

Answer: d

The radial dimension represents cumulative cost and the angular dimension represents progress made in completing each cycle of the spiral. The Spiral model is actually a meta-model for software development processes. A summary of the stages in the spiral is as follows:

- The spiral begins in the top, left-hand quadrant by determining the objectives of the portion of the product being developed, the alternative means of implementing this portion of the product, and the constraints imposed on the application of the alternatives.

- Next, the risks of the alternatives are evaluated based on the objectives and constraints. Following this step, the relative balances of the perceived risks are determined.

- The spiral then proceeds to the lower right-hand quadrant where the development phases of the projects begin. A major review completes each cycle, and then the process begins anew for succeeding phases of the project. Typical succeeding phases are software product design, integration and test plan development, additional risk analyses, operational prototype, detailed design, code, unit test, acceptance test, and implementation.

Answers a, b, and c are distracters.

30. In the Capability Maturity Model (CMM) for software, the definition "describes the range of expected results that can be achieved by following a software process" is that of:

   a. Structured analysis/structured design (SA/SD)

   b. Software process capability

   c. Software process performance

   d. Software process maturity

Answer: b

A software process is a set of activities, methods, and practices that are used to develop and maintain software and associated products. Software process capability is a means of predicting the outcome of the next software project conducted by an organization. Answer c, software process performance, is the result achieved by following a software process. Thus, software capability is aimed at expected results while software performance is focused on results that have been achieved. Software process maturity, answer d, is the extent to which a software process is:

• Defined

• Managed

• Measured

• Controlled

• Effective

Software process maturity, then, provides for the potential for growth in capability of an organization. An immature organization develops software in a crisis mode, usually exceeds budgets and time schedules, and develops software processes in an ad hoc fashion during the project. In a mature organization, the software process is effectively communicated to staff, the required processes are documented and consistent, software quality is evaluated, and roles and responsibilities are understood for the project.

Answer a is a distracter, but it is discussed in question 24.

Chapter 8

1. Which choice below is the first priority in an emergency?

   a. Communicating to employees' families the status of the emergency

   b. Notifying external support resources for recovery and restoration

   c. Protecting the health and safety of everyone in the facility

   d. Warning customers and contractors of a potential interruption of service

Answer: c

Life safety, or protecting the health and safety of everyone in the facility, is the first priority in an emergency or disaster.

2. Which choice below is NOT considered an appropriate role for senior management in the business continuity and disaster recovery process?

   a. Delegate recovery roles

   b. Publicly praise successes

   c. Closely control media and analyst communications

   d. Assess the adequacy of information security during the disaster recovery

Answer: d

The tactical assessment of information security is a role of information management or technology management, not senior management.

3. Why is it so important to test disaster recovery plans frequently?

   a. The businesses that provide subscription services might have changed ownership.

   b. A plan is not considered viable until a test has been performed.

   c. Employees might get bored with the planning process.

   d. Natural disasters can change frequently.

Answer: b

A plan is not considered functioning and viable until a test has been performed. An untested plan sitting on a shelf is useless and might even have the reverse effect of creating a false sense of security. While the other answers, especially a, are good reasons to test, b is the primary reason.

4. Which disaster recovery/emergency management plan–testing type below is considered the most cost-effective and efficient way to identify areas of overlap in the plan before conducting more demanding training exercises?

   a. Full-scale exercise

   b. Walk-through drill

   c. Table-top exercise test

   d. Evacuation drill

Answer: c

In a table-top exercise, members of the emergency management group meet in a conference room setting to discuss their responsibilities and how they would react to emergency scenarios.

5. Which type of backup subscription service will allow a business to recover quickest?

 a. A hot site

 b. A mobile or rolling backup service

 c. A cold site

 d. A warm site

Answer: a

Warm and cold sites require more work after the event occurs to get them to full operating functionality. A mobile backup site might be useful for specific types of minor outages, but a hot site is still the main choice of backup processing site.

6. Which choice below represents the most important first step in creating a business resumption plan?

 a. Performing a risk analysis

 b. Obtaining senior management support

 c. Analyzing the business impact

 d. Planning recovery strategies

Answer: b

The business resumption, or business continuity plan, must have total, highly visible senior management support.

7. What could be a major disadvantage to a mutual aid or reciprocal type of backup service agreement?

 a. It is free or at a low cost to the organization.

 b. The use of prefabricated buildings makes recovery easier.

 c. In a major emergency, the site might not have the capacity to handle the operations required.

 d. Annual testing by the Info Tech department is required to maintain the site.

Answer: c

The site might not have the capacity to handle the operations required during a major disruptive event. While mutual aid might be a good system for sharing resources during a small or isolated outage, a major natural or other type of disaster can create serious resource contention between the two organizations.

8. In developing an emergency or recovery plan, which choice below would NOT be considered a short-term objective?

    a. Priorities for restoration

    b. Acceptable downtime before restoration

    c. Minimum resources needed to accomplish the restoration

    d. The organization's strategic plan

Answer: d

The organization's strategic plan is considered a long-term goal.

9. When is the disaster considered to be officially over?

    a. When the danger has passed and the disaster has been contained

    b. When the organization has processing up and running at the alternate site

    c. When all of the elements of the business have returned to normal functioning at the original site

    d. When all employees have been financially reimbursed for their expenses

Answer: c

The disaster is officially over when all of the elements of the business have returned to normal functioning at the original site. It's important to remember that a threat to continuity exists when processing is being returned to its original site after salvage and cleanup has been done.

10. When should the public and media be informed about a disaster?

    a. Whenever site emergencies extend beyond the facility

    b. When any emergency occurs at the facility, internally or externally

    c. When the public's health or safety is in danger

    d. When the disaster has been contained

Answer: a

When an emergency occurs that could potentially have an impact outside the facility, the public must be informed, regardless of whether there is any immediate threat to public safety.

11. What is the number one priority of disaster response?

     a. Resuming transaction processing

     b. Personnel safety

     c. Protecting the hardware

     d. Protecting the software

Answer: b

The number one function of all disaster response and recovery is the protection of the safety of people; all other concerns are vital to business continuity but are secondary to personnel safety.

12. Which choice below is the BEST description of the criticality prioritization goal of the Business Impact Assessment (BIA) process?

     a. The identification and prioritization of every critical business unit process

     b. The identification of the resource requirements of the critical business unit processes

     c. The estimation of the maximum downtime the business can tolerate

     d. The presentation of the documentation of the results of the BIA

Answer: a

The three primary goals of a BIA are criticality prioritization, maximum down time estimation, and identification of critical resource requirements. Answer d is a distracter.

13. Which choice below most accurately describes a business impact analysis (BIA)?

     a. A program that implements the strategic goals of the organization

     b. A management-level analysis that identifies the impact of losing an entity's resources

     c. A prearranged agreement between two or more entities to provide assistance

     d. Activities designed to return an organization to an acceptable operating condition

Answer: b

A business impact analysis (BIA) measures the effect of resource loss and escalating losses over time in order to provide the entity with reliable data upon which to base decisions on hazard mitigation and continuity planning. Answer a is a definition of a disaster/emergency management program. Answer c describes a mutual aid agreement. Answer d is the definition of a recovery program.

14. What is considered the major disadvantage to employing a hot site for disaster recovery?

    a. Exclusivity is assured for processing at the site.

    b. Maintaining the site is expensive.

    c. The site is immediately available for recovery.

    d. Annual testing is required to maintain the site.

Answer: b

A hot site is commonly used for those extremely time-critical functions that the business must have up and running to continue operating, but the expense of duplicating and maintaining all of the hardware, software, and application elements is a serious resource drain to most organizations.

15. Which choice below is NOT considered an appropriate role for Financial Management in the business continuity and disaster recovery process?

    a. Tracking the recovery costs

    b. Monitoring employee morale and guarding against employee burnout

    c. Formally notifying insurers of claims

    d. Reassessing cash flow projections

Answer: b

Monitoring employee morale and guarding against employee burnout during a disaster recovery event is the proper role of human resources.

16. Which choice below is the MOST accurate description of a warm site?

    a. A backup processing facility with adequate electrical wiring and air conditioning but no hardware or software installed

    b. A backup processing facility with most hardware and software installed, which can be operational within a matter of days

    c. A backup processing facility with all hardware and software installed and 100% compatible with the original site, operational within hours

    d. A mobile trailer with portable generators and air conditioning

Answer: b

17. Which of the following is NOT one of the five disaster recovery plan testing types?

     a. Simulation

     b. Checklist

     c. Mobile

     d. Full Interruption

     Answer: c

18. Which choice below is an example of a potential hazard due to a technological event, rather than a human event?

     a. Sabotage

     b. Financial collapse

     c. Mass hysteria

     d. Enemy attack

     Answer: b

     A financial collapse is considered a technological potential hazard, whereas the other three are human events.

19. Which of the following is NOT considered an element of a backup alternative?

     a. Electronic vaulting

     b. Remote journaling

     c. Warm site

     d. Checklist

     Answer: d

     A checklist is a type of disaster recovery plan test. Electronic vaulting is the batch transfer of backup data to an offsite location. Remote journaling is the parallel processing of transactions to an alternate site. A warm site is a backup-processing alternative.

20. Which choice below refers to a business asset?

     a. Events or situations that could cause a financial or operational impact to the organization

     b. Protection devices or procedures in place that reduce the effects of threats

     c. Competitive advantage, credibility, or good will

     d. Personnel compensation and retirement programs

Answer: c

Answer a is a definition for a threat. Answer b is a description of mitigating factors that reduce the effect of a threat, such as a UPS, sprinkler systems, or generators. Answer d is a distracter.

21. Which statement below is NOT correct regarding the role of the recovery team during the disaster?

    a. The recovery team must be the same as the salvage team as they perform the same function.

    b. The recovery team is often separate from the salvage team as they perform different duties.

    c. The recovery team's primary task is to get predefined critical business functions operating at the alternate processing site.

    d. The recovery team will need full access to all backup media.

Answer: a

The recovery team performs different functions from the salvage team. The recovery team's primary mandate is to get critical processing reestablished at an alternate site. The salvage team's primary mandate is to return the original processing site to normal processing environmental conditions.

22. Which choice below is incorrect regarding when a BCP, DRP, or emergency management plan should be evaluated and modified?

    a. Never; once it has been fully tested it should not be changed.

    b. Annually, in a scheduled review.

    c. After training drills, tests, or exercises.

    d. After an emergency or disaster response.

Answer: a

Emergency management plans, business continuity plans, and disaster recovery plans should be regularly reviewed, evaluated, modified, and updated. At a minimum, the plan should be reviewed at an annual audit.

23. When should security isolation of the incident scene start?

    a. Immediately after the emergency is discovered

    b. As soon as the disaster plan is implemented

    c. After all personnel have been evacuated

    d. When hazardous materials have been discovered at the site

Answer: a

Isolation of the incident scene should begin as soon as the emergency has been discovered.

24. Which choice below is NOT a recommended step to take when resuming normal operations after an emergency?

   a. Reoccupy the damaged building as soon as possible.

   b. Account for all damage-related costs.

   c. Protect undamaged property.

   d. Conduct an investigation.

Answer: a

Reoccupying the site of a disaster or emergency should not be undertaken until a full safety inspection has been done, an investigation into the cause of the emergency has been completed, and all damaged property has been salvaged and restored.

25. Which choice below would NOT be a good reason to test the disaster recovery plan?

   a. Testing verifies the processing capability of the alternate backup site.

   b. Testing allows processing to continue at the database shadowing facility.

   c. Testing prepares and trains the personnel to execute their emergency duties.

   d. Testing identifies deficiencies in the recovery procedures.

Answer: b

The other three answers are good reasons to test the disaster recovery plan.

26. Which statement below is NOT true about the post-disaster salvage team?

   a. The salvage team must return to the site as soon as possible regardless of the residual physical danger.

   b. The salvage team manages the cleaning of equipment after smoke damage.

   c. The salvage team identifies sources of expertise to employ in the recovery of equipment or supplies.

   d. The salvage team may be given the authority to declare when operations can resume at the disaster site.

Answer: a

Salvage cannot begin until all physical danger has been removed or mitigated and emergency personnel have returned control of the site to the organization.

27. Which statement below is the most accurate about the results of the disaster recovery plan test?

    a. If no deficiencies were found during the test, then the plan is probably perfect.

    b. The results of the test should be kept secret.

    c. If no deficiencies were found during the test, then the test was probably flawed.

    d. The plan should not be changed no matter what the results of the test.

Answer: c

The purpose of the test is to find weaknesses in the plan. Every plan has weaknesses. After the test, all parties should be advised of the results, and the plan should be updated to reflect the new information.

28. Which statement is true regarding the disbursement of funds during and after a disruptive event?

    a. Because access to funds is rarely an issue during a disaster, no special arrangements need to be made.

    b. No one but the finance department should ever disburse funds during or after a disruptive event.

    c. In the event senior-level or financial management is unable to disburse funds normally, the company will need to file for bankruptcy.

    d. Authorized, signed checks should be stored securely off-site for access by lower-level managers in the event senior-level or financial management is unable to disburse funds normally.

Answer: d

Authorized, signed checks should be stored securely off-site for access by lower-level managers in the event senior-level or financial management is unable to disburse funds normally.

29. Which statement is true regarding company/employee relations during and after a disaster?

    a. The organization has a responsibility to continue salaries or other funding to the employees and/or families affected by the disaster.

    b. The organization's responsibility to the employee's families ends when the disaster stops the business from functioning.

    c. Employees should seek any means of obtaining compensation after a disaster, including fraudulent ones.

    d. Senior-level executives are the only employees who should receive continuing salaries during the disruptive event.

Answer: a

The organization has an inherent responsibility to its employees and their families during and after a disaster or other disruptive event. The company must be insured to the extent it can properly compensate its employees and families. Alternatively, employees do not have the right to obtain compensatory damages fraudulently if the organization cannot compensate.

30. Which choice below is the correct definition of a Mutual Aid Agreement?

  a. A management-level analysis that identifies the impact of losing an entity's resources

  b. An appraisal or determination of the effects of a disaster on human, physical, economic, and natural resources

  c. A prearranged agreement to render assistance to the parties of the agreement

  d. Activities taken to eliminate or reduce the degree of risk to life and property

Answer: c

A mutual aid agreement is used by two or more parties to provide for assistance if one of the parties experiences an emergency. Answer a describes a business continuity plan. Answer b describes a damage assessment, and answer d describes risk mitigation.

31. Which choice below most accurately describes a business continuity program?

  a. Ongoing process to ensure that the necessary steps are taken to identify the impact of potential losses and maintain viable recovery

  b. A program that implements the mission, vision, and strategic goals of the organization

  c. A determination of the effects of a disaster on human, physical, economic, and natural resources

  d. A standard that allows for rapid recovery during system interruption and data loss

Answer: a

A business continuity program is an ongoing process supported by senior management and funded to ensure that the necessary steps are taken to identify the impact of potential losses, maintain viable recovery strategies and recovery plans, and ensure continuity of services through personnel training, plan testing, and maintenance. Answer b describes a disaster/emergency management program. Answer c describes a damage assessment. Answer d is a distracter.

32. Which of the following would best describe a cold backup site?

    a. A computer facility with electrical power and HVAC, all needed applications installed and configured on the file/print servers, and enough workstations present to begin processing

    b. A computer facility with electrical power and HVAC but with no workstations or servers on-site prior to the event and no applications installed

    c. A computer facility with no electrical power or HVAC

    d. A computer facility available with electrical power and HVAC and some file/print servers, although the applications are not installed or configured and all of the needed workstations may not be on site or ready to begin processing

Answer: b

A computer facility with electrical power and HVAC, with workstations and servers available to be brought on-site when the event begins and no applications installed, is a cold site. Answer a is a hot site, and d is a warm site. Answer c is just an empty room.

Chapter 9

1. According to the Internet Activities Board (IAB), an activity that causes which of the following is considered a violation of ethical behavior on the Internet?

    a. Wasting resources

    b. Appropriating other people's intellectual output

    c. Using a computer to steal

    d. Using a computer to bear false witness

Answer: a

The correct answer is a. Answers b, c, and d are ethical considerations of other organizations.

2. Which of the following best defines social engineering?

    a. Illegal copying of software

    b. Gathering information from discarded manuals and printouts

    c. Using people skills to obtain proprietary information

    d. Destruction or alteration of data

Answer: c

The correct answer is c, using people skills to obtain proprietary information. Answer a is software piracy, answer b is dumpster diving, and answer d is a violation of integrity.

3. Because the development of new technology usually outpaces the law, law enforcement uses which traditional laws to prosecute computer criminals?

   a. Malicious mischief

   b. Embezzlement, fraud, and wiretapping

   c. Immigration

   d. Conspiracy and elimination of competition

   Answer: b

   The correct answer is b. Answer a is not a law, answer c is not applicable because it applies to obtaining visas and so on, and answer d is not correct because the laws in answer b are more commonly used to prosecute computer crimes.

4. Which of the following is NOT a category of law under the Common Law System?

   a. Criminal law

   b. Civil law

   c. Administrative/Regulatory law

   d. Derived law

   Answer: d

   The correct answer is d. It is a distracter, and all of the other answers are categories under common law.

5. A trade secret:

   a. Provides the owner with a legally enforceable right to exclude others from practicing the art covered for a specified time period

   b. Protects original works of authorship

   c. Secures and maintains the confidentiality of proprietary technical or business-related information that is adequately protected from disclosure by the owner

   d. Is a word, name, symbol, color, sound, product shape, or device used to identify goods and to distinguish them from those made or sold by others

   Answer: c

   The correct answer is c. It defines a trade secret. Answer a refers to a patent. Answer b refers to a copyright. Answer d refers to a trademark.

6. Which of the following is NOT a European Union (EU) principle?

  a. Data should be collected in accordance with the law.

  b. Transmission of personal information to locations where equivalent personal data protection cannot be assured is permissible.

  c. Data should be used only for the purposes for which it was collected and should be used only for a reasonable period of time.

  d. Information collected about an individual cannot be disclosed to other organizations or individuals unless authorized by law or by consent of the individual.

Answer: b

The correct answer is b. The transmission of data to locations where equivalent personal data protection cannot be assured is NOT permissible. The other answers are EU principles.

7. The Federal Sentencing Guidelines:

  a. Hold senior corporate officers personally liable if their organizations do not comply with the law

  b. Prohibit altering, damaging, or destroying information in a federal interest computer

  c. Prohibit eavesdropping or the interception of message contents

  d. Established a category of sensitive information called Sensitive But Unclassified (SBU)

Answer: a

The correct answer is a. Answer b is part of the U.S. Computer Fraud and Abuse Act. Answer c is part of the U.S. Electronic Communications Privacy Act. Answer d is part of the U.S. Computer Security Act.

8. What does the prudent man rule require?

  a. Senior officials to post performance bonds for their actions

  b. Senior officials to perform their duties with the care that ordinary, prudent people would exercise under similar circumstances

  c. Senior officials to guarantee that all precautions have been taken and that no breaches of security can occur

  d. Senior officials to follow specified government standards

Answer: b

The correct answer is b. Answer a is a distracter and is not part of the prudent man rule. Answer c is incorrect because it is not possible to guarantee that breaches of security can never occur. Answer d is incorrect because the prudent man rule does not refer to a specific government standard but relates to what other prudent persons would do.

9. Information Warfare is:

    a. Attacking the information infrastructure of a nation to gain military and/or economic advantages

    b. Developing weapons systems based on artificial intelligence technology

    c. Generating and disseminating propaganda material

    d. Signal intelligence

Answer: a

The correct answer is a. Answer b is a distracter and has to do with weapon systems development. Answer c is not applicable. Answer d is the conventional acquisition of information from radio signals.

10. The chain of evidence relates to:

    a. Securing laptops to desks during an investigation

    b. DNA testing

    c. Handling and controlling evidence

    d. Making a disk image

Answer: c

The correct answer is c. Answer a relates to physical security, answer b is a type of biological testing, and answer d is part of the act of gathering evidence.

11. The Kennedy-Kassebaum Act is also known as:

    a. RICO

    b. OECD

    c. HIPAA

    d. EU Directive

Answer: c

The correct answer is c. The others refer to other laws or guidelines.

12. Which of the following refers to a U.S. government program that reduces or eliminates emanations from electronic equipment?

    a. CLIPPER

    b. ECHELON

    c. ECHO

    d. TEMPEST

Answer: d

The correct answer is d. Answer a refers to the U.S. government Escrowed Encryption Standard. Answer b refers to the large-scale monitoring of RF transmissions. Answer c is a distracter.

13. Imprisonment is a possible sentence under:

    a. Civil (tort) law

    b. Criminal law

    c. Both civil and criminal law

    d. Neither civil nor criminal law

Answer: b

The correct answer is b. It is the only one of the choices where imprisonment is possible.

14. Which one of the following conditions must be met if legal electronic monitoring of employees is conducted by an organization?

    a. Employees must be unaware of the monitoring activity.

    b. All employees must agree with the monitoring policy.

    c. Results of the monitoring cannot be used against the employee.

    d. The organization must have a policy stating that all employees are regularly notified that monitoring is being conducted.

Answer: d

The correct answer is d. Answer a is incorrect because employees must be made aware of the monitoring if it is to be legal; answer b is incorrect because employees do not have to agree with the policy; and answer c is incorrect because the results of monitoring might be used against the employee if the corporate policy is violated.

15. Which of the following is a key principle in the evolution of computer crime laws in many countries?

    a. All members of the United Nations have agreed to uniformly define and prosecute computer crime.

    b. Existing laws against embezzlement, fraud, and wiretapping cannot be applied to computer crime.

    c. The definition of property was extended to include electronic information.

    d. Unauthorized acquisition of computer-based information without the intent to resell is not a crime.

Answer: c

The correct answer is c. Answer a is incorrect because all nations do not agree on the definition of computer crime and corresponding punishments. Answer b is incorrect because the existing laws can be applied against computer crime. Answer d is incorrect because in some countries, possession without intent to sell is considered a crime.

16. The concept of *due care* states that senior organizational management must ensure that:

    a. All risks to an information system are eliminated.

    b. Certain requirements must be fulfilled in carrying out their responsibilities to the organization.

    c. Other management personnel are delegated the responsibility for information system security.

    d. The cost of implementing safeguards is greater than the potential resultant losses resulting from information security breaches.

Answer: b

The correct answer is b. Answer a is incorrect because all risks to information systems cannot be eliminated; answer c is incorrect because senior management cannot delegate its responsibility for information system security under due care; and answer d is incorrect because the cost of implementing safeguards should be less than or equal to the potential resulting losses relative to the exercise of due care.

17. Liability of senior organizational officials relative to the protection of the organization's information systems is prosecutable under:

    a. Criminal law

    b. Civil law

    c. International law

    d. Financial law

Answer: b

18. Responsibility for handling computer crimes in the United States is assigned to:

    a. The Federal Bureau of Investigation (FBI) and the Secret Service

    b. The FBI only

    c. The National Security Agency (NSA)

    d. The Central Intelligence Agency (CIA)

Answer: a

The correct answer is a, making the other answers incorrect.

19. In general, computer-based evidence is considered:

    a. Conclusive

    b. Circumstantial

    c. Secondary

    d. Hearsay

Answer: d

The correct answer is d. Answer a refers to incontrovertible evidence; answer b refers to inference from other, intermediate facts; and answer c refers to a copy of evidence or oral description of its content.

20. Investigating and prosecuting computer crimes is made more difficult because:

    a. Backups may be difficult to find.

    b. Evidence is mostly intangible.

    c. Evidence cannot be preserved.

    d. Evidence is hearsay and can never be introduced into a court of law.

Answer: b

The correct answer is b. Answer a is incorrect because if backups are done, they usually can be located. Answer c is incorrect because evidence can be preserved using the proper procedures. Answer d is incorrect because there are exceptions to the hearsay rule.

21. Which of the following criteria are used to evaluate suspects in the commission of a crime?

    a. Motive, Intent, and Ability

    b. Means, Object, and Motive

    c. Means, Intent, and Motive

    d. Motive, Means, and Opportunity

Answer: d

22. Which one of the following U.S. government entities was assigned the responsibility for improving government efficiency through the application of new technologies and for developing guidance on information security for government agencies by the Paperwork Reduction Act of 1980,1995?

   a. The National Institute for Standards and Technology (NIST)

   b. The General Services Administration (GSA)

   c. The Office of Management and Budget (OMB)

   d. The National Security Agency (NSA)

Answer: c

23. What is enticement?

   a. Encouraging the commission of a crime when there was initially no intent to commit a crime

   b. Assisting in the commission of a crime

   c. Luring the perpetrator to an attractive area or presenting the perpetrator with a lucrative target after the crime has already been initiated

   d. Encouraging the commission of one crime over another

Answer: c

The correct answer is c, the definition of enticement. Answer a is the definition of entrapment. Answers b and d are distracters.

24. Which of the following is NOT a computer investigation issue?

   a. Evidence is easy to obtain.

   b. The time frame for investigation is compressed.

   c. An expert may be required to assist.

   d. The information is intangible.

Answer: a

The correct answer is a. In many instances, evidence is difficult to obtain in computer crime investigations. Answers b, c, and d are computer investigation issues.

25. Conducting a search without the delay of obtaining a warrant if destruction of evidence seems imminent is possible under:

   a. Federal Sentencing Guidelines

   b. Proximate Causation

   c. Exigent Circumstances

   d. Prudent Man Rule

Answer: c

The correct answer is c. The other answers refer to other principles, guidelines, or rules.

26. Which one of the following items is NOT TRUE concerning the Platform for Privacy Preferences (P3P) developed by the World Wide Web Consortium (W3C)?

   a. It allows Web sites to express their privacy practices in a standard format that can be retrieved automatically and interpreted easily by user agents.

   b. It allows users to be informed of site practices in human-readable format.

   c. It does not provide the site privacy practices to users in machine-readable format.

   d. It automates decision-making based on the site's privacy practices when appropriate.

Answer: c

The correct answer is c. In addition to the capabilities in answers a, b, and d, P3P does provide the site privacy practices to users in machine-readable format.

27. The 1996 Information Technology Management Reform Act (ITMRA), or Clinger-Cohen Act, did which one of the following?

   a. Relieved the General Services Administration of responsibility for procurement of automated systems and contract appeals and charged the Office of Management and Budget with providing guidance on information technology procurement

   b. Relieved the General Services Administration of responsibility for procurement of automated systems and contract appeals and charged the National Institute for Standards and Technology with providing guidance on information technology procurement

   c. Relieved the Office of Management and Budget of responsibility for procurement of automated systems and contract appeals and charged the General Services Administration with providing guidance on information technology procurement

   d. Relieved the General Services Administration of responsibility for procurement of automated systems and contract appeals and charged the National Security Agency with providing guidance on information technology procurement

Answer: a

The correct answer is a. The other answers are distracters.

28. Which one of the following U.S. Acts prohibits trading, manufacturing, or selling in any way that is intended to bypass copyright protection mechanisms?

   a. The 1999 Uniform Information Transactions Act (UCITA)

   b. The 1998 Digital Millennium Copyright Act (DMCA)

   c. The 1998 Sonny Bono Copyright Term Extension Act

   d. The 1987 U.S. Computer Security Act

Answer: b

Answers a and d are distracters. Answer c, the 1998 Sonny Bono Copyright Term Extension Act, amends the provisions concerning duration of copyright protection. The Act states that the terms of copyright are generally extended for an additional 20 years.

29. Which of the following actions by the U.S. government is NOT permitted or required by the U.S. Patriot Act, signed into law on October 26, 2001?

   a. Subpoena of electronic records

   b. Monitoring of Internet communications

   c. Search and seizure of information on live systems (including routers and servers), backups, and archives

   d. Reporting of cash and wire transfers of $5,000 or more

Answer: d

Wire and cash transfers of $10,000 or more in a single transaction must be reported to government officials. Actions in answers a, b, and c are permitted under the Patriot Act. In answers a and b, the government has new powers to subpoena electronic records and to monitor Internet traffic. In monitoring information, the government can require the assistance of ISPs and network operators. This monitoring can extend even into individual organizations. In the Patriot Act, Congress permits investigators to gather information about electronic mail without having to show probable cause that the person to be monitored had committed a crime or was intending to commit a crime. In answer c, the items cited now fall under existing search and seizure laws. A new twist is delayed notification of a search warrant. Under the Patriot Act, if it is suspected that notification of a search warrant would cause a suspect to flee, a search can be conducted before notification of a search warrant is given.

In a related matter, the U.S. and numerous other nations have signed the Council of Europe's Cybercrime Convention. In the U.S., participation in the Convention has to be ratified by the Senate. In essence, the Convention requires the signatory nations to spy on their own residents, even if the action being monitored is illegal in the country in which the monitoring is taking place.

30. Which Act required U.S. government agencies to do the following?

   • Manage information resources to protect privacy and security

   • Designate a senior official, reporting directly to the Secretary of the Treasury, to ensure that the responsibilities assigned by the Act are accomplished

   • Identify and afford security protections in conformance with the Computer Security Act of 1987 commensurate with the magnitude of harm and risk that might result from the misuse, loss, or unauthorized access relative to information collected by an agency or maintained on behalf of an agency

   • Implement and enforce applicable policies, procedures, standards, and guidelines on privacy, confidentiality, security, disclosures, and sharing of information collected or maintained by or for the agency

   a. 1994 U.S. Computer Abuse Amendments Act

   b. 1996, Title I, Economic Espionage Act

   c. 1987 U.S. Computer Security Act

   d. Paperwork Reduction Act of 1980, 1995

   Answer: d

Chapter 10

1. Which choice below is NOT a type of motion-detection system?

   a. Ultrasonic-detection system

   b. Microwave-detection system

   c. Host-based intrusion-detection system

   d. Sonic-detection system

   Answer: c

   Host-based intrusion-detection systems are used to detect unauthorized logical access to network resources, not the physical presence of an intruder.

2. Which type of personnel control below helps prevent piggybacking?

   a. Mantraps

   b. Back doors

   c. Brute force

   d. Maintenance hooks

Answer: a

The other three answers are not personnel or physical controls but are technical threats or vulnerabilities. Answer b, back doors, commonly refers to Trojan Horses used covertly to give an attacker backdoor network access. Hackers install back doors to gain network access at a later time. Answer c, brute force, is a cryptographic attack attempting to use all combinations of key patterns to decipher a message. Answer d, maintenance hooks, are undocumented openings into an application to assist programmers with debugging. Although intended innocently, these can be exploited by intruders.

3. Which choice below most accurately describes the prime benefit of using guards?

   a. Human guards are less expensive than guard dogs.

   b. Guards can exercise discretionary judgment in a way that automated systems can't.

   c. Automated systems have a greater reliability rate than guards.

   d. Guard dogs cannot discern an intruder's intent.

Answer: b

The prime advantage to using human guards is that they can exercise discretionary judgment when the need arises. For example, during an emergency guards can switch roles from access control to evacuation support, something guard dogs or automated systems cannot.

4. The recommended optimal relative humidity range for computer operations is:

   a. 10%–30%

   b. 30%–40%

   c. 40%–60%

   d. 60%–80%

Answer: c

40% to 60% relative humidity is recommended for safe computer operations. Too low humidity can create static discharge problems, and too high humidity can create condensation and electrical contact problems.

5. How many times should a diskette be formatted to comply with TCSEC Orange Book object reuse recommendations?

   a. Three

   b. Five

   c. Seven

   d. Nine

   Answer: c

   Most computer certification and accreditation standards recommend that diskettes be formatted seven times to prevent any possibility of data remanence.

6. Which of the following more closely describes the combustibles in a Class B-rated fire?

   a. Paper

   b. Gas

   c. Liquid

   d. Electrical

   Answer: c

   Paper is described as a common combustible and is therefore rated a class A fire. An electrical fire is rated Class C. Gas is not defined as a combustible.

7. Which of the following is NOT the proper suppression medium for a Class B fire?

   a. CO_2

   b. Soda Acid

   c. Halon

   d. Water

   Answer: d

   Water is not a proper suppression medium for a class B fire. The other three are commonly used.

8. What does an audit trail or access log usually NOT record?

   a. How often a diskette was formatted

   b. Who attempted access

   c. The date and time of the access attempt

   d. Whether the attempt was successful

   Answer: a

   The other three answers are common elements of an access log or audit trail.

9. A brownout can be defined as a:

   a. Prolonged power loss

   b. Momentary low voltage

   c. Prolonged low voltage

   d. Momentary high voltage

Answer: c

Answer a, prolonged power loss, is a blackout; answer b, momentary low voltage, is a sag; and d, momentary high voltage, is a spike.

10. Which statement below is NOT accurate about smoke damage to electronic equipment?

    a. Smoke exposure during a fire for a relatively short period does little immediate damage.

    b. Continuing power to the smoke-exposed equipment can increase the damage.

    c. Moisture and oxygen corrosion constitute the main damage to the equipment.

    d. The primary damage done by smoke exposure is immediate.

Answer: d

Immediate smoke exposure to electronic equipment does little damage. However, the particulate residue left after the smoke has dissipated contains active by-products that corrode metal contact surfaces in the presence of moisture and oxygen.

11. A surge can be defined as a(n):

    a. Prolonged high voltage

    b. Initial surge of power at start

    c. Momentary power loss

    d. Steady interfering disturbance

Answer: a

Answer b, initial surge of power at start or power on, is called an inrush; c, momentary power loss, is a fault; and d, a steady interfering disturbance, is called noise.

12. Which is NOT a type of a fire detector?

    a. Heat-sensing

    b. Gas-discharge

    c. Flame-actuated

    d. Smoke-actuated

Answer: b

Gas-discharge is a type of fire extinguishing system, not a fire detection system.

13. Which of the following is NOT considered an acceptable replacement for Halon discharge systems?

    a. FA200

    b. Inergen (IG541)

    c. Halon 1301

    d. Argon (IG55)

Answer: c

Existing installations are encouraged to replace Halon 1301 with one of the substitutes listed.

14. Which type of fire extinguishing method contains standing water in the pipe and therefore generally does not enable a manual shutdown of systems before discharge?

    a. Dry pipe

    b. Wet pipe

    c. Preaction

    d. Deluge

Answer: b

The other three are variations on a dry pipe discharge method with the water not standing in the pipe until a fire is detected.

15. Which type of control below is NOT an example of a physical security access control?

    a. Retinal scanner

    b. Guard dog

    c. Five-key programmable lock

    d. Audit trail

Answer: d

16. Which is NOT a recommended way to dispose of unwanted used data media?

    a. Destroying CD-ROMs

    b. Formatting diskettes seven or more times

    c. Shredding paper reports by cleared personnel

    d. Copying new data over existing data on diskettes

Answer: d

While this method might overwrite the older files, recoverable data might exist past the file end marker of the new file if the new data file is smaller than the older data file.

17. According to the NFPA, which choice below is NOT a recommended risk factor to consider when determining the need for protecting the computing environment from fire?

    a. Life safety aspects of the computing function or process

    b. Fire threat of the installation to occupants or exposed property

    c. Distance of the computing facility from a fire station

    d. Economic loss of the equipment's value

Answer: c

While the distance of the computing facility from a fire station should be considered when initially determining the physical location of a computing facility (as should police and hospital proximity), it is not considered a primary factor in determining the need for internal fire suppression systems.

18. Which choice below is NOT an example of a Halocarbon Agent?

    a. HFC-23

    b. FC-3-1-10

    c. IG-541

    d. HCFC-22

Answer: c

IG-541 is an inert gas agent, not a halocarbon agent.

19. Which statement below most accurately describes a dry pipe sprinkler system?

    a. Dry pipe is the most commonly used sprinkler system.

    b. Dry pipe contains air pressure.

    c. Dry pipe sounds an alarm and delays water release.

    d. Dry pipe may contain carbon dioxide.

Answer: b

In a dry pipe system, air pressure is maintained until the sprinkler head seal is ruptured. Answer a is incorrect; wet pipe is the most commonly used sprinkler system, dry pipe is second. Answer c describes a preaction pipe, which sounds an alarm and delays the water release. A preaction pipe may or may not be a dry pipe, but not all dry pipes are preaction. Answer d is incorrect because a dry pipe is a water release system.

20. The theft of a laptop poses a threat to which tenet of the C.I.A. triad?

    a. Confidentiality

    b. Integrity

    c. Availability

    d. All of the above

Answer: d

Confidentiality, because the data can now be read by someone outside of a monitored environment; availability, because the user has lost the computing ability provided by the unit; and integrity, because the data residing on and any telecommunications from the portable are now suspect.

21. Which is a benefit of a guard over an automated control?

    a. Guards can use discriminating judgment.

    b. Guards are cheaper.

    c. Guards do not need training.

    d. Guards do not need preemployment screening.

Answer: a

Guards can use discriminating judgment. Guards are typically more expensive than automated controls, need training as to the protection requirements of the specific site, and need to be screened and bonded.

22. Which is NOT considered a preventative security measure?

    a. Fences

    b. Guards

    c. Audit trails

    d. Preset locks

Answer: c

Audit trails are detective, rather than preventative, because they are used to piece together the information of an intrusion or intrusion attempt after the fact.

23. Which is NOT a PC security control device?

   a. A cable lock

   b. A switch control

   c. A port control

   d. A file cabinet lock

Answer: d

A cable lock is used to attach the PC to a desk; a switch control is used to prevent powering off of a unit; and a port control (such as a diskette drive lock) is used to prevent data from being downloaded from the PC.

24. Which choice below is NOT an example of a clean fire-extinguishing agent?

   a. CO_2

   b. IG-55

   c. IG-01

   d. HCFC-22

Answer: a

CO_2, carbon dioxide, leaves a corrosive residue, and is therefore not recommended for computer facility fire suppression systems.

25. What is the recommended height of perimeter fencing to keep out casual trespassers?

   a. 1' to 2' high

   b. 3' to 4' high

   c. 6' to 7' high

   d. 8' to 12' high

Answer: b

3' to 4' high fencing is considered minimal protection, for restricting only casual trespassers. Answers c and d are better protection against intentional intruders.

26. Why should extensive exterior perimeter lighting of entrances or parking areas be installed?

   a. To enable programmable locks to be used

   b. To create two-factor authentication

   c. To discourage prowlers or casual intruders

   d. To prevent data remanence

Answer: c

The other answers have nothing to do with lighting.

27. Which of the following is NOT a form of data erasure?

    a. Clearing

    b. Remanence

    c. Purging

    d. Destruction

Answer: b

Clearing refers to the overwriting of data media intended to be reused in the same organization. Purging refers to degaussing or overwriting media intended to be removed from the organization. Destruction refers to completely destroying the media.

28. Which is NOT considered a physical intrusion detection method?

    a. Audio motion detector

    b. Photoelectric sensor

    c. Wave pattern motion detector

    d. Line supervision

Answer: d

Line supervision is the monitoring of the alarm signaling transmission medium to detect tampering. Audio detectors monitor a room for any abnormal soundwave generation. Photoelectric sensors receive a beam of light from a light-emitting device. Wave pattern motion detectors generate a wave pattern and send an alarm if the pattern is disturbed.

29. Which choice below represents the BEST reason to control the humidity in computer operations areas?

    a. Computer operators do not perform at their peak if the humidity is too high.

    b. Electrostatic discharges can harm electronic equipment.

    c. Static electricity destroys the electrical efficiency of the circuits.

    d. If the air is too dry, electroplating of conductors may occur.

Answer: b

Electrostatic discharges from static electricity can damage sensitive electronic equipment, even in small amounts.

30. Which term below refers to a standard used in determining the fire safety of a computer room?

   a. Noncombustible

   b. Fire-resistant

   c. Fire retardant

   d. Nonflammable

Answer: b

Answer a, noncombustible, means material that will not aid or add appreciable heat to an ambient fire. Answer c, fire retardant, describes material that lessens or prevents the spread of a fire. Fire retardant coatings are designed to protect materials from fire exposure damage. Answer d, nonflammable, describes material that will not burn.

Chapter 11

1. Which one of the following is NOT one of the five system life cycle planning phases as defined in NIST SP 800-14?

   a. Initiation phase

   b. Requirements phase

   c. Implementation phase

   d. Disposal phase

Answer: b

The requirements phase is not one of the five system life cycle planning phases. The other two phases of the system life cycle are the Development/Acquisition phase and the Operations phase.

2. Which one of the following sets of activities BEST describes a subset of the Acquisition Cycle phases as given in NIST SP 800-64, *Security Considerations in the Information System Development Life Cycle*?

   a. Mission and business planning, acquisition planning, contract performance, disposal and contract closeout

   b. Initiation, mission and business planning, acquisition planning, contract performance

   c. Initiation, acquisition/development, contract performance, disposal and contract closeout

   d. Mission and business planning, acquisition/development, contract performance, disposal and contract closeout

Answer: a

The other answers are distracters comprising components of the SDLC and the Acquisition cycle.

3. The IATF document 3.1 stresses that information assurance relies on three critical components. Which one of the following answers correctly lists these components?

   a. People, documentation, technology

   b. People, Defense in Depth, technology

   c. People, evaluation, certification

   d. People, operations, technology

Answer: d

The other answers are distracters.

4. In the 14 Common IT Security Practices listed in NIST SP 800-14, one of the practices addresses having three types of policies in place. Which one of the following items is NOT one of these types of policies?

   a. A program policy

   b. An issue specific policy

   c. A system specific policy

   d. An enclave specific policy

Answer: d

A program policy is used to create and define a computer security program; an issue specific policy addresses specific areas and issues; and a system specific policy focuses on decisions made by management.

5. Risk management, as defined in NIST SP 800-30, comprises which three processes?

   a. Risk assessment, risk mitigation, and evaluation and assessment

   b. Risk identification, risk mitigation, and evaluation and assessment

   c. Risk assessment, risk impacts, and risk mitigation

   d. Risk assessment, risk mitigation, and risk identification

Answer: a

The other answers are distracters.

6. In the system development life cycle, SDLC, or system life cycle as it is sometimes called, in which one of the of the five phases are the system security features configured, enabled, tested, and verified?

a. Operation/maintenance

b. Development/acquisition

c. Implementation

d. Initiation

Answer: c

7. Which one of he following activities is performed in the Development/Acquisition phase of the SDLC?

a. The scope of the IT system is documented.

b. The IT system is developed, programmed, or otherwise constructed.

c. The system performs its function.

d. Disposition of information, hardware, or software.

Answer: b

Answer a refers to the Initiation phase; answer c refers to the Operation/Maintenance phase; and answer d refers to the Disposal phase.

8. In NIST SP 800-30, risk is defined as a function of which set of the following items?

a. Threat likelihood, vulnerabilities, and impact

b. Threat likelihood, mission, and impact

c. Vulnerabilities, mission and impact

d. Threat likelihood, sensitivity, and impact

Answer: a

The other answers are distracters.

9. The risk assessment methodology described in NIST SP 800-30 comprises nine primary steps. Which one of the following is NOT one of these steps?

a. System characterization

b. Control analysis

c. Impact analysis

d. Accreditation boundaries

Answer: d

Delineating accreditation boundaries is a subset of answer a, system characterization.

10. The engineering principles for information technology security (EP-ITS), described in NIST SP 800-27, are which one of the following?

    a. A list of 33 system-level security principles to be considered in the design, development, and operation of an information system

    b. A list of eight principles and 14 practices derived from OECD guidelines

    c. Part of the Common Criteria (CC)

    d. Component of the Defense in Depth strategy

Answer: a

Answer b describes the principles and practices found in NIST SP 800-14. Answers c and d are distracters.

11. Which one of the following items is NOT one of the activities of the generic systems engineering (SE) process?

    a. Discover needs

    b. Define system requirements

    c. Obtain accreditation

    d. Assess effectiveness

Answer: c

Obtain accreditation is not one of the SE process activities. The other SE process activities are Design system architecture, develop detailed design, and implement system.

12. The elements of Discover information protection needs, Develop detailed security design, and Assess information protection effectiveness are part of what process:

    a. The systems engineering (SE) process

    b. The information systems security engineering process (ISSE)

    c. The system development life cycle (SDLC)

    d. The risk management process

Answer: b

13. In the ISSE process, information domains are defined under the Discover Information Protection Needs process. Which one of the following tasks is NOT associated the information domain?

    a. Identify the members of the domain

    b. List the information entities that are under control in the domain

    c. Identify the applicable privileges, roles, rules, and responsibilities of the users in the domain

    d. Map security mechanisms to security design elements in the domain.

Answer: d

This task is performed under the Develop Detailed Security Design activity.

14. In the Discover Information Protection Needs activity of the ISSE process, the information systems security engineer must document the elements of this activity, including roles, responsibilities, threats, strengths, security services, and priorities. These items form the basis of which one of the following:

    a. Threat matrix

    b. Functional analysis

    c. Synthesis

    d. Information protection policy (IPP)

Answer: d

The other answers are distracters.

15. As part of the Define System Security Requirements activity of the ISSE process, the information systems security engineer identifies and selects a solution set that can satisfy the requirements of the IPP. Which one of the following elements is NOT a component of the solution set?

    a. Functional decomposition

    b. Preliminary security concept of operations (CONOPS)

    c. System context

    d. System requirements

Answer: a

Functional decomposition is part of the Design System Security Architecture activity of the ISSE process.

16. The information systems security engineer's tasks of cataloging candidate commercial off-the-shelf (COTS) products, government off-the-shelf (GOTS) products, and custom security products are performed in which one of the following ISSE process activities?

    a. Define System Security Requirements

    b. Develop Detailed Security Design

    c. Implement System Security

    d. Design System Security Architecture

Answer: b

17. Which ISSE activity includes conducting unit testing of components, integration testing, and developing installation and operational procedures?

    a. Assess Information Protection Effectiveness

    b. Develop Detailed Security Design

    c. Implement System Security

    d. Design System Security Architecture

Answer: c

18. Security certification is performed in which phase of the SDLC?

    a. Implementation phase

    b. Validation phase

    c. Development/Acquisition phase

    d. Operations/Maintenance phase

Answer: a

Answer b, Validation, is not a phase of the SDLC. Answers c and d are additional phases of the SDLC.

19. The certification and accreditation process receives inputs from the ISSE process. These inputs are which one of the following items?

    a. Certification documentation

    b. Certification recommendations

    c. Accreditation decision

    d. Evidence and documentation

Answer: d

Answers a, b, and c are outputs of the Certification and Accreditation process.

20. Which one of the following items is NOT part of an implementation-independent protection profile (PP) of the Common Criteria (CC)?

    a. Security objectives

    b. Information assurance requirements

    c. Security-related functional requirements

    d. Defense of the enclave boundary

Answer: d

Defense of the enclave boundary is addressed in the Defense in Depth strategy.

21. Which one of the following is NOT one of the technology focus areas of the Defense in Depth strategy?

    a. Defend the certificate management

    b. Defend the network and infrastructure

    c. Defend the computing environment

    d. Defend the supporting infrastructure

Answer: a

22. Security categorization is part of which phase of the SDLC?

    a. Initiation

    b. Acquisition/Development

    c. Implementation

    d. Requirements

Answer: a

Security categorization defines low, moderate, or high levels of potential impact on organizations as a result of a security breach. Answers b and c are other phases of the SDLC. Answer d is not a phase of the SDLC.

23. The Defense in Depth strategy identifies five types of attacks on information systems as listed in IATF document 3.1. Which one of the following types of attacks is NOT one of these five types?

    a. Passive

    b. Active

    c. Close-in

    d. Outsider

Answer: d

The other two types of attacks are insider and distribution.

24. Which one of the following items is NOT an activity under the Acquisition/Development phase of the SDLC?

    a. Preliminary risk assessment

    b. Security functional requirements analysis

    c. Cost considerations and reporting

    d. Developmental security evaluation

Answer: a

This activity is performed in the initiation phase of the SDLC. Additional activities under the acquisition/development phase of the SDLC are risk assessment, assurance requirements analysis security, security planning, and security control development.

25. Which one of the following types of enclaves is NOT of those categorized in the U.S. federal and defense computing environments?

    a. Private

    b. Public

    c. Classified

    d. Secure

Answer: d

26. According to NIST SP 800-64, which phase of the SDLC includes the activities of functional statement of need, market research, cost-benefit analysis, and a cost analysis?

    a. Initiation

    b. Acquisition/Development

    c. Implementation

    d. Operations/Maintenance

Answer: b

Additional activities under this phase include requirements analysis, alternatives analysis, and a software conversion study.

27. Which one of the following models is an evolutionary model used to represent the acquisition management process?

    a. The acquisition process model

    b. The Spiral model

    c. The Waterfall model

    d. The acquisition/development model

Answer: b

This model depicts the acquisition management process as a set of phases and decision points in a circular representation. The other answers are distracters.

28. In NIST SP 800-30, a threat is defined as which one of the following items?

    a. Intent and method targeted at the intentional exploit of a vulnerability

    b. The likelihood that a given threat-source will exercise a particular potential vulnerability, and the resulting impact of that adverse event on the organization

    c. The potential for a threat-source to exercise a specific vulnerability

    d. A flaw or weakness in system security procedures, design, implementation, or internal controls that could be exercised and result in a security breach or a violation of the system's security policy

Answer: c

Answer a is a threat-source, answer b defines risk, and answer d is the definition of vulnerability.

29. Questionnaires, on-site interviews, review of documents, and automated scanning tools are primarily used to gather information for which one of the following steps of the risk assessment process?

    a. System characterization

    b. Risk determination

    c. Vulnerability identification

    d. Control analysis

Answer: a

30. In performing an impact analysis as part of the risk assessment process, three important factors should be considered in calculating the negative impact. Which one of the following items is NOT one of these factors?

    a. The sensitivity of the system and its data

    b. The management of the system

    c. The mission of the system

    d. The criticality of the system, determined by its value and the value of the data to the organization

Answer: b

Chapter 12

1. Which statement is NOT true about the NIACAP SSAA?

a. The SSAA is used throughout the entire NIACAP process.

b. The SSAA is a formal agreement among the DAA(s), certifier, user representative, and program manager.

c. The SSAA is used only through Phase 3, Validation.

d. The SSAA documents the conditions of the C&A for an IS.

Answer: c

The SSAA is used throughout the entire NIACAP process. After accreditation, the SSAA becomes the baseline security configuration document and is maintained during Phase 4.

2. Which choice BEST describes NIACAP Phase 1, Definition?

a. The objective of Phase 1 is to ensure the fully integrated system will be ready for certification testing.

b. The objective of Phase 1 is to produce the required evidence to support the DAA in making an informed decision to grant approval to operate the system (accreditation or Interim Approval to Operate [IATO]).

c. The objective of Phase 1 is to agree on the security requirements, C&A boundary, schedule, level of effort, and resources required.

d. The objective of Phase 1 is to ensure secure system management, operation, and maintenance to preserve an acceptable level of residual risk.

Answer: c

Phase 1, Definition, is focused on understanding the IS business case, environment, and architecture to determine the security requirements and level of effort necessary to achieve certification and accreditation. The objective of Phase 1 is to agree on the security requirements, C&A boundary, schedule, level of effort, and resources required. Answer a describes the objectives of Phase 2. Answer b describes the objectives of Phase 3. Answer d describes the objectives of Phase 4.

3. Which choice BEST describes NIACAP Phase 3, Accreditation?

a. The objective of Phase 3 is to ensure the fully integrated system will be ready for certification testing.

b. The objective of Phase 3 is to agree on the security requirements, C&A boundary, schedule, level of effort, and resources required.

    c. The objective of Phase 3 is to ensure secure system management, operation, and maintenance to preserve an acceptable level of residual risk.

    d. The objective of Phase 3 is to produce the required evidence to support the DAA in making an informed decision to grant approval to operate the system (accreditation or Interim Approval to Operate [IATO]).

Answer: d

Phase 3, Validation, validates compliance of the fully integrated system with the security policy and requirements stated in the SSAA. The objective of Phase 3 is to produce the required evidence to support the DAA in making an informed decision to grant approval to operate the system. Answer a describes the objectives of Phase 2. Answer b describes the objectives of Phase 1. Answer c describes the objectives of Phase 4.

4. Which NIACAP role is also referred to as the accreditor?

    a. IS program manager

    b. Designated Approving Authority (DAA)

    c. Certification agent

    d. User representative

Answer: b

The Designated Approving Authority (DAA) is also referred to as the accreditor.

5. Which is NOT a NIACAP role?

    a. IS program manager

    b. Certifier

    c. Vendor representative

    d. User representative

Answer: c

Answer c is a distracter; the other answers are all NIACAP roles.

6. Which is NOT a NIACAP accreditation type?

    a. Site accreditation

    b. Process accreditation

    c. Type accreditation

    d. System accreditation

Answer: b

Answer b is a distracter; the NIACAP applies to each of the other three accreditation types and may be tailored to meet the specific needs of the organization and IS. Answer a, a site accreditation, evaluates the applications and systems at a specific, self-contained location. Answer c, a type accreditation, evaluates an application or system that is distributed to a number of different locations. Answer d, a system accreditation, evaluates a major application or general support system.

7. Which statement is NOT true about the Designated Approving Authority (DAA)?

   a. The DAA determines the existing level of residual risk and makes an accreditation recommendation.

   b. The DAA is the primary government official responsible for implementing system security.

   c. The DAA is an executive with the authority and ability to balance the needs of the system with the security risks.

   d. The DAA can grant an accreditation or an Interim Approval to Operate (IATO), or may determine that the system's risks are not at an acceptable level and it is not ready to be operational.

Answer: a

The certifier, not the DAA, determines the existing level of residual risk and makes the accreditation recommendation. The DAA determines the acceptable, not existing, level of risk for a system. The other answers about the DAA are true.

8. Which statement is NOT true about the certification agent?

   a. The certifier provides the technical expertise to conduct the certification throughout the system's life cycle based on the security requirements documented in the SSAA.

   b. The certifier determines the acceptable level of residual risk for a system.

   c. The certifier determines whether a system is ready for certification and conducts the certification process.

   d. The certifier should be independent from the organization responsible for the system development or operation.

Answer: b

The DAA, not the certifier, determines the acceptable level of residual risk for a system and must have the authority to oversee the budget and IS business operations of systems under his/her purview. The other statements about the certifier are true.

9. What is the task of the certifier at the completion of the certification effort?

   a. Recommends to the DAA whether or not to accredit the system based on documented residual risk.

   b. Provides details of the system and its life cycle management to the DAA.

   c. Ensures that the security requirements are integrated in a way that will result in an acceptable level of risk.

   d. Keeps all NIACAP participants informed of life cycle actions, security requirements, and documented user needs.

Answer: a

At the completion of the certification effort the certifier reports the status of certification and makes a recommendation to the DAA. The other answers are tasks assigned to the program manager.

10. Why does NIACAP have a user representative?

   a. The user representative is an executive with the authority and ability to balance the needs of the system with the security risks.

   b. The user representative is concerned with system availability, access, integrity, functionality, performance, and confidentiality as they relate to the mission environment.

   c. The user representative determines the acceptable level of residual risk for a system.

   d. The user representative is the primary government official responsible for implementing system security.

Answer: b

The operational interests of system users are vested in the user representative. In the NIACAP process, the user representative is concerned with system availability, access, integrity, functionality, performance, and confidentiality as they relate to the mission environment. Users and their representative are found at all levels of an agency. The other answers are qualities of the DAA.

11. Which is NOT a responsibility of the NIACAP user representative?

   a. The user representative is responsible for the secure operation of a certified and accredited IS.

   b. The user representative represents the user community.

   c. The user representative determines whether a system is ready for certification and conducts the certification process.

   d. The user representative functions as the liaison for the user community throughout the life cycle of the system.

Answer: c

Answer c is a task for the certifier. As noted in the SSAA, the user representative:

- Is responsible for the identification of operational requirements
- Is responsible for the secure operation of a certified and accredited IS
- Represents the user community
- Assists in the C&A process
- Functions as the liaison for the user community throughout the life cycle of the system
- Defines the system's operations and functional requirements
- Is responsible for ensuring that the user's operational interests are maintained throughout system development, modification, integration, acquisition, and deployment

12. Which is NOT an activity in NIACAP Phase 2?

    a. System Development and Integration

    b. Initial Certification Analysis

    c. Refine the SSAA

    d. Negotiation

Answer: d

Negotiation is a Phase 1 activity. The other three are the Phase 2 activities.

13. Which statement about certification and accreditation (C&A) is NOT correct?

    a. Certification is the comprehensive evaluation of the technical and non-technical security features of an information system.

    b. C&A is optional for most federal agencies' security systems.

    c. Accreditation is the formal declaration by a DAA approving an information system to operate.

    d. C&A consists of formal methods applied to ensure that the appropriate information system security safeguards are in place and that they are functioning per the specifications.

Answer: b

NSTISSP No. 6 establishes the requirement for federal departments and agencies to implement a C&A process for national security systems. The requirements of the NSTISSI No. 6 apply to all U.S. government executive branch departments, agencies, and their contractors and consultants. The other three answers are correct statements about C&A.

14. Which is NOT an activity in NIACAP Phase 1?

    a. Preparation

    b. Initial Certification Analysis

    c. Registration

    d. Negotiation

Answer: b

Initial Certification Analysis is a Phase 2 activity. The other three are the Phase 1 activities.

15. During which NIACAP phase does the Security Test and Evaluation (ST&E) occur?

    a. Phase 1

    b. Phase 2

    c. Phase 3

    d. Phase 4

Answer: c

The Security Test and Evaluation (ST&E) is a major activity in Phase 3.

16. Which choice below BEST describes the objective of the Security Test and Evaluation (ST&E)?

    a. The objective of the ST&E is to update the SSAA to include changes made during system development and the results of the certification analysis.

    b. The objective of the ST&E is to evaluate the integration of COTS software, hardware, and firmware.

    c. The objective of the ST&E is to verify that change control and configuration management practices are in place.

    d. The objective of the ST&E is to assess the technical implementation of the security design.

Answer: d

The objective of the ST&E is to assess the technical implementation of the security design; to ascertain that security software, hardware, and firmware features affecting confidentiality, integrity, availability, and accountability have been implemented as documented in the SSAA; and that the features perform properly. ST&E validates the correct implementation of identification and authentication, audit capabilities, access controls, object reuse, trusted recovery, and network connection rule compliance. The other answers are distracters.

17. Penetration Testing is part of which NIACAP phase?

    a. Phase 1

    b. Phase 2

    c. Phase 3

    d. Phase 4

Answer: c

Penetration testing assesses the system's ability to withstand intentional attempts to circumvent system security features by exploiting technical security vulnerabilities. Penetration testing may include insider and outsider penetration attempts based on common vulnerabilities for the technology being used.

18. The DAA accreditation decision is made at the last step of which phase?

    a. Phase 1

    b. Phase 2

    c. Phase 3

    d. Phase 4

Answer: c

After receipt of the certifier's recommendation, the DAA reviews the SSAA and makes an accreditation determination. This determination is added to the SSAA. The final SSAA accreditation package includes the certifier's recommendation, the DAA authorization to operate, and supporting documentation. The SSAA must contain all information necessary to support the certifier's recommended decision, including security findings, deficiencies, risks to operation, and actions to resolve any deficiencies.

19. If the DAA does not accredit the system, what happens?

    a. The NIACAP process reverts to Phase 1.

    b. The NIACAP process moves on to Phase 4.

    c. The NIACAP project is ended.

    d. The NIACAP stays in Phase 3 until the system is accredited.

Answer: a

If the decision is made to not authorize the system to operate, the NIACAP process reverts to Phase 1, and the DAA, certifier, program manager, and user representative must agree to proposed solutions to meet an acceptable level of risk. The decision must state the specific reasons for denial and, if possible, provide suggested solutions.

20. What is the main purpose of the post-accreditation phase?

   a. To initiate the risk management agreement process among the four principals: the DAA, certifier, program manager, and user representative

   b. To continue to operate and manage the system so that it will maintain an acceptable level of residual risk

   c. To ensure that the SSAA properly and clearly defines the approach and level of effort

   d. To collect Information and documentation about the system, such as capabilities and functions the system will perform

Answer: b

Phase 4 contains activities required to continue to operate and manage the system so that it will maintain an acceptable level of residual risk. Post-accreditation activities must include ongoing maintenance of the SSAA, system operations, security operations, change management, and compliance validation. The other answers relate to Phase 1.

21. How long does Phase 4 last?

   a. Until the initial certification analysis determines whether the IS is ready to be evaluated and tested

   b. Until the DAA reviews the SSAA and makes an accreditation determination

   c. Until the information system is removed from service, a major change is planned for the system, or a periodic compliance validation is required

   d. Until the responsible organizations adopt the SSAA and concur that those objectives have been reached

Answer: c

Phase 4 must continue until the information system is removed from service, a major change is planned for the system, or a periodic compliance validation is required. The other answers are distracters.

22. SSAA maintenance continues under which phase?

   a. Phase 1

   b. Phase 2

   c. Phase 3

   d. Phase 4

Answer: d

Phase 4 involves ongoing review of the SSAA to ensure it remains current. The user representative, DAA, certifier, and program manager must approve revisions to the SSAA. On approval, the necessary changes to the mission, environment, and architecture are documented in the SSAA.

23. Change management is initiated under which phase?

    a. Phase 1

    b. Phase 2

    c. Phase 3

    d. Phase 4

Answer: d

After an IS is approved for operation in a specific computing environment, changes to the IS and the computing environment must be controlled. While changes may adversely affect the overall security posture of the infrastructure and the IS, change is ongoing as it responds to the needs of the user and new technology developments. As the threats become more sophisticated or focused on a particular asset, countermeasures must be strengthened or added to provide adequate protection. Therefore, change management is required to maintain an acceptable level of residual risk.

24. How many levels of certification does NIACAP specify to ensure that the appropriate C&A is performed for varying schedule and budget limitations?

    a. Two

    b. Three

    c. Four

    d. Five

Answer: c

NIACAP has four levels of certification to ensure that the appropriate C&A is performed for varying schedule and budget limitations. To determine the appropriate level of certification, the certifier must analyze the system's business functions; national, departmental, and agency security requirements; criticality of the system to the organizational mission; software products; computer infrastructure; the types of data processed by the system, and types of users. The levels are as follows:

- *Level 1* — Basic Security Review

- *Level 2* — Minimum Analysis

- *Level 3* — Detailed Analysis

- *Level 4* — Comprehensive Analysis

25. What happens to the SSAA after the NIACAP accreditation?

    a. The SSAA becomes the baseline security configuration document.

    b. The SSAA is discarded as the project is finished.

    c. The SSAA cannot be reviewed or changed.

    d. The ISSO can revise the SSAA independently.

Answer: a

After accreditation, the SSAA becomes the baseline security configuration document. Phase 4 involves ongoing review of the SSAA to ensure it remains current. The user representative, DAA, certifier, and program manager must approve revisions to the SSAA. On approval, the necessary changes to the mission, environment, and architecture are documented in the SSAA.

26. Which policy document determines that all federal government departments and agencies establish and implement programs mandating the certification and accreditation (C&A) of national security systems under their operational control?

    a. DoD 8510.1-M, "Department of Defense Information Technology Security Certification and Accreditation Process (DITSCAP) Application Manual," July 31, 2000

    b. FIPS PUB102, "Guidelines for Computer Security Certification and Accreditation," September 27, 1983

    c. NSTISS Instruction (NSTISSI) No. 1000, "National Information Assurance Certification and Accreditation Process (NIACAP)," April 2000

    d. NSTISS Policy (NSTISSP) No. 6, "National Policy on Certification and Accreditation of National Security Telecommunications and Information Systems," 8 April 1994

Answer: d

NSTISSP No. 6 determines that all federal government departments and agencies establish and implement programs mandating the certification and accreditation (C&A) of national security systems under their operational control. These C&A programs must ensure that information processed, stored, or transmitted by national security systems is adequately protected for confidentiality, integrity, and availability.

27. Which assessment methodology below is a self-guided assessment implemented in a series of short workshops focusing on key organizational areas and conducted in three phases?

    a. Federal Information Technology Security Assessment Framework (FITSAF)

    b. Operationally Critical Threat, Asset, and Vulnerability Evaluation (OCTAVE)

c. Office of Management and Budget (OMB) Circular A-130

d. INFOSEC Assessment Methodology (IAM)

Answer: b

Carnegie Mellon University's Software Engineering Institute (SEI) created the Operationally Critical Threat, Asset, and Vulnerability Evaluation (OCTAVE). OCTAVE is a self-guided assessment implemented in a series of short workshops focusing on key organizational areas.

It is conducted in three phases:

1. Identify critical assets and the threats to those assets

2. Identify the vulnerabilities that expose those threats

3. Develop an appropriate protection strategy for the organization's mission and priorities

28. Which assessment methodology below is a 6-step comprehensive C&A guide?

   a. Federal Information Processing Standard (FIPS) 102

   b. Operationally Critical Threat, Asset, and Vulnerability Evaluation (OCTAVE)

   c. Federal Information Technology Security Assessment Framework (FITSAF)

   d. INFOSEC Assessment Methodology (IAM)

Answer: a

The Federal Information Processing Standard (FIPS) 102, the *Guideline for Computer Security Certification and Accreditation*, is a comprehensive guide explaining how to establish a C&A program and execute a complete C&A.

FIPS 102 details a 6-step approach:

1. Planning

2. Data Collection

3. Basic Evaluation

4. Detailed Evaluation

5. Report of Findings

6. Accreditation

29. Which assessment methodology below was developed by the National Security Agency to assist both assessment suppliers and consumers?

    a. Operationally Critical Threat, Asset, and Vulnerability Evaluation (OCTAVE)

    b. Federal Information Processing Standard (FIPS) 102

    c. Federal Information Technology Security Assessment Framework (FITSAF)

    d. INFOSEC Assessment Methodology (IAM)

Answer: d

The INFOSEC assessment methodology (IAM) is a detailed and systematic way of examining cyber vulnerabilities that was developed by the National Security Agency to assist both INFOSEC assessment suppliers and consumers requiring assessments. The IAM examines the mission, organization, security policies and programs, and information systems and the threat to these systems.

30. What is the order of phases in a DITSCAP assessment?

    a. Verification, Definition, Validation, and Post Accreditation

    b. Definition, Verification, Validation, and Post Accreditation

    c. Definition, Validation, Verification, and Post Accreditation

    d. Validation, Definition, Verification, and Post Accreditation

Answer: b

The DITSCAP phases are identical to the NIACAP phases:

- Phase 1, Definition
- Phase 2, Verification
- Phase 3, Validation
- Phase 4, Post Accreditation

Chapter 13

1. Which statement about the SSE-CMM is incorrect?

    a. The SSE-CMM defines two dimensions that are used to measure the capability of an organization to perform specific activities.

    b. The domain dimension consists of all of the practices that collectively define security engineering.

   c. The domain dimension represents practices that indicate process management and institutionalization capability.

   d. The capability dimension represents practices that indicate process management and institutionalization capability.

Answer: c

The SSE-CMM defines two dimensions that are used to measure the capability of an organization to perform specific activities, the domain dimension and the capability dimension. The domain dimension consists of all of the practices that collectively define security engineering. The capability dimension represents practices that indicate process management and institutionalization capability.

2. Which description of the SSE-CMM Level 5 Generic Practice is correct?

   a. Planned and Tracked

   b. Continuously Improving

   c. Quantitatively Controlled

   d. Performed Informally

Answer: b

Level 5, Continuously Improving, is the highest level. A statement characterizing this level would be: "A culture of continuous improvement requires a foundation of sound management practice, defined processes, and measurable goals."

3. Which statement about testing and evaluation is NOT true?

   a. A TEMP is required for most large programs.

   b. A DT&E is equivalent to Analytical, Type 1, and Type 2 testing.

   c. A OT&E is equivalent to Type 5 and Type 6 testing.

   d. A OT&E is equivalent to Type 3 and Type 4 testing.

Answer: c

In the Defense sector, a TEMP is required for most large programs and includes the planning and implementation of procedures for the Development Test and Evaluation (DT&E) and the Operational Test and Evaluation (OT&E). DT&E basically equates to the Analytical, Type 1, and Type 2 testing, and OT&E is equivalent to Type 3 and Type 4 testing.

4. Which attribute about the Level 1 SSE-CMM Generic Practice is correct?

   a. Performed Informally

   b. Planned and Tracked

   c. Well Defined

   d. Continuously Improving

Answer: a

The lowest level, Level 1, Performed Informally, focuses on whether an organization or project performs a process that incorporates the BPs. The attribute of this level simply requires that the BPs are performed.

5. Which choice below is NOT a true statement about good cost control?

   a. Cost control starts with the initiation of corrective action.

   b. Cost control requires good overall cost management.

   c. Cost control requires immediate initiation of corrective action.

   d. Cost control starts with the initial development of cost estimates for the program.

Answer: a

Cost control starts with the initial development of cost estimates for the program and continues with the functions of cost monitoring, the collection of cost data, the analysis of the data, and the immediate initiation of corrective action. Cost control requires good overall cost management, including:

- Cost Estimating
- Cost Accounting
- Cost Monitoring
- Cost Analysis and Reporting
- Control Functions

6. Which statement about the SE-CMM is NOT correct?

   a. The SE-CMM describes the essential elements of an organization's systems engineering process that must exist in order to ensure good systems engineering.

   b. The SE-CMM provides a reference to compare existing systems engineering practices against the essential systems engineering elements described in the model.

c. The SE-CMM goal is to improve the system- or product-engineering process.

d. The SE-CMM was created to define, improve, and assess security-engineering capability.

Answer: d

The SSE-CMM goal is to define, improve, and assess security-engineering capability, not the SE-CMM. The SE-CMM goal is to improve the system- or product-engineering process. The SE-CMM describes the essential elements of an organization's systems engineering process that must exist in order to ensure good systems engineering. It also provides a reference to compare existing systems engineering practices against the essential systems engineering elements described in the model.

7. Which statement about system security testing and evaluation (ST&E) categories is correct?

a. Type 1 testing is performed during the latter stages of the detail design and development phase.

b. Type 2 testing is design evaluation conducted early in the system life cycle.

c. Type 3 testing is performed during the latter stages of the detail design and development phase.

d. Type 4 testing is conducted during the system operational use and life cycle support phase.

Answer: d

Testing and evaluation processes often involve several stages of testing, categories, or phases, such as:

- *Analytical* — Design evaluations conducted early in the system life cycle using computerized techniques such as CAD, CAM, CALS, simulation, rapid prototyping, and other related approaches.

- *Type 1 testing* — The evaluation of system components in the laboratory using bench test models and service test models, designed to verify performance and physical characteristics.

- *Type 2 testing* — Testing performed during the latter stages of the detail design and development phase when preproduction prototype equipment and software are available.

- *Type 3 testing* — Tests conducted after initial system qualification and prior to the completion of the production or construction phase. This is the first time that all elements of the system are operated and evaluated on an integrated basis.

- *Type 4 testing* — Testing conducted during the system operational use and life-cycle support phase, intended to provide further knowledge of the system in the user environment.

8. Which choice is NOT an activity in the cost control process?

   a. Identifying potential suppliers

   b. Developing a functional cost data collection capability

   c. Developing the costs as estimated for each task

   d. Creating a procedure for cost evaluation

Answer: a

Answer a is an activity of outsourcing. The cost control process includes:

   1. Define the elements of work, as extracted from the SOW

   2. Integrate the tasks defined in the WBS

   3. Develop the costs, as estimated for each task

   4. Develop a functional cost data collection and reporting capability

   5. Develop a procedure for evaluation and quick corrective action

9. Which choice does NOT describe a common outsourcing activity?

   a. Review of proposals

   b. Develop a functional cost reporting capability

   c. Contract negotiation

   d. Development of an RFP

Answer: b

Developing a functional cost reporting capability is a function of Cost Control. The order of activities for the outsourcing process is:

   1. Identification of Potential Suppliers

   2. Development of a Request For Proposal (RFP)

   3. Review and Evaluation of Supplier Proposals

   4. Selection of Suppliers and Contract Negotiation

   5. Supplier Monitoring and Control

10. Which choice is NOT an accurate description of an activity level of the WBS?

   a. Level 1 may be used as the basis for the authorization of the program work.

   b. Program budgets are usually prepared at level 1.

   c. Level 2 identifies the various projects that must be completed.

   d. Program schedules are generally prepared at level 3.

Answer: b

The WBS structure generally includes three levels of activity:

- *Level 1*—Identifies the entire program scope of work to be produced and delivered. Level 1 may be used as the basis for the authorization of the program work.

- *Level 2*—Identifies the various projects, or categories of activity, that must be completed in response to program requirements. Program budgets are usually prepared at this level.

- *Level 3*—Identifies the activities, functions, major tasks, and/or components of the system that are directly subordinate to the Level 2 items. Program schedules are generally prepared at this level.

11. Which choice below is NOT a phase in the IDEAL model?

    a. Authorizing

    b. Learning

    c. Diagnosing

    d. Establishing

Answer: a

The five phases of the IDEAL model are:

- *Initiating*—Laying the groundwork for a successful improvement effort

- *Diagnosing*—Determining where you are relative to where you want to be

- *Establishing*—Planning the specifics of how you will reach your destination

- *Acting*—Doing the work according to the plan

- *Learning*—Learning from the experience and improving your ability

12. Which choice below best describes systems engineering, as defined in the SSE-CMM?

    a. An integrated composite of people, products, and processes that provides a capability to satisfy a need or objective.

    b. The selective application of scientific and engineering efforts to integrate the efforts of all engineering disciplines and specialties into the total engineering effort

    c. A narrative description of the work required for a given project.

    d. The contracting with one or more outside suppliers for the procurement and acquisition of materials and services.

Answer: b

The definition of systems engineering on which the SE-CMM is based is defined as the selective application of scientific and engineering efforts to:

- Transform an operational need into a description of the system configuration that best satisfies the operational need according to the measures of effectiveness

- Integrate related technical parameters and ensure the compatibility of all physical, functional, and technical program interfaces in a manner that optimizes the total system definition and design

- Integrate the efforts of all engineering disciplines and specialties into the total engineering effort

Answer a describes a system, answer c describes the SOW, and answer d describes outsourcing.

13. Which choice below is NOT a benefit of the WBS?

   a. The WBS facilitates the initial allocation of budgets.

   b. The WBS facilitates the collection and reporting of costs.

   c. The system can easily be described through the logical breakout of its elements into work packages.

   d. The WBS integrates the efforts of all engineering disciplines and specialties into the total engineering effort.

Answer: d

The WBS provides many benefits, such as:

- Provides for the reporting of system technical performance measures (TPMs)

- The entire security system can easily be defined by the breakout of its elements in to discrete work packages

- Aids in linking objectives and activities with available resources

- Facilitates budgeting and cost reporting

- Responsibility assignments can readily be identified through the assignment of tasks

- Provides a greater probability that every activity will be accounted for

Answer d describes a benefit of systems engineering.

14. Which choice is NOT an element of the Statement of Work (SOW)?

   a. An identification of the input requirements from other tasks

   b. A description of specific results to be achieved

   c. Management of security awareness, training, and education programs

   d. A proposed schedule for delivery of the product

Answer: c

The Statement of Work (SOW) is a narrative description of the work required for a given project. It includes:

• Summary statement of the tasks to be accomplished

• Identification of the input requirements from other tasks, including tasks accomplished by the customer and supplier

• References to applicable specifications, standards, procedures, and related documentation

• Description of the specific results to be achieved and a proposed schedule of delivery

Answer c is an example of an SSE-CMM Best Practice.

15. Which statement below best describes the difference between a Type 1 testing and evaluation category and a Type 2 category?

   a. Type 1 testing is the evaluation of system components in the laboratory, designed to verify performance and physical characteristics.

   b. Type 2 testing is the evaluation of system components in the laboratory, designed to verify performance and physical characteristics.

   c. Type 1 testing establishes design evaluations conducted early in the system life cycle.

   d. Type 2 testing is conducted after initial system qualification and prior to the completion of the production or construction phase.

Answer: a

Answer b describes Type 1 testing, answer c describes the Analytical stage of testing, and answer d describes Type 3 testing.

16. Which choice has the outsourcing activities listed in their proper order?

    a. Review and evaluation of supplier proposals, supplier monitoring and control, development of a Request For Proposal (RFP), and selection of suppliers.

    b. Development of a Request For Proposal (RFP), review and evaluation of supplier proposals, supplier monitoring and control, and selection of suppliers.

    c. Development of a Request For Proposal (RFP), review and evaluation of supplier proposals, selection of suppliers, and supplier monitoring and control.

    d. Review and evaluation of supplier proposals, selection of suppliers, development of a Request For Proposal (RFP), and supplier monitoring and control.

Answer: c

17. Which answer BEST describes a Statement of Work (SOW)?

    a. A narrative description of the work required for a given project.

    b. An integrated composite of people, products, and processes that provides a capability to satisfy a need or objective.

    c. The contracting with one or more outside suppliers for the procurement and acquisition of materials and services.

    d. The development of a functional cost reporting capability.

Answer: a

The Statement of Work is a narrative description of the work required for a given project. Answer b describes a system as defined by the SE-CMM, answer c describes outsourcing, and answer d describes a function of Cost Control.

18. Which statement about SSE-CMM Base Practices is correct?

    a. BPs are mandatory characteristics that must exist within an implemented security engineering process before an organization can claim satisfaction in a given PA.

    b. BPs are ordered in degrees of maturity and are grouped to form and distinguish among five levels of security engineering maturity.

    c. BPs are ordered in degrees of maturity and are grouped to form and distinguish among 22 levels of security engineering maturity.

    d. BPs are optional characteristics that must exist within an implemented security engineering process before an organization can claim satisfaction in a given PA.

Answer: a

BPs are mandatory characteristics that must exist within an implemented security engineering process before an organization can claim satisfaction in a given PA. The GPs are ordered in degrees of maturity and are grouped to form and distinguish among five levels of security engineering maturity. The other answers are distracters.

19. As per the SE-CMM, which statement defining a system is incorrect?

    a. An interacting combination of elements that are viewed in relation to function

    b. A continuous cycle of evaluating the current status of an organization, making improvements, and repeating the cycle

    c. An assembly of things or parts forming a complex or unitary whole

    d. An integrated composite of people, products, and processes that provides a capability to satisfy a need or objective

Answer: b

In the SE-CMM, a system is defined as:

    • An integrated composite of people, products, and processes that provides a capability to satisfy a need or objective.

    • An assembly of things or parts forming a complex or unitary whole; a collection of components organized to accomplish a specific function or set of functions.

    • An interacting combination of elements that are viewed in relation to function.

Answer b describes process improvement.

20. Which choice below best describes the purpose of the Learning phase of the IDEAL model?

    a. The Learning phase is the implementation phase and requires the greatest level of effort of all the phases both in terms of resources and time.

    b. The Learning phase is both the final stage of the initial process improvement cycle and the initial phase of the next process improvement effort.

    c. In the Learning phase, it is imperative that an understanding of the organization's current and desired future state of process maturity be established.

    d. In the Learning phase, a detailed plan of action based on the goals of the effort and the recommendations developed during the Diagnosing phase is developed.

Answer: b

The Learning phase is both the final stage of the initial process improvement cycle and the initial phase of the next process improvement effort. Based on the analysis of the improvement effort itself, the lessons learned are translated into recommendations for improving subsequent efforts. Answer a describes the Acting phase, answer c describes the Diagnosing phase, and answer d describes the Establishing phase.

21. Which statement about the System Engineering Management Plan (SEMP) is NOT true?

   a. Development program planning and control is a SEMP element.

   b. The goal of SEMP is to establish a continuous cycle of evaluating the current status of the organization.

   c. The SEMP contains detailed statements of how the systems security engineering functions are to be carried out during development.

   d. The security systems engineering process is a SEMP element.

Answer: b

The SEMP contains detailed statements of how the systems security engineering functions are to be carried out during development. Two elements of the SEMP are:

   • Development program planning and control

   • Security systems engineering process

Answer b describes a goal of process improvement.

22. Which choice has the correct order of activities in the IDEAL model?

   a. Learning, Initiating, Diagnosing, Establishing, and Acting

   b. Initiating, Learning, Diagnosing, Establishing, and Acting

   c. Learning, Diagnosing, Initiating, Establishing, and Acting

   d. Initiating, Diagnosing, Establishing, Acting, and Learning

Answer: d

The order of activities in the IDEAL model is Initiating, Diagnosing, Establishing, Acting, and Learning.

23. Which choice is an incorrect statement regarding the Systems Engineering Management Plan (SEMP)?

   a. The SEMP covers all management functions associated with the performance of security systems engineering activities for a given program.

   b. It starts as an outline and is updated as the security system development process goes on.

      c. It contains detailed statements of how the systems security engineering functions are to be carried out during development.

      d. The SEMP is a static document, intended to remain unchanged.

Answer: d

The SEMP is intended to be a dynamic document. It starts as an outline, is updated as the security system development process goes on, and contains detailed statements of how the systems security engineering functions are to be carried out during development. The SEMP covers all management functions associated with the performance of security systems engineering activities for a given program.

24. Which choice best describes an outsourced supplier?

      a. A broad class of external organizations that provide products, components, materials, and/or services to a producer or prime contractor.

      b. An interacting combination of elements that are viewed in relation to function.

      c. An integrated composite of people, products, and processes that provides a capability to satisfy a need or objective.

      d. Practices that indicate process management and institutionalization capability.

Answer: a

The term *suppliers* is defined here as a broad class of external organizations that provide products, components, materials, and/or services to a producer or prime contractor. Answers b and c describe a system, and answer d is a distracter.

25. Which statement below best describes the main premise of process improvement?

      a. Major changes must be sponsored by senior management.

      b. The quality of services produced is a direct function of the quality of the associated development and maintenance processes.

      c. Focus on fixing the process, not assigning blame.

      d. All suppliers must be security vetted prior to contracting.

Answer: b

The basic premise of process improvement is that the quality of services produced is a direct function of the quality of the associated development and maintenance processes. Answers a and c describe some knowledge or assumptions required to implement a successful security engineering process improvement activity, but not the main premise. Answer d is a distracter.

26. What is the main purpose of the Work Breakdown Structure (WBS)?

    a. It creates a hierarchical tree of work packages.

    b. It may be a contractual requirement in competitive bid system developments.

    c. It ensures the authorization for the program work.

    d. It ensures that all essential tasks are properly defined, assigned, scheduled, and controlled.

Answer: d

The Work Breakdown Structure (WBS) is an important technique to ensure that all essential tasks are properly defined, assigned, scheduled, and controlled. It contains a hierarchical structure of the tasks to be accomplished during the project. The WBS may be a contractual requirement in competitive bid system developments. As such, answers a, c, and d are attributes of the WBS, not its main purpose.

27. Which choice is not an activity in the Development Program Planning and Control element of the SEMP?

    a. System Test and Evaluation Strategy

    b. Scheduling and Cost Estimation

    c. Technical Performance Measurement

    d. Statement of Work

Answer: a

Development Program Planning and Control describes the security systems engineering tasks that must be implemented to manage the development phase of the security program, including:

- Statement of Work
- Organizational Structure
- Scheduling and Cost Estimation
- Technical Performance Measurement

Answer a is an activity of the Security Systems Engineering Process element of the SEMP.

28. At what point in the project is the Work Breakdown Structure (WBS) usually created?

    a. After the generation of the SOW and the identification of the organizational structure

    b. After the development of a functional cost data collection and reporting capability

    c. After the costs for each task are estimated

    d. After the development of an RFP but before the identification of the organizational structure

Answer: a

After the generation of the SOW and the identification of the organizational structure, one of the initial steps in program planning is the development of the Work Breakdown Structure (WBS). The other answers are distracters.

29. Which choice accurately lists the five levels of security engineering maturity as defined by the SSE-CMM?

    a. Planned and Tracked, Well Defined, Performed Informally, Quantitatively Controlled, and Continuously Improving

    b. Planned and Tracked, Performed Informally, Well Defined, Quantitatively Controlled, and Continuously Improving

    c. Performed Informally, Planned and Tracked, Well Defined, Quantitatively Controlled, and Continuously Improving

    d. Performed Informally, Planned and Tracked, Quantitatively Controlled, Well Defined, and Continuously Improving

Answer: c

The five levels are: Level 1, Performed Informally; Level 2, Planned and Tracked; Level 3, Well Defined; Level 4, Quantitatively Controlled; and Level 5, Continuously Improving.

30. Which choice has the correct order of activities in the security system design testing process?

    a. Acquisition, Testing, Analysis, Planning, and Correction

    b. Acquisition, Planning, Testing, Analysis, and Correction

    c. Planning, Analysis, Testing, Acquisition, and Correction

    d. Planning, Acquisition, Testing, Analysis, and Correction

Answer: d

The correct order of activities in the security system design testing process is Planning, Acquisition, Testing, Analysis, and Correction.

Chapter 14

1. Techniques and concerns that are normally addressed by management in the organization's computer security program are defined in NIST SP 800-12 as:

    a. Administrative controls

    b. Management controls

    c. Operational controls

    d. Technical controls

Answer: b.

Answer a is a distracter. Answer c, operational controls, are security controls that are usually implemented by people instead of systems. Answer d, technical controls, are security controls that the computer system executes.

2. The National Research Council publication, *Computers at Risk*, defines an element of computer security as a "requirement intended to assure that systems work properly and service is not denied to authorized users." Which one of the following elements best fits this definition?

    a. Availability

    b. Assurance

    c. Integrity

    d. Authentication

Answer: a

3. NSTISSI Publication No. 4009, "National Information Systems Security (INFOSEC) Glossary," defines the term *assurance* as:

    a. Requirement that information and programs are changed only in a specified and authorized manner

    b. Measure designed to establish the validity of a transmission, message, or originator, or a means of verifying an individual's authorization to receive specific categories of information

    c. Measure of confidence that the security features, practices, procedures, and architecture of an IS accurately mediate and enforce the security policy

    d. Requirement that private or confidential information not be disclosed to unauthorized individuals

Answer: c

Answer a is a definition of data integrity, answer b defines authentication, and answer d describes confidentiality.

4. The "National Information Systems Security (INFOSEC) Glossary," defines an information system security term as a "formal determination by an authorized adjudicative office that an individual is authorized access, on a need to know basis, to a specific level of collateral classified information." This definition refers to which one of the following terms?

    a. Sensitivity of information

    b. Classification of information

    c. Clearance

    d. Compartmentalization

Answer: c

Answers a and b are distracters. Answer d refers to a "nonhierarchical grouping of sensitive information used to control access to data more finely than with hierarchical security classification alone," as defined in NSTISSI Publication No. 4009.

5. In NSTISSI Publication No. 4009, what term is defined as a "document detailing the method, act, process, or effect of using an information system (IS)"?

    a. QUADRANT

    b. Concept of Operations (CONOPS)

    c. Evaluation Assurance Level (EAL)

    d. Information Assurance (IA) architecture

Answer: b

Answer a, QUADRANT, refers to technology that provides tamper-proof protection to cryptographic equipment. Answer c defines "a set of assurance requirements that represent a point on the Common Criteria predefined assurance scale," and answer d is a "framework that assigns and portrays IA roles and behavior among all IT assets, and prescribes rules for interaction and connection."

6. Which one of the following definitions best describes the National Information Assurance Partnership (NIAP) according to NSTISSI Publication No. 4009?

    a. Nationwide interconnection of communications networks, computers, databases, and consumer electronics that makes vast amounts of information available to users.

    b. Worldwide interconnections of the information systems of all countries, international and multinational organizations, and international commercial communications

    c. Joint initiative between NSA and NIST responsible for security testing needs of both IT consumers and producers, promoting the development of technically sound security requirements for IT products

    d. First level of the PKI Certification Management Authority that approves the security policy of each Policy Certification Authority (PCA)

Answer: c

Answer a refers to the National Information Infrastructure (NII), answer b defines the Global Information Infrastructure (GII), and answer d defines a Policy Approving Authority, (PAA).

7. TEMPEST refers to which one of the following definitions?

   a. Property whereby the security level of an object cannot change while the object is being processed by an IS

   b. Investigation, study, and control of compromising emanations from IS equipment

   c. Program established for a specific class of classified information that imposes safeguarding and access requirements that exceed those normally required for information at the same classified level

   d. Unclassified cryptographic equipment

Answer: b

Answer a refers to the concept of Tranquillity, answer c refers to a Special Access Program (SAP), and answer d is distracter.

8. Executive Order (E.O.) 13231, issued on October 16, 2001, renamed the National Security Telecommunications and Information Systems Security Committee (NSTISSC) as which one of the following committees?

   a. Committee for Information Systems Security (CISS)

   b. Committee on National Security Systems (CNSS)

   c. Committee on National Infrastructure Protection (CNIP)

   d. Committee for the Protection of National Information Systems (CPNIS)

Answer: b

The other answers are distracters.

9. In addressing the *security of systems with national security information*, E.O. 3231 assigned the responsibilities of developing government-wide policies and overseeing the implementation of government-wide policies, procedures, standards, and guidelines to the:

   a. U.S. Secretary of Defense and the Director of the FBI

   b. FBI and the Director of Central Intelligence

   c. NIST and the U.S. Secretary of Defense

   d. U.S. Secretary of Defense and the Director of Central Intelligence

Answer: d

10. Which one of the following characteristics is NOT associated with the definition of a national security system?

   a. Contains classified information

   b. Involved in industrial commerce

   c. Supports intelligence activities

   d. Involved with the command and control of military forces

Answer: b

Additional characteristics of a national information system include employing cryptographic activities related to national security, associated with equipment that is an integral part of a weapon or weapons system(s), and critical to the direct fulfillment of military or intelligence missions.

11. In 2002, the U.S. Congress enacted the E-Government Act (Public Law 107-347). Title III of the E-Government Act was written to provide for a number of protections of Federal information systems, including to "provide a comprehensive framework for ensuring the effectiveness of information security controls over information resources that support Federal operations and assets." Title III of the E-Government Act is also known as the:

   a. Computer Security Act (CSA)

   b. Computer Fraud and Abuse Act (CFAA)

   c. Federal Information Security Management Act (FISMA)

   d. Cyber Security Enhancement Act

Answer: c

12. FISMA assigned which one of the following entities the responsibility of overseeing the security policies and practices of U.S. government agencies?

   a. The FBI

   b. The U.S. Secretary of Defense

   c. The Director of the Office of Management and Budget (OMB)

   d. The Director of Central Intelligence

Answer: c

Standards associated with national defense are still the responsibility of the DoD and NSA.

13. Which information system security–related Act requires government agencies to perform periodic assessments of risk, develop policies and procedures that are based on risk assessments, conduct security awareness training, perform periodic testing and evaluation of the effectiveness of information security policies, and implement procedures for detecting, reporting, and responding to security incidents?

    a. Computer Security Act (CSA)

    b. Federal Information Security Management Act (FISMA)

    c. Computer Fraud and Abuse Act (CFAA)

    d. Cyber Security Enhancement Act

Answer: b

14. FISMA charged which one of the following entities to develop information system security standards and guidelines for federal agencies?

    a. FBI

    b. DoD

    c. NSA

    d. NIST

Answer: d

15. The general formula for categorization of an *information type* developed in FIPS Publication 199, "Standards for Security Categorization of Federal Information and Information Systems," is which one of the following?

    a. $SC_{\text{information type}}$ = {(**confidentiality**, *risk*), (**integrity**, *risk*), (**availability**, *risk*)}

    b. $SC_{\text{information type}}$ = {(**confidentiality**, *impact*), (**integrity**, *impact*), (**availability**, *impact*)}

    c. $SC_{\text{information type}}$ = {(**assurance**, *impact*), (**integrity**, *impact*), (**authentication**, *impact*)}

    d. $SC_{\text{information type}}$ = {(**confidentiality**, *controls*), (**integrity**, *controls*), (**availability**, *controls*)}

Answer: b

The other answers are distracters.

16. Circular A-130 directs that an oversight function should be performed consisting of the use of information technology planning reviews, fiscal budget reviews, information collection budget reviews, management reviews, and such other measures as deemed necessary to evaluate the adequacy and efficiency of each agency's information resources management and compliance with the Circular. Which one of the following individuals does the Circular designate as being responsible for this oversight function?

    a. The Secretary of Commerce

    b. The Director of the Office of Management and Budget

    c. The U.S. Secretary of Defense

    d. The Director of NSA

Answer: b

17. The National Computer Security Center Publication NCSC-TG-004-88 includes a definition that refers to the characteristic of a system that "performs its intended function in an unimpaired manner, free from deliberate, inadvertent, or unauthorized manipulation of the system." This characteristic defines which one of the following terms?

    a. Data integrity

    b. System integrity

    c. Enterprise integrity

    d. Risk integrity

Answer: b

18. Which one of the following terms best describes a secure telecommunications or associated cryptographic component that is unclassified but governed by a special set of control requirements, as defined in NSTISSI Publication 4009?

    a. Controlled cryptographic item (CCI) assembly

    b. Controlled cryptographic item (CCI) component

    c. Controlled cryptographic item (CCI)

    d. Crypto-ignition key (CIK)

Answer: c

Answer a refers to a device embodying a communications security (COMSEC) design that NSA has approved as a CCI. Answer b is part of a CCI that does not perform the entire COMSEC function but depends upon the host equipment, or assembly, to complete and operate the COMSEC function. Answer d is a device or electronic key used to unlock the secure mode of crypto-equipment.

19. What is a definable perimeter encompassing all hardware, firmware, and software components performing critical COMSEC functions, such as key generation and key handling and storage?

    a. COMSEC area

    b. COMSEC compartment

    c. COMSEC partition

    d. COMSEC boundary

Answer: d

Answers a, b, and c are distracters.

20. What process involves the five steps of identification of critical information, analysis of threats, analysis of vulnerabilities, assessment of risks, and application of appropriate countermeasures?

    a. Operations security

    b. Application security

    c. Administrative security

    d. Management security

Answer: a

The other answers are distracters.

21. Information that has been determined pursuant to Executive Order 12958 or any predecessor order to require protection against unauthorized disclosures is known as:

    a. Protected information (PI)

    b. National security information (NSI)

    c. Personally identifiable information (PII)

    d. Secure information (SI)

Answer: b

Answers a and d are distracters. Answer c, PII, is usually associated with privacy. An example of PII is a person's health care information.

22. An area that, when staffed, must be occupied by two or more appropriately cleared individuals who remain within sight of each other is referred to as which one of the following terms?

    a. No-lone zone

    b. Restricted area

   c. Protected occupancy zone

   d. Cleared area

Answer: a

The other answers are distracters.

23. According to NSTISSI Publication 4009, the process of identifying and applying countermeasures commensurate with the value of the assets protected based on a risk assessment is called:

   a. Vulnerability assessment

   b. Continuity planning

   c. Risk management

   d. Risk control

Answer: c

24. In the context of information systems security, the abbreviation ST&E stands for which one of the following terms?

   a. Security training and evaluation

   b. Security test and evaluation

   c. Security test and engineering

   d. Sensitivity test and evaluation

Answer: b

The other answers are distracters.

25. Which one of the following designations refers to a product that is a classified or controlled cryptographic item endorsed by the NSA for securing classified and sensitive U.S. government information, when appropriately keyed?

   a. Cleared product

   b. Type 3 product

   c. Type 1 product

   d. Type 2 product

Answer: c

Answers a and b are distracters. Answer d, a Type 2 product, defines unclassified cryptographic equipment, assemblies, or components endorsed by the NSA for use in national security systems as defined in Title 40 U.S.C. Section 1452.

26. Which one of the following items is NOT one of the responsibilities of the Committee on National Security Systems (CNSS) for the security of national security systems?

   a. Providing a forum for the discussion of policy issues

   b. Setting national policy

   c. Providing operational procedures, direction, and guidance.

   d. Requiring agencies to identify and provide information security protections commensurate with the risk and magnitude of the harm to information or information systems of government agencies

Answer: d

This responsibility is assigned to the OMB.

27. FISMA, Title III of the E-Government Act of 2002, reserves the responsibility for standards associated with the national defense establishment to which of the following entities?

   a. DoD and NSA

   b. DoD and CIA

   c. CIA and NSA

   d. CIA and NIST

Answer: a

28. FIPS Publication 199, "Standards for Security Characterization of Federal Information and Information Systems, NIST Pre-Publication Final Draft," December 2003, characterizes 3 levels of potential impact on organizations or individuals based on the objectives of confidentiality, integrity, and availability. What is the level of impact specified in Publication 199 for the following description of integrity: "The unauthorized modification or destruction of information could be expected to have a *serious* adverse effect on organizational operations, organizational assets, or individuals."?

   a. High

   b. Moderate

   c. Low

   d. Severe

Answer: b

29. Referring to question 28, the following impact description refers to which one of the three security objectives and which corresponding level of impact: "The disruption of access to or use of information or an information system could be expected to have a *limited* adverse effect on organizational operations, organizational assets, or individuals."?

    a. Confidentiality—Low

    b. Availability—Moderate

    c. Availability—Low

    d. Availability—High

Answer: c

30. DoD Directive 8500.1, "Information Assurance (IA)," October 4, 2002, specifies a defense-in-depth approach that integrates the capabilities of which set of the following entities?

    a. Personnel, operations, and technology

    b. Personnel, research and development, and technology

    c. Operations, resources, and technology

    d. Personnel, operations, and resources

Answer: a

The other answers are distracters.

✦   ✦   ✦

Glossary of Terms and Acronyms

* property (or star property) A Bell-LaPadula security model rule giving a subject write access to an object only if the security level of the object dominates the security level of the subject. Also called the *confinement property*.

1000BaseT 1,000 Mbps (1Gbps) baseband Ethernet using twisted pair wire.

100BaseT 100 Mbps baseband Ethernet using twisted pair wire.

10Base2 802.3 IEEE Ethernet standard for 10 Mbps Ethernet using coaxial cable (thinnet) rated to 185 meters.

10Base5 10 Mbps Ethernet using coaxial cable (thicknet) rated to 500 meters.

10BaseF 10 Mbps baseband Ethernet using optical fiber.

10BaseT 10 Mbps UTP Ethernet rated to 100 meters.

10Broad36 10 Mbps broadband Ethernet rated to 3,600 meters.

3DES Triple Data Encryption Standard

802.10 IEEE standard that specifies security and privacy access methods for LANs.

802.11 IEEE standard that specifies 1 Mbps and 2 Mbps wireless connectivity. Defines aspects of frequency hopping and direct-sequence spread spectrum (DSSS) systems for use in the 2.4 MHz ISM (industrial, scientific, medical) band. Also refers to the IEEE committee responsible for setting wireless LAN standards.

802.11a Specifies high-speed wireless connectivity in the 5 GHz band using orthogonal frequency division multiplexing (OFDM) with data rates up to 54 Mbps.

802.11b Specifies high-speed wireless connectivity in the 2.4 GHz ISM band up to 11 Mbps.

802.15 Specification for Bluetooth LANs in the 2.4–2.5 GHz band.

802.2 Standard that specifies the LLC (logical link control).

802.3 Ethernet bus topology using carrier sense medium access control/carrier detect (CSMA/CD) for 10 Mbps wired LANs. Currently, it is the most popular LAN topology.

802.4 Specifies a token-passing bus access method for LANs.

802.5 Specifies a token-passing ring access method for LANs.

acceptance inspection The final inspection to determine whether a facility or system meets specified technical and performance standards. Note: This inspection is held immediately after facility and software testing and is the basis for commissioning or accepting the information system.

acceptance testing A type of testing used to determine whether the network is acceptable to the actual users.

access A specific type of interaction between a subject and an object that results in the flow of information from one to the other.

access control The process of limiting access to system resources only to authorized programs, processes, or other systems (on a network). This term is synonymous with *controlled access* and *limited access*.

access control mechanism Hardware or software features, operating procedures, management procedures, and various combinations thereof that are designed to detect and prevent unauthorized access and to permit authorized access in an automated system.

access level The hierarchical portion of the security level that is used to identify the sensitivity of data and the clearance or authorization of users. Note: The access level, in conjunction with the nonhierarchical categories, forms the sensitivity label of an object. See *category*, *security level*, and *sensitivity label*.

access list A list of users, programs, and/or processes and the specifications of access categories to which each is assigned; a list denoting which users have what privileges to a particular resource.

access period A segment of time, generally expressed on a daily or weekly basis, during which access rights prevail.

access point (AP) A wireless LAN transceiver interface between the wireless network and a wired network. Access points forward frames between wireless devices and hosts on the LAN.

access port A logical or physical identifier that a computer uses to distinguish different terminal input/output data streams.

access type The nature of an access right to a particular device, program, or file (for example, read, write, execute, append, modify, delete, or create).

accountability Property that allows auditing of IT system activities to be traced to persons or processes that may then be held responsible for their actions. Accountability includes *authenticity* and *non-repudiation*.

accreditation A formal declaration by the DAA that the AIS is approved to operate in a particular security mode by using a prescribed set of safeguards. Accreditation is the official management authorization for operation of an AIS and is based on the certification process as well as other management considerations. The accreditation statement affixes security responsibility with the DAA and shows that due care has been taken for security.

accreditation authority Synonymous with *Designated Approving Authority*.

ACK Acknowledgment; a short-return indication of the successful receipt of a message.

acknowledged connectionless service A datagram-style service that includes error-control and flow-control mechanisms.

ACO Authenticated ciphering offset.

acquisition organization The Government organization that is responsible for developing a system.

adaptive routing A form of network routing whereby the path data packets traverse from a source to a destination node, depending upon the current state of the network, by calculating the best path through the network.

add-on security The retrofitting of protection mechanisms implemented by hardware or software.

Address Resolution Protocol (ARP) A TCP/IP protocol that binds logical (IP) addresses to physical addresses.

administrative security The management constraints and supplemental controls established to provide an acceptable level of protection for data. Synonymous with *procedural security*.

Advanced Encryption Standard (AES) (Rijndael) A symmetric block cipher with a block size of 128 bits in which the key can be 128, 192, or 256 bits. The Advanced Encryption Standard replaces the Date Encryption Standard (DES) and was announced on November 26, 2001, as Federal Information Processing Standard Publication (FIPS PUB 197).

AIS *Automated information system*

analog signal An electrical signal with an amplitude that varies continuously.

Application Layer The top layer of the OSI model, which is concerned with application programs. It provides services such as file transfer and email to the network's end users.

application process An entity, either human or software, that uses the services offered by the Application Layer of the OSI reference model.

application program interface A software interface provided between a specialized communications program and an end-user application.

application software Software that accomplishes functions such as database access, electronic mail, and menu prompts.

architecture As refers to a computer system, an architecture describes the type of components, interfaces, and protocols the system uses and how they fit together. The configuration of any equipment or interconnected system or subsystems of equipment that is used in the automatic acquisition, storage, manipulation, management, movement, control, display, switching, interchange, transmission, or reception of data or information; includes computers, ancillary equipment, and services, including support services and related resources.

assurance A measure of confidence that the security features and architecture of an AIS accurately mediate and enforce the security policy. Grounds for confidence that an IT product or system meets its security objectives. See *DITSCAP*.

asymmetric (public) key encryption Cryptographic system that employs two keys, a public key and a private key. The public key is made available to anyone wishing to send an encrypted message to an individual holding the corresponding private key of the public-private key pair. Any message encrypted with one of these keys can be decrypted with the other. The private key is always kept private. It should not be possible to derive the private key from the public key.

Asynchronous Transfer Mode A cell-based connection-oriented data service offering high-speed data communications. ATM integrates circuit and packet switching to handle both constant and burst information at rates up to 2.488 Gbps. Also called *cell relay*.

asynchronous transmission Type of communications data synchronization with no defined time relationship between transmission of data frames. See *synchronous transmission*.

attachment unit interface (AUI) A 15-pin interface between an Ethernet Network Interface Card and a transceiver.

attack The act of trying to bypass security controls on a system. An attack can be active, resulting in data modification, or passive, resulting in the release of data. Note: The fact that an attack is made does not necessarily mean that it will succeed. The degree of success depends on the vulnerability of the system or activity and the effectiveness of existing countermeasures.

audit trail A chronological record of system activities that is sufficient to enable the reconstruction, reviewing, and examination of the sequence of environments and activities surrounding or leading to an operation, a procedure, or an event in a transaction from its inception to its final result.

authenticate (1) To verify the identity of a user, device, or other entity in a computer system, often as a prerequisite to allowing access to system resources. (2) To verify the integrity of data that have been stored, transmitted, or otherwise exposed to possible unauthorized modification.

authentication Generically, the process of verifying "who" is at the other end of a transmission.

authentication device A device whose identity has been verified during the lifetime of the current link based on the authentication procedure.

authenticator The means used to confirm the identity or verify the eligibility of a station, originator, or individual.

authenticity The property that allows the ability to validate the claimed identity of a system entity.

authorization The granting of access rights to a user, program, or process.

automated data processing security Synonymous with *automated information systems security*.

automated information system (AIS) An assembly of computer hardware, software, and/or firmware that is configured to collect, create, communicate, compute, disseminate, process, store, and/or control data or information.

automated information system security Measures and controls that protect an AIS against Denial of Service (DoS) and unauthorized (accidental or intentional) disclosure, modification, or destruction of AISs and data. AIS security includes consideration of all hardware and/or software functions, characteristics, and/or features; operational procedures, accountability procedures, and access controls at the central computer facility, remote computers and terminal facilities; management constraints; physical structures and devices; and personnel and communication controls that are needed to provide an acceptable level of risk for the AIS and for the data and information contained in the AIS. It includes the totality of security safeguards needed to provide an acceptable protection level for an AIS and for data handled by an AIS.

automated security monitoring The use of automated procedures to ensure that security controls are not circumvented.

availability Timely, reliable access to data and information services for authorized users.

availability of data The condition in which data is in the place needed by the user, at the time the user needs it, and in the form needed by the user.

backbone network A network that interconnects other networks.

back door Synonymous with *trapdoor*.

backup plan Synonymous with *contingency plan*.

backward chaining In an expert system, the process of beginning with a possible solution and using the knowledge in the knowledge base to justify the solution based on the raw input data. Backward chaining is generally used when a large number of possible solutions exist relative to the amount of input.

bandwidth Specifies the amount of the frequency spectrum that is usable for data transfer. In other words, bandwidth identifies the maximum data rate a signal can attain on the medium without encountering significant attenuation (loss of power). Also, the amount of information one can send through a connection.

baud rate The number of pulses of a signal that occurs in one second. Thus, baud rate is the speed at which the digital signal pulses travel. Also, the rate at which data is transferred.

Bell-LaPadula model A formal state transition model of computer security policy that describes a set of access control rules. In this formal model, the entities in a computer system are divided into abstract sets of subjects and objects. The notion of a secure state is defined, and each state transition preserves security by moving from secure state to secure state, thereby inductively proving that the system is secure. A system state is defined to be secure only if the permitted access modes of subjects to objects are in accordance with a specific security policy. In order to determine whether a specific access mode is allowed, the clearance of a subject is compared to the classification of the object, and a determination is made as to whether the subject is authorized for the specific access mode. See *star property (* property)* and *simple security property*.

benign environment A nonhostile environment that might be protected from external hostile elements by physical, personnel, and procedural security countermeasures.

between-the-lines entry Unauthorized access obtained by tapping the temporarily inactive terminal of a legitimate user. See *piggyback*.

beyond A1 A level of trust, defined by the DoD Trusted Computer System Evaluation Criteria (TCSEC), that is beyond the state-of-the-art technology available at the time the criteria was developed. It includes all of the A1-level features plus additional features that are not required at the A1 level.

binary digit See *bit*.

biometrics Access control method in which an individual's physiological or behavioral characteristics are used to determine that individual's access to a particular resource.

BIOS Basic Input/Output System; The BIOS is the first program to run when the computer is turned on. BIOS initializes and tests the computer hardware, loads and runs the operating system, and manages setup for making changes in the computer.

bit Short for *binary digit*. A single digit number in binary (0 or 1).

bit rate The transmission rate of binary symbol 0s and 1s. Bit rate is equal to the total number of bits transmitted in one second.

blackboard An expert system reasoning methodology in which a solution is generated by the use of a virtual "blackboard," wherein information or potential solutions are placed on the blackboard by a plurality of individuals or expert knowledge sources. As more information is placed on the blackboard in an iterative process, a solution is generated.

blind signature A form of digital signature where the signer is not privy to the content of the message.

block cipher A symmetric key algorithm that operates on a fixed-length block of plaintext and transforms it into a fixed-length block of ciphertext. A block cipher is obtained by segregating plaintext into blocks of n characters or bits and applying the same encryption algorithm and key to each block.

Bluetooth An open specification for wireless communication of data and voice, based on a low-cost short-range radio link facilitating protected ad hoc connections for stationary and mobile communication environments.

bridge A network device that provides internetworking functionality by connecting networks. Bridges can provide segmentation of data frames and can be used to connect LANs by forwarding packets across connections at the media access control (MAC) sublayer of the OSI model's Data Link Layer.

broadband A transmission system in which signals are encoded and modulated into different frequencies and then transmitted simultaneously with other signals (that is, of a different frequency). A LAN broadband signal is commonly analog.

browsing The act of searching through storage to locate or acquire information without necessarily knowing the existence or the format of the information being sought.

BSI ISO/IEC 17799:2000,BS 7799-I: 2000, Information technology — Code of practice for information security management, British Standards Institution, London, UK A standard intended to "provide a comprehensive set of controls comprising best practices in information security." ISO refers to the International Organization for Standardization, and IEC is the International Electrotechnical Commission.

bus topology A type of network topology wherein all nodes are connected to a single length of cabling with a terminator at each end.

Business Software Alliance (BSA) An international organization representing leading software and e-commerce developers in 65 countries around the world. BSA efforts include educating computer users about software copyrights; advocating for public policy that fosters innovation and expands trade opportunities; and fighting software piracy.

byte A set of bits, usually eight, that represent a single character.

C & A Certification and Accreditation

CA Certification Authority/Agent. See *Certification Authority*.

call back A procedure for identifying a remote terminal. In a call back, the host system disconnects the caller and then dials the authorized telephone number of the remote terminal in order to reestablish the connection. Synonymous with *dial back*.

capability A protected identifier that both identifies the object and specifies the access rights allowed to the accessor who possesses the capability. In a capability-based system, access to protected objects (such as files) is granted if the would-be accessor possesses a capability for the object.

Capstone A Very Large Scale Integration (VLSI) chip that employs the Escrowed Encryption Standard and incorporates the Skipjack algorithm, similar to the Clipper Chip. As such, it has a Law Enforcement Access Field (LEAF). Capstone also supports public key exchange and digital signatures. At this time, Capstone products have their LEAF function suppressed and a certificate authority provides for key recovery.

Carnivore A device used by the U.S. FBI to monitor ISP traffic (S.P. Smith, et. al., "Independent Technical Review of the Carnivore System—Draft report," U.S. Department of Justice Contract # 00-C-328 IITRI, CR-022-216, November 17, 2000).

carrier current LAN A LAN that uses power lines within the facility as a medium for data transport.

carrier sense multiple access (CSMA) The technique used to reduce transmission contention by listening for contention before transmitting.

carrier sense multiple access/collision detection (CSMA/CD) The most common Ethernet cable access method.

category A restrictive label that has been applied to classified or unclassified data as a means of increasing the protection of the data and further restricting its access.

category 1 twisted pair wire Used for early analog telephone communications; not suitable for data.

category 2 twisted pair wire Rated for 4 Mbps and used in 802.5 token ring networks.

category 3 twisted pair wire Rated for 10 Mbps and used in 802.3 10Base-T Ethernet networks.

category 4 twisted pair wire Rated for 16 Mbps and used in 802.5 token ring networks.

category 5 twisted pair wire Rated for 100 Mbps and used in 100BaseT Ethernet networks.

CBC Cipher block chaining is an encryption mode of the Data Encryption Standard (DES) that operates on plaintext blocks 64 bits in length.

CC Common Criteria are a standard for specifying and evaluating the features of computer products and systems.

Centronics A de facto standard 36-pin parallel 200 Kbps asynchronous interface for connecting printers and other devices to a computer.

CERT Coordination Center (CERT(r)/CC) A unit of the Carnegie Mellon University Software Engineering Institute (SEI). SEI is a federally funded R&D Center. CERT's mission is to alert the Internet community to vulnerabilities and attacks and to conduct research and training in the areas of computer security, including incident response.

certification The comprehensive evaluation of the technical and nontechnical security features of an AIS and other safeguards, made in support of the accreditation process, that establishes the extent to which a particular design and implementation meets a specified set of security requirements.

certification authority (CA) The official responsible for performing the comprehensive evaluation of the technical and nontechnical security features of an IT system and other safeguards, made in support of the accreditation process, to establish the extent that a particular design and implementation meet a set of specified security requirements.

Chinese Wall model Uses internal rules to compartmentalize areas in which individuals may work to prevent disclosure of proprietary information and to avoid conflicts of interest. The Chinese Wall model also incorporates the principle of separation of duty.

CINC Commander-in-Chief

cipher A cryptographic transformation that operates on characters or bits.

ciphertext or cryptogram An unintelligible encrypted message.

circuit-switched The application of a network wherein a dedicated line is used to transmit information; contrast with *packet-switched*.

client A computer that accesses a server's resources.

client/server architecture A network system design in which a processor or computer designated as a file server or database server provides services to other client processors or computers. Applications are distributed between a host server and a remote client.

closed security environment An environment in which both of the following conditions hold true: 1) Application developers (including maintainers) have sufficient clearances and authorizations to provide an acceptable presumption that they have not introduced malicious logic, and 2) Configuration control provides sufficient assurance that applications and equipment are protected against the introduction of malicious logic prior to and during the operation of system applications.

closed shop Data processing area using physical access controls to limit access to authorized personnel.

Clustering Situation in which a plaintext message generates identical ciphertext messages using the same transformation algorithm but with different cryptovariables or keys.

CNSS Committee on National Security Systems (formerly NSTISS Committee)

coaxial cable (coax) Type of transmission cable consisting of a hollow outer cylindrical conductor that surrounds a single inner wire conductor for current flow. Because the shielding reduces the amount of electrical noise interference, coax can extend much greater lengths than twisted pair wiring.

code division multiple access (CDMA) A spread spectrum digital cellular radio system that uses different codes to distinguish users.

codes Cryptographic transformations that operates at the level of words or phrases.

collision detection The detection of simultaneous transmission on the communications medium.

Common Object Model (COM) A model that allows two software components to communicate with each other independent of their platforms' operating systems and languages of implementation. As in the object-oriented paradigm, COM works with encapsulated objects.

Common Object Request Broker Architecture (CORBA) A standard that uses the Object Request Broker (ORB) to implement exchanges among objects in a heterogeneous, distributed environment.

Communications Assistance for Law Enforcement Act (CALEA) of 1994 An act that required all communications carriers to make wiretaps possible in ways approved by the FBI.

communications security (COMSEC) Measures and controls taken to deny unauthorized persons information derived from telecommunications and to ensure the authenticity of such telecommunications. Communications security includes cryptosecurity, transmission security, emission security, and physical security of COMSEC material and information.

compartment A class of information that has need-to-know access controls beyond those normally provided for access to confidential, secret, or top secret information.

compartmented security mode See *modes of operation.*

compensating controls A combination of controls, such as physical and technical or technical and administrative (or all three).

composition model An information security model that investigates the resulting security properties when subsystems are combined.

compromise A violation of a system's security policy such that unauthorized disclosure of sensitive information might have occurred.

compromising emanations Unintentional data-related or intelligence-bearing signals that, when intercepted and analyzed, disclose the information transmission that is received, handled, or otherwise processed by any information processing equipment. See *TEMPEST.*

COMPUSEC See *Computer security.*

computer abuse The misuse, alteration, disruption, or destruction of data-processing resources. The key is that computer abuse is intentional and improper.

computer cryptography The use of a crypto-algorithm in a computer, microprocessor, or microcomputer to perform encryption or decryption in order to protect information or to authenticate users, sources, or information.

computer facility The physical structure housing data processing operations.

computer forensics Information collection from and about computer systems that is admissible in a court of law.

computer fraud Computer-related crimes involving deliberate misrepresentation, alteration, or disclosure of data in order to obtain something of value (usually for monetary gain). A computer system must have been involved in the perpetration or cover-up of the act or series of acts. A computer system might have been involved through improper manipulation of input data, output or results, applications programs, data files, computer operations, communications, computer hardware, systems software, or firmware.

computer security (COMPUSEC) Synonymous with *automated information systems security*.

computer security subsystem A device that is designed to provide limited computer security features in a larger system environment.

Computer Security Technical Vulnerability Reporting Program (CSTVRP) A program that focuses on technical vulnerabilities in commercially available hardware, firmware, and software products acquired by the DoD. CSTVRP provides for the reporting, cataloging, and discrete dissemination of technical vulnerability and corrective measure information to DoD components on a need-to-know basis.

computing environment The total environment in which an automated information system, network, or a component operates. The environment includes physical, administrative, and personnel procedures as well as communication and networking relationships with other information systems.

COMSEC See *communications security*.

concealment system A method of achieving confidentiality in which sensitive information is hidden by embedding it inside irrelevant data.

confidentiality Assurance that information is not disclosed to unauthorized persons, processes, or devices. The concept of holding sensitive data in confidence, limited to an appropriate set of individuals or organizations.

configuration control The process of controlling modifications to the system's hardware, firmware, software, and documentation that provides sufficient assurance that the system is protected against the introduction of improper modifications prior to, during, and after system implementation. Compare with *configuration management*.

configuration management The management of security features and assurances through control of changes made to a system's hardware, software, firmware, documentation, test, test fixtures, and test documentation throughout the development and operational life of the system. Compare with *configuration control*.

configuration manager The individual or organization responsible for Configuration Control or Configuration Management.

confinement The prevention of the leaking of sensitive data from a program.

confinement channel Synonymous with *covert channel*.

confinement property Synonymous with *star property (* property)*.

confusion A method of hiding the relationship between the plaintext and the ciphertext.

connection-oriented service Service that establishes a logical connection that provides flow control and error control between two stations who need to exchange data.

connectivity A path through which communications signals can flow.

connectivity software A software component that provides an interface between the networked appliance and the database or application software located on the network.

CONOPS Concept of Operations

Construction Cost Model (COCOMO), Basic version Estimates software development effort and cost as a function of the size of the software product in source instructions.

containment strategy A strategy for containment (in other words, stopping the spread) of the disaster and the identification of the provisions and processes required to contain the disaster.

contamination The intermixing of data at different sensitivity and need-to-know levels. The lower-level data is said to be contaminated by the higher-level data; thus, the contaminating (higher-level) data might not receive the required level of protection.

contingency management Establishing actions to be taken before, during, and after a threatening incident.

contingency plan A plan for emergency response, backup operations, and post-disaster recovery maintained by an activity as a part of its security program; this plan ensures the availability of critical resources and facilitates the continuity of operations in an emergency situation. Synonymous with *disaster plan* and *emergency plan*.

continuity of operations Maintenance of essential IP services after a major outage.

control zone The space, expressed in feet of radius, surrounding equipment processing sensitive information that is under sufficient physical and technical control to preclude an unauthorized entry or compromise.

controlled access See *access control*.

controlled sharing The condition that exists when access control is applied to all users and components of a system.

Copper Data Distributed Interface (CDDI) A version of FDDI specifying the use of unshielded twisted pair wiring.

cost-risk analysis The assessment of the cost of providing data protection for a system versus the cost of losing or compromising the data.

COTS Commercial off-the-shelf

countermeasure Any action, device, procedure, technique, or other measure that reduces the vulnerability of or threat to a system.

countermeasure/safeguard An entity that mitigates the potential risk to an information system.

covert channel A communications channel that enables two cooperating processes to transfer information in a manner that violates the system's security policy. Synonymous with *confinement channel*.

covert storage channel A covert channel that involves the direct or indirect writing of a storage location by one process and the direct or indirect reading of the storage location by another process. Covert storage channels typically involve a finite resource (for example, sectors on a disk) that is shared by two subjects at different security levels.

covert timing channel A covert channel in which one process signals information to another by modulating its own use of system resources (for example, CPU time) in such a way that this manipulation affects the real response time observed by the second process.

CPU The central processing unit of a computer.

criteria See *DoD Trusted Computer System Evaluation Criteria*.

CRL Certificate Revocation List

CRLCMP Computer Resources Life Cycle Management Plan

CRMP Computer Resource Management Plan

CRR Certification Requirements Review

cryptanalysis Refers to the ability to "break" the cipher so that the encrypted message can be read. Cryptanalysis can be accomplished by exploiting weaknesses in the cipher or in some fashion determining the key.

crypto-algorithm A well-defined procedure, sequence of rules, or steps used to produce a key stream or ciphertext from plaintext, and vice versa. A step-by-step procedure that is used to encipher plaintext and decipher ciphertext. Also called a *cryptographic algorithm*.

cryptographic algorithm See *crypto-algorithm*.

cryptographic application programming interface (CAPI) An interface to a library of software functions that provide security and cryptography services. CAPI is designed for software developers to call functions from the library, which makes it easier to implement security services.

cryptography The principles, means, and methods for rendering information unintelligible and for restoring encrypted information to intelligible form. The word *cryptography* comes from the Greek *kryptos,* meaning "hidden," and *graphein*, "to write."

cryptosecurity The security or protection resulting from the proper use of technically sound cryptosystems.

cryptosystem A set of transformations from a message space to a ciphertext space. This system includes all cryptovariables (keys), plaintexts, and ciphertexts associated with the transformation algorithm.

cryptovariable See *key*.

CSMA/CA Carrier sense multiple access/collision avoidance, commonly used in 802.11 Ethernet and LocalTalk.

CSMA/CD Carrier sense multiple access/collision detection, used in 802.3 Ethernet.

CSTVRP See *Computer Security Technical Vulnerability Reporting Program*.

cyclic redundancy check (CRC) A common error-detection process. A mathematical operation is applied to the data when transmitted. The result is appended to the core packet. Upon receipt, the same mathematical operation is performed and checked against the CRC. A mismatch indicates a very high probability that an error has occurred during transmission.

DAA See *designated approving authority*.

DAC See *discretionary access control*.

data dictionary A database that comprises tools to support the analysis, design, and development of software and to support good software engineering practices.

Data Encryption Standard (DES) A cryptographic algorithm for the protection of unclassified data, published in Federal Information Processing Standard (FIPS) 46. The DES, which was approved by the National Institute of Standards and Technology (NIST), is intended for public and government use.

data flow control See *information flow control*.

data integrity The attribute of data that is related to the preservation of its meaning and completeness, the consistency of its representation(s), and its correspondence to what it represents. When data meets a prior expectation of quality.

Data Link Layer The OSI level that performs the assembly and transmission of data packets, including error control.

data mart A database that comprises data or relations that have been extracted from the data warehouse. Information in the data mart is usually of interest to a particular group of people.

data mining The process of analyzing large data sets in a data warehouse to find nonobvious patterns.

data scrubbing Maintenance of a data warehouse by deleting information that is unreliable or no longer relevant.

data security The protection of data from unauthorized (accidental or intentional) modification, destruction, or disclosure.

Data service unit/channel service unit (DSU/CSU) A set of network components that reshape data signals into a form that can be effectively transmitted over a digital transmission medium, typically a leased 56 Kbps or T1 line.

data warehouse A subject-oriented, integrated, time-variant, nonvolatile collection of data in support of management's decision-making process.

database A persistent collection of data items that form relations among each other.

database shadowing A data redundancy process that uses the live processing of remote journaling but creates even more redundancy by duplicating the database sets to multiple servers.

datagram service A connectionless form of packet switching whereby the source does not need to establish a connection with the destination before sending data packets.

DB-9 A standard 9-pin connector commonly used with RS-232 serial interfaces on portable computers. The DB-9 connector does not support all RS-232 functions.

DB-15 A standard 15-pin connector commonly used with RS-232 serial interfaces, Ethernet transceivers, and computer monitors.

DB-25 A standard 25-pin connector commonly used with RS-232 serial interfaces. The DB-25 connector supports all RS-232 functions.

DCID Director of Central Intelligence Directive

de facto standard A standard based on broad usage and support but not directly specified by the IEEE.

decipher To unscramble the encipherment process in order to make the message human readable.

declassification of AIS storage media An administrative decision or procedure to remove or reduce the security classification of the subject media.

DeCSS A program that bypasses the Content Scrambling System (CSS) software used to prevent the viewing of DVD movie disks on unlicensed platforms.

dedicated security mode See *modes of operation*.

default A value or option that is automatically chosen when no other value is specified.

default classification A temporary classification reflecting the highest classification being processed in a system. The default classification is included in the caution statement that is affixed to the object.

defense information infrastructure (DII) The DII is the seamless web of communications networks, computers, software, databases, applications, data, security services, and other capabilities that meets the information processing and transport needs of DoD users in peace and in all crises, conflict, humanitarian support, and wartime roles.

Defense Information Technology Systems Certification and Accreditation Process (DITSCAP) Establishes for the defense entities a standard process, set of activities, general task descriptions, and management structure to certify and accredit IT systems that will maintain the required security posture. The process is designed to certify that the IT system meets the accreditation requirements and that the system will maintain the accredited security posture throughout the system life cycle. The four phases to the DITSCAP are Definition, Verification, Validation, and Post Accreditation.

degauss To degauss a magnetic storage medium is to remove all the data stored on it by demagnetization. A *degausser* is a device used for this purpose.

Degausser Products List (DPL) A list of commercially produced degaussers that meet National Security Agency specifications. This list is included in the NSA *Information Systems Security Products and Services Catalogue* and is available through the Government Printing Office.

degraded fault tolerance Specifies which capabilities the TOE will still provide after a system failure. Examples of general failures are flooding of the computer room, short-term power interruption, breakdown of a CPU or host, software failure, or buffer overflow. Only functions specified must be available.

Denial of Service (DoS) Any action (or series of actions) that prevents any part of a system from functioning in accordance with its intended purpose. This action includes any action that causes unauthorized destruction, modification, or delay of service. Synonymous with *interdiction*.

DES See *Data Encryption Standard*.

Descriptive Top-Level Specification (DTLS) A top-level specification that is written in a natural language (for example, English), an informal design notation, or a combination of the two.

designated approving authority The official who has the authority to decide on accepting the security safeguards prescribed for an AIS, or the official who might be responsible for issuing an accreditation statement that records the decision to accept those safeguards.

developer The organization that develops the information system.

DGSA DoD Goal Security Architecture

dial back Synonymous with *call back*.

dial-up The service whereby a computer terminal can use the telephone to initiate and effect communication with a computer.

diffusion A method of obscuring redundancy in plaintext by spreading the effect of the transformation over the ciphertext.

Digital Millennium Copyright Act (DMCA) of 1998 In addition to addressing licensing and ownership information, the DMCA prohibits trading, manufacturing, or selling in any way that is intended to bypass copyright protection mechanisms.

DII See *Defense Information Infrastructure.*

Direct-sequence spread spectrum (DSSS) A method used in 802.11b to split the frequency into 14 channels, each with a frequency range, by combining a data signal with a chipping sequence. Data rates of 1, 2, 5.5, and 11 Mbps are obtainable. DSSS spreads its signal continuously over this wide-frequency band.

disaster A sudden, unplanned, calamitous event that produces great damage or loss; any event that creates an inability on the organization's part to provide critical business functions for some undetermined period of time.

disaster plan Synonymous with *contingency plan.*

disaster recovery plan Procedure for emergency response, extended backup operations, and post-disaster recovery when an organization suffers a loss of computer resources and physical facilities.

discovery In the context of legal proceedings and trial practice, a process in which the prosecution presents information it has uncovered to the defense. This information may include potential witnesses, reports resulting from the investigation, evidence, and so on. During an investigation, discovery refers to:

- The process undertaken by the investigators to acquire evidence needed for prosecution of a case

- A step in the computer forensic process

discretionary access control A means of restricting access to objects based on the identity and need-to-know of the user, process, and/or groups to which they belong. The controls are discretionary in the sense that a subject that has certain access permissions is capable of passing that permission (perhaps indirectly) on to any other subject. Compare with *mandatory access control.*

disk image backup Conducting a bit-level copy, sector-by-sector of a disk, which provides the capability to examine slack space, undeleted clusters, and possibly, deleted files.

Distributed Component Object Model (DCOM) A distributed object model that is similar to the Common Object Request Broker Architecture (CORBA). DCOM is the distributed version of COM that supports remote objects as if the objects reside in the client's address space. A COM client can access a COM object through the use of a pointer to one of the object's interfaces and then invoke methods through that pointer.

Distributed Queue Dual Bus (DQDB) The IEEE 802.6 standard that provides full-duplex 155 Mbps operation between nodes in a metropolitan area network.

distributed routing A form of routing wherein each router on the network periodically identifies neighboring nodes, updates its routing table, and, with this information, sends its routing table to all of its neighbors. Because each node follows the same process, complete network topology information propagates through the network and eventually reaches each node.

DITSCAP See *Defense Information Technology Systems Certification and Accreditation Process.*

DoD U.S. Department of Defense

DoD Trusted Computer System Evaluation Criteria (TCSEC) A document published by the National Computer Security Center containing a uniform set of basic requirements and evaluation classes for assessing degrees of assurance in the effectiveness of hardware and software security controls built into systems. These criteria are intended for use in the design and evaluation of systems that process and/or store sensitive or classified data. This document is Government Standard DoD 5200.28-STD and is frequently referred to as "The Criteria" or "The Orange Book."

DoJ U.S. Department of Justice

domain The unique context (for example, access control parameters) in which a program is operating; in effect, the set of objects that a subject has the ability to access. See *process* and *subject.*

dominate Security level S1 is said to dominate security level S2 if the hierarchical classification of S1 is greater than or equal to that of S2 and if the non-hierarchical categories of S1 include all those of S2 as a subset.

DoS attack Denial of Service attack

DPL Degausser Products List

DT Data terminal

DTLS Descriptive Top-Level Specification

due care The care which an ordinary prudent person would have exercised under the same or similar circumstances. The terms *due care* and *reasonable care* are used interchangeably.

Dynamic Host Configuration Protocol (DHCP) A protocol that issues IP addresses automatically within a specified range to devices such as PCs when they are first powered on. The device retains the use of the IP address for a specific license period that the system administrator can define.

EAP Extensible Authentication Protocol. Cisco proprietary protocol for enhanced user authentication and wireless security management.

EBCDIC Extended Binary-Coded Decimal Interchange Code. An 8-bit character representation developed by IBM in the early 1960s.

ECC Elliptic curve cryptography

ECDSA Elliptic curve digital signature algorithm

Echelon A cooperative, worldwide signal intelligence system that is run by the NSA of the United States, the Government Communications Head Quarters (GCHQ) of England, the Communications Security Establishment (CSE) of Canada, the Australian Defense Security Directorate (DSD), and the General Communications Security Bureau (GCSB) of New Zealand.

Electronic Communications Privacy Act (ECPA) of 1986 An act that prohibited eavesdropping or the interception of message contents without distinguishing between private or public systems.

Electronic Data Interchange (EDI) A service that provides communications for business transactions. ANSI standard X.12 defines the data format for EDI.

electronic vaulting A term that refers to the transfer of backup data to an off-site location. This process is primarily a batch process of dumping the data through communications lines to a server at an alternate location.

Electronics Industry Association (EIA) A U.S. standards organization that represents a large number of electronics firms.

emanations See *compromising emanations*.

embedded system A system that performs or controls a function, either in whole or in part, as an integral element of a larger system or subsystem.

emergency plan Synonymous with *contingency plan*.

emission(s) security (EMSEC) The protection resulting from all measures taken to deny unauthorized persons information of value derived from the intercept and analysis of compromising emanations from crypto-equipment or an IT system.

EMSEC See *Emissions Security*.

encipher To make the message unintelligible to all but the intended recipients.

Endorsed Tools List (ETL) The list of formal verification tools endorsed by the NCSC for the development of systems that have high levels of trust.

end-to-end encryption Encrypted information sent from the point of origin to the final destination. In symmetric key encryption, this process requires the sender and the receiver to have the identical key for the session.

Enhanced Hierarchical Development Methodology An integrated set of tools designed to aid in creating, analyzing, modifying, managing, and documenting program specifications and proofs. This methodology includes a specification parser and typechecker, a theorem prover, and a multilevel security checker. Note: This methodology is not based upon the *Hierarchical Development Methodology*.

entrapment The deliberate planting of apparent flaws in a system for the purpose of detecting attempted penetrations.

environment The aggregate of external procedures, conditions, and objects that affect the development, operation, and maintenance of a system.

EPL Evaluated Products List

erasure A process by which a signal recorded on magnetic media is removed. Erasure is accomplished in two ways: 1) by alternating current erasure, by which the information is destroyed when an alternating high and low magnetic field is applied to the media; or 2) by direct current erasure, in which the media is saturated by applying a unidirectional magnetic field.

Ethernet An industry-standard local area network media access method that uses a bus topology and CSMA/CD. IEEE 802.3 is a standard that specifies Ethernet.

Ethernet repeater A component that provides Ethernet connections among multiple stations sharing a common collision domain. Also referred to as a *shared Ethernet hub*.

Ethernet switch More intelligent than a hub, with the capability to connect the sending station directly to the receiving station.

ETL Endorsed Tools List

ETSI European Telecommunications Standards Institute

Evaluated Products List (EPL) A list of equipment, hardware, software, and/or firmware that have been evaluated against, and found to be technically compliant at, a particular level of trust with the DoD TCSEC by the NCSC. The EPL is included in the *National Security Agency Information Systems Security Products and Services Catalogue*, which is available through the Government Printing Office (GPO).

evaluation Assessment of an IT product or system against defined security functional and assurance criteria performed by a combination of testing and analytic techniques.

Evaluation Assurance Level (EAL) In the Common Criteria, the degree of examination of the product to be tested. EALs range from EA1 (functional testing) to EA7 (detailed testing and formal design verification). Each numbered package represents a point on the CCs predefined assurance scale. An EAL can be considered a level of confidence in the security functions of an IT product or system.

evolutionary program strategies Generally characterized by design, development, and deployment of a preliminary capability that includes provisions for the evolutionary addition of future functionality and changes as requirements are further defined (DoD Directive 5000.1).

executive state One of several states in which a system can operate and the only one in which certain privileged instructions can be executed. Such instructions cannot be executed when the system is operating in other (for example, user) states. Synonymous with *supervisor state*.

exigent circumstances doctrine Specifies that a warrantless search and seizure of evidence can be conducted if there is probable cause to suspect criminal activity or destruction of evidence.

expert system shell An off-the-shelf software package that implements an inference engine, a mechanism for entering knowledge, a user interface, and a system to provide explanations of the reasoning used to generate a solution. It provides the fundamental building blocks of an expert system and supports the entering of domain knowledge.

exploitable channel Any information channel that is usable or detectable by subjects that are external to the trusted computing base, whose purpose is to violate the security policy of the system. See *covert channel*.

exposure An instance of being exposed to losses from a threat.

fail over Operations automatically switching over to a backup system when one system/application fails.

fail safe A term that refers to the automatic protection of programs and/or processing systems to maintain safety when a hardware or software failure is detected in a system.

fail secure A term that refers to a system that preserves a secure state during and after identified failures occur.

fail soft A term that refers to the selective termination of affected nonessential processing when a hardware or software failure is detected in a system.

failure access An unauthorized and usually inadvertent access to data resulting from a hardware or software failure in the system.

failure control The methodology that is used to detect and provide fail-safe or fail-soft recovery from hardware and software failures in a system.

fault A condition that causes a device or system component to fail to perform in a required manner.

fault-resilient systems Systems designed without redundancy; in the event of failure, they result in a slightly longer down time.

FCC Federal Communications Commission

FDMA Frequency division multiple access. A spectrum-sharing technique whereby the available spectrum is divided into a number of individual radio channels.

FDX Full-duplex

Federal Intelligence Surveillance Act (FISA) of 1978 An act that limited wiretapping for national security purposes as a result of the Nixon Administration's history of using illegal wiretaps.

fetch protection A system-provided restriction to prevent a program from accessing data in another user's segment of storage.

Fiber-Distributed Data Interface (FDDI) An ANSI standard for token-passing networks. FDDI uses optical fiber and operates at 100 Mbps in dual, counter-rotating rings.

Fiestel cipher An iterated block cipher that encrypts by breaking a plaintext block into two halves and, with a subkey, applying a "round" transformation to one of the halves. The output of this transformation is then XOR'd with the remaining half. The round is completed by swapping the two halves.

FIFO Acronym for "first in, first out".

file protection   The aggregate of all processes and procedures in a system designed to inhibit unauthorized access, contamination, or elimination of a file.

file security The means by which access to computer files is limited to authorized users only.

file server A computer that provides network stations with controlled access to sharable resources. The network operating system (NOS) is loaded on the file server, and most sharable devices, including disk subsystems and printers, are attached to it.

File Transfer Protocol (FTP) A TCP/IP protocol for file transfer.

FIPS Federal Information Processing Standard

firewall A network device that shields the trusted network from unauthorized users in the untrusted network by blocking certain specific types of traffic. Many types of firewalls exist, including packet filtering and stateful inspection.

firmware Executable programs stored in nonvolatile memory.

flaw hypothesis methodology A systems analysis and penetration technique in which specifications and documentation for the system are analyzed and then hypotheses are made regarding flaws in the system. The list of hypothesized flaws is prioritized on the basis of the estimated probability that a flaw exists, on the ease of exploiting it if it does exist, and on the extent of control or compromise that it would provide. The prioritized list is used to direct a penetration attack against the system.

flow control See *information flow control*.

formal access approval Documented approval by a data owner to allow access to a particular category of information.

Formal Development Methodology A collection of languages and tools that enforces a rigorous method of verification. This methodology uses the Ina Jo specification language for successive stages of system development, including identification and modeling of requirements, high-level design, and program design.

formal proof A complete and convincing mathematical argument presenting the full logical justification for each proof step for the truth of a theorem or set of theorems.

formal security policy model A mathematically precise statement of a security policy. To be adequately precise, such a model must represent the initial state of a system, the way in which the system progresses from one state to another, and a definition of a secure state of the system. To be acceptable as a basis for a TCB, the model must be supported by a formal proof that if the initial state of the system satisfies the definition of a secure state and if all assumptions required by the model hold, then all future states of the system will be secure. Some formal modeling techniques include state transition models, denotational semantics models, and algebraic specification models. See *Bell-LaPadula model*.

Formal Top-Level Specification (FTLS) A top-level specification that is written in a formal mathematical language to enable theorems showing the correspondence of the system specification to its formal requirements to be hypothesized and formally proven.

formal verification The process of using formal proofs to demonstrate the consistency between a formal specification of a system and a formal security policy model (design verification) or between the formal specification and its high-level program implementation (implementation verification).

forward chaining The reasoning approach that can be used when a small number of solutions exist relative to the number of inputs. The input data is used to reason "forward" to prove that one of the possible solutions in a small solution set is correct.

fractional T-1 A 64 Kbps increment of a T1 frame.

frame relay A packet-switching interface that operates at data rates of 56 Kbps to 2 Mbps. Frame relay is minus the error control overhead of X.25, and it assumes that a higher-layer protocol will check for transmission errors.

frequency division multiple access (FDMA) A digital radio technology that divides the available spectrum into separate radio channels. Generally used in conjunction with time division multiple access (TDMA) or code division multiple access (CDMA).

frequency hopping multiple access (FHMA) A system using frequency hopping spread spectrum (FHSS) to permit multiple, simultaneous conversations or data sessions by assigning different hopping patterns to each.

frequency hopping spread spectrum (FHSS) A method used to share the available bandwidth in 802.11b WLANs. FHSS takes the data signal and modulates it with a carrier signal that hops from frequency to frequency on a cyclical basis over a wide band of frequencies. FHSS in the 2.4 GHz frequency band will hop between 2.4 GHz and 2.483 GHz. The receiver must be set to the same hopping code.

frequency modulation (FM) A method of transmitting information over a radio wave by changing frequencies.

frequency shift keying (FSK) A modulation scheme for data communications using a limited number of discrete frequencies to convey binary information.

front-end security filter A security filter that could be implemented in hardware or software, which is logically separated from the remainder of the system in order to protect the system's integrity.

FTLS Formal Top-Level Specification

functional programming A programming method that uses only mathematical functions to perform computations and solve problems.

functional testing The segment of security testing in which the advertised security mechanisms of the system are tested, under operational conditions, for correct operation.

gateway A network component that provides interconnectivity at higher network layers.

genetic algorithms Part of the general class known as *evolutionary computing*, which uses the Darwinian principles of survival of the fittest, mutation, and the adaptation of successive generations of populations to their environment. The genetic algorithm implements this process through iteration of generations of a constant-size population of items or individuals.

gigabyte (GB, GByte) A unit of measure for memory or disk storage capacity; usually 1,073,741,824 bytes.

gigahertz (GHz) A measure of frequency; one billion hertz.

Global System for Mobile (GSM) communications The wireless analog of the ISDN landline system.

GOTS Government off-the-shelf software

governing security requisites Those security requirements that must be addressed in all systems. These requirements are set by policy, directive, or common practice set; for example, by EO, OMB, the OSD, a military service, or a DoD agency. Those requirements are typically high-level. Although implementation will vary from case to case, those requisites are fundamental and shall be addressed.

Gramm-Leach-Bliley (GLB) Act of November 1999 An act that removes Depression-era restrictions on banks that limited certain business activities, mergers, and affiliations. It repeals the restrictions on banks affiliating with securities firms contained in sections 20 and 32 of the Glass-Steagall Act. GLB became effective on November 13, 2001. GLB also requires health plans and insurers to protect member and subscriber data in electronic and other formats. These health plans and insurers will fall under new state laws and regulations that are being passed to implement GLB because GLB explicitly assigns enforcement of the health plan and insurer regulations to state insurance authorities (15 U.S.C. §6805). Some of the privacy and security requirements of Gramm-Leach-Bliley are similar to those of HIPAA.

grand design program strategies Characterized by acquisition, development, and deployment of the total functional capability in a single increment, reference (i).

granularity An expression of the relative size of a data object; for example, protection at the file level is considered coarse granularity, whereas protection at the field level is considered to be of a finer granularity.

guard A processor that provides a filter between two disparate systems operating at different security levels or between a user terminal and a database in order to filter out data that the user is not authorized to access.

Gypsy Verification Environment An integrated set of tools for specifying, coding, and verifying programs written in the Gypsy language — a language similar to Pascal that has both specification and programming features. This methodology includes an editor, a specification processor, a verification condition generator, a user-directed theorem prover, and an information flow tool.

handshaking procedure A dialogue between two entities (for example, a user and a computer, a computer and another computer, or a program and another program) for the purpose of identifying and authenticating the entities to one another.

HDX Half duplex

Hertz (Hz) A unit of frequency measurement; one cycle of a periodic event per second. Used to measure frequency.

Hierarchical Development Methodology A methodology for specifying and verifying the design programs written in the Special specification language. The tools for this methodology include the Special specification processor, the Boyer-Moore theorem prover, and the Feiertag information flow tool.

high-level data link control An ISO protocol for link synchronization and error control.

HIPAA See *Kennedy-Kassebaum Act of 1996*.

host A time-sharing computer accessed via terminals or terminal emulation; a computer to which an expansion device attaches.

host to front-end protocol A set of conventions governing the format and control of data that is passed from a host to a front-end machine.

HTTP Hypertext Transfer Protocol

Hypertext Markup Language (HTML) A standard used on the Internet for defining hypertext links between documents.

I&A Identification and authentication

IA Information Assurance

IAC Inquiry access code; used in inquiry procedures. The IAC can be one of two types: a dedicated IAC for specific devices or a generic IAC for all devices.

IASE Information Assurance Support Environment

IAW Acronym for "in accordance with".

ICV Integrity check value; In WEP encryption, the frame is run through an integrity algorithm, and the generated ICV is placed at the end of the encrypted data in the frame. Then the receiving station runs the data through its integrity algorithm and compares it to the ICV received in the frame. If it matches, the unencrypted frame is passed to the higher layers. If it does not match, the frame is discarded.

ID Common abbreviation for "identifier" or "identity".

identification The process that enables a system to recognize an entity, generally by the use of unique machine-readable user names.

Identity-Based Encryption The IBE concept proposes that any string can be used as an individual's public key, including his or her email address.

IDS Intrusion detection system

IETF Internet Engineering Task Force

IKE Internet key exchange

impersonating Synonymous with *spoofing.*

incomplete parameter checking A system design flaw that results when all parameters have not been fully examined for accuracy and consistency, thus making the system vulnerable to penetration.

incremental program strategies Characterized by acquisition, development, and deployment of functionality through a number of clearly defined system "increments" that stand on their own.

individual accountability The ability to positively associate the identity of a user with the time, method, and degree of access to a system.

industrial, scientific, and medicine (ISM) bands Radio frequency bands authorized by the Federal Communications Commission (FCC) for wireless LANs. The ISM bands are located at 902 MHz, 2.400 GHz, and 5.7 GHz. The transmitted power is commonly less than 600mw, but no FCC license is required.

inference engine A component of an artificial intelligence system that takes inputs and uses a knowledge base to infer new facts and solve a problem.

information category The term used to bound information and tie it to an information security policy.

information flow control A procedure undertaken to ensure that information transfers within a system are not made from a higher security level object to an object of a lower security level. See *covert channel, simple security property,* and *star property (* property).* Synonymous with *data flow control* and *flow control.*

information flow model Information security model in which information is categorized into classes, and rules define how information can flow between the classes.

information security policy The aggregate of public law, directives, regulations, and rules that regulate how an organization manages, protects, and distributes information. For example, the information security policy for financial data processed on DoD systems may be in U.S.C., E.O., DoD Directives, and local regulations. The information security policy lists all the security requirements applicable to specific information.

information system (IS) Any telecommunications or computer-related equipment or interconnected systems or subsystems of equipment that is used in the acquisition, storage, manipulation, management, movement, control, display, switching, interchange, transmission, or reception of voice and/or data; includes software, firmware, and hardware.

information system security officer (ISSO) The person who is responsible to the DAA for ensuring that security is provided for and implemented throughout the life cycle of an AIS, from the beginning of the concept development plan through its design, development, operation, maintenance, and secure disposal. In C&A, the person responsible to the DAA for ensuring the security of an IT system is approved, operated, and maintained throughout its life cycle in accordance with the SSAA.

Information Systems Security Products and Services Catalogue A catalogue issued quarterly by the National Security Agency that incorporates the DPL, EPL, ETL, PPL, and other security product and service lists. This catalogue is available through the U.S. Government Printing Office, Washington, D.C., 20402.

information technology (IT) The hardware, firmware, and software used as part of the information system to perform DoD information functions. This definition includes computers, telecommunications, automated information systems, and automatic data processing equipment. IT includes any assembly of computer hardware, software, and/or firmware configured to collect, create, communicate, compute, disseminate, process, store, and/or control data or information.

information technology security (ITSEC) Protection of information technology against unauthorized access to or modification of information, whether in storage, processing, or transit, and against the denial of service to authorized users, including those measures necessary to detect, document, and counter such threats. Protection and maintenance of confidentiality, integrity, availability, and accountability.

INFOSEC Information System Security

infrared (IR) light Light waves that range in length from about 0.75 to 1,000 microns; this is a lower frequency than the spectral colors but a higher frequency than radio waves.

infrastructure-centric A security management approach that considers information systems and their computing environment as a single entity.

inheritance (in object-oriented programming) When all the methods of one class, called a *superclass*, are inherited by a subclass. Thus, all messages understood by the superclass are understood by the subclass.

Institute of Electrical and Electronic Engineers (IEEE) A U.S.–based standards organization participating in the development of standards for data transmission systems. The IEEE has made significant progress in the establishment of standards for LANs, namely the IEEE 802 series.

Integrated Services Digital Network (ISDN) A collection of CCITT standards specifying WAN digital transmission services. The overall goal of ISDN is to provide a single physical network outlet and transport mechanism for the transmission of all types of information, including data, video, and voice.

integration testing Testing process used to verify the interface among network components as the components are installed. The installation crew should integrate components into the network one-by-one and perform integration testing when necessary to ensure proper gradual integration of components.

integrator An organization or individual that unites, combines, or otherwise incorporates information system components with another system(s).

integrity (1) A term that refers to a sound, unimpaired, or perfect condition (2) Quality of an IT system reflecting the logical correctness and reliability of the operating system; the logical completeness of the hardware and software implementing the protection mechanisms; and the consistency of the data structures and occurrence of the stored data. It is composed of data integrity and system integrity.

interdiction See *Denial of Service*.

Interface Definition Language (IDL) A standard interface language that is used by clients to request services from objects.

internal security controls Hardware, firmware, and software features within a system that restrict access to resources (hardware, software, and data) to authorized subjects only (persons, programs, or devices).

International Standards Organization (ISO) A non-treaty standards organization active in the development of international standards, such as the Open System Interconnection (OSI) network architecture.

International Telecommunications Union (ITU) An intergovernmental agency of the United States responsible for making recommendations and standards regarding telephone and data communications systems for public and private telecommunication organizations and for providing coordination for the development of international standards.

International Telegraph and Telephone Consultative Committee (CCITT) An international standards organization that is part of the ITU and is dedicated to establishing effective and compatible telecommunications among members of the United Nations. CCITT develops the widely used V-series and X-series standards and protocols.

Internet The largest network in the world. The successor to ARPANET, the Internet includes other large internetworks. The Internet uses the TCP/IP protocol suite and connects universities, government agencies, and individuals around the world.

Internet Protocol (IP) The Internet standard protocol that defines the Internet datagram as the information unit passed across the Internet. IP provides the basis of a best-effort packet delivery service. The Internet protocol suite is often referred to as TCP/IP because IP is one of the two fundamental protocols, the other being the *Transfer Control Protocol*.

Internetwork Packet Exchange (IPX) NetWare protocol for the exchange of message packets on an internetwork. IPX passes application requests for network services to the network drives and then to other workstations, servers, or devices on the internetwork.

IPSec Secure Internet Protocol

IS See *Information System*.

isochronous transmission Type of synchronization whereby information frames are sent at specific times.

isolation The containment of subjects and objects in a system in such a way that they are separated from one another as well as from the protection controls of the operating system.

ISP Internet service provider

ISSE Information systems security engineering/engineer

ISSO See *information system security officer*.

IT See *information technology*.

ITA Industrial Telecommunications Association

ITSEC See *information technology security*.

IV Initialization vector; for WEP encryption.

joint application design (JAD) A parallel team design process simultaneously defining requirements composed of users, sales people, marketing staff, project managers, analysts, and engineers. Members of this team are used to simultaneously define requirements.

Kennedy-Kassebaum Health Insurance Portability and Accountability Act (HIPAA) of 1996 A set of regulations that mandates the use of standards in health care record keeping and electronic transactions. The act requires that health care plans, providers, insurers, and clearinghouses do the following:

- Provide for restricted access by the patient to personal healthcare information
- Implement administrative simplification standards
- Enable the portability of health insurance
- Establish strong penalties for healthcare fraud

Kerberos A trusted, third-party authentication protocol that was developed under Project Athena at MIT. In Greek mythology, Kerberos is a three-headed dog that guards the entrance to the underworld. Using symmetric key cryptography, Kerberos authenticates clients to other entities on a network of which a client requires services.

key Information or sequence that controls the enciphering and deciphering of messages. Also known as a *cryptovariable*. Used with a particular algorithm to encipher or decipher the plaintext message.

key clustering A situation in which a plaintext message generates identical ciphertext messages by using the same transformation algorithm but with different cryptovariables.

key schedule A set of subkeys derived from a secret key.

kilobyte (KB, Kbyte) A unit of measurement of memory or disk storage capacity; a data unit of 2^{10} (1,024) bytes.

kilohertz (kHz) A unit of frequency measurement equivalent to 1,000 Hertz.

knowledge acquisition system The means of identifying and acquiring the knowledge to be entered into an expert system's knowledge base.

knowledge base Refers to the rules and facts of the particular problem domain in an expert system.

least privilege The principle that requires each subject to be granted the most restrictive set of privileges needed for the performance of authorized tasks. The application of this principle limits the damage that can result from accident, error, or unauthorized use.

legacy information system An operational information system that existed before the implementation of the DITSCAP.

Light-emitting diode (LED) Used in conjunction with optical fiber, an LED emits incoherent light when current is passed through it. Its advantages include low cost and long lifetime, and it is capable of operating in the Mbps range.

limited access Synonymous with *access control*.

limited fault tolerance Specifies against what type of failures the Target of Evaluation (TOE) must be resistant. Examples of general failures are flooding of the computer room, short-term power interruption, breakdown of a CPU or host, software failure, or buffer overflow. Requires all functions to be available if a specified failure occurs.

Link Access Procedure An ITU error correction protocol derived from the HDLC standard.

link encryption Each entity has keys in common with its two neighboring nodes in the chain of transmission. Thus, a node receives the encrypted message from its predecessor neighboring node, decrypts it, and re-encrypts it with another key that is common to the successor node. Then, the encrypted message is sent on to the successor node, where the process is repeated until the final destination is reached. Obviously, this mode provides no protection if the nodes along the transmission path are subject to compromise.

list-oriented A computer protection system in which each protected object has a list of all subjects that are authorized to access it. Compare *ticket-oriented*.

LLC Logical Link Control; the IEEE layer 2 protocol.

local area network (LAN) A network that interconnects devices in the same office, floor, building, or close buildings.

lock-and-key protection system A protection system that involves matching a key or password with a specific access requirement.

logic bomb A resident computer program that triggers the perpetration of an unauthorized act when particular states of the system are realized.

Logical Link Control layer The highest layer of the IEEE 802 reference model; provides similar functions to those of a traditional data link control protocol.

loophole An error of omission or oversight in software or hardware that permits circumventing the system security policy.

LSB Least-significant bit

MAC *Mandatory access control* if used in the context of a type of access control; MAC also refers to the *media access control* address assigned to a network interface card on an Ethernet network.

magnetic remanence A measure of the magnetic flux density that remains after removal of the applied magnetic force. Refers to any data remaining on magnetic storage media after removal of the power.

mail gateway A type of gateway that interconnects dissimilar email systems.

maintainer The organization or individual that maintains the information system.

maintenance hook Special instructions in software to enable easy maintenance and additional feature development. These instructions are not clearly defined during access for design specification. Hooks frequently enable entry into the code at unusual points or without the usual checks, so they are serious security risks if they are not removed prior to live implementation. Maintenance hooks are special types of trap doors.

maintenance organization The organization that keeps an IT system operating in accordance with prescribed laws, policies, procedures, and regulations. In the case of a contractor-maintained system, the maintenance organization is the government organization responsible for, or sponsoring the operation of, the IT system.

malicious logic Hardware, software, or firmware that is intentionally included in a system for an unauthorized purpose (for example, a Trojan horse).

MAN Metropolitan area network

management information base (MIB) A collection of managed objects residing in a virtual information store.

mandatory access control (MAC) A means of restricting access to objects based on the sensitivity (as represented by a label) of the information contained in the objects and the formal authorization (in other words, clearance) of subjects to access information of such sensitivity. Compare *discretionary access control*.

MAPI Microsoft's mail application programming interface.

masquerading See *spoofing.*

media access control (MAC) An IEEE 802 standards sublayer used to control access to a network medium, such as a wireless LAN. Also deals with collision detection. Each computer has its own unique MAC address.

Medium access The Data Link Layer function that controls how devices access a shared medium. IEEE 802.11 uses either CSMA/CA or contention-free access modes. Also, a data link function that controls the use of a common network medium.

Megabits per second (Mbps) One million bits per second

Megabyte (MB, Mbyte) A unit of measurement for memory or disk storage capacity; usually 1,048,576 bytes.

Megahertz (MHz) A measure of frequency equivalent to one million cycles per second.

middleware An intermediate software component located on the wired network between the wireless appliance and the application or data residing on the wired network. Middleware provides appropriate interfaces between the appliance and the host application or server database.

mimicking See *spoofing.*

mission The assigned duties to be performed by a resource.

Mobile IP A protocol developed by the IETF that enables users to roam to parts of the network associated with a different IP address than the one loaded in the user's appliance. Also refers to any mobile device that contains the IEEE 802.11 MAC and physical layers.

modes of operation A description of the conditions under which an AIS functions, based on the sensitivity of data processed and the clearance levels and authorizations of the users. Four modes of operation are authorized:

1. *Dedicated mode* — An AIS is operating in the dedicated mode when each user who has direct or indirect individual access to the AIS, its peripherals, remote terminals, or remote hosts has all of the following:

   a. A valid personnel clearance for all information on the system

   b. Formal access approval; furthermore, the user has signed nondisclosure agreements for all the information stored and/or processed (including all compartments, subcompartments, and/or special access programs)

   c. A valid need-to-know for all information contained within the system

2. *System-high mode* — An AIS is operating in the system-high mode when each user who has direct or indirect access to the AIS, its peripherals, remote terminals, or remote hosts has all of the following:

   a. A valid personnel clearance for all information on the AIS

   b. Formal access approval, and signed nondisclosure agreements, for all the information stored and/or processed (including all compartments, subcompartments, and/or special access programs)

   c. A valid need-to-know for some of the information contained within the AIS

3. *Compartmented mode* — An AIS is operating in the compartmented mode when each user who has direct or indirect access to the AIS, its peripherals, remote terminals, or remote hosts has all of the following:

   a. A valid personnel clearance for the most restricted information processed in the AIS

   b. Formal access approval, and signed nondisclosure agreements, for that information which he or she will be able to access

   c. A valid need-to-know for that information which he or she will be able to access

4. *Multilevel mode* — An AIS is operating in the multilevel mode when all of the following statements are satisfied concerning the users who have direct or indirect access to the AIS, its peripherals, remote terminals, or remote hosts:

   a. Some do not have a valid personnel clearance for all the information processed in the AIS.

   b. All have the proper clearance and the appropriate formal access approval for that information to which they are to have access.

   c. All have a valid need-to-know for that information to which they are to have access.

modulation The process of translating the baseband digital signal to a suitable analog form. Any of several techniques for combining user information with a transmitter's carrier signal.

MSB Most significant bit

multilevel device A device that is used in a manner that permits it to simultaneously process data of two or more security levels without risk of compromise. To accomplish this, sensitivity labels are normally stored on the same physical medium and in the same form (for example, machine-readable or human-readable) as the data being processed.

multilevel secure A class of system containing information with different sensitivities that simultaneously permits access by users with different security clearances and needs-to-know but that prevents users from obtaining access to information for which they lack authorization.

multilevel security mode See *modes of operation.*

multipath The signal variation caused when radio signals take multiple paths from transmitter to receiver.

multipath fading A type of fading caused by signals taking different paths from the transmitter to the receiver and consequently interfering with each other.

multiple access rights terminal A terminal that can be used by more than one class of users; for example, users who have different access rights to data.

multiple inheritance In object-oriented programming, a situation where a subclass inherits the behavior of multiple superclasses.

multiplexer A network component that combines multiple signals into one composite signal in a form suitable for transmission over a long-haul connection, such as leased 56 Kbps or T1 circuits.

Multi-station access unit (MAU) A multiport wiring hub for token-ring networks.

multiuser mode of operation A mode of operation designed for systems that process sensitive, unclassified information in which users might not have a need-to-know for all information processed in the system. This mode is also used for microcomputers processing sensitive unclassified information that cannot meet the requirements of the stand-alone mode of operation.

Musical Instrument Digital Interface (MIDI) A standard protocol for the interchange of musical information between musical instruments and computers.

mutually suspicious A state that exists between interacting processes (subsystems or programs) in which neither process can expect the other process to function securely with respect to some property.

MUX Multiplexing sublayer; a sublayer of the L2CAP layer.

NACK or NAK Negative acknowledgement. This can be a deliberate signal that the message was received in error or it can be inferred by a time out.

National Computer Security Assessment Program A program designed to evaluate the interrelationship of the empirical data of computer security infractions and critical systems profiles while comprehensively incorporating information from the CSTVRP. The assessment builds threat and vulnerability scenarios that are based on a collection of facts from relevant reported cases. Such scenarios are a powerful, dramatic, and concise form of representing the value of loss experience analysis.

National Computer Security Center (NCSC) Originally named the *DoD Computer Security Center,* the NCSC is responsible for encouraging the widespread availability of trusted computer systems throughout the federal government. It is a branch of the National Security Agency (NSA) that also initiates research and develops and publishes standards and criteria for trusted information systems.

National Information Assurance Certification and Accreditation Process (NIACAP) Provides a standard set of activities, general tasks, and a management structure to certify and accredit systems that will maintain the information assurance and security posture of a system or site. The NIACAP is designed to certify that the information system meets documented accreditation requirements and continues to maintain the accredited security posture throughout the system life cycle.

National Security Decision Directive 145 (NSDD 145) Signed by President Ronald Reagan on September 17, 1984, this directive is entitled "National Policy on Telecommunications and Automated Information Systems Security." It provides initial objectives, policies, and an organizational structure to guide the conduct of national activities toward safeguarding systems that process, store, or communicate sensitive information; establishes a mechanism for policy development; and assigns implementation responsibilities.

National Telecommunications and Information System Security Directives (NTISSD) NTISS directives establish national-level decisions relating to NTISS policies, plans, programs, systems, or organizational delegations of authority. NTISSDs are promulgated by the executive agent of the government for telecommunications and information systems security or by the chairman of the NTISSC when so delegated by the executive agent. NTISSDs are binding upon all federal departments and agencies.

National Telecommunications and Information Systems Security Advisory Memoranda/Instructions (NTISSAM, NTISSI) Provide advice, assistance, or information on telecommunications and systems security that is of general interest to applicable federal departments and agencies. NTISSAMs/NTISSIs are promulgated by the National Manager for Telecommunications and Automated Information Systems Security and are recommendatory.

NCSC See *National Computer Security Center.*

NDI See *non-developmental item.*

need-to-know The necessity for access to, knowledge of, or possession of specific information that is required to carry out official duties.

Network Basic Input/Output System (NetBIOS) A standard interface between networks and PCs that enables applications on different computers to communicate within a LAN. NetBIOS was created by IBM for its early PC network, was adopted by Microsoft, and has since become a de facto industry standard. It is not routable across a WAN.

network file system (NFS) A distributed file system enabling a set of dissimilar computers to access each other's files in a transparent manner.

network front end A device that implements the necessary network protocols, including security-related protocols, to enable a computer system to be attached to a network.

Network Interface Card (NIC)   A network adapter inserted into a computer that enables the computer to be connected to a network.

network monitoring A form of operational support enabling network management to view the network's inner workings. Most network-monitoring equipment is nonobtrusive and can be used to determine the network's utilization and to locate faults.

network reengineering A structured process that can help an organization proactively control the evolution of its network. Network reengineering consists of continually identifying factors influencing network changes, analyzing network modification feasibility, and performing network modifications as necessary.

network service access point (NSAP) A point in the network where OSI network services are available to a transport entity.

NIACAP See *National Information Assurance Certification and Accreditation Process*.

NIAP National Information Assurance Partnership

NIST National Institute of Standards and Technology

node Any network-addressable device on the network, such as a router or Network Interface Card. Any network station.

non-developmental item (NDI) Any item that is available in the commercial marketplace; any previously developed item that is in use by a department or agency of the federal, a state, or a local government, or a foreign government with which the United States has a mutual defense cooperation agreement; any item described above that requires only minor modifications in order to meet the requirements of the procuring agency; or any item that is currently being produced that does not meet the requirements of the definitions above solely because the item is not yet in use or is not yet available in the commercial marketplace.

noninterference model The information security model that addresses a situation wherein one group is not affected by another group using specific commands.

NSA National Security Agency

NSDD 145 See *National Security Decision Directive 145*.

NSTISS National Security Telecommunications and Information Systems Security

NTISSC The National Telecommunications and Information Systems Security Committee

Number Field Sieve (NFS) A general-purpose factoring algorithm that can be used to factor large numbers.

object A passive entity that contains or receives information. Access to an object potentially implies access to the information that it contains. Examples of objects include records, blocks, pages, segments, files, directories, directory trees, and programs, as well as bits, bytes, words, fields, processors, video displays, keyboards, clocks, printers, and network nodes.

Object Request Broker (ORB) The fundamental building block of the Object Request Architecture (ORA), which manages the communications among the ORA entities. The purpose of the ORB is to support the interaction of objects in heterogeneous, distributed environments. The objects may be on different types of computing platforms.

object reuse The reassignment and reuse of a storage medium (for example, page frame, disk sector, and magnetic tape) that once contained one or more objects. To be securely reused and assigned to a new subject, storage media must contain no residual data (data remanence) from the object(s) that were previously contained in the media.

object services Services that support the ORB in creating and tracking objects as well as performing access control functions.

OFDM Orthogonal frequency division multiplexing; a set of frequency-hopping codes that never use the same frequency at the same time. Used in IEEE 802.11a for high-speed data transfer.

OMB Office of Management and Budget

one-time pad Encipherment operation performed using each component ki of the key, K, only once to encipher a single character of the plaintext. Therefore, the key has the same length as the message. The popular interpretation of one-time pad is that the key is used only once and never used again. Ideally, the components of the key are truly random and have no periodicity or predictability, making the ciphertext unbreakable.

Open Database Connectivity (ODBC) A standard database interface enabling interoperability between application software and multivendor ODBC-compliant databases.

Open Data-Link Interface (ODI) Novell's specification for Network Interface Card device drivers, allowing simultaneous operation of multiple protocol stacks.

open security environment An environment that includes those systems in which at least one of the following conditions holds true: 1) application developers (including maintainers) do not have sufficient clearance or authorization to provide an acceptable presumption that they have not introduced malicious logic, and 2) configuration control does not provide sufficient assurance that applications are protected against the introduction of malicious logic prior to and during the operation of system applications.

Open Shortest Path First (OSPF) A TCP/IP routing protocol that bases routing decisions on the least number of hops from source to destination.

open system authentication The IEEE 802.11 default authentication method, which is a very simple, two-step process: first, the station that wants to authenticate with another station sends an authentication management frame containing the sending station's identity. The receiving station then sends back a frame indicating whether it recognizes the identity of the authenticating station.

Open System Interconnection (OSI) An ISO standard specifying an open system capable of enabling communications between diverse systems. OSI has the following seven layers of distinction: Physical, Data Link, Network, Transport, Session, Presentation, and Application. These layers provide the functions that enable standardized communications between two application processes.

operations security Controls over hardware, media, and operators who have access; protects against asset threats, baseline, or selective mechanisms.

Operations Security (OPSEC) An analytical process by which the U.S. government and its supporting contractors can deny to potential adversaries information about capabilities and intentions by identifying, controlling, and protecting evidence of the planning and execution of sensitive activities and operations.

operator An individual who supports system operations from the operator's console, monitors execution of the system, controls the flow of jobs, and mounts input/output volumes (be alert for shoulder surfing).

OPSEC See *Operations Security.*

Orange Book Alternate name for *DoD Trusted Computer Security Evaluation Criteria.*

original equipment manufacturer (OEM) A manufacturer of products for integration in other products or systems.

OS Commonly used abbreviation for "operating system".

OSD Office of the Secretary of Defense

other program strategies Strategies intended to encompass variations and/or combinations of the grand design, incremental, evolutionary, or other program strategies (DoD Directive 5000.1)

overt channel A path within a computer system or network that is designed for the authorized transfer of data. Compare with *covert channel.*

overwrite procedure A stimulation to change the state of a bit followed by a known pattern. See *magnetic remanence.*

packet A basic message unit for communication across a network. A packet usually includes routing information, data, and (sometimes) error-detection information.

packet-switched (1) A network that routes data packets based on an address contained in the data packet is said to be a *packet-switched network.* Multiple data packets can share the same network resources. (2) A communications network that uses shared facilities to route data packets from and to different users. Unlike a circuit-switched network, a packet-switched network does not set up dedicated circuits for each session.

PAD Acronym for "packet assembly/disassembly".

partitioned security mode A mode of operation wherein all personnel have the clearance but not necessarily the formal access approval and need-to-know for all information contained in the system. Not to be confused with *compartmented security mode*.

password A protected/private character string that is used to authenticate an identity.

PCMCIA Personal Computer Memory Card International Association. The industry group that defines standards for PC cards (and the name applied to the cards themselves). These roughly credit card–sized adapters for memory and modem cards come in three thicknesses: 3.3, 5, and 10.5 mm.

PDN Public data network

PED Personal electronic device

Peer-to-peer network A network in which a group of devices can communicate among a group of equal devices. A peer-to-peer LAN does not depend upon a dedicated server but allows any node to be installed as a nondedicated server and share its files and peripherals across the network.

pen register A device that records all the numbers dialed from a specific telephone line.

penetration The successful act of bypassing a system's security mechanisms.

penetration signature The characteristics or identifying marks that might be produced by a penetration.

penetration study A study to determine the feasibility and methods for defeating the controls of a system.

penetration testing The portion of security testing in which the evaluators attempt to circumvent the security features of a system. The evaluators might be assumed to use all system design and implementation documentation, which can include listings of system source code, manuals, and circuit diagrams. The evaluators work under the same constraints that are applied to ordinary users.

performance modeling The use of simulation software to predict network behavior, allowing developers to perform capacity planning. Simulation makes it possible to model the network and impose varying levels of utilization to observe the effects.

performance monitoring Activity that tracks network performance during normal operations. Performance monitoring includes real-time monitoring, during which metrics are collected and compared against thresholds; recent-past monitoring, in which metrics are collected and analyzed for trends that may lead to performance problems; and historical data analysis, in which metrics are collected and stored for later analysis.

periods processing The processing of various levels of sensitive information at distinctly different times. Under periods processing, the system must be purged of all information from one processing period before transitioning to the next, when there are different users who have differing authorizations.

permissions A description of the type of authorized interactions that a subject can have with an object. Examples of permissions types include read, write, execute, add, modify, and delete.

permutation A method of encrypting a message, also known as transposition; operates by rearranging the letters of the plaintext.

personnel security (1) The procedures that are established to ensure that all personnel who have access to sensitive information possess the required authority as well as appropriate clearances. (2) Procedures to ensure a person's background; provides assurance of necessary trustworthiness.

PGP Pretty Good Privacy; a form of encryption.

Physical Layer (PHY) The layer of the OSI model that provides the transmission of bits through a communication channel by defining electrical, mechanical, and procedural specifications. It establishes protocols for voltage and data transmission timing and rules for "handshaking."

physical security The application of physical barriers and control procedures as preventive measures or countermeasures against threats to resources and sensitive information.

piconet A collection of devices connected via Bluetooth technology in an ad hoc fashion. A piconet starts with two connected devices, such as a portable PC and a cellular phone, and can grow to eight connected devices.

piggyback Gaining unauthorized access to a system via another user's legitimate connection. See *between-the-lines entry*.

pipelining In computer architecture, a design in which the decode and execution cycles of one instruction are overlapped in time with the fetch cycle of the next instruction.

PKI Public key infrastructure

plain old telephone system (POTS) The original analog telephone system, which is still in widespread use today.

plaintext Message text in clear, human-readable form.

Platform for Privacy Preferences (P3P) Proposed standards developed by the World Wide Web Consortium (W3C) to implement privacy practices on Web sites.

Point-to-Point Protocol (PPP) A protocol that provides router-to-router and host-to-network connections over both synchronous and asynchronous circuits. PPP is the successor to SLIP.

portability Defines network connectivity that can be easily established, used, and then dismantled.

PPL See *Preferred Products List*.

PRBS Pseudorandom bit sequence

Preferred Products List (PPL) A list of commercially produced equipment that meets TEMPEST and other requirements prescribed by the National Security Agency. This list is included in the NSA *Information Systems Security Products and Services Catalogue*, issued quarterly and available through the Government Printing Office.

Presentation Layer The layer of the OSI model that negotiates data transfer syntax for the Application Layer and performs translations between different data types, if necessary.

print suppression Eliminating the displaying of characters in order to preserve their secrecy; for example, not displaying a password as it is keyed at the input terminal.

private key encryption See *symmetric (private) key encryption*.

privileged instructions A set of instructions (for example, interrupt handling or special computer instructions) to control features such as storage protection features that are generally executable only when the automated system is operating in the executive state.

PRNG Pseudorandom number generator

procedural language Implies sequential execution of instructions based on the von Neumann architecture of a CPU, memory, and input/output device. Variables are part of the sets of instructions used to solve a particular problem, and therefore, the data is not separate from the statements.

procedural security Synonymous with *administrative security*.

process A program in execution. See *domain* and *subject*.

program manager The person ultimately responsible for the overall procurement, development, integration, modification, operation, and maintenance of the IT system.

Protected Health Information (PHI) Individually identifiable health information that is:

- Transmitted by electronic media
- Maintained in any medium described in the definition of electronic media (under HIPAA)
- Transmitted or maintained in any other form or medium

protection philosophy An informal description of the overall design of a system that delineates each of the protection mechanisms employed. A combination, appropriate to the evaluation class, of formal and informal techniques is used to show that the mechanisms are adequate to enforce the security policy.

Protection Profile (PP)   In the Common Criteria, an implementation-independent specification of the security requirements and protections of a product that could be built.

protection ring   One of a hierarchy of privileged modes of a system that gives certain access rights to user programs and processes authorized to operate in a given mode.

protection-critical portions of the TCB   Those portions of the TCB whose normal function is to deal with access control between subjects and objects. Their correct operation is essential to the protection of the data on the system.

protocols   A set of rules and formats, semantic and syntactic, that permits entities to exchange information.

prototyping   A method of determining or verifying requirements and design specifications. The prototype normally consists of network hardware and software that support a proposed solution. The approach to prototyping is typically a trial-and-error experimental process.

pseudoflaw   An apparent loophole deliberately implanted in an operating system program as a trap for intruders.

PSTN   Public-switched telephone network; the general phone network.

public key cryptography   See *asymmetric key encryption*.

Public Key Cryptography Standards (PKCS)   A set of public key cryptography standards that supports algorithms such as Diffie-Hellman and RSA, as well as algorithm-independent standards.

Public Law 100-235 (P.L. 100-235)   Also known as the Computer Security Act of 1987, this law creates a means for establishing minimum acceptable security practices for improving the security and privacy of sensitive information in federal computer systems. This law assigns responsibility to the National Institute of Standards and Technology for developing standards and guidelines for federal computer systems processing unclassified data. The law also requires establishment of security plans by all operators of federal computer systems that contain sensitive information.

pump   In a multilevel security system, or MLS, a one-way information flow device or data diode. In an analog to a pump operation, it permits information flow in one direction only, from a lower level of security classification or sensitivity to a higher level. The pump is a convenient approach to multilevel security in that it can be used to put together systems with different security levels.

purge   The removal of sensitive data from an AIS, AIS storage device, or peripheral device with storage capacity at the end of a processing period. This action is performed in such a way that there is assurance proportional to the sensitivity of the data that the data cannot be reconstructed. An AIS must be disconnected from any external network before a purge. After a purge, the medium can be declassified by observing the review procedures of the respective agency.

Quantum Computer A quantum computer is based on the principles of quantum mechanics. One principle is that of superposition, which states that atomic particles can exist in multiple states at the same time. Thus the fundamental unit of information in a quantum computer, the qubit, can exist in both the 0 and 1 states simultaneously. The ability of a qubit to represent a 0 or 1 simultaneously coupled with another quantum phenomenon called quantum interference permits a quantum computer to perform calculations at drastically higher speeds than conventional computers. Quantum computers have the potential of solving problems in polynomial time that now require exponential time or are currently unsolvable.

Quantum Cryptography Quantum cryptography provides the means for two users of a common communication channel to create a body of shared and secret information. This data is usually a random string of bits than can be used as a secret key for secure communication. Because of its basis in quantum mechanics, quantum cryptography theoretically guarantees that the communications will always be secure and that the transmitted information cannot be intercepted.

RADIUS Remote Authentication Dial-In User Service

RC4 RSA cipher algorithm 4

read A fundamental operation that results only in the flow of information from an object to a subject.

read access Permission to read information.

recovery planning The advance planning and preparations that are necessary to minimize loss and to ensure the availability of the critical information systems of an organization.

recovery procedures The actions that are necessary to restore a system's computational capability and data files after a system failure or outage/disruption.

Red Book A document of the United States National Security Agency (NSA) defining criteria for secure networks.

Reduced Instruction Set Computer (RISC) A computer architecture designed to reduce the number of cycles required to execute an instruction. A RISC architecture uses simpler instructions but makes use of other features, such as optimizing compilers and large numbers of general-purpose registers in the processor and data caches, to reduce the number of instructions required.

reference monitor concept An access-control concept that refers to an abstract machine that mediates all accesses to objects by subjects.

reference-validation mechanism An implementation of the reference monitor concept. A security kernel is a type of reference-validation mechanism.

reliability The probability of a given system performing its mission adequately for a specified period of time under expected operating conditions.

remote bridge A bridge connecting networks separated by longer distances. Organizations use leased 56 Kbps circuits, T1 digital circuits, and radio waves to provide such long-distance connections among remote sites.

remote journaling Refers to the parallel processing of transactions to an alternate site, as opposed to a batch dump process such as electronic vaulting. A communications line is used to transmit live data as it occurs. This enables the alternate site to be fully operational at all times and introduces a very high level of fault tolerance.

repeater A network component that provides internetworking functionality at the Physical Layer of a network's architecture. A repeater amplifies network signals, extending the distance they can travel.

residual risk The portion of risk that remains after security measures have been applied.

residue Data left in storage after processing operations are complete but before degaussing or rewriting has taken place.

resource encapsulation The process of ensuring that a resource not be directly accessible by a subject but that it be protected so that the reference monitor can properly mediate access to it.

restricted area Any area to which access is subject to special restrictions or controls for reasons of security or safeguarding of property or material.

RFC Acronym for "request for comment."

RFP Acronym for "request for proposal."

ring topology A topology in which a set of nodes are joined in a closed loop.

risk (1) A combination of the likelihood that a threat will occur, the likelihood that a threat occurrence will result in an adverse impact, and the severity of the resulting impact. (2) The probability that a particular threat will exploit a particular vulnerability of the system.

risk analysis The process of identifying security risks, determining their magnitude, and identifying areas needing safeguards. Risk analysis is a part of risk management. Synonymous with *risk assessment*.

risk assessment Process of analyzing threats to an IT system, vulnerabilities of a system, and the potential impact that the loss of information or capabilities of a system would have on security. The resulting analysis is used as a basis for identifying appropriate and effective measures.

risk index The disparity between the minimum clearance or authorization of system users and the maximum sensitivity (for example, classification and categories) of data processed by a system. See the publications CSC-STD-003-85 and CSC-STD-004-85 for a complete explanation of this term.

risk management The total process of identifying, controlling, eliminating, or minimizing uncertain events that might affect system resources. It includes risk analysis, cost-benefit analysis, selection, implementation, tests, a security evaluation of safeguards, and an overall security review.

ROM Read-only memory

router A network component that provides internetworking at the Network Layer of a network's architecture by allowing individual networks to become part of a WAN. A router works by using logical and physical addresses to connect two or more separate networks. It determines the best path by which to send a packet of information.

Routing Information Protocol (RIP) A common type of routing protocol. RIP bases its routing path on the distance (number of hops) to the destination. RIP maintains optimum routing paths by sending out routing update messages if the network topology changes.

RS-232 (1) A serial communications interface. (2) The ARS-232n EIA standard that specifies up to 20 Kbps, 50 foot, serial transmission between computers and peripheral devices. Serial communication standards are defined by the Electronic Industries Association (EIA).

RS-422 An EIA standard specifying electrical characteristics for balanced circuits (in other words, both transmit and return wires are at the same voltage above ground). RS-422 is used in conjunction with RS-449.

RS-423 An EIA standard specifying electrical characteristics for unbalanced circuits (in other words, the return wire is tied to the ground). RS-423 is used in conjunction with RS-449.

RS-449 An EIA standard specifying a 37-pin connector for high-speed transmission.

RS-485 An EIA standard for multipoint communications lines.

S/MIME A protocol that adds digital signatures and encryption to Internet MIME (Multipurpose Internet Mail Extensions).

safeguards See *security safeguards*.

SAISS Subcommittee on Automated Information Systems Security of the NTISSC

sandbox An access control–based protection mechanism. It is commonly applied to restrict the access rights of mobile code that is downloaded from a Web site as an applet. The code is set up to run in a "sandbox" that blocks its access to the local workstation's hard disk, thus preventing the code from malicious activity. The sandbox is usually interpreted by a virtual machine such as the Java Virtual Machine (JVM).

SBU Abbreviation for "sensitive but unclassified"; an information designation.

scalar processor A processor that executes one instruction at a time.

scavenging Searching through object residue to acquire unauthorized data.

SCI Sensitive Compartmented Information

SDLC Synchronous data link control

secure configuration management The set of procedures that are appropriate for controlling changes to a system's hardware and software structure for the purpose of ensuring that changes will not lead to violations of the system's security policy.

secure state A condition in which no subject can access any object in an unauthorized manner.

secure subsystem A subsystem that contains its own implementation of the reference monitor concept for those resources it controls. The secure subsystem, however, must depend on other controls and the base operating system for the control of subjects and the more primitive system objects.

security Measures and controls that ensure the confidentiality, integrity, availability, and accountability of the information processed and stored by a computer.

security critical mechanisms Those security mechanisms whose correct operation is necessary to ensure that the security policy is enforced.

security evaluation An evaluation that is performed to assess the degree of trust that can be placed in systems for the secure handling of sensitive information. One type, a product evaluation, is an evaluation performed on the hardware and software features and assurances of a computer product from a perspective that excludes the application environment. The other type, a system evaluation, is made for the purpose of assessing a system's security safeguards with respect to a specific operational mission; it is a major step in the certification and accreditation process.

security fault analysis A security analysis, usually performed on hardware at the gate level, to determine the security properties of a device when a hardware fault is encountered.

security features The security-relevant functions, mechanisms, and characteristics of system hardware and software. Security features are a subset of system security safeguards.

security filter A trusted subsystem that enforces a security policy on the data that pass through it.

security flaw An error of commission or omission in a system that might enable protection mechanisms to be bypassed.

security flow analysis A security analysis performed on a formal system specification that locates the potential flows of information within the system.

Security functional requirements Requirements, preferably from the Common Criteria, Part 2, that when taken together specify the security behavior of an IT product or system.

security inspection Examination of an IT system to determine compliance with security policy, procedures, and practices.

security kernel The hardware, firmware, and software elements of a Trusted Computer Base (TCB) that implement the reference monitor concept. The security kernel must mediate all accesses, must be protected from modification, and must be verifiable as correct.

security label A piece of information that represents the security level of an object.

security level The combination of a hierarchical classification and a set of nonhierarchical categories that represents the sensitivity of information.

security measures Elements of software, firmware, hardware, or procedures that are included in a system for the satisfaction of security specifications.

security objective A statement of intent to counter specified threats and/or satisfy specified organizational security policies and assumptions.

security perimeter The boundary where security controls are in effect to protect assets.

security policy The set of laws, rules, and practices that regulates how an organization manages, protects, and distributes sensitive information.

security policy model A formal presentation of the security policy enforced by the system. It must identify the set of rules and practices that regulate how a system manages, protects, and distributes sensitive information. See *Bell-LaPadula model* and *formal security policy model*.

security process The series of activities that monitor, evaluate, test, certify, accredit, and maintain the system accreditation throughout the system life cycle.

security range The highest and lowest security levels that are permitted in or on a system, system component, subsystem, or network.

security requirements The types and levels of protection that are necessary for equipment, data, information, applications, and facilities to meet security policy.

security requirements baseline A description of minimum requirements necessary for a system to maintain an acceptable level of security.

security safeguards The protective measures and controls that are prescribed to meet the security requirements specified for a system. Those safeguards can include (but are not necessarily limited to) the following: hardware and software security features, operating procedures, accountability procedures, access and distribution controls, management constraints, personnel security, and physical structures, areas, and devices. Also called *safeguards*.

security specifications A detailed description of the safeguards required to protect a system.

Security Target (ST) (1) In the Common Criteria, a listing of the security claims for a particular IT security product. (2) A set of security functional and assurance requirements and specifications to be used as the basis for evaluating an identified product or system.

Security Test and Evaluation (ST&E) Examination and analysis of the safeguards required to protect an IT system, as they have been applied in an operational environment, to determine the security posture of that system.

security testing A process that is used to determine that the security features of a system are implemented as designed. This process includes hands-on functional testing, penetration testing, and verification.

sensitive information Information which, if lost, misused, modified, or accessed by unauthorized individuals, could affect the national interest or the conduct of federal programs or the privacy to which individuals are entitled under Section 552a of Title 5, U.S. Code, but that has not been specifically authorized under criteria established by an executive order or an act of Congress to be kept classified in the interest of national defense or foreign policy. The concept of sensitive information can apply to private-sector entities as well.

sensitivity label A piece of information that represents the security level of an object. Sensitivity labels are used by the TCB as the basis for mandatory access control decisions.

serial interface An interface to provide serial communications service.

Serial Line Internet Protocol (SLIP) An Internet protocol used to run IP over serial lines and dial-up connections.

Session Layer One of the seven OSI model layers. Establishes, manages, and terminates sessions between applications.

SETA Systems Engineering, Testing, and Analysis

shared key authentication A type of authentication that assumes each station has received a secret shared key through a secure channel, independent from an 802.11 network. Stations authenticate through shared knowledge of the secret key. Use of shared key authentication requires implementation of the 802.11 Wired Equivalent Privacy (WEP) algorithm.

Simple Mail Transfer Protocol (SMTP) The Internet email protocol.

Simple Network Management Protocol (SNMP) The network management protocol of choice for TCP/IP-based Internets. Widely implemented with 10BASE-T Ethernet. A network management protocol that defines information transfer among *management information bases (MIBs)*.

simple security condition See *simple security property*.

simple security property A Bell-LaPadula security model rule enabling a subject read access to an object only if the security level of the subject dominates the security level of the object. Synonymous with *simple security condition*.

single user mode An OS loaded without Security Front End.

single-level device An automated information systems device that is used to process data of a single security level at any one time.

SMS Short (or small) message service

SNR Signal-to-noise ratio

software development methodologies Methodologies for specifying and verifying design programs for system development. Each methodology is written for a specific computer language. See *Enhanced Hierarchical Development Methodology*, *Formal Development Methodology*, *Gypsy Verification Environment*, and *Hierarchical Development Methodology*.

software engineering The science and art of specifying, designing, implementing, and evolving programs, documentation, and operating procedures whereby computers can be made useful to man.

software process A set of activities, methods, and practices that are used to develop and maintain software and associated products.

software process capability Describes the range of expected results that can be achieved by following a software process.

software process maturity The extent to which a software process is defined, managed, measured, controlled, and effective.

software process performance The result achieved by following a software process.

software security General-purpose executive, utility, or software development tools and applications programs or routines that protect data that are handled by a system.

software system test and evaluation process A process that plans, develops, and documents the quantitative demonstration of the fulfillment of all baseline functional performance and operational and interface requirements.

spoofing An attempt to gain access to a system by posing as an authorized user. Synonymous with *impersonating*, *masquerading*, or *mimicking*.

SSAA See *System Security Authorization Agreement*.

SSL Secure Sockets Layer

SSO System security officer

ST connector An optical fiber connector that uses a bayonet plug and socket.

ST&E See *Security Test and Evaluation*.

standalone (shared system) A system that is physically and electrically isolated from all other systems and is intended to be used by more than one person, either simultaneously (for example, a system that has multiple terminals) or serially, with data belonging to one user remaining available to the system while another user uses the system (for example, a personal computer that has nonremovable storage media, such as a hard disk).

standalone (single-user system) A system that is physically and electrically isolated from all other systems and is intended to be used by one person at a time, with no data belonging to other users remaining in the system (for example, a personal computer that has removable storage media, such as a floppy disk).

star property See ** property (or star property)*.

star topology A topology wherein each node is connected to a common central switch or hub.

State Delta Verification System A system that is designed to give high confidence regarding microcode performance by using formulae that represent isolated states of a computation to check proofs concerning the course of that computation.

state variable A variable that represents either the state of the system or the state of some system resource.

storage object An object that supports both read and write access.

Structured Query Language (SQL) An international standard for defining and accessing relational databases.

STS Subcommittee on Telecommunications Security of NTISSC

Subcommittee on Automated Information Systems Security The SAISS is composed of one voting member from each organization that is represented on the NTISSC.

Subcommittee on Telecommunications Security (STS) NSDD-145 authorizes and directs the establishment, under the NTISSC, of a permanent subcommittee on Telecommunications Security. The STS is composed of one voting member from each organization that is represented on the NTISSC.

subject An active entity, generally in the form of a person, process, or device, that causes information to flow among objects or that changes the system state. Technically, a process/domain pair.

subject security level A subject's security level is equal to the security level of the objects to which it has both read and write access. A subject's security level must always be dominated by the clearance of the user with which the subject is associated.

superscalar processor A processor that allows concurrent execution of instructions in the same pipelined stage. The term *superscalar* denotes multiple, concurrent operations performed on scalar values, as opposed to vectors or arrays that are used as objects of computation in array processors.

supervisor state See *executive state*.

Switched Multimegabit Digital Service (SMDS) A packet-switching connectionless data service for WANs.

symmetric (private) key encryption Cryptographic system in which the sender and receiver both know a secret key that is used to encrypt and decrypt a message.

Synchronous Optical NETwork (SONET) A fiber-optic transmission system for high-speed digital traffic. SONET is part of the B-ISDN standard.

Synchronous transmission A type of communications data synchronization whereby frames are sent within defined time periods. It uses a clock to control the timing of bits being sent. See *asynchronous transmission*.

system A set of interrelated components consisting of mission, environment, and architecture as a whole. Also, a data processing facility.

system development methodologies Methodologies developed through software engineering to manage the complexity of system development. Development methodologies include software engineering aids and high-level design analysis tools.

system entity A system subject (user or process) or object.

system high security mode A system and all peripherals protected in accordance with (IAW) requirements for the highest security level of material in the system; personnel with access have security clearance but not a need-to-know. See *modes of operation*.

system integrity A characteristic of a system when it performs its intended function in an unimpaired manner, free from deliberate or inadvertent unauthorized manipulation of the system.

system low security mode The lowest security level supported by a system at a particular time or in a particular environment.

System Security Authorization Agreement (SSAA) A formal agreement among the DAA(s), the CA, the IT system user representative, and the program manager. It is used throughout the entire DITSCAP to guide actions, document decisions, specify ITSEC requirements, document certification tailoring and level-of-effort, identify potential solutions, and maintain operational systems security.

System Security Officer (SSO) See *Information System Security Officer*.

system testing A type of testing that verifies the installation of the entire network. Testers normally complete system testing in a simulated production environment, simulating actual users in order to ensure the network meets all stated requirements.

Systems Network Architecture (SNA) IBM's proprietary network architecture.

Systems Security Steering Group The senior government body established by NSDD-145 to provide top-level review and policy guidance for the telecommunications security and automated information systems security activities of the United States government. This group is chaired by the assistant to the President for National Security Affairs and consists of the Secretary of State, Secretary of Treasury, Secretary of Defense, Attorney General, Director of the Office of Management and Budget, and Director of Central Intelligence.

T1 A standard specifying a time division–multiplexing scheme for point-to-point transmission of digital signals at 1.544 Mbps.

TAFIM Technical Architecture Framework for Information Management

tampering An unauthorized modification that alters the proper functioning of an equipment or system in a manner that degrades the security or functionality that it provides.

Target of Evaluation (TOE) In the Common Criteria, TOE refers to the product to be tested.

TCB See *Trusted Computing Base*.

TCSEC See *DoD Trusted Computer System Evaluation Criteria*.

technical attack An attack that can be perpetrated by circumventing or nullifying hardware and software protection mechanisms, rather than by subverting system personnel or other users.

technical vulnerability A hardware, firmware, communication, or software flaw that leaves a computer processing system open for potential exploitation, either externally or internally — thereby resulting in a risk to the owner, user, or manager of the system.

TELNET A virtual terminal protocol used in the Internet, enabling users to log in to a remote host. TELNET is defined as part of the TCP/IP protocol suite.

TEMPEST The short name referring to the investigation, study, and control of spurious compromising emanations emitted by electrical equipment.

terminal identification The means used to uniquely identify a terminal to a system.

test case An executable test with a specific set of input values and a corresponding expected result.

threat Any circumstance or event with the potential to cause harm to an IT system in the form of destruction, disclosure, adverse modification of data, and/or denial of service.

threat agent A method that is used to exploit a vulnerability in a system, operation, or facility.

threat analysis The examination of all actions and events that might adversely affect a system or operation.

threat assessment Formal description and evaluation of threat to an IT system.

threat monitoring The analysis, assessment, and review of audit trails and other data that are collected for the purpose of searching for system events that might constitute violations or attempted violations of system security.

ticket-oriented A computer protection system in which each subject maintains a list of unforgeable bit patterns called tickets, one for each object the subject is authorized to access. Compare with *list-oriented*.

time-dependent password A password that is valid only at a certain time of day or during a specified interval of time.

time-domain reflectometer (TDR) Mechanism used to test the effectiveness of network cabling.

TLA Top-level architecture

TLS Transport Layer security

token bus A network that uses a logical token-passing access method. Unlike a token passing ring, permission to transmit is usually based on the node address rather than the position in the network. A token bus network uses a common cable set, with all signals broadcast across the entire LAN.

token ring A local area network (LAN) standard developed by IBM that uses tokens to control access to the communication medium. A token ring provides multiple access to a ring-type network.. FDDI and IEEE 802.5 are token ring standards.

top-level specification A nonprocedural description of system behavior at the most abstract level; typically, a functional specification that omits all implementation details.

topology A description of the network's geographical layout of nodes and links.

tranquility A security model rule stating that an object's security level cannot change while the object is being processed by an AIS.

transceiver A device for transmitting and receiving packets between the computer and the medium.

Transmission Control Protocol (TCP) A commonly used protocol for establishing and maintaining communications between applications on different computers. TCP provides full-duplex, acknowledged, and flow-controlled service to upper-layer protocols and applications.

Transmission Control Protocol/ Internet Protocol (TCP/IP) A de facto, industry-standard protocol for interconnecting disparate networks. TCP/IP are standard protocols that define both the reliable full-duplex transport level and the connectionless, best effort unit of information passed across an internetwork.

Transport Layer OSI model layer that provides mechanisms for the establishment, maintenance, and orderly termination of virtual circuits while shielding the higher layers from the network implementation details.

trapdoor A hidden software or hardware mechanism that can be triggered to permit system protection mechanisms to be circumvented. It is activated in a manner that appears innocent — for example, a special "random" key sequence at a terminal. Software developers often introduce trap doors in their code to enable them to re-enter the system and perform certain functions. Synonymous with *back door*.

Trojan horse A computer program that has an apparently or actually useful function but contains additional (hidden) functions that surreptitiously exploit the legitimate authorizations of the invoking process to the detriment of security or integrity.

trusted computer system A system that employs sufficient hardware and software assurance measures to enable its use for simultaneous processing of a range of sensitive or classified information.

Trusted Computing Base (TCB) The totality of protection mechanisms within a computer system, including hardware, firmware, and software, the combination of which is responsible for enforcing a security policy. A TCB consists of one or more components that together enforce a unified security policy over a product or system. The ability of a TCB to correctly enforce a unified security policy depends solely on the mechanisms within the TCB and on the correct input of parameters by system administrative personnel (for example, a user's clearance level) related to the security policy.

trusted distribution A trusted method for distributing the TCB hardware, software, and firmware components, both originals and updates, that provides methods for protecting the TCB from modification during distribution and for the detection of any changes to the TCB that might occur.

trusted identification forwarding An identification method used in networks whereby the sending host can verify that an authorized user on its system is attempting a connection to another host. The sending host transmits the required user authentication information to the receiving host. The receiving host can then verify that the user is validated for access to its system. This operation might be transparent to the user.

trusted path A mechanism by which a person at a terminal can communicate directly with the TCB. This mechanism can be activated only by the person or by the TCB and cannot be imitated by untrusted software.

trusted process A process whose incorrect or malicious execution is capable of violating system security policy.

trusted software The software portion of the TCB.

twisted-pair wire Type of medium using metallic-type conductors twisted together to provide a path for current flow. The wire in this medium is twisted in pairs to minimize the electromagnetic interference between one pair and another.

UART Universal asynchronous receiver transmitter. A device that either converts parallel data into serial data for transmission or converts serial data into parallel data for receiving data.

untrusted process A process that has not been evaluated or examined for adherence to the security policy. It might include incorrect or malicious code that attempts to circumvent the security mechanisms.

user (1) A person or process that is accessing an AIS either by direct connections (for example, via terminals), or by indirect connections (in other words, preparing input data or receiving output that is not reviewed for content or classification by a responsible individual) (2) Person or process authorized to access an IT system.

user representative The individual or organization that represents the user or user community in the definition of information system requirements.

User Datagram Protocol UDP uses the underlying Internet protocol (IP) to transport a message. This is an unreliable, connectionless delivery scheme. It does not use acknowledgments to ensure that messages arrive and does not provide feedback to control the rate of information flow. UDP messages can be lost, duplicated, or arrive out of order.

user ID A unique symbol or character string that is used by a system to identify a specific user.

user profile Patterns of a user's activity that can be used to detect changes in normal routines.

U.S Federal Computer Incident Response Center (FedCIRC) FedCIRC provides assistance and guidance in incident response and provides a centralized approach to incident handling across U.S. government agency boundaries.

U.S. Patriot Act of October 26, 2001 A law that permits the following:

- Subpoena of electronic records

- Monitoring of Internet communications

- Search and seizure of information on live systems (including routers and servers), backups, and archives

- Reporting of cash and wire transfers of $10,000 or more

Under the Patriot Act, the government has new powers to subpoena electronic records and to monitor Internet traffic. In monitoring information, the government can require the assistance of ISPs and network operators. This monitoring can even extend into individual organizations.

U.S. Uniform Computer Information Transactions Act (UCITA) of 1999 A model act that is intended to apply uniform legislation to software licensing.

utility An element of the DII providing information services to DoD users. Those services include Defense Information Systems Agency Mega-Centers, information processing, and wide-area network communications services.

V.21 An ITU standard for asynchronous 0–300 bps full-duplex modems.

V.21FAX An ITU standard for facsimile operations at 300 bps.

V.34 An ITU standard for 28,800 bps modems.

validation (in DITSCAP) Determination of the correct implementation in the completed IT system with the security requirements and approach agreed on by the users, acquisition authority, and DAA.

validation (in software engineering) To establish the fitness or worth of a software product for its operational mission.

vaulting Running mirrored data centers in separate locations.

verification The process of determining compliance of the evolving IT system specification, design, or code with the security requirements and approach agreed on by the users, acquisition authority, and the DAA. Also, the process of comparing two levels of system specification for proper correspondence (for example, a security policy model with top-level specification, top-level specification with source code, or source code with object code). This process might or might not be automated.

very-long-instruction word (VLIW) processor A processor in which multiple, concurrent operations are performed in a single instruction. The number of instructions is reduced relative to those in a scalar processor. However, for this approach to be feasible, the operations in each VLIW instruction must be independent of each other.

VIM Lotus' vendor-independent messaging system.

virus A self-propagating Trojan horse composed of a mission component, a trigger component, and a self-propagating component.

vulnerability A weakness in system security procedures, system design, implementation, internal controls, and so on that could be exploited to violate system security policy.

vulnerability analysis A measurement of vulnerability that includes the susceptibility of a particular system to a specific attack and the opportunities that are available to a threat agent to mount that attack.

vulnerability assessment Systematic examination of an information system or product to determine the adequacy of security measures, identify security deficiencies, provide data from which to predict the effectiveness of proposed security measures, and confirm the adequacy of such measures after implementation.

WAP Wireless Application Protocol. A standard commonly used for the development of applications for wireless Internet devices.

wide area network (WAN) A network that interconnects users over a wide area, usually encompassing different metropolitan areas.

Wired Equivalency Privacy (WEP) The algorithm of the 802.11 wireless LAN standard that is used to protect transmitted information from disclosure. WEP is designed to prevent the violation of the confidentiality of data transmitted over the wireless LAN. WEP generates secret shared encryption keys that both source and destination stations use to alter frame bits to avoid disclosure to eavesdroppers.

wireless Describes any computing device that can access a network without a wired connection.

wireless metropolitan area network (wireless MAN) Provides communications links between buildings, avoiding the costly installation of cabling or leasing fees and the downtime associated with system failures.

WLAN Wireless local area network

work breakdown structure (WBS) A diagram of the way a team will accomplish the project at hand by listing all tasks the team must perform and the products they must deliver.

work factor An estimate of the effort or time needed by a potential intruder who has specified expertise and resources to overcome a protective measure.

work function (factor) The difficulty in recovering plaintext from ciphertext, as measured by cost and/or time. The security of the system is directly proportional to the value of the work function. The work function need only be large enough to suffice for the intended application. If the message to be protected loses its value after a short period of time, the work function need only be large enough to ensure that the decryption would be highly infeasible in that period of time.

write A fundamental operation that results only in the flow of information from a subject to an object.

write access Permission to write to an object.

X.12 An ITU standard for EDI.

X.121 An ITU standard for international address numbering.

X.21 An ITU standard for a circuit-switching network.

X.25 An ITU standard for an interface between a terminal and a packet-switching network. X.25 was the first public packet-switching technology, developed by the CCITT and offered as a service during the 1970s. It is still available today. X.25 offers connection-oriented (virtual circuit) service; it operates at 64 Kbps, which is too slow for some high-speed applications.

X.400 An ITU standard for OSI messaging.

X.500 An ITU standard for OSI directory services.

X.75 An ITU standard for packet switching between public networks.

✦   ✦   ✦

Sample SSAA

The System Security Authorization Agreement (SSAA) is a formal agreement among the DAA(s), certifier, user representative, and program manager. The objective of the SSAA is to establish an evolving yet binding agreement on the level of security required before the system development begins or changes to a system are made.

The SSAA is used throughout the entire C&A process to guide actions, document decisions, specify IA requirements, document certification tailoring and level of effort, identify possible solutions, and maintain operational systems security. After accreditation, the SSAA becomes the baseline security configuration document.

Both the DITSCAP and NIACAP SSAAs are very similar, with only minor differences.

SSAA OUTLINE

The SSAA is a living document that represents the formal agreement among the DAA, the CA, the user representative, and the program manager. The SSAA is developed in phase 1 and updated in each phase as the system development progresses and new information becomes available.

At minimum, the SSAA should contain the information in the following sample format:

1. Mission Description and System Identification

    1.1. System name and identification

    1.2. System description

    1.3. Functional description

    1.3.1. System capabilities

5. System Security Requirements

5.1. National and DoD security requirements

5.2. Governing security requisites

5.3. Data security requirements

5.4. Security CONOPS

5.5. Network connection rules

5.5.1. To connect to this system

5.5.2. To connect to the other systems defined in the CONOPS

5.6. Configuration and change-management requirements

5.7. Reaccreditation requirements

6. Organizations and Resources

6.1. Identification of organizations

6.1.1. Identification of the DAA

6.1.2. Identification of the CA

6.1.3. Identification of the user representative

6.1.4. Identification of the organization responsible for the system

6.1.5. Identification of the program manager or system manager

6.2. Resources

6.2.1. Staffing requirements

6.2.2. Funding requirements

6.3. Training for certification team

6.4. Roles and responsibilities

6.5. Other supporting organizations or working groups

7. C&A Plan

7.1. Tailoring factors

7.1.1. Programmatic considerations

7.1.2. Security environment

7.1.3. IT system characteristics

7.1.4. Reuse of previously approved solutions

7.1.5. Tailoring summary

7.2. Tasks and milestones

7.3. Schedule summary

7.4. Level of effort

7.5. Roles and responsibilities

Additional Material

Appendices shall be added to include system C&A artifacts. Optional appendices may be added to meet specific needs. Include all documentation that will be relevant to the systems' C&A.

APPENDIX A. Acronym list

APPENDIX B. Definitions

APPENDIX C. References

APPENDIX D. Security requirements and/or requirements traceability matrix

APPENDIX E. Security test and evaluation plan and procedures

APPENDIX F. Certification results

APPENDIX G. Risk assessment results

APPENDIX H. CA's recommendation

APPENDIX I. System rules of behavior

APPENDIX J. Contingency plan(s)

APPENDIX K. Security awareness and training plan

APPENDIX L. Personnel controls and technical security controls

APPENDIX M. Incident response plan

APPENDIX N. Memorandums of agreement—system interconnect agreements

APPENDIX O. Applicable system development artifacts or system documentation

APPENDIX P. Accreditation documentation and accreditation statement

✦   ✦   ✦

Excerpts from the Common Criteria

Below are excerpts from the Common Criteria, version 2.1, from August 1999, ISO International Standard 15408 (Source: http://csrc.nist.gov/cc/index.html. Used by permission.). We feel these sections are the most relevant to the ISSEP candidate.

Scope

This multipart standard, the Common Criteria (CC), is meant to be used as the basis for evaluation of security properties of IT products and systems. By establishing such a common criteria base, the results of an IT security evaluation will be meaningful to a wider audience.

The CC will permit comparability between the results of independent security evaluations. It does so by providing a common set of requirements for the security functions of IT products and systems and for assurance measures applied to them during a security evaluation. The evaluation process establishes a level of confidence that the security functions of such products and systems and the assurance measures applied to them meet these requirements. The evaluation results may help consumers to determine whether the IT product or system is secure enough for their intended application and whether the security risks implicit in its use are tolerable.

The CC is useful as a guide for the development of products or systems with IT security functions and for the procurement of commercial products and systems with such functions. During evaluation, such an IT product or system is known as a Target of Evaluation (TOE). Such TOEs include, for example, operating systems, computer networks, distributed systems, and applications.

The CC addresses protection of information from unauthorised disclosure, modification, or loss of use. The categories of protection relating to these three types of failure of security are commonly called confidentiality, integrity, and availability, respectively. The CC may also be applicable to aspects of IT security outside of these three. The CC concentrates on threats to that information arising from human activities, whether malicious or otherwise, but may be applicable to some non-human threats as well. In addition, the CC may be applied in other areas of IT, but makes no claim of competence outside the strict domain of IT security.

The CC is applicable to IT security measures implemented in hardware, firmware or software. Where particular aspects of evaluation are intended only to apply to certain methods of implementation, this will be indicated within the relevant criteria statements.

Certain topics, because they involve specialised techniques or because they are somewhat peripheral to IT security, are considered to be outside the scope of the CC. Some of these are identified below.

a) The CC does not contain security evaluation criteria pertaining to administrative security measures not related directly to the IT security measures. However, it is recognised that a significant part of the security of a TOE can often be achieved through administrative measures such as organisational, personnel, physical, and procedural controls. Administrative security measures in the operating environment of the TOE are treated as secure usage assumptions where these have an impact on the ability of the IT security measures to counter the identified threats.

b) The evaluation of technical physical aspects of IT security such as electromagnetic emanation control is not specifically covered, although many of the concepts addressed will be applicable to that area. In particular, the CC addresses some aspects of physical protection of the TOE.

c) The CC addresses neither the evaluation methodology nor the administrative and legal framework under which the criteria may be applied by evaluation authorities. However, it is expected that the CC will be used for evaluation purposes in the context of such a framework and such a methodology.

d) The procedures for use of evaluation results in product or system accreditation are outside the scope of the CC. Product or system accreditation is the administrative process whereby authority is granted for the operation of an IT product or system in its full operational environment. Evaluation focuses on the IT security parts of the product or system and those parts of the operational environment that may directly affect the secure use of IT elements. The results of the evaluation process are consequently a valuable input to the accreditation process. However, as other techniques are more appropriate for the assessments of non-IT related product or system security properties and their relationship to the IT security parts, accreditors should make separate provision for those aspects.

e) The subject of criteria for the assessment of the inherent qualities of cryptographic algorithms is not covered in the CC. Should independent assessment of mathematical properties of cryptography embedded in a TOE be required, the evaluation scheme under which the CC is applied must make provision for such assessments.

Overview

Information held by IT products or systems is a critical resource that enables organisations to succeed in their mission. Additionally, individuals have a reasonable expectation that their personal information contained in IT products or systems remain private, be available to them as needed, and not be subject to unauthorised modification. IT products or systems should perform their functions while exercising proper control of the information to ensure it is protected against hazards such as unwanted or unwarranted dissemination, alteration, or loss. The term IT security is used to cover prevention and mitigation of these and similar hazards.

Many consumers of IT lack the knowledge, expertise or resources necessary to judge whether their confidence in the security of their IT products or systems is appropriate, and they may not wish to rely solely on the assertions of the developers. Consumers may therefore choose to increase their confidence in the security measures of an IT product or system by ordering an analysis of its security (i.e. a security evaluation).

The CC can be used to select the appropriate IT security measures and it contains criteria for evaluation of security requirements.

Target audience of the CC

There are three groups with a general interest in evaluation of the security properties of IT products and systems: TOE consumers, TOE developers, and TOE evaluators. The criteria presented in this document have been structured to support the needs of all three groups. They are all considered to be the principal users of this CC. The three groups can benefit from the criteria as explained in the following paragraphs.

Consumers

The CC plays an important role in supporting techniques for consumer selection of IT security requirements to express their organisational needs. The CC is written to ensure that evaluation fulfils the needs of the consumers as this is the fundamental purpose and justification for the evaluation process.

Consumers can use the results of evaluations to help decide whether an evaluated product or system fulfils their security needs. These security needs are typically identified as a result of both risk analysis and policy direction. Consumers can also use the evaluation results to compare different products or systems. Presentation of the assurance requirements within a hierarchy supports this need.

The CC gives consumers — especially in consumer groups and communities of interest — an implementation-independent structure termed the Protection Profile (PP) in which to express their special requirements for IT security measures in a TOE.

Developers

The CC is intended to support developers in preparing for and assisting in the evaluation of their products or systems and in identifying security requirements to be satisfied by each of their products or systems. It is also quite possible that an associated evaluation methodology, potentially accompanied by a mutual recognition agreement for evaluation results, would further permit the CC to support someone, other than the TOE developer, in preparing for and assisting in the evaluation of a developer's TOE.

The CC constructs can then be used to make claims that the TOE conforms to its identified requirements by means of specified security functions and assurances to be evaluated. Each TOE's requirements are contained in an implementation dependent construct termed the Security Target (ST). One or more PPs may provide the requirements of a broad consumer base.

The CC describes security functions that a developer could include in the TOE. The CC can be used to determine the responsibilities and actions to support evidence that is necessary to support the evaluation of the TOE. It also defines the content and presentation of that evidence.

Evaluators

The CC contains criteria to be used by evaluators when forming judgements about the conformance of TOEs to their security requirements. The CC describes the set of general actions the evaluator is to carry out and the security functions on which to perform these actions. Note that the CC does not specify procedures to be followed in carrying out those actions.

Others

While the CC is oriented towards specification and evaluation of the IT security properties of TOEs, it may also be useful as reference material to all parties with an interest in or responsibility for IT security. Some of the additional interest groups that can benefit from information contained in the CC are:

a) system custodians and system security officers responsible for determining and meeting organisational IT security policies and requirements;

b) auditors, both internal and external, responsible for assessing the adequacy of the security of a system;

c) security architects and designers responsible for the specification of the security content of IT systems and products;

d) accreditors responsible for accepting an IT system for use within a particular environment;

e) sponsors of evaluation responsible for requesting and supporting an evaluation; and

f) evaluation authorities responsible for the management and oversight of IT security evaluation programmes.

Evaluation context

In order to achieve greater comparability between evaluation results, evaluations should be performed within the framework of an authoritative evaluation scheme that sets the standards, monitors the quality of the evaluations and administers the regulations to which the evaluation facilities and evaluators must conform.

The CC does not state requirements for the regulatory framework. However, consistency between the regulatory frameworks of different evaluation authorities will be necessary to achieve the goal of mutual recognition of the results of such evaluations.

Use of a common evaluation methodology contributes to the repeatability and objectivity of the results but is not by itself sufficient. Many of the evaluation criteria require the application of expert judgement and background knowledge for which consistency is more difficult to achieve. In order to enhance the consistency of the evaluation findings, the final evaluation results could be submitted to a certification process. The certification process is the independent inspection of the results of the evaluation leading to the production of the final certificate or approval. The certificate is normally publicly available. It is noted that the certification process is a means of gaining greater consistency in the application of IT security criteria.

The evaluation scheme, methodology, and certification processes are the responsibility of the evaluation authorities that run evaluation schemes and are outside the scope of the CC.

Organisation of the Common Criteria

The CC is presented as a set of distinct but related parts as identified below. Terms used in the description of the parts are explained in the General Model clause.

a) **Part 1, Introduction and general model,** is the introduction to the CC. It defines general concepts and principles of IT security evaluation and presents a general model of evaluation. Part 1 also presents constructs for expressing IT security objectives, for selecting and defining IT security requirements, and for writing high-level specifications for products and systems. In addition, the usefulness of each part of the CC is described in terms of each of the target audiences.

b) **Part 2, Security functional requirements,** establishes a set of functional components as a standard way of expressing the functional requirements for TOEs. Part 2 catalogues the set of functional components, families, and classes.

c) **Part 3, Security assurance requirements,** establishes a set of assurance components as a standard way of expressing the assurance requirements for TOEs. Part 3 catalogues the set of assurance components, families and classes. Part 3 also defines evaluation criteria for PPs and STs and presents evaluation assurance levels that define the predefined CC scale for rating assurance for TOEs, which is called the Evaluation Assurance Levels (EALs).

In support of the three parts of the CC listed above, it is anticipated that other types of documents will be published, including technical rationale material and guidance documents.

General model

This clause presents the general concepts used throughout the CC, including the context in which the concepts are to be used and the CC approach for applying the concepts. Part 2 and Part 3 expand on the use of these concepts and assume that the approach described is used. This clause assumes some knowledge of IT security and does not propose to act as a tutorial in this area.

The CC discusses security using a set of security concepts and terminology. An understanding of these concepts and the terminology is a prerequisite to the effective use of the CC. However, the concepts themselves are quite general and are not intended to restrict the class of IT security problems to which the CC is applicable.

Security context

General security context

Security is concerned with the protection of assets from threats, where threats are categorised as the potential for abuse of protected assets. All categories of threats should be considered; but in the domain of security greater attention is given to those threats that are related to malicious or other human activities.

Safeguarding assets of interest is the responsibility of owners who place value on those assets. Actual or presumed threat agents may also place value on the assets and seek to abuse assets in a manner contrary to the interests of the owner. Owners will perceive such threats as potential for impairment of the assets such that the value of the assets to the owners would be reduced. Security specific impairment commonly includes, but is not limited to, damaging disclosure of the asset to unauthorised recipients (loss of confidentiality), damage to the asset through unauthorised modification (loss of integrity), or unauthorised deprivation of access to the asset (loss of availability).

The owners of the assets will analyse the possible threats to determine which ones apply to their environment. The results are known as risks. This analysis can aid in the selection of countermeasures to counter the risks and reduce it to an acceptable level.

Countermeasures are imposed to reduce vulnerabilities and to meet security policies of the owners of the assets (either directly or indirectly by providing direction to other parties). Residual vulnerabilities may remain after the imposition of countermeasures. Such vulnerabilities may be exploited by threat agents representing a residual level of risk to the assets. Owners will seek to minimise that risk given other constraints.

Owners will need to be confident that the countermeasures are adequate to counter the threats to assets before they will allow exposure of their assets to the specified threats. Owners may not themselves possess the capability to judge all aspects of the countermeasures, and may therefore seek evaluation of the countermeasures. The outcome of evaluation is a statement about the extent to which assurance is gained that the countermeasures can be trusted to reduce the risks to the protected assets. The statement assigns an assurance rating of the countermeasures, assurance being that property of the countermeasures that gives grounds for confidence in their proper operation. This statement can be used by the owner of the assets in deciding whether to accept the risk of exposing the assets to the threats.

Owners of assets will normally be held responsible for those assets and should beagle to defend the decision to accept the risks of exposing the assets to the threats. This requires that the statements resulting from evaluation are defensible. Thus, evaluation should lead to objective and repeatable results that can be cited as evidence.

Information technology security context

Many assets are in the form of information that is stored, processed and transmitted by IT products or systems to meet requirements laid down by owners of the information. Information owners may require that dissemination and modification of any such information representations (data) be strictly controlled. They may demand that the IT product or system implement IT specific security controls as part of the overall set of security countermeasures put in place to counteract the threats to the data.

IT systems are procured and constructed to meet specific requirements and may, for economic reasons, make maximum use of existing commodity IT products such as operating systems, general purpose application components, and hardware platforms. IT security countermeasures implemented by a system may use functions of the underlying IT products and depend upon the correct operation of IT product security functions. The IT products may, therefore, be subject to evaluation as part of the IT system security evaluation.

Where an IT product is incorporated or being considered for incorporation in multiple IT systems, there are cost advantages in evaluating the security aspects of such a product independently and building a catalogue of evaluated products. The results of such an evaluation should be expressed in a manner that supports incorporation of the product in multiple IT systems without unnecessary repetition of work required to examine the product's security.

An IT system accreditor has the authority of the owner of the information to determine whether the combination of IT and non-IT security countermeasures furnishes adequate protection for the data, and thus to decide whether to permit the operation of the system. The accreditor may call for evaluation of the IT countermeasures in order to determine whether the IT countermeasures provide adequate protection and whether the specified countermeasures are properly implemented by the IT system. This evaluation may take various forms and degrees of rigour, depending upon the rules imposed upon, or by, the accreditor.

Common Criteria approach

Confidence in IT security can be gained through actions that may be taken during the processes of development, evaluation, and operation.

Development

It is essential that the security requirements imposed on the IT development be effective in contributing to the security objectives of consumers. Unless suitable requirements are established at the start of the development process, the resulting end product, however well engineered, may not meet the objectives of its anticipated consumers.

The process is based on the refinement of the security requirements into a TOE summary specification expressed in the security target. Each lower level of refinement represents a design decomposition with additional design detail. The least abstract representation is the TOE implementation itself.

The CC does not mandate a specific set of design representations. The CC requirement is that there should be sufficient design representations presented at a sufficient level of granularity to demonstrate where required:

> a) that each refinement level is a complete instantiation of the higher levels (i.e. all TOE security functions, properties, and behaviour defined at the higher level of abstraction must be demonstrably present in the lower level);

> b) that each refinement level is an accurate instantiation of the higher levels (i.e. there should be no TOE security functions, properties, and behaviour defined at the lower level of abstraction that are not required by the higher level).

The CC assurance criteria identify the design abstraction levels of functional specification, high-level design, low-level design, and implementation. Depending upon the assurance level specified, developers may be required to show how the development methodology meets the CC assurance requirements.

TOE evaluation

The TOE evaluation process may be carried out in parallel with development, or it may follow. The principal inputs to TOE evaluation are:

> a) the set of TOE evidence, which includes the evaluated ST as the basis for TOE evaluation;

> b) the TOE for which the evaluation is required;

> c) the evaluation criteria, methodology and scheme.

In addition, informative material (such as application notes of the CC) and the IT security expertise of the evaluator and the evaluation community are likely to be used as inputs to the evaluation.

The expected result of the evaluation process is a confirmation that the TOE satisfies its security requirements as stated in the ST with one or more reports documenting the evaluator findings about the TOE as determined by the evaluation criteria. These reports will be useful to actual and potential consumers of the product or system represented by the TOE as well as to the developer.

The degree of confidence gained through an evaluation depends on the assurance requirements (e.g. Evaluation Assurance Level) met.

Evaluation can lead to better IT security products in two ways. Evaluation is intended to identify errors or vulnerabilities in the TOE that the developer may correct, thereby reducing the probability of security failures in future operation. Also in preparing for the rigours of evaluation, the developer may take more care in TOE design and development. Therefore, the evaluation process can exert a strong, though indirect, positive effect on the initial requirements, the development process, the end product, and the operational environment.

Operation

Consumers may elect to use evaluated TOEs in their environments. Once a TOE is in operation, it is possible that previously unknown errors or vulnerabilities may surface or environmental assumptions may need to be revised. As a result of operation, feedback could be given that would require the developer to correct the TOE or redefine its security requirements or environmental assumptions. Such changes may require the TOE to be re-evaluated or the security of its operational environment to be strengthened. In some instances this may only require that the needed updates are evaluated in order to regain confidence in the TOE. Although the CC contains criteria to cover assurance maintenance, detailed procedures for reevaluation, including reuse of evaluation results, are outside the scope of the CC.

Security concepts

Evaluation criteria are most useful in the context of the engineering processes and regulatory frameworks that are supportive of secure TOE development and evaluation. This subclause is provided for illustration and guidance purposes only and is not intended to constrain the analysis processes, development approaches, or evaluation schemes within which the CC might be employed.

The CC is applicable when IT is being used and there is concern about the ability of the IT element to safeguard assets. In order to show that the assets are secure, the security concerns must be addressed at all levels from the most abstract to the final IT implementation in its operational environment. These levels of representation, as described in the following subclauses, permit security problems and issues to be characterised and discussed but do not, of themselves, demonstrate that the final IT implementation actually exhibits the required security behaviour and can, therefore, be trusted.

The CC requires that certain levels of representation contain a rationale for the representation of the TOE at that level. That is, such a level must contain a reasoned and convincing argument that shows that it is in conformance with the higher level, and is itself complete, correct and internally consistent. Statements of rationale demonstrating conformance with the adjacent higher level representation contribute to the case for TOE correctness. Rationale directly demonstrating compliance with security objectives supports the case that the TOE is effective in countering the threats and enforcing the organisational security policy.

The CC layers the different levels of representation. All TOE security requirements ultimately arise from consideration of the purpose and context of the TOE. This chart is not intended to constrain the means by which PPs and STs are developed, but illustrates how the results of some analytic approaches relate to the content of PPs and STs.

Security environment

The security environment includes all the laws, organisational security policies, customs, expertise and knowledge that are determined to be relevant. It thus defines the context in which the TOE is intended to be used. The security environment also includes the threats to security that are, or are held to be, present in the environment.

To establish the security environment, the PP or ST writer has to take into account:

a) the TOE physical environment which identifies all aspects of the TOE operating environment relevant to TOE security, including known physical and personnel security arrangements;

b) the assets requiring protection by the element of the TOE to which security requirements or policies will apply; this may include assets that are directly referred to, such as files and databases, as well as assets that are indirectly subject to security requirements, such as authorisation credentials and the IT implementation itself;

c) the TOE purpose, which would address the product type and the intended usage of the TOE.

Investigation of the security policies, threats and risks should permit the following security specific statements to be made about the TOE:

a) A statement of assumptions which are to be met by the environment of the TOE in order for the TOE to be considered secure. This statement can be accepted as axiomatic for the TOE evaluation.

b) A statement of threats to security of the assets would identify all the threats perceived by the security analysis as relevant to the TOE. The CC characterises a threat in terms of a threat agent, a presumed attack method, any vulnerabilities that are the foundation for the attack, and identification of the asset under attack. An assessment of risks to security would qualify each threat with an assessment of the likelihood of such a threat developing into an actual attack, the likelihood of such an attack proving successful, and the consequences of any damage that may result.

c) A statement of applicable organisational security policies would identify relevant policies and rules. For an IT system, such policies may be explicitly referenced, whereas for a general purpose IT product or product class, working assumptions about organisational security policy may need to be made.

Security objectives

The results of the analysis of the security environment could then be used to state the security objectives that counter the identified threats and address identified organisational security policies and assumptions. The security objectives should be consistent with the stated operational aim or product purpose of the TOE, and any knowledge about its physical environment.

The intent of determining security objectives is to address all of the security concerns and to declare which security aspects are either addressed directly by the TOE or by its environment. This categorisation is based on a process incorporating engineering judgement, security policy, economic factors and risk acceptance decisions.

The security objectives for the environment would be implemented within the IT domain, and by non-technical or procedural means.

Only the security objectives for the TOE and its IT environment are addressed by IT security requirements.

IT security requirements

The IT security requirements are the refinement of the security objectives into a set of security requirements for the TOE and security requirements for the environment which, if met, will ensure that the TOE can meet its security objectives.

The CC presents security requirements under the distinct categories of functional requirements and assurance requirements.

The functional requirements are levied on those functions of the TOE that are specifically in support of IT security, and define the desired security behaviour. Part 2 defines the CC functional requirements. Examples of functional requirements include requirements for identification, authentication, security audit and non-repudiation of origin.

When the TOE contains security functions that are realised by a probabilistic or permutational mechanism (e.g. a password or hash function), the assurance requirements may specify that a minimum strength level consistent with the security objectives is to be claimed. In this case, the level specified will be one of the following SOF-basic, SOF-medium, SOF-high. Each such function will be required to meet that minimum level or at least an optionally defined specific metric.

The degree of assurance can be varied for a given set of functional requirements; therefore it is typically expressed in terms of increasing levels of rigour built with assurance components. Part 3 defines the CC assurance requirements and a scale of evaluation assurance levels (EALs) constructed using these components. The assurance requirements are levied on actions of the developer, on evidence produced and on the actions of the evaluator. Examples of assurance requirements include constraints on the rigour of the development process and requirements to search for and analyse the impact of potential security vulnerabilities.

Assurance that the security objectives are achieved by the selected security functions is derived from the following two factors:

> a) confidence in the correctness of the implementation of the security functions, i.e., the assessment whether they are correctly implemented; and

> b) confidence in the effectiveness of the security functions, i.e., the assessment whether they actually satisfy the stated security objectives.

Security requirements generally include both requirements for the presence of desired behaviour and requirements for the absence of undesired behaviour. It is normally possible to demonstrate, by use or testing, the presence of the desired behaviour. It is not always possible to perform a conclusive demonstration of absence of undesired behaviour. Testing, design review, and implementation review contribute significantly to reducing the risk that such undesired behaviour is present. The rationale statements provide further support to the claim that such undesired behaviour is absent.

TOE summary specification

The TOE summary specification provided in the ST defines the instantiation of the security requirements for the TOE. It provides a high-level definition of the security functions claimed to meet the functional requirements, and assurance measures taken to meet the assurance requirements.

TOE implementation

The TOE implementation is the realisation of the TOE based on its security functional requirements and the TOE summary specification contained in the ST. TOE implementation is accomplished using a process of applying security and IT engineering skills and knowledge. The TOE will meet the security objectives if it correctly and effectively implements all the security requirements contained in the ST.

CC descriptive material

The CC presents the framework in which an evaluation can take place. By presenting the requirements for evidence and analysis, a more objective, and hence useful evaluation result can be achieved. The CC incorporates a common set of constructs and a language in which to express and communicate the relevant aspects of IT security, and permits those responsible for IT security to benefit from the prior experience and expertise of others.

Expression of security requirements

The CC defines a set of constructs that combine into meaningful assemblies of security requirements of known validity, which can be used in establishing security requirements for prospective products and systems. The relationships among the various constructs for requirements expression are described below.

The organisation of the CC security requirements into the hierarchy of class–family–component is provided to help consumers to locate specific security requirements.

The CC presents requirements for functional and assurance aspects in the same general style and uses the same organisation and terminology for each.

Class

The term class is used for the most general grouping of security requirements. All the members of a class share a common focus, while differing in coverage of security objectives.

The members of a class are termed families.

Family

A family is a grouping of sets of security requirements that share security objectives but may differ in emphasis or rigour.

The members of a family are termed components.

Component

A component describes a specific set of security requirements and is the smallest selectable set of security requirements for inclusion in the structures defined in the CC. The set of components within a family may be ordered to represent increasing strength or capability of security requirements that share a common purpose. They may also be partially ordered to represent related non-hierarchical sets. In some instances, there is only one component in a family so ordering is not applicable.

The components are constructed from individual elements. The element is the lowest level expression of security requirements, and is the indivisible security requirement that can be verified by the evaluation.

Dependencies between components

Dependencies may exist between components. Dependencies arise when a component is not self sufficient and relies upon the presence of another component. Dependencies may exist between functional components, between assurance components, and between functional and assurance components.

Component dependency descriptions are part of the CC component definitions. In order to ensure completeness of the TOE requirements, dependencies should be satisfied when incorporating components into PPs and STs where appropriate.

Permitted operations on components

CC components may be used exactly as defined in the CC, or they may be tailored through the use of permitted operations in order to meet a specific security policy or counter a specific threat. Each CC component identifies and defines any permitted operations of assignment and selection, the circumstances under which these operations may be applied to the component, and the results of the application of the operation. The operations of iteration and refinement can be performed for any component. These four operations are described as follows:

> a) **iteration**, which permits the use of a component more than once with varying operations;
>
> b) **assignment**, which permits the specification of a parameter to be filled in when the component is used;
>
> c) **selection**, which permits the specification of items that are to be selected from a list given in the component;
>
> d) **refinement**, which permits the addition of extra detail when the component is used.

Some required operations may be completed (in whole or part) in the PP or may be left to be completed in the ST. Nevertheless, all operations must be completed in the ST.

Use of security requirements

The CC defines three types of requirement constructs: package, PP and ST. The CC further defines a set of IT security criteria that can address the needs of many communities and thus serve as a major expert input to the production of these constructs. The CC has been developed around the central notion of using wherever possible the security requirements components defined in the CC, which represent a well-known and understood domain.

Package

An intermediate combination of components is termed a package. The package permits the expression of a set of functional or assurance requirements that meet an identifiable subset of security objectives. A package is intended to be reusable and to define requirements that are known to be useful and effective in meeting the identified objectives. A package may be used in the construction of larger packages, PPs, and STs.

The evaluation assurance levels (EALs) are predefined assurance packages contained in Part 3. An EAL is a baseline set of assurance requirements for evaluation. EALs each define a consistent set of assurance requirements. Together, the EALs form an ordered set that is the predefined assurance scale of the CC.

Protection Profile

The PP contains a set of security requirements either from the CC, or stated explicitly, which should include an EAL (possibly augmented by additional assurance components). The PP permits the implementation independent expression of security requirements for a set of TOEs that will comply fully with a set of security objectives. A PP is intended to be reusable and to define TOE requirements that are known to be useful and effective in meeting the identified objectives, both for functions and assurance. A PP also contains the rationale for security objectives and security requirements.

A PP could be developed by user communities, IT product developers, or other parties interested in defining such a common set of requirements. A PP gives consumers a means of referring to a specific set of security needs and facilitates future evaluation against those needs.

Security Target

An ST contains a set of security requirements that may be made by reference to a PP, directly by reference to CC functional or assurance components, or stated explicitly. An ST permits the expression of security requirements for a specific TOE that are shown, by evaluation, to be useful and effective in meeting the identified objectives.

An ST contains the TOE summary specification, together with the security requirements and objectives, and the rationale for each. An ST is the basis for agreement between all parties as to what security the TOE offers.

Sources of security requirements

TOE security requirements can be constructed by using the following inputs:

a) Existing PPs. The TOE security requirements in an ST may be adequately expressed by, or are intended to comply with, a pre-existing statement of requirements contained in an existing PP. Existing PPs may be used as a basis for a new PP.

b) Existing packages. Part of the TOE security requirements in a PP or ST may have already been expressed in a package that may be used. A set of predefined packages is the EALs defined in Part 3. The TOE assurance requirements in a PP or ST should include an EAL from Part 3.

c) Existing functional or assurance requirements components. The TOE functional or assurance requirements in a PP or ST may be expressed directly, using the components in Part 2 or 3.

d) Extended requirements. Additional functional requirements not contained in Part 2 and/or additional assurance requirements not contained in Part 3 may be used in a PP or ST.

Existing requirements material from Parts 2 and 3 should be used where available. The use of an existing PP will help to ensure that the TOE will meet a well known set of needs of known utility and thus be more widely recognised.

Types of evaluation

PP evaluation

The PP evaluation is carried out against the evaluation criteria for PPs contained in Part 3. The goal of such an evaluation is to demonstrate that the PP is complete, consistent, and technically sound and suitable for use as a statement of requirements for an evaluatable TOE.

ST evaluation

The evaluation of the ST for the TOE is carried out against the evaluation criteria for STs contained in Part 3. The goal of such an evaluation is twofold: first to demonstrate that the ST is complete, consistent, and technically sound and hence suitable for use as the basis for the corresponding TOE evaluation; second, in the case where an ST claims conformance to a PP, to demonstrate that the ST properly meets the requirements of the PP.

TOE evaluation

The TOE evaluation is carried out against the evaluation criteria contained in Part 3 using an evaluated ST as the basis. The goal of such an evaluation is to demonstrate that the TOE meets the security requirements contained in the ST.

Assurance maintenance

TOE assurance maintenance is carried out against the evaluation criteria contained in Part 3 using a previously evaluated TOE as the basis. The goal is to derive confidence that assurance already established in a TOE is maintained and that the TOE will continue to meet its security requirements as changes are made to the TOE or its environment.

Functional requirements paradigm

This part of the CC is a catalogue of security functional requirements that can be specified for a *Target of Evaluation (TOE)*. A TOE is an IT product or system (along with user and administrator guidance documentation) containing resources such as electronic storage media (e.g. disks), peripheral devices (e.g. printers), and computing capacity (e.g. CPU time) that can be used for processing and storing information and is the subject of an evaluation.

TOE evaluation is concerned primarily with ensuring that a defined *TOE Security Policy (TSP)* is enforced over the TOE resources. The TSP defines the rules by which the TOE governs access to its resources, and thus all information and services controlled by the TOE.

The TSP is, in turn, made up of multiple *Security Function Policies (SFPs)*. Each SFP has a scope of control, that defines the subjects, objects, and operations controlled under the SFP. The SFP is implemented by a *Security Function (SF)*, whose mechanisms enforce the policy and provide necessary capabilities.

Those portions of a TOE that must be relied on for the correct enforcement of the TSP are collectively referred to as the *TOE Security Functions (TSF)*. The TSF consists of all hardware, software, and firmware of a TOE that is either directly or indirectly relied upon for security enforcement.

A *reference monitor* is an abstract machine that enforces the access control policies of a TOE. A *reference validation mechanism* is an implementation of the reference monitor concept that possesses the following properties: tamperproof, always invoked, and simple enough to be subjected to thorough analysis and testing. The *TSF* may consist of a reference validation mechanism and/or other security functions necessary for the operation of the TOE.

The TOE may be a monolithic product containing hardware, firmware, and software.

Alternatively a TOE may be a distributed product that consists internally of multiple separated parts. Each of these parts of the TOE provides a particular service for the TOE, and is connected to the other parts of the TOE through an *internal communication channel*. This channel can be as small as a processor bus, or may encompass a network internal to the TOE.

When the TOE consists of multiple parts, each part of the TOE may have its own part of the TSF which exchanges user and TSF data over internal communication channels with other parts of the TSF. This interaction is called *internal TOE transfer*. In this case the separate parts of the TSF abstractly form the composite TSF, which enforces the TSP.

TOE interfaces may be localised to the particular TOE, or they may allow interaction with other IT products over *external communication channels*. These external interactions with other IT products may take two forms:

a) The security policy of the 'remote trusted IT product' and the TSP of the local TOEs have been administratively coordinated and evaluated. Exchanges of information in this situation are called *inter-TSF transfers*, as they are between the TSFs of distinct trusted products.

b) The remote IT product may not be evaluated, therefore its security policy is unknown. Exchanges of information in this situation are called *transfers outside TSF control*, as there is no TSF (or its policy characteristics are unknown) on the remote IT product.

The set of interactions that can occur with or within a TOE and are subject to the rules of the TSP is called the *TSF Scope of Control (TSC)*. The TSC encompasses a defined set of interactions based on subjects, objects, and operations within the TOE, but it need not encompass all resources of a TOE.

The set of interfaces, whether interactive (man-machine interface) or programmatic (application programming interface), through which resources are accessed that are mediated by the TSF, or information is obtained from the TSF, is referred to as the *TSF Interface (TSFI)*. The TSFI defines the boundaries of the TOE functions that provide for the enforcement of the TSP.

Users are outside of the TOE, and therefore outside of the TSC. However, in order to request that services be performed by the TOE, users interact with the TOE through the TSFI. There are two types of users of interest to the CC Part 2 security functional requirements: *human users* and *external IT entities*. Human users are further differentiated as *local human users*, meaning they interact directly with the TOE via TOE devices (e.g. workstations), or *remote human users*, meaning they interact indirectly with the TOE through another IT product.

A period of interaction between users and the TSF is referred to as a user *session*. Establishment of user sessions can be controlled based on a variety of considerations, for example: user authentication, time of day, method of accessing the TOE, and number of allowed concurrent sessions per user.

This part of the CC uses the term *authorised* to signify a user who possesses the rights and/or privileges necessary to perform an operation. The term *authorised user*, therefore, indicates that it is allowable for a user to perform an operation as defined by the TSP.

To express requirements that call for the separation of administrator duties, the relevant CC Part 2 security functional components (from family FMT_SMR) explicitly state that administrative *roles* are required. A role is a pre-defined set of rules establishing the allowed interactions between a user and the TOE. A TOE may support the definition of any number of roles. For example, roles related to the secure operation of a TOE may include "Audit Administrator" and "User Accounts Administrator".

TOEs contain resources that may be used for the processing and storing of information. The primary goal of the TSF is the complete and correct enforcement of the TSP over the resources and information that the TOE controls.

TOE resources can be structured and utilised in many different ways. However, CC Part 2 makes a specific distinction that allows for the specification of desired security properties. All entities that can be created from resources can be characterised in one of two ways. The entities may be active, meaning that they are the cause of actions that occur internal to the TOE and cause operations to be performed on information. Alternatively, the entities may be passive, meaning that they are either the container from which information originates or to which information is stored.

Active entities are referred to as *subjects*. Several types of subjects may exist within a TOE:

a) those acting on behalf of an authorised user and which are subject to all the rules of the TSP (e.g. UNIX processes);

b) those acting as a specific functional process that may in turn act on behalf of multiple users (e.g. functions as might be found in client/server architectures); or

c) those acting as part of the TOE itself (e.g. trusted processes).

CC Part 2 addresses the enforcement of the TSP over types of subjects as those listed above.

Passive entities (i.e. information containers) are referred to in the CC Part 2 security functional requirements as *objects*. Objects are the targets of operations that may be performed by subjects. In the case where a subject (an active entity) is the target of an operation (e.g. interprocess communication), a subject may also be acted on as an object.

Objects can contain *information*. This concept is required to specify information flow control policies as addressed in the FDP class.

Users, subjects, information and objects possess certain *attributes* that contain information that allows the TOE to behave correctly. Some attributes, such as file names, may be intended to be informational (i.e. to increase the user-friendliness of the TOE) while others, such as access control information, may exist specifically for the enforcement of the TSP. These latter attributes are generally referred to as *'security attributes'*. The word attribute will be used as a shorthand in this part of the CC for the word 'security attribute', unless otherwise indicated. However, no matter what the intended purpose of the attribute information, it may be necessary to have controls on attributes as dictated by the TSP.

Data in a TOE is categorised as either user data or TSF data. *User Data* is information stored in TOE resources that can be operated upon by users in accordance with the TSP and upon which the TSF places no special meaning. For example, the contents of an electronic mail message is user data. *TSF Data* is information used by the TSF in making TSP decisions. TSF Data may be influenced by users if allowed by the TSP. Security attributes, authentication data and access control list entries are examples of TSF data.

There are several SFPs that apply to data protection such as *access control SFPs* and *information flow control SFPs*. The mechanisms that implement access control SFPs base their policy decisions on attributes of the subjects, objects and operations within the scope of control. These attributes are used in the set of rules that govern operations that subjects may perform on objects.

The mechanisms that implement information flow control SFPs base their policy decisions on the attributes of the subjects and information within the scope of control and the set of rules that govern the operations by subjects on information. The attributes of the information, which may be associated with the attributes of the container (or may not, as in the case of a multi-level database) stay with the information as it moves.

Two specific types of TSF data addressed by CC Part 2 can be, but are not necessarily, the same. These are *authentication data* and *secrets*.

Authentication data is used to verify the claimed identity of a user requesting services from a TOE. The most common form of authentication data is the password, which depends on being kept secret in order to be an effective security mechanism. However, not all forms of authentication data need to be kept secret. Biometric authentication devices (e.g. fingerprint readers, retinal scanners) do not rely on the fact that the data is kept secret, but rather that the data is something that only one user possesses and that cannot be forged. The term secrets, as used in CC Part 2 functional requirements, while applicable to authentication data, is intended to also be applicable to other types of data that must be kept secret in order to enforce a specific SFP. For example, a trusted channel mechanism that relies on cryptography to preserve the confidentiality of information being transmitted via the channel can only be as strong as the method used to keep the cryptographic keys secret from unauthorised disclosure.

Therefore, some, but not all, authentication data needs to be kept secret and some, but not all, secrets are used as authentication data.

Security functional components

This clause defines the content and presentation of the functional requirements of the CC, and provides guidance on the organisation of the requirements for new components to be included in an ST. The functional requirements are expressed in classes, families, and components.

Class structure

Each functional class includes a class name, class introduction, and one or more functional families.

Class name

The class name subclause provides information necessary to identify and categorise a functional class. Every functional class has a unique name. The categorical information consists of a short name of three characters. The short name of the class is used in the specification of the short names of the families of that class.

Class introduction

The class introduction expresses the common intent or approach of those families to satisfy security objectives. The definition of functional classes does not reflect any formal taxonomy in the specification of the requirements.

The class introduction provides a figure describing the families in this class and the hierarchy of the components in each family, as explained in subclause 2.2.

Family structure

Family name

The family name subclause provides categorical and descriptive information necessary to identify and categorise a functional family. Every functional family has a unique name. The categorical information consists of a short name of seven characters, with the first three identical to the short name of the class followed by an underscore and the short name of the family as follows XXX_YYY. The unique short form of the family name provides the principal reference name for the components.

Family behaviour

The family behaviour is the narrative description of the functional family stating its security objective and a general description of the functional requirements. These are described in greater detail below:

  a) The *security objectives* of the family address a security problem that may be solved with the help of a TOE that incorporates a component of this family;

  b) The description of the *functional requirements* summarises all the requirements that are included in the component(s). The description is aimed at authors of PPs, STs and functional packages who wish to assess whether the family is relevant to their specific requirements.

Component levelling

Functional families contain one or more components, any one of which can be selected for inclusion in PPs, STs and functional packages. The goal of this section is to provide information to users in selecting an appropriate functional component once the family has been identified as being a necessary or useful part of their security requirements.

This section of the functional family description describes the components available, and their rationale. The exact details of the components are contained within each component.

The relationships between components within a functional family may or may not be hierarchical. A component is hierarchical to another if it offers more security.

As explained in Subclause 2.2 the descriptions of the families provide a graphical overview of the hierarchy of the components in a family.

Management

The *management* requirements contain information for the PP/ST authors to consider as management activities for a given component. The management requirements are detailed in components of the management class (FMT).

A PP/ST author may select the indicated management requirements or may include other management requirements not listed. As such the information should be considered informative.

Audit

The *audit* requirements contain auditable events for the PP/ST authors to select, if requirements from the class FAU, Security audit, are included in the PP/ST. These requirements include security relevant events in terms of the various levels of detail supported by the components of the FAU_GEN Security audit data generation family. For example, an audit note might include actions that are in terms of: Minimal—successful use of the security mechanism; Basic—any use of the security mechanism as well as relevant information regarding the security attributes involved; Detailed—any configuration changes made to the mechanism, including the actual configuration values before and after the change.

It should be observed that the categorisation of auditable events is hierarchical. For example, when Basic Audit Generation is desired, all auditable events identified as being both Minimal and Basic should be included in the PP/ST through the use of the appropriate assignment operation, except when the higher level event simply provides more detail than the lower level event. When Detailed Audit Generation is desired, all identified auditable events (Minimal, Basic and Detailed) should be included in the PP/ST.

In the class FAU the rules governing the audit are explained in more detail.

Component structure

The component identification subclause provides descriptive information necessary to identify, categorise, register and cross-reference a component. The following is provided as part of every functional component:

A *unique name*. The name reflects the purpose of the component.

A *short name*. A unique short form of the functional component name. This short name serves as the principal reference name for the categorisation, registration and cross-referencing of the component. This short name reflects the class and family to which the component belongs and the component number within the family.

A *hierarchical-to* list. A list of other components that this component is hierarchical to and for which this component can be used to satisfy dependencies to the listed components.

Functional elements

A set of elements is provided for each component. Each element is individually defined and is self-contained.

A functional element is a security functional requirement that if further divided would not yield a meaningful evaluation result. It is the smallest security functional requirement identified and recognised in the CC.

When building packages, PPs and/or STs, it is not permitted to select only one or more elements from a component. The complete set of elements of a component must be selected for inclusion in a PP, ST or package.

A unique short form of the functional element name is provided. For example the requirement name FDP_IFF.4.2 reads as follows: F—functional requirement, DP—class "User data protection", _IFF—family "Information flow control functions", .4—4th component named "Partial elimination of illicit information flows", .2—2nd element of the component.

Dependencies

Dependencies among functional components arise when a component is not self sufficient and relies upon the functionality of, or interaction with, another component for its own proper functioning.

Each functional component provides a complete list of dependencies to other functional and assurance components. Some components may list "No dependencies". The components depended upon may in turn have dependencies on other components. The list provided in the components will be the direct dependencies. That is only references to the functional requirements that are required for this requirement to perform its job properly. It is noted that in some cases the dependency is optional in that a number of functional requirements are provided, where each one of them would be sufficient to satisfy the dependency.

The dependency list identifies the minimum functional or assurance components needed to satisfy the security requirements associated with an identified component. Components that are hierarchical to the identified component may also be used to satisfy the dependency.

The dependencies indicated in CC Part 2 are normative. They must be satisfied within a PP/ST. In specific situations the indicated dependencies might not be applicable. The PP/ST author, by providing the rationale why it is not applicable, may leave the depended upon component out of the package, PP or ST.

Permitted functional component operations

The functional components used in the definition of the requirements in a PP, an ST or a functional package may be exactly as specified in clauses 3 to 13 of this part of the CC, or they may be tailored to meet a specific security objective. However, selecting and tailoring these functional components is complicated by the fact that identified component dependencies must be considered. Thus, this tailoring is restricted to an approved set of operations.

A list of permitted operations is included with each functional component. Not all operations are permitted on all functional components.

The permitted operations are selected from the following set:

> iteration: allows a component to be used more than once with varying operations,
>
> assignment: allows the specification of an identified parameter,
>
> selection: allows the specification of one or more elements from a list,
>
> refinement: allows the addition of details.

Iteration

Where necessary to cover different aspects of the same requirement (e.g. identification of more than one type of user), repetitive use of the same component from this part of the CC to cover each aspect is permitted.

Assignment

Some functional component elements contain parameters or variables that enable the PP/ST author to specify a policy or a set of values for incorporation into the PP or ST to meet a specific security objective. These elements clearly identify each parameter and constraint on values that may be assigned to that parameter.

Any aspect of an element whose acceptable values can be unambiguously described or enumerated can be represented by a parameter. The parameter may be an attribute or rule that narrows the requirement to a specific value or range of values. For instance, based on a specified security objective, the functional component element may state that a given operation should be performed a number of times. In this case, the assignment would provide the number, or range of numbers, to be used in the parameter.

Selection

This is the operation of picking one or more items from a list in order to narrow the scope of a component element.

Refinement

For all functional component elements the PP/ST author is permitted to limit the set of acceptable implementations by specifying additional detail in order to meet a security objective. Refinement of an element consists of adding these technical details.

Within a ST, the meanings of the terms subject and object might need to be explained for the TOE to be meaningful, and are therefore subject to refinement.

Like the other operations, refinement does not levy any completely new requirements. It applies an elaboration, interpretation, or a special meaning to a requirement, rule, constant or condition based on security objectives. Refinement shall only further restrict the set of possible acceptable functions or mechanisms to implement the requirements, but never increase it. Refinement does not allow new requirements to be created, and therefore does not increase the list of dependencies associated with a component. The PP/ST author must be careful that the dependency needs of other requirements that depend on this requirement, are satisfied.

Security assurance requirements

Structures

The following subclauses describe the constructs used in representing the assurance classes, families, components, and EALs along with the relationships among them.

Note that the most abstract collection of assurance requirements is referred to as a class. Each class contains assurance families, which then contain assurance components, which in turn contain assurance elements. Classes and families are used to provide a taxonomy for classifying assurance requirements, while components are used to specify assurance requirements in a PP/ST.

Class structure

Each assurance class is assigned a unique name. The name indicates the topics covered by the assurance class.

A unique short form of the assurance class name is also provided. This is the primary means for referencing the assurance class. The convention adopted is an "A" followed by two letters related to the class name.

Class introduction

Each assurance class has an introductory subclause that describes the composition of the class and contains supportive text covering the intent of the class.

Assurance families

Each assurance class contains at least one assurance family. The structure of the assurance families is described in the following subclause.

Assurance family structure

Family name

Every assurance family is assigned a unique name. The name provides descriptive information about the topics covered by the assurance family. Each assurance family is placed within the assurance class that contains other families with the same intent.

A unique short form of the assurance family name is also provided. This is the primary means used to reference the assurance family. The convention adopted is that the short form of the class name is used, followed by an underscore, and then three letters related to the family name.

Objectives

The objectives subclause of the assurance family presents the intent of the assurance family.

This subclause describes the objectives, particularly those related to the CC assurance paradigm, that the family is intended to address. The description for the assurance family is kept at a general level. Any specific details required for objectives are incorporated in the particular assurance component.

Component levelling

Each assurance family contains one or more assurance components. This subclause of the assurance family describes the components available and explains the distinctions between them. Its main purpose is to differentiate between the assurance components once it has been determined that the assurance family is a necessary or useful part of the assurance requirements for a PP/ST.

Assurance families containing more than one component are levelled and rationale is provided as to how the components are levelled. This rationale is in terms of scope, depth, and/or rigour.

Application notes

The application notes subclause of the assurance family, if present, contains additional information for the assurance family. This information should be of particular interest to users of the assurance family (e.g. PP and ST authors, designers of TOEs, evaluators). The presentation is informal and covers, for example, warnings about limitations of use and areas where specific attention may be required.

Assurance components

Each assurance family has at least one assurance component. The structure of the assurance components is provided in the following subclause.

Assurance component structure

The relationship between components within a family is highlighted using a bolding convention. Those parts of the requirements that are new, enhanced or modified beyond the requirements of the previous component within a hierarchy are bolded. The same bolding convention is also used for dependencies.

Component identification

The component identification subclause provides descriptive information necessary to identify, categorise, register, and reference a component.

Every assurance component is assigned a unique name. The name provides descriptive information about the topics covered by the assurance component. Each assurance component is placed within the assurance family that shares its security objective.

A unique short form of the assurance component name is also provided. This is the primary means used to reference the assurance component. The convention used is that the short form of the family name is used, followed by a period, and then a numeric character. The numeric characters for the components within each family are assigned sequentially, starting from 1.

Objectives

The objectives subclause of the assurance component, if present, contains specific objectives for the particular assurance component. For those assurance components that have this subclause, it presents the specific intent of the component and a more detailed explanation of the objectives.

Application notes

The application notes subclause of an assurance component, if present, contains additional information to facilitate the use of the component.

Dependencies

Dependencies among assurance components arise when a component is not selfsufficient, and relies upon the presence of another component.

Each assurance component provides a complete list of dependencies to other assurance components. Some components may list "No dependencies", to indicate that no dependencies have been identified. The components depended upon may have dependencies on other components.

The dependency list identifies the minimum set of assurance components which are relied upon. Components which are hierarchical to a component in the dependency list may also be used to satisfy the dependency.

In specific situations the indicated dependencies might not be applicable. The PP/ST author, by providing rationale for why a given dependency is not applicable, may elect not to satisfy that dependency.

Assurance elements

A set of assurance elements is provided for each assurance component. An assurance element is a security requirement which, if further divided, would not yield a meaningful evaluation result. It is the smallest security requirement recognised in the CC.

Each assurance element is identified as belonging to one of the three sets of assurance elements:

a) Developer action elements: the activities that shall be performed by the developer. This set of actions is further qualified by evidential material referenced in the following set of elements. Requirements for developer actions are identified by appending the letter "D" to the element number.

b) Content and presentation of evidence elements: the evidence required, what the evidence shall demonstrate, and what information the evidence shall convey. Requirements for content and presentation of evidence are identified by appending the letter "C" to the element number.

c) Evaluator action elements: the activities that shall be performed by the evaluator. This set of actions explicitly includes confirmation that the requirements prescribed in the content and presentation of evidence elements have been met. It also includes explicit actions and analysis that shall be performed in addition to that already performed by the developer. Implicit evaluator actions are also to be performed as a result of developer action elements which are not covered by content and presentation of evidence requirements. Requirements for evaluator actions are identified by appending the letter "E" to the element number.

The developer actions and content and presentation of evidence define the assurance requirements that are used to represent a developer's responsibilities in demonstrating assurance in the TOE security functions. By meeting these requirements, the developer can increase confidence that the TOE satisfies the functional and assurance requirements of a PP or ST.

The evaluator actions define the evaluator's responsibilities in the two aspects of evaluation. The first aspect is validation of the PP/ST, in accordance with the classes APE and ASE in clauses 4 and 5. The second aspect is verification of the TOE's conformance with its functional and assurance requirements. By demonstrating that the PP/ST is valid and that the requirements are met by the TOE, the evaluator can provide a basis for confidence that the TOE will meet its security objectives.

The developer action elements, content and presentation of evidence elements, and explicit evaluator action elements, identify the evaluator effort that shall be expended in verifying the security claims made in the ST of the TOE.

Assurance elements

Each element represents a requirement to be met. These statements of requirements are intended to be clear, concise, and unambiguous. Therefore, there are no compound sentences: each separable requirement is stated as an individual element.

The elements have been written using the normal dictionary meaning for the terms used, rather than using a number of predefined terms as shorthand which results in implicit requirements. Therefore, elements are written as explicit requirements, with *no reserved terms*.

In contrast to CC Part 2, neither assignment nor selection operations are relevant for elements in CC Part 3; however, refinements may be made to Part 3 elements as required.

EAL structure

Each EAL is assigned a unique name. The name provides descriptive information about the intent of the EAL.

A unique short form of the EAL name is also provided. This is the primary means used to reference the EAL.

Objectives

The objectives subclause of the EAL presents the intent of the EAL.

Application notes

The application notes subclause of the EAL, if present, contains information of particular interest to users of the EAL (e.g. PP and ST authors, designers of TOEs targeting this EAL, evaluators). The presentation is informal and covers, for example, warnings about limitations of use and areas where specific attention may be required.

Assurance components

A set of assurance components have been chosen for each EAL. A higher level of assurance than that provided by a given EAL can be achieved by:

a) including additional assurance components from other assurance families; or

b) replacing an assurance component with a higher level assurance component from the same assurance family.

Relationship between assurances and assurance levels

While assurance components further decompose into assurance elements, assurance elements cannot be individually referenced by assurance levels.

Component taxonomy

This Part 3 contains classes of families and components that are grouped on the basis of related assurance. The assurance families in this Part 3 are all linearly hierarchical, although linearity is not a mandatory criterion for assurance families that may be added in the future.

Protection Profile and Security Target evaluation criteria class structure

The requirements for protection profile and security target evaluation are treated as assurance classes and are presented using the similar structure as that used for the other assurance classes, described below. One notable difference is the absence of a component levelling subclause in the associated family descriptions. The reason is that each family has only a single component and therefore no levelling has occurred.

Narrative summaries for the APE families can be found in CC Part 1, annex B, subclauses B.2.2 through B.2.8, whereas narrative summaries for the ASE families can be found in CC Part 1, annex C, subclauses C.2.2 through C.2.9.

Evaluation assurance levels

The Evaluation Assurance Levels (EALs) provide an increasing scale that balances the level of assurance obtained with the cost and feasibility of acquiring that degree of assurance. The CC approach identifies the separate concepts of assurance in a TOE at the end of the evaluation, and of maintenance of that assurance during the operational use of the TOE.

It is important to note that not all families and components from CC Part 3 are included in the EALs. This is not to say that these do not provide meaningful and desirable assurances. Instead, it is expected that these families and components will be considered for augmentation of an EAL in those PPs and STs for which they provide utility.

Evaluation assurance level (EAL) overview

As outlined in the next subclause, seven hierarchically ordered evaluation assurance levels are defined in the CC for the rating of a TOE's assurance. They are hierarchically ordered inasmuch as each EAL represents more assurance than all lower EALs. The increase in assurance from EAL to EAL is accomplished by *substitution* of a hierarchically higher assurance component from the same assurance family (i.e. increasing rigour, scope, and/or depth) and from the *addition* of assurance components from other assurance families (i.e. adding new requirements).

These EALs consist of an appropriate combination of assurance components as described in clause 2 of Part 3. More precisely, each EAL includes no more than one component of each assurance family and all assurance dependencies of every component are addressed.

While the EALs are defined in the CC, it is possible to represent other combinations of assurance. Specifically, the notion of "augmentation" allows the addition of assurance components (from assurance families not already included in the EAL) or the substitution of assurance components (with another hierarchically higher assurance component in the same assurance family) to an EAL. Of the assurance constructs defined in the CC, only EALs may be augmented. The notion of an "EAL minus a constituent assurance component" is not recognised by the standard as a valid claim. Augmentation carries with it the obligation on the part of the claimant to justify the utility and added value of the added assurance component to the EAL. An EAL may also be extended with explicitly stated assurance requirements.

Evaluation assurance level details

The following subclauses provide definitions of the EALs, highlighting differences between the specific requirements and the prose characterisations of those requirements using bold type.

Evaluation assurance level 1 (EAL1) – functionally tested

EAL1 is applicable where some confidence in correct operation is required, but the threats to security are not viewed as serious. It will be of value where independent assurance is required to support the contention that due care has been exercised with respect to the protection of personal or similar information.

EAL1 provides an evaluation of the TOE as made available to the customer, including independent testing against a specification, and an examination of the guidance documentation provided. It is intended that an EAL1 evaluation could be successfully conducted without assistance from the developer of the TOE, and for minimal outlay.

An evaluation at this level should provide evidence that the TOE functions in a manner consistent with its documentation, and that it provides useful protection against identified threats.

Assurance components

EAL1 provides a basic level of assurance by an analysis of the security functions using a functional and interface specification and guidance documentation, to understand the security behaviour. The analysis is supported by independent testing of the TOE security functions.

This EAL provides a meaningful increase in assurance over an unevaluated IT product or system.

Evaluation assurance level 2 (EAL2) – structurally tested

EAL2 requires the co-operation of the developer in terms of the delivery of design information and test results, but should not demand more effort on the part of the developer than is consistent with good commercial practice. As such it should not require a substantially increased investment of cost or time.

EAL2 is therefore applicable in those circumstances where developers or users require a low to moderate level of independently assured security in the absence of ready availability of the complete development record. Such a situation may arise when securing legacy systems, or where access to the developer may be limited.

Assurance components

EAL2 provides assurance by an analysis of the security functions, using a functional and interface specification, guidance documentation and the high-level design of the TOE, to understand the security behaviour.

The analysis is supported by independent testing of the TOE security functions, evidence of developer testing based on the functional specification, selective independent confirmation of the developer test results, strength of function analysis, and evidence of a developer search for obvious vulnerabilities (e.g. those in the public domain).

EAL2 also provides assurance through a configuration list for the TOE, and evidence of secure delivery procedures.

This EAL represents a meaningful increase in assurance from EAL1 by requiring developer testing, a vulnerability analysis, and independent testing based upon more detailed TOE specifications.

Evaluation assurance level 3 (EAL3) – methodically tested and checked

EAL3 permits a conscientious developer to gain maximum assurance from positive security engineering at the design stage without substantial alteration of existing sound development practices.

EAL3 is applicable in those circumstances where developers or users require a moderate level of independently assured security, and require a thorough investigation of the TOE and its development without substantial re-engineering.

Assurance components

EAL3 provides assurance by an analysis of the security functions, using a functional and interface specification, guidance documentation, and the high-level design of the TOE, to understand the security behaviour.

The analysis is supported by independent testing of the TOE security functions, evidence of developer testing based on the functional specification and high-level design, selective independent confirmation of the developer test results, strength of function analysis, and evidence of a developer search for obvious vulnerabilities (e.g. those in the public domain).

EAL3 also provides assurance through the use of development environment controls, TOE configuration management, and evidence of secure delivery procedures.

This EAL represents a meaningful increase in assurance from EAL2 by requiring more complete testing coverage of the security functions and mechanisms and/or procedures that provide some confidence that the TOE will not be tampered with during development.

Evaluation assurance level 4 (EAL4) — methodically designed, tested, and reviewed

EAL4 permits a developer to gain maximum assurance from positive security engineering based on good commercial development practices which, though rigorous, do not require substantial specialist knowledge, skills, and other resources. EAL4 is the highest level at which it is likely to be economically feasible to retrofit to an existing product line.

EAL4 is therefore applicable in those circumstances where developers or users require a moderate to high level of independently assured security in conventional commodity TOEs and are prepared to incur additional security-specific engineering costs.

Assurance components

EAL4 provides assurance by an analysis of the security functions, using a functional and complete interface specification, guidance documentation, the high-level and low-level design of the TOE, and a subset of the implementation, to understand the security behaviour. Assurance is additionally gained through an informal model of the TOE security policy.

The analysis is supported by independent testing of the TOE security functions, evidence of developer testing based on the functional specification and high-level design, selective independent confirmation of the developer test results, strength of function analysis, evidence of a developer search for vulnerabilities, and an independent vulnerability analysis demonstrating resistance to penetration attackers with a low attack potential.

EAL4 also provides assurance through the use of development environment controls and additional TOE configuration management including automation, and evidence of secure delivery procedures.

This EAL represents a meaningful increase in assurance from EAL3 by requiring more design description, a subset of the implementation, and improved mechanisms and/or procedures that provide confidence that the TOE will not be tampered with during development or delivery.

Evaluation assurance level 5 (EAL5) — semiformally designed and tested

EAL5 permits a developer to gain maximum assurance from security engineering based upon rigorous commercial development practices supported by moderate application of specialist security engineering techniques. Such a TOE will probably be designed and developed with the intent of achieving EAL5 assurance. It is likely that the additional costs attributable to the EAL5 requirements, relative to rigorous development without the application of specialised techniques, will not be large.

EAL5 is therefore applicable in those circumstances where developers or users require a high level of independently assured security in a planned development and require a rigorous development approach without incurring unreasonable costs attributable to specialist security engineering techniques.

Assurance components

EAL5 provides assurance by an analysis of the security functions, using a functional and complete interface specification, guidance documentation, the high-level and low-level design of the TOE, and all of the implementation, to understand the security behaviour. Assurance is additionally gained through a formal model of the TOE security policy and a semiformal presentation of the functional specification and high-level design and a semiformal demonstration of correspondence between them. A modular TOE design is also required.

The analysis is supported by independent testing of the TOE security functions, evidence of developer testing based on the functional specification, high-level design and low-level design, selective independent confirmation of the developer test results, strength of function analysis, evidence of a developer search for vulnerabilities, and an independent vulnerability analysis demonstrating resistance to penetration attackers with a moderate attack potential. The analysis also includes validation of the developer's covert channel analysis.

EAL5 also provides assurance through the use of a development environment controls, and comprehensive TOE configuration management including automation, and evidence of secure delivery procedures.

This EAL represents a meaningful increase in assurance from EAL4 by requiring semiformal design descriptions, the entire implementation, a more structured (and hence analysable) architecture, covert channel analysis, and improved mechanisms and/or procedures that provide confidence that the TOE will not be tampered with during development.

Evaluation assurance level 6 (EAL6) — semiformally verified design and tested

EAL6 permits developers to gain high assurance from application of security engineering techniques to a rigorous development environment in order to produce a premium TOE for protecting high value assets against significant risks.

EAL6 is therefore applicable to the development of security TOEs for application in high risk situations where the value of the protected assets justifies the additional costs.

Assurance components

EAL6 provides assurance by an analysis of the security functions, using a functional and complete interface specification, guidance documentation, the high-level and low-level design of the of the TOE, and a structured presentation of the implementation, to understand the security behaviour. Assurance is additionally gained through a formal model of the TOE security policy, a semiformal presentation of the functional specification, high-level design, and low-level design and a semiformal demonstration of correspondence between them. A modular and layered TOE design is also required.

The analysis is supported by independent testing of the TOE security functions, evidence of developer testing based on the functional specification, high-level design and low-level design, selective independent confirmation of the developer test results, strength of function analysis, evidence of a developer search for vulnerabilities, and an independent vulnerability analysis demonstrating resistance to penetration attackers with a high attack potential. The analysis also includes validation of the developer's systematic covert channel analysis.

EAL6 also provides assurance through the use of a structured development process, development environment controls, and comprehensive TOE configuration management including complete automation, and evidence of secure delivery procedures.

This EAL represents a meaningful increase in assurance from EAL5 by requiring more comprehensive analysis, a structured representation of the implementation, more architectural structure (e.g. layering), more comprehensive independent vulnerability analysis, systematic covert channel identification, and improved configuration management and development environment controls.

Evaluation assurance level 7 (EAL7) – formally verified design and tested

EAL7 is applicable to the development of security TOEs for application in extremely high risk situations and/or where the high value of the assets justifies the higher costs. Practical application of EAL7 is currently limited to TOEs with tightly focused security functionality that is amenable to extensive formal analysis.

Assurance components

EAL7 provides assurance by an analysis of the security functions, using a functional and complete interface specification, guidance documentation, the high-level and low-level design of the TOE, and a structured presentation of the implementation, to understand the security behaviour. Assurance is additionally gained through a formal model of the TOE security policy, a formal presentation of the functional specification and high-level design, a semiformal presentation of the low-level design, and formal and semiformal demonstration of correspondence between them, as appropriate. A modular, layered and simple TOE design is also required.

The analysis is supported by independent testing of the TOE security functions, evidence of developer testing based on the functional specification high-level design, low-level design and implementation representation, complete independent confirmation of the developer test results, strength of function analysis, evidence of a developer search for vulnerabilities, and an independent vulnerability analysis demonstrating resistance to penetration attackers with a high attack potential. The analysis also includes validation of the developer's systematic covert channel analysis.

EAL7 also provides assurance through the use of a structured development process, development environment controls, and comprehensive TOE configuration management including complete automation, and evidence of secure delivery procedures.

This EAL represents a meaningful increase in assurance from EAL6 by requiring more comprehensive analysis using formal representations and formal correspondence, and comprehensive testing.

✦   ✦   ✦

The Cost Analysis Process

Many of our day-to-day decisions, as they pertain to the design and development of new systems and the reengineering of existing systems, are based on technical performance-related factors alone. Economic considerations, if addressed at all, have dealt primarily with initial, procurement and acquisition costs only, and not the "downstream" costs associated with system operation and maintenance support. Yet these downstream costs, which often constitute a significant portion of the total life-cycle cost of a system, are highly influenced by the decisions made in the early phases of system development. In other words, the early decision-making process must consider the total spectrum of costs if economic benefits are to be gained in the long term. The consequences of the short-term approach often practiced in the past have been rather detrimental overall, as conveyed in Section 1.2 (Chapter 1 of Benjamin S. Blanchard, *System Engineering Management, 3rd Edition*, New York, NY: Wiley Publishing, Inc., 2003). Total cost visibility, as illustrated in Figure E-1, is a must if the risks associated with the decision-making process are to be properly assessed.

Life-cycle costing includes the consideration of all future costs associated with research and development (i.e., design), construction, production, distribution, system operation, sustaining maintenance and support, system retirement, and material disposal and/or recycling. It involves the costs of all technical and management activities throughout the system life cycle; that is, customer activities, producer and/or contractor activities, supplier activities, and consumer or user activities. Although the influencing of these costs can best be realized during the early phases in the development of a new system, as conveyed in Figure E-2, benefits can also be gained through the identification and evaluation of high-cost contributors for existing systems already in use. In other words, the applications and benefits that can be gained through the accomplishment of life cycle cost analyses are numerous, as shown in Figure 3.40 (Chapter 3 of Benjamin S. Blanchard, *System Engineering Management, 3rd Edition*).

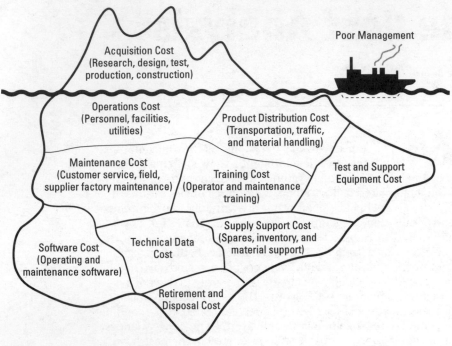

Figure E-1: Total cost visibility.

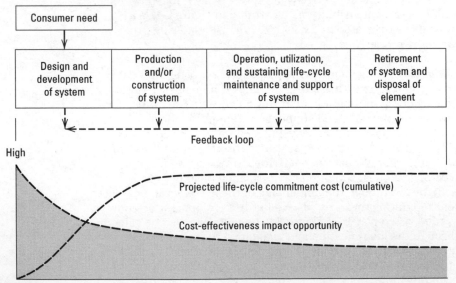

Figure E-2: Opportunity for impacting cost-effectiveness in the system life cycle.

In performing a life cycle cost analysis, there is a series of steps one may follow. These steps are briefly described in Figure 3.38 and are conveyed in the context of the overall process in Figure 3.41. The purpose of this appendix is to provide some additional explanation covering each of the steps identified in Figure 3.38 (Chapter 3 of Benjamin S. Blanchard, *System Engineering Management, 3rd Edition*).

Define System Requirements

The first step in the performance of a life-cycle cost analysis is to define the problem, identify the proposed technical solution, describe the operational requirements and the maintenance concept for the system, identify the critical technical performance measures (TPMs), and describe the system configuration in functional terms; that is, the process described in Sections 2.1 through 2.7 (Chapter 2 of Benjamin S. Blanchard, *System Engineering Management, 3rd Edition*). Depending on where one is in the system life cycle, the definition may be rather cursory or more in-depth. In any event, the basic system requirements must be defined in order to provide the necessary structure for the analysis, and the assumptions that are made at this point may have a significant impact on the results.

In Figure E-3, it is assumed that a ground vehicle in development requires the incorporation of a communications capability. Multiple quantities of the vehicle will be deployed to three different geographical locations, (i.e., 20, 20, and 25 at each location, respectively), performing a variety of missions. Although there are variations from one location to the next, it is assumed that each vehicle will be utilized on the average of 4 hours per day, 360 days per year. The equipment must enable communication with other vehicles at a range of at least 200 miles, overhead aircraft at an altitude of up to 10,000 feet, and with a centralized area communications facility. The system must have a reliability mean time between failure (MTBF) of 450 hours, a corrective maintenance downtime (M̄ct) of 30 minutes, a maintenance labor hours per system operating hour (MLH/OH) requirement of 0.2, and a unit life-cycle cost not to exceed $20,000. The equipment will be functionally packaged in units (i.e., Units A, B, and C) and, in the event of failure, the problem will be isolated to the unit level, faulty units will be removed and replaced with spares and sent back to the intermediate level of maintenance for corrective action, and so on.

In the figure, the system operational requirements and the maintenance concept have been defined to the depth that will allow for the accomplishment of a life-cycle cost analysis during the late conceptual design or early preliminary design phase. The next step is to describe the system, and the mission(s) that is to be performed, in functional terms by accomplishing a top-level functional analysis. See Figure 2.12 (Chapter 2 of Benjamin S. Blanchard, *System Engineering Management, 3rd Edition*). The communication system can be described in a similar manner, followed with an evaluation of each functional block to determine the resource requirements that will provide the basis for functional costing; see Figure 2.17 (Chapter 2 of Benjamin S. Blanchard, *System Engineering Management, 3rd Edition*).

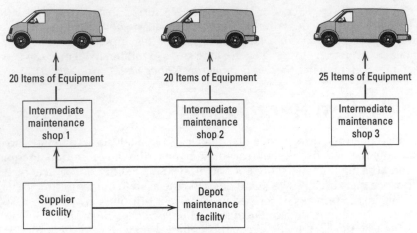

20 Items of Equipment   20 Items of Equipment   25 Items of Equipment

Intermediate maintenance shop 1   Intermediate maintenance shop 2   Intermediate maintenance shop 3

Supplier facility   Depot maintenance facility

Deployment: Three geographical areas (flat and mountainous terrain)
Utilization: Four (4) hr/day throughout year (average)

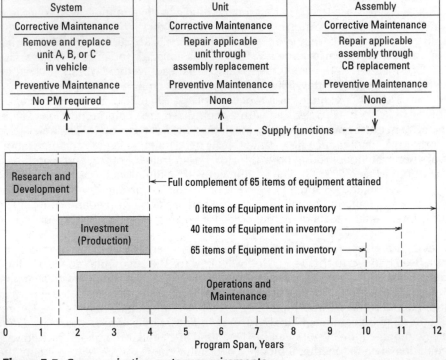

Organizational	Intermediate	Depot
System	Unit	Assembly
Corrective Maintenance	Corrective Maintenance	Corrective Maintenance
Remove and replace unit A, B, or C in vehicle	Repair applicable unit through assembly replacement	Repair applicable assembly through CB replacement
Preventive Maintenance	Preventive Maintenance	Preventive Maintenance
No PM required	None	None

Supply functions

Research and Development

Full complement of 65 items of equipment attained

0 items of Equipment in inventory

Investment (Production)

40 items of Equipment in inventory

65 items of Equipment in inventory

Operations and Maintenance

0 1 2 3 4 5 6 7 8 9 10 11 12
Program Span, Years

Figure E-3: Communication system requirements.

Describe the System Life Cycle and Identify the Major Activities in Each Phase

Given the definition of system requirements and the identification of functions, it is appropriate to provide a time line for these requirements in terms of the life cycle. In Figure E-3, the planned life cycle is 12 years. In other words, it is assumed that there is a need for the communication system and the functions that are to be performed for a 12-year period. Although this planning horizon may change (as requirements change), a baseline must be established. Thus, the 12-year period and the major activities identified in the figure will be assumed herein. The activity categories identified in the figure (i.e., research and development, investment/production, and operations and maintenance) form the basis for the development of a cost breakdown structure (CBS).

Develop a Cost Breakdown Structure (CBS)

The functions described through the functional analysis can be broken down into subfunctions, categories of work, work packages, and, ultimately, the identification of physical elements. From a planning and management perspective, it is necessary to establish a top-down framework that will allow for the initial allocation and subsequent collecting, accumulating, organizing, and computing of costs. For a typical project, this may lead to the development of a work breakdown structure (WBS) prepared to show, in a hierarchical manner, all of the elements of work that are necessary to complete a given program. As shown in Section 6.2.4 (Figure 6.12), a summary work breakdown structure (SWBS) may be developed initially, followed by one or more individual contract work breakdown structures (CWBS) designed to address specific elements of work that are covered through some form of a contractual arrangement (Chapter 6 of Benjamin S. Blanchard, *System Engineering Management, 3rd Edition*). It is the SWBS that provides a good basis for the development of a cost breakdown structure (CBS) used in life-cycle cost analyses, primarily because its intent is to cover all future activities and associated costs; that is, research and development, construction/production, distribution, operation and maintenance support, and retirement activities.

The CBS is intended to show all future functions/activities, broken down to the depth necessary to provide the appropriate level of visibility and tailored to the system configuration in question. Ultimately, the CBS will lead to the identification of a product and/or a process, with the objective of establishing a structure that can be initially used for the top-down allocation of costs during the conceptual design phase (refer to Section 2.8) and subsequently for the bottom-up collection of costs for the purposes of accomplishing a life-cycle cost analysis (Chapter 2 of Benjamin S. Blanchard, *System Engineering Management, 3rd Edition*). Figure E-4 provides an illustration of a sample cost breakdown structure (CBS), and Figure E-5 provides an abbreviated example showing how each category of the CBS should be

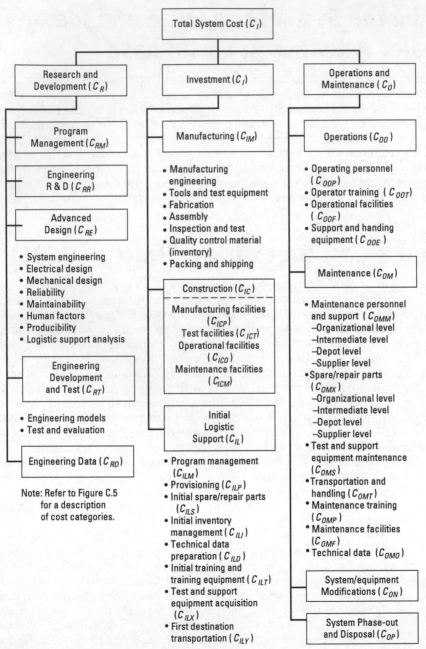

Figure E-4: Cost breakdown structure (CBS).

Source: Logistics Engineering and Management 4/E by Blanchard, Benjamin S., © Reprinted with permission of Pearson Education, Inc., Upper Saddle River, NJ.

Cost Category (Figure C.4)	Method of Determination (Quantitive Expression)	Cost Category Description and Justification
Total system cost (C)	$C = C_R + C_I + C_0$ $C_R = R$ and D cost C_I = Investment cost C_0 = Operations and maintenance cost	Includes all future costs associated with the acquisition, utilization, and subsequent disposal of system/equipment.
Research and development (C_R)	$CR = C_{RM} + C_{RR} + C_{RE} + C_{RT} + C_{RD}$ C_{RM} = Program management cost C_{RR} = Advanced R&D cost C_{RE} = Engineering design cost C_{RT} = Equipment development/ test cost C_{RD} = Engineering data cost	Includes all costs associated with conceptual/feasibility studies, basic research, advanced research and development, engineering design, fabrication and test of engineering prototype models (hardware) and associated documentation. Also covers all related program management functions. These cost are basically nonrecurring.
Investment (C_I)	$C_I = C_{IM} + C_{IC} + C_{IL}$ C_{IM} = System/equipment manufacturing cost C_{IC} = System construction cost C_{IL} = Cost of initial logistic support	Includes all costs associated with the acquisition of systems/ equipment (once design and development have been completed). Specifically, this covers manufacturing (recurring and nonrecurring), manufacture-ing management, system construction, and initial logistic support.
Operations and maintenance (C_0)	$C_0 = C_{OO} + C_{OM} + C_{ON} + C_{OP}$ C_{OO} = Cost of system/equipment life-cycle operations C_{OM} = Cost of system/equipment life-cycle maintenance C_{ON} = Cost of system/equipment life-cycle modifications C_{OP} = Cost of system/equipment phase-out and disposal	Includes all costs associated with the operation and maintenance support of the system throughout its life cycle subsequent to equipment delivery in the field. Specific categories cover the cost of system operation, maintenance, sustaining logic support, equipment modifications, and system/ equipment phase-out and disposal. Costs are generally determined for each year throughout the life cycle.

Figure E-5: Description of cost categories (partial).

Cost Category (Reference Figure C.4)	Method of Determination (Quantitive Expression)	Cost Category Description and Justification
Transportation and handling cost (C_{OMT})	$C_{OMT} = [(C_T)(Q_T) + (C_P)(Q_T)]$ C_T = Cost of transportation C_P = Cost of packing Q_T = Quantity of one-way shipments $C_T = [(W)(C_{TS})]$ W = Weight of item (lb) C_{TS} = Shipping cost ($/lb) C_{TS} will, of course, vary with the distance (in miles) of the one-way shipment. $C_P = [(W)(C_{TP})]$ C_{TP} = Packing cost ($/lbs) Packing cost and weight will vary depending on whether reuseable containers are employed.	Initial (first destination) transportation and handling costs are covered in C_{ILY}. This category includes all sustaining transportation and handling (or packing and shipping) between organizational, intermediate, depot, and supplier facilities in support of maintenance operations. This includes the return of faulty material items to a higher echelon; the transportation of items to a higher echelon for preventive maintenance (overhaul, calibration); and the shipment of spare/repair parts, personnel, data, etc., from the supplier to forward echelons.
Maintenance training cost (C_{OMP})	$C_{OMP} = [(Q_{SM})(T_T)(C_{TOM})]$ Q_{SM} = Quantity of maintenance students C_{TOM} = Cost of maintenance training ($/student-week) T_T = Duration of training program (weeks)	Initial maintenance training cost is included in C_{ILT}. This category covers the *formal* training of personnel assigned to maintain the prime equipment, test and support equipment, and training equipment. Such training is accomplished on a periodic basis throughout the system life-cycle to cover personnel replacements due to attrition. Total costs include instructor time; supervision; student pay and allowances while in school; training facilities (allocation of portion of facility required specifically for formal training); training aids and data; and student transportation as applicable.
Operational facilities cost (C_{OOF})	$C_{OOF} = [(C_{PPE} + C_U)(\% \text{ Allocation}) \times (N_{OS})]$ C_{PPE} = Cost of operational facility support ($/site) C_U = Cost of utilities ($/site) N_{OS} = Number of operational sites *Alternative Approach* $C_{OOF} = [(C_{PPF})(N_{OS})(S_0)]$ C_{PPF} = Cost of operational facility space ($/square foot/site). Utility cost allocation is included. S_0 = Facility space requirements (square feet)	Initial acquisition cost for operational facilities is included in C_{ICO}. This category covers the annual recurring costs associated with the occupancy and maintenance (repair, paint, etc.) of operational facilities throughout the system life-cycle. Utility costs are also included. Facility and utility costs are proportionately allocated to each system.

Figure E-5: Description of cost categories (partial).

described in terms of what is included, how the costs are calculated, and the basis for accomplishing such. The CBS provides a vehicle for looking at costs from a functional perspective. As one proceeds with the life-cycle cost analysis, costs are estimated for each year in the planned life cycle and are summarized for each category in the CBS.[1]

Estimate the Costs for Each Phase of the Life Cycle

The next step is to estimate the costs, by category in the CBS, for each year in the system life cycle. Such estimates must consider the effects of inflation, learning curves when repetitive processes or activities occur, and any other factors that are likely to cause changes in cost, either upward or downward. Cost estimates may be derived from a combination of accounting records, cost projections, supplier proposals, and predictions in one form or another.

In Figure E-2, the early stages in the system life cycle is the preferred time to commence with the estimation of costs, because it is at this point when the greatest impact on total system life-cycle cost can be realized. However, the availability of good historical cost data at this time is almost nonexistent in most organizations, particularly the type of data that pertain to the downstream activities of operations and support for similar systems in the past. Thus, one must depend heavily on the use of various cost-estimating methods in order to accomplish the end objectives.

As shown in Figure E-6, as the system configuration becomes better defined in a developmental effort, the use of direct engineering and manufacturing standard factors based on past experience can be applied, as is the case for any "cost-to-complete" projection on a typical project today (e.g., cost per labor hour). On the other hand, in the earlier stages of the life cycle when the system configuration has not been well defined, the analyst must rely on the use of a combination of analogous and/or parametric methods developed from experience with similar systems in the past. The objective is to collect data on a "known entity," identify the major functions that have been accomplished and the costs associated with these functions, relate the costs in terms of some functional or physical parameter of the system, and then use this relationship in attempting to estimate the costs for a new system.

---

[1] The cost breakdown structure (CBS) should be tailored to the system in question. In Figure 3.39, another example is presented. If the system is very "software-intensive," then Category Crs should be broken down to show more detail. If the system is very "operator-intensive" (e.g., a ground radar tracking station requiring a large number of operating personnel), then Category Cop should be expanded. On the other hand, if Category Cin is too detailed for the purposes of a given analysis, then one can summarize the costs accordingly. The objective is to provide visibility relative to key functional activities.

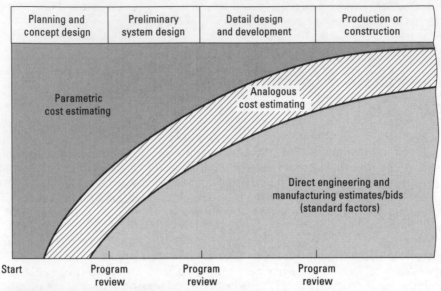

Planning and concept design	Preliminary system design	Detail design and development	Production or construction

Parametric cost estimating

Analogous cost estimating

Direct engineering and manufacturing estimates/bids (standard factors)

Start   Program review   Program review   Program review

Figure E-6: Cost estimation by program phase.

A goal is to identify the applicable technical performance measures (TPMs) for the system in question and estimate the cost per a given level of performance (e.g., cost per unit of product output, cost per mile of range, cost per unit of weight, cost per volume of capacity used, cost per unit of acceleration, cost per functional output, etc.). Costs can be related to the appropriate blocks in the functional description of the system. Figures E-7 and E-8 provide some simple illustrations of considerations in cost estimating. However, care must be exercised to ensure that the historical information used in the development of cost-estimating relationships (CERs) is relevant to the system configuration being evaluated today. CERs based on the mission and performance characteristics of one system may not be appropriate for another system configuration, even if the configuration is similar in a physical sense. Thus, costs must be related from a functional perspective.

To be effective in total cost management (and in the accomplishment of cost-effectiveness analyses) requires full-cost visibility allowing for the traceability of all costs back to the activities, processes, and/or products that generate these costs. In the traditional accounting structures employed in most organizations, a large percentage of the total cost cannot be traced back to the "causes." For example, "overhead" or "indirect" costs, which often constitute more than 50% of the total, include a lot of management costs, supporting organization costs, and other costs that are difficult to trace and assign to specific objects (refer to the overhead costs in Figure 6.27).

(Chapter 6 of Benjamin S. Blanchard, *System Engineering Management, 3rd Edition*.)
With these costs being allocated across the board, it is impossible to identify the
actual "causes" and to pinpoint the true high-cost contributors. As a result, the concept of activity-based costing (ABC) has been introduced.[2]

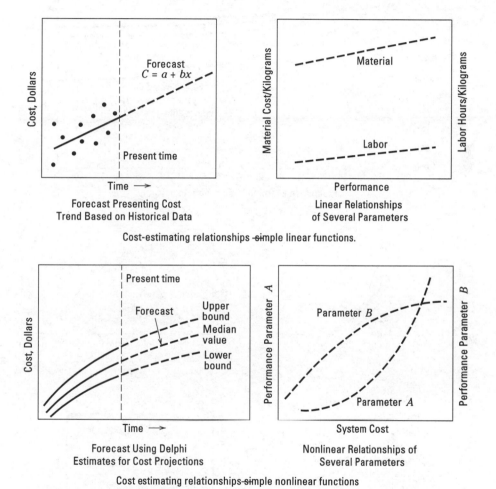

Cost-estimating relationships ~~simple~~ linear functions.

Cost estimating relationships ~~simple~~ nonlinear functions

Figure E-7: Cost-estimating relationships (CERs).

[2] J. R. Canada, W. G. Sullivan, and J. A. White, *Capital Investment Analysis for Engineering and
Management, 2d ed.* (Upper Saddle River, NJ: Prentice-Hall, 1996); and P. T. Kidd, *Agile
Manufacturing: Forging New Frontiers* (Reading, MA: Addison-Wesley, 1994).

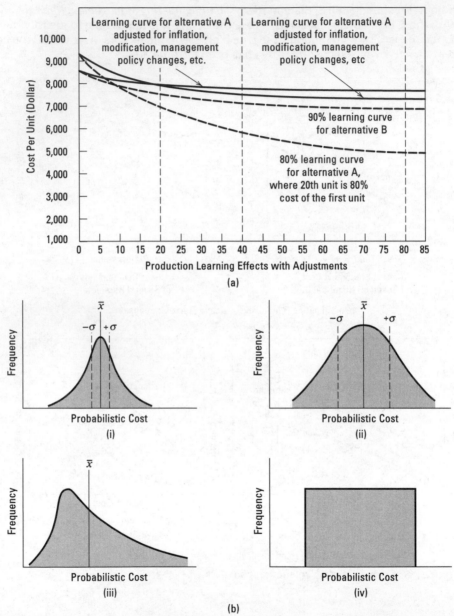

Figure E-8: (a) Learning curves and (b) the probabilistic aspects of costs.

Activity-based costing is a methodology directed toward the detailing and assignment of costs to the items that cause them to occur. The objective is to enable the "traceability" of all applicable costs to the process or product that generates these costs. The ABC approach allows for the initial allocation and later assessment of costs by function. It was developed to deal with the shortcomings of the traditional management accounting structure whereby large overhead factors are assigned to all elements of the enterprise across the board without concern for whether they directly apply or not. More specifically, the principles of ABC include the following:

1. Costs are directly traceable to the applicable cost-generating process, product, and/or a related object. Cause-and effect relationships are established between a cost factor and a specific process or activity.

2. There is no distinction between direct and indirect (or overhead) costs. Generally, 80 to 90% of all costs are traceable, and nontraceable costs are not allocated across the board, but are allocated directly to the organizational unit(s) involved in the project.

3. Costs can be easily allocated on a functional basis; that is, according to the functions identified in Figures 2.13 and 2.16 (Chapter 2 of Benjamin S. Blanchard, *System Engineering Management, 3rd Edition*, 0-471-29176-5). It is relatively easy to develop cost-estimating relationships in terms of the cost of activities per some activity measure (i.e., the cost per unit output).

4. The emphasis in ABC is on "resource consumption" (versus "spending"). Processes and products consume activities, and activities consume resources. With resource consumption being the focus, the ABC approach facilitates the evaluation of day-to-day decisions in terms of their impact on resource consumption downstream.

5. The ABC approach fosters the establishment of cause-and-effect relationships and, as such, enables the identification of the "high-cost contributors." Areas of risk can be identified with some specific activity and the decisions that are being made associated with this activity.

6. The ABC approach tends to eliminate some of the cost doubling (or double counting) that occurs in attempting to differentiate as to what should be included as a "direct" cost or as an "indirect" cost. Without the necessary visibility, there is the potential for including the same costs in both categories.

Implementation of the ABC approach, or something of an equivalent nature, is essential if one is to do a good job of total cost management. Costs are tied to objects and viewed over the long term, and such a perspective facilitates the life-cycle cost-analysis process. An objective for the future is to persuade the accounting organizations in various companies/agencies to supplement their current end-of-year financial reporting structure to include the objectives of ABC.

Select a Computer-Based Model to Facilitate the Analysis Process

In the selection of a computer-based model, one must ensure that the tool selected does what is expected, is sensitive to the problem at hand, and allows for the visibility needed in addressing the system as an entity, as well as any of its major components on an individual-by-individual basis. The model must enable the comparison of many different alternatives and aid in selecting the best among them rapidly and efficiently. The model must be comprehensive, allowing for the integration of many different parameters; flexible in structure, enabling the analyst to look at the system as a whole or any part of the system; reliable, in terms of repeatability of results; and user-friendly. So often, one selects a computer model based on the material in the advertising brochure alone, purchases the necessary equipment and software, uses the model to manipulate data, and believes in the output results without having any idea as to how the model was put together, the internal analytical relationships established, whether it is sensitive to the variation of input parameters in terms of output results, and so on. The results of a recent survey indicate that there are more than 350 computer-based tools available in the commercial marketplace and intended for use in accomplishing different levels of analysis. Each was developed on a relatively "independent" or "isolated" basis in terms of selected platform, language used, input data needs, and interface requirements. In general, the models do not "talk to each other," are not user-friendly, and are too complex for use in early system design and development.

When using a model, it is essential that the analyst become thoroughly familiar with the tool, know how it was put together, and understand what it can do. For the purposes of accomplishing a life-cycle cost analysis, it may be appropriate to select a group of models, combined as illustrated in Figure E-9 and integrated in such a manner that will enable the analyst to look not only at the cost for the system overall, but at some of the key functional areas representing potential high-cost contributors. The model(s) must be structured around the cost breakdown structure (CBS) and in such a way that will allow the analyst to look at the costs associated with each of the major functions. Further, it must be adaptable for use during the early stages of conceptual design as well as in the detail design and development phase.

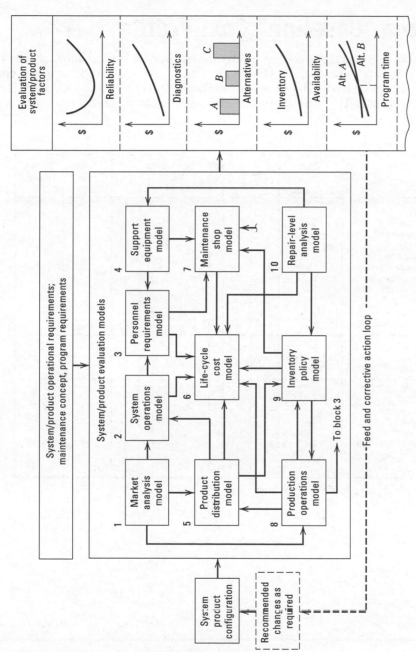

Figure E-9: Example models in life cycle costing.

Develop a "Baseline" Cost Profile

Through the application of various estimating methods, the costs for each CBS category and for each year in the system life cycle are projected in the form of a cost profile. The worksheet format presented in Figure E-10 can serve as a vehicle for recording costs, and the profile shown in Figure E-11 can represent the anticipated cost stream.

Program Activity	Cost Category Designation	Cost by Program Year ($)												Total cost ($)	Percent Contr. (%)
		1	2	3	4	5	6	7	8	9	10	11	12		
Alternative A 1. Research and development cost a. Program management b. Engineering design c. Electrical design d. Engineering data 2. 3. Others	C_R C_{RM} C_{RE} C_{RED} C_{RD}														
Total Actual Cost	C														
Total P. V. Cost (10%)	$C_{(10)}$														
Alternative B 1. Research and development cost a. Program management b. Engineering design Etc.	C_R C_{RM} C_{RE}														

Figure E-10: Cost collection worksheet.

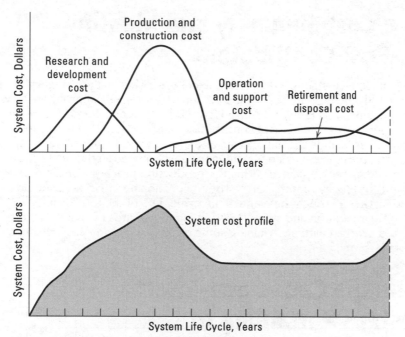

Figure E-11: Development of a cost profile.

In developing profiles, it may be feasible to start out with one presented in terms of constant dollars first (i.e., the costs for each year in the future presented in terms of today's dollars) and then develop a second profile by adding the appropriate inflationary factors for each year to reflect a budgetary stream. In comparing alternative profiles, the appropriate economic analysis methods must be applied in converting the various alternative cost streams to the present value or to the point in time when the decision is to be made in selecting a preferred approach. It is necessary to evaluate alternative profiles on the basis of some form of equivalence.[3]

---

[3] The treatment of cost streams considering the "time value of money" is presented in most texts dealing with engineering economy. Two good references are (1) G. J. Thuesen, and W. J. Fabrycky, *Engineering Economy, 9th ed.* (Prentice-Hall, 2001); and (2) W. J. Fabrycky, G. J. Thuesen, and D. Verma, *Economic Decision Analysis* (Upper Saddle River, NJ: Prentice-Hall, 1997). See Appendix A of Benjamin S. Blanchard, *System Engineering Management, 3rd edition*, for additional references.

Develop a Cost Summary and Identify the High-Cost Contributors

In order to gain some insight pertaining to the costs for each major category in the CBS and to readily identify the high-cost contributors, it may be appropriate to view the results presented in a tabular form. In Figure E-12, the costs for each category are identified along with the percent contribution of each. Note that in this example, the high-cost areas include the initial costs associated with "facilities" and "capital equipment" and the operating and maintenance costs related to the "inspection and test" function being accomplished within the production process. For the purposes of product and/or process improvement, the "inspection and test" area should be investigated further. Through the planned life cycle, 17% of the total cost is attributed to the operation and support of this functional area of activity, and the analyst should proceed with determining some of the reasons for this high cost.

Determine the Cause-and-Effect Relationships Pertaining to High-Cost Areas

Given the presentation of costs (and the percent contribution) as shown in Figure E-12, the next step is to determine the likely "causes" for these costs. The analyst will need to revisit the CBS, the assumptions made leading to the determination of the costs, and the cost-estimating relationships utilized in the process. It is to be hoped that an activity-based costing (ABC) approach was used, or something of an equivalent nature, to ensure the proper traceability. The application of an Ishikawa cause-and-effect diagram, as illustrated in Figure B.4 (Appendix B of Benjamin S. Blanchard, *System Engineering Management, 3rd Edition*)), may be used to assist in pinpointing the actual "causes." The problem may relate to an unreliable product requiring a lot of maintenance, an inadequate procedure or poor process, a supplier problem, or other such factors.

Conduct a Sensitivity Analysis

To properly assess the results of the life cycle cost analysis, the validity of the data presented in Figure E-12, and the associated risks, the analyst needs to conduct a sensitivity analysis. One may challenge the accuracy of the input data (i.e., the factors used and the assumptions made in the beginning) and determine their impact

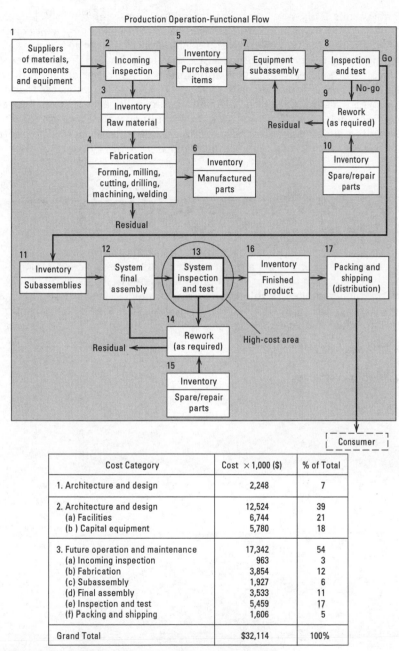

Figure E-12: Life cycle cost breakdown summary.

Cost Category	Cost × 1,000 ($)	% of Total
1. Architecture and design	2,248	7
2. Architecture and design	12,524	39
(a) Facilities	6,744	21
(b) Capital equipment	5,780	18
3. Future operation and maintenance	17,342	54
(a) Incoming inspection	963	3
(b) Fabrication	3,854	12
(c) Subassembly	1,927	6
(d) Final assembly	3,533	11
(e) Inspection and test	5,459	17
(f) Packing and shipping	1,606	5
Grand Total	$32,114	100%

on the analysis results. This may be accomplished by identifying the critical factors at the input stage (i.e., those parameters that are suspected as having a large impact on the results), introducing variations over a designated range at the input stage, and determining the differences in output. For example, if the initially predicted reliability MTBF value is "suspect," it may be appropriate to apply variations at the input stage and determine the changes in cost at the output. The object is to identify those areas in which a small variation at the input stage will cause a large delta cost at the output. This, in turn, leads to the identification of potential high-risk areas, a necessary input to the risk management program described in Section 6.7 (Chapter 6 of Benjamin S. Blanchard, *System Engineering Management, 3rd Edition*).

Conduct a Pareto Analysis to Identify Major Problem Areas

With the objective of implementing a program for continuous process improvement, the analyst may wish to rank the problem areas on the basis of relative importance, the higher-ranked problems requiring immediate attention. This may be facilitated through the conductance of a Pareto analysis and the construction of a diagram, as shown in Figure E-13.

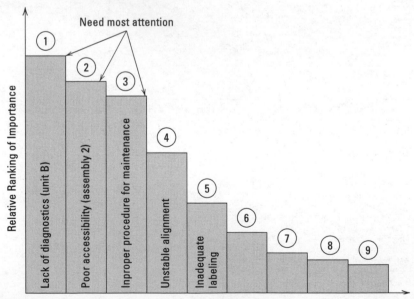

Figure E-13: Pareto ranking of major problem areas.

Identify and Evaluate Feasible Alternatives

In referring to the requirements for the communication system described in the "Define System Requirements" section, two potential suppliers were considered through a feasibility analysis; that is, Configuration A and Configuration B. Figure E-14 presents a budgetary profile for each of three configurations, with Configuration C being eliminated for noncompliance. For the purposes of comparison on an equivalent basis, the two remaining profiles have been converted to reflect present value costs. Figure E-15 presents a breakdown summary of these present value costs by major CBS category and identifies the relative percent contribution of each category in terms of the total. A 10% interest rate was used in determining present value costs.

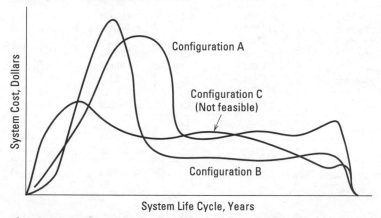

Figure E-14: Alternative cost profiles.

Although a review of Figure E-15 might lead one to immediately select Configuration A as being preferable, prior to making such a decision the analyst needs to project the two cost streams in terms of the life cycle and determine the point in time when Configuration A assumes the position of preference. Figure E-16 shows the results of a break-even analysis, and it appears that A is preferable after approximately 6.5 years into the future. The question arises as to whether this break-even point is reasonable in considering the type of system and its mission, the technologies being utilized, the length of the planned life cycle, and the possibilities of obsolescence. For systems in which the requirements are changing constantly and obsolescence may become a problem 2 to 3 years hence, the selection of Configuration B may be preferable. On the other hand, for larger systems with longer life cycles (e.g., 10 to 15 years and greater), the selection of Configuration A may be the best choice.

In this case, it is assumed that Configuration A is preferable. However, when the cost profile for this alternative is converted back to a budgetary projection, it is realized that a further reduction of cost is necessary. This, in turn, leads the analyst to Figure E-15 and the identification of potential high-cost contributors. Given that a large percentage of the total cost of a system is often in the area of maintenance and support,

Cost Category	Configuration A		Configuration B	
	Present Cost	% of Total	Present Cost	% of Total
1. Research and development	$70,219	7.8	$53,246	4.2
(a) Management	9,374	1.1	9,252	0.8
(b) Engineering	45.552	5.0	28,731	2.3
(c) Test and evaluation	12,176	1.4	12,153	0.9
(d) Technical data	3,117	0.3	3,110	0.2
2. Production (investment)	407,114	45.3	330,885	26.1
(a) Construction	45,553	5.1	43,227	3.4
(b) Manufacturing	362,261	40.2	287,658	22.7
3. Operations and maintenance	422,217	46.7	883,629	69.4
(a) Operations	37,811	4.2	39,301	3.1
(b) Maintenance	382,106	42.5	841,108	66.3
-maintenance personnel	210,659	23.4	407,219	32.2
-spares/repair parts	103,520	11.5	228,926	18.1
-Test equipment	47,713	5.3	131,747	10.4
-Transportation	14,404	1.6	51,838	4.1
-Maintenance training	1,808	0.2	2,125	0.1
-Facilities	900	0.1	1,021	Neg.
-Field data	3,102	0.4	18,232	1.4
4. Phaseout and disposal	2,300	0.2	3,220	0.3
Grand Total	$900,250	100%	$1,267,760	100%

Figure E-15: Life cycle cost breakdown (evaluation of two alternative configurations).

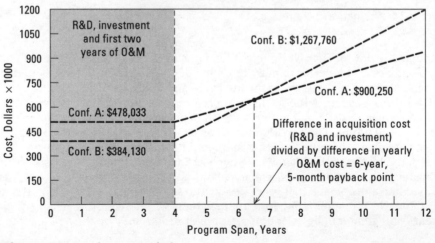

Figure E-16: Break-even analysis.

one might investigate the categories of "maintenance personnel" and "spares/repair parts," representing 23.4% and 11.5% of the total cost, respectively. The next step is to identify the applicable cause-and-effect relationships and to determine the actual causes for such high costs. This may be accomplished by being able to trace the costs back to a specific function, process, product design characteristic, or a combination thereof. The analyst also needs to refer back to the CBS and review how the costs were initially derived and the assumptions that were made at the input stage. In any event, the problem may be traced back to a specific function in which the resource consumption is high, a particular component of the system with low reliability and requiring frequent maintenance, a specific system operating function that requires a lot of highly skilled personnel, or something of an equivalent nature. Various design tools can be effectively utilized to aid in making visible these causes and to help identify areas where improvement can be made; for example, the failure mode, effects, and criticality analysis, the detailed task analysis, and so on.

As a final step, the analyst needs to conduct a sensitivity analysis to properly assess the risks associated with the selection of Configuration A. Figure E-17 illustrates this approach as it applies to the "maintenance personnel" and "spares/repair parts" categories addressed earlier. The objective is to identify those areas where a small variation at the input stage will cause a large delta cost at the output. This, in turn, leads to the identification of potential high-risk areas, a necessary input to the risk management program described in Section 6.7 (Chapter 6 of Benjamin S. Blanchard, *System Engineering Management, 3rd Edition*).

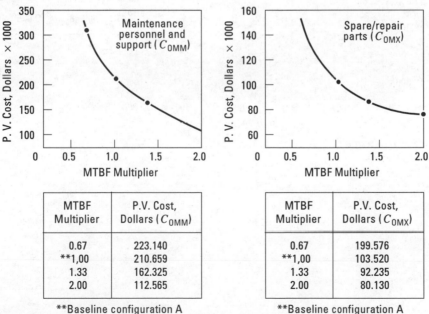

MTBF Multiplier	P.V. Cost, Dollars (C_{OMM})
0.67	223.140
**1,00	210.659
1.33	162.325
2.00	112.565

**Baseline configuration A

MTBF Multiplier	P.V. Cost, Dollars (C_{OMX})
0.67	199.576
**1,00	103.520
1.33	92.235
2.00	80.130

**Baseline configuration A

Figure E-17: Sensitivity analysis.

Select a Preferred Design Approach

The cost issue having been addressed, it is necessary to view the results in the context of the overall cost-effectiveness balance illustrated in Figure 1.24 (Chapter 1 of Benjamin S. Blanchard, *System Engineering Management, 3rd Edition*). Although the emphasis here has been on cost, the ultimate decision-making process must consider both sides of the spectrum; that is, cost and effectiveness. For example, the two alternative communication system configurations discussed earlier must meet the reliability and cost goals described in the "Define System Requirements" section. In Figure E-18, the shaded area represents the allowable design trade-off "space," and the alternatives must be viewed not only in terms of cost, but in terms of reliability as well. As indicated in Section 3.4.12, the ultimate decision may be based on an overall cost-effectiveness ratio or some equivalent metric (Chapter 3 of Benjamin S. Blanchard, *System Engineering Management, 3rd Edition*).

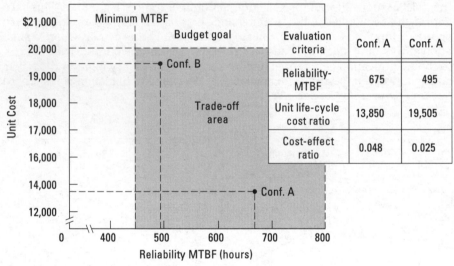

Evaluation criteria	Conf. A	Conf. A
Reliability-MTBF	675	495
Unit life-cycle cost ratio	13,850	19,505
Cost-effect ratio	0.048	0.025

Figure E-18: Reliability versus unit life cycle cost.

✦   ✦   ✦

National Information Assurance (IA) Glossary

CNSS Instruction No. 4009 (www.nstissc.gov/Assets/pdf/4009.pdf). Used by permission.

Revised May 2003

THIS DOCUMENT PROVIDES MINIMUM STANDARDS. FURTHER IMPLEMENTATION MAY BE REQUIRED BY YOUR DEPARTMENT OR AGENCY.

FOREWORD

1. The CNSS Glossary Working Group recently convened to review terms submitted by the CNSS membership since the Glossary was last published in September 2000. This edition incorporates those terms.

2. We recognize that, to remain useful, a glossary must be in a continuous state of coordination, and we encourage your review and welcome your comments. The goal of the Glossary Working Group is to keep pace with changes in information assurance terminology and to meet regularly for consideration of comments.

3. The Working Group would like your help in keeping this glossary up to date as new terms come into being and old terms fall into disuse or change meaning. Some terms from the previous version were deleted, others updated or added, and some are identified as candidates

for deletion (C.F.D.). If a term you still find valuable and need in your environment has been deleted, please resubmit the term with a definition based on the following criteria: (a) specific relevance to the security of information systems; (b) economy of words; (c) accuracy; and (d) clarity. Use these same criteria to recommend any changes to existing definitions or suggest new terms. In all cases, send your suggestions to the CNSS Secretariat via e-mail or fax at the numbers found below.

4. Representatives of the CNSS may obtain additional copies of this instruction at the address listed below.

/s/

MICHAEL V. HAYDEN

Lieutenant General, USAF

National Manager

Committee on National Security Systems

CNSS Secretariat (I42) . National Security Agency . 9800 Savage Road . STE 6716 . Ft Meade MD 20755-6716 (410) 854-6805 . UFAX: (410) 854-6814 nstissc@radium.ncsc.mil **CNSS Instruction No. 4009**

SECTION I

TERMS AND DEFINITIONS

A

A1 Highest level of trust defined in the Orange Book (C.F.D.) (Department of Defense Trusted Computer System Evaluation Criteria, DoD 5200.28-STD).

access Opportunity to make use of an information system (IS) resource.

access control Limiting access to information system resources only to authorized users, programs, processes, or other systems.

access control list (ACL) Mechanism implementing discretionary and/or mandatory access control between subjects and objects.

access control mechanism Security safeguard designed to detect and deny unauthorized access and permit authorized access in an IS.

access control officer (ACO) Designated individual responsible for limiting (C.F.D.) access to information systems resources.

access level Hierarchical portion of the security level used to identify the sensitivity of IS data and the clearance or authorization of users. Access level, in conjunction with the nonhierarchical categories, forms the sensitivity label of an object. See category.

access list (IS) Compilation of users, programs, or processes and the access levels and types to which each is authorized. (COMSEC) Roster of individuals authorized admittance to a controlled area.

access period Segment of time, generally expressed in days or (C.F.D.) weeks, during which access rights prevail.

access profile Associates each user with a list of protected objects the user may access.

access type Privilege to perform action on an object. Read, write, execute, append, modify, delete, and create are examples of access types.

accountability (IS) Process of tracing IS activities to a responsible source. (COMSEC) Principle that an individual is entrusted to safeguard and control equipment, keying material, and information and is answerable to proper authority for the loss or misuse of that equipment or information.

accounting legend code (ALC) Numeric code used to indicate the minimum accounting controls required for items of accountable COMSEC material within the COMSEC Material Control System.

accounting number Number assigned to an item of COMSEC material to facilitate its control.

accreditation Formal declaration by a Designated Accrediting Authority (DAA) that an IS is approved to operate in a particular security mode at an acceptable level of risk, based on the implementation of an approved set of technical, managerial, and procedural safeguards.

accreditation boundary See security perimeter.

accreditation package Product comprised of a System Security Plan (SSP) and a report documenting the basis for the accreditation decision.

accrediting authority Synonymous with Designated Accrediting Authority (DAA).

add-on security Incorporation of new hardware, software, or firmware safeguards in an operational IS.

advanced encryption (AES) standard FIPS approved cryptographic algorithm that is a symmetric block cypher using cryptographic key sizes of 128, 192, and 256 bits to encrypt and decrypt data in blocks of 128 bits.

advisory Notification of significant new trends or developments regarding the threat to the IS of an organization. This notification may include analytical insights into trends, intentions, technologies, or tactics of an adversary targeting ISs.

alert Notification that a specific attack has been directed at the IS of an organization.

alternate COMSEC custodian Individual designated by proper authority to perform the duties of the COMSEC custodian during the temporary absence of the COMSEC custodian.

alternative work site Government-wide, national program allowing Federal employees to work at home or at geographically convenient satellite offices for part of the work week (e.g., telecommuting).

anti-jam Measures ensuring that transmitted information can be received despite deliberate jamming attempts.

anti-spoof Measures preventing an opponent's participation in an IS.

application Software program that performs a specific function directly for a user and can be executed without access to system control, monitoring, or administrative privileges.

assembly (COMSEC) Group of parts, elements, subassemblies, or circuits that are removable items of COMSEC equipment.

assurance Measure of confidence that the security features, practices, procedures, and architecture of an IS accurately mediates and enforces the security policy.

attack Attempt to gain unauthorized access to an IS's services, resources, or information, or the attempt to compromise an IS's integrity, availability, or confidentiality.

Attack Sensing and Warning (AS&W) Detection, correlation, identification, and characterization of intentional unauthorized activity with notification to decision makers so that an appropriate response can be developed.

attention character (C.F.D.) In Trusted Computing Base (TCB) design, a character entered from a terminal that tells the TCB the user wants a secure communications path from the terminal to some trusted code to provide a secure service for the user.

audit Independent review and examination of records and activities to assess the adequacy of system controls, to ensure compliance with established policies and operational procedures, and to recommend necessary changes in controls, policies, or procedures.

audit trail Chronological record of system activities to enable the reconstruction and examination of the sequence of events and/or changes in an event.

authenticate To verify the identity of a user, user device, or other entity, or the integrity of data stored, transmitted, or otherwise exposed to unauthorized modification in an IS, or to establish the validity of a transmission.

authentication Security measure designed to establish the validity of a transmission, message, or originator, or a means of verifying an individual's authorization to receive specific categories of information.

authentication system Cryptosystem or process used for authentication.

authenticator Means used to confirm the identity of a station, originator, or individual.

authorization Access privileges granted to a user, program, or process.

authorized vendor Manufacturer of INFOSEC equipment authorized to produce quantities in excess of contractual requirements for direct sale to eligible buyers. Eligible buyers are typically U.S. Government organizations or U.S. Government contractors.

Authorized Vendor Program (AVP) Program in which a vendor, producing an INFOSEC product under contract to NSA, is authorized to produce that product in numbers exceeding the contracted requirements for direct marketing and sale to eligible buyers. Eligible buyers are typically U.S. Government organizations or U.S. Government contractors. Products approved for marketing and sale through the AVP are placed on the Endorsed Cryptographic Products List (ECPL).

automated security monitoring Use of automated procedures to ensure security controls are not circumvented or the use of these tools to track actions taken by subjects suspected of misusing the IS.

automatic remote rekeying Procedure to rekey a distant crypto-equipment electronically without specific actions by the receiving terminal operator.

availability Timely, reliable access to data and information services for authorized users.

B

back door Hidden software or hardware mechanism used to circumvent security controls. Synonymous with trap door.

backup Copy of files and programs made to facilitate recovery, if necessary.

banner Display on an IS that sets parameters for system or data use.

Bell-La Padula security model (C.F.D.) Formal-state transition model of a computer security policy that describes a formal set of access controls based on information sensitivity and

subject authorizations See star (*) property and simple security property.

benign Condition of cryptographic data that cannot be compromised by human access.

benign environment Nonhostile environment that may be protected from external hostile elements by physical, personnel, and procedural security countermeasures.

beyond A1 (C.F.D.) Level of trust defined by the DoD Trusted Computer System Evaluation Criteria (TCSEC) to be beyond the state-of-the-art technology. It includes all the A1-level features plus additional ones not required at the A1-level.

binding Process of associating a specific communications terminal with a specific cryptographic key or associating two related elements of information.

biometrics Automated methods of authenticating or verifying an individual based upon a physical or behavioral characteristic.

bit error rate Ratio between the number of bits incorrectly received and the total number of bits transmitted in a telecommunications system.

BLACK Designation applied to information systems, and to associated areas, circuits, components, and equipment, in which national security information is encrypted or is not processed.

boundary Software, hardware, or physical barrier that limits access to a system or part of a system.

brevity list List containing words and phrases used to shorten messages.

browsing Act of searching through IS storage to locate or acquire information, without necessarily knowing the existence or format of information being sought.

bulk encryption Simultaneous encryption of all channels of a multichannel telecommunications link.

C

call back Procedure for identifying and authenticating a remote IS terminal, whereby the host system disconnects the terminal and reestablishes contact. Synonymous with dial back.

canister Type of protective package used to contain and dispense key in punched or printed tape form.

capability (C.F.D.) Protected identifier that both identifies the object and specifies the access rights to be allowed to the subject who possesses the capability. In a capability-based system, access to protected objects such as files is granted if the would-be subject possesses a capability for the object.

cascading Downward flow of information through a range of security levels greater than the accreditation range of a system network or component.

category Restrictive label applied to classified or unclassified information to limit access.

CCI assembly Device embodying a cryptographic logic or other COMSEC design that NSA has approved as a Controlled Cryptographic Item (CCI). It performs the entire COMSEC function, but depends upon the host equipment to operate.

CCI component Part of a Controlled Cryptographic Item (CCI) that does not perform the entire COMSEC function but depends upon the host equipment, or assembly, to complete and operate the COMSEC function.

CCI equipment Telecommunications or information handling equipment that embodies a Controlled Cryptographic Item (CCI) component or CCI assembly and performs the entire COMSEC function without dependence on host equipment to operate.

central office of record (COR) Office of a federal department or agency that keeps records of accountable COMSEC material held by elements subject to its oversight.

certificate Digitally signed document that binds a public key with an identity. The certificate contains, at a minimum, the identity of the issuing Certification Authority, the user identification information, and the user's public key.

certificate management Process whereby certificates (as defined above) are generated, stored, protected, transferred, loaded, used, and destroyed.

certificate revocation list (CRL) List of invalid certificates (as defined above) that have been revoked by the issuer.

certification Comprehensive evaluation of the technical and nontechnical security safeguards of an IS to support the accreditation process that establishes the extent to which a particular design and implementation meets a set of specified security requirements.

certification authority (CA) Trusted entity authorized to create, sign, and issue public key certificates. By digitally signing each certificate issued, the user's identity is certified, and the association of the certified identity with a public key is validated.

certification authority workstation (CAW) Commercial-off-the-shelf (COTS) workstation with a trusted operating system and special purpose application software that is used to issue certificates.

certification package Product of the certification effort documenting the detailed results of the certification activities.

certification test and evaluation (CT&E) Software and hardware security tests conducted during development of an IS.

certified TEMPEST authority (CTTA) technical An experienced, technically qualified U.S. Government employee who has met established certification requirements in accordance with CNSS (NSTISSC)-approved criteria and has been appointed by a U.S. Government Department or Agency to fulfill CTTA responsibilities.

certifier Individual responsible for making a technical judgment of the system's compliance with stated requirements, identifying and assessing the risks associated with operating the system, coordinating the certification activities, and consolidating the final certification and accreditation packages.

challenge and reply authentication Prearranged procedure in which a subject requests authentication of another and the latter establishes validity with a correct reply.

checksum Value computed on data to detect error or manipulation during transmission. See hash total.

check word Cipher text generated by cryptographic logic to detect failures in cryptography.

cipher Any cryptographic system in which arbitrary symbols or groups of symbols, represent units of plain text, or in which units of plain text are rearranged, or both.

cipher text Enciphered information.

cipher text auto-key (CTAK) Cryptographic logic that uses previous cipher text to generate a key stream.

ciphony Process of enciphering audio information, resulting in encrypted speech.

classified information Information that has been determined pursuant to Executive Order 12958 or any predecessor Order, or by the Atomic Energy Act of 1954, as amended, to require protection against unauthorized disclosure and is marked to indicate its classified status.

clearance Formal security determination by an authorized adjudicative office that an individual is authorized access, on a need to know basis, to a specific level of collateral classified information (TOP SECRET, SECRET, CONFIDENTIAL).

clearing Removal of data from an IS, its storage devices, and other peripheral devices with storage capacity, in such a way that the data may not be reconstructed using common system capabilities (i.e., keyboard strokes); however, the data may be reconstructed using laboratory methods. Cleared media may be reused at the same classification level or at a higher level. Overwriting is one method of clearing.

client Individual or process acting on behalf of an individual who makes requests of a guard or dedicated server. The client's requests to the guard or dedicated server can involve data transfer to, from, or through the guard or dedicated server.

closed security environment Environment providing sufficient assurance that applications and equipment are protected against the introduction of malicious logic during an IS life cycle. Closed security is based upon a system's developers, operators, and maintenance personnel having sufficient clearances, authorization, and configuration control.

code (COMSEC) System of communication in which arbitrary groups of letters, numbers, or symbols represent units of plain text of varying length.

code book Document containing plain text and code equivalents in a systematic arrangement, or a technique of machine encryption using a word substitution technique.

code group Group of letters, numbers, or both in a code system used to represent a plain text word, phrase, or sentence.

code vocabulary Set of plain text words, numerals, phrases, or sentences for which code equivalents are assigned in a code system.

cold start Procedure for initially keying crypto-equipment.

collaborative computing Applications and technology (e.g. , whiteboarding, group conferencing) that allow two or more individuals to share information real time in an inter- or intra-enterprise environment.

command authority Individual responsible for the appointment of user representatives for a department, agency, or organization and their key ordering privileges.

Commercial COMSEC Evaluation Program (CCEP) Relationship between NSA and industry in which NSA provides the COMSEC expertise (i.e., standards, algorithms, evaluations, and guidance) and industry provides design, development, and production capabilities to produce a type 1 or type 2 product. Products developed under the CCEP may include modules, subsystems, equipment, systems, and ancillary devices.

Common Criteria Provides a comprehensive, rigorous method for specifying security function and assurance requirements for products and systems. (International Standard ISO/IEC 5408, Common Criteria for Information Technology Security Evaluation [ITSEC])

common fill device One of a family of devices developed to read-in, transfer, or store key.

communications cover Concealing or altering of characteristic communications patterns to hide information that could be of value to an adversary.

communications deception Deliberate transmission, retransmission, or alteration of communications to mislead an adversary's interpretation of the communications. See imitative communications deception and manipulative communications deception.

communications profile Analytic model of communications associated with an organization or activity. The model is prepared from a systematic examination of communications content and patterns, the functions they reflect, and the communications security measures applied.

communications security (COMSEC) Measures and controls taken to deny unauthorized individuals information derived from telecommunications and to ensure the authenticity of such telecommunications. Communications security includes cryptosecurity, transmission security, emission security, and physical security of COMSEC material.

community risk Probability that a particular vulnerability will be exploited within an interacting population and adversely impact some members of that population.

compartmentalization A nonhierarchical grouping of sensitive information used to control access to data more finely than with hierarchical security classification alone.

compartmented mode Mode of operation wherein each user with direct or indirect access to a system, its peripherals, remote terminals, or remote hosts has all of the following: (a) valid security clearance for the most restricted information processed in the system; (b) formal access approval and signed nondisclosure agreements for that information which a user is to have access; and (c) valid need-to-know for information which a user is to have access.

compromise Type of incident where information is disclosed to unauthorized individuals or a violation of the security policy of a system in which unauthorized intentional or unintentional disclosure, modification, destruction, or loss of an object may have occurred.

compromising emanations Unintentional signals that, if intercepted and analyzed, would disclose the information transmitted, received, handled, or otherwise processed by information systems equipment. See TEMPEST.

computer abuse Intentional or reckless misuse, alteration, disruption, or destruction of information processing resources.

computer cryptography Use of a crypto-algorithm program by a computer to authenticate or encrypt/decrypt information.

computer security Measures and controls that ensure confidentiality, integrity, and availability of IS assets including hardware, software, firmware, and information being processed, stored, and communicated.

computer security incident See incident.

computer security subsystem Hardware/software designed to provide computer security features in a larger system environment.

computing environment Workstation or server (host) and its operating system, peripherals, and applications.

COMSEC account Administrative entity, identified by an account number, used to maintain accountability, custody, and control of COMSEC material.

COMSEC account audit Examination of the holdings, records, and procedures of a COMSEC account ensuring all accountable COMSEC material is properly handled and safeguarded.

COMSEC aid COMSEC material that assists in securing telecommunications and is required in the production, operation, or maintenance of COMSEC systems and their components. COMSEC keying material, callsign/frequency systems, and supporting documentation, such as operating and maintenance manuals, are examples of COMSEC aids.

COMSEC boundary Definable perimeter encompassing all hardware, firmware, and software components performing critical COMSEC functions, such as key generation and key handling and storage.

COMSEC chip set Collection of NSA approved microchips.

COMSEC control program Computer instructions or routines controlling or affecting the externally performed functions of key generation, key distribution, message encryption/decryption, or authentication.

COMSEC custodian Individual designated by proper authority to be responsible for the receipt, transfer, accounting, safeguarding, and destruction of COMSEC material assigned to a COMSEC account.

COMSEC end-item Equipment or combination of components ready for use in a COMSEC application.

COMSEC equipment Equipment designed to provide security to telecommunications by converting information to a form unintelligible to an unauthorized interceptor and, subsequently, by reconverting such information to its original form for authorized recipients; also, equipment designed specifically to aid in, or as an essential element of, the conversion process. COMSEC equipment includes crypto-equipment, crypto-ancillary equipment, cryptoproduction equipment, and authentication equipment.

COMSEC facility Authorized and approved space used for generating, storing, repairing, or using COMSEC material.

COMSEC incident See incident.

COMSEC insecurity COMSEC incident that has been investigated, evaluated, and determined to jeopardize the security of COMSEC material or the secure transmission of information.

COMSEC manager Individual who manages the COMSEC resources of an organization.

COMSEC material Item designed to secure or authenticate telecommunications. COMSEC material includes, but is not limited to key, equipment, devices, documents, firmware, or software that embodies or describes cryptographic logic and other items that perform COMSEC functions.

COMSEC Material Control System (CMCS) Logistics and accounting system through which COMSEC material marked "CRYPTO" is distributed, controlled, and safeguarded. Included are the COMSEC central offices of record, cryptologistic depots, and COMSEC accounts. COMSEC material other than key may be handled through the CMCS.

COMSEC modification See information systems security equipment modification.

COMSEC module Removable component that performs COMSEC functions in a telecommunications equipment or system.

COMSEC monitoring Act of listening to, copying, or recording transmissions of one's own official telecommunications to analyze the degree of security.

COMSEC profile Statement of COMSEC measures and materials used to protect a given operation, system, or organization.

COMSEC survey Organized collection of COMSEC and communications information relative to a given operation, system, or organization.

COMSEC system data Information required by a COMSEC equipment or system to enable it to properly handle and control key.

COMSEC training Teaching of skills relating to COMSEC accounting, use of COMSEC aids, or installation, use, maintenance, and repair of COMSEC equipment.

concept of operations (CONOP) Document detailing the method, act, process, or effect of using an IS.

confidentiality Assurance that information is not disclosed to unauthorized individuals, processes, or devices.

configuration control Process of controlling modifications to hardware, firmware, software, and documentation to ensure the IS is protected against improper modifications prior to, during, and after system implementation.

configuration management Management of security features and assurances through control of changes made to hardware, software, firmware, documentation, test, test fixtures, and test documentation throughout the life cycle of an IS.

confinement channel See covert channel.

confinement property (C.F.D.) Synonymous with star (*) property.

contamination Type of incident involving the introduction of data of one security classification or security category into data of a lower security classification or different security category.

contingency key Key held for use under specific operational conditions or in support of specific contingency plans.

contingency plan Plan (C.F.D.) maintained for emergency response, backup operations, and post-disaster recovery for an IS, to ensure the availability of critical resources and to facilitate the continuity of operations in an emergency situation.

continuity of operations plan (COOP) Plan for continuing an organization's (usually a headquarters element) essential functions at an alternate site and performing those functions for the duration of an event with little or no loss of continuity before returning to normal operations.

controlled access protection The C2 level of protection described in the Trusted Computer System Evaluation Criteria (Orange Book). Its major characteristics are: individual accountability, audit, access control, and object reuse. These characteristics will be embodied in the NSA produced, Controlled Access Protection Profile (and its related follow-on profiles).

controlled cryptographic item (CCI) Secure telecommunications or information handling equipment, or associated cryptographic component, that is unclassified but governed by a special set of control requirements. Such items are marked "CONTROLLED CRYPTOGRAPHIC ITEM" or, where space is limited, "CCI."

controlled interface Mechanism that facilitates the adjudication of different interconnected system security policies (e.g., controlling the flow of information into or out of an interconnected system).

controlled security mode (C.F.D.) See multilevel security.

controlled sharing (C.F.D.) Condition existing when access control is applied to all users and components of an IS.

controlled space Three-dimensional space surrounding IS equipment, within which unauthorized individuals are denied unrestricted access and are either escorted by authorized individuals or are under continuous physical or electronic surveillance.

controlling authority Official responsible for directing the operation of a cryptonet and for managing the operational use and control of keying material assigned to the cryptonet.

cooperative key generation Electronically exchanging functions of locally generated, random components, from which both terminals of a secure circuit construct traffic encryption key or key encryption key for use on that circuit.

cooperative remote rekeying Synonymous with manual remote rekeying.

correctness proof A mathematical proof of consistency between a specification and its implementation.

countermeasure Action, device, procedure, technique, or other measure that reduces the vulnerability of an IS.

covert channel Unintended and/or unauthorized communications path that can be used to transfer information in a manner that violates an IS security policy. See overt channel and exploitable channel.

covert channel analysis Determination of the extent to which the security policy model and subsequent lower-level program descriptions may allow unauthorized access to information.

covert storage channel Covert channel involving the direct or indirect writing to a storage location by one process and the direct or indirect reading of the storage location by another process. Covert storage channels typically involve a finite resource (e.g., sectors on a disk) that is shared by two subjects at different security levels.

covert timing channel Covert channel in which one process signals information to another process by modulating its own use of system resources (e.g., central processing unit time) in such a way that this manipulation affects the real response time observed by the second process.

credentials Information, passed from one entity to another, used to establish the sending entity's access rights.

critical infrastructures Those physical and cyber-based systems essential to the minimum operations of the economy and government.

cryptanalysis Operations performed in converting encrypted messages to plain text without initial knowledge of the crypto-algorithm and/or key employed in the encryption.

CRYPTO Marking or designator identifying COMSEC keying material used to secure or authenticate telecommunications carrying classified or sensitive U.S. Government or U.S. Government-derived information.

crypto-alarm Circuit or device that detects failures or aberrations in the logic or operation of crypto-equipment. Crypto-alarm may inhibit transmission or may provide a visible and/or audible alarm.

crypto-algorithm Well-defined procedure or sequence of rules or steps, or a series of mathematical equations used to describe cryptographic processes such as encryption/decryption, key generation, authentication, signatures, etc.

crypto-ancillary equipment Equipment designed specifically to facilitate efficient or reliable operation of crypto-equipment, without performing cryptographic functions itself.

crypto-equipment Equipment that embodies a cryptographic logic.

cryptographic Pertaining to, or concerned with, cryptography.

cryptographic component Hardware or firmware embodiment of the cryptographic logic. A cryptographic component may be a modular assembly, a printed wiring assembly, a microcircuit, or a combination of these items.

cryptographic equipment room (CER) Controlled-access room in which cryptosystems are located.

cryptographic initialization Function used to set the state of a cryptographic logic prior to key generation, encryption, or other operating mode.

cryptographic logic The embodiment of one (or more) crypto-algorithm(s) along with alarms, checks, and other processes essential to effective and secure performance of the cryptographic process(es).

cryptographic randomization Function that randomly determines the transmit state of a cryptographic logic.

cryptography Art or science concerning the principles, means, and methods for rendering plain information unintelligible and for restoring encrypted information to intelligible form.

crypto-ignition key (CIK) Device or electronic key used to unlock the secure mode of crypto-equipment.

cryptology Field encompassing both cryptography and cryptanalysis.

cryptonet Stations holding a common key.

cryptoperiod Time span during which each key setting remains in effect.

cryptosecurity Component of COMSEC resulting from the provision of technically sound cryptosystems and their proper use.

cryptosynchronization Process by which a receiving decrypting cryptographic logic attains the same internal state as the transmitting encrypting logic.

cryptosystem Associated INFOSEC items interacting to provide a single means of encryption or decryption.

cryptosystem analysis Process of establishing the exploitability of a cryptosystem, normally by reviewing transmitted traffic protected or secured by the system under study.

cryptosystem evaluation Process of determining vulnerabilities of a cryptosystem.

cryptosystem review Examination of a cryptosystem by the controlling authority ensuring its adequacy of design and content, continued need, and proper distribution.

cryptosystem survey Management technique in which actual holders of a cryptosystem express opinions on the system's suitability and provide usage information for technical evaluations.

cyclic redundancy check Error checking mechanism that checks data integrity by computing a polynomial algorithm based checksum.

D

dangling threat (C.F.D.) Set of properties about the external environment for which there is no corresponding vulnerability and therefore no implied risk.

dangling vulnerability (C.F.D.) Set of properties about the internal environment for which there is no corresponding threat and, therefore, no implied risk.

data aggregation Compilation of unclassified individual data systems and data elements that could result in the totality of the information being classified or of beneficial use to an adversary.

data encryption standard (DES) Cryptographic algorithm, designed for the protection of unclassified data and published by the National Institute of Standards and Technology (NIST) in Federal Information Processing Standard (FIPS) Publication 46.

data flow control Synonymous with information flow control.

data integrity Condition existing when data is unchanged from its source and has not been accidentally or maliciously modified, altered, or destroyed.

data origin authentication Corroborating the source of data is as claimed.

data security Protection of data from unauthorized (accidental or intentional) modification, destruction, or disclosure. 20

data transfer device (DTD) Fill device designed to securely store, transport, and transfer electronically both COMSEC and TRANSEC key, designed to be backward compatible with the previous generation of COMSEC common fill devices, and programmable to support modern mission systems.

decertification Revocation of the certification of an IS item or equipment for cause.

decipher Convert enciphered text to plain text by means of a cryptographic system.

decode Convert encoded text to plain text by means of a code.

decrypt Generic term encompassing decode and decipher.

dedicated mode IS security mode of operation wherein each user, with direct or indirect access to the system, its peripherals, remote terminals, or remote hosts, has all of the following: a. valid security clearance for all information within the system; b. formal access approval and signed nondisclosure agreements for all the information stored and/or processed (including all compartments, subcompartments, and/or special access programs); and c. valid need-to-know for all information contained within the IS. When in the dedicated security mode, a system is specifically and exclusively dedicated to and controlled for the processing of one particular type or classification of information, either for full-time operation or for a specified period of time.

default classification Temporary classification reflecting the highest classification being processed in an IS. Default classification is included in the caution statement affixed to an object.

defense-in-depth IA strategy integrating people, technology, and operations capabilities to establish variable barriers across multiple layers and dimensions of networks.

degaussing Procedure that reduces the magnetic flux to virtual zero by applying a reverse magnetizing field. Also called demagnetizing.

delegated development program INFOSEC program in which the Director, NSA, delegates, on a case by case basis, the development and/or production of an entire telecommunications product, including the INFOSEC portion, to a lead department or agency.

denial of service Type of incident resulting from any action or series of actions that prevents any part of an IS from functioning.

depot maintenance See full maintenance.

descriptive top-level specification Top-level specification written in a natural language (e.g., English), an informal design notation, or a combination of the two. Descriptive top-level specification, required for a class B2 and B3 (as defined in the Orange Book, Department of Defense Trusted Computer System Evaluation Criteria, DoD 5200.28-STD) information system, completely and accurately describes a trusted computing base. See formal top-level specification.

design documentation (C.F.D.) Set of documents, required for Trusted Computer System Evaluation Criteria (TCSEC) classes C1 and above (as defined in the Orange Book, Department of Defense Trusted Computer System Evaluation Criteria, DoD 5200.28-STD), whose primary purpose is to define and describe the properties of a system. As it relates to TCSEC, design documentation provides an explanation of how the security policy of a system is translated into a technical solution via the Trusted Computing Base (TCB) hardware, software, and firmware.

designated accrediting authority (DAA) Official with the authority to formally assume responsibility for operating a system at an acceptable level of risk. This term is synonymous with designated approving authority and delegated accrediting authority.

dial back Synonymous with call back.

digital signature Cryptographic process used to assure message originator authenticity, integrity, and nonrepudiation.

digital signature algorithm Procedure that appends data to, or performs a cryptographic transformation of, a data unit. The appended data or crypto-graphic transformation allows reception of the data unit and protects against forgery, e.g., by the recipient.

direct shipment Shipment of COMSEC material directly from NSA to user COMSEC accounts.

disaster recover plan Provides for the continuity of system operations after a disaster.

discretionary access control (DAC) Means of restricting access to objects based on the identity and need-to-know of users and/or groups to which the object belongs. Controls are discretionary in the sense that a subject with a certain access permission is capable of passing that permission (directly or indirectly) to any other subject. See mandatory access control.

distinguished name Globally unique identifier representing an individual's identity.

DMZ (Demilitarized Zone) Perimeter network segment that is logically between internal and external networks. It purpose is to enforce the internal network's IA policy for external information exchange and to provide external, untrusted sources with restricted access to releasable information while shielding the internal networks from outside attacks. A DMZ is also called a "screened subnet".

DoD Trusted Computer System Evaluation Criteria (TCSEC) Document con-taining basic requirements and evaluation classes for assessing degrees of C.F.D. effectiveness of hardware and software security controls built into an IS. This document, DoD 5200.28 STD, is frequently referred to as the Orange Book.

domain Unique context (e.g., access control parameters) in which a program is operating; in effect, the set of objects a subject has the privilege to access.

dominate (C.F.D.) Term used to compare IS security levels. Security level S1 is said to dominate security level S2, if the hierarchical classification of S1 is greater than, or equal to, that of S2 and the non-hierarchical categories of S1 include all those of S2 as a subset.

drop accountability Procedure under which a COMSEC account custodian ini-tially receipts for COMSEC material, and then provides no further accounting for it to its central office of record. Local accountability of the COMSEC mate-rial may continue to be required. See accounting legend code.

E

electronically generated key Key generated in a COMSEC device by introducing (either mechanically or electronically) a seed key into the device and then using the seed, together with a software algorithm stored in the device, to produce the desired key.

Electronic Key Management System (EKMS) Interoperable collection of systems being developed by services and agencies of the U.S. Government to automate the planning, ordering, generating, distributing, storing, filling, using, and destroying of electronic key and management of other types of COMSEC material.

electronic messaging services Services providing interpersonal messaging capability; meeting specific functional, management, and technical requirements; and yielding a business-quality electronic mail service suitable for the conduct of official government business.

electronic security (ELSEC) Protection resulting from measures designed to deny unauthorized individuals information derived from the interception and analysis of noncommunications electromagnetic radiations.

electronic signature See digital signature.

element Removable item of COMSEC equipment, assembly, or subassembly; normally consisting of a single piece or group of replaceable parts.

embedded computer Computer system that is an integral part of a larger system.

embedded cryptography Cryptography engineered into an equipment or system whose basic function is not cryptographic.

embedded cryptographic system Cryptosystem performing or controlling a function as an integral element of a larger system or subsystem.

emissions security Protection resulting from measures taken to deny unauthorized individuals information derived from intercept and analysis of compromising emanations from crypto-equipment or an IS.

encipher Convert plain text to cipher text by means of a cryptographic system.

enclave Collection of computing environments connected by one or more internal networks under the control of a single authority and security policy, including personnel and physical security.

enclave boundary Point at which an enclave's internal network service layer connects to an external network's service layer, i.e., to another enclave or to a Wide Area Network (WAN).

encode Convert plain text to cipher text by means of a code.

encrypt Generic term encompassing encipher and encode.

encryption algorithm Set of mathematically expressed rules for rendering data unintelligible by executing a series of conversions controlled by a key.

end-item accounting Accounting for all the accountable components of a COMSEC equipment configuration by a single short title.

end-to-end encryption Encryption of information at its origin and decryption at its intended destination without intermediate decryption.

end-to-end security Safeguarding information in an IS from point of origin to point of destination.

endorsed for unclassified cryptographic item (EUCI) Unclassified cryptographic equipment that embodies a U.S. Government classified cryptographic logic and is endorsed by NSA for the protection of national security information. See type 2 product.

endorsement NSA approval of a commercially developed product for safeguarding national security information.

entrapment Deliberate planting of apparent flaws in an IS for the purpose of detecting attempted penetrations.

environment Aggregate of external procedures, conditions, and objects affecting the development, operation, and maintenance of an IS.

erasure Process intended to render magnetically stored information irretrievable by normal means.

Evaluated Products List (EPL) (C.F.D.) Equipment, hardware, software, and/or firmware evaluated by the National Computer Security Center (NCSC) in accordance with DoD TCSEC and found to be technically compliant at a particular level of trust. The EPL is included in the NSA Information Systems Security Products and Services Catalogue.

evaluation assurance level (EAL) Set of assurance requirements that represent a point on the Common Criteria predefined assurance scale.

event Occurrence, not yet assessed, that may affect the performance of an IS.

executive state One of several states in which an IS may operate, and the only one in which certain privileged instructions may be executed. Such privileged instructions cannot be executed when the system is operating in other states. Synonymous with supervisor state.

exercise key Key used exclusively to safeguard communications transmitted over-the-air during military or organized civil training exercises.

exploitable channel Channel that allows the violation of the security policy governing an IS and is usable or detectable by subjects external to the trusted computing base. See covert channel.

extraction resistance Capability of crypto-equipment or secure telecommunications equipment to resist efforts to extract key.

extranet Extension to the intranet allowing selected outside users access to portions of an organization's intranet.

F

fail safe Automatic protection of programs and/or processing systems when hardware or software failure is detected.

fail soft Selective termination of affected nonessential processing when hardware or software failure is determined to be imminent.

failure access Type of incident in which unauthorized access to data results from hardware or software failure.

failure control Methodology used to detect imminent hardware or software failure and provide fail safe or fail soft recovery.

fetch protection (C.F.D.) IS hardware provided restriction to prevent a program from accessing data in another user's segment of storage.

file protection Aggregate of processes and procedures designed to inhibit unauthorized access, contamination, elimination, modification, or destruction of a file or any of its contents.

file security Means by which access to computer files is limited to authorized users only.

fill device COMSEC item used to transfer or store key in electronic form or to insert key into a crypto-equipment.

FIREFLY Key management protocol based on public key cryptography.

firewall System designed to defend against unauthorized access to or from a private network.

firmware Program recorded in permanent or semipermanent computer memory.

fixed COMSEC facility COMSEC facility located in an immobile structure or aboard a ship.

flaw Error of commission, omission, or oversight in an IS that may allow protection mechanisms to be bypassed.

flaw hypothesis methodology System analysis and penetration technique in which the specification and documentation for an IS are analyzed to produce a list of hypothetical flaws. This list is prioritized on the basis of the estimated probability that a flaw exists on the ease of exploiting it, and on the extent of control or compromise it would provide. The prioritized list is used to perform penetration testing of a system.

flooding Type of incident involving insertion of a large volume of data resulting in denial of service.

formal access approval Process for authorizing access to classified or sensitive information with specified access requirements, such as Sensitive Compartmented Information (SCI) or Privacy Data, based on the specified access requirements and a determination of the individual's security eligibiity and need-to-know.

formal development Software development strategy that proves security methodology design specifications.

formal proof Complete and convincing mathematical argument presenting the full logical justification for each proof step and for the truth of a theorem or set of theorems.

formal security policy model Mathematically precise statement of a security policy. Such a model must define a secure state, an initial state, and how the model represents changes in state. The model must be shown to be secure by proving the initial state is secure and all possible subsequent states remain secure.

formal top-level specification Top-level specification written in a formal mathematical language to allow theorems, showing the correspondence of the system specification to its formal requirements, to be hypothesized and formally proven.

formal verification Process of using formal proofs to demonstrate the consistency between formal specification of a system and formal security policy model (design verification) or between formal specification and its high-level program implementation (implementation verification).

frequency hopping Repeated switching of frequencies during radio transmission according to a specified algorithm, to minimize unauthorized interception or jamming of telecommunications.

front-end security filter Security filter logically separated from the remainder of an IS to protect system integrity. Synonymous with firewall.

full maintenance Complete diagnostic repair, modification, and overhaul of COMSEC equipment, including repair of defective assemblies by piece part replacement. Also known as depot maintenance. See limited maintenance.

functional proponent See network sponsor.

functional testing Segment of security testing in which advertised security mechanisms of an IS are tested under operational conditions.

G

gateway Interface providing a compatibility between networks by converting transmission speeds, protocols, codes, or security measures.

global information infrastructure (GII) Worldwide interconnections of the information systems of all countries, international and multinational organizations, and international commercial communications.

granularity (C.F.D.) Relative fineness to which an access control mechanism can be adjusted.

guard Mechanism limiting the exchange of information between systems.

Gypsy verification environment (C.F.D.) Integrated set of software tools for specifying, coding, and verifying programs written in the Gypsy language.

H

hacker Unauthorized user who attempts to or gains access to an IS.

handshaking procedures Dialogue between two ISs for synchronizing, identifying, and authenticating themselves to one another.

hard copy key Physical keying material, such as printed key lists, punched or printed key tapes, or programmable, read-only memories (PROM).

hardwired key Permanently installed key.

hash total Value computed on data to detect error or manipulation. See checksum.

hashing Computation of a hash total.

hashword Memory address containing hash total.

high assurance guard (HAG) Device comprised of both hardware and software that is designed to enforce security rules during the transmission of X.400 message and X.500 directory traffic between enclaves of different classification levels (e.g., UNCLASSIFIED and SECRET).

I

IA architecture Framework that assigns and portrays IA roles and behavior among all IT assets, and prescribes rules for interaction and interconnection.

IA-enabled information technology product Product or technology whose primary role is not security, but which provides security services as an associated feature of its intended operating capabilities. Examples include such products as security-enabled web browsers, screening routers, trusted operating systems, and security-enabled messaging systems.

identification Process an IS uses to recognize an entity.

identity token Smart card, metal key, or other physical object used to authenticate identity.

identity validation Tests enabling an IS to authenticate users or resources.

imitative communications Introduction of deceptive messages or signals into deception an adversary's telecommunications signals. See communications deception and manipulative communications deception.

impersonating Form of spoofing.

implant Electronic device or electronic equipment modification designed to gain unauthorized interception of information-bearing emanations.

inadvertent disclosure Type of incident involving accidental exposure of information to an individual not authorized access.

incident (IS) Assessed occurrence having actual or potentially adverse effects on an IS. (COMSEC) Occurrence that potentially jeopardizes the security of COMSEC material or the secure electrical transmission of national security information or information governed by 10 U.S.C. Section 2315.

incomplete parameter checking System flaw that exists when the operating system does not check all parameters fully for accuracy and consistency, thus making the system vulnerable to penetration.

indicator Recognized action, specific, generalized, or theoretical, that an adversary might be expected to take in preparation for an attack.

individual accountability Ability to associate positively the identity of a user with the time, method, and degree of access to an IS.

information assurance (IA) Measures that protect and defend information and information systems by ensuring their availability, integrity, authentication, confidentiality, and non-repudiation. These measures include providing for restoration of information systems by incorporating protection, detection, and reaction capabilities.

information assurance manager (IAM) See information systems security manager.

information assurance officer (IAO) See information systems security officer.

information assurance product Product or technology whose primary purpose is to provide security services (e.g., confidentiality, authentication, integrity, access control, non-repudiation of data) correct known vulnerabilities; and/or provide layered defense against various categories of non-authorized or malicious penetrations of information systems or networks. Examples include such products as data/network encryptors, firewalls, and intrusion detection devices.

information environment Aggregate of individuals, organizations, or systems that collect, process, or disseminate information, also included is the information itself.

information flow control Procedure to ensure that information transfers within an IS are not made from a higher security level object to an object of a lower security level.

information operations (IO) Actions taken to affect adversary information and ISs while defending one's own information and ISs.

information owner Official with statutory or operational authority for specified information and responsibility for establishing the controls for its generation, collection, processing, dissemination, and disposal.

information security policy Aggregate of directives, regulations, rules, and practices that prescribe how an organization manages, protects, and distributes information.

information system (IS) Set of information resources organized for the collection, storage, processing, maintenance, use, sharing, dissemination, disposition, display, or transmission of information.

information systems security (INFOSEC) Protection of information systems against unauthorized access to or modification of information, whether in storage, processing or transit, and against the denial of service to authorized users, including those measures necessary to detect, document, and counter such threats.

information systems security engineering (ISSE) Process that captures and refines information protection requirements and ensures their integration into IT acquisiton processes through purposeful security design or configuration.

information systems security Modification of any fielded hardware, firmware, equipment modification software, or portion thereof, under NSA configuration control. There are three classes of modifications: mandatory (to include human safety); optional/special mission modifications; and repair actions. These classes apply to elements, subassemblies, equipment, systems, and software packages performing functions such as key generation, key distribution, message encryption, decryption, authentication, or those mechanisms necessary to satisfy security policy, labeling, identification, or accountability.

information systems security manager (ISSM) Individual responsible for a program, organization, system, or enclave's information assurance program.

information systems security officer (ISSO) Individual responsible to the ISSM for ensuring the appropriate operational IA posture is maintained for a system, program, or enclave.

information systems security product Item (chip, module, assembly, or equipment), technique, or service that performs or relates to information systems security.

initialize Setting the state of a cryptographic logic prior to key generation, encryption, or other operating mode.

inspectable space Three dimensional space surrounding equipment that process classified and/or sensitive information within which TEMPEST exploitation is not considered practical or where legal authority to identify and/or remove a potential TEMPEST exploitation exists. Synonymous with zone of control.

integrity Quality of an IS reflecting the logical correctness and reliability of the operating system; the logical completeness of the hardware and software implementing the protection mechanisms; and the consistency of the data structures and occurrence of the stored data. Note that, in a formal security mode, integrity is interpreted more narrowly to mean protection against unauthorized modification or destruction of information.

integrity check value Checksum capable of detecting modification of an IS.

interconnection security Written management authorization to interconnect agreement information systems based upon acceptance of risk and implementatin of established controls.

inter-domain connections Connections between domains of different classifications for the purpose of transferring data through controlled interfaces.

interface Common boundary between independent systems or modules where interactions take place.

interface control document Technical document describing interface controls and identifying the authorities and responsibilities for ensuring the operation of such controls. This document is baselined during the preliminary design review and is maintained throughout the IS lifecycle.

interim approval Temporary authorization granted by a DAA for an IS to process information based on preliminary results of a security evaluation of the system.

internal security controls Hardware, firmware, or software features within an IS that restrict access to resources only to authorized subjects.

internetwork private line Network cryptographic unit that provides secure interface connections, singularly or in simultaneous multiple connections, between a host and a predetermined set of corresponding hosts.

internet protocol (IP) Standard protocol for transmission of data from source to destinations in packet-switched communications networks and interconnected systems of such networks.

intrusion Unauthorized act of bypassing the security mechanisms of a system.

K

key Usually a sequence of random or pseudorandom bits used initially to set up and periodically change the operations performed in crypto-equipment for the purpose of encrypting or decrypting electronic signals, or for determining electronic counter-countermeasures patterns, or for producing other key.

key-auto-key (KAK) Cryptographic logic using previous key to produce key.

key distribution center (KDC) COMSEC facility generating and distributing key in electrical form.

key-encryption-key (KEK) Key that encrypts or decrypts other key for transmission or storage.

key exchange Process of exchanging public keys (and other information) in order to establish secure communications.

key list Printed series of key settings for a specific cryptonet. Key lists may be produced in list, pad, or printed tape format.

key management infrastructure (KMI) Framework and services that provide the generation, production, storage, protection, distribution, control, tracking, and destruction for all cryptographic key material, symmetric keys as well as public keys and public key certificates.

key pair Public key and its corresponding private key as used in public key cryptography.

key production key (KPK) Key used to initialize a keystream generator for the production of other electronically generated key.

key recovery Mechanisms and processes that allow authorized parties to retrieve the cryptographic key used for data confidentiality.

key stream Sequence of symbols (or their electrical or mechanical equivalents) produced in a machine or auto-manual cryptosystem to combine with plain text to produce cipher text, control transmission security processes, or produce key.

key tag Identification information associated with certain types of electronic key.

key tape Punched or magnetic tape containing key. Printed key in tape form is referred to as a key list.

key updating Irreversible cryptographic process for modifying key.

keying material Key, code, or authentication information in physical or magnetic form.

L

label See security label.

labeled security protections Elementary-level mandatory access control protection features and intermediate-level discretionary access control features in a TCB that uses sensitivity labels to make access control decisions.

laboratory attack Use of sophisticated signal recovery equipment in a laboratory environment to recover information from data storage media.

least privilege Principle requiring that each subject be granted the most restrictive set of privileges needed for the performance of authorized tasks. Application of this principle limits the damage that can result from accident, error, or unauthorized use of an IS.

level of concern Rating assigned to an IS indicating the extent to which protection measures, techniques, and procedures must be applied. High, Medium, and Basic are identified levels of concern. A separate Level-of-Concern is assigned to each IS for confidentiality, integrity, and availability.

level of protection Extent to which protective measures, techniques, and procedures must be applied to ISs and networks based on risk, threat, vulnerability, system interconnectivity considerations, and information assurance needs. Levels of protection are: 1. Basic: IS and networks requiring implementation of standard minimum security countermeasures. 2. Medium: IS and networks requiring layering of additional safeguards above the standard minimum security countermeasures. 3. High: IS and networks requiring the most stringent protection and rigorous security countermeasures.

limited maintenance COMSEC maintenance restricted to fault isolation, removal, and replacement of plug-in assemblies. Soldering or unsoldering usually is prohibited in limited maintenance. See full maintenance.

line conditioning Elimination of unintentional signals or noise induced or conducted on a telecommunications or IS signal, power, control, indicator, or other external interface line.

line conduction Unintentional signals or noise induced or conducted on a telecommunications or IS signal, power, control, indicator, or other external interface line.

link encryption Encryption of information between nodes of a communications system.

list-oriented IS protection in which each protected object has a list of all subjects authorized to access it. See also ticket-oriented.

local authority Organization responsible for generating and signing user certificates.

Local Management Device/ Key Processor (LMD/KP) EKMS platform providing automated management of COMSEC material and generating key for designated users.

lock and key protection system Protection system that involves matching a key or password with a specific access requirement.

logic bomb Resident computer program triggering an unauthorized act when particular states of an IS are realized.

logical completeness measure Means for assessing the effectiveness and degree to which a set of security and access control mechanisms meets security specifications.

long title Descriptive title of a COMSEC item.

low probability of detection Result of measures used to hide or disguise intentional electromagnetic transmissions.

low probability of intercept Result of measures to prevent the intercept of intentional electromagnetic transmissions.

M

magnetic remanence Magnetic representation of residual information remaining on a magnetic medium after the medium has been cleared. See clearing.

maintenance hook Special instructions (trapdoors) in software allowing easy maintenance and additional feature development. Since maintenance hooks frequently allow entry into the code without the usual checks, they are a serious security risk if they are not removed prior to live implementation.

maintenance key Key intended only for in-shop use.

malicious applets Small application programs automatically downloaded and executed that perform an unauthorized function on an IS.

malicious code Software or firmware intended to perform an unauthorized process that will have adverse impact on the confidentiality, integrity, or availability of an IS.

malicious logic Hardware, software, or firmware capable of performing an unauthorized function on an IS.

mandatory access control (MAC) Means of restricting access to objects based on the sensitivity of the information contained in the objects and the formal authorization (i.e., clearance, formal access approvals, and need-to-know) of subjects to access information of such sensitivity. See discretionary access control.

mandatory modification Change to a COMSEC end-item that NSA requires to be completed and reported by a specified date. See optional modification.

manipulative communications Alteration or simulation of friendly deception telecommunications for the purpose of deception. See communications deception and imitative communications deception.

manual cryptosystem Cryptosystem in which the cryptographic processes are performed without the use of crypto-equipment or auto-manual devices.

manual remote rekeying Procedure by which a distant crypto-equipment is rekeyed electrically, with specific actions required by the receiving terminal operator.

masquerading Form of spoofing.

master crypto-ignition key Key device with electronic logic and circuits providing the capability for adding more operational CIKs to a keyset (maximum of seven) any time after fill procedure is completed. The master CIK can only be made during the fill procedure as the first CIK.

memory scavenging The collection of residual information from data storage.

message authentication code Data associated with an authenticated message allowing a receiver to verify the integrity of the message.

message externals Information outside of the message text, such as the header, trailer, etc.

message indicator Sequence of bits transmitted over a communications system for synchronizing crypto-equipment. Some off-line cryptosystems, such as the KL-51 and one-time pad systems, employ message indicators to establish decryption starting points.

mimicking Form of spoofing.

mobile code Software modules obtained from remote systems, transferred across a network, and then downloaded and executed on local systems without explicit installation or execution by the recipient.

mode of operation Description of the conditions under which an IS operates based on the sensitivity of information processed and the clearance levels, formal access approvals, and need-to-know of its users. Four modes of operation are authorized for processing or transmitting information: dedicated mode, system-high mode, compartmented/partitioned mode, and multilevel mode.

multilevel device Equipment trusted to properly maintain and separate data of different security categories.

multilevel mode INFOSEC mode of operation wherein all the following statements are satisfied concerning the users who have direct or indirect access to the system, its peripherals, remote terminals, or remote hosts: a. some users do not have a valid security clearance for all the information processed in the IS; b. all users have the proper security clearance and appropriate formal access approval for that information to which they have access; and c. all users have a valid need-to-know only for information to which they have access.

multilevel security (MLS) Concept of processing information with different classifications and categories that simultaneously permits access by users with different security clearances and denies access to users who lack authorization.

multi-security level (MSL) Capability to process information of different security classifications or categories by using periods processing or peripheral sharing.

mutual suspicion Condition in which two ISs need to rely upon each other to perform a service, yet neither trusts the other to properly protect shared data.

N

National Information Assurance Partnership (NIAP) Joint initiative between NSA and NIST responsible for security testing needs of both IT consumers and producers and promoting the development of technically sound security requirements for IT products and systems and appropriate measures for evaluating those products and systems.

National Information Infrastructure (NII) Nationwide interconnection of communications networks,computers, databases, and consumer electronics that make vast amount of information available to users. It includes both public and private networks, the internet, the public switched network, and cable, wireless, and satellite communications.

national security information (NSI) Information that has been determined, pursuant to Executive Order 12958 or any predecessor order, to require protection against unauthorized disclosure.

national security system Any telecommunications or information system operated by the United States Government, the function, operation, or use of which: 1. involves intelligence activities; 2. involves cryptologic activities related to national security; 3. involves command and control of military forces; 4. involves equipment that is an integral part of a weapon or weapon system; or 5. is critical to the direct fulfillment of military or intelligence missions and does not include a system that is to be used for routine administrative and business applications (including payroll, finance, logistics, and personnel management applications). (Title 40 U.S.C. Section1452, Information Technology Management Reform Act of 1996.)

need-to-know Necessity for access to, or knowledge or possession of, specific official information required to carry out official duties.

need to know determination Decision made by an authorized holder of official information that a prospective recipient requires access to specific official information to carry out official duties.

network IS implemented with a collection of interconnected nodes.

network front-end Device implementing protocols that allow attachment of a computer system to a network.

network reference monitor See reference monitor.

network security See information systems security.

network security architecture Subset of network architecture specifically addressing security-relevant issues.

network security officer See information systems security officer.

network sponsor Individual or organization responsible for stating the security policy enforced by the network, designing the network security architecture to properly enforce that policy, and ensuring the network is implemented in such a way that the policy is enforced.

network system System implemented with a collection of interconnected components. A network system is based on a coherent security architecture and design.

network trusted computing base (NTCB) (C.F.D.) Totality of protection mechanisms within a network, including hardware, firmware, and software, the combination of which is responsible for enforcing a security policy. See trusted computing base.

network trusted computing base Totality of mechanisms within a single network

(NTCB) partition (C.F.D.) component for enforcing the network policy, as allocated to that component; the part of the NTCB within a single network component.

network weaving Penetration technique in which different communication networks are linked to access an IS to avoid detection and trace-back.

no-lone zone Area, room, or space that, when staffed, must be occupied by two or more appropriately cleared individuals who remain within sight of each other. See two-person integrity.

nonrepudiation Assurance the sender of data is provided with proof of delivery and the recipient is provided with proof of the sender's identity, so neither can later deny having processed the data.

null Dummy letter, letter symbol, or code group inserted into an encrypted message to delay or prevent its decryption or to complete encrypted groups for transmission or transmission security purposes.

O

object Passive entity containing or receiving information. Access to an object implies access to the information it contains.

object reuse Reassignment and re-use of a storage medium containing one or more objects after ensuring no residual data remains on the storage medium.

official information All information in the custody and control of a U.S. Government department or agency that was acquired by U.S. Government employees as a part of their official duties or because of their official status and has not been cleared for public release.

off-line cryptosystem Cryptosystem in which encryption and decryption are performed independently of the transmission and reception functions.

one-part code Code in which plain text elements and their accompanying code groups are arranged in alphabetical, numerical, or other systematic order, so one listing serves for both encoding and decoding. One-part codes are normally small codes used to pass small volumes of low-sensitivity information.

one-time cryptosystem Cryptosystem employing key used only once.

one-time pad Manual one-time cryptosystem produced in pad form.

one-time tape Punched paper tape used to provide key streams on a one-time basis in certain machine cryptosystems.

on-line cryptosystem Cryptosystem in which encryption and decryption are performed in association with the transmitting and receiving functions.

open storage Storage of classified information within an accredited facility, but not in General Services Administration approved secure containers, while the facility is unoccupied by authorized personnel.

operational key Key intended for use over-the-air for protection of operational information or for the production or secure electrical transmission of key streams.

operational waiver Authority for continued use of unmodified COMSEC end-items pending the completion of a mandatory modification.

operations code Code composed largely of words and phrases suitable for general communications use.

operations security (OPSEC) Systematic and proven process by which potential adversaries can be denied information about capabilities and intentions by identifying, controlling, and protecting generally unclassified evidence of the planning and execution of sensitive activities. The process involves five steps: identification of critical information, analysis of threats, analysis of vulnerabilities, assessment of risks, and application of appropriate countermeasures.

optional modification NSA-approved modification not required for universal implementation by all holders of a COMSEC end-item. This class of modification requires all of the engineering/doctrinal control of mandatory modification but is usually not related to security, safety, TEMPEST, or reliability.

Orange Book (C.F.D) DoD Trusted Computer System Evaluation Criteria (DoD 5200.28-STD).

organizational maintenance Limited maintenance performed by a user organization.

organizational registration authority (ORA) Entity within the PKI that authenticates the identity and the organizational affiliation of the users.

over-the-air key distribution Providing electronic key via over-the-air rekeying, over-the-air key transfer, or cooperative key generation.

over-the-air key transfer Electronically distributing key without changing traffic encryption key used on the secured communications path over which the transfer is accomplished.

over-the-air rekeying (OTAR) Changing traffic encryption key or transmission security key in remote crypto-equipment by sending new key directly to the remote crypto-equipment over the communications path it secures.

overt channel Communications path within a computer system or network designed for the authorized transfer of data. See covert channel.

overwrite procedure Process of writing patterns of data on top of the data stored on a magnetic medium.

P

parity Bit(s) used to determine whether a block of data has been altered.

partitioned security mode IS security mode of operation wherein all personnel have the clearance, but not necessarily formal access approval and need-to-know, for all information handled by an IS.

password Protected/private string of letters, numbers, and special characters used to authenticate an identity or to authorize access to data.

penetration See intrusion.

penetration testing Security testing in which evaluators attempt to circumvent the security features of a system based on their understanding of the system design and implementation.

per-call key Unique traffic encryption key generated automatically by certain secure telecommunications systems to secure single voice or data transmissions. See cooperative key generation.

periods processing Processing of various levels of classified and unclassified information at distinctly different times. Under the concept of periods processing, the system must be purged of all information from one processing period before transitioning to the next.

permuter Device used in crypto-equipment to change the order in which the contents of a shift register are used in various nonlinear combining circuits.

plain text Unencrypted information.

policy approving authority (PAA) First level of the PKI Certification Management Authority that approves the security policy of each PCA.

policy certification authority (PCA) Second level of the PKI Certification Management Authority that formulates the security policy under which it and its subordinate CAs will issue public key certificates.

positive control material Generic term referring to a sealed authenticator system, permissive action link, coded switch system, positive enable system, or nuclear command and control documents, material, or devices.

preproduction model Version of INFOSEC equipment employing standard parts and suitable for complete evaluation of form, design, and performance. Preproduction models are often referred to as beta models.

print suppression Eliminating the display of characters in order to preserve their secrecy.

privacy system Commercial encryption system that affords telecommunications limited protection to deter a casual listener, but cannot withstand a technically competent cryptanalytic attack.

privileged access (C.F.D.) Explicitly authorized access of a specific user, process, or computer to a computer resource(s).

privileged user Individual who has access to system control, monitoring, or administration functions (e.g., system administrator, system ISSO, maintainers, system programmers, etc.)

probe Type of incident involving an attempt to gather information about an IS for the apparent purpose of circumventing its security controls.

production model INFOSEC equipment in its final mechanical and electrical form.

proprietary information Material and information relating to or associated with a company's products, business, or activities, including but not limited to financial information; data or statements; trade secrets; product research and development; existing and future product designs and performance specifications; marketing plans or techniques; schematics; client lists; computer programs; processes; and know-how that has been clearly identified and properly marked by the company as proprietary information, trade secrets, or company confidential information. The information must have been developed by the company and not be available to the Government or to the public without restriction from another source.

protected distribution systems (PDS) Wire line or fiber optic distribution system used to transmit unencrypted classified national security information through an area of lesser classification or control.

protection philosophy Informal description of the overall design of an IS delineating each of the protection mechanisms employed. Combination of formal and informal techniques, appropriate to the evaluation class, used to show the mechanisms are adequate to enforce the security policy.

protection profile Common Criteria specification that represents an implementation-independent set of security requirements for a category of Target of Evaluations that meets specific consumer needs.

protection ring One of a hierarchy of privileged modes of an IS that gives certain access rights to user programs and processes that are authorized to operate in a given mode.

protective packaging Packaging techniques for COMSEC material that discourage penetration, reveal a penetration has occurred or was attempted, or inhibit viewing or copying of keying material prior to the time it is exposed for use.

protective technologies Special tamper-evident features and materials employed for the purpose of detecting tampering and deterring attempts to compromise, modify, penetrate, extract, or substitute information processing equipment and keying material.

protocol Set of rules and formats, semantic and syntactic, permiting ISs to exchange information.

proxy Software agent that performs a function or operation on behalf of another application or system while hiding the details involved.

public domain software Software not protected by copyright laws of any nation that may be freely used without permission of, or payment to, the creator, and that carries no warranties from, or liabilities to the creator.

public key certificate Contains the name of a user, the public key component of the user, and the name of the issuer who vouches that the public key component is bound to the named user.

public key cryptography (PKC) Encryption system using a linked pair of keys. What one key encrypts, the other key decrypts.

public key infrastructure (PKI) Framework established to issue, maintain, and revoke public key certificates accommodating a variety of security technologies, including the use of software.

purging Rendering stored information unrecoverable. See sanitize.

Q

QUADRANT Short name referring to technology that provides tamper-resistant protection to crypto-equipment.

R

randomizer Analog or digital source of unpredictable, unbiased, and usually independent bits. Randomizers can be used for several different functions, including key generation or to provide a starting state for a key generator.

read Fundamental operation in an IS that results only in the flow of information from an object to a subject.

read access Permission to read information in an IS.

real time reaction Immediate response to a penetration attempt that is detected and diagnosed in time to prevent access.

recovery procedures Actions necessary to restore data files of an IS and computational capability after a system failure.

RED Designation applied to an IS, and associated areas, circuits, components, and equipment in which unencrypted national security information is being processed.

RED/BLACK concept Separation of electrical and electronic circuits, components, equipment, and systems that handle national security information (RED), in electrical form, from those that handle non-national security information (BLACK) in the same form.

Red team Independent and focused threat-based effort by an interdisciplinary, simulated adversary to expose and exploit vulnerabilities as a means to improve the security posture of ISs.

RED signal Any electronic emission (e.g., plain text, key, key stream, subkey stream, initial fill, or control signal) that would divulge national security information if recovered.

reference monitor Concept of an abstract machine that enforces Target of Evaluation (TOE) access control policies.

reference validation mechanism Portion of a trusted computing base whose normal function is to control access between subjects and objects and whose correct operation is essential to the protection of data in the system.

release prefix Prefix appended to the short title of U.S.-produced keying material to indicate its foreign releasability. "A" designates material that is releasable to specific allied nations and "U.S." designates material intended exclusively for U. S. use.

remanence Residual information remaining on storage media after clearing. See magnetic remanence and clearing.

remote access Access for authorized users external to an enclave established through a controlled access point at the enclave boundary.

remote rekeying Procedure by which a distant crypto-equipment is rekeyed electrically. See automatic remote rekeying and manual remote rekeying.

repair action NSA-approved change to a COMSEC end-item that does not affect the original characteristics of the end-item and is provided for optional application by holders. Repair actions are limited to minor electrical and/or mechanical improvements to enhance operation, maintenance, or reliability. They do not require an identification label, marking, or control but must be fully documented by changes to the maintenance manual.

reserve keying material Key held to satisfy unplanned needs. See contingency key.

residual risk Portion of risk remaining after security measures have been applied.

residue Data left in storage after information processing operations are complete, but before degaussing or overwriting has taken place.

resource encapsulation Method by which the reference monitor mediates accesses to an IS resource. Resource is protected and not directly accessible by a subject. Satisfies requirement for accurate auditing of resource usage.

risk Possibility that a particular threat will adversely impact an IS by exploiting a particular vulnerability.

risk analysis Examination of information to identify the risk to an IS.

risk assessment Process of analyzing threats to and vulnerabilities of an IS, and the potential impact resulting from the loss of information or capabilities of a system. This analysis is used as a basis for identifying appropriate and cost-effective security countermeasures.

risk index Difference between the minimum clearance or authorization of IS users and the maximum sensitivity (e.g., classification and categories) of data processed by the system.

risk management Process of identifying and applying countermeasures commensurate with the value of the assets protected based on a risk assessment.

S

safeguard 1.) Protection included to counteract a known or expected condition. 2.) Incorporated countermeasure or set of countermeasures within a base release.

safeguarding statement Statement affixed to a computer output or printout that states the highest classification being processed at the time the product was produced and requires control of the product, at that level, until determination of the true classification by an authorized individual. Synonymous with banner.

sanitize Process to remove information from media such that data recovery is not possible. It includes removing all classified labels, markings, and activity logs. See purging.

scavenging Searching through object residue to acquire data.

secure communications Telecommunications deriving security through use of type 1 products and/or PDSs.

secure hash standard Specification for a secure hash algorithm that can generate a condensed message representation called a message digest.

secure state Condition in which no subject can access any object in an unauthorized manner.

secure subsystem Subsystem containing its own implementation of the reference monitor concept for those resources it controls. Secure subsystem must depend on other controls and the base operating system for the control of subjects and the more primitive system objects.

security fault analysis (SFA) Assessment, usually performed on IS hardware, to determine the security properties of a device when hardware fault is encountered.

security features users guide (SFUG) (C.F.D.) Guide or manual explaining how the security mechanisms in a specific system work.

security filter IS trusted subsystem that enforces security policy on the data passing through it.

security inspection Examination of an IS to determine compliance with security policy, procedures, and practices.

security kernel Hardware, firmware, and software elements of a trusted computing base implementing the reference monitor concept. Security kernel must mediate all accesses, be protected from modification, and be verifiable as correct.

security label Information representing the sensitivity of a subject or object, such as its hierarchical classification (CONFIDENTIAL, SECRET, TOP SECRET) together with any applicable nonhierarchical security categories (e.g., sensitive compartmented information, critical nuclear weapon design information).

security net control station Management system overseeing and controlling implementation of network security policy.

security perimeter All components/devices of an IS to be accredited. Separately accredited components generally are not included within the perimeter.

security range Highest and lowest security levels that are permitted in or on an IS, system component, subsystem, or network.

security requirements Types and levels of protection necessary for equipment, data, information, applications, and facilities to meet IS security policy.

security requirements baseline Description of the minimum requirements necessary for an IS to maintain an acceptable level of security.

security safeguards Protective measures and controls prescribed to meet the security requirements specified for an IS. Safeguards may include security features, management constraints, personnel security, and security of physical structures, areas, and devices. See accreditation.

security specification Detailed description of the safeguards required to protect an IS.

security target Common Criteria specification that represents a set of security requirements to be used as the basis of an evaluation of an identified Target of Evaluation (TOE).

security test and evaluation (ST&E) Examination and analysis of the safeguards required to protect an IS, as they have been applied in an operational environment, to determine the security posture of that system.

security testing Process to determine that an IS protects data and maintains functionality as intended.

seed key Initial key used to start an updating or key generation process.

sensitive compartmented (SCI) Classified information concerning or derived from information intelligence sources, methods, or analytical processes, which is required to be handled within formal access control systems established by the Director of Central Intelligence.

sensitive compartmented (SCIF) Accredited area, room, or group of rooms, information facility buildings, or installation where SCI may be stored, used, discussed, and/or processed.

sensitive information Information, the loss, misuse, or unauthorized access to or modification of, that could adversely affect the national interest or the conduct of federal programs, or the privacy to which individuals are entitled under 5 U.S.C. Section 552a (the Privacy Act), but that has not been specifically authorized under criteria established by an Executive Order or an Act of Congress to be kept classified in the interest of national defense or foreign policy. (Systems that are not national security systems, but contain sensitive information, are to be protected in accordance with the requirements of the Computer Security Act of 1987 (P.L.100-235).)

sensitivity label Information representing elements of the security label(s) of a subject and an object. Sensitivity labels are used by the trusted computing base (TCB) as the basis for mandatory access control decisions.

shielded enclosure Room or container designed to attenuate electromagnetic radiation.

short title Identifying combination of letters and numbers assigned to certain COMSEC materials to facilitate handling, accounting, and controlling.

simple security property (C.F.D.) Bell-La Padula security model rule allowing a subject read access to an object, only if the security level of the subject dominates the security level of the object.

single point keying Means of distributing key to multiple, local crypto-equipment or devices from a single fill point.

sniffer Software tool for auditing and identifying network traffic packets.

software system test and evaluation process Process that plans, develops, and documents the quantitative demonstration of the fulfillment of all baseline functional performance, operational, and interface requirements.

special access program (SAP) Program established for a specific class of classified information that imposes safeguarding and access requirements that exceed those normally required for information at the same classified level.

special access program facility (SAPF) Facility formally accredited by an appropriate agency in accordance with DCID 1/21 in which SAP information may be proceced.

split knowledge Separation of data or information into two or more parts, each part constantly kept under control of separate authorized individuals or teams so that no one individual or team will know the whole data.

spoofing Unauthorized use of legitimate Indentification and Authentication (I&A) data, however it was obtained, to mimic a subject different from the attacker. Impersonating, masquerading, piggybacking, and mimicking are forms of spoofing.

spread spectrum Telecommunications techniques in which a signal is transmitted in a bandwidth considerably greater than the frequency content of the original information. Frequency hopping, direct sequence spreading, time scrambling, and combinations of these techniques are forms of spread spectrum.

star (*) property (C.F.D.) Bell-La Padula security model rule allowing a subject write access to an object only if the security level of the object dominates the security level of the subject.

start-up KEK Key-encryption-key held in common by a group of potential communicating entities and used to establish ad hoc tactical networks.

state variable Variable representing either the state of an IS or the state of some system resource.

storage object Object supporting both read and write accesses to an IS.

strong authentication Layered authentication approach relying on two or more authenticators to establish the identity of an originator or receiver of information.

subassembly Major subdivision of an assembly consisting of a package of parts, elements, and circuits that perform a specific function.

subject Generally an individual, process, or device causing information to flow among objects or change to the system state.

subject security level Sensitivity label(s) of the objects to which the subject has both read and write access. Security level of a subject must always be dominated by the clearance level of the user associated with the subject.

superencryption Process of encrypting encrypted information. Occurs when a message, encrypted off-line, is transmitted over a secured, on-line circuit, or when information encrypted by the originator is multiplexed onto a communications trunk, which is then bulk encrypted.

supersession Scheduled or unscheduled replacement of a COMSEC aid with a different edition.

supervisor state Synonymous with executive state of an operating system.

suppression measure Action, procedure, modification, or device that reduces the level of, or inhibits the generation of, compromising emanations in an IS.

surrogate access See discretionary access control.

syllabary List of individual letters, combination of letters, or syllables, with their equivalent code groups, used for spelling out words or proper names not present in the vocabulary of a code. A syllabary may also be a spelling table.

symmetric key Encryption methodology in which the encryptor and decryptor use the same key, which must be kept secret.

synchronous crypto-operation Method of on-line crypto-operation in which crypto-equipment and associated terminals have timing systems to keep them in step.

system administrator (SA) Individual responsible for the installation and maintenance of an IS, providing effective IS utilization, adequate security parameters, and sound implementation of established IA policy and procedures.

system assets Any software, hardware, data, administrative, physical, communications, or personnel resource within an IS.

system development Methodologies developed through software methodologies engineering to manage the complexity of system development. Development methodologies include software engineering aids and high-level design analysis tools.

system high Highest security level supported by an IS.

system high mode IS security mode of operation wherein each user, with direct or indirect access to the IS, its peripherals, remote terminals, or remote hosts, has all of the following: a. valid security clearance for all information within an IS; b. formal access approval and signed nondisclosure agreements for all the information stored and/or processed (including all compartments, subcompartments and/or special access programs); and c. valid need-to-know for some of the information contained within the IS.

system indicator Symbol or group of symbols in an off-line encrypted message identifying the specific cryptosystem or key used in the encryption.

system integrity Attribute of an IS when it performs its intended function in an unimpaired manner, free from deliberate or inadvertent unauthorized manipulation of the system.

system low Lowest security level supported by an IS.

system profile Detailed security description of the physical structure, equipment component, location, relationships, and general operating environment of an IS.

system security See information systems security.

system security engineering See information systems security engineering.

system security officer See information system security officer.

system security plan Formal document fully describing the planned security tasks required to meet system security requirements.

T

tampering Unauthorized modification altering the proper functioning of INFOSEC equipment.

target of evaluation IT product or system and its associated administrator and user guidance documentation that is the subject of an evaluation.

telecommunications Preparation, transmission, communication, or related processing of information (writing, images, sounds, or other data) by electrical, electromagnetic, electromechanical, electro-optical, or electronic means.

telecommunications security (TSEC) (C.F.D.) See information systems security.

TEMPEST Short name referring to investigation, study, and control of compromising emanations from IS equipment.

TEMPEST test Laboratory or on-site test to determine the nature of compromising emanations associated with an IS.

TEMPEST zone Designated area within a facility where equipment with appropriate TEMPEST characteristics (TEMPEST zone assignment) may be operated.

test key Key intended for testing of COMSEC equipment or systems.

threat Any circumstance or event with the potential to adversely impact an IS through unauthorized access, destruction, disclosure, modification of data, and/or denial of service.

threat analysis Examination of information to identify the elements comprising a threat.

threat assessment Formal description and evaluation of threat to an IS.

threat monitoring Analysis, assessment, and review of audit trails and other information collected for the purpose of searching out system events that may constitute violations of system security.

ticket-oriented IS protection system in which each subject maintains a list of unforgeable bit patterns called tickets, one for each object a subject is authorized to access. See list-oriented.

time bomb Resident computer program that triggers an unauthorized act at a predefined time.

time-compliance date Date by which a mandatory modification to a COMSEC end-item must be incorporated if the item is to remain approved for operational use.

time-dependent password Password that is valid only at a certain time of day or during a specified interval of time.

TOE Security Functions (TSF) Set consisting of all hardware, software, and firmware of the TOE that must be relied upon for the correct enforcement of the TSP.

TOE Security Policy (TSP) Set of rules that regulate how assets are managed, protected, and distributed within the TOE.

traditional INFOSEC program Program in which NSA acts as the central procurement agency for the development and, in some cases, the production of INFOSEC items. This includes the Authorized Vendor Program. Modifications to the INFOSEC end-items used in products developed and/or produced under these programs must be approved by NSA.

traffic analysis (TA) Study of communications patterns.

traffic encryption key (TEK) Key used to encrypt plain text or to superencrypt previously encrypted text and/or to decrypt cipher text.

traffic-flow security (TFS) Measure used to conceal the presence of valid messages in an on-line cryptosystem or secure communications system.

traffic padding Generation of spurious communications or data units to disguise the amount of real data units being sent.

tranquility Property whereby the security level of an object cannot change while the object is being processed by an IS.

transmission security (TRANSEC) Component of COMSEC resulting from the application of measures designed to protect transmissions from interception and exploitation by means other than cryptanalysis.

trap door Synonymous with back door.

trojan horse Program containing hidden code allowing the unauthorized collection, falsification, or destruction of information. See malicious code.

trusted channel Means by which a TOE Security Function (TSF) and a remote trusted IT product can communicate with necessary confidence to support the TOE Security Policy (TSP)

trusted computer system IS employing sufficient hardware and software assurance measures to allow simultaneous processing of a range of classified or sensitive information.

trusted computing base (TCB) Totality of protection mechanisms within a computer system, including hardware, firmware, and software, the combination responsible for enforcing a security policy.

trusted distribution Method for distributing trusted computing base (TCB) hardware, software, and firmware components that protects the TCB from modification during distribution.

trusted facility manual (C.F.D.) Document containing the operational requirements; security environment; hardware and software configurations and interfaces; and all security procedures, measures, and contingency plans.

trusted identification Identification method used in IS networks whereby forwarding the sending host can verify an authorized user on its system is attempting a connection to another host. The sending host transmits the required user authentication information to the receiving host.

trusted path Means by which a user and a TOE Security Function (TSF) can communicate with necessary confidence to support the TOE Security Policy (TSP).

trusted process Process that has privileges to circumvent the system security policy and has been tested and verified to operate only as intended.

trusted recovery Ability to ensure recovery without compromise after a system failure.

trusted software Software portion of a trusted computing base (TCB).

TSEC nomenclature System for identifying the type and purpose of certain items of COMSEC material.

tunneling Technology enabling one network to send its data via another network's connections. Tunneling works by encapsulating a network protocol within packets carried by the second network.

two-part code Code consisting of an encoding section, in which the vocabulary items (with their associated code groups) are arranged in alphabetical or other systematic order, and a decoding section, in which the code groups (with their associated meanings) are arranged in a separate alphabetical or numeric order.

two-person control Continuous surveillance and control of positive control material at all times by a minimum of two authorized individuals, each capable of detecting incorrect and unauthorized procedures with respect to the task being performed, and each familiar with established security and safety requirements.

two-person integrity (TPI) System of storage and handling designed to prohibit individual access to certain COMSEC keying material by requiring the presence of at least two authorized individuals, each capable of detecting incorrect or unauthorized security procedures with respect to the task being performed. See no-lone zone.

type certification The certification acceptance of replica information systems based on the comprehensive evaluation of the technical and non-technical security features of an IS and other safeguards, made as part of and in support of the accreditation process, to establish the extent to which a particular design and implementation meet a specified set of security requirements.

type 1 product Classified or controlled cryptographic item endorsed by the NSA for securing classified and sensitive U.S. Government information, when appropriately keyed. The term refers only to products, and not to information, key, services, or controls. Type 1 products contain approved NSA algorithms. They are available to U.S. Government users, their contractors, and federally sponsored non-U.S. Government activities subject to export restrictions in accordance with International Traffic in Arms Regulation.

type 2 product Unclassified cryptographic equipment, assembly, or component, endorsed by the NSA, for use in national security systems as defined in Title 40 U.S.C. Section 1452.

type 3 algorithm Cryptographic algorithm registered by the National Institute of Standards and Technology (NIST) and published as a Federal Information Processing Standard (FIPS) for use in protecting unclassified sensitive information or commercial information.

type 4 algorithm Unclassified cryptographic algorithm that has been registered by the National Institute of Standards and Technology (NIST), but not published as a Federal Information Processing Standard (FIPS).

U

unauthorized disclosure Type of event involving exposure of information to individuals not authorized to receive it.

unclassified Information that has not been determined pursuant to E.O. 12958 or any predecessor order to require protection against unauthorized disclosure and that is not designated as classified.

untrusted process Process that has not been evaluated or examined for adherence to the security policy. It may include incorrect or malicious code that attempts to circumvent the security mechanisms.

updating Automatic or manual cryptographic process that irreversibly modifies the state of a COMSEC key, equipment, device, or system.

user Individual or process authorized to access an IS. (PKI) Individual defined, registered, and bound to a public key structure by a certification authority (CA).

user ID Unique symbol or character string used by an IS to identify a specific user.

User Partnership Program (UPP) Partnership between the NSA and a U.S. Government agency to facilitate development of secure IS equipment incorporating NSA-approved cryptography. The result of this program is the authorization of the product or system to safeguard national security information in the user's specific application.

user representative Individual authorized by an organization to order COMSEC keying material and interface with the keying system, provide information to key users, and ensure the correct type of key is ordered.

U.S.-controlled facility Base or building to which access is physically controlled by U.S. individuals who are authorized U.S. Government or U.S. Government contractor employees.

U.S.-controlled space Room or floor within a facility that is not a U.S.-controlled facility, access to which is physically controlled by U.S. individuals who are authorized U.S. Government or U.S. Government contractor employees. Keys or combinations to locks controlling entrance to U.S.-controlled spaces must be under the exclusive control of U.S. individuals who are U.S. Government or U.S. Government contractor employees.

U.S. person U.S. citizen or a permanent resident alien, an unincorporated association substantially composed of U.S. citizens or permanent resident aliens, or a corporation incorporated in U.S., except for a corporation directed and controlled by a foreign government or governments.

V

validated products list List of validated products that have been successfully evaluated under the National Information Assurance Partnership (NIAP) Common Criteria Evaluation and Validation Scheme (CCEVS).

validation Process of applying specialized security test and evaluation procedures, tools, and equipment needed to establish acceptance for joint usage of an IS by one or more departments or agencies and their contractors.

variant One of two or more code symbols having the same plain text equivalent.

verification Process of comparing two levels of an IS specification for proper correspondence (e.g., security policy model with top-level specification, top-level specification with source code, or source code with object code).

virtual private network (VPN) Protected IS link utilizing tunneling, security controls (see information assurance), and end-point address translation giving the impression of a dedicated line.

virus Self-replicating, malicious code that attaches itself to an application program or other executable system component and leaves no obvious signs of its presence.

vulnerability Weakness in an IS, system security procedures, internal controls, or implementation that could be exploited.

vulnerability analysis Examination of information to identify the elements comprising a vulnerability.

vulnerability assessment Formal description and evaluation of vulnerabilities of an IS.

W

web risk assessment Process for ensuring websites are in compliance with applicable policies.

work factor Estimate of the effort or time needed by a potential perpetrator, with specified expertise and resources, to overcome a protective measure.

worm See malicious code.

write Fundamental operation in an IS that results only in the flow of information from a subject to an object. See access type.

write access Permission to write to an object in an IS.

z

zero fill To fill unused storage locations in an IS with the representation of the character denoting "0."

zeroize To remove or eliminate the key from a crypto-equipment or fill device.

zone of control Synonymous with inspectable space.

SECTION II

COMMONLY USED ABBREVIATIONS AND ACRONYMS

ACL Access Control List

ACO (C.F.D.) Access Control Officer

AES Advanced Encryption standard

AIG Address Indicator Group

AIN Advanced Intelligence Network

AK Automatic Remote Rekeying

AKD/RCU Automatic Key Distribution/Rekeying Control Unit

ALC Accounting Legend Code

AMS 1. Auto-Manual System 2. Autonomous Message Switch

ANDVT Advanced Narrowband Digital Voice Terminal

ANSI American National Standards Institute

APC Adaptive Predictive Coding

APU Auxiliary Power Unit

ASCII American Standard Code for Information Interchange

ASSIST Program Automated Information System Security Incident Support Team Program

ASU (C.F.D.) Approval for Service Use

ATM Asynchronous Transfer Mode

AUTODIN Automatic Digital Network

AVP Authorized Vendor Program

C2 1. Command and Control 2. Controlled Access Protection (C.F.D.)

C3 Command, Control, and Communications

C3I Command, Control, Communications and Intelligence

C4 Command, Control, Communications and Computers

CA 1. Controlling Authority 2. Cryptanalysis 3. COMSEC Account 4. Command Authority 5. Certification Authority

C&A Certification and Accreditation

CAW Certificate Authority Workstation

CC Common Criteria

CCEP Commercial COMSEC Evaluation Program

CCEVS Common Criteria Evaluation and Validation Scheme

CCI Controlled Cryptographic Item

CCO Circuit Control Officer

CEOI Communications Electronics Operating Instruction

CEPR Compromising Emanation Performance Requirement

CER 1. Cryptographic Equipment Room 2. Communication Equipment Room

CERT Computer Security Emergency Response Team

CFD Common Fill Device

CIAC Computer Incident Assessment Capability

CIK Crypto-Ignition Key

CIRT Computer Security Incident Response Team

CKG Cooperative Key Generation

CMCS COMSEC Material Control System

CNA Computer Network Attack

CNCS (C.F.D.) Cryptonet Control Station

CND Computer Network Defense

CNK (C.F.D.) Cryptonet Key

CNSS Committee on National Security Systems

COMPUSEC Computer Security

COMSEC Communications Security

CONOP Concept of Operations

COOP Continuity of Operations Plan

COR 1. Central Office of Record (COMSEC) 2. Contracting Officer Representative

COTS Commercial-off-the-shelf

CPS (C.F.D.) COMSEC Parent Switch

CPU Central Processing Unit

CRL Certificate Revocation List

CRP (C.F.D.) COMSEC Resources Program (Budget)

Crypt/Crypto Cryptographic-related

CSE Communications Security Element

CSS 1. COMSEC Subordinate Switch 2. Constant Surveillance Service (Courier) 3. Continuous Signature Service (Courier) 4. Coded Switch System

CSSO Contractor Special Security Officer

CSTVRP Computer Security Technical Vulnerability Report Program

CTAK Cipher Text Auto-Key

CT&E Certification Test and Evaluation

CTTA Certified TEMPEST Technical Authority

CUP COMSEC Utility Program

DAA 1. Designated Accrediting Authority 2. Delegated Accrediting Authority

DAC Discretionary Access Control

DAMA Demand Assigned Multiple Access

DCID Director Central Intelligence Directive

DCS 1. Defense Communications System 2. Defense Courier Service

DDS Dual Driver Service (courier)

DES Data Encryption Standard

DISN Defense Information System Network

DITSCAP DoD Information Technology Security Certification and Accreditation Process

DoD TCSEC (C.F.D.) Department of Defense Trusted Computer System Evaluation Criteria

DMA Direct Memory Access

DMS Defense Message System

DSA Digital Signature Algorithm

DSN Defense Switched Network

DSVT Digital Subscriber Voice Terminal

DTLS Descriptive Top-Level Specification

DTD Data Transfer Device

DTS Diplomatic Telecommunications Service

DUA Directory User Agent

EAM Emergency Action Message

ECCM Electronic Counter-Countermeasures

ECM Electronic Countermeasures

ECPL Endorsed Cryptographic Products List (a section in the Information Systems Security Products and Services Catalogue)

EDAC Error Detection and Correction

EFD Electronic Fill Device

EFTO Encrypt For Transmission Only

EKMS Electronic Key Management System

ELINT Electronic Intelligence

E Model Engineering Development Model

EPL Evaluated Products List (a section in the INFOSEC Products and Services Catalogue)

ERTZ Equipment Radiation TEMPEST Zone

ETPL Endorsed TEMPEST Products List

FDIU Fill Device Interface Unit

FIPS Federal Information Processing Standard

FOCI Foreign Owned, Controlled or Influenced

FOUO For Official Use Only

FSRS Functional Security Requirements Specification

FSTS Federal Secure Telephone Service

FTS Federal Telecommunications System

FTAM File Transfer Access Management

FTLS Formal Top-Level Specification

GCCS Global Command and Control System

GETS Government Emergency Telecommunications Service

GOTS Government-off-the-Shelf

GPS Global Positioning System

GTS Global Telecommunications Service

GWEN Ground Wave Emergency Network

IA Information Assurance

I&A Identification and Authentication

IBAC Identity Based Access Control

ICU Interface Control Unit

IDS Intrusion Detection System

IEMATS Improved Emergency Message Automatic Transmission System

IFF Identification, Friend or Foe

IFFN Identification, Friend, Foe, or Neutral

ILS Integrated Logistics Support

INFOSEC Information Systems Security

IO Information Operations

IP Internet Protocol

IPM Interpersonal Messaging

IPSO Internet Protocol Security Option

IS Information System

ISDN Integrated Services Digital Network

ISO International Standards Organization

ISSE Information Systems Security Engineering

ISSM Information Systems Security Manager

ISSO Information Systems Security Officer

IT Information Technology

ITAR International Traffic in Arms Regulation

ITSEC Information Technology Security Evaluation Criteria

KAK Key-Auto-Key

KDC Key Distribution Center

KEK Key Encryption Key

KG Key Generator

KMC Key Management Center

KMI Key Management Infrastructure

KMID Key Management Identification Number

KMODC Key Management Ordering and Distribution Center

KMP Key Management Protocol

KMS Key Management System

KP Key Processor

KPK Key Production Key

KSD Key Storage Device

LEAD Low-Cost Encryption/Authentication Device

LMD Local Management Device

LMD/KP Local Management Device/Key Processor

LOCK Logical Co-Processing Kernel

LPC Linear Predictive Coding

LPD Low Probability of Detection

LPI Low Probability of Intercept

LRIP Limited Rate Initial Preproduction

LSI Large Scale Integration

MAC 1. Mandatory Access Control 2. Message Authentication Code

MAN 1. Mandatory Modification 2. Metropolitan Area Network

MER Minimum Essential Requirements

MHS Message Handling System

MI Message Indicator

MIB Management Information Base

MIJI (C.F.D.) Meaconing, Intrusion, Jamming, and Interference

MINTERM Miniature Terminal

MISSI Multilevel Information Systems Security Initiative

MLS Multilevel Security

MSE Mobile Subscriber Equipment

NACAM National COMSEC Advisory Memorandum

NACSI National COMSEC Instruction

NACSIM National COMSEC Information Memorandum

NAK Negative Acknowledge

NCCD Nuclear Command and Control Document

NCS 1. National Communications System 2. National Cryptologic School 3. Net Control Station

NCSC National Computer Security Center

NISAC National Industrial Security Advisory Committee

NIST National Institute of Standards and Technology

NLZ No-Lone Zone

NSA National Security Agency

NSD National Security Directive

NSDD National Security Decision Directive

NSEP National Security Emergency Preparedness

NSI National Security Information

NSTAC National Security Telecommunications Advisory Committee

NSTISSAM National Security Telecommunications and Information Systems Security Advisory/Information Memorandum

NSTISSC National Security Telecommunications and Information Systems Security Committee

NSTISSD National Security Telecommunications and Information Systems Security Directive

NSTISSI National Security Telecommunications and Information Systems Security Instruction

NSTISSP National Security Telecommunications and Information Systems Security Policy

NTCB Network Trusted Computing Base

NTIA National Telecommunications and Information Administration

NTISSAM National Telecommunications and Information Systems Security Advisory/Information Memorandum

NTISSD National Telecommunications and Information Systems Security Directive

NTISSI National Telecommunications and Information Systems Security Instruction

NTISSP National Telecommunications and Information Systems Security Policy

OADR Originating Agency's Determination Required

OPCODE Operations Code

OPSEC Operations Security

ORA Organizational Registration Authority

OTAD Over-the-Air Key Distribution

OTAR Over-the-Air Rekeying

OTAT Over-the-Air Key Transfer

OTP One-Time Pad

OTT One-Time Tape

PAA Policy Approving Authority

PAL Permissive Action Link

PC Personal Computer

PCA Policy Certification Authority

PCIPB President's Critical Infrastructure Protection Board

PCMCIA Personal Computer Memory Card International Association

PDR Preliminary Design Review

PDS 1. Protected Distribution Systems 2. Practices Dangerous to Security

PES Positive Enable System

PKC Public Key Cryptography

PKI Public Key Infrastructure

PKSD Programmable Key Storage Device

P model Preproduction Model

PNEK Post-Nuclear Event Key

PPL Preferred Products List (a section in the INFOSEC Products and Services Catalogue)

PRBAC (C.F.D.) Partition Rule Base Access Control

PROPIN Proprietary Information

PWDS Protected Wireline Distribution System

RAMP Rating Maintenance Program

SA System Administrator

SABI Secret and Below Interoperability

SAO Special Access Office

SAP 1. System Acquisition Plan 2. Special Access Program

SARK SAVILLE Advanced Remote Keying

SBU Sensitive But Unclassified

SCI Sensitive Compartmented Information

SCIF Sensitive Compartmented Information Facility

SDNS Secure Data Network System

SDR System Design Review

SFA Security Fault Analysis

SHA Secure Hash Algorithm

SFUG Security Features Users Guide

SI Special Intelligence

SISS Subcommittee on Information Systems Security

SMU Secure Mobile Unit

SPK Single Point Key(ing)

SRR Security Requirements Review

SSO Staff Security Officer

SSP System Security Plan

ST&E Security Test and Evaluation

STE Secure Terminal Equipment

STS Subcommittee on Telecommunications Security

STU Secure Telephone Unit

TA Traffic Analysis

TACTERM Tactical Terminal

TAG TEMPEST Advisory Group

TCB Trusted Computing Base

TCP/IP Transmission Control Protocols

TED Trunk Encryption Device

TEK Traffic Encryption Key

TEP TEMPEST Endorsement Program

TFM Trusted Facility Manual

TFS Traffic Flow Security

TLS Top-Level Specification

TPC Two-Person Control

TPEP Trusted Products Evaluation Program

TPI Two-Person Integrity

TRANSEC Transmission Security

TRB Technical Review Board

TRI-TAC Tri-Service Tactical Communications System

TSABI Top Secret and Below Interoperability

TSCM Technical Surveillance Countermeasures

TSEC Telecommunications Security

TTAP Trust Technology Assessment Program

UA User Agent

UIRK (C.F.D.) Unique Interswitch Rekeying Key

UIS User Interface System

UPP User Partnership Program

USDE (C.F.D.) Undesired Signal Data Emanations

V model (C.F.D.) Advanced Development Model

VPN Virtual Private Network

XDM/X Model (C.F.D.) Experimental Development Model/Exploratory Development Model

SECTION III

REFERENCES

a. National Security Directive 42, National Policy for the Security of National Security Telecommunications and Information Systems, 5 July 1990.

b. Executive Order 12958, National Security Information, dated 29 September 1995.

c. Executive Order 12333, United States Intelligence Activities, dated 4 December 1981.

d. Public Law 100-235, Cmputer Security Act of 1987, dated 8 January 1988.

e. 10 United States Codes Section 2315.

f. 44 United States Code Section 3502(2), Public Law 104-13, Paperwork Reduction Act of 1995, dated 22 May 1995.

g. Information Technology Management Reform Act of 1996 (within Public Law 104-106, DoD Authorization Act of 1996).

h. NSA Information Systems Security Organization Regulation 90-16, dated 29 October 1996.

i. Federal Information Processing Standards Publication 46-2, Data Encryption Standard, dated 30 December 1993.

j. Federal Information Processing Standards Publication 140 Security Requirements for Cryptographic Modules, dated 10 October 2001.

k. Title 40 United States Code Section 1452, National Security System Defined.

l. Title 5 United States Code Section 552a, The Privacy Act, Records Maintained on Individuals.

m. Executive Order (E.O.) 13231, Critical Infrastructure Protection in the Information Age, 16 October 2001.

n. P.O. 107-347, E-Government Act of 2002, Title III, Federal Information Security Management Act (FISMA) of 2002, dated 17 December 2002.

o. International Standard of Common Criteria for Information Technology Security Evaluation 15408, dated August 1999

✦   ✦   ✦

What's on the CD-ROM

This appendix provides you with information on the contents of the CD that accompanies this book. For the latest and greatest information, please refer to the ReadMe file located at the root of the CD. Here is what you will find:

- ✦ System Requirements
- ✦ Using the CD with Windows
- ✦ What's on the CD
- ✦ Troubleshooting

System Requirements

Make sure that your computer meets the minimum system requirements listed in this section. If your computer doesn't match up to most of these requirements, you may have a problem using the contents of the CD.

For Windows 9x, Windows 2000, Windows NT4 (with SP 4 or later), Windows Me, or Windows XP:

- ✦ PC with a Pentium processor running at 120 Mhz or faster
- ✦ At least 32 MB of total RAM installed on your computer; for best performance, we recommend at least 64 MB
- ✦ A CD-ROM drive

Using the CD with Windows

To install the items from the CD to your hard drive, follow these steps:

1. Insert the CD into your computer's CD-ROM drive.

2. A window will appear with the following options:

   Install — Gives you the option to install the supplied software and/or the author-created samples on the CD-ROM.

   Explore — Allows you to view the contents of the CD-ROM in its directory structure.

   Exit — Closes the autorun window.

If you do not have autorun enabled or if the autorun window does not appear, follow the steps below to access the CD:

1. Click Start ⇨ Run.

2. In the dialog box that appears, type d:\setup.exe, where d is the letter of your CD-ROM drive. This will bring up the autorun window described above.

3. Choose the desired option from the menu. (See Step 2 in the preceding list for a description of these options.)

What's on the CD

Included on the CD-ROM is a testing engine that is powered by Boson Software. This program resembles the testing engine that will be used by the testing center where you will be taking your exam. The goal of the testing engine is to make you comfortable with the testing interface so that when you take your exam it will not be the first time you see that style of exam.

The testing engine uses questions that are presented in the book, and it covers all 10 domains of the CISSP exam and the four areas of the ISSEP exam. When installed and run, the test engine presents you with a multiple-choice, question-and-answer format. Each question deals directly with exam-related material.

There are two tests available: One covers CISSP questions from Chapters 1 through 10, and the other contains ISSEP questions from Chapters 11 through 14.

Once you select what you believe to be the correct answer for each question, the test engine not only notes whether you are correct, but also provides information as to why the right answer is right and the wrong answers are wrong, providing you with valuable information for further review. Thus, the test engine gives valuable simulated exam experience and useful tutorial direction as well.

Troubleshooting

If you have difficulty installing or using any of the materials on the companion CD, try the following solutions:

Turn off any anti-virus software that you may have running — Installers sometimes mimic virus activity and can make your computer incorrectly believe that it is being infected by a virus. (Be sure to turn the anti-virus software back on later.)

Close all running programs — The more programs you're running, the less memory is available to other programs. Installers also typically update files and programs; if you keep other programs running, installation may not work properly.

Reference the ReadMe — Please refer to the ReadMe file located at the root of the CD-ROM for the latest product information at the time of publication.

If you have trouble with the CD-ROM, please call the Wiley Product Technical Support phone number: (800) 762-2974. Outside the United States, call 1 (317) 572-3994. You can also contact Wiley Product Technical Support at www.wiley.com/techsupport. Wiley will provide technical support only for installation and other general quality control items; for technical support on the applications themselves, consult the program's vendor or author.

To place additional orders or to request information about other Wiley products, please call (800) 225-5945.

✦   ✦   ✦

Wiley Publishing, Inc.
End-User License Agreement

READ THIS. You should carefully read these terms and conditions before opening the software packet(s) included with this book "Book". This is a license agreement "Agreement" between you and Wiley Publishing, Inc. "WPI". By opening the accompanying software packet(s), you acknowledge that you have read and accept the following terms and conditions. If you do not agree and do not want to be bound by such terms and conditions, promptly return the Book and the unopened software packet(s) to the place you obtained them for a full refund.

1. **License Grant.** WPI grants to you (either an individual or entity) a nonexclusive license to use one copy of the enclosed software program(s) (collectively, the "Software") solely for your own personal or business purposes on a single computer (whether a standard computer or a workstation component of a multi-user network). The Software is in use on a computer when it is loaded into temporary memory (RAM) or installed into permanent memory (hard disk, CD-ROM, or other storage device). WPI reserves all rights not expressly granted herein.

2. **Ownership.** WPI is the owner of all right, title, and interest, including copyright, in and to the compilation of the Software recorded on the disk(s) or CD-ROM "Software Media". Copyright to the individual programs recorded on the Software Media is owned by the author or other authorized copyright owner of each program. Ownership of the Software and all proprietary rights relating thereto remain with WPI and its licensers.

3. **Restrictions on Use and Transfer.**

   (a) You may only (i) make one copy of the Software for backup or archival purposes, or (ii) transfer the Software to a single hard disk, provided that you keep the original for backup or archival purposes. You may not (i) rent or lease the Software, (ii) copy or reproduce the Software through a LAN or other network system or through any computer subscriber system or bulletin-board system, or (iii) modify, adapt, or create derivative works based on the Software.

   (b) You may not reverse engineer, decompile, or disassemble the Software. You may transfer the Software and user documentation on a permanent basis, provided that the transferee agrees to accept the terms and conditions of this Agreement and you retain no copies. If the Software is an update or has been updated, any transfer must include the most recent update and all prior versions.

4. **Restrictions on Use of Individual Programs.** You must follow the individual requirements and restrictions detailed for each individual program in the About the CD-ROM appendix of this Book. These limitations are also contained in the individual license agreements recorded on the Software Media. These limitations may include a requirement that after using the program for a specified period of time, the user must pay a registration fee or discontinue use. By opening the Software packet(s), you will be agreeing to abide by the licenses and restrictions for these individual programs that are detailed in the About the CD-ROM appendix and on the Software Media. None of the material on this Software Media or listed in this Book may ever be redistributed, in original or modified form, for commercial purposes.

5. Limited Warranty.

(a) WPI warrants that the Software and Software Media are free from defects in materials and workmanship under normal use for a period of sixty (60) days from the date of purchase of this Book. If WPI receives notification within the warranty period of defects in materials or workmanship, WPI will replace the defective Software Media.

(b) **WPI AND THE AUTHOR(S) OF THE BOOK DISCLAIM ALL OTHER WARRANTIES, EXPRESS OR IMPLIED, INCLUDING WITHOUT LIMITATION IMPLIED WARRANTIES OF MERCHANTABILITY AND FITNESS FOR A PARTICULAR PURPOSE, WITH RESPECT TO THE SOFTWARE, THE PROGRAMS, THE SOURCE CODE CONTAINED THEREIN, AND/OR THE TECHNIQUES DESCRIBED IN THIS BOOK. WPI DOES NOT WARRANT THAT THE FUNCTIONS CONTAINED IN THE SOFTWARE WILL MEET YOUR REQUIREMENTS OR THAT THE OPERATION OF THE SOFTWARE WILL BE ERROR FREE.**

(c) This limited warranty gives you specific legal rights, and you may have other rights that vary from jurisdiction to jurisdiction.

6. Remedies.

(a) WPI's entire liability and your exclusive remedy for defects in materials and workmanship shall be limited to replacement of the Software Media, which may be returned to WPI with a copy of your receipt at the following address: Software Media Fulfillment Department, Attn.: *The CISSP Prep Guide, Second Edition: Mastering the CISSP and ISSEP Exams,* Wiley Publishing, Inc., 10475 Crosspoint Blvd., Indianapolis, IN 46256, or call 1-800-762-2974. Please allow four to six weeks for delivery. This Limited Warranty is void if failure of the Software Media has resulted from accident, abuse, or misapplication. Any replacement Software Media will be warranted for the remainder of the original warranty period or thirty (30) days, whichever is longer.

(b) In no event shall WPI or the author be liable for any damages whatsoever (including without limitation damages for loss of business profits, business interruption, loss of business information, or any other pecuniary loss) arising from the use of or inability to use the Book or the Software, even if WPI has been advised of the possibility of such damages.

(c) Because some jurisdictions do not allow the exclusion or limitation of liability for consequential or incidental damages, the above limitation or exclusion may not apply to you.

7. U.S. Government Restricted Rights. Use, duplication, or disclosure of the Software for or on behalf of the United States of America, its agencies and/or instrumentalities "U.S. Government" is subject to restrictions as stated in paragraph (c)(1)(ii) of the Rights in Technical Data and Computer Software clause of DFARS 252.227-7013, or subparagraphs (c) (1) and (2) of the Commercial Computer Software - Restricted Rights clause at FAR 52.227-19, and in similar clauses in the NASA FAR supplement, as applicable.

8. General. This Agreement constitutes the entire understanding of the parties and revokes and supersedes all prior agreements, oral or written, between them and may not be modified or amended except in a writing signed by both parties hereto that specifically refers to this Agreement. This Agreement shall take precedence over any other documents that may be in conflict herewith. If any one or more provisions contained in this Agreement are held by any court or tribunal to be invalid, illegal, or otherwise unenforceable, each and every other provision shall remain in full force and effect.

Index

A

abbreviations and acronyms, list of, 976–984

absolute addressing, 267

acceptability, 59–60

access control attacks, 50–55
    back door, 51, 174
    brute force, 53, 233, 682
    countermeasures, 334
    data scavenging, 334, 335
    defined, 74, 664
    denial of service/distributed denial of service
        (DoS/DDoS), 50–51, 159–160, 174, 411, 682
    dictionary attack, 53, 664
    dumpster diving, 53, 327, 334, 412
    eavesdropping, 163–164, 173–174, 334, 412, 680
    factoring, 234
    insertion, 161
    laboratory, 335
    man-in-the-middle, 51, 175, 233
    password guessing, 53, 63
    PDAs and, 165
    replay, 52
    rogue access points, 161–162
    service set identifier (SSID) issues, 163
    social engineering, 52–53, 327, 334, 412, 717
    software exploitation, 54
    spoofing, 51, 178, 412
    system scanning, 54–55, 75, 665
    TCP hijacking, 52
    Trojan Horses, 54, 186
    WAP GAP, 160–161, 252
    war driving, 164, 174, 685
    on Wired Equivalent Privacy (WEP), 162–163
    wireless packet sniffers, 164–165

access control devices
    biometric devices, 472
    digital-coded cards, 470–471
    photo-image cards, 470
    wireless proximity card, readers, 471

access control list (ACL), 47, 114, 286

access control models
    access matrix, 286, 701
    Bell-LaPadula, 287–290, 699–700, 702
    Take-Grant, 287, 701

access control systems
    accountability, 72
    attacks on, 50–55
    authentication, 57

    availability and, 46
    biometrics, 58–60
    centralized, 66
    confidentiality and, 45, 72
    content-dependent, 48, 705
    context-dependent, 48, 705
    controls, 46–50
    cost of, 72
    data normalization, 69
    decentralized/distributed, 66
    entity and referential integrity, 68
    identification, 57
    integrity and, 45–46
    intrusion detection, 70–72
    Kerberos, 61–65
    KryptoKnight, 65
    media security, 323
    methodologies, 65–66
    models for, 47–50
    object-oriented databases (OODB), 70
    object-relational databases, 70
    passwords, 57–58
    penetration testing, 56–72
    reasons for, 45–46
    relational database model, 66–69
    risk and, 46, 667
    SESAME, 65
    Single Sign-On (SSO), 60–61
    SQL, 70
    threats and, 46, 667
    violations of, compensatory measures, 72
    vulnerability and, 46, 667

access log, 456–457, 755

access matrix, 286, 701

access point (AP), 154

access rights, 286

access servers, 129

accidental loss, 333

account administration, 717

accountability, 6, 33
    and access control, 72
    controls and, 47
    two-man control and, 309

accreditation, defined, 280, 551. *See also* certification,
        defined

active eavesdropping, 173

active monitor, 95

adaptive chosen ciphertext attack, 233

Continued

Continued

Continued

transparent bridging, 108
Virtual Local Area Networks, 111–112
neural networks, 363–364, 720
New Technology File System (NTFS), 192
NIACAP. *See* National Information Assurance
  Certification and Accreditation Process
NIST. *See* National Institute of Standards and
  Technology
Nmap scans, 181, 182
no-lone zone, 628, 803
noise, 100, 334, 458–459
nonce, 52
non-discretionary access control, 48
non-interference model, 293
non-persistent carrier sense, 104
non-privileged instructions, 268
NSTISSP No. 6, 552, 580, 775, 780
NT Security Accounts Manager (SAM), 183
Nybergrueppel's signature algorithm, 229

O

object, 286
object code, 271, 368
object orientation, 358–359
Object Request Architecture (ORA), 359–360
Object Request Brokers (ORBs), 359
object reuse, 318–319, 477, 712, 755
Object Services, 360
Object-Oriented Analysis (OOA), 359
object-oriented database (OODB), 70, 78, 670
Object-Oriented Design (OOD), 359
Object-Oriented Programming (OOP), 359
Object-Oriented Requirements Analysis (OORA), 359
object-oriented systems, 357–360, 727–728
  behavior, 358
  class, 358
  delegation, 358
  examples of, 360
  inheritance, 358
  instance, 358
  message, 358
  method, 358, 722
  multiple inheritance, 358
  polyinstantiation, 358–359
  polymorphism, 358, 722
object-relational database, 70
Office of Management and Budget (OMB)
  Circular A-130 (Management of Federal Information
    Resources), 10, 40, 581, 635, 654, 801
  Memorandum 99-18 (Private Policies on Federal
    Web Sites), 581
  and Paperwork Reduction Acts, 427, 750

one-time pad, 208, 214, 697
one-way functions, 224–225
On-Line Analytical Processing (OLAP), 365
open box penetration test, 56, 665
Open Database Connectivity (ODBC), 365
Open Group, 61
Open Shortest Path First (OSPF), 85, 110, 686
open systems, 272
Open Systems Interconnection (OSI) model, 83–86, 120
  application layer, 83
  data link layer, 85
  network layer, 85, 687
  physical layer, 86
  presentation layer, 84
  purpose of, 83
  security services and mechanisms, 86
  session layer, 84
  transport layer, 85, 687
  trusted facility management, 307–310
  trusted recovery, 310–311
open view, 18
operating state, 268
operating system (OS)
  defined, 272
  using scanning to identify, 180–181
operational assurance, defined, 713
operational controls, defined, 624
Operationally Critical Threat, Asset, and Vulnerability
    Evaluation (OCTAVE), 578, 781
operations controls, 319–326
  defined, 319
  degaussing, 323–324
  destruction, 324
  hardware controls, 321
  media resource protection, 322
  media security controls, 323
  media viability controls, 324–325
  overwriting, 323
  physical access controls, 325–326
  privileged entity controls, 322
  resource protection, 320–321
  restricting hardware instructions, 323
  software controls, 321–322
  transparency of controls, 322
operations job functions, 318
Operations Security (OPSEC)
  application controls, 303
  asset, 302
  auditing, 329–332
  availability, 302
  change controls, 304

Continued

Continued

Continued